CW01021943

THE ROUTLEDGE HANDB(
SUBNATIONAL CONSTITUTIONS AND
CONSTITUTIONALISM

This handbook provides a toolbox of definitions and typologies to develop a theory of multi-level constitutionalism and subnational constitutions.

The volume examines systems with subnational entities that have full subnational constituent autonomy and systems where subnational constituent powers, while claimed by subnational governments, are incomplete or non-existent. Understanding why complete subnational constituent power exists or is denied sheds significant light on the status and functioning of subnational constitutions. The book deals with questions of how constitutions at multiple levels of a political system can co-exist and interact. The term 'multilevel constitutionalism', recognized as explaining how a supranational European constitution can exist alongside those of the Member States, is now used to capture dynamics between constitutions at the national, subnational and, where applicable, supranational levels. Broad in scope, the book encompasses many different types of multi-tiered systems world-wide to map the possible meanings, uses and challenges of subnational or state constitutions in a variety of political and societal contexts.

The book develops the building blocks of an explanatory theory of subnational constitutionalism and as such will be an essential reference for all those interested in comparative constitutional law, federalism and governance.

Patricia Popelier is Full Professor of Constitutional Law at the University of Antwerp, director of the Research Group on Government and Law, Senior Research Fellow at the University of Kent, Centre for Federal Studies and co-promoter of the Centre of Excellence GOVTRUST.

Giacomo Delledonne is Assistant Professor of Constitutional Law at the Scuola Superiore Sant'Anna, Pisa, Italy.

Nicholas Aroney is Professor of Constitutional Law and Fellow of the Centre for Public, International and Comparative Law at the University of Queensland.

THE ROUTLEDGE HANDBOOK OF SUBNATIONAL CONSTITUTIONS AND CONSTITUTIONALISM

Edited by
Patricia Popelier, Giacomo Delledonne
and Nicholas Aroney

Routledge
Taylor & Francis Group

LONDON AND NEW YORK

First published 2022
by Routledge
2 Park Square, Milton Park, Abingdon, Oxon OX14 4RN

and by Routledge
605 Third Avenue, New York, NY 10158

Routledge is an imprint of the Taylor & Francis Group, an informa business

British Library Cataloguing-in-Publication Data
A catalogue record for this book is available from the British Library

Library of Congress Cataloging-in-Publication Data
A catalog record has been requested for this book

ISBN: 978-0-367-51015-2 (hbk)
ISBN: 978-0-367-51017-6 (pbk)
ISBN: 978-1-003-05211-1 (ebk)

DOI: 10.4324/9781003052111

Typeset in Galliard
by SPi Technologies India Pvt Ltd (Straive)

CONTENTS

v

Contents

Contents

TABLES

These maps and tables are elaborated by the authors

ACKNOWLEDGEMENTS

This book is the outcome of activities in the International Association of Constitutional Law's standing research group on subnational constitutions in federal and quasi-federal systems.

It was written with the support of the FWO funding agency and the University of Antwerp, which sponsored a co-editor's sabbatical.

CONTRIBUTORS

Editors

Nicholas Aroney is Professor of Constitutional Law and Fellow of the Centre for Public, International and Comparative Law at the University of Queensland. He is the author of over 140 articles, book chapters and books on constitutional law, comparative federalism, and law and religion, and he has held visiting positions at Oxford, Cambridge, Paris, Edinburgh, Sydney, Emory and Tilburg universities. His sole-authored and joint publications include: *The Constitution of a Federal Commonwealth* (Cambridge, 2009), *Shari'a in the West* (Oxford, 2010), *The Future of Australian Federalism* (Cambridge, 2012), *The Constitution of the Commonwealth of Australia* (Cambridge, 2015), *Courts in Federal Systems* (Toronto, 2017) and *Christianity and Constitutionalism* (forthcoming, Oxford, 2021).

Giacomo Delledonne is Assistant Professor of Constitutional Law at the Scuola Superiore Sant'Anna, Pisa, Italy. He is qualified as Full Professor of Comparative Law and as Associate Professor of Constitutional Law. His research covers comparative and Italian constitutional law, with a strong focus on comparative federalism and the judicialization of politics. His first monograph, *L'omogeneità costituzionale degli ordinamenti composti* (2017), was awarded the 10th 'Opera Prima—Sergio P. Panunzio Prize', organised by the Italian Association of Constitutional Law Scholars.

Patricia Popelier is Full Professor of Constitutional Law at the University of Antwerp, director of the Research Group on Government and Law, Senior Research Fellow at the University of Kent, Centre for Federal Studies and co-promoter of the Centre of Excellence GOVTRUST. She is the author of *Dynamic Federalism* (Routledge, 2021) and publishes widely in the field of federalism, constitutional courts, legal certainty and legislative studies. She is convenor of the standing research group on subnational constitutions in federal and quasi-federal systems of the International Association of Constitutional Law, of which this edited volume is a product.

Authors

Eva Maria Belser holds a Chair for Constitutional and Administrative Law at the University of Fribourg and a UNESCO Chair in Human Rights and Democracy. She is Co-Director of the Institute of Federalism and heads its international centre. She is also a Board Member of the Swiss Centre of Expertise in Human Rights and responsible for the cluster dealing with the institutional aspects of human rights implementation. She teaches and publishes in the field of Swiss and comparative constitutional law, federalism, decentralisation and globalisation, human and minority rights and democracy, as well as constitution making and conflict resolution. Eva Maria Belser regularly accepts mandates to serve as a Swiss expert in international cooperation and consultancy projects. Her recent consultancy activities were related to Iraq, the Maldives, Myanmar, Sri Lanka and Syria. She was awarded the Swiss federalism prize in 2019.

Gonzalo Gabriel Carranza (LLM, PhD) is currently Professor of Constitutional Law at the *Universidad Internacional de La Rioja* (Spain). He was Visiting Researcher at the *Universität-Wien* (Austria) and, as DAAD fellow, at the *Humboldt-Universität zu Berlin* and the *Ludwig-Maximilians-Universität München* (Germany). His research interests lie in the theory and practice of federalism, the intergovernmental relations, and the judicial protection of the right to health.

Yonatan Tesfaye Fessha (LLB, LLM, PhD) is a Professor of Law at the University of the Western Cape in South Africa. His teaching and research focuses on examining the relevance of constitutional design in dealing with the challenges of divided societies. He has published widely on matters pertaining to but not limited to federalism, constitutional design, autonomy and politicized ethnicity. His publications include the books *Ethnic Diversity and Federalism: Constitution making in South Africa and Ethiopia* (Ashgate, 2010) and *Federalism and Courts in Africa: Design and impact in comparative perspective* (co-edited, Routledge, 2020). He has contributed to constitution-building projects, including in Sudan, South Sudan and Yemen. He was a Michigan Grotius Research Scholar at the University of Michigan. He is currently a Marie-Curie fellow at the Institute for Comparative Federalism at Eurac Research (Italy).

Richard Foo (BSc, LLB, PhD) practised as an advocate and solicitor in Malaysia and is now a Teaching Associate in the Faculty of Law at Monash University. His research, which focuses on constitutional change and reform in Malaysia, recently contributed to the report of the Institutional Reforms Committee commissioned by the Malaysian government in 2018. He has written for the *Singapore Journal of Legal Studies*, the *Journal of International and Comparative Law* and the *Journal of Comparative Law*.

Anna Gamper (Unv-Prof. Dr.) is Full Professor of Public Law at the Institut für Öffentliches Recht, Staats- und Verwaltungslehre, University of Innsbruck, Austria. Her research interests lie in Austrian and comparative constitutional law, constitutional theory, federalism and university law. Her recent key publications deal with constitutional courts and constitutional interpretation.

James A. Gardner is Bridget and Thomas Black SUNY Distinguished Professor of Law, and Research Professor of Political Science, at the State University of New York, University at

Buffalo School of Law. His research focuses on federalism, electoral law and democratic theory. He is the author of *Interpreting State Constitutions* (University of Chicago Press, 2005); co-editor, with Jim Rossi, of *New Frontiers of State Constitutional Law: Dual Enforcement of Norms* (Oxford, 2011); and the author of more than 30 articles and chapters on federalism and American and comparative subnational constitutional law.

Benjamen Franklen Gussen is the President of the Australian Law and Economics Association (AustLEA), and a tenured constitutional jurist at the Swinburne School of Law, Melbourne, Victoria. He was admitted to the legal profession in New Zealand in 2011, and in Australia in 2014. He has been a member of the International Association of Constitutional Law (IACL) since 2014. His main area of research is comparative constitutional law and constitutional economics, with emphasis on the three Anglo-American federations (the United States, Canada and Australia). His latest monograph (Axial Shift: City Subsidiarity and the World System in the 21st Century, Palgrave Macmillan, 2019) predicts the emergence of a new world system where sovereign cities replace nation-states as the dominant polity.

Antonio María Hernández is Professor of Constitutional Law and State Constitutional and Municipal Law at the National University of Cordoba, Honorary Professor of the University of Buenos Aires and Postdoctoral Senior Fellow, State University of New York at Buffalo Law School. He is Director of the Institute of Federalism of the National Academy of Law and Social Sciences of Cordoba and Member of the Board of Directors of the IACFS. He was Member of the Constitutional Conventions of the Nation (1994), the Province of Cordoba (1987) and the City of Cordoba (1995). He is author of several books on federalism, including *Studies in Comparative Federalism. Argentina, the United States and Mexico* (e-book, Universidad Nacional de Cordoba, 2019).

Marcelo Labanca Corrêa de Araújo (LLM, PhD) is a full Professor of Constitutional Law at the Catholic University of Pernambuco in Brazil. He held a fellow postdoctoral research at University of Pisa, Italy (2012–2013). His research focus is on state constitutional law, federalism, courts and state fundamental rights, and his publications include books *Jurisdição Constitucional e Federação* (Elsevier, 2009) and *Il futuro dei diritti fondamentali* (co-edited with Roberto Romboli, Pisa University Press, 2020). He is also the director of The Brazilian Center for Constitutional Studies in State Law (ConState Center), contributing to several projects with the state governors, parliaments and courts in Brazil.

Hoong Phun ('HP') Lee is Emeritus Professor and a Teaching Associate in the Faculty of Law at Monash University. He held the Sir John Latham Chair of Law from 1995 to 2014, and served as Deputy Dean for a number of years. He is the author of *Constitutional Conflicts in Contemporary Malaysia* (2nd edn, Oxford University Press, 2017). His extensive publications include *Emergency Powers in Australia* (2nd edn, Cambridge University Press, 2019) (co-author) and *The Australian Judiciary* (2nd edn, Cambridge University Press, 2013) (co-author).

Giuseppe Martinico is currently Full Professor of Comparative Public law at the Scuola Superiore Sant'Anna, Pisa. Prior to joining the Scuola Sant'Anna, he was García Pelayo Fellow at the Centro de Estudios Politicos y Constitucionales (CEPC), Madrid, and Max Weber Fellow at the European University Institute, Florence.

Matteo Monti is Postdoctoral Fellow in Comparative Constitutional Law, Department of Law, University of Pisa, Italy. His research interests cover both comparative and Italian constitutional law, especially fundamental rights (freedom of expression and information and non-discrimination), Internet and new technologies, asymmetrical federalism, and the problem of secession in national and international law.

Werner Reutter has worked as a research fellow at the Social Science Research Centre Berlin, the Free University, and as an assistant professor at the Humboldt University Berlin. He was a visiting professor in Berlin, Bonn and Jena, and a visiting associate professor at the University of Minnesota (USA). Currently, he is a research fellow at the Humboldt University Berlin and works on subnational constitutional adjudication. He has published books and articles on interest groups, the international trade union movement, constitutional politics, German politics, German *state* parliaments and German *state* constitutional courts. One of his most recent books is *Verfassungsgerichtsbarkeit in Bundesländern. Theoreitsche Perspektiven, methodische Probleme und empirische Befunde* (2020).

Maja Sahadžić is Research Fellow and Visiting Professor at the University of Antwerp. Her research revolves around the concepts of constitutional asymmetry, multinationalism and multi-level governance, dynamic legitimacy, dynamic stability, constitutional values and principles, fundamental rights, legal theory and constitutionalism (under extreme measures). She often applies her research in the fields of alternative conflict solution, diplomacy and security. She is the author of a monography on *Asymmetry, Multinationalism and Constitutional Law: Managing Legitimacy and Stability in Federalist States* (Routledge, 2020) and many other publications in books and journals.

Rekha Saxena is a Professor at the Department of Political Science, University of Delhi. She is also Honorary Senior Advisor, Forum of Federations, Ottawa, and Honorary Vice Chairperson, Centre for Multilevel Federalism, Delhi. She specializes in the study of comparative federal political institutions. Her publications include: *New Dimensions in Federal Discourse in India*, Routledge (2021, edited), *The Value of Comparative Federalism*, Routledge (2021, coedited), *Varieties of Federal Governance: Major Contemporary Models*, Foundation: Cambridge University Press, India (2010).

José Ma. Serna de la Garza is a Researcher at the Institute of Legal Research and Professor at the Law School, both of the National University of Mexico. He was a visiting professor at the Law School of the University of Texas (at Austin), and a visiting scholar at the Max Planck Institute for Comparative Public Law and International Law. He is president to the Mexican section of the Ibero-American Institute of Constitutional Law. He holds a PhD in Government (University of Essex) and a PhD in Law (National University of Mexico). Key publications include: *El Sistema federal mexicano, un análisis jurídico* (Porrúa, México, 2009); and *The Constitution of Mexico, a contextual analysis* (Hart, UK, 2013).

M.P. Singh is presently a National Fellow in Political Science at the Indian Institute of Advanced Study, Shimla 171005, India. He was formerly a Professor and Head of the Political Science Department in the University of Delhi. His fields of specialization are party system and Indian and comparative federalism. His publications include *Federalizing India in the Age of Globalization* (with Rekha Saxena) (Delhi: Primus Books, 2013); and *Federalism in South Asia* (with Veena Kukreja) (New Delhi: Routledge, 2016).

Nikos Skoutaris is an Associate Professor in EU Law at the University of East Anglia. His research interests lie in the intersection between EU law, comparative constitutional law and conflict resolution theory. He is the author of Territorial Pluralism in Europe: Vertical separation of powers in the EU and its Member States (Oxford, Bloomsbury (Hart Publishing), forthcoming in 2021). He has acted as an adviser to the European parliamentary group of the European United Left/Nordic Green Left for Brexit related issues. His Report on a special designated status for Northern Ireland post-Brexit has shaped the position of this party and has been praised as an 'imaginative way forward' while his work on the Cyprus conflict has been extensively used by both communities. His website focuses on secessions, constitutions and EU law.

Nico Steytler is the South African Research Chair in Multilevel Government, Law and Development at the Dullah Omar Institute of Constitutional Law, Governance and Human Rights of the University of the Western Cape. He was a technical advisor to the Constitutional Assembly during the drafting of the 1996 South African Constitution as well as a technical advisor to the Western Cape Provincial Legislature on the drafting of a provincial constitution (1996–1997). His research focus is multilevel government, principally in South Africa and Africa, but also further afield. His recent publications include: Steytler, Arora and Saxena (eds) *The Value of Comparative Federalism: The legacy of Ronald L. Watts* (Routledge, 2021); Fombad and Steytler (eds) *Corruption and Constitutionalism: Revisiting control measures and strategies* (OUP, 2020); and Fombad and Steytler (eds) *Decentralisation and Constitutionalism in Africa* (OUP, 2019).

FOREWORD

Comparative subnational constitutional law

Robert F. Williams[1]

1 Introduction

It seems clear from the recent rise of interest in *subnational* constitutions in federal states that they present an important and interesting sub-branch of comparative constitutional law.

Professor Vicki Jackson has suggested four goals of comparative constitutional study: 1) developing a better intellectual understanding of other systems; 2) enhancing the capacity for self-reflection on one's own system; 3) developing a normative understanding of best practices; and 4) responding to domestic questions that are comparative in nature.[2]

1 Distinguished Emeritus Professor of Law, Rutgers Law School Director, Center for State Constitutional Studies, www.camlaw.rutgers.edu/statecon/.

This is an updated and expanded version of my article 'Teaching and Researching Comparative Subnational Constitutional Law', 115 *Penn St. L. Rev.* 1109 (2011). It is used with permission. See also Robert F. Williams, 'Comparative State Constitutional Law: A Research Agenda on Subnational Constitutions in Federal Systems', in *Law In Motion* 339 (Roger Blanpain, ed., 1997).

I dedicate this foreword to my colleagues and former students at the University of Graz, Austria. Their law faculty and Rutgers Law School in Camden, New Jersey, have had a faculty exchange programme now for over 30 years.

2 See, e.g., Vicki C. Jackson, 'Methodological Challenges in Comparative Constitutional Law', 28 *Penn. St. Int'l L. Rev.* 319 (2010). Ran Hirschl criticized comparative constitutional law scholarship because it is 'under-theorized and lacks a coherent methodology'. Ran Hirschl, 'The Question of Case Selection in Comparative Constitutional Law', 53 *Am. J. Comp. L.* 125, 125 (2005). If that is true for comparative constitutional law it must be an even more accurate description of comparative *subnational* constitutional law. Hirschl continued:

> I begin by identifying four main types of scholarship labeled as comparative in the field of constitutional law and politics: (1) freestanding, single-country studies mistakenly characterized as comparative only by virtue of dealing with any country other than the author's own; (2) comparative reference aimed at self-reflection through analogy, distinction, and contrast; (3) comparative research aimed at generating 'thick' concepts and thinking tools through multi-faceted descriptions; and (4) studies that draw upon controlled comparison and inference-oriented case selection principles in order to assess change, explain dynamics, and make inferences about cause and effect through systematic case selection and analysis of data. While the study of comparative constitutional law by legal academics has contributed significantly to concept formation and the accumulation of knowledge drawing upon the former three categories of comparative analysis, it has, for the most part, fallen short of advancing knowledge through inference-oriented, controlled comparison.

Id. at 125–6.

All of these seem to apply equally to comparative subnational constitutional law.

Together with my Rutgers political science colleague, and then-Director of the Center for State Constitutional Studies, Dr G. Alan Tarr,[3] we initiated a study of 'subnational' constitutions in other countries that are organized on the basis of constitutional federalism. This investigation began with a tentative, nonexhaustive set of questions that could be asked about the constitutions of component units in federal countries as a basis for comparative evaluation:

> First, what is the theoretical function of subnational constitutions? Do they limit residual governmental power, or grant enumerated powers? Are there records of the debates on adoption, amendment, and revision of such constitutions? Is there anything in the national constitution that mandates certain provisions or matters be contained in the state constitutions? What is the role of popular sovereignty or constituent power in the process of adopting, amending, and revising the subnational constitution, and does constituent power (initiative, referendum, approval of borrowing, etc.) come into play in the operation of governmental systems under the subnational constitutions?

> Second, how similar are the subnational constitutions to each other? Is there evidence that provisions in some constitutions have been modeled from others, either within the country or from outside? What have been the processes of evolution of subnational constitutions over the years, both within the subnational polity and, more generally, within each federal system? Are governmental institutions, rights protections, distribution of powers, and other matters different from or similar to those contained in the national constitution? Is there a standard set of matters and issues—a checklist—that should be dealt with in any subnational constitution? Which governmental institutions provide authoritative interpretation of the subnational constitutions? Is there a subnational judiciary that interprets the subnational constitution, and, if so, can such interpretations be reviewed by the national judiciary? Were there important proposals put forward during consideration of subnational constitutions that were not adopted and, if so, were they adopted later?

> Third, what are the politics of subnational constitutional change? Is the constitution frequently amended or revised, as a normal part of the component unit's politics, or are constitutional politics outside the scope of 'normal politics'?

> Fourth, how have the federal system's origins as integrative (leaving subnational constitutional space) or as devolutionary (creating subnational constitutional space) affected such issues as whether the component units' constitutions primarily limit or grant power? Have preexisting subnational constitutions served as models or provided experience for drafting the national constitution or for other, more recently admitted or created component units?[4]

We believed that these and other questions about the subnational constitutions within a federal state would begin to reveal the variety of characteristics of these heretofore low-visibility constitutions.

---

3 G. Alan Tarr, *Understanding State Constitutions* (1998).

4 Robert F. Williams and G. Alan Tarr, 'Subnational Constitutional Space: A View From the States, Provinces, Regions, Länder, and Cantons', in *Federalism, Subnational Constitutions, and Minority Rights* (G. Alan Tarr, Robert F. Williams and Josef Marko, eds, 2004) 3, 13–14.

2 Subnational constitutional space: Top-down

We contend that a careful study of the subnational constitutions of component units[5] must proceed, first, from a top-down (or centre-periphery) view to determine the quantity and quality of 'subnational constitutional space' permitted by the national constitution to the component units.[6] This would involve a determination of *legal* or *de jure* questions concerning the competency of component units to enact their own constitutions. We suggest that this space would be either wider or narrower depending on the range of discretion the national constitution provided for component units to adopt their own constitutions. Alan Tarr has provided a perceptive review of the factors that may contribute to either a wider or narrower subnational constitutional space within a federal country.[7]

Subnational constitutional space might also be accordion-like, expanding and contracting over the years through changes to the text of the national constitution or judicial interpretation of it. For example, in Austria, the national constitution was amended in 1999 *to permit Länder* constitutions to include audit offices which could examine financial management of *Land* governments, after substantial doubt was expressed over whether such institutions exceeded the allotted subnational constitutional space.[8] Countries like the United States and Germany provide a fairly wide space in which component units may exercise competency to adopt their own constitutions (their national constitutions are less 'complete').[9] Countries like Mexico, South Africa and Austria, on the other hand, provide only a relatively narrow range of such subnational constitutional competency (their national constitutions are more 'complete'). India, except for the special case (recent events cast doubt on this) of the Muslim-majority state of Jammu and Kashmir, does not permit any state constitutional space because all of the structural and other

---

5 More than a dozen countries organized on the basis of constitutional federalism utilize subnational constitutions. Robert F. Williams, 'Comparative Subnational Constitutional Law: South Africa's Provincial Constitutional Experiments', 40 *S. Tex. L. Rev.* 625, 630 (1999). There are many good articles on subnational constitutionalism in *Perspectives on Federalism*.

6 Williams and Tarr, *supra* note 4, at 4–5. For a survey of top-down changes in federal countries, see Nathalie Behnke and Arthur Benz, 'The Politics of Constitutional Change Between Reform and Evolution', 39 *Publius: The Journal of Federalism* 213 (Spring 2009). See also Richard Simeon, 'Constitutional Design and Change in Federal Systems: Issues and Questions', 39 *Publius: The Journal of Federalism* 241 (Spring 2009).

7 G. Alan Tarr, *Explaining Sub-national Constitutional Space*, 115 *Penn. St. L. Rev.* 1133 (2011).

8 Peter Bussjäger, 'Constitutional Autonomy Versus Centralizing Powers: The Case of Austria', in Michael Burgess and G. Alan Tarr, *Constitutional Dynamics in Federal Systems: Sub-National Perspectives* 88 (2012).

9 Donald Lutz, 'The United States Constitution as an Incomplete Text', 496 *Annals Am. Acad. Pol. & Soc. Science* 23, 32 (Mar. 1988):

> The Constitution is incomplete because a significant number of questions we can bring to it are not answerable using the one document alone. The general question of what the Founders intended, depending upon the specific topic, almost always takes us beyond the national Constitution for resolution. The prominence of states in 42 separate sections of the Constitution is one reason. Another is that the term 'Founders', given the relationship of the Constitution to the state constitutions, Declaration of Independence, and Articles of Confederation, must include far more than those who attended the Philadelphia convention in 1787.

elements of state competency are contained in the national constitution itself.[10] Canada does not have formal, written provincial constitutions.[11]

Federal countries bracket their subnational constitutional space in different ways. Subnational constitutional space may have both substantive and procedural elements. In other words the national constitution may not only specify the areas in which the component units may exercise their constitution-making competency and discretion, but also mandate the processes by which that discretion is exercised.

In addition, of course, these matters may be dealt with in the national constitution in either a symmetrical or an asymmetrical manner. Some federal countries, by contrast to the United States, treat their component units differently with respect to their substantive and procedural subnational constitutional space. Interestingly, Francesco Palermo contends that asymmetry has been increasing in federal countries.[12] On the other hand, James Gardner and Antoni Abad i Ninet argue, based on Madisonian views, for an effective federalism where the component units can resist federal power, and where asymmetry encourages competition *among* component units rather than *between* the component units in common competition with the federal government.[13]

We suggest that these questions concerning subnational constitutional space are *legal* in nature, and require a method of federal (usually judicial) policing to ensure that the subnational constitutional space is not *exceeded* by the component units, on the one hand, nor is it *invaded* by national authorities, on the other.[14]

3 Subnational constitutional space: Bottom-up

Next, however, we opined that if one were to look at the subnational constitutions themselves in a federal country, this would constitute a bottom-up (or periphery-centre) analysis. From this point of view, the evaluation would not be a *legal* one, but rather an evaluation of the *political, de facto* choices made by each subnational unit as to how and to what extent to utilize its subnational constitutional space or constitution-making competency.[15] From this comparative perspective, in virtually all federal countries, a much wider variety of subnational constitution-making,

---

10 Akhtar Majeed, *Republic of India*, in Constitutional Origins, Structure, and Change in Federal Countries 180, 188 (John Kincaid and G. Alan Tarr eds., 2005); Arshi Khan, *Federalism and Nonterritorial Minorities in India*, in Tarr, Williams and Marko, *supra* note 4, at 199, 201. See also Harihar Bhattacharyya, *Federalism in Asia: India, Pakistan and Malaysia* 28 (2010) ('Although it is the only State in the Indian Federation to have a Constitution of its own, its Constitution is governed by Article 370 of the Indian Constitution, which does not allow it to establish a theocracy').

11 G. Alan Tarr, 'Subnational Constitutions and Minority Rights: A Perspective on Canadian Provincial Constitutionalism', 40 *Rutgers L.J.* 767, 770 (2009). See also *id.*, at 783–4:

> Bill 196, introduced in the Quebec National Assembly in 2007 … acknowledges the identity of Quebecers as a French-speaking nation and affirms that 'it is the prerogative of the Québec nation to express its identity through the adoption of a Québec Constitution.'

On the 'unentrenched constitution of Quebec, see James F. Mchugh, 'The Quebec Constitution', 28 *Que'bec Studies* 3 (1999).

12 Francesco Palermo, 'Asymmetries in Constitutional Law—an Introduction', in *Asymmetries in Constitutional Law: Recent Developments in Federal and Regional Systems* 11, 12–13 (Franchesco Palermo, Carolin Zwilling and Karl Kössler, eds, 2009).

13 James A. Gardner and Antoni Abad i Ninet, 'Sustainable Decentralization: Power, Extraconstitutional Influence, and Subnational Symmetry in the United States and Spain', 59 *Am. J. Comp. L.* 491 (2011).

14 Williams and Tarr, *supra* note 4, at 7.

15 *Id.*, at 11.

or asymmetry, would come into focus. One of our early conclusions, however, was that many component units in federal countries do not fully utilize (a political decision) the subnational constitutional space allotted them as a matter of law under the national constitution.[16] The political explanations of this 'underutilization thesis' present a fertile area of research.[17,18]

Peter Quint noted that, at the time of German reunification, when the five former East German Länder revised their subnational constitutions, this was a very important step:

> Even the most modest of these new state constitutions reflect the lessons of the GDR past and the 1989 revolution, and—with all their similarities to the Basic Law [national constitution]—can still be said to represent a distinctly different, and distinctly eastern constitutional consciousness.[19]

Australia considered the inclusion of a new state, the Northern Territory, with its attendant state constitution-making possibilities.[20] Australian comparative constitutional law expert Cheryl Saunders noted, in 2000, that: 'A revival of interest in state constitutions in Australia would be consistent with developments elsewhere in the world'.[21] Even in the Sudan, at least in the southern portion, state constitutions were adopted earlier in a very important exercise of subnational constitution-making.[22] An important question is whether component units in federal states *should* utilize their allotted subnational constitutional space.[23] Nigeria considered this question

16 *Id.* at 14–15; Gerard Carney, *The Constitutional Systems of the Australian States and Territories* 29 (2006) ('While the States enjoy the capacity to amend their Constitutions by ordinary legislation, to experiment and to innovate, they have largely neglected to do this'); Juan Marcos Gutiérrez González, 'United Mexican States', in 1 *A Global Dialogue on Federalism: Constitutional Origins, Structure and Change in Federal Countries* 209, 215 (John Kincaid and G. Alan Tarr, eds, 2005) ('Although state constitutions [in Mexico] can create institutions and procedures that are not regulated by the federal Constitution, they usually deal with matters of minor importance, such as simple administrative organization and some alternative legal ways of implementing federal regulations'). See Helen Hershkoff and Stephen Loffredo, *State Courts and Constitutional Socio-economic Rights: Exploring the Underutilization Thesis*, 115 *Penn St. L. Rev.* 923, 924 (2011):

> [T]he nascent comparative literature on subnationalism suggests that constitutive units do not always develop the political space that their constitution-making authority affords them. Rather, commentators observe that 'subnational units in federal systems more often underutilize their constitution-making competency than they overutilize it.' Some commentators further argue that because of agency costs, subnational rights may tend to be under-protected or only weakly entrenched in the sense of being subject to easy amendment, reversed by popular referendum, or diluted through legislative backlash.

17 Astrid Lorenz and Werner Reutter, 'Subconstitutionalism in a Multilayered System: A Comparative Analysis of Constitutional Politics in the German *Länder*', 4 *Perspectives on Federalism* E-148 (2012).
18 Bussjäger, *supra* note 8.
19 Peter E. Quint, *In Perfect Union: Constitutional Structures of German Unification* 99 (1997).
20 Cheryl Saunders, 'Australian State Constitutions', 31 *Rutgers L.J.* 999, 999–1000, 1014–18 (2000).
21 *Id.* At 1000. For discussion on Australian state constitutions, see Anne Twomey, 'Australia Subnational Constitutional Law', in *Vol. Sub-Nat'l Const. L.* 1 *International Encyclopaedia of Laws* 13 (Roger Blanpain et al., eds, 2004).
22 Christina Murray and Catherine Maywald, 'Subnational Constitution-Making in Southern Sudan', 37 *Rutgers L.J.* 1203 (2006).
23 On this question in South Africa, see Ralph Lawrence, 'Where There's Political Will There Might Be a Way: Subnational Constitutions and the Birth of Democracy in South Africa', in *Seminar Report: Subnational Constitutional Governance* 87 (Konrad-Adenauer-Stiftung 1999). See also Jonathan L. Marshfield, 'Authorizing Subnational Constitutions in Transitional Federal States: South Africa, Democracy, and the KwaZulu-Natal Constitution', 41 *Vand. J. Transitional L.* 585 (2008). On the national political influence on this question in South Africa, see Williams, *supra* note 5 at 643.

in 1977 and decided not even to permit state constitutions to be adopted there because they might prove too 'divisive'.[24] John Marshfield has provided a detailed consideration to the question of the benefits of permitting subnational constitutions in federal countries, including accommodation of multiple political communities, providing checks and balances to protect liberty and improving the deliberative quality of democracy.[25]

In some countries the increased interest in the importance of subnational constitutions has led to the assertion of 'subnational identity constitutionalism', often at the urging of local political parties, where 'formulas like "nation," "nationality," "historical nationality," "national identity" or "historical community" are used, and many provisions are devoted to the local idioms'.[26] In Spain, for example, there were major adjustments in the 'autonomy statutes' (not referred to as 'constitutions') that govern the regional, autonomous communities.[27] Similar developments have been taking place with Italy's regional statutes (*Statuti regionali*) which, somewhat like those in Spain, are not called 'constitutions', but share a number of the characteristics of subnational constitutions.[28] The Italian Constitutional Court has ruled, as a legal matter, that the regional *statuti* are not 'constitutions' and cannot have the legal effect of constitutions.[29] The Spanish Constitutional Court, in 2010, in a very controversial decision, struck down several provisions, some of which reflected 'subnational identity constitutionalism', of the revised Autonomy Statute of Catalonia.[30] An important controversy, before the fundamental issues now concerning Hong Kong, had already been taking place in China over the question whether the organic statutes for Hong Kong and Macau may properly be referred to as subnational constitutions.[31] The High Court in Hong Kong did, in fact, refer to these as 'constitutions', only to be rebuffed by the Standing Committee of the National People's Congress and forced to clarify its position.[32] So, the developments in Spain, Italy and China raise the question as to what really counts as a *constitution* at the subnational level, as well as the limits of subnational 'constitutional' space.[33]

---

24 Jonathan Marshfield, 'Models of Subnational Constitutionalism', 115 *Penn. St. L. Rev.* 1151 (2011). See also L. Adele Jinadu, 'The Constitutional Situation of the Nigerian States', 12 *Publius: The J. Federalism* 155, 163–4 (Winter 1982).

25 Marshfield, *supra* note 24.

26 Giacomo Delledonne and Giuseppe Martinico, 'Legal Conflicts and Subnational Constitutionalism', 42 *Rutgers L.J.* 881, 881–2 (2011).

27 César Colino, 'Constitutional Change Without Constitutional Reform: Spanish Federalism and the Revision of Catalonia's Statute of Autonomy', 39 *Publius: The Journal of Federalism* 262 (Spring 2009). See also Giuseppe Martinico, 'The New "Estatutos de autonomia" in Spain: A brief overview of the literature', 2 *Perspectives in Federalism* R-1 (Issue No. 1, 2010).

28 Giacomo Delledonne and Giuseppe Martinico, 'Handle with Care! The Regional Charters and Italian Constitutionalism's "Grey Zone"', 5 *European Const. Rev.* 218, 219–22 (2009).

29 *Id.*, at 223. See also Delledonne and Martinico, *supra* note 26, at 894.

30 Delledonne and Martinico, *supra* note 26 at 904. Interestingly, it was *other* Autonomous Communities that challenged the provisions of its fellow component unit's 'constitution'. Gardner and Abad i Ninet *supra* note 13, at 518–20.

31 Han Bing, 'The Basic Laws of HK and Macao SARs Aren't Subnational Constitutions in China', paper delivered at the Workshop on Subnational Constitutions of the World Congress of the International Association of Constitutional Law, Mexico City, 7 December 2010.

32 Wang Zhenjun, 'On the Hierarchy of Constitution and Basic Law in the SAR—from the Perspective of Decision of Hong Kong's "Ng Ka Ling Case"', paper delivered at the Workshop, *supra* note 31. See generally *One Country, Two Systems, Three Legal Orders—Perspectives of Evolution: Essays on Macau's Autonomy After The Resumption of Sovereignty By China* (Jorge Oliveira and Paulo Cardinal, eds, 2009). Of course, the German national 'constitution', the Basic Law, has intentionally never been referred to as a 'constitution'.

33 See generally Cheryl Saunders, 'The Constitutional Credentials of State Constitutions', 42 *Rutgers L.J.* 853 (2011).

4 Policing the boundaries of subnational constitutional space

In Austria the national Constitutional Court struck down a provision in the constitution of one of the *Länder*,Vorarlberg, because the subnational constitution purported to authorize a form of direct democracy that would require the Land parliament to enact a statute that it otherwise refused to enact.[34] This ruling, purportedly based on the requirements of the 'Homogeneity Principle' of the Austrian Constitution,[35] was not based on any explicit limit, relied on a judge-made, implied federal constitutional *limit* on subnational constitutions, and was the subject of substantial academic criticism.[36]

There was a similar decision in South Africa, where the South African Constitutional Court rendered a grudging interpretation of the already extremely narrow subnational constitutional space granted to the provinces in the South African Constitution.[37] Despite the fact that the national constitution permitted the provinces to enact constitutions that varied the 'default' or 'complete' provisions in the national constitution for the structure of their legislative and executive branches, the Court struck down a provision in the proposed Western Cape Provincial Constitution that adopted a different electoral system for the provincial legislature. This decision, like the one in Austria, lead to significant academic criticism as being too conservative or narrow a federal judicial view of the constitutional space accorded the component units.[38]

To give a comparative, American example of these issues, one might refer to the fairly grudging, narrow interpretation of the power of states to ratify proposed federal constitutional amendments under Article V of the United States Constitution. The United States Supreme Court, even in the absence of any explicit limits on state legislatures contained in Article V of the US Constitution, struck down a variety of procedural steps that states inserted in their constitutions before state legislatures may vote to ratify proposed federal constitutional amendments.[39] Of course, the case of *Bush v. Gore*[40] comes to mind as an example of an implied limit on state election mechanisms in presidential elections, partly based on the fact that the Florida Supreme Court relied not only on state statutes (from the legislature) but also alluded to the Florida Constitution.[41] These could be seen as American examples of the top-down judicial 'overenforcement thesis'. Of course, also in the United States, it is common for provisions in state constitutions to be struck down because they have more clearly 'exceeded their subnational constitutional space', or in American constitutional terms, because they violate federal law.[42]

---

34 Anna Gamper, 'Homogeneity and Democracy in Austrian Federalism: The Constitutional Court's Ruling on Direct Democracy in Vorarlberg', 33 *Publius: The Journal of Federalism* 45 (Winter 2003).

35 *Id.*, at 46–52.

36 *Id.* at 52–57; Bussjäger, *supra* note 8.

37 Ex Parte Speaker of the Western Cape Provincial Legislature: In re Certification of the Constitution of the Western Cape, 1997 (9) BCLR 1167 (CC) 1997 (4) SA 795 (CC).

38 Dirk Brand, 'The Western Cape Provincial Constitution', 31 *Rutgers L.J.* 961, 966–7 (2000). *See also* Williams, *supra* note 5, at 654–9; Rassie Malherbe and Dirk Brand, 'South Africa Sub-national Constitutional Law', in *Vol. Sub-Nat'l Const. L.* 1 *International Encyclopaedia of Laws* 98–100 (Roger Blanpain et al., eds, 2001).

39 Hawke v. Smith, 253 US 221 (1920); Leser v. Garnett, 258 US 130 (1922). Several more recent federal court decisions concerned the defeat of the federal Equal Rights Amendment in Florida and Illinois. See Trombetta v. Florida, 353 F. Supp. 575 (M.D. Fla. 1973); Dyer v. Blair, 390 F. Supp. 1291 (N.D. Ill. 1975).

40 531 US 98 (2000).

41 See James A. Gardner, 'The Regulatory Role of State Constitutional Structural Constraints in Presidential Elections', 29 *Fla. St. U.L. Rev.* 625 (2001); Robert A. Schapiro, *Conceptions and Misconceptions of State Constitutional Law in Bush v. Gore*, 29 *Fla. St. U.L. Rev.* 661 (2001).

42 See, e.g., Romer v. Evans, 517 US 620 (1996); Reitman v. Mulkey, 387 US 369 (1967); Hunter v. Underwood, 471 US 222 (1985); Honda Motor Co. v. Oberg, 512 US 415 (1994); Rice v. Cayetano, 528 US 495 (2000).

Brazil presents an example of an extreme overenforcement of the top-down states' subnational constitutional space. Despite the 1989 process of state constitutional replacement, the Supreme Court has been extremely aggressive in striking down even the slightest deviation from the federal model.[43] The Court bases its rulings on Article 25 of the national constitution: 'The states are organized and governed by the Constitutions and laws they may adopt, in accordance with the principles of this Constitution.

Paragraph 1. All powers that this Constitution does not prohibit the states from exercising shall be conferred on them.'

Cases such as those described in Italy, Spain, Austria, South Africa, China and Brazil, as well as those in Mexico and the United States,[44] may begin to form the basis for a top-down, federal judicial 'overenforcement thesis', where national judicial review results in an unnecessarily narrow and grudging view of subnational constitutional space. This may be particularly true with respect to 'subnational identity constitutionalism',[45] where largely symbolic provisions are struck down. Interestingly, in an important book Yonathan Fessha argues that such expressions of subnational constitutional identity are very important to a healthy and effective federal system.[46]

Despite national constitutional authorization, albeit narrow, only two of South Africa's nine provinces have engaged in subnational constitution-making. The only province other than the Western Cape to do so, KwaZulu-Natal, submitted a provincial constitution that was struck down by the Constitutional Court because it *far exceeded* the allocated subnational constitutional space.[47] Interestingly, however, in the course of these decisions by the South African Constitutional Court it expressed the view that it would be proper for a province to include a bill of rights, even providing rights beyond (but not in conflict with) the national constitution, in its

---

43 Virgílio Alfonso Da Silva, *The Constitution of Brazil: A Contextual Analysis* 206–09 (2019); Cláudio Gonsalves Conto and Gabriel Luan Absher-Bellon, 'Imitation or coercion? State Constitutions and federative centralization in Brazil', 52 *Brazilian J. Pub. Admn.* 321 (2018); Breno Baia Magalhaes, 'Subnational Constitutionalism and Constitutional Change in Brazil: The Impact of Federalism in Constitutional Stability', in Richard Albert, Calos Bernal and Juliano Zaiden (eds), *Constitutional Change and Transformation in Latin America* 269 (2019).

44 See *supra* text accompanying n. 34–43. For Mexican examples, see Hector Fix-Fierro, 'Judicial Reform and the Supreme Court of Mexico: The Trajectory of Three Years', 6 *U.S.-Mex. L.J.* 1, 10–12 (1998).

45 Delledonne and Martinico, *supra* note 26. Antoni Abad I Ninet and James A. Gardner investigate this possibility in 'Distinctive identity claims in federal systems: Judicial policing of subnational variance', 14 *I-CON* 378 (2016).

46 Yonathan Fessha, *Ethnic Diversity and Federalism: Constitution Making in South Africa and Ethiopia* (2010):

> The book contends that a multi-ethnic state must somehow recognize the ethnic plurality that characterizes its society. It presents recognition of ethnic diversity as an important institutional principle of a state that seeks to respond to the challenges of ethnic diversity. It advances this argument based on two points. First, an empirical examination of the experiences of multi-ethnic states suggest that states that are predicated on suppressing ethnic diversity have not succeeded in achieving their goal of creating a common national identity. In fact, the empirical evidence suggests that most of these countries are plagued by ethnic-based conflicts. Second, a state cannot remain neutral in so far as ethnic relationships are concerned, although this, admittedly, is the best strategy to build a state that does not create a hierarchical relationship among the different ethnic groups. The upshot of this argument is that the state has no choice but to recognize its multi-ethnic character.

47 Certification of the Constitution of the Province of KwaZulu-Natal, 1996 (Case CCT 15/96, September 6, 1996); Williams, *supra* note 5, at 648–54; Marshfield, *supra* note 23, at 613–20.

provincial constitution.[48] This is not explicitly authorized. So, just as there may be implied *limits* on subnational constitutional space, as illustrated by the Austrian, American and earlier South African examples, there may also be implied *competence* beyond the space explicitly created in the national constitution. To what extent is this true in other federal systems?[49]

One additional point, noted earlier, about federal judicial policing of the legal contours of subnational constitutional space should be made: *process* as well as substance may be involved. Therefore, in South Africa the national constitution permits provincial (subnational) constitutions to be made only by the provincial parliament, with a two-thirds majority vote of the elected members. When the Province of KwaZulu-Natal purported to adopt a constitution that permitted further constitutional provisions to be adopted at a later point in time, *by statute*, the Constitutional Court noted this as one of the grounds for refusing to certify the provincial constitution.[50]

As noted, it is not only possible for subnational constitutions to *exceed* their allotted space, but the opposite is also true. The national authorities may *intrude* into protected subnational constitutional space and the legal policing mechanisms must operate here as well. In the words of the Ronald Watts, a leading scholar of federalism:

> Federations have varied enormously in the range of powers assigned to each order of government, but common to them all is the *constitutional* guarantee to the subnational governments of noncentralization, i.e., autonomy, in at least some fields of jurisdiction.[51]

Another South African example provides an important lesson. The very narrow subnational constitutional space allocated to the provinces in the South African Constitution still permits ('guarantees') them to vary the legislative or executive 'structures' provided in the national constitution. The Western Cape province's constitution specified that the provincial legislature would be composed of 42 members, but the national election authorities, purporting to rely on their federal authority, determined that the Western Cape Provincial Parliament should have 39 seats. When this dispute could not be resolved, the Constitutional Court had to step in and *protect* the Western Cape's utilization of its narrow, albeit legitimate, subnational constitution-making space.[52] An interesting inquiry would be to evaluate the extent that judicial or other *protection* of subnational constitutional space takes place in other federal systems and the types of argument that are made.

Dr John Dinan conducted an important comparative study of subnational constitutions in federal countries.[53] His study was aimed particularly at the extent to which subnational constitutional structures differ (political decisions about the use of subnational constitutional space)

48 Williams, *supra* note 5, at 650–1. The Court also ruled that several other, less important, matters could be included in provincial constitutions even though not specifically authorized. In Italy, by contrast, the Constitutional Court ruled that the regional charters could not contain enforceable rights guarantees. Stopping short of declaring such provisions unconstitutional, the Court 'rescued', or kept them 'alive' by creating a middle ground of 'cultural statements'. Delledonne and Martinico, *supra* note 28, at 222–4.
49 In Mexico, the Constitution of the state of Oaxaca provided protection for indigenous peoples before the federal Constitution. González, *supra* note 16 at 214.
50 Williams supra note 5 at 657.
51 Ronald L. Watts, 'Foreword: States, Provinces, Länder, and Cantons: International Variety Among Subnational Constitutions', 31 *Rutgers L.J.* 941, 949 (2000).
52 Premier of the Province of the Western Cape v. the Electoral Commission, 1999 (11) BCLR 1209 (CC) (S. Afr.).
53 John Dinan, 'Patterns of Subnational Constitutionalism in Federal Countries', 39 *Rutgers L.J.* 837 (2008).

from those of the national constitution of the country. Dinan found that federal countries did not show variance between national and subnational constitutions with respect to presidentialism or parliamentarism. On this vertical issue, subnational constitutions almost always mirror the national constitution. He continued:

> However, in three other areas, subnational constitution-makers have departed from their national counterparts in important and patterned ways that suggest distinctive traits of subnational constitutionalism. Although all but a few federations have bicameral national legislatures, unicameralism is increasingly the norm in subnational constitutions. Subnational constitutions are invariably easier to amend than their national counterparts. Subnational constitutions also generally provide more opportunities for direct democracy.[54]

The ease of change is true for subnational constitutions in other countries that utilize constitutions within their federal constitution.[55]

5 Subnational rights guarantees

Another comparative approach, of course, would be to see horizontally how the subnational constitutions within a country compare to each other, or to evaluate how subnational constitutions within one federal country compare to those in another federal country or countries. Comparative subnational constitutional law research obviously could be expanded to cover many other questions such as whether subnational constitutions provide, or are interpreted to provide, rights guarantees beyond national minimum standards. Céline Fercot has provided an interesting introduction to such analysis, comparing Germany, Switzerland and the United States.[56]

This area of subnational constitutional rights protection beyond the national minimum constitutional guarantees is potentially very important.[57] As noted earlier, the South African Constitutional Court has ruled that provincial constitutions there may contain rights guarantees beyond those in the national constitution. There is at least one example of a judicial ruling in Germany, by a *Land* constitutional court, interpreting language in the *Land* constitution to be more protective than similar language in the national Basic Law as interpreted by the Constitutional Court.[58] This is an important area for both subnational constitutional textual innovation and evolution as well as judicial interpretation.[59] As John Kincaid observed:

> The new judicial federalism, however, suggests a model that would enable rights advocates to continue pressing for vigorous national and even international rights

54 *Id.*, at 841.
55 Jonathan L. Marshfield, 'Dimensions of Constitutional Change', 43 *Rutgers L.J.* 593, 598 (2013); Tom Ginsburg and Eric A. Posner, 'Subconstitutionalism', 62 *Stan. L. Rev.* 1583, 1600, 1618–19 (2010). See Werner Reutter and Astrid Lorenz, 'Explaining the Frequency of Constitutional Change in the German *Länder*: Institutional and Party Factors', 46 *Publius: The Journal of Federalism* 103 (2016).
56 Céline Fercot, 'Diversity of Constitutional Rights in Federal Systems: A Comparative Analysis of German, American and Swiss Law', 4 *European Const. L. Rev.* 302 (2008).
57 Williams and Tarr, *supra* note 4, at 15–16. This is, of course, one of the primary features of state constitutional law in the United States.
58 Jörn Ipsen, 'Relations Between Subnational and Local Governments Structured by Subnational Constitutions', in *Seminar Report*, *supra* note 23, at 59, 64.
59 In Germany, the 1946 constitution of the Land Hesse outlawed lockouts even though the Basic Law did not. Delledonne and Martinico, *supra* note 26, at 882.

protections, while also embedding in regional constitutions and local charters rights that cannot be embedded in the national constitution, effectively enforced by the national government, or enforced only at minimal levels. Such an arrangement would produce peaks and valleys of rights protection within a nation, but this rugged rights terrain is surely preferable to a flat land of minimal or ineffectual national rights protection. The peak jurisdictions can function, under democratic conditions, as rights leaders for a leveling-up process. In an emerging democracy culturally hostile to women's rights, for example, such an arrangement could embolden at least one subnational jurisdiction to institutionalize women's rights, thus establishing a rights peak visible to the entire society without plunging the nation into civil war or back into reactionary authoritarianism.[60]

6 Subnational constitutions as instruments of policymaking

Another interesting area of inquiry might evaluate the extent to which subnational constitutions are utilized, as in the United States, as tools or instruments of policymaking to supplement, or supplant, ordinary lawmaking.[61] For example, after Mexico's Supreme Court upheld Mexico City's statute legalizing first-trimester abortion, many of the state constitutions in Mexico are being amended to ban abortion altogether. As one journalist observed:

> But three months after the Supreme Court upheld Mexico City's law, the state of Morelos amended its own constitution to decree that life begins at conception, granting embryos the same rights and protections as the mothers who carry them. Within a year, 14 more of Mexico's 31 states had passed similar amendments. (Three more are expected to join them soon.) Some of the amendments even outlaw the IUD, a popular birth control method.[62]

By contrast, in Argentina the constitution of Buenos Aires (a capital autonomous region) was amended to protect same-sex marriage. Of course, many American states amended their constitutions to ban same-sex marriage, including California's Proposition 8 which overturned the California Supreme Court's decision that a ban on same-sex marriage violated the California Constitution's equality provision.[63] John Dinan analysed this use of state constitutional amendments to attain policies that cannot be achieved at the federal level.[64] To what extent have such processes been taking place in other federal countries?

---

60 John Kincaid, 'Foreword: The New Federalism Context of The New Judicial Federalism', 26 *Rutgers L.J.* 913, 946–7 (1995).

61 Robert F. Williams, *The Law of American State Constitutions* 21–5 (2009).

62 Mary Cuddehe, 'Mexico's Abortion Wars', *The Atlantic*, 29 October 2009. See also Ken Ellingwood, 'Antiabortion Forces are Sweeping Mexico', *Phil. Inquirer*, 10 January 2010, p. A24.

63 See, e.g., Vikram David Amar, 'California Constitutional Conundrums—State Constitutional Quirks Exposed by the Same-Sex Marriage Experience', 40 *Rutgers L.J.* 741 (2009).

64 John Dinan, 'Subnational Constitutional Amendment Processes and the Safeguards of Federalism: The U.S. in Comparative Context', 115 *Penn. St. L. Rev.* 1007 (2011).

Comparative subnational constitutional research is now covering both theoretical aspects[65] as well as practical lessons from subnational constitutions in one country to another.[66] It still seems clear, however, that the 'Renaissance' of comparative constitutional law[67] has not included much of a focus on subnational constitutions. Subnational constitutional law, however, is here to stay despite globalization[68] and scepticism about its ability to foster genuine 'subnational constitutionalism'.[69] This new book demonstrates that this is clearly the case.

65 Ginsberg and Posner, *supra* note 55 Marshfield, *supra* note 24; Tarr, *supra* note 7; James A. Gardner, 'In Search of Sub-National Constitutionalism', 4 *European Const. Rev.* 325 (2008); Robert A. Schapiro, 'Foreword: In the Twilight of The Nation-State: Subnational Constitutions in the New World Order', 39 *Rutgers L.J.* 801 (2008).

66 Anne Twomey, 'Dangerous Democracy: Citizens' Initiated Referenda in California', 21 *Public L. Rev.* 70 (2010) (reviewing direct democracy in California for Australian audience). Alan Tarr's important book, *Understanding State Constitutions* had now been translated into Spanish by Daniel A. Barceló Rojas: *Comprendiendo Las Constituciones Estatales* (2009). *See also* Vicki Jackson, 'Constitutional Dialogue and Human Dignity: States and Transnational Constitutional Discourse', 65 *Mont. L. Rev.* 15 (2004).

67 A.E. Dick Howard, 'A Traveler from an Antique Land: The Modern Renaissance of Comparative Constitutionalism', 50 *Va. J. Int'l L.* 3 (2009).

68 Schapiro, *supra* note 65, at 804, 834–5:

Nation-states are losing their monopoly on international influence, but some need for a framework continues. States and state constitutions are well positioned to fill that gap. States can provide a mediating structure to allow a variety of subnational bodies to participate in governance with less danger of conflict and confusion. States and state constitutions also offer a mechanism to provide political legitimacy within a post-Westphalian regime. As compared with the national political system, the state governmental process provides a means to incorporate international law that is more accountable to the electorate and more likely to ensure the appropriate adaptation of global norms within the domestic system. In this way, states can make the globalizing process more democratic and more authentic.

★ ★ ★ ★

Globalization has led to a proliferation of intersecting legal institutions, thus heightening the need for conceptions of legitimacy and for coordinating structures.

States and state constitutions have a central role in this project of legitimation and coordination. States always have existed in a liminal space, mediating between the national government and the localities. Moreover, states long have functioned as non-Westphalian sovereigns. They are not nation-states, but polities that act within a complex web of legal institutions. Their legitimacy comes not from their identification with the 'people' of the state, but through adhering to certain transparent processes and providing numerous means of democratic accountability. States are well suited to provide key nodes of power in the new world order, and an understanding of their role will be critical to responding to the challenges that globalization poses.

69 Gardner, *supra* note 65. Gardner notes that in countries other than the United States factors such as much easier access to constitutional change at the national level, as well as the advent of supranational institutions for rights protection, may actually result in declining importance for subnational constitutions.

1

SUBNATIONAL CONSTITUTIONALISM

Defining subnational constitutions and self-constituent capacity

Patricia Popelier, Nicholas Aroney and Giacomo Delledonne

We are witnessing a trend towards decentralization, leading to a rise of multi-tiered systems that, characterized by devolution, fragmentation and multinationalism, differ substantially from traditional federal systems. This new category of (quasi-) federal systems puts a spotlight on the phenomenon of subnational constitutions. Subnational constitutions, considered as a matter of course in traditional federal theory (and there conceived not as 'subnational' but rather as constituent 'state' constitutions), have become a bone of contention in contemporary, devolutionary federalism, as a symbol of self-rule for one group, and as a prelude to secession for the other. As the foundational expression of subnational autonomy, subnational constitutions put their finger on the tension between state unity and subnational claims for autonomy. The extent to which sub-national entities are able to determine the content of their subnational constitutions, and the extent to which those constitutions affirm the capacity of the subnational entity to engage in its own local self-governance, are key indicators of the autonomy enjoyed by subnational entities. As such, they are crucial for the understanding of all multi-tiered systems, whether classified as federal or devolutionary.

Yet, constitutional theory has remained centred on national constitutions. Constitutional theory, with its focus on the legitimation of public power and the protection of individual rights and liberties against abuse of power, is mostly interested in the functioning of the nation-state. Despite the spread of subnational constitutions worldwide, little attention has been given to the development of subnational or state constitutional law, and its interaction with national or federal constitutional law. Yet, this interaction between federal and state constitutions was always present in the literature. Elazar, for example, pointed out that federal constitutions usually focus on frame-of-government issues, leaving state constitutions to concentrate on moral and socioeconomic principles.[1] The idea was most forcefully promoted under the labels of 'multilevel constitutionalism', introduced by Pernice to explain how a supranational European constitution

---

1 Daniel J. Elazar, 'Foreword: The Moral Compass of State Constitutionalism' (1998–99) 30 *Rutgers Law Journal* 849, at 850.

DOI: 10.4324/9781003052111-1

can be conceived next to those of the Member States.[2] Again, the focus was on national constitutions, but the term can be used to capture the dynamics between constitutions at national, subnational and supranational levels. This has resulted in theories of constitutional pluralism, which are mostly concerned with questions of ultimate power and how to resolve conflicts between constitutional norms of connected legal orders.[3] However, within a federalised state, the real issue lies elsewhere, namely: how to address the tensions between subnational claims for autonomy and self-organization without affecting the integrity of the political system as a whole.

The purpose of this volume is to provide an up-to-date handbook on subnational or constituent state constitutions that gives a general understanding of the notion and functions of such constitutions and identifies the particularities and controversies related to subnational or state constitutional law. In this introduction, we attempt to define subnational constitutions and distinguish their functions. In doing so, we highlight the particularities of subnational or state constitutions compared to national or federal constitutions. Based on our current knowledge, we formulate nine expectations or working hypotheses that serve as the main threads throughout the volume. These expectations are tested in the country reports to see whether they are helpful to build a theoretical account of the emergence and functioning of subnational constitutions in federal, quasi-federal or multi-tiered systems (MTS). We will return to these hypotheses in the concluding chapter to establish whether or under what circumstances they are confirmed, and to refine them where possible.

1.1 Definition

In this volume, we define subnational or state constitutions as basic documents for given subnational entities which lay down entrenched basic rules on subnational identity, representative structures, organization of powers, fundamental rights and/or policy principles, and require the approval of the people or representatives of the subnational entity.

To explain this definition, we begin with a very basic and generally accepted working definition: subnational or state constitutions are constitutions adopted by subnational or constituent state entities. In this definition, subnational/state constitutions are distinguished from national/ federal constitutions simply by the constituent body to which they owe their existence. However, as soon as we try to classify subnational constitutional documents under this definition, problems come to the surface related to the three main components of the definition: (i) what are constitutions, (ii) what are subnational or state entities, and (iii) what does it mean for a constitution to be 'adopted' by a subnational or constituent state entity? Dealing with these problems brings us to our more nuanced definition.

---

2 Ingolf Pernice, 'Multilevel Constitutionalism and the Treaty of Amsterdam: European Constitution-Making Revisited?' (1999) 36 *Common Market Law Review* 703 and 'Multilevel Constitutionalism in the European Union' (2002) 27 *European Law Review* 511.

3 See, for example, Matej Avbelj and Jan Komárek (eds), *Constitutional Pluralism in the EU and Beyond* (Hart Publishing 2012); Nico Krisch, *Beyond Constitutionalism. The Pluralist Structure of Postnational Law* (Oxford University Press 2010); Klemen Jaklic, *Constitutional Pluralism in the EU* (Oxford University Press 2014); Armin von Bogdandy, 'Pluralism, Direct Effect, and the Ultimate Say: On the Relationship Between International and Domestic Constitutional Law' (2008) 6 *Int'l J. Const. Law* 397. See also, under different terminology, Leonard F.M. Besselink, 'National Parliaments in the EU's composite constitution: a plea for a shift in paradigm' in Philipp Kiiver (ed.), *National and Regional Parliaments in the European Constitutional Order* (Europa Law Publishing 2006) 117; Mattias Kumm, 'How does European Union Law Fit into the World of Public Law? Costa, Kadi and Three Conceptions of Public Law' in Jürgen Neyer and Antje Wiener (eds) *Political Theory of the European Union* (Oxford University Press 2011) 111.

1.1.1 What do we mean by 'constitutions'?

We cannot escape the existential question of what defines a constitution as such, because sub-national/state constitutions are necessarily integrated into a national/federal constitutional framework, and subnational constituent powers may often be derivative, partial or limited. According to Gardner, constitutions are 'a framework for self-governance consisting of a set of written instructions issued by a sovereign people to their governmental agents'.[4] In his view, subnational constitutions do not result from reasoned deliberation on issues of self-governance or express the fundamental values or unique character of distinct policies, and therefore differ essentially from this traditional definition of constitutions. However, we can debate whether this is true for all subnational or state constitutions. In integrative federations, the constituent states existed as self-governing communities operating independently under their own constitutions prior to the existence of the federation. In devolved federal systems, by contrast, claims for autonomy are typically inspired by an aspiration for self-governance and the expression of the fundamental traits that distinguish a subnational group. Nonetheless, once a federal system is established, even in integrative systems, the subnational or state constitutions are conditioned, at least to some extent, by the structure and principles of the national/federal constitution. In some devolutionary systems the fundamental rules that define the institutions and powers of the sub-national units are enactments of the originally unitary state. At which point, then, is the 'constitutional space'[5] available to subnational entities too insignificant to be recognized as constitutional autonomy?

National/federal constitutions usually consist of four components: the fundamental identifying marks of the state, the organization of public authority, the relations of public bodies with individuals, and the determination of some basic policy principles. As 'identity cards', constitutions describe the basic structure of society and articulate or imply basic values; they identify national symbols; and they define relationships with the global legal space. To organize public authority, they identify the source of all powers, whether this be the people, the nation or God; they establish the main institutions to exercise public authority and they lay down basic rules as to their composition and functioning. Relations with individuals and groups within the society are regulated by rules that define nationality or citizenship, enumerate individual and group rights and, in some cases, the duties of citizens towards the state. Policy principles may include, for instance, basic rules on private and public property, or goals of health policy, environment protection or budgetary discipline. Constitutions of the most diverse political systems—let's say Germany and Saudi Arabia—have these components in common, even though they are very different in material content and in the relative weight they attach to each element. For example, the German Constitution mentions democracy, the social state, federalism and the protection of fundamental rights as basic principles and commits itself to environmental protection and to the European Union integration project,[6] whereas the Saudi Arabian Constitution describes the Kingdom of Saudi Arabia as an essentially Arab Islamic State, sums up the basic values of Saudi society, focused on family, religion and national unity, and obliges the State to 'nourish the aspirations of Arab and Muslim nations in solidarity and harmony and strengthen relations with friendly states'.[7] The first determines the

---

4 James Gardner, 'What is a State Constitution' (1993) 24 *Rutgers L.J.* 1025. See also J.A. Gardner, 'The Failed Discourse of State Constitutionalism' (1992) 90 *Michigan L. Rev.* 761, at 812–18.
5 Michael Burgess and G. Alan Tarr, 'Introduction: Sub-national Constitutionalism and Constitutional Development' in Michael Burgess and G. Alan Tarr (eds), *Constitutional Dynamics in Federal Systems* (Mc Gill-Queen's University Press 2012) 1, at 4.
6 Art. 1, 20, 20a and 23 German Basic Law.
7 Art. 1, Chapter 3 and Art. 25 Saudi Arabian Constitution.

colours of the German flag (black, red and gold),[8] whereas the latter describes the flag in more detail as well as the State's emblem.[9]

By contrast, subnational or state constitutions do not necessarily address all these issues. At most, subnational or state entities have the power to determine all aspects of their constitutional fundamentals, provided they adhere to the basic principles that underpin the national system— for example that they have a republican form of government,[10] or adhere to principles of free trade.[11] More often, subnational constitutional powers (as distinct from constituent state powers) are limited to certain aspects of constitutional ordering. In Belgium, for example, subnational constituent powers are confined to a detailed and conditional list of provisions regarding the composition and functioning of Parliament and the Executive, and the organization of elections, but they do not include the power to draft their own bill of rights. At the extreme, subnational claims to regulate specific aspects are conflictual. This is exemplified by two of the most ambitious attempts to reform regional charters (*Estatutos de Autonomía*) of the Spanish Autonomous Communities. In Spain, the failed Ibarrexte Plan for a new regional charter for the Basque Country, ultimately aiming to establish a 'free association' with Spain, illustrated the instrumental role of subnational constitutionalism against the background of identity politics. Some years later, the attempt of the Catalan government to enact a new, all-encompassing regional *Estatut* and the ensuing reaction of national political parties and the Constitutional Court played a key role in exacerbating conflicts between the government of Spain and Catalonia.

Subnational constitutional powers, then, are relative and gradual, but rarely complete. They always move within the space agreed to pursuant to the federal constitution, or provided for by it. Obviously, neither do national constitutions live in a void. The European Court of Justice, for example, has declared the superiority of European Union law over the national constitutions of the Member States.[12] It is, however, the Member State national constitutions that provide the legal foundation for the outsourcing of powers with the EU and therefore determine in an ultimate sense, the relation between national and international law.[13] This is different for subnational constitutions. This makes it difficult to pin down at which point subnational powers develop from 'embryonic' to 'mature', or from 'mature' to 'full'—or decline in the opposite direction. For these reasons, in this book we distinguish five components of constitution-making: constituent identity, representative structures, organization of powers, fundamental rights and policy principles. Subnational constitutions are distinguished according to whether they cover the entire spectrum of these elements, or only some of them, or some of them to a limited extent.

This leads to a first correction of the working definition that subnational/state constitutions are constitutions adopted by subnational/state entities. Rather, subnational constitutions are documents adopted by *or for* subnational entities that lay down basic rules on subnational identity, representative structures, organization of powers, fundamental rights and/or policy principles. This revised definition leaves room for gradation. Subnational constitutional autonomy is not something that SNEs necessarily have or have not. Instead, it is a matter of degree: SNEs can have limited, moderate or strong constitutional autonomy, depending on which of the five components in the definition fall within their constituent powers, and to what extent this is the case.

8 Art. 22(2) German Basic Law.
9 Art. 3 and 4 Saudi Arabian Constitution.
10 Art. IV, Section 4 of the US Constitution; Art. 28(1) German Basic Law.
11 Sec. 92 Australian Constitution.
12 European Court of Justice, case 11/70, *Internationale Handelsgesellschaft* case.
13 As asserted by the German Constitutional Court, BVerfGE 89, 155 (1993), 33 I.L.M. 395 (1994), *Maastricht* case.

This is a technical, formal definition: it does not determine the content of subnational constitutions but rather indicates their essential elements and range of possibilities.

As such, the definition does not tell us much about the strengths or weaknesses of subnational constitutions. Constitutions are most effective when they offer a constitutional narrative that illuminates a polity's identity, gives effect to its basic values, and enables the polity to develop and thrive. In the US, where states enjoy considerable constitutional autonomy, state constitutional discourse has been called 'impoverished'.[14] Obviously, subnational constitutionalism requires more than formal constituent authority and the trappings of a legal document. It is also in need of an interpretative community that is ready to participate in constitutional conversations. Courts are functionally vital institutions, but even more important is the underlying subnational entity whose identity is affirmed and reflected in the constitution. As Gardner put it: what matters is the attitude of the subnational people toward their constitution, and whether they treat it as constitutive of their society.[15]

At the same time, it is not the strength or weakness of subnational constitutions, or whether they lend themselves to constitutional narratives, that is decisive of whether a subnational document is a 'real' constitution. At the national level as well, constitutions are sometimes weak. For example, in the Netherlands, the constitution has conceded its narrative power to international treaties, and to the European Convention of Human Rights in particular. This results from the fact that courts are denied the power to review statutes against the constitution, but granted the power to review them against self-executing international treaties.[16] The insignificance of the Dutch Constitution in constitutional discourse—to the point that a Commission was established in 2009 to discuss how to update and revive the constitution[17]—has not led to questioning whether it is still a 'real' constitution.

Likewise, our revised definition does not imply that each subnational constitution must serve the same function. In one system it may serve as the expression of self-governance, even if this is within the boundaries of a more global constitutional system. In another system it may serve as a check on the exercise of central power, a potential power that only needs to be put into effect in the case of federal abuse of power.[18] Much depends on the way in which federalism is understood and implemented within a given country, and the constitutional narratives derived from that. In the US, the notion of checks and balances is a dominating justification for federalism, whereas elsewhere, it can be a means of local self-government,[19] a tool for multinational conflict management,[20] a practical device for effective governance considering the large

---

14 Gardner, 'The Failed Discourse of State Constitutionalism' (n 4), at 761–805.

15 Gardner, 'What is a State Constitution' (n 4), at 1032.

16 Art. 120 resp. 94 Dutch Constitution.

17 Barbara Oomen, 'Strengthening Constitutional Identity Where There Is None: The Case of the Netherlands' (2016) *Revue interdisciplinaire d'études juridiques* no. 77, 235.

18 Gardner, 'What is a State Constitution' (n 4), at 1045; 1050; 1053.

19 This is the heart of Jefferson's notion of federalism; see Charles D. Tarlton, 'Symmetry and Asymmetry as Elements of Federalism: A Theoretical Speculation' (1965) 27(4) *The Journal of Politics* 861, at 864.

20 Sujit Choudry and Nathan Hume, 'Federalism, Devolution and Secession: From classical to post-conflict federalism' in Tom Ginsburg and Rosalind Dixon (eds) *Comparative Constitutional Law* (Edward Elgar 2011) 356, at 366. For example, in Ethiopia, where the right to self-determination or the ethnic groups is considered the cornerstone of the federal system, essential to ward off disintegration, see Gedion T. Hessebon and Abduletif K. Idris, 'The Supreme Court of Ethiopia: Federalism's Bystander' in Nicholas Aroney and John Kincaid (eds), *Courts in Federal Countries. Federalists or Unitarists?* (Univ. of Toronto Press 2017) 165, at 167; or Bosnia and Herzegovina as a model of 'ethnic federalism', see Jens Woelk, 'Bosnia-Herzegovina: Trying to Build a Federal State on Paradoxes', in Burgess and Tarr (n 5) 109, at 114.

territorial size of the country,[21] or it can be instituted to secure an efficient system of government administration, prominent in forms of executive federalism.[22] Within each federal country, particular narratives tend to predominate, but not without contest. Whatever the prevailing understandings of federalism, they tend to shape the space for subnational constitutions and the functions they serve.

1.1.2 What do we mean by subnational or constituent state entities?

Defining subnational entities—whether they are called 'states', 'cantons', 'provinces', 'communities', 'regions' or otherwise—implies defining the structure within which they operate. As subnational constitutions are most contentious in multi-tiered systems that fall beyond the traditional definition of federalism, we are interested in the broader category of multi-tiered systems (MTS). This book therefore also covers systems that do not self-define as 'federal', such as Italy, or that are more confederal, such as Bosnia and Herzegovina, where the range of central powers is limited and the constituent entities have veto powers. MTS come into being as dynamic responses to tensions borne out of conflicting claims for autonomy by territorial sub-entities on the one hand and state integrity on the other.[23]

On this view, there is only a difference of gradation between administratively decentralized systems, federal systems and confederal systems. All depends on the centre of gravity: systems that are more concerned with mechanisms that secure national integrity are situated on one end of the scale, whereas systems that are concentrated on securing subnational autonomy rather than mechanisms of cohesion are situated at the other extreme. Actual federal systems are a middle category, balancing subnational autonomy with concerns for national integrity. Although administrative decentralization is an important sub-category of MTS, this book only covers MTS with subnational or state entities that have representative legislative assemblies vested with lawmaking powers. In highly centralized systems, where subnational entities only act as administrative agents of the central authority, subnational or state constitutionalism is not in issue.

Even when confined to subnational entities with lawmaking powers, multi-tiered systems may have different types of territorial entities. In Bosnia-Herzegovina, for example, the federation consists of a republic and a federation, each with their own constitution, and the sub-state federation, in turn, also consists of subnational entities, each with their own constitutions. The country reports will point to this complexity but will focus on what they consider the most important level to understand the functioning of subnational constitutions in the multi-tiered system.

By moving away from traditional federal theory to embrace a broader concept of dynamic federalism, this volume is not in search of a theory that advocates subnational constitutionalism as a normative device. While in the Hamiltonian tradition the classification of forms of state is based upon defining institutional features,[24] we by no means hold that subnational or constituent state autonomy is the defining element of true federations, let alone of MTS at large, or that, in the absence of substantial constitutional autonomy, federations are not yet 'mature'. Instead,

---

21 Burgess and Tarr (n 5), at 13 refer to Argentina, Brazil and the US.

22 Burgess and Tarr (n 5), at 14.

23 See Patricia Popelier, 'Subnational Multilevel Constitutionalism' (2014) 6(2) *Perspectives of Federalism* E1, at E3–5.

24 John Pinder, 'Multinational federations. Introduction' in Michael Burgess and John Pinder (eds), *Multinational Federations* (Routledge 2007) 1, at 2. For arguments against defining subnational constitutionalism as an essential feature of federal systems: Patricia Popelier, 'The need for subnational constitutions in theory and practice' (2012) 4(2) *Perspectives on Federalism* E36, at E43–4.

subnational constitutional autonomy is considered one of several indicators by which subnational autonomy can be measured; along with integrative mechanisms, subnational autonomy is only one component in the balancing exercise that constitutes a federal system.

1.1.3 *What do we mean by the adoption of a constitution?*

If constitutions are frameworks for self-governance issued by a sovereign people, then they are necessarily adopted, revised and amended by the people of the self-governing polity.

One could easily be led to conclude from this that subnational constitutions that require the approval of the central authorities, as is the case in Switzerland,[25] or are negotiated instruments adopted by the central authorities, such as the Statutes of Autonomy of the Autonomous Communities in Spain,[26] should be excluded from the definition. However, this would have the unexpected result that the Statutes of Autonomy adopted by the Italian ordinary regions are subnational constitutions, whereas the statutes of the more autonomous special regions are not, since they are adopted by the national parliament as constitutional law.[27] As a matter of fact, the latter are more entrenched than the former, enjoy formal constitutional status, and cannot be altered without the consent of the affected SNE.[28]

Yet, even national constitutions are often in some way or other 'imposed' by conquering nations, international organizations or political elites.[29] The authority of the constituent power may often be constrained by external agents; the supremacy of EU law over national constitutions is one of the more obvious examples. Perhaps even more importantly, although most national constitutions attribute the constituent power to the sovereign people of the nation, federal constitutions are a different matter.[30] For federations, the question of 'the people' is a complex one. Although the US Constitution, for example, attributes sovereign power to 'We the people', that term is immediately pluralized by the prepositional phrase 'of the United States'.[31] As James Madison acknowledged, the US Constitution derived its binding force from a decision of representatives of the peoples of the several constituent states.[32] In integrative federations, therefore, it is a question not merely of 'We the people', but of 'We the peoples'.[33] From this point of view, the involvement of central authorities in subnational constitution-making can be seen as the counterpart of subnational involvement in central constitution-making. If central and subnational constitutions are interrelated in this way, then central authorities may have an

---

25 Art. 51(2) Swiss Constitution.
26 In this sense Pau Bossacoma Busquets and Marc Sanjaume-Calvet, 'Asymmetry as a Device for Equal Recognition and Reasonable Accommodations of Majority and Minority Nations' in Patricia Popelier and Maja Sahadzic, *Constitutional Asymmetry in Multinational Federalism* (Palgrave MacMillan 2019) 429, at 449.
27 Art. 116(1) Italian Constitution.
28 Francesco Palermo and Alice Valdesalici, 'Irreversibly Different. A Country Study of Constitutional Asymmetry in Italy' in Popelier and Sahadzic (n 26) 287, at 294–5.
29 See most recently on this concept: Richard Albert, Xenophon Contiades and Alkmene Fotiadou (eds), *The Law and Legitimacy of Imposed Constitutions* (Routledge 2018).
30 Olivier Beaud, *Théorie De La Fédération* (Presses Universitaires de France 2009).
31 The Australian Constitution is similar. See Nicholas Aroney, *The Constitution of a Federal Commonwealth: The Making and Meaning of the Australian Constitution* (Cambridge University Press 2009).
32 James Madison, 'The Federalist No. 39' (1788) in Clinton Rossiter (ed.), *The Federalist Papers* (New American Library, 1961).
33 Henry Paul Monaghan, 'We the People[s], Original Understanding, and Constitutional Amendment' (1996) 96(1) *Columbia Law Review* 121; Kalypso Nicolaïdis, 'We, the Peoples of Europe…' (2004) 83(6) *Foreign Affairs* 97; Stephen Tierney, '"We the Peoples": Constituent Power and Constitutionalism in Plurinational States' in Martin Loughlin and Neil Walker (eds), *The Paradox of Constitutionalism* (Oxford University Press 2008) 229.

interest in the content of subnational constitutions to secure the integrity of the system as a whole, just as SNEs have an interest in the content of the central constitution in order to protect their autonomy. The question is, again, *where to draw the line*.

Involvement of the people of the SNEs or their representatives in the adoption, amendment or revision of at least some aspects of the process of subnational constitution-making seems a minimum requirement for the existence of genuine self-constituent capacity. However, within a certain range, subnational constituent powers can range from weak to medium to strong. At the most centralist extreme, there are national constitutions that contain provisions determining how aspects of the subnational entities should be organized, but which require the approval of each SNE concerned, through their legislative assembly or a referendum, before such provisions in the national constitution can be amended. At the other extreme we find subnational documents adopted by each SNE without central involvement. In between lie a variety of mechanisms such as: negotiated bilateral agreements adopted by the national legislature (Spain); approval by the central parliament (Switzerland); consistency-check by a constitutional court (South Africa); or ex post judicial review for consistency with the national constitution (United States).

Self-constituent capacity and subnational constitutions do not make for a one-to-one relationship however. At which point can we consider a document dealing with subnational arrangements a subnational constitution rather than an aspect of the central constitution or derived therefrom? At a minimum, we might require that the putative subnational document— whether it is, in the end, adopted as a central or a subnational act—is identified as a basic statute or fundamental law for a given SNE. This will most likely not be the case if provisions are included in the central constitution: even if SNEs play a role in their amendment, they live under the label of the central constitution. This, however, is different when it comes to bilateral agreements adopted by the central legislature: even when they are ultimately approved by the national parliament, as is the case in Spain, they are often perceived as subnational documents.

Another question is how entrenched the document must be to qualify as a constitution. Systems with a written constitution adopt rigid procedures for amendment or revision of the constitution. There is a great variety of procedural requirements, including special voting thresholds, approval at the national and/or subnational levels, direct referendums, electoral preconditions, temporal requirements, etc.[34] The precise balance between rigidity and flexibility, as well as the particular mechanisms adopted, are country-specific and highly variable. In general, however, subnational constitutions are usually less rigid than their national counterpart.[35] One reason is that there is less distance between principal and agent and, in many cases, more central supervision, and therefore less need for safeguards.[36] Nonetheless, as a basic law, we may at least expect that the adoption and amendment of the subnational constitution will involve relatively more exacting procedures than those which are required for ordinary subnational legislation.[37] After all, it is this added rigidity that contributes to the character of constitutions as superior

---

34 Richard Albert, 'The Structure of Constitutional Amendment Rules' (2014) 49 *Wake Forest L. Rev.* 913, at 949; Xenophon Contiades and Alkmene Fotiadou (eds), *Engineering Constitutional Change: A Comparative Perspective on Europe, Canada and the USA* (Routledge 2013).

35 John Dinan, 'Patterns of Subnational Constitution-Making in Federal Countries' (2008) 39 *Rutgers L. Journal* 837, at 841–7; Tom Ginsburg and Eric A. Posner, 'Subconstitutionalism' (2010) 62 *Stanford L. Rev.* 1583, at 1600.

36 For a more detailed theoretical justification, see Ginsburg and Posner (n 35), at 1586, 1596, 1600.

37 Likewise, Francesco Palermo and Karl Kössler, *Comparative Federalism* (Hart 2017) 129: 'to be considered as such, a (subnational) constitution generally needs to differ from (substantial) ordinary legislation in both form and substance'.

law.[38] Yet, as rigidity is a matter of degree and may descend to a relatively low threshold, an ordinary law may qualify as 'constitutional' if at least some special conditions attach to its amendment or repeal, or by convention or practice they play a fundamental stabilising and defining role within the polity.

Approaching the matter in this way leaves open the question of which level should determine the procedure for amending the subnational constitution. This is not a definitional question, but a question of content. While full subnational constitutional self-determination implies control over the content of the amendment procedure, such power may in practice be extracted from the SNE's powers and transferred to the central constitution.

1.1.4 Conclusion

On the basis of the foregoing we arrive at a revised definition in which subnational or constituent state constitutions are described as *basic documents for given subnational entities which lay down entrenched fundamental rules on one or more of the categories of subnational identity, representative structures and organization of powers, fundamental rights and policy principles, and require the approval of the people or representatives of the subnational entity.*

This definition places subnational/state constitutions on a continuum,[39] with two indicators that measure the strength of subnational constituent power, namely content and procedure.[40] As to content, the power is strong if it comprises all or most of the five aspects of substantive constitution-making contained in the definition, and weak if it only relates to one or two aspects, or when it covers most of the aspects, but only in relation to a limited number of minor issues. As to procedure, the power will be at its strongest in circumstances where SNEs take the initiative and adopt the constitution with little or no involvement of the central authorities, and it will be at its weakest when the central authority or the other SNEs have a veto right over proposed changes, or where changes are dependent upon the central authorities for approval.

This allows us to categorize subnational constitutions in terms of the discretional constitutional space available to SNEs, taking into account their control over content and procedure. The perspective is bottom-up, which means that in Table 1.1 the analysis allows the comparison of subnational constitutions within multi-tiered systems and with asymmetrical arrangements, as well as within the more traditional federations. In asymmetrical systems, for example, particular SNEs may have considerably more or less constitutional autonomy than others.

Table 1.1 Measuring the strength of the power to adopt subnational constitutions

Procedure ↑

SW Strong – Weak	SM Strong – Medium	SS Strong – Strong
MW Medium – Weak	MM Medium – Medium	MS Medium – Strong
WW Weak – Weak	WM Weak – Medium	WS Weak – Strong
		Content ⟶

---

38 Ginsburg and Posner (n 35), at 1586.
39 Burgess and Tarr (n 5), at 6.
40 For a more detailed index to measure subnational constitutional autonomy, see Patricia Popelier, *Dynamic Federalism* (Routledge 2021).

The analysis also needs to distinguish: (1) subnational/state constitutionalism, (2) self-constituent capacity, and (3) subnational/state constitutions:

(1) The fact that there are no written subnational or state constitutions in a particular country does not necessarily mean the absence of subnational *constitutionalism*, i.e. the idea that sub-national governance is legitimized and limited by certain fundamental principles and fundamental rights that are recognized as a matter of convention or practice. Subnational constitutionalism does not require that limits are imposed in a written document adopted by the subnational community: they may be contained in a national constitution, an international treaty, or unwritten principles and conventions.

(2) *Self-constituent capacity* means the power to influence the constitutional arrangements applied to subnational or state governments. Even if they do not have their own subnational constitutions, SNEs may still have self-constituent capacity if they can veto amendments to subnational arrangements within the national constitution.

(3) The capacity of a SNE to adopt a *subnational constitution* is additional to the existence of subnational/state constitutionalism and self-constituent power as such. Such a capacity means that the subnational community has a dominant voice in the creation, revision and amendment of its subnational constitutional arrangements and that these arrangements are acknowledged as belonging to each SNE.

These distinctions mean that even if SNEs have weak subnational constitutions, they may still have strong self-constituent capacity. Canada illustrates the three features of subnational constitutionalism. Firstly, subnational constitutional arrangements in Canada are mostly contained within the national constitution, although supplemented by ordinary subnational legislation and supported by important unwritten conventions. Together, these constitute a form of subnational constitutionalism, legitimizing and limiting provincial governance. Secondly, the Canadian provinces have self-constituent capacity even in relation to the constitutional requirements that are laid down in the national constitution, as several of these provisions can only be amended with the consent of the SNEs concerned.[41] Also, while the provinces have not felt the urge to entrench subnational constitutional arrangements, they arguably have the power to do so.[42] Thirdly and finally, some provincial laws have supra-statutory authority, meaning that other laws can only deviate from them if they expressly indicate the intention to do so.[43] These statutes can therefore be identified as subnational constitutions.

1.2 Structure

In this book, we explore the forms and meaning of subnational/state constitutions in a wide range of multi-tiered systems. Our aim is to explain why such constitutions are a self-evident given in some systems, and a bone of contention in others. Understanding the use, purpose, status and dynamics of subnational or state constitutions provides insight into the federal dynamics of each multi-tiered system considered as a whole. To capture these elements of purpose, use, status and dynamics, we have developed nine hypotheses to guide the authors in the writing of their country reports for this volume. Such a template will allow us to test and, as necessary,

---

41 Art. 41 and 43 Constitution.
42 Gerald Baier, 'Canada: Federal and Sub-national Constitutional Practices' in Burgess and Tarr (n 5) 174, at 186: with the exception of requiring a binding referendum.
43 For example, the Quebec's Charter of Human Rights and Freedoms. See Baier (n 42), at 184–5.

revise and refine the hypotheses, but in a manner which we hope will enable comparative insights to be generated in respect of all and any of the topics discussed.

While we are not able to include all relevant multi-tiered systems in our selection of case studies, we have maintained variety as to geographical scope, type of system and societal characteristics. A first criterion we used to determine the countries to be examined was the scope of subnational powers: we only selected countries where subnational entities have lawmaking powers. Secondly, we excluded systems with only one subnational entity or with overseas or disputed territories. As these systems are very specific, we leave them for follow-up research. Finally, the hypotheses served as a guide to identify the types of systems and societies that were examined. On this basis, we have included more and less centralized systems, displaying either fragmenting or centralizing dynamics, and covering multinational, multicultural, as well as homogeneous countries. Consistently with this plan, the country reports in this book elaborate on each of the following matters in turn:

(1) *Context of the MTS.* This section will explain whether the system operates in a 'coming together' or 'devolving' context, and the extent to which the country as a whole and the component SNEs are homogeneous, multicultural or multinational in nature. Following Alfred Stepan, we take a multinational society to be defined as a country in which significant groups voice important political autonomy claims for territorially related entities based on linguistic, religious, cultural or ethnic identities.[44] This section will also discuss the pre-existence of subnational constitutions or any striving for subnational constitutional autonomy within the country, and it will report on the principal arguments in debates over the use, purpose or status of subnational or state constitutions and subnational constitutionalism, or else explain why this debate is limited, muted or entirely absent. Based on the first three hypotheses, explained below, we expect such debates to be linked with the form or type of multi-tiered system. For example, reluctance towards the granting of subnational constituent autonomy may be related to multinational conflicts within the political system.

(2) *The extent of the subnational constituent autonomy.* This section will discuss the trichotomy discussed above—subnational constitutionalism, self-constituent capacity, and the power to adopt subnational constitutions—in relation to the country under discussion in each chapter. After discussing how the constitutional organization of the SNEs is embedded in the wider constitutional system, the section will assess the power of SNEs to adopt their own constitutions, in terms of both content and procedure, using the 'weak, medium and strong' scheme of analysis set out in Table 1.1 above. These results will then be discussed in terms of the internal debates within the country concerning the desirability of subnational or state constitutions, as reported in Section 1.1. The goal will be to explain why the particular degree of SNE constituent power is acknowledged within the country, and why certain limitations are in place and certain powers are restricted or controlled. In jurisdictions where no subnational constituent powers are granted at all, this debate will be dealt with more extensively. In those jurisdictions where subnational constituent powers are distributed on an asymmetric basis, the reasons for asymmetry will also be discussed and explained as far as possible.

---

44 Alfred Stepan, 'Towards a New Comparative Politics of Federalism, Multinationalism, and Democracy: Beyond Rikerian Federalism' in Edward L. Gibson (ed.), *Federalism and Democracy in Latin America* (Johns Hopkins University Press 2004) 29, at 39.

(3) *Position of the subnational or state constitutions.* In those jurisdictions with full or incomplete subnational or state constitutions, details will be given as to both the form and use of those constitutions. As to form, the question is whether subnational constitutional provisions are concentrated in one document or spread over several documents, and how these instruments relate to other juristic documents and legal principles extant within the jurisdiction. For example, is the subnational or state constitution substantially more entrenched than the ordinary or organic laws adopted by the subnational entity? As to use, a discussion of the purpose and symbolic value of the subnational constitution will tie in with the debate, discussed in the previous sections, concerning the desirability of or dangers posed by a subnational constitution. Next, each country report will assess the visibility of the subnational or state constitution within civil society and consider how it is used by societal and political actors in constitutional debate. Where little or no subnational constitutional autonomy is acknowledged, it is anticipated that country debate will revolve around mostly political claims for subnational constituent autonomy. The discussion of the political use of subnational constitutions will also be situated in the political party landscape of the country. For example, if political parties are regionalized, this may strengthen demands for subnational constituent autonomy.

(4) *Content.* Section 1.4 will offer an overview of the content of the subnational or state constitutions within the country. The section will reveal the matters over which constituent powers are acknowledged and those in which they are not. Where no subnational constituent autonomy is granted and yet drafts or blueprints have been adopted by SNEs as political statements without legal force, these documents will also be discussed. The particular categories into which the content of subnational constitutions will be classified and analysed will be those identified in our definition of subnational constitutions above. These are, firstly, subnational identity, a category which includes questions of nationhood and citizenship; secondly, the representative structures adopted for the SNEs; thirdly, the organization of powers within the SNEs of the country; fourthly, the protection of fundamental rights; and fifthly, the enunciation of policy principles intended to guide the regulation of matters over which the entity has lawmaking powers. Any other important matters addressed within a subnational constitution or claimed for inclusion will be discussed in additional subsections as necessary. This section will also compare the content of particular subnational constitutional arrangements among themselves and with those of the central government. The degree to which subnational arrangements are different from each other and from the central arrangements is relevant to the assessment of the value added by the existence of subnational constitutions. Such differences may support or counter arguments that subnational constitutions are necessary to address the specific needs or preferences of subnational entities.

(5) *Multilevel constitutionalism.* In this section, the link between the subnational constitutional order and the central constitution, as well as with the wider regional and international environment, will be examined. First, it will be established whether constitutions within the country function as communicating vessels between the constitutional orders at a central and subnational level. If, for a specific jurisdiction, subnational constituent power is incomplete, the question arises whether the federal constitution addresses the gap and whether it does so in a uniform way, or whether different arrangements are made for different subnational entities according to their needs. Where overlap is detected—in particular if fundamental rights are protected at both levels—this section will reveal how conflicts involving such matters are resolved. Next, this section will examine whether, and if so how, subnational entities participate in the revision of the central constitution. This will be of

particular importance where subnational constituent power is restricted and subnational constitutional arrangements are regulated at the central level.

At a broader level, provisions in supranational and international treaties will be examined to determine their impact on subnational or state constitutions. For example, if fundamental rights are protected in international treaties, and the dynamics between international and national fundamental rights charters secure continuous improvement in the level of protection, then what is the added value of including fundamental rights in subnational constitutions? And yet, perhaps this may not be the case, and a strong argument for SNE protection may exist. By way of further example, if subnational entities have exclusive power over matters that are regulated by EU directives and regulations, and if EU law has priority over subnational constitutions, do subnational entities have tools to participate in the EU decision-making process and protect the integrity of their constitutions?

(6) *Constitutional review.* The last section will address the reviewability of subnational constitutions within the country. The starting point will be the expectation that constitutional review helps to bring the constitution to life and ensure its application in practice. One question will be whether constitutional review is available to protect or else control the country's subnational constitutions and whether this takes place at the central or the subnational level. This inquiry will also address the question whether observance of procedural requirements for the amendment of the subnational constitution can be reviewed by courts. This will give rise to the general question of whether the subnational constitution itself can be reviewed by the courts to check whether they remain within the limits imposed by the central authorities.

The hypotheses to be tested and, as necessary revised and refined, are as follows.

1.3 Hypotheses

Hypothesis 1. Strong SNE powers to adopt subnational constitutions is mainly a feature of coming-together federations (Section1.1–1.2).

Subnational constitutional autonomy is often regarded to be a natural and essential component of genuine federalism. This is echoed in the case law of courts that are invited to assess state reforms in the light of an enshrined federalism clause in the constitution. For example, the Austrian Constitutional Court has defined the constitutional federalism principle on the basis of three components, including subnational constitutional autonomy.[45] Yet, as this edited volume makes clear, subnational constitutional autonomy is not as self-evident in other federations.

The expectation in federal theory is that 'coming-together' federations acknowledge more subnational constitutional space for SNEs than 'devolving' multi-tiered systems.[46] The reasons are clear: in aggregative federations, the constitutions were pre-existent, while in devolutionary systems, they were part of a negotiated bargain by representatives of merely nascent SNEs. We therefore expect that in coming-together federations, SNEs have strong subnational constituent power, both as to content and procedure.

We expect coming-together federations to display strong subnational constituent power in relation to the content of subnational constitutions because the SNEs already had full

---

45 See Peter Bussjäger, 'Sub-national Constitutions and the Federal Constitution in Austria' in Burgess and Tarr (n 5) 88, at 89.

46 Burgess and Tarr (n 5), at 11; Palermo and Kössler (n 37), at 129.

pre-existent constitutions under which the SNE exercised effective self-governing powers. Also, in such systems, SNEs have mostly residual powers, including constituent powers. In this context, the residual character of the powers is testament to their 'original' rather than 'derivative' status within the federation.[47] One can add to this that the detail or brevity with which powers are defined and regulated also impacts upon the subnational constitutional space. For example, the brevity of the US federal constitution, concentrated mainly on federal arrangements, is said to contribute to the liveliness of subnational constitutionalism in the US.[48] But this can also be turned around, since the fact that the US states already had fully-fledged constitutions may explain why the federal constitution was kept so short. In addition, the 'silence' of the federal constitution as to the content of state powers can have the largely unintended effect of placing the national government at an interpretive advantage over the states because there is no acknowledged core of constitutionally guaranteed state power.[49]

As to the question of procedure, because they were already in place before the central authorities were established, the subnational constitutions in integrative federations will have come into being through procedures internal to the SNEs, with no dependence on a central government that did not yet exist. At most within such federations, there may be power, most probably ex post judicial power, to ensure the consistency of subnational constitutions with central constitutional requirements. Larger control is only likely to be exercised when new entities apply for admission to the federation, in which case the central authorities are in a position to impose minimum standards as to the content of the subnational constitution.[50]

> Hypothesis 2. The power to adopt subnational constitutions in divided multinational states is likely to be weak: incomplete, restricted and submitted to central oversight (Section 1.1–1.2).

This is the counterpart of the first hypothesis, since divided multinational federations are typically falling apart or holding together systems. As these types of systems are usually under fragmenting pressure, this runs counter to the expectations put forward by Ginsburg and Posner, that subnational constitutionalism is stronger in devolving states to compensate for the loss of central state power and restrictions on the exercise of such power.[51] We expect that in these systems, having subnational constitutional powers is desired for their symbolic value (see further, hypothesis 3). Central authorities will be less inclined to give in on this point in negotiations on state reform, and if they do, we expect them to maintain more control over the content and procedures of subnational constitutions. Moreover, multinational systems are prone to constitutional asymmetry,[52] so we expect that some SNEs will have more, and others will have fewer constituent powers.

> Hypothesis 3. The symbolic value and visibility of subnational constitutions is higher in divided multinational states (Section 1.3).

---

47 Nicholas Aroney, 'Formation, Representation and Amendment in Federal Constitutions' (2006) 54(1) *American Journal of Comparative Law* 277.

48 John Dinan, 'State Constitutions and American Political Development' in Burgess and Tarr (n 5) 43, at 44.

49 Koen Lenaerts, 'Constitutionalism and the Many Faces of Federalism' (1990) 38 *American Journal of Comparative Law* 205.

50 Burgess and Tarr (n 5), at 8.

51 Ginsburg and Posner (n 35), at 1601.

52 Maja Sahadzic, *Constitutional Asymmetry in Multi-tiered Multinational Systems* (Doctoral thesis, University of Antwerp 2019) 85–114.

When SNEs have strong constitutional powers, subnational constitutional discourse often remains dispassionate and subnational constitutions go largely unnoticed. What brings the constitution to life is what has been called an 'interpretive community'. This can be built by a constitutional court (hypothesis 9) or even by political elites and their willingness to resort to arguments drawn from the subnational or state constitution in public discussion. However, what it requires in the first place is a people with its own identity reflected in the constitution (hypothesis 4). We can therefore expect that when a group of people are tied by a common regional identity they will be more passionate and insistent about constitutional self-expression than subnational groups in a homogeneous society.

This may be the reason why subnational autonomy is granted so sparingly in divided, fragmenting systems, whereas detailed subnational constitutions in traditional federations with a strong national identity are fading away. There, the integrity and stability of the system is at stake, especially if subnational groups build constitutional narratives about regional identity that potentially alienate them from a sense of national belonging. Also, where secessionist sentiments are brewing below the surface, subnational constitutions, together with subnational parliaments, executives and courts, add to the institutional capacity that facilitates actual secession.[53]

> Hypothesis 4. The subnational constitutional entrenchment of regional identity is the most crucial, and at the same time the most contentious, aspect of constitutional autonomy in divided multinational states (Section 4.1.).

This hypothesis focuses on the type of provisions that are most contested, for example by the central authorities that have to approve the subnational constitution, or by the court that tests its legality. Identity clauses are contentious because they can challenge the integrity of the nation state. Delledonne and Martinico refer to Italy and Spain as examples of countries where subnational constitutions have been used for the purpose of 'claiming sovereignty rather than simple authority, or to challenge in a way the central sovereignty of the super-state'.[54] Considering the potentially destabilizing effect of emergent regional identities as building blocks of a 'nation' within the nation, we expect that identity clauses are more liable to contestation than other provisions.

One example concerns the Statute of Autonomy of Catalonia, adopted in 2006, which referred in its preamble to the definition of Catalonia as 'a nation' by the Catalonian Parliament. The Constitutional Court interpreted this statement, along with other provisions referring to subnational symbols and historical rights, as subject to the national Constitution, thereby reducing their scope.[55] Another example can be found in Italy, where the name given to the Sardinian Commission 'for drafting the new statute on autonomy and sovereignty of the Sardinian people' was deliberately provocative, and the idea of Sardinian sovereignty was rejected by the Constitutional Court in light of the indivisibility of sovereignty vested at the national level.[56] However, an inherent risk in the neutralizing techniques deployed by the constitutional courts in Italy and Spain is that identity-related conflicts may be merely postponed.[57]

---

53 See Lawrence M. Anderson, 'The Institutional Basis of Secessionist Politics: Federalism and Secession in the United States' (2004) 34(2) *Publius: The Journal of Federalism* 1, at 7–10; John McGarry and Brendan O'Leary, 'Federation and managing nations' in Burgess and Pinder (n 24) 180, at 192.

54 Giacomo Delledonne and Giuseppe Martinico, 'Legal Conflict and subnational constitutionalism' (2011) 42 *Rutgers Law Journal* 881, at 885.

55 Spanish Const. Court, sentencia no. 31/2010 of 28 June 2010.

56 See Francesco Palermo, 'Italy: A Federal Country without Federalism?' in Burgess and Tarr (n 5) 237, at 247.

57 Delledonne and Martinico (n 54), at 911.

Not only identity clauses are contested. If fear of destabilization explains the conflictual nature of identity clauses, then other provisions may also have that potential. For example, in Switzerland, a very rare example where the federal parliament refused to give its guarantee to a subnational constitution concerned the canton of Jura, which 'welcomed' any part of the Jurassian territory that had regularly seceded. Although a constitution-consistent reading could be offered, the Federal Assembly refused its approval for fear that this would encourage three neighbouring districts to secede from the canton of Bern.[58] Similar observations may be made about claims for greater autonomy for Scotland, Wales and Northern Ireland in the United Kingdom, particularly through calls for a formal statement declaring that the devolutionary arrangements are a 'permanent part of the United Kingdom's constitutional arrangements',[59] noting that the relevant constitutional documents are in the form of statutes enacted by the British Parliament, but amended as a matter of convention only with the consent of the devolved governments.[60]

> Hypothesis 5. Subnational constitutions organize powers in the same way as the federal constitution, with the exception of the organization of the legislature, direct participation and the revision of the constitution (Section 4.2.).

In the literature it is argued that subnational constitutions diverge little from national constitutions,[61] and where they diverge, this most often concerns the constitutional amendment procedure (which is typically easier), direct participation (of which there is usually more), and the design of the legislature (a tendency towards unicameral instead of bicameral systems).[62] Importantly, these are only tendencies, and there are several important exceptions, such as the fact that most subnational legislatures in the United States and Australia are bicameral.[63] Further differences may in turn result from the fact that subnational constitutions are easier to amend, making them more likely to adopt novel approaches to institutional design or new forms of fundamental rights protection.[64] This is linked with their function as laboratories of constitutional and political change (see further, hypothesis 6).

The similarity between national and subnational constitutions may be explained in homogeneous countries by the fact that political culture and institutional preferences are similar throughout the country.[65] And even when preferences differ, the homogeneity principle may have a coercive influence towards similar government designs.[66] This is particularly true when new territorial units join an already existing coming-together federation and acquire the status of SNEs: in order to do so, they generally have to comply with these homogeneity principles.[67]

---

58 Nicolas Schmitt, 'New Constitutions for All Swiss Cantons: A Contemporary Challenge' in Burgess and Tarr (n 5) 140, at 154–5.

59 Scotland Act s 63A(1).

60 See Nicholas Aroney, 'Devolutionary Federalism within a Westminster-Derived Context' in Aileen McHarg et al (eds), *The Scottish Independence Referendum: Constitutional and Political Implications* (Oxford University Press 2016) 295.

61 See, from a theoretical point of view, also the assumption of Ginsburg and Posner (n 35), at 1597.

62 Dinan (n 35), at 841; Palermo and Kössler (n 37), at 137.

63 Samuel Charles Patterson and Anthony Mughan, *Senates: Bicameralism in the Contemporary World* (Ohio State University Press 1999); Jörg Luther, Paolo Passaglia and Rolando Tarchi (eds), *A World of Second Chambers* (Giuffrè Editore 2006).

64 For the US, see Dinan (n 48), at 49.

65 Gardner, 'What is a State Constitution' (n 4), at 1028.

66 Palermo and Kössler (n 37), at 137.

67 Charles O. Lerche, Jr., 'The Guarantee of a Republican Form of Government and the Admission of New States', (1949) 11 *The Journal of Politics* 579; Eric Biber, 'The Price of Admission: Causes, Effects, and Patterns of Conditions Imposed on States Entering the Union' (2004), 46 *The American Journal of Legal History* 119.

Where differences occur, national constitutions may, over time, follow subnational leads and close the gap. One reason is that in coming-together federations, original federal arrangements may be inspired by pre-existing subnational constitutions and systems of government. This was the case in the US, Canada and Australia.[68]

One question is whether this also holds true for fragmenting, multinational states, where subnational entities may have specific preferences. Also, in asymmetrical arrangements, we may expect particular SNEs with broader subnational constituent powers to make more use of these powers for particular arrangements that reflect their regional identities.[69] Then again, linked with our expectation, articulated in hypothesis 2, that in divided multinational states subnational autonomy is restricted and placed under central supervision, there might not be much opportunity for SNEs to use subnational constitutions to confirm and strengthen regional identities.

> Hypothesis 6. Subnational constitutions serve as laboratories for fundamental rights and/or institutional arrangements (Section 4.3.).

The idea that subnational entities serve as laboratories for innovation is ascribed to Justice Louis Brandeis.[70] New arrangements can be tested on a smaller scale and, if successful, adopted by other SNEs or at the central level. Brandeis did not formulate this metaphor with regard to constitutional arrangements; he was concerned with social and economic experiments only.[71] Still, the fact that subnational constitutions are usually easier to amend makes them more capable of innovative experimentation.[72] As Palermo and Kössler observe, this makes federalism a catalyst rather then a driver of institutional innovation.[73]

Adoption of such innovations by other SNEs presupposes that they have sufficient if not identical constitutive powers, which is not necessarily the case in asymmetrical systems. Adoption at the centre level requires sufficient power and political will to do so. While the necessary constituent power is usually available, the rigidity of central constitutions may make innovation less likely. Nonetheless, intra-federation borrowing is more likely than borrowing from experiences in other countries, as political units within a particular country are more likely to face similar challenges and to operate within a similar political and cultural contexts.

A prominent example of these mechanisms can be found in the US, where state constitutions were used to test institutional arrangements, and accelerated the expansion of the suffrage and the protection of individual rights.[74] In Germany, the unification brought an impetus for the new *Länder* to adopt institutional arrangements of the old *Länder*, and for the old *Länder* to copy constitutional provisions on direct democracy, social rights and policy goals.[75] Subnational constitutions, however, are not by definition more progressive than their federal counterpart. Also in the US, several subnational constitutions have inserted requirements to lift thresholds for the exercise of the right to vote designed to exclude African Americans from the suffrage.[76] In

---

68 Dinan (n 48), at 48.
69 See also Palermo and Kössler (n 37), at 137.
70 *New State Ice Co. V. Liebmann*, 285 U.S. 262, 311 (1932).
71 G. Alan Tarr, 'Laboratories of Democracy? Brandeis, Federalism, and Scientific Management' (2001) 31(1) *Publius: the Journal of Federalism* 37, at 41.
72 Burgess and Tarr (n 5), at 4.
73 Palermo and Kössler (n 37), at 122.
74 Dinan (n 48), at 43–4, 50–3.
75 Arthur B. Gunlicks, '*Land* Constitutions in Germany' (1998) 28(4) *Publius: the Journal of Federalism* 105.
76 Dinan (n 48), at 50.

Switzerland, some of the cantons have been remarkably slower in removing obstacles for women's suffrage.[77]

Again, these phenomena of experimentation and borrowing are less evident in divided multinational states. If subnational constitutions are justified by the need to accommodate specific preferences within a subnational entity that are linked with regional identity claims, diffusion of such arrangements is less likely to occur.[78] Also, the laboratory metaphor disguises the ultimate goal of centralization:[79] if the experiment is successful, the central authority is expected to adopt the policy on a wider scale. This goes counter to the fragmenting dynamics that usually define divided multinational systems. Also, it is questionable whether subnational constitutions serve this function in global or regional multi-layered systems, with enforceable fundamental rights catalogues at a supranational level. The constitutional dialogue between national states and supranational organizations and courts such as the European Court of Human Rights is likely to overshadow intra-federal dynamics.

> Hypothesis 7. The constitutional dimension of policy principles is the strongest where they contribute to subnational identity-building by freezing ideological preferences (Section 4.4.).

Subnational constitutions seem more prone to the articulation of policy principles than federal constitutions.[80] Several factors may explain this. For example, in the US, the fact that state constitutions, unlike the federal constitution, tend to give constitutional status to policy principles is explained by the fact that they are easier to amend and that the Jeffersonian view that constitutions should only last for a generation and then be adapted to new developments, prevails in the subnational constitutional culture.[81] In Austria, the elevation of social, economic and environmental goals to constitutional status has been criticized for its lack of binding effect. Inserting non-enforceable policy programmes was considered a cultural shift away from legal positivism. This shift was implemented in the subnational constitutions first, as they are easier to amend than the federal constitution.[82]

A second relevant factor is the partisan capture of state government for longer periods, which creates favourable conditions for the entrenchment of policy preferences of the parties in the majority. In this respect, the constitutionalization of policy principles allows governments to secure ideological preferences over time. For example, in the US, constitutional amendments have been used to secure conservative policy goals in some states—for example, to protect property rights, limit property taxes, or insert balanced budget requirements—and liberal rights in others—for example, in the field of education or minimum wages.[83] In this way, subnational constitutions are identity cards reflecting the ideological preferences of a community within the larger nation-state.

> Hypothesis 8. Weak subnational constitutional autonomy is compensated through representation (Section 5).

77 Max Frenkel, 'The Communal Basis of Swiss Liberty' (1993) 23(2) *Publius: the Journal of Federalism* 61, at 68.
78 Burgess and Tarr (n 5), at 19.
79 See Tarr (n 71), at 42.
80 For the US, see G Alan Tarr, *Understanding State Constitutions* (Princeton University Press 1998) 20–3.
81 Dinan (n 48), at 45–6; 53–6.
82 Bussjäger (n 45), at 94.
83 Dinan (n 48), at 54–5.

In systems where the power of SNEs to adopt their own constitutions is weak as to content, we expect substantial subnational involvement in the subnational institutional arrangements adopted at the central level. The hypothesis presupposes the ideal of a federal system, in which there is a balancing of subnational autonomy claims with national integrity concerns. In more centralized systems, the 'balance' may be somewhat lopsided, to the detriment of subnational autonomy. The question, then, is under what conditions weak subnational constitutional autonomy and weak representation are likely to be the most common feature. The hypothesis does not imply, in reverse, that a low involvement in central constitution-making is expected from SNEs with strong powers to adopt their own constitution.

> Hypothesis 9. Constitutional review is vital to ensure that subnational state constitutions are practically applied (Section 6).

Courts develop constitutional narratives based on constitutional principles and adapt constitutional provisions to new needs and developments. Judicial interpretation and compliance checks bring constitutions to life. For example, in the US, the vitality of state constitutions is considered to be partly due to the fact that they are interpreted by state courts, which are not bound by the federal court's interpretation of federal fundamental rights, as long as they allow a broader, and not a lesser, degree of fundamental rights protection.[84] The structure of the judicial system is thus of vital importance in federal and multilevel systems: it makes a difference whether the judiciary is organized dualistically into separate federal and state systems, or integrated into a single, continuous hierarchy.[85]

Having subnational constitutions and subnational (constitutional) courts to interpret them does not suffice in itself, however. Where central courts have supervisory powers—for example, where parts of the subnational constitutions are mandatory reproductions of provisions in the central constitution, as is the case in Brazil—subnational courts are more easily placed in the straitjacket of the central constitutional narrative.

1.4 Conclusion

In what follows, we present 18 country reports that follow the template introduced above to allow for comparative analysis. They are spread over five continents, and include a wide set of multi-tiered systems that vary in many ways: some are multinational systems, others are multi-cultural or even homogeneous; some are traditional federations whereas others are more recent, devolving systems; some have fully-fledged subnational constitutions while others only allow for them in embryonic form. The template is designed to enable us to test each hypothesis against the evidence adduced in each country report. In the concluding chapter, we seek to develop more general insights based upon the country reports and the revision of the hypotheses based on those reports.

---

84 Dinan (n 48), at 47.
85 Aroney and Kincaid (n 20).

2

SUBNATIONAL CONSTITUTIONALISM IN ARGENTINA

Provincial autonomy in a uninational federation

Antonio María Hernández

2.1 Context

2.1.1 Argentine federalism

Subnational constitutionalism[1] in Argentina is a very important ingredient of the institutional and political federal system of the country. Juan Bautista Alberdi[2] pointed out that provincial constitutionalism was the richest part of Argentinian Public Law.[3] The Argentinian experience verifies Justice Brandeis's observation that states are the laboratory of federal institutions.[4] The provinces, the Autonomous City of Buenos Aires and the autonomous municipal governments are important and decisive institutions of Argentine subnational constitutionalism,[5] and provincial constitutionalism has influenced federal constitutionalism in several respects.

Argentina has three normative versions of federalism, the original 1853 Constitution, the constitutional reform of 1860 and the constitutional reform of 1994.[6] The basic model was the American Constitution of 1787. The Argentine Federation includes several grand principles inspired by the American example, namely the distribution of powers between the federal government and the provinces, the allotment to the federal government of only those powers that are expressly or implicitly delegated, while the provinces have residual powers, also retaining

---

1 See Alan Tarr, 'Explaining sub-national constitutional space' (2011) 115 *Penn State Law Review* 1133.

2 Considered the father of Argentine public law. Author of *Bases y puntos de partida para la organización política de la República Argentina* (in *Obras completas de Juan Bautista Alberdi*, vol. 3 (La Tribuna Nacional 1886) 371), a book which influenced the 1853 constituents who enacted the National Constitution. See Antonio María Hernández, *Studies in comparative federalism. Argentina, The United States and Mexico* (E-Book, UNC Press 2019) Ch. 2

3 Juan Bautista Alberdi, 'Elementos de derecho público provincial' in *Obras completas de Juan Bautista Alberdi*, vol. 5 (La Tribuna Nacional 1886) 5, at 6–7.

4 Regarding the expression of Justice Brandeis' dissent in New State Ice Co. V. Liebmann, 285, U.S., 262, 311 (1932), see James A. Gardner, 'The States as laboratories Metaphor in State Constitutional Law' (1996) 30 *Valparaiso University Law Review* 475.

5 See Hernández (n 2), at Ch. 2, Part 3, and Antonio María Hernández, *Federalismo y Constitucionalismo Provincial* (Abeledo Perrot 2009).

6 For a deeper analysis, see Antonio María Hernández, 'Argentina Subnational Constitutional Law' in *International Encyclopaedia of Laws*, Constitutional Law, Suppl. 142 (Kluwer Law International 2019) and *Federalismo y Constitucionalismo provincial* (n 5).

DOI: 10.4324/9781003052111-2   20

autonomy in constituent, institutional, political, financial and administrative matters. However, the Argentinian system moved away from that model towards a more centralized federation, under the influence of Alberdi.[7]

The 1860 constitutional reform had special importance because it modified certain articles of the original 1853 text, with the purpose of establishing a greater decentralization of power. It abrogated the articles that established review by Congress of provincial constitutions, the impeachment of provincial governors before the Congress and the competence of the Supreme Court of Justice to resolve internal conflicts between authorities of a province. This Reform affirmed the rights of the provinces, with a focus on greater decentralization, following the thinking of Sarmiento.[8]

Finally, the 1994 constitutional reform[9] had as one of its main objectives the deepening of the decentralization of power, in three aspects: a) strengthening the institutional, political, financial, economic and social aspects of provinces; b) recognizing the principle of municipal autonomy; and (c) granting a new status to the Autonomous City of Buenos Aires.[10] The Reform established four levels of government in the Argentine federation: the federal government, the provincial governments, the Autonomous City of Buenos Aires, and municipal governments, with their respective competences and autonomies.

Argentine federal society is thus composed of the federal government, 23 provinces and the Autonomous City of Buenos Aires, now the seat of the federal capital. The Reform also added regions within the Constitution (Article 124), established as unions of provinces, but only for economic and social development and not as new political entities.[11]

On the distribution of competences, the Reform increased the exclusive powers of the provinces,[12] and it was established that only Congress could declare the federal intervention[13] of provinces or of the Autonomous City of Buenos Aires.[14]

---

7 In Chapters 17 to 24 of his book *Bases y puntos de partida para la organización política de la República Argentina,* 1852, he proposed a centralized federalism.

8 Sarmiento was another great Argentine constitutionalist who was president of the republic (1868–74) and previously had a decisive role in the constitutional reform of 1860. He argued strongly against Alberdi, postulating modifications to correct the centralist aspects of the original text of 1853 and to return to the more decentralized American model of federalism. See Hernández (n 2), at Ch. 2.

9 This was the most legitimate and democratic reform in Argentine constitutional history, the result of a National Constituent Convention of 305 delegates of 19 political blocs, representing the entire spectrum of Argentine politics, after free elections. It was also the most important, because it included 61 norms: 20 new, 24 reformed and 17 transitory provisions. The reform achieved a notable modernization of Argentine public law. See our book *A 25 años de la reforma constitucional de 1994. Legitimidad, ideas fuerza, diseño constitucional, modernización e incumplimientos* (Editorial de la Universidad Nacional de Córdoba 2019).

10 I participated as vice president of the Drafting Committee of the National Constituent Convention. See Hernández, *Federalismo y Constitucionalismo Provincial* (n 5), Hernández (n 2), and Hernández (n 6), Suppl. 139.

11 Although four regions were established (Gran Norte Argentino, Centro, Nuevo Cuyo and Patagonia), this process is practically stopped. The province of Buenos Aires and the Autonomous City of Buenos Aires are not part of any region. See our Seminar: 'Federalismo y Regiones en la Constitución Nacional', co-organised with the Senate of the Nation in 2017 on YouTube.

12 María Celia Castorina de Tarquini, 'El régimen federal y la reforma constitucional' in Dardo Pérez Guilhou and Felipe Seisdedos, *Derecho constitucional de la reforma de 1994* (Depalma 1995) 337, at 351–2 and 353.

13 Art. 6 of the Constitution reads as follows: 'The federal government intervenes in the territory of the provinces to guarantee the republican form of government or repel external invasions'. There have been over 170 interventions, of which two-thirds were decreed by the president of the republic and the others by a law of Congress. The reform established that Congress can approve or revoke any intervention decreed by the president during recess of Congress. Art. 99, Sec. 20, established that if the executive branch decrees an intervention during the recess, then it must simultaneously call for extraordinary sessions to discuss the measure.

14 See Art. 75 Sec. 31.

Throughout the history of Argentina, there has been a profound centralization process, which has produced notable inconsistencies between the formal Constitution and reality.[15] There are two primary ways in which this has occurred. Firstly, Argentina is characterized by an abuse of states of emergency such as federal interventions, states of siege, legislation delegated by the Congress to the president in emergencies and Decrees of Necessity and Urgency (DNU).[16] Secondly, a culture of 'hyperpresidentialism' has developed, through which the powers of the presidency have expanded at the expense of the other branches of government, without adequate political control by the Congress, and without any substantial judicial review by the judiciary. This pathology of the system has undermined not only the operation of republican principles but also federalism as a form of government.

Argentina displays profound problems of inequality, injustice and inequity, which are exacerbated by this centralization of the country and the weakness of the constitutional and political culture.[17] These problems affect the country's subnational constitutionalism, particularly by making the provinces and municipalities politically and economically dependent on the federal government.

Political centralization in Argentina is complemented by economic centralization, as revealed by the fact that nearly 35 per cent of the population is concentrated in less than 1 per cent of the territory surrounding the metropolitan area of Buenos Aires and that nearly 80 per cent of Argentine production originates in a radius that is hardly more than 700km from that area.

Several centralizing features of the Argentinian political system continue today, such as: a) the tax co-participation agreement law, according to Art. 75 Sec. 2 of the National Constitution, has not been enacted—this is fundamental for fiscal federalism and, according to the sixth transitory clause of the Constitution, should have been established by the end of 1996; b) budget laws continue to be issued that do not conform to the mandates of Art. 75 Sec. 8, regarding the federal principles for public spending; c) there is still a notable insufficiency in the progress of regional integration within the country, and in some cases it is halted; d) there is no full autonomy for the Autonomous City of Buenos Aires; e) there are violations of municipal autonomy, especially in fiscal aspects and the exercise of policing power; and f) an inadequate Argentine territorial planning, with its central axis in the overpopulation of the metropolitan area of Buenos Aires, is unchanged.[18] These require urgent solutions.

---

15 See Pedro J. Frías et al., *Derecho Público Provincial* (Depalma 1987), where he analysed the process of defederalization in Argentina.
16 See Antonio María Hernández, *Las emergencias y el orden constitucional* (Instituto de Investigaciones Juridicas de la UNAM 2003). Again, in the Covid crisis, Art. 4 of the DNU N° 457 issued by the president on May 10, 2020, authorizes the Chief of the Cabinet of Ministers to modify up to 100 per cent of the budget items. The official previously had power under Art. 37 of the Financial Administration Law to modify up to 5 per cent of the items. This decision is unconstitutional, advancing over the most important budgetary powers of Congress. This consolidates hyperpresidentialism and government by decree. In the grave economic situation of the country, provincial and municipal governments are increasingly dependent on financial support from the federal government. The arbitrariness of this support explains why the governors, whatever their political alignment, must go along with the presidential policy, See also Antonio María Hernández, 'Federalismo y COVID-19', *Clarín* newspaper (Buenos Aires, 24 April 2020).
17 See Antonio María Hernández, 'The distribution of competences and the tendency toward centralization in the Argentine Federation' in *Decentralizing and Re-centralizing Trends in the Distribution of Powers within Federal Countries*, Institut d'Estudis Autonòmics, 2008 IACFS Conference, Barcelona, September 19/20, (Government of Catalonia 2010) 71 and Antonio María Hernández, Daniel Zovatto and Eduardo Fidanza (eds), *Segunda Encuesta de Cultura Constitucional. Argentina: una sociedad anómica* (Eudeba 2016).
18 See Antonio María Hernández, 'Argentina Federal Report 2017' in *Cuaderno de Federalismo*, Tomo XXXI (Instituto de Federalismo, Academia Nacional de Derecho y Ciencias Sociales de Córdoba 2018).

2.1.2 *Characteristics of Argentine federalism*

The Republic of Argentina is located at the southernmost extreme of South America, and its continental area is 2,791,810 km², with approximately 44 million inhabitants. The country received waves of immigration, mainly from Spain and Italy, at the end of the nineteenth and the beginning of the twentieth centuries. The population is homogeneous, and overwhelmingly shares a common language, religion and culture. There are about 900,000 aboriginal people, located in the northern and in the southern provinces. It is a federal state composed of 24 subnational entities: 23 provinces, the Autonomous City of Buenos Aires, which is the federal capital, and approximately 2,300 local governments.

Argentine federalism may be defined as integrative, asymmetrical, dual and coordinate, and centralized.

2.1.2.1 *Integrative*

'Integrative' federalisms are the result of an aggregation of previously independent states giving rise to the new state. In fact, the 14 original provinces created the federation through the National Constitution of 1853 and the reform of 1860.

2.1.2.2 *Asymmetrical*

In Argentina, there are clear political asymmetries, e.g. in terms of GDP per capita and human development between the provinces of Neuquén, Tierra del Fuego or the Autonomous City of Buenos Aires, and the provinces of Chaco, Formosa or Santiago del Estero, and also in population, between the province of Buenos Aires with its approximately 17 million inhabitants and that of Tierra del Fuego, with about 250,000.

From a constitutional point of view, the Argentine federation was symmetrical until the constitutional reform of 1994, which introduced asymmetry to the system to recognize special status for the newly Autonomous City of Buenos Aires.[19]

2.1.2.3 *Dual and coordinate*

Argentina was initially organized as a form of 'dual' federalism, characterized by a clear division of powers in the original 1853 Constitution between the federal government and the provinces. Cooperative federalism began to take effect in the 1950s, with different interjurisdictional treaties, and was incorporated into the 1994 reform of the federal Constitution and in provincial constitutions produced since 1986, which inserted federal clauses to this effect.

2.1.2.4 *Centralized*

Throughout its history, Argentina has undergone profound centralization processes that have produced a marked discontinuity between the formal Constitution and the reality.[20] This obliges

---

19 For an analysis of asymmetrical federalism, see Peter Pernthaler, 'Asymmetric Federalism as a Comprehensive Framework of Regional Autonomy' in Ann L. Griffiths (ed.), *Handbook of Federal Countries 2002* (McGill-Queens' University Press 2002) 472.

20 See Hernández (n 2), at 66.

a reconsideration of federalism from a realistic or sociological point of view, since its applicability is being put into question.

There are multiple reasons for this, which Frías has summarized as: (a) the advance of the federal government without adequate resistance from the provinces; (b) the development of centralizing aspects within the Constitution itself; and (c) the concentration of social and economic infrastructure in the metropolitan area of Buenos Aires to the detriment of the provinces and the balance of the country.[21] I would add: (d) the coups d'état of 1930, 1943, 1955, 1962, 1966 and 1976, which contravened the Constitution and republican and federal principles, and undermined the autonomy of provinces and municipalities; (e) the number of states of emergency, in different political, economic and social orders, centralizing powers in the federal level of government and, especially in the presidency; and (f) the hyperpresidentialism, which means that the advance of the presidency over the other branches of government is accepted without adequate political control from the Congress, and practically without review from the judiciary. This pathology has affected not only republican principles but also federalism as a form of state and government.[22]

2.1.2.5 With presidential government

Federations can also be distinguished by their form of government, whether presidential or parliamentary. The former has given rise to the denomination of 'executive' federalisms, although great differences can be seen between such different countries as the United States, Argentina, Nigeria and Russia, which have this form of government.[23] As mentioned, in Argentina the original constitutional model was the Philadelphia Constitution of 1787 but, over time, centralization has resulted in hyperpresidentialism.[24] The power of the president can be seen, for example, in the management of public revenues, since more than 80 per cent corresponds to the federal government, showing the degree of dependency of the provincial and municipal governments.[25]

2.2 Autonomy

2.2.1 Scope

The autonomy[26] of each province is acknowledged in the federal Constitution and includes institutional, political, financial and administrative aspects. Its Art. 122 states: 'They determine their local institutions and are self-governed by these. They elect their governors, legislators, and other provincial officers, without the intervention of the federal government.'

21 Frías (n 15), at 389.
22 See Antonio María Hernández, *Fortalezas y debilidades constitucionales. Una lectura crítica en el Bicentenario* (Abeledo Perrot 2012), and *Las emergencias y el orden constitucional* (n 16).
23 See Cheryl Saunders, 'Legislative, Executive and Judicial Institutions: A synthesis' in Katy Le Roy, Cheryl Saunders and John Kincaid (eds), *Legislative, Executive and Judicial Governance in Federal Countries* (Forum of Federations 2006) 344, at 353, where she describes the differences between American presidentialism, subject to constitutional limits, and other cases of 'hyperpresidentialism', as it is called in Argentina, or 'super-presidentialism', in Russia, where it affects the correct functioning of the federations.
24 See Antonio María Hernández, 'Poder Ejecutivo' in Antonio María Hernández (ed.), *Derecho Constitucional*, vol. 2 (La Ley 2012) Ch. 17; *A 25 años de la reforma constitucional de 1994* (n 9); *Constitutional Law in Argentina* (3rd edition, Kluwer Law International 2018).
25 See Hernández (n 9).
26 Discussing the nature of the provinces, we argue that, as well as autonomous, they are sovereign in all residual powers not delegated to the federal government. See my article: 'Soberanía y autonomía provinciales en la doctrina y jurisprudencia de la Corte Suprema de Justicia de la Nación Argentina' (2015) *Cuestiones constitucionales, Revista Mexicana de Derecho Constitucional* no. 31, 247.

Their exercise of constituent power is set forth in Art. 5:

> Each province shall enact its own Constitution under the republican, representative system, in accordance with the principles, statements and guarantees of the federal Constitution; ensuring its administration of justice, municipal regime, and elementary education. Under these conditions, the federal government shall guarantee each province the full exercise of its institutions.

Art. 123 adds: 'Each province enacts its own constitution as stated in Art. 5, ensuring municipal autonomy, and ruling its scope and content in institutional, political, administrative, economic and financial aspects'.

Provincial Constitutions are the Supreme Law of the Provinces. In general, their constitutions are longer and more detailed than the federal Constitution, since they regulate the fundamental rights, the organization of the provincial government, and the competences and regime of local governments.

The provinces enacted their original constitutions, immediately after the enactment of the federal Constitution and, from then on, exercise derived constituent powers when reforming these constitutions. The Federal Supreme Court of Justice is responsible for monitoring the constitutionality of provincial constitutions and must ensure the supremacy of the federal Constitution.

Fourteen provinces already existed when independence from Spain was declared in 1810. They exercised constituent power long before the national Constitution was enacted in 1853. The provinces of Santa Fe in 1819, Tucumán in 1820, Córdoba and Corrientes in 1821, Entre Rios in 1822, Catamarca in 1823, San Juan in 1825, Santiago del Estero in 1830, San Luis in 1832 and Jujuy in 1835 enacted their own provincial constitutions.[27] These, together with interprovincial pacts, were institutional antecedents of the national Constitution of 1853. The provinces considered themselves sovereign and it was they who organized the country as a confederation through the Federal Pact of 1831. In 1852, they signed the San Nicolás Agreement, which gave rise to the federal state in compliance with pre-existing pacts and was the immediate antecedent of the national Constitution of 1853.

2.2.2 *The provincial constitutions—reform and amendment processes*

All the provincial constitutions provide for their own total or partial reform. In general, the method is similar to that used at the federal level, i.e. a pre-constituent stage, in which the respective legislatures declare the need for constitutional reform, and then the Constitutional Assembly itself, directly elected by the people.

The current provincial constitutional reform systems may be synthesized as follows:[28]

(a) Reforms through Constitutional Assemblies, the most generally used system in Argentine subnational constitutional law. The legislature declares the need for total or partial reform of the Constitution, which in general must be approved by a majority of two-thirds of each house in bicameral systems, or of the house when the system is unicameral.[29]

---

27 See Hernández (n 2), at 50.
28 Rodolfo Berardo, 'Poder Constituyente en las Provincias' in Frías et al. (n 15), at 35–53.
29 The province of Mendoza includes a referendum on whether to call an Assembly, and San Juan a referendum on the need for reform.

(b) Several provincial constitutions, with different modalities,[30] admit the possibility that the legislatures themselves reform one or two articles, but '*ad referendum*' of the people. This is known as the *enmienda* (amendment) system. The amendment must be approved by the vote of two-thirds of the legislature.[31]

(c) In the Constitution for the province of Buenos Aires, the law declaring the need of reform must establish whether or not to call a Constitutional Assembly and, if not, the law must contain the amendment which is then submitted to a referendum and, if approved by the people, is included in the Constitution.[32]

Several constitutions require that the law declaring the need for constitutional reform must include the subjects, items or articles proposed to the Assembly to be reformed.[33]

The composition, and the eligibility, incompatibilities, immunities and privileges of the members of the Constitutional Assembly are established by the constitutions or by the law declaring the need for reform, and likewise the venue of the Assembly and the term fixed to complete the reform.

There are formal and material restrictions to the reforming powers of the Assembly arising from the federal Constitution, from national laws and international treaties (Articles 5, 31 and 75, Section 22 of the federal Constitution), the provincial constitutions and the laws declaring the need of the reform.

Table 2.1 shows the year of passing of their first Constitution and number of the constitutional reforms that the entities have had since the 1853 federal Constitution.

Table 2.1 Subnational constitutional reforms in Argentina

Provinces		Year of the first constitution	Total constitutional reforms	Most recent reform to date
1.	Buenos Aires	1854	6	1994
2.	Catamarca	1855	4	1988
3.	Córdoba	1855	8	2001
4.	Corrientes	1855	7	2007
5.	Chaco	1951	2	1994
6.	Chubut	1957	4	1994
7.	Entre Ríos	1860	6	2008
8.	Formosa	1957	2	2003
9.	Jujuy	1855	6	1986
10.	La Pampa	1952	3	1998
11.	La Rioja	1855	8	2008
12.	Mendoza	1854	10	1965
13.	Misiones	1958	1	1964

(Continued)

30 For further detail, see Eduardo Luna, 'Poder Constituyente y Reforma Constitucional en el Derecho Público Provincial' in Dardo Pérez Guilhou et al., *Derecho Público Provincial y Municipal* (La Ley 2003) 535.
31 Except for the Province of Formosa in which its Constitution (Art. 226) establishes a majority of four-fifths of the legislature members.
32 Gabino Adolfo Ziulu, 'Algunas reflexiones acerca del procedimiento de reforma de la Constitución de la Provincia de Buenos Aires' (1991) *Jurisprudencia Argentina* 830.
33 Buenos Aires, Art. 206, s. a; Corrientes, Art. 78; Catamarca, Art. 282; Córdoba, Art. 196; Chaco, Art. 210; Chubut, Art. 266; Entre Ríos, Art. 217; Formosa, Art. 124; Jujuy, Art. 97; La Rioja, Art. 161; Río Negro, Art. 111; Salta, Art. 178; San Luis, Art. 281; Santa Cruz, Art. 154; Santa Fe, Art. 114; Tucumán, Art. 128; Santiago del Estero, Art. 224.

Table 2.1 (Continued)

Provinces		Year of the first constitution	Total constitutional reforms	Most recent reform to date
14.	Neuquén	1957	2	2006
15.	Río Negro	1957	1	1988
16.	Salta	1855	9	2003
17.	San Juan	1856	6	1986
18.	San Luis	1855	7	1987
19.	Santa Cruz	1957	2	1998
20.	Santa Fe	1856	8	1962
21.	Santiago del Estero	1856	11	2002
22.	Tierra del Fuego, Antártida e Islas del Atlántico Sur	1991	0	1991
23.	Tucumán	1856	5	2006

The Autonomous City of Buenos Aires, created under the 1994 constitutional reform, in accordance with Art. 129, enacted its own Constitution in 1996, so far without reforms. Fourteen provinces existed prior to the formation of the nation. In 1951, the new provinces of Chaco and La Pampa were formed, in 1953 Misiones, in 1955 Chubut, Neuquén, Rio Negro, Santa Cruz and Formosa, and in 1990 Tierra del Fuego.

The chart shows a good exercise of constituent powers by the provinces in terms of content and procedure, especially since 1986, after the reinstation of democracy. The result of these reforms was a marked modernization of Argentine subnational constitutional law.

2.3 The position of the provincial constitutions

Provincial constitutions are very important as the Supreme Law of the Provinces, acknowledging the citizens' rights, organizing the powers and establishing the bases of the municipal regime. The provinces exercise reserved or residual powers, in addition to those concurrent with the federal government. Consequently, they cannot exercise powers delegated explicitly or implicitly to the federal government. Their constitutions may also be considered as power-limiting, in accordance with the democratic, republican, federal principles of the national Constitution.

In Argentine Constitutional Law, both at federal and at provincial level, there have been three different stages: 1) liberal or classic constitutionalism, which gave rise to the liberal state and acknowledged first generation (civil and political) human rights; 2) social constitutionalism, which sought a 'welfare' state and acknowledged second generation (social) human rights; and 3) constitutionalism of the internationalization of human rights, which gave constitutional status to certain international human rights treaties, acknowledging third generation human rights.[34]

At federal level, the first stage started in 1853, social constitutionalism was incorporated in the 1949 and 1957 constitutional reforms, and the third stage in the 1994 constitutional reform. The initial provincial constitutions showed liberal characteristics, but later most of them incorporated social constitutionalism. In this, several provincial constitutions were more advanced than federal constitutionalism; for example, the constitutions of Mendoza (1916), San Juan (1927) and Entre Ríos (1933) acknowledged the rights of workers and the vote of women. This

34 See Antonio María Hernández, 'Teoría Constitucional' in Antonio María Hernández (ed.), *Derecho Constitucional*, vol. 1 (La Ley 2012) Ch 1.

change was confirmed with the enactment of the constitutions of the new provinces as from 1957 and the reforms made until 1966. Unfortunately, these principles and rights in most cases are not in effect, because they require a level of political, economic and social development in the provinces and in the republic that does not exist.

In respect of the third stage of constitutionalism, three provincial constitutions, Neuquén (1957), San Juan (1986) and Córdoba (1987), incorporated some international human rights treaties as a supplement.[35]

2.4 Content

2.4.1 Constitutional protection of native peoples

The issue of native peoples has been included with varying depth and scope in provincial constitutions.[36] At federal level, the former Article 67, Section 15, of the Constitution of 1853/1860 ordered Congress 'to provide for the security of borders, to preserve peaceful treatment with Indians and to promote their conversion to Catholicism'. This paternalist formula implied the acknowledgement of the same rights for native peoples as those enjoyed by the rest of the population, except for freedom of worship.[37]

The current federal Constitution, in Article 75, Section 17, includes among the powers of Congress:

> To acknowledge the ethnic and cultural pre-existence of Argentine native peoples; to assure respect for their identity and the right to a bilingual and intercultural education; to acknowledge the legal status of their communities and the possession and title to the lands they have traditionally occupied; and to regulate the granting of other land suitable and adequate for human development; none of them may be sold, transferred or subject to liens or attachments. To assure their participation in the management of their natural resources and other interests affecting them. The provinces may concurrently exercise these powers.

Thus, provinces exercise these powers together with the federal government, and to this effect those provinces recording natives among their inhabitants may issue specific rules regulating these matters. This rule appears as the condensation of principles and rights previously contemplated in provincial constitutional law. Thus, prior to the enactment of Art. 75, Section 17 of the federal Constitution, the pre-existence of these peoples,[38] respect for their identity,[39] the right to a bilingual and intercultural education,[40] title to their lands[41] of a community nature[42] and that these cannot be sold, transferred or attached,[43] the right to granting of other lands,[44] and the

---

35 See Hernández *Federalismo y Constitucionalismo Provincial* (n 5), at Ch. XV.
36 Jujuy (Art. 50), Río Negro (Art. 42), Formosa (Art. 79), Buenos Aires (Art. 36, item 9), Chaco (Art. 37), La Pampa (Art. 6), Neuquén (Art. 23, item d), Chubut (Arts 34 and 95) and Salta (Art. 15).
37 See Paulina Chiacchiera Castro, 'Los derechos indígenas en la Constitución Nacional' (2004) 15 *Foro de Córdoba* no. 89, 33.
38 Constitutions of Río Negro (1988), Salta (1986) and La Pampa (1994).
39 Constitutions of Chubut (1994), Río Negro (1988), Salta (1986), Buenos Aires (1994) and Formosa (1991).
40 Constitutions of Chubut (1994) and Salta (1986).
41 Constitutions of Río Negro (1988) and Salta (1986).
42 Constitutions of Formosa (1991), Chubut (1994) and Buenos Aires (1994).
43 Constitutions of Salta (1986), Formosa (1991) and Chubut (1994).
44 Constitution of Salta (1986).

right to the participation of their communities in the interests that may affect them[45] had already been acknowledged. However, it has been difficult to put such rights into practice, as Chiacchiera Castro stated,[46] as with other articles of the federal and provincial constitutions, due to lack of compliance and the weakness of the culture of legality.

2.4.2 *The international, federal and provincial sources of fundamental rights*[47]

The 1994 reform of the Argentine Constitution granted constitutional status to several international human rights instruments, and these are applicable in the provinces through their subordination to the federal Constitution. These instruments, under Art. 75, Section 22 of the federal Constitution, 'in the full force of their provisions, have constitutional status, do not repeal any Article of the First Part of this Constitution and are to be understood as supplementary to the rights and guarantees recognised herein'. In consequence, in Argentina there are three sources of rights: international, federal and provincial.

The provincial constitutions show a humanist and personalist philosophy in their broad and deep acknowledgement of human rights, affirming that 'all inhabitants' or 'all persons' enjoy these rights, thus preventing any discrimination.[48] Rights and guarantees safeguard civil liberty (conscience, physical integrity, defence in trial, privacy of correspondence and papers, communications, etc.), equality, freedom of speech, work and the exercise of a profession, religious freedom, the right to hold meetings, to request, to associate, to teach and learn, to hold property, among other rights inherent in classic constitutionalism.

As in Art. 33 of the federal Constitution, they also acknowledge non-enumerated rights, with various formulas.[49] This is within the framework of respect for fundamental legal order arising from Arts 5 and 31 of the federal Constitution. There are explicit references to the rights and guarantees of the federal Constitution in provincial constitutions.[50]

The provincial constitutions expressly enshrine the political rights of democracy, republicanism, and the principle of popular sovereignty, in compliance with Art. 5 of the federal Constitution. Rules are incorporated which regulate positive actions to take gender into account, to ensure the admission of women to elective public bodies.[51]

All the provincial constitutions include rules regarding due process, defence in trial, evidence, natural judge and the protection of personal freedom, and the inviolability of domicile,

---

45 Constitutions of Formosa (1991), Salta (1986) and Chubut (1994).

46 See Paulina Chiacchiera Castro, 'Los pueblos indígenas en la jurisprudencia nacional e internacional de derechos humanos' in Silvia B. Caeiro (ed.), *Tratados de Derechos Humanos y su influencia en el derecho argentino* (La Ley 2015) 1371.

47 See Antonio María Hernández, 'Judicial federalism and the protection of fundamental rights in Argentina' (2010) 41 *Rutgers Law Journal* 907.

48 Constitutions of: Córdoba, Art. 18; Jujuy, Art. 16; La Rioja, Art. 19; Salta, Art. 17; San Juan, Art. 15; San Luis, Art. 11; and Santiago del Estero, Art. 17.

49 For example, the Constitution of Córdoba, in Art. 20, provides for those which 'derive from the democratic form of government and from the natural condition of man'; Jujuy, in Art. 17, '…which are related to liberty, dignity and safety of human beings, to the essence of democracy and to the republican system of government'.

50 Córdoba, Art. 18; Jujuy, Art. 16, item 1; La Rioja, Art. 28; Salta, Art. 84; San Juan, Art. 40; San Luis, Art. 11; and Santiago del Estero, Art. 38.

51 Positive actions in relation to gender extend to other situations, such as the labour market. See Alberto Calandrino et al., 'El caso "Freddo" y las conductas patronales como "categorías sospechosas"' (2003) *Revista AADC* no. 192, 112.

communications and private papers. Some of these rules expressly regulate guarantees such as the amparo, habeas corpus and habeas data.

They also acknowledge economic, cultural and social rights for workers, women, children, people with disabilities, elderly people and consumers, clearly responding to social constitutionalism. The richness of provincial constitutionalism is shown in the notable development of rights and guarantees.[52]

However, many of these norms do not in reality have full and sufficient force. I have already remarked on the distance between norm and reality as a mark of the weak culture of the constitution and legality, a principal cause of Argentine underdevelopment, as Nino[53] noted. Argentina has suffered emergencies of every kind, institutional, political, economic, and social, which have severely harmed the rule of law, the republican system and the full force of individual rights and guarantees, as mentioned previously.[54]

2.4.3 *Organization of powers*

All the provinces and the Autonomous City of Buenos Aires established a republican system with legislative, executive, and judicial branches, just as in the federal sphere. They also have a presidential system, with a governor in charge of the executive branch and a legislature in charge of the legislative branch, all directly elected by the people.

2.4.3.1 *The legislature*

Fifteen provinces and the Autonomous City of Buenos Aires have a unicameral system and eight provinces a bicameral system. In general, the smaller and less populous provinces adopted unicameralism, except for the larger province of Córdoba which adopted this system in its 2001 constitutional reform. The other more populated provinces have a bicameral legislature, with a House of Representatives representing the people of the province and the Senate representing the districts.[55]

The legislatures have important powers in connection with the federal system since they must approve the tax sharing law agreement, interprovincial treaties, agreements with the federal government or with the other governmental entities, and in general, the laws of a provincial sphere within the federation.

In relation to the governors, the same problems appear in the provinces as in the federal government, i.e. the functioning of the republican system tends to be inadequate, with the legislative and judicial powers effectively renouncing their control powers over the executive branch.

Legislators are elected directly by the people, but their number and forms of election vary. Most of the provinces and the Autonomous City of Buenos Aires adopt the D'Hondt proportional system; other provinces adopt a mixed or combined system for the election of legislators by department and by a sole list for the whole province. A few provinces have a system of circumscription and uninominal vote.

---

52 See Hernández *Federalismo y Constitucionalismo Provincial* (n 5), at Ch. XV; Antonio María Hernández and Guillermo Barrera Buteler (eds), *Derecho Público Provincial* (2nd edition, Lexis Nexis 2011).

53 See Carlos Santiago Nino, *Un país al margen de la ley* (Emecé 1992).

54 See Hernández, *Fortalezas y debilidades constitucionales* (n 22) and *Las emergencias y el orden constitucional* (n 16).

55 Each province is divided into districts, and senators are generally elected in representation of those districts. In general, they do not coincide with local government areas.

2.4.3.2 *The executive branch*

The governors are the highest provincial officers, exercising the executive branch, like the president at the federal level. In general, the executive branch is considered as a single member body, although the governors may have the cooperation of other important officers. There is no doubt that, due to the hyperpresidential culture in the country, the governors wield the political power in the provinces. All the provinces also have a vice-governor, directly elected with the governor, whom they succeed in the event of acephaly, in addition to presiding over the provincial legislatures.

As I mentioned regarding the legislative branch, the governors also have important powers in connection with federalism, under the provisions of the federal Constitution and the provincial constitutions, but throughout history they have failed to successfully defend provincial autonomies against advances made by the federal government. They have, in general, responded to the political directives of the president and the federal political parties in detriment to provincial interests and powers, because they are economically heavily dependent on the federal executive branch. Together with the president, they hold the true political power in the country.

Governors are elected directly by the people by simple majority, except in the case of the province of Corrientes and the Autonomous City of Buenos Aires, where double voting is required. The term of office is four years. The election is judged by the legislative power, which has the final decision in the event of a tie. There are some provincial constitutions that prohibit the immediate re-election of governors,[56] while the majority allow immediate election for one period,[57] and exceptionally for two periods.[58] Some recently reformed constitutions allow indefinite re-elections,[59] which is a disadvantage for the Argentine republican system since, in almost all these provinces, this has consolidated political hegemonies, evidence of their democratic political sub-development.

2.4.3.3 *The judicial branch*

Each provincial constitution organizes its judicial branch, normally consisting of a provincial High Court of Justice,[60] and lower courts according to the different matters. Article 5 of the federal Constitution obliges the provinces to ensure the administration of justice and the republican regime. But it does not include any specific organization and structure of the judicial branch. Therefore, all the provincial constitutional powers have broad freedom to institute the system that they deem most suitable for this function. The provincial constitutions mention maximum provincial jurisdictional bodies (higher tribunals or courts). Others refer to Courts of Appeal—collegiate lower courts—judges, justices of peace or simply use the formula 'and other courts established by the law'. The judicial branch in Argentina also hears electoral matters, creating the respective electoral tribunals for this purpose. The Public Prosecutor's Office is also organized under the judicial branch.

---

56 Mendoza and Santa Fe.
57 Buenos Aires, Córdoba, Corrientes, Chaco, Chubut, Entre Ríos, Jujuy, La Pampa, La Rioja, Neuquén, Río Negro, San Luis, San Juan, Santiago del Estero, Tierra del Fuego and Tucumán, and the Autonomous City of Buenos Aires.
58 Salta.
59 Catamarca, Formosa and Santa Cruz.
60 Called Tribunales Superiores de Justicia, or Cortes Supremas de Justicia, in some provinces.

The functional independence of the members of the judicial branch depends on the appointment proceedings.[61] The issue involves the effectiveness of the separation and balance of branches as distinctive elements of the republican principle of government. It must be remembered that in the Argentine constitutional system any judge exercises the control of constitutionality. In several Argentine provinces, such as Córdoba, the appointment of judges by the executive branch with the agreement of the legislative branch follows the model of the 1853 federal Constitution, which adopted the US model.[62]Approximately half the provincial Constitutions[63] created a Magistrate Council, consisting of representatives of the lawyers, judges, the legislative branch and the executive branch, with powers to select judges and officers by contest, just as occurs at federal level for the appointment of the lower judges since the 1994 constitutional reform. Among other functions, the Council may propose lists of three candidates binding on the executive branch so that the latter can appoint one, with legislative agreement. It also decides, as appropriate, the opening of disqualification proceedings of judicial magistrates.

2.4.4 *Constitutional policy principles*

As I mentioned previously, each provincial state and the Autonomous City of Buenos Aires forms part of the Argentine federal society. The institutional, political, financial and administrative autonomy of each is acknowledged, according to the provisions of Articles 5, 122, 123 and 129 of the federal Constitution. Argentina's federal, republican and presidential government system is reproduced in the provincial territories, following the guidelines of Article 5 of the federal Constitution. Article 121 of the federal Constitution states that they keep 'all the power not delegated by this Constitution to the Federal Government …', but they must respect the federal supremacy principle of its Article 31 and the basis of Article 5 above.

2.5 **Multilevel constitutionalism**

2.5.1 *The relation between the federal and subnational constitutions*

As mentioned, provincial constitutions in certain cases were ahead of the federal Constitution as regards the incorporation of principles of social constitutionalism and internationalization of human rights. They were also a significant source for the 1994 reform of the federal Constitution. After democracy was reinstated in 1983, the provinces began in 1986 to reform their provincial constitutions, which resulted in marked modernization, such as in the so-called 'federal clauses' regarding the limitation of federal intervention, the ownership of natural resources, the possibility of regionalization, federal tax sharing, etc., with a clear idea of a consensus, modern and in-depth federalism. The great majority of provincial constitutions also implemented municipal autonomy in all its aspects. New institutions were included, such as the Ombudsman, to make possible the effectiveness of citizenship rights and control over the state, and the Magistrate Council, to ensure the independence of the judicial branch. In addition, significant progress was made in acknowledging new rights and guarantees, such as the rights of users and consumers, environment and amparo.

---

61 I refer to judicial independence with respect to the political powers, i.e. to the most usual sense of the term. By political powers of the province, I only refer to the executive and the legislative branches (without ignoring the political function that the judicial branch exercises in certain circumstances, in its capacity as final interpreter of the Constitution). (See Roberto Gargarella, *La justicia frente al gobierno* (Ariel 1996) 231–2).

62 See Alexander Hamilton, *El Federalista*, LXXVI (6th printing, Fondo de Cultura Económica 1998) 322–5.

63 Santa Fe, Art. 86; Tucumán, Art. 99; Entre Ríos, Art. 154; Corrientes, Art. 142.

All this constitutional change notably influenced the federal reform in 1994. This precedence of provincial reforms, and the enactment of municipal constitutions prior to the federal reform, must be noted as an affirmation of federalism, because most of the time the process has been the inverse: a reform at the federal level was followed by constitutional change in the provinces. Thus, after the 1994 reform of the federal Constitution, corresponding provincial constitutional reforms were enacted to update their institutions and their catalogue of rights and guarantees.

2.5.2 *The impact of international and American legal space on subnational constitutionalism in Argentina*

Argentina belongs to the United Nations and the Organization of American States (OAS) and the International and Regional System of Human Rights, under Articles 75, Sections 22 and 24 of the federal Constitution. While the Argentine Supreme Court of Justice is the final and irrevocable interpreter of the federal Constitution, Argentina is subject to the legal provisions of the American Convention on Human Rights (Pact of San José, Costa Rica) under two institutions: the Interamerican Commission and Inter-American Court of Human Rights.

Under Article 64.2 of the Pact, the Inter-American Court, in exercise of its consultative competence at the request of a state member of the OAS, may give opinions on the compatibility between any of its domestic laws—for instance, a provincial constitution—and the interpretation of the Pact or of other treaties regarding the protection of human rights in American states. It may also pass judgments obliging resolutions issued by state members to be modified.

Article 28 of the Pact,[64] known as the 'federal clause', deals with the issue of federal states and prescribes the following:

> 1. Where a State Party is constituted as a federal state, the national government of such State Party shall implement all the provisions of the Convention over whose subject matter it exercises legislative and judicial jurisdiction; 2. With respect to the provisions over whose subject matter the constituent units of the federal state have jurisdiction, the national government shall immediately take suitable measures, in accordance with its constitution and its laws, to the end that the competent authorities of the constituent units may adopt appropriate provisions for the fulfilment of this Convention; 3. Whenever two or more State Parties agree to form a federation or other type of association, they shall take care that the resulting federal or other compact contains the provisions necessary for continuing and rendering effective the standards of this Convention in the new State that is organised.

2.6 Constitutional review of provincial constitutions

An issue that has divided the opinion of legal authors and on which there have been some contradictory judicial decisions is the question of whether courts have the power to declare a constitutional reform unconstitutional.[65] According to the classifications of constituent power, there are different orders in the federation and the provinces are in second place after the federal Constitution. This implies that, when exercising their constituent power, the provinces must

---

64 For a deeper analysis, see Antonio María Hernández, 'La cláusula federal del Pacto de San José de Costa Rica' in Daniel Sabsay (ed.), Pablo Manili (coord.), Constitución de la Nación Argentina, vol. 5 (Hammurabi 2016) 284.

65 On this issue, see Antonio María Hernández, *El Caso Fayt* (Abeledo Perrot 2012).

comply with the bases set forth in Articles 5 and 123 and related provisions of the federal Constitution. Consequently, it is clear that the Argentine Supreme Court may declare the unconstitutionality of a provincial constitution for lack of compliance with the bases set forth in the federal Constitution, to ensure the latter's supremacy.

The Supreme Court of Justice is the most federal and national of the constituted powers, since it may review acts under provincial and municipal public law to ensure respect for the federal Constitution, the rights contained therein and the republican form of government. Spota (h)[66] recalled that, historically, the Supreme Court has authorized its instance to invalidate provincial constitutions only when they affected the federal distribution of competences, in particular to secure the monopoly of enacting substantive legislation by Congress, since the provinces cannot exercise the delegated powers. This case law persists, as shown by the declaration of the unconstitutionality of Article 58 of the Córdoba Constitution with respect to the non-attachable nature of the housing, since the determination of assets subject to the property execution power of the creditor is a matter of common legislation, and as such, an exclusive prerogative of the Congress.[67] As from the 1980s, the Supreme Court modified its inhibitory case law with respect to Article 5,[68] and it even declared the unconstitutionality of provincial constitutions because they were not compatible with the central government republican system[69] or affected federal rights and guarantees.[70]

Likewise, the High Courts of Justice of the provinces must exercise the same function when reviewing the constitutionality of Municipal Charters, which are true local constitutions, resulting from a constituent power of a lower degree. But additionally, there are precedents by virtue of which provincial High Courts of Justice heard cases related to control of the constitutionality of provincial constitutional reform processes. Thus, the High Court of Justice of the province of Mendoza, in a decision of 1989 in Unión del Centro Democrático v. Gobierno de la Provincia de Mendoza, stated that the issue was judiciable and decided that the decree convening the Constitutional Assembly was unconstitutional.

More recently, the High Court of Justice of Córdoba, in the event of a constitutional reform process in the province, stated that '… the High Court of Justice is the body authorised to decide on conflicts that may arise between the Legislature and the Constitutional Assembly'.[71] This is so, because the provincial constitution is, like the whole legal system, subject to control of constitutionality by the judicial branch.[72]

In the case Iribarren Casiano Rafael v. Santa Fe, the Argentine Supreme Court of Justice on 22 June 1999[73] declared the unconstitutionality of Article 88 of the Constitution of the province of Santa Fe, since it provides for the termination of the non-removal of justices as from the age of 65 if they are eligible for ordinary retirement. In the grounds of the majority vote, clause No. 8 reads: 'The transcendence of effects of Article 88 of the Constitution of the Province of Santa

---

66 Alberto Spota (h), 'El control de constitucionalidad sobre las Constituciones de Provincia'; 'Debates de Actualidad' (2003) *Magazine of the Argentine Association of Constitutional Law* no. 191, 86.

67 Banco del Suquía v. Tomassini, Juan C. CSJN: 325:428 (2002).

68 CSJN, Fallos: 308:490, 961 and 1745; 310:804; 311:2484 and 317:1162.

69 CSJN; Fallos: 311:460; 322:1253 (1999) and Alvarez, Raúl José v. Province of Santa Fe. Declaratory action, Decision of the Argentine Supreme Court of Justice, 14 October 1999.

70 CSJN, Fallos, 308:934; 324:3143.

71 See Superior Tribunal of Justice of Córdoba (T.S.J.) in 'García', Sent. No. 8 (17 August 2001) *Foro de Córdoba* No. 70, 2001, pp. 201 et seq.

72 See T.S.J. de Córdoba in 'Sesma', A.I. No. 54 (17-09-01) *Foro de Córdoba* No. 71, 2001, pp. 172 et seq.

73 With the majority vote of Justices Nazareno, Moliné O'Connor, Boggiano, Petracchi, Bossert and Vásquez (the last three according to their respective votes) and dissenting vote of Belluscio.

Fe exceed the scope of local public law and project themselves to the scope of effectiveness of the Federal Constitution'. However, I agree with Justice Belluscio's dissenting opinion, based on the following:

> 6. That Article 5 of the Federal Constitution obliges the Provinces to enact their respective constitutions under the representative and republican system according to the principles, statements and guarantees of such Federal Constitution, and to assure the administration of justice. It is obvious that this does not imply that Provinces are forced to copy exactly the national institutions, nor even to follow them as models more than in essential aspects ... To broaden the extension of the supremacy of the Argentine basic text would imply the nullification of federalism.

The Iribarren case is thus another mistaken decision of the Supreme Court, causing deep harm to Argentine federalism.

2.7 Conclusion

Argentina has an adequate constitutional design in terms of federalism and subnational constitutionalism, with a very important recognition of the autonomy of the provinces, the Autonomous City of Buenos Aires and the municipal governments. But it has a serious problem with the weakness of its constitutional and political culture which facilitates non-compliance with the national and provincial constitutions. A complex and decisive debate on federalism and subnational constitutionalism is urgent, based on the established constitutional principles, with an agenda on federal, regional, provincial and municipal matters. It is essential to build an overarching policy that overcomes partisan antagonisms, strengthens interjurisdictional relations and enables a balanced development of the country in accordance with the federal project of the Constitution. Argentina must reverse the trend towards centralization and the weakening of constitutional culture.[74]

---

74 See Hernández, 'The distribution of competences and the tendency toward centralization in the Argentine Federation' (n 17) and Hernández, Zovatto and Fidanza, *Segunda Encuesta de Cultura Constitucional* (n 17).

3

SUBNATIONAL CONSTITUTIONALISM IN AUSTRALIA

State autonomy in a uninational federation

Nicholas Aroney

3.1 Context

The Commonwealth of Australia is an integrative federation formed in 1901 through the 'coming together' of six mutually independent self-governing colonies under the ultimate authority of the British Parliament.[1] Prior to federation, each colony had its own constitutional statute enacted by its Parliament pursuant to authority conferred by the British Parliament. These constitutional statutes defined the legislative, executive and judicial institutions of each colony and conferred powers upon them. Although the oldest of the Australian colonies were initially established as penal settlements governed under the autocratic powers of governors appointed by the British government, by the mid-nineteenth century all but one of the colonies had become fully self-governing. This entailed the establishment of representative legislatures and executive governments responsible to those legislatures, operating in accordance with the conventions of parliamentary responsible government as understood within the British Westminster tradition. The one exception, Western Australia, attained full self-governing status in the late nineteenth century, a decade prior to the federation of the colonies in 1901.

These powers of local self-governance included a large degree of constitutional self-determination, subject only to the ultimate authority of the British Parliament and the continuing status of the colonies as parts of the British Empire. In a decisively important statute passed by the British Parliament in 1865, all representative legislatures within the Empire were given full power to amend their own constitutions subject only to such 'manner and form' procedural requirements as might be imposed by an Imperial statute, Order in Council or statute enacted by the colonial legislature itself.[2] This enabled the colonial legislatures to place procedural constraints on their ability to amend their own constitutions. At the time of federation, each colonial legislature was therefore in the position of a sovereign-like parliament exercising a plenitude of

1 For a general account, see Nicholas Aroney, *The Constitution of a Federal Commonwealth: The Making and Meaning of the Australian Constitution* (Cambridge University Press 2009).
2 Colonial Laws Validity Act 1865 (UK), s 5.

DOI: 10.4324/9781003052111-3

legislative power similar in scope to that exercised by the British Parliament itself, but applying only to the governance of the colony, with limited extraterritorial effect.[3]

In this context, the federation of the colonies was authorized locally by statutes passed by each of the colonial parliaments. A federal convention consisting of members directly elected by the voters in five of the six colonies was held in 1897–98.[4] Each colony was regarded as a constituent equal in the negotiating process and therefore represented by an equal number of delegates. The convention debated and drafted a constitution which was referred to the legislatures of the colonies for comment. Next the constitution was finalized by the convention and then referred to the voters in each colony for approval at a referendum. Only once the voters approved the scheme of federation was the colony committed to federation. Eventually the voters in all six colonies approved the proposed constitution and it was referred to the British Parliament for formal enactment. Although the Parliament possessed the legislative authority to determine the final content of the constitution, only minor changes concerning matters of immediate concern to the Empire as a whole were made. The *Commonwealth of Australia Constitution Act 1900* (UK), which contains the Constitution of the Commonwealth of Australia, authorized the Queen to declare by proclamation that the Australian colonies would be formed as constituent states into one indissoluble federal commonwealth under the crown.

Consistent with the scheme of federation, the Commonwealth Constitution presupposes the prior existence of the six constituent states as pre-existing self-governing political communities each governed under their respective State Constitutions. The Commonwealth Constitution confirmed that each State Constitution would 'continue' to operate, subject to the Commonwealth Constitution, until amended in accordance with the State Constitution (section 106). It also affirmed that each State Parliament would continue to exercise the legislative powers it had prior to federation, subject only to a relatively small number of restrictions.[5] The general principle was that each State Parliament would continue to have the power to determine the content of its own Constitution and to legislate as it deemed fit.

3.2 Autonomy

The transformation of the Australian colonies from penal settlements to self-governing political communities was largely a result of advocacy by the governments and peoples of the colonies themselves.[6] The original colony of New South Wales initially encompassed almost two-thirds of the Australian continent. Only over time were separate colonies established in Van Diemen's Land (Tasmania) in 1825, South Australia in 1836, Western Australia in 1829, and the colonies of Victoria and Queensland were carved out of the territory of New South Wales in 1851 and 1859 respectively. The colonies were transformed into self-governing political communities in gradual steps involving the establishment of local systems of courts, local legislative councils and assemblies, democratically responsible governments and, eventually, full power to amend their own constitutions and therefore determine the composition and powers of their institutions of government. These developments reflected aspirations for local self-government and constitutional self-determination that were widespread in the colonies.

Federation only occurred when the governments, legislatures and people of the colonies considered it to be in their best interests to do so, and the terms of federation were calculated to

---

3 *Powell v Apollo Candle Co* (1885) 10 App Cas 282, 290.
4 The Western Australian delegates were appointment by the colonial Parliament.
5 For more detail, see Part 3.2 below.
6 Aroney (n 1), at 134–8.

ensure that each colony would continue to exercise powers of local self-government and constitutional self-determination, subject only to those limitations and restrictions that were necessary in order to establish a federal commonwealth.[7] The colonies were therefore in a position to insist on five interlocking principles:

- the Constitution of each state would continue to operate, subject to the Commonwealth Constitution, until amended in accordance with the Constitution of the state (section 106);
- the powers of each State Parliament would continue, except to the extent that particular powers were exclusively vested in the Commonwealth Parliament or specifically withdrawn from the state (section 107);
- every existing state law, even if on topics over which the Commonwealth Parliament was given concurrent power to make laws, would continue to operate until amended by the state (section 108);
- even though state laws inconsistent with Commonwealth laws would be invalid to the extent of the inconsistency (section 109), the legislative powers of the Commonwealth Parliament were limited to specific topics (sections 51 and 52), thereby ensuring that the states would continue to be able to legislate on all other topics;
- by way of further safeguard, the Commonwealth Parliament would consist of two houses, one of which (the Senate) would be composed of an equal number of representatives of each state directly chosen by the people of each state (section 7).

The combined effect of these provisions was to guarantee to the states a very high degree of constitutional autonomy. Although it could be said that it is the Commonwealth Constitution which confirms that the constitutions of the states are to continue subject to the Commonwealth Constitution, the states arguably have a constitutional status that is more fundamental and certainly more original than the Commonwealth itself. All of this reflects the integrative nature of the Australian federation as a consensual 'coming together' of six mutually independent self-governing colonies.[8]

Indeed, so important are the states to the federal design of the system as a whole, amendments to the Commonwealth Constitution can generally only occur through processes that involve, in various ways, the approval of the states. Thus, the Commonwealth Constitution as a whole can only be formally altered by a statute enacted by both houses of the Commonwealth Parliament which has received the approval of a majority of the people of the Commonwealth as a whole and a majority of the people in a majority of states (section 128, paragraphs 1–4). Moreover, changes to the rights of the people of each state to be represented in the two houses of the Commonwealth Parliament,[9] as well as the territorial boundaries of each state, cannot be altered without the consent of the people of the affected state (section 128, paragraph 5). Likewise, the State Parliaments can confer additional legislative powers on the Commonwealth Parliament, but any Commonwealth law enacted pursuant to such powers extends only to states by whose

---

7 Ibid. ch 9.

8 Alfred Stepan, 'Toward a New Comparative Politics of Federalism, (Multi)Nationalism, and Democracy: Beyond Rikerian Federalism' in *Arguing Comparative Politics* (Oxford University Press 2001) 315.

9 Section 7 of the Commonwealth constitution provides that each of the Original States is represented in the Senate by an equal number of senators, notwithstanding substantial differences in the populations of the various states. Section 24 provides that the people of the states are represented in the House of Representatives in proportion to their respective populations, subject to the right of each state to a minimum representation of five members.

Parliaments the matter is referred, or which afterwards themselves confer the power as well (section 51(xxxvii)).

The constitutional status of the Australian states is underscored when they are compared with the position of the territories. The two self-governing territories, the Australian Capital Territory and the Northern Territory, are governed under statutes enacted and controlled by the Commonwealth Parliament.[10] The constitutional status of the other territories is even weaker, as illustrated by the recent disestablishment of representative institutions in the Territory of Norfolk Island.[11] The Commonwealth's power to legislate for the territories, including the power to establish their governing institutions, is plenary in nature (section 122). A Commonwealth law on any topic will overrule an inconsistent territory law, and the Commonwealth can deliberately target its legislation to overrule territory laws if it wishes.[12]

Since federation, the constitutional autonomy of the Australian states has substantially increased in one respect, and has decreased in another important respect. The first of these changes is that the ultimate authority of the British Parliament to legislate for each Australian state, as well as for the Australian Commonwealth as a whole, was brought to an end in 1986.[13] This was achieved in two ways. A provision of the Commonwealth Constitution authorizes the Commonwealth to exercise any power which at the time of federation could be exercised only by the British Parliament, provided this is done at the request or with the concurrence of all the State Parliaments directly concerned (section 51(xxxviii)). Pursuant to this provision, the State Parliaments enacted laws authorising the Commonwealth to enact a law that would terminate the power of the British Parliament to legislate for Australia.[14] At the same time, following the process required by the *Statute of Westminster*,[15] the Commonwealth requested the British Parliament to enact an identical statute likewise terminating the power of the British Parliament to legislate Australia.[16]

The second way in which the constitutional autonomy of the Australian states has changed since federation concerns the practical capacity of the states to exercise their legislative, executive and judicial powers independently of the Commonwealth. Over time, the Commonwealth has pressed the scope of its laws, executive actions and judicial decisions to the outermost limits of the Constitution, and arguably beyond those limits. Moreover, these efforts to expand the powers of the Commonwealth have been largely confirmed by decisions of the High Court of Australia.[17] These decisions have reduced the effective range of the autonomous governing powers of the states through three key mechanisms:

- a wider range of validly enacted Commonwealth laws, which prevail over inconsistent state laws to the extent of the inconsistency (section 109);

---

10 *Northern Territory (Self-Government) Act 1978* (Cth); *Australian Capital Territory (Self-Government) Act 1988* (Cth).
11 *Norfolk Island Legislation Amendment Act 2015* (Cth).
12 *Northern Territory v GPAO* (1999) 196 CLR 553; *Commonwealth v Australian Capital Territory* (2013) 88 ALJR 118.
13 See generally, Anne Twomey, *The Australia Acts 1986: Australia's Statutes of Independence* (Federation Press 2010).
14 *Australia Act 1986* (Cth).
15 *Statute of Westminster 1931* (UK), s 4.
16 *Australia Act 1986* (UK).
17 James Allan and Nicholas Aroney, 'An Uncommon Court: How the High Court of Australia has undermined Australian Federalism' (2008) 30 *Sydney Law Review* 245.

- Commonwealth monopolization of personal and corporate income taxes, thus limiting the financial resources available to the states and making them more reliant on Commonwealth grants;[18]
- financial grants to states that require the states to comply with terms and conditions imposed by the Commonwealth (section 96).[19]

Decisions of the High Court interpreting the Constitution have also placed restrictions on the capacity of the states to determine certain matters fundamental to their respective State Constitutions, particularly in relation to the functions and procedures of their judicial institutions and measures that burden communications about political matters.[20] Apart from these limitations, however, the fundamental principle remains that the State Parliaments have plenary power to enact, repeal and amend their own constitutions.

3.2.1 Scope

The power of the State Parliaments to determine the content of their own constitutions is in principle unlimited as to subject matter.[21] The composition, procedures and powers of the core legislative, executive and judicial institutions of each state are determined in the first instance by the constitutional statutes of each state, as well as by particular statutes regulating other matters of constitutional importance, such as the establishment of government departments, integrity agencies, and public corporations.

The only limitations on the power of the State Parliaments to determine the content of their own constitutions are derived from the Commonwealth Constitution. Here, the general principle is that the State Constitutions continue, subject to the Commonwealth Constitution (section 106). This means that there is nothing the states can do by way of amendments to their constitutions that modify or alter the relevant effect of the Commonwealth Constitution or the exercise of constitutional powers by the legislative, executive and judicial institutions of the Commonwealth. The states cannot prevent the Commonwealth from enacting a law that is inconsistent with a state law and therefore prevails to the extent of the inconsistency (section 109). The states cannot legislate on topics that are within the exclusive power of the Commonwealth, such as the imposition of excise duties and customs duties (section 90) or the enactment of laws concerning the seat of government of the Commonwealth or Commonwealth government departments (section 52). They are also prohibited from raising or maintaining any naval or military force without the consent of the Commonwealth Parliament (section 114) and from coining money or making anything other than gold or silver legal tender in payment of debts (section 115).

The most radical indicator of the constitutional autonomy of a constituent state concerns its capacity to withdraw from the federation.[22] The framers of the Australian Constitution, knowing the history of the United States and, in particular, the American Civil War, deliberately framed the Australian Constitution in a way that would foreclose the possibility of a lawful, unilateral secession by a state. This was achieved in two ways. Firstly, the preamble to the

18 *South Australia v Commonwealth* (1942) 65 CLR 373; *Victoria v Commonwealth* (1957) 99 CLR 575.
19 *Victoria v Commonwealth* (1926) 38 CLR 399; *Deputy Federal Commissioner of Taxation v W R Moran Pty Ltd* (1939) 61 CLR 735.
20 For more detail, see Parts 3.4.2 and 3.4.3 below.
21 *Union Steamship Co of Australia Pty Ltd v King* (1988) 166 CLR 1; *Durham Holdings Pty Ltd v New South Wales* (2001) 205 CLR 399.
22 See generally, Gregory Craven, *Secession: The Ultimate States Right* (Melbourne University Press 1986).

Constitution recorded the agreement of the people of the Australian colonies to be united in an *indissoluble* federal commonwealth. Although the preamble is not directly enforceable, this statement reflected the prevailing view and intention of the framers. Secondly, the Constitution was contained in a British statute which applied by paramount force in Australia and continues to bind the Commonwealth and the states after the passage of the *Australia Acts*.[23] It is beyond the powers of the Commonwealth and the states to legislate in a manner that is inconsistent with the *Commonwealth of Australia Constitution Act* and the Constitution which it contains. The *Constitution Act* provided in covering clause 3 that the Queen had authority to declare by proclamation that the Australian colonies would be united into a federal commonwealth. Nothing in the *Constitution Act* or the Constitution expressly affirms or confers power on a state to secede unilaterally from the federation. To remove a state from the federation pursuant to the *Constitution Act* would require a formal amendment of that Act, arguably with the consent of the Commonwealth and the state concerned, and possibly with the consent of all of the states.[24]

3.2.2 Procedure

The general principle is that the State Constitutions are nothing but ordinary statutes of the State Parliaments and can therefore be amended or repealed in any respect by an ordinary statute enacted by the Parliament.[25] In the five states where the Parliament is bicameral, this means that an amendment to the Constitution must be passed by both houses of the Parliament and then receive the royal assent, which is ordinarily given by the State Governor on the advice of the Premier, Attorney General or other relevant government minister.[26]

As mentioned, the powers of each State Parliament are limited by any 'manner and form' procedural requirements laid down for the enactment of laws that alter the 'constitution, powers and procedures' of the Parliament. The original source of such requirements was section 5 of the *Colonial Laws Validity Act 1865* (UK). This section, which affirmed the powers of colonial legislatures to establish and amend their own constitutions, distinguished between colonial legislatures generally and those that were 'representative' in character. Every colonial legislature, whether representative or not, was given full power to establish, abolish and reconstitute its system of courts. Each representative legislature was, in addition, given full power to make laws respecting the constitution, powers and procedures of the legislature itself. However, this latter power was also subject to any 'manner and form' procedural requirement that might be required by an Act of the British Parliament, Letters Patent, or an Order in Council, or by any relevant statute enacted by the colonial legislature itself.

The *Colonial Laws Validity Act* thus presupposed and affirmed the continuing power of the British Parliament to legislate for the Australian colonies and to determine, ultimately, the content of the colonial constitutions. However, it also affirmed the power of the colonial legislatures to determine the content of their constitutions. The authority of the British Parliament to legislate for the colonies continued through the period of federation and well into the twentieth century. Following the First World War, however, a landmark statement of the 1926 Imperial Conference affirmed that several of the former colonies, including Australia, had 'Dominion'

---

23 *Statute of Westminster 1931* (UK), ss 8 and 9; *Australia Acts 1986* (UK) and (Cth), ss 5, 12, 15.
24 For some of the complexities and range of views on the question, see Nicholas Aroney, 'A Public Choice? Federalism and the Prospects of a Republican Preamble' (1999) 21 *University of Queensland Law Journal* 205.
25 *McCawley v The King* [1920] AC 691. See, further, Nicholas Aroney, 'Politics, Law and the Constitution in McCawley's Case' (2006) 30(3) *Melbourne University Law Review* 605.
26 For more detail, see Part 3.4.2 below.

status, meaning they were no longer directly under the authority of the British government. They were described as 'autonomous Communities within the British Empire, equal in status, in no way subordinate one to another in any aspect of their domestic or external affairs, though united by a common allegiance to the Crown'.[27]

A further important step was taken by the *Statute of Westminster 1931* (UK). Section 2 provided, among other things, that no law of a Dominion would henceforth be void or inoperative on the ground that it is repugnant to the law of England or to the provisions of any existing or future British statute. Section 4 further provided that no Act of the British Parliament would henceforth apply to a Dominion unless it was expressly declared that the Dominion had requested and consented to its enactment. Neither of these developments directly affected the Australian states directly. However, it was recognized that the former colonies were now substantially independent states operating in world affairs.

When the *Australia Acts* were enacted in 1986, bringing the authority of the British Parliament to legislate for Australia to an end, this had profound constitutional implications. Section 1 of the *Australia Acts* provided that no British statute would henceforth apply to the Commonwealth, to a state or to a territory. Other provisions affirmed that each State Parliament would have power to make laws that have extraterritorial operation and would also have all of the legislative powers that the British Parliament could have exercised in relation to the state.[28] It was also provided that no law of a state would henceforth be void or inoperative on the ground that it is repugnant to the law of England or to the provisions of any existing or future British statute. Section 6 of the *Australia Acts* also affirmed, in terms similar to the *Colonial Laws Validity Act*, that any state statute dealing with 'the constitution, powers or procedure' of the State Parliament would be of 'no force or effect' unless enacted in accordance with any applicable 'manner and form' requirement.

One of the most common procedural requirements is that a proposed law must be approved by the people voting in a referendum.[29] Others require that proposed laws must be passed by an absolute majority or a special majority of the houses of Parliament, rather than merely by simple majority.[30] Notably, however, manner and form requirements apply only to laws respecting the 'constitution, powers or procedures' of the Parliament; they do not apply to other constitutional institutions such as the courts or the executive government.[31] While some State Constitutions contain manner and form requirements that apply to the executive and the courts, it is questionable whether they are constitutionally effective.[32]

3.3 Status

The status of the State Constitutions and their relationship to the Commonwealth Constitution is encapsulated in section 106 of the Commonwealth Constitution, which affirms that they are to *continue* as at the establishment of the Commonwealth and that they are *subject to* the Commonwealth Constitution.

27 Inter-Imperial Relations Committee, Imperial Conference 1926, *Report, Proceedings and Memoranda* (1926) 2.
28 *Australia Acts 1986*, s 2. On the extra-territorial powers of the states generally, see Nicholas Aroney et al., *The Constitution of the Commonwealth of Australia: History, Principle and Interpretation* (Cambridge University Press 2015) 621–5
29 Eg, *Constitution Act 1889* (WA), s 73(2); *Constitution Act 1902* (NSW), s 7A and 7B; *Constitution Act 1867* (Qld), s 53; *Constitution Act 1975* (Vic), s 18(1B); *Constitution Act 1934* (SA), s 10A.
30 E.g., *Constitution Act 1889* (WA), s 73(1); *Constitution Act 1975* (Vic), s 18(2), (2AA).
31 *Attorney-General (NSW) v Trethowan* (1931) 44 CLR 394; *Attorney-General (WA) v Marquet* (2003) 217 CLR 545.
32 See further, Aroney et al. (n 28), at 625–32.

There are some judicial statements suggesting that the State Constitutions derive their authority *from* the Commonwealth Constitution.[33] However, these statements are difficult to reconcile with the affirmation in section 106 that the Constitutions would 'continue', a term which suggests that the juridical sources from which they derive their authority must have predated the establishment of the Commonwealth.[34] As a matter of historical record, this is indeed the case: each of the State Constitutions can be traced to independent Imperial sources such as Instructions to the Colonial Governor, Letters Patent, Orders in Council and Acts of the British Parliament.[35] Each state has a unique constitutional history and relationship with the British sources from which its governing institutions derived their authority. As noted, the cessation of the power of the British Parliament to legislate for Australia effected by the *Australia Acts* was premised on statutes enacted by the states and the Commonwealth. The Commonwealth, the states and the territories were treated as distinct entities with particular provisions tailored to their specific constitutional circumstances.[36]

While each State Constitution continues until altered in accordance with the requirements contained in the State Constitution itself, each State Constitution is also *subject to* the Commonwealth Constitution. This not only means that it is subject to the provisions contained in the Commonwealth Constitution at the time that it came into force, but also any new provisions introduced by way of alteration to the Commonwealth Constitution. In this respect, when the people of the states agreed to be united in a federal commonwealth they committed themselves to a joint constitutional destiny that would be determined pursuant to the principles and procedures contained in the Commonwealth Constitution concerning its amendment. As noted, changes to the Commonwealth Constitution can only be made with the consent of a majority of the people of the Commonwealth and a majority of people in a majority of states (section 128). This means that people of each state have an equal voice in determining whether proposed amendments should be approved, but it also means that a minority of states can be outvoted. Notwithstanding this potential, only eight of 44 proposed amendments have been successful, and many of these failed proposals would have increased the powers of the Commonwealth at the expense of the states.[37] In principle, state powers are therefore vulnerable to diminution through changes to Commonwealth Constitution, but it is doubtful whether the states themselves can be abolished without the consent of the people of the states. The states 'are welded into the very structure and essence of the Commonwealth; ... they are inseparable from it and as enduring and indestructible as the Commonwealth itself'.[38]

The position of any new state admitted to the Commonwealth is slightly different from the six Original States. When establishing new states the Commonwealth may impose such terms and conditions, including the extent of representation in either house of the Parliament, as it thinks fit (section 121). Unlike the Original States, therefore, any new state will not necessarily

---

33 *Victoria v Commonwealth* (1970) 122 CLR 353, 371 (Barwick CJ); *New South Wales v Commonwealth* (1975) 135 CLR 337, 372 (Barwick CJ), *Bistricic v Rokov* (1976) 135 CLR 552, 566 (Murphy J); *Western Australia v Wilsmore* (1981) 149 CLR 79, 86 (Murphy J); *McGinty v Western Australia* (1996) 186 CLR 140, 171–2 (Brennan CJ), 208 (Toohey J).
34 *Western Australia v Wilsmore* (1981) 51 FLR 348, 351–3 (Burt CJ).
35 Gerard Carney, *The Constitutional Systems of the Australian States and Territories* (Cambridge University Press 2006) ch 2.
36 *Australia Acts 1986*, ss 1, 13, 14.
37 See further, George Williams and David Hume, *People Power: The History and Future of the Referendum in Australia* (UNSW Press 2010).
38 John Quick and Robert Randolph Garran, *The Annotated Constitution of the Australian Commonwealth* (Angus and Robertson 1901) 336.

be entitled to equal representation in the Senate. New states can also be formed by separation from the territory of a state, but only with the consent of the State Parliament (section 124), and any alteration to the territorial limits or boundaries of a state must be approved by the voters of that state (section 123).

3.4 Content

3.4.1 *Identity*

Australia is a relatively homogenous federation: there are no politically significant regional concentrations of people sharing particular identities along ethnic, cultural, religious or linguistic lines.[39] All the larger Australian cities are highly diverse and multicultural, but in all the major cities and regions, English remains the most commonly spoken language, Christianity is the most common religious affiliation, and the majority of the population has a British or European ancestry.[40] Australia's diversity is more subtle. This is suggested by the fact that the second and third most commonly spoken languages and the second and third most common religious affiliations vary considerably among the states and territories.[41] Differences in population size, density and age, as well as different geographies and economies, and an underlying belief in local self-government, contribute to sometimes significantly different political environments. The fundamental features of each State Constitution are broadly very similar, but there are underlying and sometimes important differences.

Each State Constitution expressly affirms or impliedly presupposes the identity of the state as a distinct and constitutionally independent political community. Some of the State Constitutions now refer expressly to the people of the state. The *Constitution of Queensland 2001* records, for example, that 'the people of Queensland, free and equal citizens of Australia … adopt the principle of the sovereignty of the people, under the rule of law, and the system of representative and responsible government, prescribed by this Constitution'.[42] Like most of the other State Constitutions it also acknowledges the prior occupation of Australia by indigenous peoples.[43] The *Constitution Act 1889* of Western Australia records that the two houses of the Parliament are 'chosen directly by the people' and requires that any proposed law that would change this must be approved by the electors at a referendum.[44] While these are not express declarations that constituent power is vested in the people of the state, they do seem to presuppose something of this idea. However, how much of this is a genuine reflection of the constitutional reality may be doubted because, as a matter of law, it is the Parliament that has the authority to alter the State Constitution, and changes to only particular aspects of the State Constitutions must be approved referendum. Although hopes were expressed in the late nineteenth century that each State

---

39 Nicholas Aroney, 'Australia' in Luis Moreno and César Colino (eds.), *Diversity and Unity in Federal Countries* (McGill-Queens University Press 2010).

40 There are many remote regions in the states and territories, however, where Indigenous languages are widely spoken.

41 See further, Nicholas Aroney, Scott Prasser and Alison Taylor, 'Federal Diversity in Australia—a Counter Narrative' in Gabrielle Appleby, Nicholas Aroney and Thomas John (eds), *The Future of Australian Federalism: International and Comparative Perspectives* (Cambridge University Press 2012) 272.

42 *Constitution of Queensland 2001* (Qld), Preamble. Remarkably, there was no referendum to approve the inclusion of this language in the Queensland Constitution. It was simply enacted by the Queensland Parliament.

43 E.g., *Constitution Act 1902* (NSW), s 2; *Constitution Act 1975* (Vic), s 1A; *Constitution Act 1934* (SA), s 2.

44 *Constitution Act 1889* (WA), Preamble and s 73(2)(c).

Constitution might one day be submitted to the approval of the people, this has not eventuated.[45]

Each state and territory has its own flag, coat of arms, and other symbols, while Australian citizenship, the national flag and the national anthem are determined at a Commonwealth level.[46] A person who is a citizen of the Commonwealth has citizenship rights throughout the country. Apart from some particular grounds of exclusion, such as serving a sentence for conviction of a serious crime, all Australian citizens over 18 are entitled to enrol to vote at a Commonwealth, state and territory level, depending on their place of residence, and voting is compulsory. Each state has its own electoral laws and electoral commission.[47]

The Australian State Constitutions, although they provide the essential constitutional foundations for the political institutions of each state, do not have a particularly strong symbolic value in mainstream political or popular consciousness.

3.4.2 *Organization of powers*

The State Constitutions each establish legislative, executive and judicial institutions and confer legislative, executive and judicial power on them respectively. In all the states except Queensland, the Parliament is bicameral and consists of a Legislative Council (upper house) and Legislative Assembly (lower house). The Queensland Parliament is unicameral,[48] as are the two self-governing territories. In all of the states except Tasmania, each member of the lower house represents a particular electorate in the state, and all states use a preferential voting system. In all bicameral states except Tasmania, the upper house is elected on the basis of multi-member districts and a proportional system of voting.[49] Accordingly, just as the Commonwealth Senate is designed to represent the people of the states, the State Legislative Councils are, with the exception of Tasmania, designed to represent the people of the various regions of the state.[50]

In some states there are special procedures for the enactment of financial bills and special procedures to avoid deadlocks between the two houses. The Tasmanian Constitution, for example, requires that financial bills must originate in the lower house and the upper house may not amend an appropriation bill.[51] The Victorian Constitution provides that bills over which the two houses cannot agree may be referred to a dispute resolution committee and that persistently deadlocked bills can ultimately be approved at a joint sitting of both houses.[52] The New South Wales Constitution provides that appropriation bills passed by the lower house which the upper house rejects can receive the royal assent and become law without being passed by the upper house.[53]

---

45 Nicholas Aroney, 'Popular ratification of the state constitutions' in Paul Kildea, Andrew Lynch and George Williams (eds), *Tomorrow's Federation: Reforming Australian Government* (Federation Press 2012) 210.

46 *Flags Act 1953* (Cth); *Australian Citizenship Act 2007* (Cth).

47 E.g., *Electoral Act 1992* (Qld).

48 Gerard Carney, 'Abolition and Restoration of a Legislative Council: Queensland and the other States' in Nicholas Aroney, Scott Prasser and John Nethercote (eds), *Restraining Elective Dictatorship: The Upper House Solution?* (University of Western Australia Press 2008) 262.

49 In Tasmania, the electoral composition of the upper and lower houses is the reverse of the other bicameral states.

50 Nicholas Aroney, 'Four Reasons for an Upper House: Representative Democracy, Public Deliberation, Legislative Outputs and Executive Accountability' (2008) 29(2) *Adelaide Law Review* 205, at 213–20.

51 *Constitution Act 1934* (Tas), ss 37, 42.

52 *Constitution Act 1975* (Vic), Pt II, Div 9A.

53 *Constitution Act 1902* (NSW), s 5A.

The executive power of each state is vested in the Queen and exercised by a Governor appointed by the Queen on the advice of the State Premier. The Premier is appointed by the Governor on the basis of his or her ability to command the support of a majority of members of the lower house of the Parliament. Other members of the government are appointed as Ministers by the Governor on the advice of the Premier. If a Premier loses the confidence of the lower house, he or she is obliged to resign and an alternative person who has the support of the house will be appointed or a general election will be held, following which a Premier who has the support of the house will be appointed.

Each state and territory has a Supreme Court and a Court of Appeal, which preside over a system of lower district and local courts. The High Court of Australia, which is established by the Commonwealth Constitution, has jurisdiction to decide appeals from the Supreme Court of each state and territory, but in practice only gives leave to appeal in significant cases. The Commonwealth is authorized to make laws investing state courts with federal jurisdiction (section 77(iii)). When it does so, the Commonwealth must accept the state courts as it finds them, because the establishment, empowerment and appointment of state courts and judges is a matter for each state.[54] However, state courts, being potential repositories of federal jurisdiction, must comply with the constitutional description of a 'court'.[55] The State Parliaments cannot confer functions on state courts incompatible with their exercise of federal judicial power because to do so could lead to a loss of public confidence in courts exercising federal jurisdiction.[56]

The constitution of each state is not exhausted by the formal *Constitution Act* enacted by its legislature. There are other statutes in each state that address particular matters of constitutional significance, such as the right to access government information and the establishment of special agencies, commissions or corporations charged with responsibility to undertake functions of public importance.[57] For example, most of the states have established permanent institutions responsible to investigate allegations of mismanagement, misconduct and corruption in government departments and agencies. However, the composition, organization, powers and functions of these bodies vary considerably among the states.[58]

3.4.3 *Fundamental rights and policy principles*

The Australian Constitutions, both Commonwealth and state, are unusual in that they contain little or no statements or guarantees of fundamental rights. Three of the four most important protections contained in the Commonwealth Constitution apply only to the Commonwealth.[59] The only significant Commonwealth provision that binds the states is the requirement that trade, commerce and intercourse between the states must be 'absolutely free' (section 92).[60] However, the High Court has also held that the system of representative or democratic

54 *Le Mesurier v Connor* (1929) 42 CLR 481; *Commonwealth v Hospital Contribution Fund of Australia* (1982) 150 CLR 49.
55 *Forge v Australian Securities & Investments Commission* (2006) 228 CLR 45; *South Australia v Totani* (2010) 242 CLR 1.
56 *Kable v Director of Public Prosecutions (NSW)* (1996) 189 CLR 51.
57 E.g., *Right to Information Act 2009* (Qld).
58 Compare, e.g.: *Independent Commission Against Corruption Act 1988* (NSW); *Independent Broad-based Anti-corruption Commission Act 2011* (Vic); *Crime and Corruption Act 2001* (Qld).
59 Commonwealth Constitution, s 51(xxxi) (acquisition of property on just terms), s 80 (trial by jury), s 116 (freedom of religion).
60 *Cole v Whitfield* (1988) 165 CLR 360. There are also provisions that prohibit discrimination on the basis of state residence (sections 51(ii), 117).

government established by the Commonwealth Constitution necessarily requires that communications about political matters must be not be unjustifiably burdened, and that this requirement binds both the Commonwealth and the states, as well as the territories.[61]

The only state that provides express constitutional protection for fundamental rights is Tasmania, the Constitution of which offers limited protection to freedom of conscience and the free profession and practice of religion.[62] The states of Victoria and Queensland and the Australian Capital Territory have enacted human rights charters which also provide a level of protection for human rights.[63] These statutes do not limit the legislative powers of the State or Territory Parliament. Rather, they require that proposed laws are scrutinized by a parliamentary committee which prepares a report on whether the proposed law unjustifiably interferes with human rights. The courts are also instructed to interpret statutes in a manner that is consistent with human rights, and when this is not possible, a court may issue a statement of incompatibility. The intention is to create a dialogue between the court and the legislature over the best approach to protecting human rights and achieving other objectives.[64] In these and other ways, the Australian states and territories engage in significant constitutional and regulatory experimentation.

Nonetheless in Australia generally, there remains, at least for the time being, a prevailing belief that fundamental rights are best protected through democratically elected legislatures which deliberate in the context of robust public debate. In practice, Australia's human rights record is generally no worse, and in some respects very much better, than many countries that have constitutional guarantees of fundamental rights. Advocates for better protection of rights draw attention to significant lapses that occur from time to time, but there remains a lively debate as to whether the introduction of judicially enforced constitutional guarantees would tip the balance of power too much in favour of unelected judges and too much against democratically elected legislatures.[65]

This orientation to parliamentary authority in the Australian political system is also expressed in the fact that the legislative powers of the Australian Parliaments are not guided or circumscribed by directive or mandatory policy principles contained in their respective constitutions. The underlying principle is that the Parliaments have general and unfettered power to make laws within their respective spheres. The policy goals and content of laws are matters for determination by the Parliaments, recognizing that they are electorally accountable to the people.

3.5 Multilevel constitutionalism

Only the Commonwealth of Australia, and not the states and territories, has international personality and capacity to enter treaties with other countries. The states and territories are free to enter into agreements with political and non-political entities outside Australia, but these agreements are not in the nature of public international law treaties and have effect in Australia subject to ordinary Australian domestic law. The decision to negotiate, sign and ratify an international

---

61 *Lange v Australian Broadcasting Corporation* (1997) 189 CLR 520.

62 *Constitution Act 1934* (Tas), s 46.

63 *Human Rights Act 2004* (ACT); *Charter of Human Rights and Responsibilities Act 2006* (Vic); *Human Rights Act 2019* (Qld).

64 For a critique, see James Allan, 'The Victorian Charter of Human Rights and Responsibilities: Exegesis and Criticism' (2006) 30 *Melbourne University Law Review* 906.

65 See further, Tom Campbell, Jeffrey Goldsworthy and Adrienne Stone, *Protecting human rights: Instruments and institutions* (Oxford University Press 2003).

treaty is a matter for the Commonwealth government alone. However, due to concerns of excessive concentration of power in the Commonwealth Executive, treaties are tabled in both houses of the Parliament and are accompanied by a national interest assessment drafted in consultation with key stakeholders, including the state and territory governments. There is also a Commonwealth–State–Territory Standing Committee on Treaties which consists of representatives of the Premier or Chief Minister of each state and territory which facilities intergovernmental discussions about treaties that have been signed or are being negotiated by the Commonwealth.[66]

When the Commonwealth signs and ratifies a treaty, it does not have effect in Australian domestic law except to the extent that it is implemented by legislation.[67] Under the Commonwealth Constitution, the Parliament has power to make laws with respect to 'external affairs' (section 51(xxix)) and this has been held to include laws implementing treaties the subject matter of which would not otherwise fall within the Commonwealth's law-making powers.[68] This does not prevent a state or territory from legislating to implement Australia's treaty obligations, but this is usually done by the Commonwealth. Some of the cases have involved laws implementing international human rights treaties.[69] The High Court has held that the Commonwealth must implement treaties in a manner that conforms to the specific obligations contained in the treaty; it does not provide authority to legislate generally on the subject matter of the treaty.[70] In exercise of this power, the Commonwealth has enacted laws prohibiting discrimination on the basis of race, sex and disability and has established the Australian Human Rights Commission, which is responsible to monitor the protection of human rights in Australia and to conciliate complaints of unlawful discrimination.[71] The Commonwealth has also legislated inconsistently with particular state laws that have been determined by the UN Human Rights Committee to be inconsistent with Australia's human rights obligations, thus rendering the state law invalid to the extent of the inconsistency (section 109).[72]

3.6 Constitutional review

Because each State Constitution is an ordinary statute of the State Parliament, it is liable to be amended by the State Parliament by ordinary legislation unless a legally effective manner and form procedural requirement applies. The role of the courts is therefore limited to determining whether any applicable manner and form requirements have been complied with. If those requirements of not been met, then the purported amendment is not legally effective and the courts will make declarations to that effect.[73] If, however, there are no relevant manner and form requirements with which the state law is inconsistent, then the state law will be fully enforced by the courts. There is no legal basis upon which the courts might review such statutes on the ground that they do not comply with the State Constitution. Nonetheless, in practice, the State

66 Australian Department of Foreign Affairs and Trade, *Treaty Making Process*, <https://dfat.gov.au/international-relations/treaties/treaty-making-process/Pages/treaty-making-process.aspx#constitution> (accessed 12 February 2020).
67 *Brown v Lizars* (1905) 2 CLR 837.
68 *R v Burgess; Ex parte Henry* (1936) 55 CLR 608; *Commonwealth v Tasmania* (1983) 158 CLR 1.
69 E.g., *Koowarta v Bjelke-Petersen* (1982) 153 CLR 168.
70 *Commonwealth v Tasmania* (1983) 158 CLR 1; *Victoria v Commonwealth* (1996) 187 CLR 416.
71 E.g., *Racial Discrimination Act 1975* (Cth); *Sex Discrimination Act 1984* (Cth); *Human Rights Commission Act 1986* (Cth); *Disability Discrimination Act 1992* (Cth).
72 *Croome v Tasmania* (1996–97) 191 CLR 119.
73 *Attorney-General (NSW) v Trethowan* (1931) 44 CLR 394; *Attorney-General (WA) v Marquet* (2003) 217 CLR 545.

Constitutions are generally respected as setting out the fundamental features of the political system of each state, and are generally not amended without considerable deliberation and public debate.

The status and effect of the Commonwealth Constitution is fundamentally different. Covering clause 5 of the *Commonwealth of Australia Constitution Act* provides that the Act, including the Constitution of the Commonwealth contained in the Act, is 'binding on the courts, judges, and people of every State and of every part of the Commonwealth, notwithstanding anything in the laws of any State'. The hierarchically superior status of the Commonwealth Constitution has led Australian courts, and in particular the High Court of Australia, to conclude that they have jurisdiction to determine the constitutionality of statutes enacted by the Commonwealth, State and Territory Parliaments, the including the Constitution Acts enacted by the states. Accordingly, a State Constitution and a state law cannot contain anything inconsistent with the Commonwealth Constitution or constitutionally valid Commonwealth law. Furthermore, the High Court has held that a Commonwealth law will be unconstitutional if, among other things, it unduly interferes with the capacity of a state to function as an independent government or exercise its constitutional powers.[74] It has also been held that a state is constitutionally entitled to maintain its own independent judicial system without undue Commonwealth interference.[75]

3.7 Conclusions

Several of the hypotheses developed and tested in this book are confirmed by the Australian case. Consistently with Hypothesis 1, Australia is an integrative or coming-together federation in which the constituent states have full constitutional autonomy. Australia is not a multinational state, and therefore Hypotheses 2, 3 and 4 are not directly applicable. Nonetheless, as a relatively homogenous federation, the Australian case provides indirect support for those hypotheses in three respects: the constitutional autonomy of Australia's states is not subjected to significant central oversight, the State Constitutions do not have a particularly strong symbolic value in mainstream political or popular consciousness, and the constitutional entrenchment of regional identity is not regarded as especially important or contentious within the country. Rather, the constitutional autonomy of the states is largely taken for granted.

Consistently with Hypothesis 5, the Australian State and Territory Constitutions organize powers in generally the same way as the Commonwealth Constitution, except in relation to the legislature and the revision of the constitution. Both the Commonwealth, State and Territory Constitutions establish legislative, executive and judicial institutions along similar lines, but the Parliaments of the two self-governing territories and the state of Queensland are unicameral, and the amendment of State Constitutions can, apart from special manner and form requirements, be secured by simple enactment by the State Parliament and the Territory Constitutions can be amended by ordinary enactments of the Commonwealth Parliament.

Consistently with Hypothesis 6, there is significant experimentation among the Australian states in relation to the protection of fundamental rights and other institutional arrangements. Consistently also with Hypothesis 7, given that the identity of the states is constitutionally well established, policy principles are not a feature of state constitutional law. Consistently with Hypothesis 8, Australia has moderate representation of the states in the Commonwealth

---

74 *Melbourne Corporation v Commonwealth* (1947) 74 CLR 31; *Austin v Commonwealth* (2003) 215 CLR 185.
75 *Re Tracey: Ex parte Ryan* (1988–89) 166 CLR 518.

Parliament (i.e., the Senate represents the people of the states, not the governments or legislatures of the states) and consequently relatively stronger protection for the autonomy of the states. Finally, also consistently with Hypothesis 9, because there is only a relatively minor degree of constitutional review occurring at a state level, the State Constitutions generally perform the central functions intended for them, but their significance in general public debate and deliberation is generally very minimal.

4

SUBNATIONAL CONSTITUTIONALISM IN AUSTRIA

The pluralization of homogeneity

Anna Gamper

4.1 Context

Exactly 101 years ago, the Austrian Federal Constitutional Act of 1920 (*Bundes-Verfasssungsgesetz*, hence: B-VG) was enacted. It was the new constitution of the federal Republic of Austria, drafted mainly by *Hans Kelsen* together with the political parties and the Austrian *Länder*.[1]

The *Länder* had already declared their will to 'accede' to the new Republic shortly after the proclamation of the Republic in late 1918.[2] Even now, it is controversial whether they actually co-founded the Austrian federal state or whether their declarations were legally irrelevant: some consider the proclamations of 1918 as the big bang of Austrian federalism, while others regard the enactment of the B-VG of 1920 as the only relevant 'federal constitutional moment'.[3,4] As a consequence, Austria may or may not be seen as a coming-together federation.[5] At any rate, however, the B-VG established federalism as a leading constitutional principle from its very beginning so that it can be regarded as an 'original' federal constitution.

Most of the *Länder*[6] had enacted their own provisional constitutions in 1918/1919, i.e. even earlier to the B-VG. The existence of *Land* constitutions was not new at that time, since the Imperial Law of 26 February 1861[7] had already contained a number of such Acts called *Landes-Ordnungen* for the former Crown *Länder* which included, *inter alia*, the later republican *Länder*

---

1 While the new republic had been already established in late 1918, a set of provisional laws of constitutional character had been in force during the interim period.
2 Anna Gamper, 'Entstehung und Constitutional Engineering des Bundesstaats' in Peter Bußjäger (ed.), *3. November 1918—Die Länder und der neue Staat* (new academic press 2019) 17.
3 Stephen Tierney, 'Federalism and constitutional theory' in Gary Jacobsohn and Miguel Schor (eds), *Comparative Constitutional Theory* (Edward Elgar Publishing 2018) 45, at 59.
4 See Anna Gamper, '100 Years of Austrian Republicanism—100 Years of Austrian Federalism?' (*Blog of the International Journal of Constitutional Law*, 30 October 2018) <www.iconnectblog.com/2018/10/100-years-of-austrian-republicanism-100-years-of-austrian-federalism> accessed 17 September 2019.
5 A 'hybrid' is the term used by Peter Bußjäger, *Föderale Systeme* (Jan Sramek 2017) 34 and Francesco Palermo and Karl Kössler, *Comparative Federalism* (Hart Publishing 2017) 43.
6 Vienna and Lower Austria became separate *Länder* in 1922, and the Burgenland joined Austria in 1921.
7 RGBl 1861/20.

     DOI: 10.4324/9781003052111-4

Lower Austria, Salzburg, Styria, Tyrol, Upper Austria and Vorarlberg. However, the Crown *Länder* of the monarchy had not been the constituent units of a federal system, but the decentralized regions of a unitary state. Accordingly, the *Landes-Ordnungen* had not been constitutional laws enacted by the Crown *Länder* themselves, but national laws enacted by the Emperor. In contrast, the republican *Land* constitutions of 1918 and 1919 had been passed by the *Länder* through resolutions of their respective assemblies.

The B-VG of 1920 settled the issue of the *Land* constitutions through its Art 99. This provision[8] has since determined how *Land* constitutions are enacted and that they must not 'touch' federal constitutional law. According to *Kelsen*'s positivistic approach, both ordinary laws and constitutional laws of the *Länder* were thus 'based only on a delegation by the federal constitution'.[9]

In accordance with the generally homogeneous design of Austrian federalism, neither Art 99 B-VG nor any other federal constitutional provision distinguishes between different degrees of constitutional autonomy per *Land*.[10] Nor was the early debate on Austrian federalism and the *Land* constitutions respectively centred on issues of asymmetry, but on whether the new system should be federal or unitary in nature and whether Austria could survive at all in terms of territory.[11] The end of the monarchy and the severe territorial losses even of the remaining Crown *Länder* rather triggered the conception of a homogeneous 'Austrian' society, despite slight differences in identity[12] with regard to history, folklore, dialects or the urban-rural gradient.

The landscape of Austrian federalism has not changed radically over time. The B-VG established full-fledged federalism, though with a centralistic profile. Powers are highly fragmented and mostly attributed to the federal level.[13] The Federal Council as the Federal Parliament's second chamber has relatively little to say in terms of law, and less even politically.[14] The *Länder* have hardly any taxing autonomy, but receive the larger share of revenues from the federation.[15] However, formal and informal cooperation plays a major role in Austrian federalism.[16] The political discussion on federalism hardly deals with the *Land* constitutions, but stays focused on competences and financial resources. Still, the existence of subnational constitutional autonomy is widely considered to form an essential element of federalism as one of the leading constitutional principles.[17] According to the Constitutional Court, subnational constitutional autonomy is necessarily linked to this principle; it is essential for the *Länder* and their parliaments to

8 Slightly amended by BGBl 1929/392.
9 Hans Kelsen, Georg Froehlich and Adolf Merkl, *Die Bundesverfassung vom 1. Oktober 1920* (Deuticke 1922) 195.
10 Vienna has a special status as the Austrian capital, as a *Land* and a municipality (Art 108-112 B-VG). Nevertheless, also Vienna enjoys constitutional autonomy under Art 99 B-VG.
11 This did not only concern the territorial losses after the war but also secessionist tendencies in the Western Austrian *Länder*.
12 Peter Bußjäger, Ferdinand Karlhofer and Günther Pallaver (eds), *Föderalistisches Bewusstsein in Österreich* (Braumüller 2010).
13 Peter Pernthaler, *Österreichisches Bundesstaatsrecht* (Verlag Österreich 2004) 313–48; Peter Bußjäger, 'Die bundesstaatliche Kompetenzverteilung in Österreich' in Anna Gamper and others (eds), *Föderale Kompetenzverteilung in Europa* (Nomos 2016) 523.
14 Peter Bußjäger, 'The Austrian Bundesrat—Imperfect and Unreformed' (2018) 10(2) *Perspectives on Federalism* 182.
15 Theo Öhlinger and Harald Eberhard, *Verfassungsrecht* (12th edn, Facultas 2019) 128–31.
16 See, for example, Peter Bußjäger (ed.), *Kooperativer Föderalismus in Österreich* (Braumüller 2010).
17 Cf., for example, Richard Novak, 'Art 99 B-VG' in Karl Korinek and others (eds), *Österreichisches Bundesverfassungsrecht* (Springer Verlag 2005) no 3; Heinz Peter Rill, 'Die österreichische Bundesstaatlichkeit und die Gesamtänderungsschwelle des Art 44 Abs 3 B-VG' in Metin Akyürek and others (eds), *Staat und Recht in europäischer Perspektive: Festschrift Heinz Schäffer* (Manz 2006) 717, at 730.

regulate their organization as independently as possible.[18] Being an 'essential element' of a leading constitutional principle entails that this element cannot be abolished or seriously amended by an ordinary amendment of the Federal Constitution, but additionally needs to be submitted to a referendum because of a 'total revision' of the Federal Constitution (Art 44 para 3 B-VG). Moreover, subnational constitutional autonomy is but a particular species of legislative power of the *Länder* and thus an important aspect of the general distribution of competences, which is an acknowledged 'essential element' of the principle of Austrian federalism.[19]

4.2 Autonomy

4.2.1 Scope

Art 99 para 1 B-VG sets out that the *Land* Constitution, which is to be enacted through a *Land* Constitutional Act, may be amended by a *Land* Constitutional Act inasmuch as this does not 'touch' the Federal Constitution. According to Art 99 para 2 B-VG, a *Land* Constitutional Act may only be passed with half of the members of the *Land* Parliament present and a majority of two-thirds of the votes cast.

Several corollaries result from this provision: first, the legal existence of *Land* constitutions is acknowledged and even demanded from the *Länder*. Second, the legal source of a *Land* constitution is determined and vested with a particular constitutional rank. Third, the procedure of how a *Land* constitution is enacted is determined. Fourth, the hierarchical position of *Land* constitutions is inferior to the Federal Constitution which they must not 'touch'. But the *Land* constitutions are constitutions in their own right; they are not only genuine laws of the *Länder*, but are vested with formal constitutional rank. They are neither (just) called statutes nor decrees nor are they federal (constitutional) laws enacted for particular *Länder*.

The entrenchment chosen by Art 99 B-VG resembles that of a subnational residuary competence which is usual in most federal states including Austria.[20] Here, it is not a general residuary power that is complementary to all enumerated powers, but the technique is similar: subnational constitutional autonomy is established not in a piecemeal fashion but through a general clause.

Thus, it would appear that the *Länder* have 'full' constitutional autonomy which is genetically connoted with a coming together or at least an 'original' federal system. This resembles the idea that a general residuary competence suggests broad powers of units that originally made up the federal system. In both cases, however, the strength or 'fullness' of power does not necessarily follow from the choice of a general clause.[21] Whether such autonomy is established under a general clause or in a piecemeal way is mostly a technical matter. While it is true that a general clause contains all non-enumerated matters without the risk of forgetting matters or defining them too narrowly, the actual scope of a general or a piecemeal entrenchment of autonomy ultimately depends on the scope of enumerated powers that are used to delimit this autonomy.

Indeed, the Federal Constitution already determines much that limits *Land* constitutional autonomy: it does not only regulate the distribution of powers—which prohibits the *Länder* from enacting *Land* constitutional law outside their competence—but also the essential

18 VfSlg 16.241/2001.
19 VfSlg 1030/1928; 2455/1952; 8161/1977; 8831/1980; 12.949/1991; 13.235/1992; 14.783/1997. See also Anna Gamper, 'Länder ohne Gesetzgebung: Was bliebe von der Bundesverfassung?' (forthcoming).
20 From comparative perspective, Palermo and Kössler (n 5), at 139–40; for Austria, see Art 15 para 1 B-VG.
21 See also Ronald L Watts, *Comparing Federal Systems* (3rd edn, McGill–Queen's University Press 2008) 89; Palermo and Kössler (n 5), at 139–40.

elements of the organization of the *Länder* (in particular, Art 95 ff B-VG). Moreover, it regulates many other constitutional features, such as fundamental rights or policy principles, in a way from which the *Länder* are not allowed to deviate. As a consequence, the degree to which the *Land* constitutions are coined by the Federal Constitution is rather high at least with regard to some constitutional matters. As early as in 1922, even *Kelsen* admitted that the fact that the Federal Constitution regulated the basic elements of the *Land* constitutions was, 'from the perspective of the principle of federalism, a certain anomaly'.[22]

In the early republican phase up to the 1960s, this 'anomaly' even entailed the concept that the *Land* constitutions were nothing but the 'implementing laws' of the Federal Constitution.[23] Since the texts of the *Land* constitutions were very similar, the general presumption was that they had been formulated after a pattern that chiefly repeated the relevant Federal Constitution's provisions and added some minor details, which was often scorned to be but a copying process.[24]

The notion of a *Land* constitution's scope changed in the 1960s, when *Friedrich Koja* published a leading book on the constitutional law of the *Länder*.[25] His concept of a 'relative constitutional autonomy' of the *Länder* was positively received into both academia and constitutional practice.[26] Accordingly, subnational constitutions may not only repeat[27] or implement in detail what the Federal Constitution states. They may also regulate additional issues as far as the Federal Constitution is not violated. The term 'touch' used by Art 99 B-VG has since been construed widely: the *Land* constitutions are not prevented from establishing their own rules on 'constitutional' matters just because anything 'constitutional' touches upon the Federal Constitution, but they are allowed to regulate anything and everything as far as this does not violate the Federal Constitution. Accordingly, the *Länder* began to enrich their constitutions, e.g. with regard to policy principles, direct democracy or even fundamental rights. As a consequence, more asymmetry emerged between them—not prescribed by the Federal Constitution, but stemming from the very possibility for a *Land* to enact its own constitution in accordance with its own political preferences.

Apart from the general clause entrenched in Art 99 B-VG, however, the B-VG[28] deals with the *Land* constitutions also in a piecemeal fashion. Thus, the *Länder* may base their constitutions not just on the general clause embedded in Art 99 B-VG, but also on more specific enabling provisions. According to these provisions, *Land* constitutional law may be passed, e.g., with

---

22 Kelsen, Froehlich and Merkl (n 9), at 194.
23 VfSlg 3134/1956; 6103/1969.
24 See, on the 'uniformity', 'conformity' and 'lack of imagination' of the older *Land* constitutions already Richard Novak, 'Ist ein "Vollzugsföderalismus" noch föderalistisch?' in Richard Novak, Berthold Sutter and Gernot D Hasiba (eds), *Historische und aktuelle Probleme des Föderalismus in Österreich* (Böhlau 1977) 27, at 54–5.
25 Friedrich Koja, *Das Verfassungsrecht der österreichischen Bundesländer* (1st edn, Verlag Österreich 1967); the second edition was published in 1988.
26 See, for example, Richard Novak, 'Bundes-Verfassungsgesetz und Landesverfassungsrecht' in Herbert Schambeck (ed.), *Das österreichische Bundes-Verfassungsgesetz und seine Entwicklung* (Duncker & Humblot 1980) 111; Peter Pernthaler, 'Die Verfassungsautonomie der österreichischen Bundesländer' (1986) *Juristische Blätter* 477, at 477–87; Pernthaler (n 13), at 459–62; Novak (n 17), at no 13–14; Erich Pürgy, 'Bundesverfassungsrecht und Landesrecht' in Erich Pürgy (ed.), *Das Recht der Länder*, vol 1 (Jan Sramek 2012) 1, at 17–19.
27 See also VfSlg 16.593/2002.
28 Apart from the B-VG, hardly any other piece of the fragmented Austrian federal constitutional law has specific impact on the *Land* constitutions. An exception is the Federal Constitutional Act on Principles for the Establishment and Management of the Offices of the *Land* Governments except Vienna (BGBl 1925/289 as amended by BGBl I 2019/14) which determines an important part of internal organization of the *Land* governments.

regard to the direct election of mayors,[29] to *Land* courts of auditors[30] and *Land* Ombudsmen,[31] several issues regarding *Land* parliamentary elections,[32] the *Land* law-making process,[33] *Land* emergency decrees,[34] the establishment of bodies that cannot be bound to instructions,[35] certain supervisory rules regarding *Land* employees,[36] the replacement of organs by *Land* functionaries in the context of schools and education,[37] as well as additional possibilities to challenge *Land* regulations[38] or laws[39] or accuse supreme *Land* functionaries[40] before the Constitutional Court. Lastly, if the *Länder* were to lose certain approval rights regarding boundary changes or if the territorial existence of a *Land* were threatened, this would require a 'combined' federal and a *Land* constitutional law.[41] In all these cases, the *Länder* are empowered and, in some cases, even obliged to enact constitutional law in order to determine the respective matter. While some of these empowerments are extremely detailed, others, such as the empowerment to regulate the *Land* lawmaking process (for which the B-VG, however, already contains essential rules), have a much broader scope. Mostly, these empowerment provisions were intended to clarify whether the *Land* constitutions were allowed to enact rules on a certain matter—accordingly, that they in these cases did not 'touch' the Federal Constitution which they would have done otherwise.[42]

Apart from Art 99 B-VG and the specific empowerment provisions, the Federal Constitution silently limits *Land* constitutional autonomy either by general principles, such as democracy or equality,[43] or provisions that literally refer to the federal level only but are applied to the *Länder* as well. It is not always easy for the *Länder* to anticipate if and how far such 'hidden' principles or provisions apply to them. For example, the Constitutional Court repealed a provision of the Vorarlberg Constitution because it allowed for stronger plebiscitarian democracy than the Federal Constitution did concerning plebiscites at federal level.[44]

According to Austrian positivistic understanding, the *Länder* could also enact constitutional law regulating a substantively non-constitutional matter provided that it passes the formal

---

29 Art 117 para 6 B-VG.
30 Art 127 para 7; Art 127c B-VG.
31 Art 148i B-VG.
32 Art 95 paras 1 and 5; Art 100 para 2 B-VG.
33 Art 97 para 1 B-VG.
34 Art 97 para 4 B-VG.
35 Art 20 para 2 B-VG.
36 Art 21 para 3 B-VG.
37 Art 113 para 2 B-VG.
38 Art 139 para 1 subpara 6 B-VG.
39 Art 140 para 1 subpara 3 B-VG.
40 Art 142 para 2 subpara d B-VG.
41 Art 2 para 3 B-VG. This suggests the idea that federal and *Land* constitutions are, even though under this aspect only, on equal level; still, however, it is the *Federal* Constitution that regulates this specificity. See Anna Gamper, 'Hierarchiefragen der Verfassungsänderung' in Clemens Jabloner and others (eds), *Scharfsinn im Recht* (Jan Sramek 2019) 161, at 178–82. 'Combined' *Land* constitutional laws can be passed for the purposes of Art 15a para 3 B-VG.
42 For instance, the specific empowerment with regard to the direct election of mayors (Art 117 para 6 B-VG) was entrenched in an amendment to the Federal Constitution after the Constitutional Court had repealed former *Land* legislation on the direct election of mayors (VfSlg 13.500/1993); see also VfSlg 15.302/1998. Six *Länder* (excluding Lower Austria, Styria and Vienna [for which Art 112 B-VG excludes a direct election of the mayor]) have decided for a direct election system.
43 On their limiting function for the *Land* constitutions, see VfSlg 11.669/1988; 12.229/1989; 13.076/1992.
44 VfSlg 16.241/2001. See Anna Gamper, 'The Principle of Homogeneity and Democracy in Austrian Federalism: The Constitutional Court's Ruling on Direct Democracy in Vorarlberg' (2003) 33(1) Publius: *The Journal of Federalism* 45.

constitutional lawmaking procedure and that its content does not violate the Federal Constitution.[45] However, the explicit enabling provisions all relate to matters that have a more or less 'constitutional' nature—inasmuch as they refer to supreme bodies, elections, direct democracy, the legislative process and other matters that, bearing an eminently political character, are typical of constitutional law in Austria and elsewhere. In some cases, the Federal Constitution even requires the *Land* constitutional lawmaker to enact certain pieces of law—e.g., regarding the legislative process at *Land* level. The Constitutional Court also held that 'provisions on the election of members of the *Land* government [...]—as norms that regulate the organisation of the *Land*—form typically 'substantive' *Land* constitutional law and should be entrenched in the *Land* Constitution'.[46] In practice, the *Land* constitutions regularly deal with substantively 'constitutional' matters only.

In rare cases, however, the Federal Constitution expressly empowers the *Länder* to enact ordinary legislation on matters that are considered 'substantively constitutional'.[47]

4.2.2 Procedure

As already mentioned, Art 99 para 2 B-VG provides that a *Land* Constitutional Act may only be passed with half of the members of the *Land* Parliament present and a majority of two-thirds of the votes cast. This provision resembles that regulating ordinary amendments to the Federal Constitution to which the same quorum and majority apply in the National Council (Art 44 para 1 B-VG). However, federal constitutional law, in order to be formally created, needs also to be officially denominated as 'federal constitutional law'. Although Art 99 para 2 B-VG does not explicitly provide a similar requirement for the creation of the *Land* constitutions, all *Land* constitutions stipulate the requirement of denominating *Land* constitutional law as '*Land* constitutional law'. The *Länder* have full procedural power to enact their own constitutions without interference from the federal level.

Two *Land* constitutions distinguish between ordinary and qualified amendments of the respective constitution, while the other seven just establish a uniform constitutional amendment procedure according to Art 99 para 2 B-VG: Art 35 para 2 Vorarlberg Constitution stipulates that *Land* constitutional amendments which would abolish Vorarlberg's position as an autonomous *Land*, reduce the *Land*'s territory, abolish the right of equal and direct vote or the rights of citizens and municipalities to launch popular initiatives as well as binding and advisory referendums, are to be submitted to a binding referendum.[48] Art 23 para 2 Salzburg Constitution provides that all 'total revisions' of the Salzburg Constitution need to be submitted to a binding referendum.[49] Even though both provisions—which have never been applied in practice—go beyond the standard amendment procedure as established by Art 99 para 2 B-VG, they are considered to be in line with the Federal Constitution since they to some extent reflect the two-layered structure of the federal constitutional order and the federal amendment procedures.[50] While the Vorarlberg Constitution exhaustively enumerates several contents that are particularly protected, the Salzburg Constitution adopts the Federal Constitution's term of a 'total revision' (Art 44 para 3

---

45 Wolfgang Pesendorfer, 'Art 99 B-VG' in Benjamin Kneihs and Georg Lienbacher (eds), *Rill-Schäffer-Kommentar Bundesverfassungsrecht* (Verlag Österreich 2002) no 11.

46 VfSlg 11.669/1988.

47 See Art 95 para 2 B-VG according to which the ordinary election laws of the *Länder* are empowered to regulate the more detailed conditions for the right to vote and to be elected in *Land* parliamentary elections.

48 Peter Pernthaler and Georg Lukasser, *Das Verfassungsrecht der österreichischen Bundesländer: 8. Vorarlberg* (Heinz Schäffer ed., Verlag Österreich 1995) 142–3.

49 Friedrich Koja, 'Bedeutet die Einführung des Mehrheitswahlrechts für die Bestellung der Landesregierung eine Gesamtänderung der Salzburger Landesverfassung?' (1998) *Journal für Rechtspolitik* 287.

50 Art 44 para 3 B-VG.

B-VG). Since *Land* constitutions have, in case of doubt, to be interpreted consistently with the Federal Constitution,[51] it appears that a 'total revision' of the Salzburg Constitution analogously needs to be understood as an amendment that abolishes or seriously interferes with a leading *Land* constitutional principle. Whether they are the same as the Federal Constitution's leading principles is questionable, since a *Land* does not even have full power to entrench all of them; at least, the leading principles of a *Land* constitution must not contravene them.[52]

4.3 Position of the subnational constitution within the subnational entity

It is, moreover, possible for the *Länder* not only to pass one incorporated *Land* constitution, but several *Land* constitutional acts or even single constitutional provisions in ordinary *Land* Acts. Even though the constitutional law of the *Länder* is not nearly as fragmented as federal constitutional law—which consists of several hundred different parts belonging to different legal sources—it often consists of more than just one 'Constitution' or 'Constitutional Act', i.e. the main constitutional document may be accompanied by one or two other constitutional *Land* laws or constitutional provisions in ordinary *Land* laws as well—e.g. with regard to electoral law, participation in EU matters, changes made to *Land* borders or budgetary matters; all these additional pieces of *Land* constitutional law have the same constitutional status and are not inferior by-laws. Still, all *Länder* have enacted one central constitutional document as their main constitution which is mostly referred to when speaking of '*Land* constitutions'. These 'main' constitutions are called *(Landes-)Verfassungsgesetz* in most of the *Länder*, *Stadtverfassung* in case of Vienna, which is both the capital, a *Land* and a municipality, and *Landesordnung* in case of the Tyrolean Constitution.

It is also up to the *Länder* constitutions to determine whether they want to give constitutional rank also to other legal acts. They could decide to vest international *Land* treaties—which the *Länder* may conclude under very restricted conditions, although they have never done so in practice[53]—or 'internal' treaties[54] with other *Länder* or the federation with constitutional rank.

Apart from Vorarlberg and Salzburg, whose constitutions, as mentioned before, establish a two-layered constitutional system, neither the Federal Constitution nor the *Land* constitutions distinguish between different layers of constitutional law of the *Länder*. In the legal hierarchy of the *Länder*, however, *Land* constitutional law is always superior to ordinary *Land* legislation. There is no intermediate level, such as that of organic laws, as in some other countries.

The *Land* constitutions are not merely symbolic documents. They serve as effective yardsticks for all legal acts of the *Länder* that are not only bound to observe the Federal Constitution, but also the respective *Land* constitution which, in turn, is itself bound to the Federal Constitution.

Unlike other (quasi-)federal systems, where subnational constitutions are crucial issues on the political agenda, serving particularly as a projection screen for regional identities, the Austrian *Land* constitutions are neither contested nor much discussed in civil society. The number of constitutional amendments varies between several amendments per year to one amendment every two or three years which shows that the *Land* constitutions are living documents that are regularly updated. *Land* constitutional amendments that have received some public attention in recent years related, e.g., to a specific protection clause regarding the Slovene national minority

---

51 See below n 65.
52 With more detail, Koja (n 49), at 287.
53 Art 16 B-VG.
54 Art 15a B-VG.

in Carinthia,[55] new policy principles such as climate protection,[56] whereas the whole *Land* constitution was re-enacted in Styria in 2010. Other recent amendments dealt with, *inter alia*, investigation committees, the *Land* budget and auditing, electoral law or direct democracy.

4.4 Content

4.4.1 Identity

All *Land* constitutions, except that of Vienna, include provisions regarding the respective *Land*'s identity at their beginning:[57] these provisions deal with symbolic issues of the *Länder* such as regional flags, coats of arms, anthems, language, capital, citizenship, territory and even saints.[58] While German as the official language is already determined by Art 8 para 1 B-VG, which is repeated by the *Land* constitutions, Art 5 Vorarlberg Constitution particularly protects the dialects spoken in Vorarlberg. Art 5 para 2 Carinthian Constitution repeats the provision entrenched in Art 8 para 2 B-VG concerning the linguistic and cultural pluralism of the 'autochthonous' national minorities in Austria, and adds 'as this is expressed in Carinthia by the Slovene national minority'.

In contrast to all other *Land* constitutions as well as the Federal Constitution, the Tyrolean Constitution features a preamble. The Tyrolean preamble is not legally binding, but expresses certain values that may be of relevance for the interpretation of the *Land* constitution or other pieces of *Land* legislation.[59] These values refer, *inter alia*, to the 'faith in God', 'the historical heritage' and 'spiritual and cultural unity of the whole *Land*' (an allusion to the division of Tyrol after the First World War between Austria and Italy), but the preamble also 'recognizes' the 'accession' of Tyrol to the Austrian federal state as well as the Federal Constitution.

No *Land* constitution uses the term 'nation' or 'national' with regard to the respective *Land*, but most constitutions stress the term 'autonomous Land' or call themselves a 'state' within the federal state of Austria. In these provisions, some constitutions reflect more self-consciousness of the *Land*'s political identity than others, such as the constitutions of Vorarlberg and Tyrol, which is typical of the Western *Länder*.[60] *Land* citizenship is already determined by Art 6 B-VG and has only limited relevance, namely with regard to the right to vote and to be elected in *Land* parliamentary elections and to the number of each *Land*'s delegates to the Federal Council.

4.4.2 Organization of powers and representative structures

The main part of the *Land* constitutions deals with the organization of powers—mainly, representative structures—both at *Land* and local level. However, this is also the part that is most

---

55 Inserted into Art 5 Carinthian Constitution by LGBl 2017/25.

56 As recently entrenched in the Carinthian, Lower Austrian and Tyrolean Constitution as well as in the Vorarlberg Constitution.

57 For an overview, Anna Gamper, 'Allgemeine Bestimmungen des Landesverfassungsrechts' in Pürgy (n 26) 61, at 75–80.

58 According to Art 7 para 6 Lower Austrian Constitution, Saint Leopold is the Land's patron saint.

59 See Anna Gamper, 'Präambel' in Peter Bußjäger, Anna Gamper and Christian Ranacher (eds), *Kommentar zum Tiroler Landesverfassungsrecht* (forthcoming); Peter Pernthaler, 'Die Präambel zur Tiroler Landesordnung' in Hans Walther Kaluza and others (eds), *Pax et Iustitia* (Duncker & Humblot 1990) 143.

60 On the political role and identity of the Western *Länder* Peter Bußjäger, 'Starke Westachse gegen Wien?' in Europäisches Zentrum für Föderalismus-Forschung Tübingen (ed.), *Jahrbuch des Föderalismus 2014* (Nomos 2014) 333; Peter Bußjäger, Ferdinand Karlhofer and Günther Pallaver (eds), *Die Besten im Westen?* (Braumüller 2008).

intensely determined by the Federal Constitution which entails that the *Land* constitutions hardly have any considerable structural differences in this respect.[61] In particular, Art 95 ff B-VG provides the basic elements of the organization of powers at *Land* level, e.g. how the *Land* parliaments and the *Land* governments are elected, what their functions are, what the position of the *Land* governor is and how *Land* legislation is passed. Other pieces of federal constitutional law regulate the internal organization of the *Land* government and its bureaucratic apparatus, the district administrative authorities, the administrative courts of the *Länder* and the basic principles of local government. Even though the *Länder* are competent to regulate these issues in their constitutions and, with even more detail, in their ordinary legislation, they must not deviate from what the Federal Constitution already establishes in this regard.

Usually, the *Land* constitutions regulate organizational issues such as, in particular, elections to the *Land* parliaments, the length of the parliamentary period, the number of parliamentary delegates, their immunity, incompatibility and loss of function, the lawmaking process, the presidency and dissolution of a *Land* parliament, the election of delegates to the Federal Council by the *Land* parliament, the election of the *Land* governments and the members of the *Land* governments and their functions. They also regulate instruments of parliamentary scrutiny that mostly resemble those that apply at federal level.[62] A particularly narrow scope applies to the electoral law regarding the *Land* parliaments, which has to follow the principles applied to the election of the National Council in accordance with the 'principle of electoral homogeneity'.[63] The margin is wider in case of the election of the *Land* government which has to be elected by the respective *Land* parliament in accordance with the Federal Constitution but for which the *Land* constitutions are free to choose a majoritarian or a proportional electoral system; in recent years, a majority of the *Länder* (except Lower Austria, Upper Austria and Vienna) decided for a majoritarian system.[64]

Since the Federal Constitution does not explicitly regulate direct democracy at *Land* level, the *Land* constitutions are thus free to decide on whether and how they establish forms of direct democracy. There are, however, implicit limits that the Constitutional Court derives from the federal constitutional principle of (mainly, representative) democracy.[65] Still, the *Land* constitutions regulate numerous instruments pertaining to direct democracy at *Land* and sometimes also at local level.[66]

---

61 See, for an overview, Pernthaler (n 13), at 462–3; Friedrich Koja, *Das Verfassungsrecht der österreichischen Bundesländer* (2nd edn, Springer Verlag 1988) 91–435; Novak (n 17), at no 8–12; Pürgy (n 26).

62 The *Länder* were, however, more innovative regarding investigation committees; Peter Bußjäger, 'Untersuchungsausschüsse im Bund und bei den Ländern' (2016) *Österreichische Juristen-Zeitung* 348, at 355.

63 Cf, most recently, VfSlg 20.139/2017. See, *inter alia*, Walter Hacksteiner and Christian Ranacher, 'Wahlrechtliche Homogenität und Landesbürgerschaft' in Anna Gamper (ed.), *Entwicklungen des Wahlrechts am europäischen Fallbeispiel* (Springer Verlag 2010) 417; Thomas Müller, 'Art 95/1–4 B-VG' in Karl Korinek and others (eds), *Österreichisches Bundesverfassungsrecht* (Springer Verlag 2006) no 5.

64 The Constitutional Court stresses the 'wide organizational scope' of the *Land* constitutions (e.g. VfSlg 11.669/1988). This assessment is, however, highly relative. While it is true that the *Land* constitutions may regulate a large variety of organizational details, the very basic elements of the *Land* lawmaking procedure as well as the election of the *Land* parliaments and the *Land* governments including their bureaucratic bodies are prescribed by the Federal Constitution.

65 VfSlg 16.241/2001.

66 For an overview, see Michael Mayrhofer, 'Landtagswahlen und Direkte Demokratie' in Pürgy (n 26) 153, at 206–12.

4.4.3 Fundamental rights

The possibility for *Land* constitutions to entrench fundamental rights is one of the most interesting fields of subnational constitutional autonomy. In accordance with the concept that the *Land* constitutions must not violate the Federal Constitution, the *Länder* may repeat fundamental rights that are already entrenched by the Federal Constitution, they may extend them or they may entrench additional fundamental rights.[67] They are, however, not allowed to reduce an existing federal constitutional right with regard to scope or apply a more restrictive reservation clause.[68] Moreover, the entire Federal Constitution—i.e. not only the fundamental rights entrenched therein—needs to be obeyed: the *Länder* could, for example, not entrench an additional fundamental right in a field where they have no competence because they could not require the competent federal legislature to enact legislation bound to this respective right.

So far, the *Länder* have made use of this possibility only in a limited way given also that the Federal Constitution already stipulates a large variety of fundamental rights; only social rights are, more or less, missing at federal constitutional level, but the *Länder* have as yet not filled the lacuna either, for lack of competence or because of general problems accompanied by the entrenchment of social rights at any level. Although the *Land* constitutions often repeat federal constitutional rights, such as the equality principle or the right to petition, and generously provide policy principles, only few genuine fundamental rights that either go beyond the respective federal constitutional right or are altogether 'new' rights were entrenched;[69] an exception are political rights such as electoral rights, the right to petition or plebiscitarian rights which are regularly entrenched in the *Land* constitutions.

However, the constitutions of Salzburg, Vorarlberg and Tyrol provide the right to compensation in case of an expropriation caused by a *Land* law while the federal constitutional right to property provides such compensation only under certain conditions.[70] The Tyrolean and Upper Austrian Constitution, moreover, oblige the respective *Land* to support people with disabilities, ill people or other people in need 'in accordance with *Land* legislation'.[71] Social welfare is a shared competence under Art 12 B-VG where the federation is responsible for framework legislation while the *Länder* have the competence to enact implementing laws and execute them. As long as the federation enacts no framework law on social welfare, the *Länder* are allowed to enact 'full' laws in this field. Until very recently, the federation had indeed not enacted a framework law on social welfare so that the *Länder* could and did enact full-fledged social welfare laws themselves which framed the Tyrolean and Upper Austrian fundamental right to social support. In 2019, however, the newly enacted federal framework law on social welfare[72] set uniform standards with regard to social benefits that had to be considered by the relevant *Länder* laws, but

---

67 See, for example, Palermo and Kössler (n 5), at 321–45; Matteo Monti, 'Subnational constitutions between asymmetry in fundamental rights protection and the principle of non-discrimination: a comparison between Belgium (Charter for Flanders) and Switzerland' (2019) 11(1) *Perspectives on Federalism* 1, at 13–16; Anna Gamper, 'Federalism and the Rule of Law' (forthcoming).

68 Gamper (n 67).

69 See Koja (n 61), at 71–81; Heinrich Kienberger, 'Grundrechtsverbürgungen in den österreichischen Landesverfassungen' in Rudolf Machacek, Willibald Pahr and Gerhard Stadler (eds), *40 Jahre EMRK. Grund- und Menschenrechte in Österreich*, vol 2 (N. P. Engel Verlag 1992) 27; Helmut Schreiner, 'Grundrechte und Landesverfassungen' (1999) 54 *Zeitschrift für öffentliches Recht* 89; Gamper (n 57), at 71–5.

70 Art 10 para 3 Salzburg Constitution; Art 11 paras 3 and 4 Tyrolean Constitution; Art 11 paras 2 and 3 Vorarlberg Constitution. See Gamper, 'Bestimmungen' (n 57), at 71–5.

71 Art 13 Tyrolean Constitution; Art 12 Upper Austrian Constitution. See Gamper (n 57), at 74.

72 BGBl I 2019/41.

part of this new law was repealed by the Constitutional Court because it was considered to violate fundamental rights guaranteed in the Federal Constitution.[73]

4.4.4 *Policy principles*

Perhaps the richest diversity of *Land* constitutional law can be found in respect of policy principles. It is remarkable that in the early period of both the Federal Constitution and the *Land* constitutions policy principles were absent due to the concept that a constitution should only establish 'the rules of the game', i.e. mainly organizational law and fundamental rights, instead of programmatic value principles. This concept has changed over time so that today both the Federal Constitution and most *Land* constitutions, apart from the constitutions of Burgenland, Styria and Vienna, contain a number of policy principles. In recent years, some *Länder* have even entrenched such a plethora of policy principles that one may almost question their relevance.

Provisions on policy principles normally use the phrasing 'the *Land* commits itself/acknowledges/recognizes/respects'. While these principles do not entrench any fundamental rights, they nevertheless establish guidelines that bind all organs of the *Länder*, i.e. both legislatures, governments and courts.[74] Since their wording is usually very general and vague, the margin of appreciation on how to implement them is wide. Only in excessive cases, interference with or non-implementation of such a principle would be found to be unconstitutional, but this is more or less theoretical. Nonetheless, the policy principles have a guiding function with regard to the interpretation of inferior law that needs to be construed in the light of these principles. In practice, this has mostly happened in the case of environmental and nature protection which is particularly often entrenched at *Land* constitutional level and includes many aspects, such as, most recently, climate protection.[75] Also a vast number of other policy principles has been entrenched, such as: an efficient economy,[76] subsidiarity and solidarity in civil society,[77] the protection of families, children and youth,[78] of elderly, people with disabilities, ill or dying people,[79] the protection of sciences, education and folklore,[80] of dialects,[81] of the importance of non-working days,[82] of adequate housing,[83] of citizen-closeness and deregulation,[84] of work and

---

73 VfGH 12 December 2019, G 164/2019-25, G 171/2019-24.

74 Gamper (n 57), at 69–71.

75 Art 7a and 7b Carinthian Constitution; Art 4 paras 2 and 3 Lower Austrian Constitution; Art 9 Salzburg Constitution; Art 7 para 2 Tyrolean Constitution; Art 10 Upper Austrian Constitution; Art 7 paras 6 and 7 Vorarlberg Constitution.

76 Art 7b Carinthian Constitution; Art 4 paras 2 and 3 Lower Austrian Constitution; Art 9 Salzburg Constitution; Art 7 paras 2-4 Tyrolean Constitution; Art 11 Upper Austrian Constitution.

77 Art 4 para 1 Lower Austrian Constitution; Art 7 para 1 Tyrolean Constitution; Art 1a and Art 9 paras 1 and 2 Upper Austrian Constitution; Art 7 para 1 Vorarlberg Constitution.

78 Art 7b Carinthian Constitution; Art 4 para 4 Lower Austrian Constitution; Art 9 Salzburg Constitution; Art 9 Tyrolean Constitution; Art 13 Upper Austrian Constitution; Art 8 Vorarlberg Constitution.

79 Art 7b Carinthian Constitution; Art 4 para 4 Lower Austrian Constitution; Art 9 Salzburg Constitution; Art 12 and Art 13 para 4 Upper Austrian Constitution; Art 7 paras 3 and 4 Vorarlberg Constitution.

80 Art 7b Carinthian Constitution; Art 4 para 5 Lower Austrian Constitution; Art 9 Salzburg Constitution; Art 10 Tyrolean Constitution; Art 14 and Art 15 para 1 Upper Austrian Constitution; Art 9 Vorarlberg Constitution.

81 Art 5 Vorarlberg Constitution.

82 Art 7b Carinthian Constitution; Art 4 para 3 Lower Austrian Constitution; Art 9 Salzburg Constitution; Art 15 para 4 Upper Austrian Constitution; Art 7 para 5 Vorarlberg Constitution.

83 Art 7b Carinthian Constitution; Art 9 Salzburg Constitution; Art 7 para 2 Tyrolean Constitution; Art 15 Aara 2 Upper Austrian Constitution.

84 Art 4 para 7 Lower Austrian Constitution; Art 9 para 5 Upper Austrian Constitution.

working conditions,[85] of volunteer work,[86] of leisure and sport,[87] of a unified Europe[88] and of legally recognized religious communities with regard to the religious and moral foundation of human life.[89] Sometimes, also direct and participatory democracy,[90] federalism,[91] local government,[92] national minorities,[93] the rule of law[94] or the social welfare state[95] are mentioned as political programmes of the respective *Land*. In some cases, the *Land* constitutions just repeat and fortify principles already established at federal constitutional level, while in other cases they establish additional principles, all of which, however, can only relate to the limited sphere of *Land* competences. While the majority of policy principles entrenches a particular state aim, some constitutions also give very general guidelines how to implement these aims—e.g. through subsidiarity, efficiency, proportionality or other principles. Even though the *Länder* have been highly innovative in developing policy principles, they have only modest impact since they are hardly justiciable and do not entrench any subjective rights.

4.4.5 Other issues

Apart from the content described above, the *Land* constitutions regulate numerous other issues. These include the *Land* budget, international treaties of the *Land*, internal treaties with other *Länder* and/or the federation, municipalities, *Land* participation in EU matters, *Land* emergency decrees, the administrative court of the *Land*, the *Land* court of auditors, the *Land* ombudsman (in Tyrol and Vorarlberg; or the empowerment of the Federal Ombudsman to scrutinize *Land* administration in all other *Land* constitutions respectively) and some other minor issues. A specific case is constituted by the Vienna Constitution which regulates both the status of Vienna as a *Land* and as a municipality and is thus split into two parts.

4.5 Multilevel constitutionalism

The degree of federal constitutional pre-determination of subconstitutional autonomy is not homogeneous: while, with regard to organizational matters, the Federal Constitution leaves little to the *Land* constitutions but to regulate the details, there is much more scope with regard to identity provisions or policy principles that, however, sometimes do not go beyond mere constitutional symbolism. But whatever the Federal Constitution requires applies symmetrically to all *Länder*, with only some exceptions for Vienna.

---

85 Art 7b Carinthian Constitution; Art 4 para 3 Lower Austrian Constitution; Art 9 Salzburg Constitution; Art 11 para 1 Upper Austrian Constitution.
86 Art 7 para 1 Tyrolean Constitution; Art 15 para 3 Upper Austrian Constitution; Art 7 para 1 Vorarlberg Constitution.
87 Art 15 para 5 Upper Austrian Constitution.
88 Art 1 para 3 Carinthian Constitution; Art 1a Upper Austrian Constitution.
89 Art 1 para 1 Vorarlberg Constitution.
90 Art 1 para 4 Carinthian Constitution; Art 5 para 5 Salzburg Constitution; Art 1 para 4 Vorarlberg Constitution.
91 Art 1 para 2 Carinthian Constitution; Art 1 para 2 Salzburg Constitution; preamble Tyrolean Constitution; Art 1a Upper Austrian Constitution; Art 1 para 1 Vorarlberg Constitution.
92 Art 1 para 2 Salzburg Constitution.
93 Art 5 para 2 Carinthian Constitution.
94 Art 1 para 1 Burgenland Constitution; 1 para 3 Carinthian Constitution; Art 1 para 2 Salzburg Constitution; Art 1a Upper Austrian Constitution; Art 1 para 1 Vorarlberg Constitution.
95 Art 1 para 1 Burgenland Constitution; Art 12 para 3 Upper Austrian Constitution.

The *Länder* cannot directly participate in the amendment procedure of the Federal Constitution, but are mediated by the Federal Council in which the *Länder* are represented asymmetrically. In most cases, however, the Federal Council commands only a suspensive veto power that could be overruled by the National Council. Since the reduction of subnational constitutional autonomy would imply the reduction of a particular legislative *Land* power, in which case the Federal Council commands an absolute veto power under Art 44 para 2 B-VG, subconstitutional autonomy is better protected, but the Federal Council hardly ever uses this power, especially not when political majorities in both chambers overlap. Moreover, it is the informal Conference of the *Land* Governors that expresses political concerns of the *Länder*, which in most cases leads to prior compromises before the Federal Council is at all approached in the federal constitutional amendment process.[96]

Supranational and international law, in their turn, have relatively little impact on the *Land* constitutions because they do not touch on organizational or identity issues at regional level. As to fundamental rights, Austria is the only Council of Europe (CoE) member state that gave the European Convention on Human Rights (ECHR) and most of its protocols the rank of federal constitutional law.[97] The *Land* constitutions are thus bound to the Convention rights as well, because they are part of the federal constitutional yardstick. However, they may extend them in accordance with Art 53 ECHR. In a few cases, the *Land* constitutions even explicitly mention international treaties, such as the ECHR[98] or the Convention on the Rights of the Child[99] to which they regard themselves committed within their competence.

Some *Land* constitutions refer to EU notification requirements[100] or to European regionalism within a united Europe: the constitutions of Carinthia and Upper Austria stress that the respective *Land* feels committed to a Europe that recognizes the autonomy of regions and secures their participation in EU decision-making.[101] The Styrian and Tyrolean Constitution explicitly prohibit a binding referendum on laws that are required by EU law.[102] Other *Land* constitutions contain, *inter alia*, provisions on EU committees of the *Land* parliaments[103] or the collaboration of the *Land* court of auditors within the EU system of financial control.[104] In some *Länder*, constitutional provisions apply according to which the *Land* parliament may deliver statements on planned EU projects which are binding to the *Land* government unless for compelling reasons that lie in the interest of the *Land* or integration policy.[105] Such a statement is important inasmuch as the *Länder*, represented by the *Länder* governors, can thus bind the federal

---

96 Andreas Rosner, *Koordinationsinstrumente der österreichischen Bundesländer* (Braumüller 2000); Andreas Rosner and Peter Bußjäger (eds), *Im Dienste der Länder—im Interesse des Gesamtstaates* (Braumüller 2011).

97 With more detail, Anna Gamper, 'Austria: Endorsing the Convention System, Endorsing the Constitution' in Patricia Popelier, Sarah Lambrecht and Koen Lemmens (eds), *Criticism of the European Court of Human Rights* (Intersentia 2016) 75, at 75–7.

98 Art 9 para 4 Upper Austrian Constitution.

99 Art 4 para 4 Lower Austrian Constitution; Art 13 para 2 Upper Austrian Constitution; Art 8 para 3 Vorarlberg Constitution.

100 Art 29 para 2 Burgenland Constitution; Art 32 para 1 Carinthian Constitution; Art 25a and Art 45a para 2 Lower Austrian Constitution.

101 Art 1 para 3 Carinthian Constitution; Art 1a Upper Austrian Constitution.

102 Art 72 para 2 subpara 3 Styrian Constitution; Art 39 para 2 subpara b Tyrolean Constitution.

103 Art 42b Burgenland Constitution; § 2 Tyrolean Constitutional Act on the Participation of the *Land* Tyrol in Issues of European Integration; Art 2 Upper Austrian Constitutional Act on the Participation of the *Land* Upper Austria in European Integration; Art 55 para 4 Vorarlberg Constitution.

104 Art 74 para 2 subpara 8 Burgenland Constitution; Art 47 para 1 subpara 5 and Art 58 Styrian Constitution; Art 67 para 4 subpara k Tyrolean Constitution; § 73b para 5 Vienna Constitution.

105 Art 83 para 3 Burgenland Constitution; Art 55 para 3 Vorarlberg Constitution; similarly, § 4 para 4 Tyrolean Constitutional Act (n 103); Art 5 paras 1 and 2 Upper Austrian Constitutional Act (n 103).

government (unless compelling reasons of foreign and integration policy apply) if planned EU projects touch upon *Länder* competences. The *Land* constitutions thus provide the (otherwise missing) link between the *Land* parliament and the *Land* government/governor respectively when it comes to the ascending phase of EU decision-making. Moreover, Art 55 Constitution Vorarlberg implements Art 23g para 3 B-VG which empowers every *Land* parliament to deliver non-binding statements to the Federal Council with regard to EU subsidiarity monitoring.[106]

However, most of the internal arrangements regarding the ascending or descending phase of EU decision-making is already determined by the B-VG, by a formal agreement between the federation and the *Länder* which itself has federal constitutional rank[107] and by a formal agreement between the *Länder* themselves.[108] The *Land* constitutions can thus only marginally contribute to these arrangements inasmuch as they determine the arrangements between the respective *Land* institutions.

4.6 Constitutional review

In accordance with Art 140 B-VG, the Austrian Constitutional Court may examine laws and repeal them if they are unconstitutional. Accordingly, the Constitutional Court will repeal ordinary *Land* laws that violate the *Land* constitutions, but also the *Land* constitutions themselves if they violate the Federal Constitution. The *Land* constitutions are thus protected by as well as themselves subject to constitutional review.

In practice, the Constitutional Court has dealt with the *Land* constitutions under both aspects. In some cases, the Constitutional Court even repealed provisions of a *Land* constitution because they violated the Federal Constitution.[109] This shows that *Land* constitutions are both fully justiciable and reviewable. The perhaps most prominent case where a provision of a *Land* constitution was repealed has already been mentioned: in its judgment on direct democracy in Vorarlberg, the Constitutional Court was, however, criticized by many academics for a too restrictive application of the democratic principle to a *Land* constitution.[110]

A recent case concerned the building of a third runway of Vienna airport in which the Constitutional Court held that policy principles of the *Land* constitutions—such as 'environmental and climate protection' according to the Lower Austrian Constitution—could only have effect within the competence of the *Land* and thus not be used as a yardstick of the interpretation of a federal law.[111] In another case concerning crosses in Lower Austrian nursery schools the Court argued that also the policy principles of the Lower Austrian Constitution regarding children and their accommodation in a democratic, free and tolerant society pleaded for the non-doctrinal character of crosses on the wall which therefore were not held to interfere with religious freedom.[112]

---

106 Anna Gamper, 'Mitwirkung des nationalen Parlaments an der Subsidiaritätskontrolle' in Stefan Griller and others (eds), *20 Jahre EU-Mitgliedschaft Österreichs* (Verlag Österreich 2015) 339, at 348–53.
107 See, for example, BGBl 1992/775 as amended by BGBl I 2008/2.
108 See, for example, Tir LGBl 1993/17.
109 See, for example, the overview by Novak (n 17), at no. 4–25.
110 VfSlg 16.241/2001. See, for example, Theo Öhlinger, 'Bundesverfassungsrechtliche Grenzen der Volksgesetzgebung' (2000) *Montfort* 402; Theo Öhlinger, 'Direkte Demokratie: Möglichkeiten und Grenzen' (2012) *Österreichische Juristen-Zeitung* 1054; Peter Pernthaler, 'Demokratische Identität oder bundesstaatliche Homogenität der Demokratiesysteme in Bund und Ländern' (2000) *Juristische Blätter* 808; Anna Gamper, 'Parlamentarische Rechtsetzung und direkte Demokratie: Verfassungsrechtliche Grenzen' in Georg Lienbacher and Erich Pürgy (eds), *Parlamentarische Rechtsetzung in der Krise* (Jan Sramek 2014) 101.
111 VfSlg 20.185/2017.
112 VfSlg 19.349/2011.

The Constitutional Court also holds that rights established by a *Land* constitution, such as electoral rights, are 'constitutionally recognized rights' against violations of which complaints under Art 144 B-VG may be made.[113] Further, the Constitutional Court applies the unwritten interpretive method of 'consistent interpretation'[114] inasmuch as an ambiguous ordinary law has to be given a meaning that is consistent with the constitution; although this mainly concerns the Federal Constitution as a consistency yardstick, the Court also found that, in case of doubt, a *Land* ordinary law has to be given a meaning that is consistent with the *Land* constitution.[115]

4.7 Conclusion

In the early period, the constitutions of the Austrian *Länder* led a life in the shadow, being understood as little more than implementing laws of the Federal Constitution. For many decades, however, a new concept has prevailed according to which the *Länder* have some scope for regulating their own constitutional issues; a growing interest for the *Land* constitutions can also be observed in academia.[116] Although their constitutions are, by and large, structurally and substantively similar, more institutional innovation and differentiation between them has become visible in recent years. This is not only due to differences in respect of state symbols and policy principles, but also in respect of institutional issues. Still, however, subnational constitutional autonomy has a symmetric character, and differences between the *Land* constitutions cannot be attributed to divided societies but to (relatively) minor differences arising from territory, budget, economy, historical identity or party politics.

The *Land* constitutions are full-fledged constitutions with a high hierarchical status, being subject only to the Federal Constitution itself. Even though the Federal Constitution predetermines some *Land* constitutional issues intensely, there still remain several fields where the *Länder* have wide constitutional space. This allows a classification of their constitutional autonomy into the medium-strong (MS) category outlined in this book: full procedural autonomy of the *Länder* to enact their own constitutions and a varying degree of autonomy regarding their content. Even though still remote from being constitutional high-tech laboratories, the *Land* constitutions thus are a solid pillar of constitutional law and a distinctive feature of federalism in Austria.

---

113 VfSlg 19.454/2011.

114 With more detail, Anna Gamper, *Regeln der Verfassungsinterpretation* (Springer Verlag 2012) 216–32.

115 VfSlg 7725/1975.

116 See, for example, Koja (n 61); Pernthaler (n 13), at 459–82. Detailed commentaries were and are written on the constitutions of Styria, Tyrol and Vorarlberg (Christoph Grabenwarter (ed.), *Steiermärkische Landesverfassung* (Verlag Österreich 2013); Siegbert Morscher, *Das Verfassungsrecht der österreichischen Bundesländer: 7. Tirol* (Heinz Schäffer ed, Verlag Österreich 1991); Peter Bußjäger, Anna Gamper and Christian Ranacher (eds), *Kommentar zum Tiroler Landesverfassungsrecht* (forthcoming); Pernthaler and Lukasser (n 48)). See also Pürgy (n 26).

5

SUBNATIONAL CONSTITUTIONALISM IN BELGIUM

A matter of abstained maturity

Patricia Popelier

5.1 Context

Subnational constitutionalism is a delicate topic in Belgium: of little relevance in daily life, but touching some nerves as a symbol of (Flemish) autonomy. It is of little practical relevance because most aspects that define a constitutional system are regulated in federal laws, and the few constituent powers that are granted to the subnational entities (SNEs) are often exercised in a way that is similar to the federal arrangements. Nonetheless, talk of subnational constitutionalism is contentious, because the francophone part easily interprets the claims for a Flemish Constitution that regularly arise as an agenda for Flemish separatism.

The embryonic level of subnational constitutionalism, as well as the symbolic value attached to it, have to be understood within the context of Belgian federalism in a divided state. Belgian federalism is fragmenting, multinational, dyadic, overlapping and asymmetric. All these traits impact on how subnational constitutionalism in Belgium is conceived.

(i)   *Fragmenting.* Throughout the years, Belgium devolved from a unitary state into a federal system. Its purpose was to accommodate autonomy claims from the two major language groups. While initially French was the official language, Flemings in the north sought protection of the Dutch language and the Flemish culture. In turn, after World War II, when the once prosperous Wallonia entered economically more difficult waters and found the Flemings unwilling to subsidize the old coal and steel industry, Walloons in the south aspired for economic autonomy. For these reasons, communities with powers in cultural and language-related matters as well as regions with more economy and territory-based powers were created. Besides the Flemish Community and Region and the French Community and Walloon Region, a small German-speaking Community and a bilingual Brussels Region took form. Along the way, the transfer of powers to the SNEs became the way out every time the distrust that prevailed between the two language groups blocked federal decision-making.[1]

---

1 Wouter Pas, 'A Dynamic Federalism Built on Static Principles: The Case of Belgium' in G. Alan Tarr, Robert F. Williams and Josef Marko (eds), *Federalism, Subnational Constitutions, and Minority Rights* (Praeger 2004) 157, at 160 and 167.

DOI: 10.4324/9781003052111-5   66

Hence, subnational constitutions did not pre-exist. Instead, the transfer of constituent powers is part of the package that is to be negotiated in the process of a state reform.

(ii) *Multinational.* The subordination of Dutch-speaking Flemings in the nineteenth century gave rise to the Flemish Movement, which created a Flemish identity to support demands for the protection of the Flemish language and culture through self-government. Once SNEs were created, the Flemish government took over this task of Flemish identity creation.[2] The Walloon identity is less explicit and controlled and developed more as part of the socioeconomic emancipation of the Walloon region.[3] However, as the Walloon economy grew increasingly dependent upon Belgian financial inputs, the Walloons identified more with a (franco-)Belgian state. The linguistic divide, reinforced by socioeconomic and ideological cleavages along the same fault lines, shaped the Belgian state structure.[4] Federalism became the device for managing multinational conflicts.

While multinationalism is at the foundation of the Belgian federalization process, at the same time it explains the reluctance to grant subnational constitutional autonomy. The reason is that federalism is a tool to facilitate co-existence within a multinational state, but also sows seeds for more radical autonomy claims, that may culminate in separatism. In Belgium, the Flemings push hard for more autonomy, whereas the Walloons, for economic reasons, remain more attached to the Belgian federal state. The Walloons therefore tend to interpret the Flemish claim for their own constitution as a sign of a hidden agenda of Flemish separatism. This is not far-fetched: institutional capacity appears to be one of the building blocks that facilitate separatism.[5] Walloon distrust of the French-speaking parties explains why the constitutional autonomy of the SNEs has remained rather limited.[6]

(iii) *Dyadic.* Although Belgium consists of six SNEs[7]—three Communities and three Regions— Belgian federalism in fact revolves around the two major language groups. This is reflected in the institutional design of the constitution, with a French and a Dutch language group in the House of Representatives and the Senate; linguistic parity in the federal government; and linguistic parity in the composition of the apex courts. As a result, the federal decision-making process in Belgium shows confederal traits, as each language group has a *de jure* or *de facto* veto right.

Dyadic federalism, however, is a conflictual and therefore unstable form of state.[8] This adds to the atmosphere of distrust and ensures that the demand for subnational

---

2 Jaak Billiet, Bart Maddens and André-Paul Frognier, 'Does Belgium (Still) Exist? Differences in Political Culture between Flemings and Walloons' (2006) 29 *West European Politics* 912, at 920.

3 Billiet, Maddens and Frognier (n 2), at 915.

4 For more detail, see Patricia Popelier, 'Asymmetry and Complexity as a Device for Multinational Conflict Management. A Country Study of Constitutional Asymmetry in Belgium' in Patricia Popelier and Maja Sahadzic (eds), *Constitutional Asymmetry in Multinational Federalism* (Palgrave Macmillan 2019) 17.

5 Lawrence M. Anderson, 'The Institutional Basis of Secessionist Politics: Federalism and Secession in the United States' (2004) 34 *Publius* 1, 7–10.

6 Patrick Peeters, 'Grondwet en "Staatlichkeit". Over institutionele, constitutieve en grondwetgevende autonomie van de gemeenschappen en de gewesten' in Frank Judo (ed.), *Van Vlaanderen tot Europa: wie vraagt om een Grondwet* (Larcier 2005) 37, at 39; Marc Uyttendaele, 'L'autonomie constitutive en droit fédéral belge' (1993) 17 *Administration Publique Trim.* 221.

7 Plus two unofficial entities in Brussels with Community competences: the Joint Community Commission and the French Community Commission. See Patricia Popelier and Koen Lemmens, *The Constitution of Belgium: A Contextual Analysis* (Hart 2015) 98–100.

8 Ivo D. Duchacek, 'Dyadic Federations and Confederations' (1988) 18 *Publius: The Journal of Federalism* 5, at 10. See also Daniel J. Elazar, *Exploring Federalism* (University of Alabama Press 1987) 244; Ronald L. Watts, *Comparing Federal Systems* (3rd edn Institute of Intergovernmental Relations, Queens' University 2008) 234.

constitutional powers ends up part of a difficult negotiating package. Also, dyadic federalism explains why constitutional powers were granted to the Brussels Region with some delay. The reasons are that the Flemish minority in Brussels needs special protection,[9] and that Flemish political parties feared that the strengthening of the Brussels Region, which is officially bilingual but predominantly French-speaking in fact, would lead to francophone dominance in the overall federal system.[10]

(iv) *Overlapping.* The Belgian federation consists of six official SNEs with several territorial overlaps. For example, the Flemish Community and the Flemish Region have jurisdiction in the Flemish linguistic area, but the Flemish Community also covers the territory of the Brussels bilingual area. The French Community and the Walloon Region have jurisdiction in the French linguistic area, but the French Community also covers the territory of the Brussels bilingual area, whereas the Walloon Region also covers the territory of the German linguistic area. The most complex situation can be found in Brussels, where the Brussels Region, the French Community as well as the Flemish Community have jurisdiction.

These overlaps create obstacles for the granting and exercise of subnational constituent powers. For example, while the Constitution prescribes a term of five years with the elections of subnational parliaments taking place on the same day as the European Parliament, it holds up the prospect for the Regions to be granted the power to change the term and day of elections.[11] The special majority law, required to make this effective, has not yet been enacted. Even if that were the case, it would be very difficult for the Flemish legislator to implement this. The composition of the Flemish Parliament—which is also responsible for community affairs in Brussels—includes six representatives from Brussels. In the absence of subnationality that distinguishes Brussels residents as belonging to the Flemish or French Community, the Flemish electoral system is hooked on to Brussels: only those Brussels voters who opt for a Flemish list for the Brussels Parliament also have the option of electing representatives for the Flemish Parliament. Hence, if the Flemish Parliament chose a separate date, it would be difficult to identify the Brussels voters.[12] Because of the overlap, institutional autonomy is often granted on a conditional basis, requiring respect for institutional and linguistic balances.

(v) *Asymmetric.* The Belgian federal system is characterized by constitutional asymmetry: variation in the status and powers of the different SNEs. The determinant for this asymmetry is multinationalism (variations in identity), reinforced by variations in economy, territory and the size of the population that correspond with the division in linguistic communities.[13] Again, this feature is reflected in the Belgian arrangement of subnational constitutionalism. Initially, subnational constitutional powers were granted to the Flemish Community (which merged with the Flemish Region), the French Community and the Walloon Region only. The Brussels Region was excluded for reasons explained above, based on the Flemish fear of francophone dominance. The German Community was excluded because, with a

---

9 Claudine Mertes, 'L'autonomie constitutive des communautés et des régions' (1999) *Courrier hebdomadaire du CRISP* Nos 1650–1, 1, at 14.

10 Marc Nihoul and François-Xavier Bárcena, 'Le principe de l'autonomie constitutive: le commencement d'un embryon viable' in Alexander De Becker and Emmanuel Vandenbossche (eds), *Eléments charnières ou éléments clés en droit constitutionnel* (die Keure 2011) 211, at 219.

11 Art. 117 and art. 118, par. 2 of the Constitution. The Constitution now also ties federal elections to this date, but the organic law to implement this principle has not (yet) been enacted.

12 Michiel Elst and Jeroen Van Nieuwenhove, *De zelfinrichtingsbevoegdheden van de deelstaten* (die Keure 2016) 144–5; Jan Velaers, *De Grondwet. Een artikelsgewijze commentaar* (die Keure, 2019, part II) 633–4.

13 Popelier (n 4), at 40–1.

population share of less than 1 per cent, it lacked the political power to claim this competence.[14] The sixth state reform of 2012–13 extended the subnational constituent powers to the Brussels Region and the German Community, but with several restrictions for the Brussels Region for the sake of linguistic and institutional balances.[15] The Joint Community Commission and the French Community Commission, two unofficial SNEs with a limited set of community powers in Brussels, are still deprived of constitutional powers.

5.2 Autonomy

5.2.1 Scope

The composition and functioning of subnational institutions as well as the recognition of fundamental rights are for the most part regulated by the federal Constitution and federal laws. The federal Constitution allows the SNEs to deviate from certain provisions, subject to two conditions. First, deviation is only possible for the election, composition and functioning of the subnational parliament, and the composition and functioning of the subnational government, and only to the extent designated by the federal lawmaker in an ordinary law (for the German-speaking Community) or in special majority laws (for the other SNEs).[16] In exceptional cases, subnational constitutional powers derive directly from the federal Constitution, such as the power of the Regions to organize an advisory referendum within their domain of exclusive powers.[17] And while residual powers rest with the federal authorities,[18] some self-organizing competences are considered to result from the very existence of SNEs with autonomous powers.[19] Most constitutional powers, however, take the form of deviations from specific provisions in the federal organic law, which gives a fragmented impression of the subnational constitution.

Several of the constitutional powers granted to the SNEs concern minor issues, such as the date for the opening of the parliamentary session[20] or the localization of the central office of an electoral district.[21] Other powers are subjected to substantial limitations or conditions, mostly in order to safeguard institutional and linguistic balances. For example, the French Community Parliament is composed of members of the Walloon Parliament and members of the French language group in the Brussels Parliament. If the French Community Parliament decides to change the number of MPs, it has to respect the proportion of Brussels and Walloon representatives, and it can only augment the number of representatives following the decision of the Walloon Parliament to augment its number of representatives first.[22]

As the federal law ultimately determines the scope of subnational constitutional powers, one might argue that the federal lawmaker, in theory, may also withdraw these powers afterwards.[23]

---

14 Nihoul and Bárcena (n 10), at 219; Pas (n 1), at 168.
15 For more detail, see Elst and Van Nieuwenhove (n 12), at 69–72.
16 Art. 118, par. 2 and art. 123, par. 2 Constitution.
17 Art. 39*bis* Constitution. For the Brussels Region, a federal majority law must lay down additional procedural requirements, to protect the Flemish minority in Brussels.
18 Art. 35 Constitution states otherwise, but has not yet come into force. This would, according to the transitional provision, require the adoption of a special majority law, but also a revision of the Constitution to include a provision that lists the federal competences.
19 For an overview: Elst and Van Nieuwenhove (n 12), at 47–59.
20 Art. 32, par. 1 Special Law on the Reform of the Institutions.
21 Art. 26*quater* Special Law on the Reform of the Institutions.
22 For more detail, Elst and Van Nieuwenhove (n 12), at 101–4.
23 Peeters (n 6), at 53. *Contra*: Karel Rimanque, 'De instellingen van Vlaanderen, de Franse Gemeenschap en het Vlaamse Gewest' in André Alen and Louis Paul Suetens (eds), *Het federale België na de vierde staatshervorming* (die Keure 1993) 165, at 186.

Special majority laws, however, require a majority in each (Dutch and French) language group, and a two-thirds majority overall. Considering the fact that the territorial division in Communities and Regions largely overlaps with the two major language groups, and that political parties are region based and therefore accountable to electors in their own linguistic region,[24] the phasing out of transferred constitutional powers is very unlikely.

5.2.2 Procedure

The procedure for changing subnational constitutional provisions is more flexible than the procedure for amending the federal Constitution or for amending special majority laws, which often have a quasi-constitutional character.

The revision of the federal Constitution requires that a majority indicates which provisions are open for amendment, followed by elections, and the newly elected constituent can only amend the provisions included in that list, with a two-thirds majority.[25] For special majority laws, as mentioned, a majority in each language group and an overall two-thirds majority is required.

By contrast, a two-thirds majority of the votes cast suffices for the use of subnational constitutional powers. Only in the Brussels Region, because of its bilingual character, a majority in each language group is an additional requirement. Here, the amendment procedure is as rigid as the procedure for amending federal special majority laws.

The two-thirds majority requirement for the German-speaking Parliament, however, is more rigid than the organic laws that determine the design of the German-speaking Community and the scope of its powers. As there is no German language group in the federal Parliament, the institutional arrangements can be amended by an ordinary majority in both the House of Representatives and the Senate. The involvement of the German-speaking Community is reduced to the presence of one community senator in the upper house.

The two-thirds majority requirement applies even to some minor issues that fall within the range of subnational constitutional autonomy. By contrast, some more important institutional matters have been transferred to the Communities and Regions in the form of subject-matter competencies rather than as constitutional powers, or are considered inherent powers linked to the entities' very existence, so that a simple majority is sufficient. An example is the control of election expenses.[26] Finally, some issues related to the functioning of the Parliament or the government are handled by internal rules of the Parliament or the government alone.

Within the scope of their subnational powers, the SNEs have full autonomy to initiate and adopt constitutional provisions, without involvement or supervision of the central authorities. Hence, from a procedural point of view, they have strong subnational constitutional powers. This agrees with the fundamental design of Belgian federalism, based on exclusive competences: once competences are transferred, they fall within the exclusive domain of that entity, without the involvement of other entities. Shared powers are extremely rare in the Belgian system of division of powers, leading to fragmentation in the distribution of powers.

---

24 With the exception of the marxist PTB-PVDA.
25 Art. 195 Constitution.
26 For more detail, see Elst and Van Nieuwenhove (n 12), at 11–12.

5.3 Position of the subnational constitution within the SNE

The way subnational constitutionalism is shaped, with punctual deviations to federal provisions, makes for fragmentation and therefore little transparency. The Flemish Community has on several occasions made efforts to strengthen the visibility of the Flemish constitutional provisions, by collecting them in one coordinated document. This resulted in a special majority law on the Flemish institutions.[27] Observers consider this Act illustrative for a more comprehensive vision on constitutional policy in Flanders, compared to the casuistic approach in Wallonia.[28] Be that as it may, the Flemish 'Special Decree', with barely 28 articles on the Flemish Parliament and government, shows how meagre and dispersed subnational constitutional autonomy in Belgium really is.

Flemish parties hold that the transfer of subnational constitutional powers is the logical consequence of any federalization process.[29] Yet, in public debate, subnational constitutionalism is not high on the priority list.

Flare-ups are at regular intervals observed in Flemish political debate, where the desire for obtaining full-fledged subnational powers is most strongly expressed, but this has not yet led to tangible results. The Flemish Parliament and government have taken several initiatives[30] to construct a more significant Flemish Constitution, in the form of discussion papers,[31] resolutions,[32] a special parliamentary commission on the Flemish Constitution, expert reports and drafts for constitutional charters.[33] Some scholars have argued for full subnational constitutional powers because of its symbolic function,[34] where it expresses the 'fundamental choices of a society'.[35] A competition was established inviting scholarly designs for a Flemish Constitution,[36] which was then discussed in the Flemish Parliament.[37] The most recent draft constitutional charter referred in its preamble to Flanders as a 'nation' within the federal state of Belgium, with its own language and culture.[38] The draft was never even discussed in Parliament. The coalition parties were reproached for keeping the process closed: neither the opposition nor the Flemish people were involved in the drafting.[39]

---

27 Special Decree on the Flemish Institutions of 7 July 2006, *Official Gazette* 17 October 2006.

28 Nihoul and Bárcena, *supra* n. 10 at p. 232.

29 This view was expressed by the Flemish government in 2008, see S. Lambrecht, 'Movement towards a Flemish Constitution: The Charter for Flanders, another failed attempt?' (2014) 6 *Perspectives on Federalism* 141, at 152. For a critical discussion, see Patricia Popelier, 'The need for subnational constitutions in federal theory and practice. The Belgian case' (2012) 4 *Perspectives on Federalism* 36.

30 For an overview, see Lambrecht (n 29), at 144–5.

31 Discussion paper on further state reform, approved by the Flemish government on 29 February 1996 and discussed in the Flemish Parliament: *Parl.Doc.* Flemish Parliament (1995–96) No. 253/1 at p. 14.

32 *Parl. Doc.* Flemish Parliament (1998–99) No. 1339.

33 Handvest van Vlaanderen, *Parl.Doc.* Flemish Parliament (2002–03) No. 46; Handvest voor Vlaanderen, *Parl. Doc.* (2011–12) No. 1643.

34 Cathy Berx, 'Een grondwet voor de Belgische deelstaten?' in Bruno Peeters and Jan Velaers (eds), *De Grondwet in groothoeksperspectief* (Intersentia 2007) 239, at 254.

35 Pas (n 1), at 169

36 This was awarded to Jan Clement et al., *Proeve van Grondwet voor Vlaanderen* (die Keure 1996).

37 Hearing, *Parl.Doc.* Flemish Parliament 1996–97, No. 527/1.

38 Handvest voor Vlaanderen, *Parl.Doc.* (2011–12) No. 1643. The use of the term 'nation' seems nevertheless to have sparked some discussion between the Flemish-nationalist N-VA and the other political parties: Guy Tegenbos, 'Vlaams Handvest struikelt nog over één woord', *De Standaard* 4 July 2011, 5.

39 See Lambrecht (n 29), at 146–7.

On the francophone side, a short-lived initiative by the socialist party for a Walloon Constitution met with little enthusiasm by the other parties, who feared that this would strengthen the position of Flemings in their demands for institutional reform.[40]

An argument has been made that if a subnational Parliament adopted a resolution establishing a constitutional charter, and if it was regularly referred to in legal or political practice, it would become a so-called 'para-legal' text that impacts on the constitutional system.[41] However, the legal reality is that subnational powers are only fragmentarily transferred to the SNEs, with the result that constitutional charters that go beyond the mere coordination of subnational constitutional provisions remain without legal force. Moreover, SNEs have only made limited use of the constitutional autonomy that they do have.[42]

5.4 Content[43]

5.4.1 Identity

The Belgian Constitution designates the 'nation' as the source of all powers.[44] This invokes the concept of national sovereignty developed by French constitutionalists such as Emmanuel Sieyès[45] and Raymond Carré de Malberg,[46] based on the abstract notion of an indivisible entity as holder of sovereignty. To symbolize this nation, the Constitution determines the Belgian flag and device: 'The Belgian Nation adopts red, yellow and black colors, and as arms of the kingdom the Lion of Belgium with the motto: Union is strength'.[47]

The concept of national sovereignty became outdated as soon as the Constitution, in 1970, lay the foundation for the multinational organization of political institutions in a divided state. The SNEs are called 'Communities' and 'Regions', avoiding the term 'States'. The use of the term 'nation' to describe Flanders in the draft constitutional charter was discussed amongst Flemish parties but not agreed on. Nevertheless, there is no principled discussion in Belgium concerning the meaning of nationhood or where sovereignty rests. Thus, despite the absence of an explicit constitutional ground, the Council of State[48] argued that Communities and Regions are public legal bodies that carry part of the sovereignty, and therefore have an inherent competence to regulate symbols of 'public collectivities', such as flags and anthems.[49] Initially, the Council derived this authority from the Communities' powers in cultural matters,[50] but,

40 'Un accueil tiède pour le projet de constitution wallonne, *La Libre,* 4 May 2006. See the proposal for a Walloon Constitution, *Parl.Doc.* Walloon Parliament, 2005–06, No. 367.
41 Olivier Van der Noot, 'Subnational constitutions: The Belgian case in the light of the Swiss experience' (2014) 6 *Perspectives on Federalism* 272, at 277–9.
42 Frank Judo, 'Deelstatelijk staatsrecht in België: theorie en praktijk van constitutieve autonomie en bijzondere decreten' (2006) 10 *Chroniques de Droit Public—Publiekrechtelijke Kronieken* 250, at 279.
43 For a comprehensive and detailed overview of constitutive powers, see Elst and Van Nieuwenhove (n 12), at 209.
44 Art. 33 Constitution.
45 Sieyès, *Ecrits politiques* and *Qu'est-ce que c'est le Tiers état?* On Sieyès thoughts, see Paul Bastid, *Sieyès et sa pensée* (Hachette 1970).
46 Raymond Carré de Malberg, *Contribution à la théorie générale de l'Etat* (Sirey 1920).
47 Art. 193 Constitution.
48 A legal body with a Division Legislation that gives obligatory, advisory opinions on draft laws and government decisions to both federal and subnational parliaments and governments.
49 Council of State, advisory opinion No. 23.800/8 of 7 November 1995, *Parl.Doc.* Flemish Parliament 1995–96, No. 266/1, 12.
50 Council of State, advisory opinion No. 12.294/2 of 30 April 1975, *Parl.Doc.* French Cultural Community Council 1974–75, No. 47/2, 7–8.

considering the principle of exclusive powers, this would lead to the 'absurd' result that the federal authority and the Regions would not be able to determine their own collective symbols.[51] As a result, the Regions and Communities determine their flags, arms, anthems and collective holidays in laws adopted by a simple majority. Although they symbolize subnational 'nationhood', they are not formally part of the set of subnational constitutional provisions.

Apart from these symbols, Belgian constitutionalism is shaped by pragmatism, rather than rhetoric. The Belgian Constitution has no preamble, and while the provisions designate Belgium as a federal state, no other state principles are mentioned. There is only an old constitutional decree, enacted after Belgium declared its independence, according to which Belgium is declared to be a constitutional, representative, hereditary monarchy.[52] The organization of the Belgian state as a democracy under the rule of law follows from the practical design of its institutions. In the same way, the federal arrangements organize the SNEs as representative governments, governed by a prime minister. The SNEs call the latter 'Minister-President', although the official federal texts speak of the 'chair of the government' and the SNEs have no authority to set up a real presidential system, with a president elected by the people. In the absence of real subnational constitutional power, there is not much room for the constitutional confirmation of subnational identity. So far, the most far-reaching expression of this is a draft Flemish constitutional charter, without legal force, the preamble and text of which proclaim adherence to the principles of democracy, the rule of law and solidarity.[53]

5.4.2 *Organization of powers*

The SNEs have their own parliaments and governments. The federal Constitution and laws determine their basic composition and functioning, but there is room for the SNEs to introduce their own details. By contrast, the judiciary in Belgium is an exclusive federal power and is therefore not discussed under this section.

5.4.2.1 *The exercise of competences*

The Constitution allows the Parliaments of the Flemish and French Communities, and their governments, to exercise the competences of the Flemish and the Walloon Regions respectively.[54] Only the Flemish Community has made use of this opportunity to merge the institutions into one Flemish Parliament and one Flemish government for both the Flemish Community and Region.

The French Community did make use of this power to delegate, in common agreement, competences to the Walloon Region and to the French linguistic group of the Brussels Region.[55] As only the French Community was a requesting party for the transfer of community competences to the region, it alone has this capacity under the Constitution.

The Walloon Region and the German-speaking Community can agree to transfer the exercise of regional competences within the German-speaking area to the German-speaking

---

51 Council of State, advisory opinion No. 23.800/8, at p. 12.
52 Decree of 22 November 1830 on the form of government of Belgium, *Bull. Off.* No. XLI.
53 The Charter for Flanders was initiated in the Parliament in 2012 as a proposal for a non-binding resolution, *Parl.Doc.* Flemish Parliament 2011–12, No 1643/1. It lost momentum when the government did not manage to find the two-thirds majority which it aspired for, even though a simple majority was sufficient for the adoption of a resolution.
54 Art. 137 Constitution.
55 Art. 138 Constitution.

Community. In this way, the German-speaking Community has expanded its sphere of competences to include, for instance, monuments, tourism and employment.

5.4.2.2 The parliaments

The composition and functioning of the subnational parliaments is largely determined by federal constitutional law. The Constitution states that the Communities and Regions have their own parliaments, composed of elected representatives.[56] The Constitution provides for a term of five years, with elections taking place on the same day as elections for the European Parliament.[57] It also gives the members of the subnational parliaments the right to free travel on all means of transport operated or funded by public authorities;[58] creates incompatibility with membership of the federal Chamber of Representative or co-opted membership of the Senate;[59] gives them immunity from prosecution with regards to opinions expressed or votes cast in the exercise of their duties; and protects them against arrest, referral to a court or coercive investigation measures except in the case of a flagrant offence or with the authorization of their parliament.[60] The Constitution confers power on the federal lawmaker to make more detailed arrangements, but it also allows the federal lawmaker to specify on which matters relating to the election, composition and functioning of the parliaments the subnational parliaments may depart from the federal arrangement.

As a result, all aspects concerning the election, composition and functioning of the parliaments are regulated by federal law, but the SNEs can deviate on some topics identified by the federal lawmaker. Often, this concerns only matters of detail and remains subject to federally imposed limitations.

As to *elections*, the SNEs[61] can determine the electoral districts, but these cannot cross linguistic borders,[62] and cannot be made so small that the electoral scheme becomes, in effect, a majority system with only one seat available for each electoral district.[63] The SNEs can also decide whether to adopt party-list or name-voting systems, as well as electoral gender quotas. With the exception of the German-speaking Community and the Brussels Region,[64] they can also determine the detailed rules under which surplus votes are weighted and combined. All other aspects, including whether a proportionality or majority system is adopted, the distribution of parliamentary seats and the determination of electoral thresholds, are federal competences.

As to *parliaments* themselves, the Communities and Regions have the power to increase or decrease the number of members, subject to several limitations aimed at protecting the Brussels representatives in the French and the Flemish Communities, and taking into account the effects on the composition of the French-speaking Parliament whose members are elected in the Walloon and the Brussels Parliaments.[65] The Brussels Region is excluded from this competence:

---

56 Art. 115–6 Constitution.
57 Art. 117 Constitution.
58 Art. 118*bis* Constitution.
59 Art. 119 Constitution. The Senate is composed of representatives of the SNEs and a few co-opted senators.
60 Art. 120 Constitution.
61 With the exception of the French Community Parliament, which is not conceived as a directly elected body because it is composed of members of the Walloon and Brussels Parliament.
62 So the Flemish Community cannot create one district for Brussels and the neigbouring province Flemish-Brabant, Elst and Van Nieuwenhove (n 12), at 130.
63 Const. Court No. 90/94, 22 December 1994.
64 See Elst and Van Nieuwenhove (n 12), at 142.
65 For more detail, see Elst and Van Nieuwenhove (n 12), at 100–4.

for the sake of institutional and linguistic balances, the Brussels Parliament has a fixed number of seats assigned to each language group. The SNEs[66]—with the exception of the French Community Parliament, whose members are not directly elected—have the power to add incompatibilities[67] to the long federal list, or to regulate some aspects of federal incompatibilities. In addition, parliaments and, respectively, governments can decide upon their own pensions and financial arrangements. Also, a subnational Act of Parliament, adopted by a single majority, can organize the parliament's right to hold an inquiry. Subnational parliaments have the power to determine the meeting and closure of the parliamentary session. More fundamentally, the Constitution directly grants the Regions the power to organize advisory referendums on matters within their sphere of exclusive competences, and to regulate these referendums by a statute adopted by a two-thirds majority.[68]

The SNEs have made little use of their constitutional competences, and mostly copy the federal arrangements. The Flemish Parliament has increased the size of the constituencies, but only to align them with the electoral districts that are delineated for the election of the federal House of Representatives.[69] The SNEs added incompatibilities for ministers and MPs, but these are similar to those that apply to their federal counterparts. They also made use of their powers to advance the opening of the parliamentary year by a few weeks and to regulate the bureau.

5.4.2.3 The government

The composition and functioning of the subnational governments are regulated in detail in the federal Constitution and federal laws enacted by special majority. In broad terms,[70] the SNEs may replace this with their own arrangements with regard to the maximum number of ministers in the government; incompatibilities; and the functioning of the government, such as the rules of deliberation, the political accountability before parliament and the modes and consequences of resignation. This is restricted for the Brussels Region, which has no power to change the rules of deliberation and the rules for resignation, because of the linguistic balances safeguarded by the current federal regulation.

The French Community and the Walloon Region have made use of their powers to augment the number of ministers in their governments. Most SNEs have added incompatibilities. The Flemish Community has replaced the federal provisions on deliberation, accountability and resignation with her own Special Act, but only to copy the federal regulation.[71]

5.4.3 Fundamental rights

The Belgian Constitution contains a list of fundamental rights. In addition, the human rights treaties to which Belgium is party apply with direct effect and in priority over domestic law.[72] The Constitutional Court connects them to the rights included in the Constitution.

---

66 Again with the exception of the French Community Parliament. Critical: Mertes (n 9), at 25–6.
67 That is, a list of functions and mandates that are deemed irreconcilable with the mandate of MP or minister.
68 Art. 39*bis* Constitution. With the exception of matters relating to finances or budget, or matters that require a two-thirds majority. The requirement of a majority in each language group is added in Art. 28 par. 4 of the federal special majority law for the regulation of advisory referendums in the Brussels Region, to protect the Dutch-speaking minority in this region.
69 For more detail, see Elst and Van Nieuwenhove (n 12), at 136–7.
70 For more detail, see Elst and Van Nieuwenhove (n 12), at 167–83.
71 Art 22–7 Special Decree on the Flemish Institutions of 7 July 2006, *Official Gazette* 17 October 2006.
72 Since Cass. 27 May 1971, Arr. *Cass.* 1971, 959

The SNEs, for their part, do not have the power to guarantee fundamental rights. They do, however, have the power to concretize and limit fundamental rights within the domain of their substantive powers.[73] In Flemish political circles there is nonetheless a desire to incorporate fundamental rights in a Flemish Constitution. The draft constitutional charter contained a list of fundamental rights, copied from the federal Constitution and international treaties, with the Charter of Fundamental Rights of the European Union as the most important frame of reference. Considering that these rights apply in Belgium in any case, the question remains what added value an additional subnational catalogue could bring. In scholarship, it has been argued that its symbolic value suffices, but also that transversal clauses could be added that are now absent in the federal catalogue.[74]

5.4.4 Policy principles

The Belgian federal Constitution was designed in 1831 as a pragmatic text, devoid of grand principles or political goals. Policy principles were added only recently. One example is Art. 7*bis*, which requires both the federal and the subnational authorities to 'pursue the objectives of sustainable development in its social, economic and environmental aspects, taking into account the solidarity between the generations'.

As the SNEs in Belgium only have the power to deviate from the federal Constitution on particular topics, they cannot add further policy principles that have constitutional status. They do have the power to formulate these within their sphere of competences, but only in an Act that can be amended by a simple majority, like any other subnational law.

5.5 Multilevel constitutionalism

5.5.1 The relation between the federal and subnational constitutions

The self-constituent capacity of SNEs in Belgium is broader than what at first sight can be deduced from the limited and fragmented constitutional powers that are assigned to them. This is because the federal and state constitutional provisions are linked.

Initially, the subnational institutions are organized at the level of the federal Constitution and, for the most part, federal special majority laws. Subsequently, SNEs may use their constitutional powers to deviate from certain federal provisions. The fact that most fundamental constitutional matters are regulated at the federal level does not necessarily prevent tailor-made design. For example, the Constitution takes into account the Flemish preference for a Community-based federal system and the francophone preference for a Region-based federal system, by providing the basis for a merger of the institutions of the Flemish Community and the Flemish Region, and for the transfer of powers from the French Community to the Walloon Region and the French Community Commission in Brussels.[75]

The SNEs are involved in federal arrangements of state institutions. A two-thirds majority of the Senate must approve any revision of the Constitution, enabling the SNEs to participate through their representatives in fundamental decisions of this kind. For the revision of the special majority laws, the French and the Dutch language groups each have veto rights. As

---

73 Karel Rimanque, 'Voorstel van Resolutie van het Vlaams Parlement houdende het Handvest van Vlaanderen' (2003–04) 67 *Rechtskundig Weekblad* 1001. This was confirmed by the Constitutional Court, No. 124/2000, 29 November 2000.
74 Van der Noot (n. 41), at 285.
75 Art. 137 and 138 Constitution.

mentioned, language groups are not identical to territorial SNEs, but they largely overlap in practice due to the absence of nation-wide political parties. By contrast, the self-constituent capacity of the German-speaking Community is weak. In the absence of a German-speaking language group in the federal Parliament, federal constitutional arrangements for the German-speaking Community are inserted in ordinary laws. In relation to those arrangements that are entrenched in the Constitution, the German-speaking Community, with only one representative in the Senate, has no control and little say over any revisions. The German-speaking Community therefore has to rely on consultation and lobbying to have influence upon federal arrangements that concern its own constitution.

Even where SNEs are involved in the federal arrangements, the fact remains that if they have specific preferences that do not fall under their range of constitutional competences, they have to negotiate possible changes.[76] In sensitive cases, the fragility of dyadic and multinational federalism explains the situation. Even the name-giving of institutions may turn out to be a sensitive matter. For example, although the SNEs do not have the power to determine their own names, the French Community unilaterally changed its name into 'Féderation Wallonie-Bruxelles'. This was met with great indignation by Flemish parties, who regarded this as a provocative francophone claim on Brussels.[77]

5.5.2 *The impact of the international and European legal space on subnational constitutionalism in Belgium*

Belgium is a Member State of the European Union (EU) and a Contracting Party to the European Convention of Human Rights (ECHR) system. This European legal space also impacts upon the Belgian constitutional order. The Belgian Constitutional Court frequently refers to EU and ECHR case law, and combines constitutional provisions with European and international law. European law may also impact on the federal system. For example, while the Belgian system of division of powers is based upon residence as a criterion for subnational competence, in the *Social Care Insurance Case*, the European Court of Justice undermined the integrity of this system by imposing employment as a criterion for matters within EU jurisdiction.[78] European and international law also impact upon the subnational sphere of autonomy. Treaties that are concluded by the federal government may include obligations that fall within the subnational sphere of competences and therefore bind the subnational authorities.

Subnational constitutional autonomy includes the capacity of SNEs to define their stance towards foreign, international and supranational entities.[79] In this respect, Belgian SNEs have surprisingly more far-reaching self-constituent capacity compared to other countries.[80]

First, they have the power to conclude international treaties within their sphere of competences.[81] The federal government can interfere only in exceptional circumstances, to safeguard the coherence of foreign policy.

---

76 Critical for this reason: Berx (n 34), at 249; Uyttendaele (n 6).
77 Toon Moonen, 'Wallobrux', *Juristenkrant* of 15 June 2011, 16.
78 Case C-212/6, Government of the French Community and Walloon Government v Flemish Government, 1 April 2008.
79 Patricia Popelier, 'Subnational Multilevel Constitutionalism' (2014) 6 *Perspectives on Federalism* 8; Nikos Skoutaris, 'Comparing the Subnational Space of the European Sub-State Entities in the Area of Foreign Relations' (2012) 4 *Perspectives on Federalism* 239, at 241.
80 For a comparative study, see Popelier (n 80), at 9–18.
81 Art. 167, para. 3 Constitution.

Second, they have a veto right in relation to so-called 'mixed' international treaties concluded by the federal government, i.e. treaties that contain provisions within the federal as well as within the subnational sphere of competence, since the federal as well as the subnational parliaments have to give approval.[82] This means that, theoretically, the German-speaking Community Parliament, representing less than 1 per cent of the Belgian population, may obstruct the coming into force of an EU treaty. In 2016, the Walloon government (with the Brussels government) threatened to block the CETA trade agreement between the EU and Canada. The agreement was finally signed, after some concessions were made.[83]

Third, in most matters that fall within the sphere of exclusive subnational competences, Belgium is represented in the European Council by subnational ministers.[84] In mixed matters, a mixed delegation is led by the federal or the regional minister, depending on the subject-matter.[85] In either case, coordination meetings precede the Council meetings where a binding stance is taken in consensus.[86]

Finally, the Belgian Declaration No. 51 states that subnational parliaments in the Belgian legal order have to be regarded on an equal footing with 'national' parliaments for the application of EU treaties. Under the Early Warning System, Member States may uphold the lawmaking procedure if they consider a draft to be contrary to the subsidiarity principle.[87] To this end, two votes are assigned to each Member State for submitting a so-called 'reasoned statement'. Under the Belgian scheme,[88] each subnational parliament can submit a reasoned statement and votes are cast in such a way that federal and subnational opinions are positioned next to each other, without fostering institutional dialogue.[89]

5.6 Constitutional review

Justice and the organization and functioning of the ordinary judiciary is somewhat fragmented but an essentially exclusive federal power, with only few aspects in which the Communities and Regions have parallel powers. The same applies to constitutional courts. Art. 142 of the Constitution establishes the Constitutional Court and assigns its organization—composition, competences and functioning—to the federal Parliament. SNEs do not have the power to establish their own constitutional courts.

The power of the federal Constitutional Court is, however, limited. It has the power to review federal and subnational Acts of Parliament against all provisions that allocate powers between the federal and subnational authorities and against certain provisions of the Constitution that concern education, taxes and fundamental rights. But it does not have the power to review subnational acts against subnational constitutional provisions.

---

82 Art. 167, para. 4 Constitution and cooperation agreement of 8 March 1994.

83 For a discussion, see Michaël Tatham, 'The Rise of Regional Influence in the EU—from Soft Policy Lobbying to Hard Vetoing' (2018) 56 *Journal of Common Market Studies* 672, at 680–3.

84 Cooperation agreement of 8 March 1994.

85 Cooperation agreement of 8 March 1994, Annex I.

86 Art. 2–6 Cooperation agreement of 8 March 1994. In the absence of consensus, Belgium will have to abstain in the Council of Ministers.

87 Protocol No. 2 on the application of subsidiarity and proportionality.

88 The last version is the parliamentary cooperation agreement of 29 March 2017.

89 Patricia Popelier and Werner Vandenbruwaene, 'The subsidiarity mechanism as a tool for inter-level dialogue in Belgium: on 'regional blindness' and cooperative flaws' (2011) 7 *European Constitutional Law Review* 204, at 223.

By contrast, ordinary and administrative courts do have the power to review lower acts against Acts of Parliament. In this way, they can, for example, assess whether government decrees are compatible with subnational constitutional provisions. In a much-discussed judgment, the Belgian Supreme Court indicated that it might review Acts of Parliament against all superior rules in so far as this task is not assigned to the Constitutional Court.[90] This might mean that ordinary and administrative courts can also review subnational Acts of Parliament against subnational constitutional provisions adopted by a two-thirds majority. However, this is not of sufficient significance to initiate the level of constitutional discourse that could bring life to subnational constitutions.

In academia, proposals were made to let Communities and Regions organize decentralized constitutional review.[91] The establishment of sub-state constitutional courts, however, has not been a topic of political discussion.

5.7 Conclusion

The features of Belgian federalism as a fragmenting, multinational, dyadic, overlapping and asymmetric system have shaped the contours of Belgian subnational constitutionalism. On the one hand, this means that SNEs only have embryonic powers to adopt constitutional provisions, and only in a fragmented way. As a result, SNEs have not made much use of their constitutional powers. This has been called a form of 'anemia', caused by the limited scope of subnational constitutional autonomy.[92] On the other hand, the self-constituent capacity of SNEs is considerable, at least for the two major language groups. The Flemish Community, the Walloon Region and the French Community have a decisive say on how federal law arranges their institutions, because the political parties in the federal government are region-based and the language groups can veto organic laws. They will have to negotiate with the other language group, but this does not alter the fact that they are strongly involved in the institutional arrangement. By contrast, the German-speaking Community hardly has a say in the federal design of its own constitutional system. Yet, all Communities and Regions have a strong position with regard to international and EU rules that impact their autonomy.

The conclusion is that Belgian SNEs have only weak powers to adopt their own constitutions, but strong procedural powers in relation to those matters that are assigned to them. This is compensated by strong self-constituent powers for the largest SNEs, while the German-speaking Community can only influence the federal arrangements that shape its constitution through informal, political means. All Regions and Communities, however, have a strong position when it comes to the conclusion of international treaties or the participation in the EU lawmaking process. In this way, all SNEs to some extent guard the gateway to international rules that are likely to put limits on their autonomy.

---

90 Cass. 21 April 2011.
91 Matthias Storme, 'De defederalisering van het gerecht in België' in Marc Taeymans (ed.), *Defederalisering van justitie* (Larcier 2003) 55, at 70–2 and 85–7.
92 Judo (n 42), at 249–50.

6

SUBNATIONAL CONSTITUTIONALISM IN BOSNIA AND HERZEGOVINA

Towering subnational autonomy and a loose clamp of the central level to all intents and purposes

Maja Sahadžić[1]

6.1 Context

The 1995 General Framework Agreement for Peace in Bosnia and Herzegovina (the Dayton Peace Agreement)[2] defines Bosnia and Herzegovina (B&H) as a compound of the Federation of B&H (FB&H) and the Republic of Srpska (RS) (the Entities)[3,4]. The FB&H consists of ten cantons, while the RS is a unitary subnational entity. The Brčko District (BD), a small subnational entity in north-eastern B&H, emerged in 1999 following an arbitration process.[5] Apart from the Constitution of B&H, the Entities and cantons have their own constitutions. The BD has a statute, which is not far from a constitution.[6] Added to this, the constitutional system of B&H is based on the principle of parity of three ethnic groups called constituent peoples—the Bosniaks, Croats and Serbs—in all tiers of government.

---

1 This paper is part of a research project funded by the Fundamental Research Foundation Flanders (Fonds Wetenschappelijk Onderzoek—FWO).
2 *The General Framework Agreement for Peace in B&H* (UN Doc. A/50/790 and S/1995/999 from 30/11/1995). The agreement was signed by Bosnia and Herzegovina, Croatia, and at that time Yugoslavia. It was witnessed by government officials from France, Germany, Spain, Russia, the United Kingdom, the United States of America and the European Union Special Negotiator. The United States played a crucial role in negotiations. Annex 4 of the Dayton Peace Agreement is the Constitution of B&H. It has never been adopted by the central level legislature and it has never been translated to the three official languages (Bosniak, Croat, and/or Serb).
3 The term 'Entities' is used in the Constitution of B&H to refer to the FB&H and the RS.
4 Article I 3. Constitution of B&H.
5 The process is described further in text.
6 The statute is not an ordinary law but calling it a constitution requires some caution. The statute has all elements of a constitution. However, the BD is a subnational entity in the joint ownership of the Entities, it is under the sovereignty of the central level government, and it displays the qualities of local self-government. See: Nedim Kulenović, 'Skupština Brčko Distrikta BiH: parlament ili općinsko vijeće?' in Saša Gavrić and Damir Banović (eds), *Parlamentarizam u Bosni i Hercegovini* (Sarajevski otvoreni centar/Fondacija Friedrich Ebert 2012).

DOI: 10.4324/9781003052111-6

There have been several ill-fated proposals to simplify the tangled framework, mainly initiated by domestic and international non-governmental actors. Some suggest repealing all subnational entities and their constitutions. Some propose replacing all subnational entities and their constitutions with a number of purely administrative regions or a number of regions with constitutions. Some argue for consolidation of the FB&H. Instead of ten cantons, they propose a smaller number of cantons with or without constitutions.[7] However, subnational constitutional reform has been opposed by all three constituent peoples. While the Bosniaks perceive that the present constitutional design increases the prospect of more autonomy for the Croats and the likelihood of independence for the Serbs, the Croats and Serbs fear the Bosniaks' aspirations for a renascence of the unitary system of government.[8] Hence, the status quo is likely to remain in place. The fragmented, multinational and asymmetrical features of the system are likely to continue.

6.1.1 A fragmenting coming-together fragmenting compound

To determine whether B&H constitutes a fragmenting or coming-together system is a formidable task. The process of constitutional (re) construction has been from the bottom-up and has occurred in several phases.

Following the dissolution of Yugoslavia[9] at the beginning of the 1990s, the unitary system of B&H started to collapse under the burden of ethnic differences. During 1992, the predominantly Serb-populated territory of B&H organized itself into the Republic of the Serb people[10] (later renamed the RS) and adopted its own constitution.[11] Following the conflict between the Bosniaks and Croats, the two sides signed the 1994 Washington Agreement.[12] This agreement established the FB&H (based on ten cantons) in the parts of B&H populated by the Bosniaks and Croats. The constitution of this subnational entity[13] was adopted as a part of the Washington Agreement, while the ten cantons subsequently adopted their own constitutions.

After the extensive peace process, the Dayton Peace Agreement established the new Constitution of B&H. Under the Constitution, B&H continued its legal existence as a state under international law.[14] But at the same time, the constitutional recognition of the previously established subnational entities and their respective constitutions[15] was also of a great moment. The Constitution implies that B&H has simply decentralized, while the bottom-up

---

7 A comprehensive set of proposals can be found at: Fondacija Centar za javno parvo, 'Ustavne inicijative' <http://fcjp.ba/index/php/-79214> accessed 18 December 2019. See also: Valery Perry, 'Constitutional Reform in Bosnia and Herzegovina: Does the Road to Confederation go through the EU?' (2015) 22 *International Peacekeeping* 490, at 491.

8 See also: Zarije Seizović, *Političke stranputice postdaytonske Bosne i Hercegovine* (Fakultet političkih nauka Univerzita u Sarajevu 2017) 7.

9 See: Pau Bossacoma Busquets, *Morality and Legality of Secession, A Theory of Natioanl Self-Determination* (Palgrave Macmillan 2020) 197.

10 *Declaration on Proclamation of the Republic of the Serb people of B&H* (Official gazette of the Serb people in B&H 2/92).

11 *The Constitution of the Serb Republic* (Official Gazette of the Serb people in B&H 3/92). Later on, this became *The Constitution of RS* (Official Gazette of RS 21/92, 28/94, 8/96, 13/96, 15/96, 16/96, 21/96, 21/02, 26/02, 30/02, 31/02, 69/02, 31/03, 98/03, 115/05, and 117/05).

12 *The Washington Framework Agreement* (Official Gazette of the FB&H 1/94).

13 *The Constitution of the Federation of B&H* (Official Gazette of the FB&H 1/94, 13/97, 16/02, 22/02, 52/02, 63/03, 9/94, 20/04, 33/04, 71/05, 72/05, and 88/08).

14 Article I 1. Constitution of B&H.

15 Article I 3. Constitution of B&H.

reconstruction suggests that the FB&H and the RS were combined to form B&H. This leaves enough space for the discussion of whether B&H has only devolved, or is an aggregate formed by combining the FB&H and the RS.

Added to this, in academic discussions, the BD remains as marginal as ever. The status of Brčko was a final stumbling block during the Dayton Peace Agreement negotiations. The city has always been multiethnic and it has existed without domination of any constituent people. During the negotiations, the sides in conflict could not agree about the status of the city. To move forward with the Dayton Peace Agreement, the sides agreed to subsequently determine the status of Brčko by arbitration. In 1999, the Arbitral Tribunal for Dispute Over the Inter-Entity Boundary in Brčko (the Arbitral Tribunal) defined the BD as a single administrative unit under the sovereignty of B&H. After that, Amendment I to the Constitution of B&H defined the Brčko District as a territory in the joint ownership of the Entities.[16] The BD features its own statute.[17]

The present state of affairs is a complex intermediate state in which the conflicting sides have substituted the battlefield for the institutions of government and their respective procedures. Repeated threats of organizing independence referendums coming from the RS,[18] steady calls for organizing a third subnational entity for the Croats[19] and ongoing unitaristic inclinations of the Bosniaks[20] are emblematic of the highly strained relations among the constituent peoples.

At first glance, and based on the constitutional provision that specifies the legal continuity of B&H, one could be tempted to mark it simply as a fragmenting system. But, such an assessment would ignore the fact that the constitutions of the Entities were in force before the Constitution of B&H. It would also ignore the fact that the Constitution of B&H (Annex 4 to the Dayton Peace Agreement) was not only approved by B&H. The Entities also approved the Constitution by signing declarations attached to Annex 4 to the Dayton Peace Agreement. The legal continuity of B&H is rather a legal fiction used to the recognition of the previously established FB&H and RS as two subnational entities.[21] After the unitary system collapsed due to identity differences, the Entities developed independently of one another. The Dayton Constitution ultimately recognized their pre-constitutional quality and bundled them together. The simultaneously fragmenting and coming-together characteristics of the system may be a portent of the future, as the three constituent peoples continue to coexist in a mutually distrustful and constitutionally conflicting environment.

---

16 *Amendment I to the Constitution of B&H* (Official Gazette of B&H 25/09).

17 *The Statute of the Brčko District of B&H* (Official Gazette of the BD of B&H 17/08, 39/09, and 02/10).

18 See, for example: Barbara Surk, 'Milorad Dodik Wants to Carve Up Bosnia. Peacefully, if Possible' (*New York Times* 2018) <https://www.nytimes.com/2018/02/16/world/Europe/dodik-republika-srpska-bosnia.html> accessed 14 April 2020; Danijel Kovacevic, 'Republika Srpska Postpones State Judiciary Referendum' (*BalkanInsight* 2017) <https://balkaninsight.com/2017/11/07/republika-srpska-postpones-state-judiciary-referendum-11-07-2017/> accessed 14 April 2020. On this note see also: Soeren Keil, 'Federalism as a Tool of Conflict-Resolution: The Case of Bosnia and Herzegovina' (2012) 1 *L'Europe en Formation* 205, at 214.

19 Mladen Lakic, 'Izetbegovic: Bosnian Croat Entity "Impossible Without War"' (*BalkanInsight* 2018) <https://balkaninsight.com/2018/02/05/third-entity-in-bosnia-not-possible-without-war-02-05-2018/> accessed 18 December 2019; Gordana Knezevic, 'Bosnia0s Postelection Blues' (RadioFreeEurope, RadioLiberty, 2018) <https://www.rferl.org/a/bosnia-s-postelection-blues/29555500.html> accessed 18 December 2019.

20 Srecko Latal, 'Bosnia Remains Hostage to Old, Obsolete Narratives' (*BalkanInsight*, 2019) <https://balkaninsight.com/2019/10/28/bosnia-remains-hostage-to-old-obsolete-narratives/> accessed 18 December 2019.

21 Joseph Marko, 'Problems of State-and-Nation-Building in Post-Conflict Situations: The Case of Bosnia-Herzegovina' (2006) 30 *Vermont Law Review* 503, at 518.

6.1.2 *Multinationalism at the core*

The Dayton Peace Agreement ended the Bosnian War[22] among the three ethnic groups in B&H. The result is an excessively complex system in which territorial formation is based on identity differences.[23] During the conflict, the three constituent peoples acquired equal power ratio among themselves.[24] This generated the principle of parity as the overriding principle that upholds a delicate ethnic equilibrium among the constituent peoples. Given that the constituent people evenly take part in all tiers of government, the multi-tiered structure of B&H and the principle of parity overlap.[25]

The principle of parity is reinforced by the party system that is based on ethnic party lines. Political parties in B&H link to identity markers and their territorial affiliation. They often feature the political leaders who advocate for two types of aspirations: centralizing (the Bosniaks) and decentralizing (the Croats and Serbs).[26] Compared to the identity of the Bosniaks, the identity of the Croats and Serbs is less associated with B&H. This is because their identity was already established and recognized in the former Yugoslavia. Added to this, they relate to neighboring Croatia and Serbia through their religious affiliation and languages. The Bosniaks had to build their distinct identity under unfortunate and difficult conditions.[27] The term Bosniak was officially first introduced in the Washington Agreement to mark the Bosnian Muslims.[28] The Bosnian language emerged as one of the three official languages by the end of the Bosnian War. However, unlike the Croats and Serbs, the Bosniaks have only B&H to relate to.[29]

22 The term 'Bosnian War' refers to an armed conflict that took place in B&H between 1992 and 1995.
23 See: Zarije Seizović, *Constituent Peoples and Constitutional Changes* (Dobra knjiga 2014) 15; Zarije Seizović, 'Političko pravni uzroci nacionalne mobilizacije i dekonstitucionalizacije u Bosni i Hercegovini' in *Paradigma Bosna, juče, danas, sutra* (Dobra knjiga 2014) 121. The linguistic split is recognized in the Constitution of Bosnia and Herzegovina, but it is somewhat disputed by linguists.
24 Soeren Keil and Anastasija Kudlenko, 'Bosnia and Herzegovina 20 Years after Dayton: Complexity Born of Paradoxes' (2015) 22 *International Peacekeeping* 471, at 480; Nurko Pobrić, *Ustavno pravo* (Slovo 2000) 320.
25 Maja Sahadžić, *Ustav Republike Srpske o ljudskim pravima i slobodama i 'Ostalim': O mogućnostima obvezujućeg i dozvoljenog narušavanja konstitutivne ravnoteže na normativnoj razini u korist nekonstitutivnih* (Edicija (ne)konstitutivni centra za političke studije, Centar za političke studije 2013) 15; Maja Sahadžić, 'Priroda političkog sistema u Bosni i Hercegovini' in Damir Banović and Saša Gavrić (eds), *Država, politika i društvo u Bosni i Hercegovini—Analiza postdejtonskog političkog sistema* (University Press, Magistrat izdanja 2011) 18. For better understanding how the concepts of the constituent peoples and parity emerged from the historical perspective see: Sven Pearson, 'The "national key" in Bosnia and Herzegovina: a historical perspective' (2015) 43 *Nationalities Papers* 213.
26 For further elaboration on how party lines link to ethnic traits see: Dino Abazović, 'Religious claims during the War and Post-War Bosnia and Herzegovina' (2015) 14 *borderlands* 1. Also, on political dynamics in B&H see: Jasmin Hasić, '"Deviating" Party Leadership Strategies in Bosnia and Herzegovina: A Comparison of Milorad Dodik and Dragan Čović' in Sergiu Gherghina (ed.), *Party Leaders in Eastern Europe, Personality, Behavior and Consequences* (Palgrave Macmillan 2020).
27 See: Dino Abazović, 'Rethinking Ethnicity, Religion, and Politics: The Case of Bosnia and Herzegovina' (2010) 7 *European Yearbook of Minority Issues* 321, at 327; James O'Brien, 'The Dayton constitution of Bosnia and Herzegovina' in Laurel E. Miller (ed.), *Framing the State in Times of Transition, Case Studies in Constitution Making* (United States Institute of Peace Press 2010) 333.
28 Sahadžić (n 25).
29 See: Maja Sahadžić, 'Mild Asymmetry and Ethnoterritorial Overlap in Charge of the Consequences of Multinationalism. A Country Study of Constitutional Asymmetry in Bosnia and Herzegovina' in Patricia Popelier and Maja Sahadžić (eds), *Constitutional Asymmetry in Multinational Federalism, Managing Multinationalism in Multi-tiered Systems* (Palgrave Macmillan 2019) 55.

6.1.3 *Asymmetries as a by-product*

The constitutional system of B&H is defined by constitutional asymmetries in status and powers and competences between and among different tiers of government. This can be explained by (1) the bottom-up constitutional (re)construction of B&H and (2) multinationalism.

As already mentioned, the system combines territorial and ethnic features. The territorial features link to the Entities, cantons, and the District. The ethnic features link to the principle of parity of the constituent peoples. As noted previously, the FB&H incorporates ten cantons (organized as unitary subnational entities) with the majority of either Bosniaks or Croats including two cantons with mixed population. The RS is organized as a unitary subnational entity populated predominantly by the Serbs. The BD is established as a multiethnic condominium.

Ethnicity is a key ingredient of constitutional asymmetries. When combined with territorial features, it interferes with territorial representation, voting, and veto mechanisms because it is reinforced with variations in size of population and variations in territory. Although the subnational entities captured vast (residual) powers and made their position towards the central level fairly symmetrical, the territorial and institutional structure embedded in subnational entities' constitutions made the distribution of competences differently prescribed and exercised.[30]

6.2 Autonomy

6.2.1 *Scope*

Subnational autonomy in B&H is high and the limitations of the central level are low (almost non-existent). This is associated with the bottom-up reconstruction of the constitutional system. While the Constitution of B&H assigns exclusive powers to the central level, these are confined to a limited number.[31] The Entities and the BD retain vast residual powers. The Constitution of B&H defines that all governmental powers and functions that are not expressly assigned to the central level belong to the Entities.[32] After the BD was established it assumed powers and functions almost identical to those of the Entities. Added to this, the Constitution of B&H explicitly allows the Entities to enter special parallel relationships with neighbouring states consistent with the sovereignty and territorial integrity of B&H. It also allows the Entities to enter into agreements with states and international organizations with the consent of the central level legislature.[33] Also, the Constitution of the FB&H allows the cantons to enter into international agreements, but with the consent of the FB&H and the central level.[34]

The Constitution of B&H is quiet about the composition and functioning of subnational institutions. Per contra, the constitutions of the Entities and the Statute of the BD shape their power to organize subnational legislative, executive, and judicial bodies.[35] However, it cannot be ignored that the composition and functioning of subnational institutions are tied to (1) the asymmetrical internal design that determines the institutional framework of the Entities and the

---

30 For a comprehensive evaluation of constitutional asymmetries in B&H see: ibid.
31 Article III 1. Constitution of B&H: foreign policy, foreign trade policy, customs policy, monetary policy, finances of the institutions and for the international obligations of B&H, international law, immigration, refugee, and asylum policy and regulation, international and inter-Entity criminal law enforcement, including relations with Interpol, establishment and operation of common and international communications facilities, regulation of inter-Entity transportation, and air traffic control.
32 Article III 3.a) Constitution of B&H.
33 Article III 2.a) and d) Constitution of B&H.
34 Article V.1.2.3) Constitution of the FB&H.
35 Sahadžić (n 29).

BD; and (2) multinationalism through the principle of parity of the constituent peoples. For example, while the Parliament of the FB&H is bicameral, the National Assembly of the RS, all cantonal assemblies and the Brčko District Assembly are unicameral. Also, the president and two vice-presidents of the FB&H and the RS have to be from different constituent peoples. Further, constitutional powers are not symmetrically consumed among the Entities and the BD. This is because differences in territorial and institutional frameworks of each subnational entity influence the way in which the subnational entities absorb constitutional powers. The decentralized FB&H and the centralized RS are the examples of how the local competences are differently consumed.

Finally, the central level is entitled to assume additional powers over the matters necessary to preserve the sovereignty, territorial integrity, political independence and international personality of B&H, respecting the distribution of powers and mutual agreement of the Entities.[36] However, transferring powers and competences from the subnational entities to the central level has been highly objectionable in the RS because the Serbs fear this would weaken the RS.[37] This makes the mutual agreement of the Entities almost impossible.[38] To bypass this obstacle, the Office of the High Representative (OHR) of B&H[39] took several initiatives when decision-making was deadlocked. So far the OHR has imposed several laws[40] in order to transfer more powers to the central level. Simultaneously, the central level established so-called 'parallel competences' with the aim of introducing policies in specific fields.[41] Whether and how the Entities can recover the transferred powers raises a question mark since the existing constitutional design of B&H does not foresee procedures for this.

Considering the analysis above, B&H features a weak central level and very strong subnational entities. This is because the narrow exclusive powers of the central level are counterbalanced by the broad residual powers of the Entities and the BD.[42]

6.2.2 Procedure

The procedure for changing the Constitution of B&H is more flexible than the procedure for changing the constitutions of the Entities. While the amendment procedure of the Constitution of B&H requires a two-thirds majority of those present and voting in the House of Representatives,[43] the procedures at the subnational level require double majorities. To amend the Constitution of the FB&H, the revision in the House of Representatives requires a two-thirds majority, while in the House of Peoples it requires a simple majority, including a majority

36 Article III 5.a) Constitution of B&H.
37 Gabriele Quattrocchi, 'Bosnia: Republika Srpska referendum and the threat of secession' (*mediterranean affairs* 2016) accessed 16 December 2019.
38 Interestingly enough, an agreement was reached about establishing unified armed forces at the central level.
39 The OHR (together with the High Representative for B&H) were created in 1995 to supervise the implementation of the Dayton Peace Agreement. Among other, the High Representative for B&H can adopt and enforce decisions when there is a deadlock in decision-making. On the powers of the OHR see: Keil and Kudlenko (n 24).
40 For example, the laws that establish the High Judicial and Prosecutorial Council and VAT.
41 The laws regulating the Armed Forces of B&H, the Intelligence-security Agency of B&H, the State Investigation and Protection Agency, the Court of Bosnia and Herzegovina, the High Judicial and Prosecutorial Council, VAT, the framework laws on primary, secondary and higher education.
42 Heleen Touquet and Peter Vermeersch, 'Bosnia and Herzegovina: Thinking Beyond Institution-Building' (2008) 14 *Nationalism and Ethnic Politics* 266, at 270. See also: Sahadžić (n 29).
43 Article X 1. Constitution of B&H.

of delegates from each constituent people.[44] Similarly, in the RS, the revision requires a two-thirds majority in the National Assembly of the RS and a majority of members from each constituent people and the Others[45] from the Council of Peoples of RS.[46][47] The revisions in the BD and cantons are less rigid than at the Entities' level since the amendment of the Statute of the BD requires a three-fourths majority[48] while in the cantons the requirement is a two-thirds majority.[49]

A reason to resort to the flexible amendment procedure at the central level may be explained by the circumstances under which the Constitution of B&H (Annex 4 to the Dayton Peace Agreement) appeared. Before the Dayton Peace Agreement negotiations, there were several unsuccessful plans to stop the Bosnian War.[50] In the meantime, ethnic cleansing and destruction intensified, which increased pressure to end the war. The Dayton negotiations opened the door to opportunity for conflict resolution. Given the urgency, the brevity of the negotiations and the existence of the two already established entities, the Dayton Peace Agreement was envisaged as a transitional document, while the Constitution of B&H was envisaged as a constitution for peace. The Agreement, together with the Constitution, laid down foundations for the state-building process and left enough space for constitutional amendments to ease future constitutional reforms. Unfortunately, so far the state-building process has barely even started.

With regard to the Entities and the BD, a quick glance at the constitutions and the Statute reveals that they enjoy full autonomy to revise their constitutional and statutory provisions. However, two observations are important: firstly, a different institutional framework among the subnational entities dictates procedural differences; and secondly, the obligatory involvement of the constituent peoples determines the majorities required for the revisions.

6.3 Position of the subnational constitutions

The fragmented process of constitutional (re)construction in B&H determined the *form* of the Entities' constitutions and the Statute of the BD. In each subnational entity in B&H, constitutional and statutory provisions are concentrated in a single document (the Constitution of the FB&H, the Constitution of the RS, ten cantonal constitutions, and the Statute of the BD). Yet, the Constitution of B&H defines that any subdivisions and their constitutions and laws shall fully comply with the Constitution.[51] This indicates the supremacy of the Constitution of B&H.

The *use* of subnational constitutionalism for political purposes differs among the subnational entities. The general public in the RS seems to have a heightened awareness of the importance of subnational constitutionalism. The reason for this is that, regardless of their political orientation, political leaders in the RS hold that a unitary and autonomous position of the RS is a

44 Article VII 1.2.a) and b) Constitution of the FB&H.
45 Those who are are not declaring as one of the constituent peoples are usually defined as national minorities and the nationally undeclared, or simply as the Others.
46 This body was established by the intervention of the Office of the High Representative of B&H during 2002 and 2003 to enable the so-called vital national interest procedure in RS. This is a safety mechanism for the protection of the interests of the constituent peoples in cases when consensus cannot be reached. This body is not involved into any other legislative procedure.
47 Article 135 paragraph 2 Constitution of the RS.
48 Article 33 paragraph 3 Statute of the BD.
49 See, for example: *The Constitution of the Sarajevo Canton* (Official gazette of the Sarajevo Canton 1/96, 2/96, 3/96, 16/97, 14/00, 4/01, 28/4, 6/13, 31/17). Article 42 paragraph 3 Constitution of the CS.
50 These include the following plans: Carrington-Cutileiro Plan, Vance-Owen Peace Plan, Owen-Stoltenberg Plan, Contact Group Plan, and plans introduced by the Bosniaks, Croats, and Serbs.
51 Article III 3.b) Constitution of B&H.

pressing matter for the Serbs in B&H. This standpoint is heavily promoted and widely accepted among the Serbs thanks to the Constitution of the RS. This type of emphasis on subnational constitutionalism has never emerged in FB&H. This is because the FB&H is a shared territory of the Bosniaks and Croats. Political leaders among the Bosniaks have repeatedly endorsed centralization and have stressed the importance of the Constitution of B&H, while political leaders among the Croats have been vocal about the absence of the 'third' or 'Croat' entity, but not necessarily about having its constitution.[52] The issue of subnational constitutionalism is rather unknown in the BD, most likely due to its small size and multiethnic composition.

More often than not, the general public in all subnational entities relies on political actors for the interpretation of subnational constitutionalism, its purpose and value.[53] One reason is that the system is perceived to be too complex and the amount of generated information is too high.[54] This is especially true in the FB&H that features the Constitution of the FB&H and ten cantonal constitutions. Another reason is that political parties in B&H are predominantly established along ethnoterritorial lines, which coincides with the fragmented political system of B&H.[55] Bosniak political parties tend to be influential at the central level and in the cantons that are predominantly populated by the Bosniaks, Croat political parties keep their foothold in the cantons that are predominantly populated by the Croats, and Serb political parties have the upper hand in the RS.[56] This simply points out that 'the unwillingness of political elites to think and to mobilize populations outside an ethnopolitical framework is a reflection of how the population at large 'thinks' in ethnopolitical terms'.[57] In other words, the political leadership of each constituent people provides their opinion on how to consume subnational constitutionalism and the constituent peoples follow their input.

6.4 Content

6.4.1 Identity

The previous sections explained that the constituent peoples and the principle of parity are essential features of B&H. This originates from the Constitution of B&H that implicitly determines that the source of constituent powers is vested in the constituent peoples. The preamble of the Constitution designates the Bosniaks, Croats and Serbs (along with Others), and citizens of B&H as the custodians of the system.[58] However, the normative part of the Constitution reveals that the constituent peoples permeate through the constitutional design. The Constitution does not mention a Bosnian-Herzegovinian nation.[59] Instead, it refers to 'a mechanical sum of the three constituent peoples who have been projected as holders of sovereignty'.[60] The Others

---

52 For similar arguments, consult: Perry (n 7).
53 Touquet and Vermeersch (n 42).
54 Generally, this is linked to transparency. See: Onora O'Neill, *A Question of Trust* (Cambridge University Press 2002) 73, cited in: Albert Meijer, 'Transparency' in Mark Bovens, Robert E. Goodin and Thomas Schillemans (eds.), *The Oxford Handbook of Public Accountability* (Oxford University Press 2014) 520.
55 See also: Seizović, 'Političko pravni uzroci nacionalne mobilizacije i dekonstitucionalizacije u Bosni i Hercegovini' (n 23). Vlade Simović, 'Političke partije u Bosni i Hercegovini' in Banović and Gavrić (n 25).
56 Sahadžić (n 29).
57 Touquet and Vermeersch (n 42).
58 Preamble Constitution of B&H.
59 See: Pobrić (n 24).
60 Group of authors, *Primjer BiH održivi koncept ili stranputice međunarodne zajednice?* (Fondacija Heinrich Boell 2007) 26.

have been (almost)[61] excluded from the system of government despite several decisions of the European Court of Human Rights (ECtHR) that highlighted a need to amend the Constitution of B&H.[62] Finally, the term 'citizens' has no relevance to the matter in hand. Those who are not declaring as one of the constituent peoples are automatically considered to be the Others.

The Constitution of B&H addresses only the central level of government by the term 'state'.[63] The FB&H and the RS are 'Entities',[64] while other subnational entities are 'cantons'[65] and 'District'.[66] This diverse terminology is an attempt to counteract the ramifications of the bottom-up approach by providing at least some ground for the top-down consolidation of the system. While this terminology is primarily introduced to emphasize the overarching role of the central level and to avoid situations in which the Entities would be considered a state, one specificity is striking. Apart from the citizenship of B&H, the Constitution of B&H recognizes the citizenship of each Entity.[67] This is rather a symbolic act since the citizenship of the Entities has no importance in international relations.

The Constitution of B&H is silent about the state symbols. After the 1992–95 conflict ended, the existing symbols were exclusively associated with the Bosniaks.[68] Since ethnic political elites were unable to reach an agreement about a new flag and national anthem, the OHR imposed laws regulating the points of dispute.[69] The national anthem of B&H is simply instrumental as it has no official lyrics. This is, again, because ethnic political bastions have persistently and firmly declined to adopt various proposals. On a different note, the constitutions of the Entities and cantons determine their respective flags and anthems while the BD uses the symbols of B&H.[70] Interestingly, the FB&H also uses the symbols of B&H. In 2006 the Constitutional

61 For example, article 6 paragraph 3 *Law on the Council of Ministers* (Official Gazette of the B&H 30/03, 42/03, 81/06, 76/07, 81/07, 94/07 and 24/08) reserves at least one position for the members of the Others in the Council of Ministers of B&H, either the position of Minister or the position of Secretary General. More often than not, this requirement has not been met, either because of the small number of the Others or because of the so-called 'pseudo-constitutive' peoples (those who choose to declare as the Others only to win a nomination for the position or those who shift from being a member of the constituent peoples to being a member of the Others to win the nomination).

62 In 2009, the European Court of Human Rights, deciding in the case of Sejdić and Finci v. B&H established that the constitutional provisions by which the persons who do not identify themselves as one of the constituent peoples stand ineligible for election to the Presidency of B&H are discriminatory. In 2014, in the case of Zornić v. BaH, the European Court reinforced the previous decision. In 2016, in the case of Pilav v. B/H, the European Court held that the applicant (a Bosniak living in RS) is prevented from being entitled to stand for the election to the Presidency and therefore the Court found it to be discriminatory. See: *Sejdić and Finci v. Bosnia and Herzegovina* (App. no. 27996/06 and 34836/06 to the ECtHR), *Zornić v. Bosnia and Herzegovina* (App. no. 681/06 to the ECtHR), and *Pilav v. Bosnia and Herzegovina* (App. no. 41939/07 to the ECtHR). Also, for a brief explanation of how the Others are positioned within the system see: Maja Sahadžić, *Bosnia and Herzegovina Approaching European Union Membership, A miniature plea on behalf of the non-constituent peoples* (eurac research 2019). Importantly, this discriminatory framework fabricated by the Constitution of B&H is the subject of wide and major research that cannot be fitted within this paper due to its large scope.

63 Article I 2. Constitution of B&H.

64 Article I 3. Constitution of B&H.

65 Article I 2. Constitution of FB&H.

66 Article IV 4. Constitution of B&H.

67 Article I 7. Constitution of B&H.

68 Jelena Džankić, *Citizenship in Bosnia and Herzegovina, Macedonia and Montenegro, Effects of Statehood and Identity Challenges* (Ashgate 2015) 101.

69 Goran Marković, 'Ustavne promjene u Bosni i Hercegovini' in Banović and Gavrić (n 25), 85. See also: *The Law on the State Flag of Bosnia and Herzegovina* (Official Gazette of B&H 19/1 and 23/4) and *The Law on the National Anthem* of B&H (Official Gazette of B&H 19/1 and 17/4).

70 Article I 5.(1) Constitution of the FB&H, Article 8 paragraph 1 Constitution of the RS, and Article 3 Statute of the BD.

Court of B&H declared the insignia of both Entities unconstitutional since they represented only the Bosniaks and Croats in the FB&H and only the Serbs in the RS. The Court concluded that this was against the principle of the constituent peoples and the principle of parity.[71] In the meanwhile, the National Assembly of the RS adopted new symbols. However, the Parliament of the FB&H has failed to complete this task due to an ongoing standstill in the decision-making process.

Generally, the constitutional entrenchment of subnational identity is crucial in the RS. On one side, the RS has a more compact internal organization and its population, for the most part, consists of the Serbs, compared to the FB&H. This helps political leaders to create daily political narratives about autonomy claims. On the other side, the Bosniaks and Croats have to share their multi-tiered territorial slot. Added to that, the Bosniaks are numerous and pro-centralization oriented, while the Croats are small in number and in favor of decentralization. These differences disable or at least weaken the importance of their subnational identity.

6.4.2 *The organization of powers*

In B&H, the strong subnational entities that occupy vast residual powers outweigh the weak central level that has only a handful of exclusive powers.[72] Transferring powers and competences from the subnational entities to the central level is possible, although it requires a mutual agreement of the Entities, meaning that both the FB&H and the RS have to opt in.[73] So far, the Entities have rarely been ready to give up on their powers and competences. Most of the powers that were transferred to the central level were in fact imposed by the OHR.[74] Transferring powers and competences is especially objectionable in the RS. For example, the RS has highly disapproved of the establishment of the Court of B&H, the Prosecutor's Office of B&H, and the High Judicial and Prosecutorial Council of B&H. Because of the imposition, the work of these institutions has been opposed to the point that the RS has threatened to organize a referendum to abolish the institutions.[75] In the FB&H, transferring powers and competences has been complicated by the fact that the FB&H itself applies different techniques in the allocation of powers and competences between the Entity and the cantons (exclusive and shared).[76] Further, after the Constitution of B&H was adopted, it was decided that the central level will regulate relations between the central level and the BD.[77] However, this is still pending. In conclusion, unlike the central level, all subnational entities enjoy a wide range of powers and competences and surrendering those to the central level is highly unlikely either for principled or practical reasons.

All subnational entities in B&H have their own parliaments, government and judiciary. Their composition and functioning are defined entirely by their respective constitutions and the Statute.

As noted previously, the Parliament of the FB&H is bicameral, the National Assembly of the RS, all cantonal assemblies and the Brčko District Assembly are unicameral. The parliaments are

---

71 The decision of the Constitutional Court of B&H U-4/04.
72 For comprehensive explanations on the power-sharing in B&H see: Marko (n 21). Soeren Keil and Jens Woelk, 'In Search of Functionality and Acceptance: The Distribution of Competence in Bosnia and Herzegovina' in Günther Pallaver and Ferdinand Karlhofer (eds), *Federal Power-Sharing in Europe* (Nomos 2017) 119.
73 Article IV 4.d) Constitution of B&H.
74 Keil (n 18).
75 Perry (n 7).
76 Article III paragraphs 1–4 of the Constitution of the FB&H.
77 Sahadžić (n 29).

composed of elected representatives (the lower house of the Parliament of the FB&H, the National Assembly, the cantonal assemblies and the BD Assembly) and delegates (the upper house of the Parliament of the FB&H is composed of members delegated from cantonal assemblies). Their term is four years.

The Election Law of B&H defines the principles governing elections.[78] The Election Law applies to all levels of authority in B&H. Because it was adopted at the central level, this law is a way for the central level to interfere in subnational entities' affairs.[79] In 2016, the Constitutional Court of B&H ruled that certain provisions of the Election Law were not in conformity with the Constitution of B&H,[80] including the provision that 'each of the constituent peoples shall be allocated one seat in every canton' and the provisions that define the number and ethnic belonging of the delegates in the upper house of the Parliament of the FB&H based on the census from 1991. Because the Parliamentary Assembly failed to comply with the decision, in 2017 the Constitutional Court rendered the provisions ineffective.[81] Pressured, the Central Election Commission of B&H issued an instruction to regulate the division of mandates in the upper house of the Parliament of the FB&H according to the 2013 census. However, the Constitution of the FB&H defines that the constituent peoples and Others shall be proportionately represented following the 1991 census until Annex 7 to the Dayton Peace Agreement is fully implemented. Importantly, a comparison between the 1991 census and the 2013 census underlines differences in ethnic composition of specific parts of the territory before and after the Bosnian War. While the census from 1991 is certainly outdated and artificial, the census from 2013 confirms the consequences of ethnic cleansing. Essentially, each census differently affects the distribution of mandates. Added to this, Annex 7 has not been implemented. It is necessary that the OHR, in line with Annex 10 to the Dayton Peace Agreement, delivers a decision confirming this. Needless to say, the OHR has not delivered such a decision yet. Also in 2017, the Election Law was challenged under similar terms but the Constitutional Court upheld its previous decision.[82]

6.4.3 *Human rights and fundamental freedoms*

The Constitution of B&H enumerates internationally recognized human rights and fundamental freedoms ensured in B&H.[83] The relevance of international human rights standards is further emphasized. The Constitution specifically sets out that rights and freedoms contained in the European Convention for the Protection of Human Rights and Fundamental Freedoms (ECtHR) and its Protocols apply directly in B&H and have priority over all other law.[84] Due to its specific formulation, this constitutional provision has initiated numerous discussions about

---

78 Article 1.1 *Election Law of Bosnia and Herzegovina* (Official Gazette of B&H 23/01, 7/02, 9/02, 20/02, 25/02, 4/04, 20/04, 25/05, 52/05, 65/05, 77/05, 11/06, 24/06, 32/07, 33/08, 37/08, 32/10, 18/13, 7/14, and 31/16).
79 For detailed observations on the issues discussed further in text consult: Maja Sahadžić, '2019 Global Review of Constitutional Law: Bosnia and Herzegovina' (2020) 18 *International Journal of Constitutional Law* 591.
80 The decision of the Constitutional Court of B&H U-23/14. For the commentary of the decision see: Nurko Pobrić, 'Izbor delegate u Dom naroda Parlamenta Federacije Bosne i Hercegovine: Odluka Ustavnog suda Bosne i Hercegovine U-23/14 od 1. decembra 2016' (Fondacija Centar za javno parvo 2016) <http://www.fcjp.ba/templates/ja_avian_ii_d/images/green/Nurko_Pobric15.pdf> accessed 23 December 2019.
81 The decision of the Constitutional Court of B&H.
82 The decision of the Constitutional Court of B&H U-3/17.
83 Article II 3. Constitution of B&H.
84 Article II 2. Constitution of B&H.

whether the Convention has the above constitutional character.[85] Added to this, the general principles of international law are also an integral part of the law of B&H and the Entities.[86] Finally, the Constitution lists 15 human rights agreements applied in B&H.[87]

The subnational entities in B&H also have the power to guarantee human rights and fundamental freedoms. For example, the Constitution of the FB&H incorporates 22 international human rights agreements.[88] Cantonal constitutions rather mention the obligation to take measures for the protection of human rights and fundamental freedoms, since guarantees and implementation are the responsibility of the FB&H. The Constitution of the RS contains a detailed chapter on human rights and fundamental freedoms.[89] The Statute of BD modestly defines the subject, but throughout the text, the Statute reserves an important place for the ECtHR in the BD. While the Constitution of B&H provides enough guarantees to protect human rights and freedoms in B&H a rationale behind the overly stressed importance of human rights and fundamental freedoms in subnational entities is lacking. The question about its added value remains.

6.4.4 Policy principles

The constitutions and the Statute avoid stipulating policy principles. However, they do define who is competent to formulate policy principles.

6.5 Multilevel constitutionalism

6.5.1 Domestic legal space

The constitutions and the Statute of the BD do not interact as communicating vessels. This is because each subnational entity has full constituent powers. Importantly, the Constitution of B&H defines that the Entities and any subdivisions have to fully comply with the Constitution and ensure the conformity of their law with the Constitution of B&H.[90] After the Dayton Peace Agreement entered into force, the constitutions of the Entities had to be amended to comply with the Constitution. Although the constitutions of the Entities received an extensive overhaul, some inconsistencies remained. Because the Constitution of B&H does not define a further link to the Entities' constitutions, it was the Constitutional Court of B&H that settled remaining inconsistencies between the constitutions. The Constitutional Court was particularly compelled to disable the territorial separation of the constituent peoples between the Entities in the system of government. To that end, the Court confirmed the principle of the constituency of peoples regardless of the Entity.[91]

The Constitution of B&H barely defines its own revision. Apart from the provision that defines that no amendment may eliminate or diminish any of the rights and freedoms referred to in the Constitution,[92] there is only one provision about the amendment procedure. According

---

85 For the opinions on the discussions see: Andrea Zubović, 'Ljudska prava u kontekstu političkog sistema' in Banović and Gavrić (n 25), 107; Enida Turkušić, 'Ljudska prava u kontekstu političkog sistema' in Saša Gavrić, Damir Banović and Christina Krause (eds), *Uvod u politički sistem Bosne i Hercegovine—Izabrani aspekti* (Sarajevski otvoreni centar i Fondacija Konrad Adenauer 2009) 88.
86 Article III 3.b) Constitution of B&H.
87 Annex I to the Constitution of B&H.
88 Annex I to the Constitution of FB&H.
89 Chapter 2 of the Constituton of RS.
90 Article III 3.b) and article XII 2. Constitution of B&H.
91 See the decision of the Constitutional Court of B&H U-5/98.
92 Article X 2. Constitution of B&H.

to this provision, the Constitution can be amended by a decision of the central level legislature, including a two-thirds majority of those present and voting in the House of Representatives.[93] It is striking that despite the constitutional structure, which is almost entirely based on ethnoterritorial traits, the Constitution does not require specific involvement of the constituent peoples or the subnational entities in the amendment procedure. It could be argued, however, that their involvement is rather indirect. The House of Representatives of the Parliamentary Assembly of B&H consists of 42 representatives. Two-thirds of representatives (the Bosniaks and Croats) are elected from FB&H and one-third (the Serbs) from RS.[94] Remarkably, the Constitution can be revised without the actual decision of the House of Representatives. Based on their mutual agreement, the Entities can transfer powers and competences to the central level and produce the revision without the actual change of the constitutional text.[95]

6.5.2 International legal space

As already mentioned, B&H is a contracting party to the ECtHR and its Protocols. Although B&H gives special constitutional significance to the ECtHR, the central level has been struggling to implement several decisions of the ECtHR (Sejdić and Finci v. B&H, Zornić v. B&H, Pilav v. B&H, etc.).[96] This not only proves the consistent failure of B&H to comply with the decisions of the judicial authority in Strasbourg, but it also shows that not even *a priori* commitment to international standards can pierce through the ethnoterritorial trenches.

Regarding the Entities and cantons, they also have the capacity to conclude international agreements, subject to central level oversight. Agreements concluded by the cantons undergo additional oversight by the Parliament of the FB&H. This capacity of the Entities and cantons is broadened by the right to establish special parallel relationships with neighboring states. In this case, the cantons undergo an oversight procedure. Such provisions do not exist for the BD.

6.6 Constitutional review

The Constitution of B&H is silent about the organization and functioning of the ordinary judiciary. In 2002, the ORH helped to establish the Court of B&H at the central level.[97] However, this has not compensated for the absence of a supreme court at the central level. On the one hand, considering its narrowly defined jurisdiction[98] the Court can only judge on the basis of the legal regulations adopted at the central level—which are scarce. On the other hand, there is no hierarchical relationship between the Court and the courts in the subnational entities.[99] It is a rather specialized court that is independent of the rest of the judicial system.

93 Article X 1. Constitution of B&H.
94 Article IV 2. Constitution of B&H. The BD is not represented. Rather, in parliamentary elections their inhabitants vote from FB&H or RS.
95 Marković (n 69).
96 For a more detailed reflection see: Sahadžić (n 62).
97 *The Law on the Court of B&H* (Official Gazette of B&H 29/00, 16/02, 24/02, 3/03, 37/03, 42/03, 4/04, 9/04, 35/04, 61/04, 32/07, 49/09, 74/09 and 97/09).
98 Criminal and administrative matters plus appellate jurisdiction. Article 7–9 Law on the Court of B&H.
99 Maja Sahadžić, 'Uspostavljanje Vrhovnog suda BiH, Aktualna pravna misao o teoretskoj nedosljednosti u praksi' (2011) *Sveske za javno parvo/Blätter für Öffentliches Recht* 17.

The subnational entities have full constitutional powers to establish their own judicial systems.[100] Based on these powers, each Entity and the BD feature complete and individual judiciaries.[101] But, as previously mentioned, there is no hierarchical relationship between these judicial systems and the judicial system established at the central level.

The Constitutional Court of B&H is, however, found in the Constitution of FB&H.[102] The composition of the Court is rather a peculiarity. The Constitution defines that four judges are selected by the House of Representatives of the Parliament of the FB&H, two by the National Assembly of the RS.[103] It is a custom that the principle of parity applies to the selection of domestic judges (two judges from each constituent people). The remaining three judges are selected by the President of the ECtHR after consultation with the Presidency of B&H. Comparatively, this is a unique feature.[104] The Court has exclusive jurisdiction to solve disputes arising under conflicts of jurisdiction and in constitutional review. This means that the Court decides on any dispute arising between the subnational entities (the Entities and the BD), between the central level and the subnational entities, and between institutions at the central level.[105] This includes positive and negative conflicts of jurisdiction or any other dispute including the decision to establish special parallel relationships with the neighboring states. To this end, the Court decides whether the Entities' constitutions, the Statute of the BD, and laws in all subnational entities are in compliance with the Constitution of B&H.[106] The Constitution does not contain an explicit provision about its jurisdiction to review the laws of B&H. However, this is implicit from the general obligation of the Court to uphold the Constitution of B&H.[107] For example, during 2000, the Constitutional Court of B&H adopted four partial decisions about the compliance of the Constitution of the FB&H and the Constitution of the RS. These decisions confirmed the constituency of peoples on the entire territory of B&H.[108] The Constitutional Court of B&H also partly compensates for the lack of a supreme court at the central level, given that it has appellate jurisdiction over issues arising from the judgment of any other court in B&H.[109] Practically, this means that any final judgment of all ordinary courts in B&H can be reviewed in case of a violation of the rights and freedoms guaranteed by the Constitution. Linked to this, the Constitutional Court also has jurisdiction over issues referred by any court in B&H concerning whether a law is compatible with the Constitution of B&H, with the ECtHR, or with the laws of B&H, or concerning the existence of or the scope of a general rule of public international law pertinent to the court's decision.[110] Importantly, the lack of a supreme court at the central level seemingly compelled the Constitutional Court of B&H to go beyond its defined jurisdiction to review the decisions of the ordinary courts regarding the application of

---

100 Article IV C Constitution of the FB&H, Article 121–31 Constitution of the RS, Article 66–75 Statute of the BD. *The Law on the Courts in FB&H* (Official Gazette of FB&H 38/05, 22/06, and 63/10), *The Law on the Courts in RS* (Official Gazette of RS 111/04, 109/05, 37/06, 17/08, 119/08, 58/09, and 72/09), and *The Law on the Courts in BD* (Official Gazette of BD 19/07, 20/07, and 39/09).

101 Sahadžić (n 99).

102 Article VI Constitution of B&H.

103 Article VI 1.a) Constitution of B&H.

104 See: Nedžad Smailagić, 'Constitutional Court of Bosnia and Herzegovina' in Rainer Grote, Frauke Lachenmann and Rüdiger Wolfgrum (eds), *Max Planck Encyclopedia of Comparative Constitutional Law* (Oxford Constitutional Law 2019).

105 Article VI 3.a) Constitution of B&H.

106 Article VI 3.b) and Amendment I Constitution of B&H.

107 Article VI 3. Constitution of B&H.

108 The decision of the Constitutional Court of B&H, U-5/98.

109 Article VI 3.b) Constitution of B&H.

110 Article VI 3.c) Constitution of B&H.

the law. For example, in a highly discussed decision, the Constitutional Court of B&H deliberated on how the courts interpreted and applied the laws.[111]

The Entities also have the power to establish constitutional courts.[112] The Constitutional Court of FB&H maintains exclusive jurisdiction to solve disputes arising under conflicts of jurisdiction and in constitutional review. This means that the Court decides on any dispute arising between the levels of government (the FB&H, the cantons, municipalities, cities) and between the institutions.[113] It also performs a constitutional review of the legislation adopted by any level of government in FB&H.[114] The Constitutional Court of FB&H decides on constitutional issues referred to it by the Supreme Court of FB&H or by a cantonal court, which arise in the course of proceedings before that court.[115] The jurisdiction of the Constitutional Court of the RS is similar, notwithstanding the differences in its internal organization that reflect on how the Court decides, for example, in disputes between the levels of government.[116]

Since the BD emerged after the Constitution of B&H was adopted, its access to the Constitutional Court of B&H was left undefined regarding the disputes over the protection of its status and powers which can appear between the Entities and the District. Amendment I to the Constitution of B&H defined the BD as a territory in the joint ownership of two entities thus giving the Constitutional Court of B&H the jurisdiction to make decisions in the disputes.

6.7 Conclusion

Under the assumption that B&H is considered an aggregate, the paper confirms that full subnational constitutional autonomy is an inherent attribute of coming-together systems. Full subnational constitutional autonomy suggests that the power of the subnational entities in B&H to adopt the constitutions and the Statute, with reference to content and procedure, can be marked as strong. This goes against the expectation that full subnational constitutional autonomy is rather carefully granted in multi-tiered systems. The unusual process of constitutional (re)construction from the bottom-up can be blamed for this. Identity is undeniably the crucial and the most contentious aspect of B&H. Indeed, identity differences caused the bottom-up (re)construction of the system. The differences in identity allowed the subnational entities to capture full constituent powers. This left the central level deprived of necessary tools to address specific issues linked to the subnational entities. For example, the RS underlines the symbolic value of subnational constitutions mainly because the Serbs managed to attach their identity to a specific territory during and after the Bosnian War. The Constitution of the RS is exploited as a tool to prove its statehood and as a foundation for independence claims and there is little that the central level can do to counteract.

Further, the central level appears to be more progressive regarding the guarantees of human rights and fundamental freedoms. However, the inability to implement the decisions of the ECtHR implies that this is only a decorative feature. At the same time, the subnational entities are more successful regarding the implementation. Regrettably, none of the levels is ready yet to experiment with policy principles.

---

111 The decision of the Constitutional Court of B&H AP 775/08.
112 Article IV C.3, and Article 115–20 Constitution of the RS.
113 Article IV C.3.10.1 Constitution of FB&H.
114 Article IV C.3.10.2 Constitution of FB&H.
115 Article IV C.3.10.4 Constitution of FB&H.
116 Article 115 Constitution of RS.

Contrary to the expectations, the strong powers of all subnational entities to adopt the constitutions and the Statute seem to determine their low involvement in constitution-making at the central level. Since subnational constitutional autonomy is broad, there is no need to compensate through representation. Nevertheless, the incoherent structure of the judicial system somewhat reflects on the constitutional review in B&H. Considering that the judiciaries are organized as separate systems, the Constitutional Court of B&H still maintains the upper hand when it comes to the reviewability of subnational constitutional texts.

7

SUBNATIONAL CONSTITUTIONALISM IN BRAZIL

The space of state constitutions for improving Brazilian federalism

Marcelo Labanca Corrêa de Araújo

7.1 Context

Brazil is a federation in the classic sense of the term. It has a constitution that expressly stipulates the federative structure of the system of government, with 26 member states, such as Rio de Janeiro, São Paulo, Bahia, Amazonas and Pernambuco, in addition to the Federal District. Each state has a state constitution. However, in order to better understand the role played by these Brazilian state constitutions and, consequently, to better understand subnational constitutionalism in Brazil, it is necessary to explain how Brazilian society was formed and the paths taken in the formation of the federal system.

Brazilian society was never and remains not entirely homogeneous, since it was originally composed of Portuguese colonizers, native peoples and those who arrived from Africa in slave ships. Down to this day Brazilian indigenous peoples and Afro-descendants organize themselves to defend their rights and form social movements in search of racial equality. This, however, does not imply that the construction of Brazilian federalism was due to this ethnic diversity or that the system of political and territorial decentralization was created to accommodate the ethnic differences of a people.

To the extent ethnic diversities exist, they are 'homogeneous differences' from the territorial aspect, since they are not concentrated in specific parts of the country. Ethnic differences are therefore not linked to territorial claims for political autonomy based on territorially located linguistic, religious, cultural or ethnic identities. Rather, the Brazilian federation was created in 1889 as a means of granting greater autonomy to the old provinces established during the colonial era, which came to be called States. While ethnic diversity is not a relevant element in the construction of Brazilian federalism, it is possible to recognize a plurality from the point of view of political capacity.

DOI: 10.4324/9781003052111-7

Oliveira Viana has observed that Brazil is a discontinuous, ganglionic country, composed of several nuclei or ganglia when considered in political-sociological terms.[1]

Brazil was formed through colonization by Portugal commencing in the year 1500. It found a land occupied by indigenous people and started a colonization process with the use of slave labor of Afro-descendants. The name of the country came from the exploitation of a red-coloured wood called 'Pau-Brasil', removed from the forests for exportation to Europe. To enable Portugal to maintain control over such a vast territory of continental size, a system of 'hereditary captaincies' was implemented. Through the so-called 'Capitanias', lots of land were handed over to be managed by nobles chosen by the Portuguese government in order to better explore the territory and prevent foreign invasion. These were the harbingers of what, centuries later, would become the states of the Brazilian federation. The captaincies were called 'hereditary' captaincies because they passed from father to son. It was from this system of administrative-territorial division that the map of Brazil was drawn up with internal subdivisions. However, there were important changes in the administrative and territorial structure over the years. The captaincies ceased being hereditary and later became provinces, a particular kind of subnational entity.[2]

In the year 1822, Brazil officially ceased to be a colony of Portugal through a declaration of independence which established the country as a unitary and imperial (monarchical) state.[3] While officially the first Brazilian Constitution of 1824 was imperial and unitary,[4] the constitutional text devoted several articles to the organization of territorially decentralized subnational provinces which lacked political autonomy. The presidents of the provinces were chosen by the Emperor (art. 165). But there was also a kind of subnational legislative body that the Constitution of 1824

---

1 Francisco José Oliveira Viana, *Instituições Políticas Brasileiras*, vol. 2 (EdUSP; EDUFF 1987). Viana says that Brazilian federalism's mistake has a lot to do with treating states uniformly when, according to him, even in the colonial period there was no uniform treatment of powers for provincial governors: 'Whoever studies the history of our local administration in the Colony will see, in effect, that—in the Regiments granted by the Metropolis—the attributions given to the captaincy governors did not have uniformity; on the contrary, they were sometimes enlarged, sometimes restricted, depending on the economic, social or political situation of each captaincy or even the degree of confidence or capacity of the delegate ' (p. 136) (free translation). However, the first federal constitution (1891) and the following ones treated uniformly the powers of states. The principle of equality between states (in the point of their competencies) is, in Brazil, a constitutional dogma (unlike Italy, despite not being a federation).

2 The transformation of captaincies into provinces, still in the colonial period, took place from 1821 in the context of increasing parliamentary control over the Portuguese crown. See Roderick Barman, *Brazil: The Forging of a Nation, 1798–1852* (Stanford University Press 1988) and see Maria Aparecida Silva de Souza, *Bahia: de capitania a província*, 1808–23 (PhD Thesis, University of São Paulo 2008). <https://teses.usp.br/teses/disponiveis/8/8138/tde-08102009-165107/publico/MARIA_APARECIDA_SILVA_DE_SOUSA.pdf > accessed 25 September 2020.

3 Two timely clarifications: first, independence took place as a transition process, without ruptures. In fact, the Brazilian emperor Dom Pedro First was the son of the King of Portugal at that time, Dom João Sixth; second, the name used was 'Emperor', instead of 'King'. The choice of the name 'emperor' and 'empire' ended with a reference to the well-known Roman Empire whose characteristic was unity and centralization. This can be explained by the revolts and insurrections that were beginning to appear in the vast Brazilian mainland. The strength of the expression 'empire', therefore, is an attempt to reinforce central authority.

4 I used the expression 'officially' because before that it was already possible to identify constitutional documents, such as, for example, the organic law of the Pernambuco revolution of 1817 (a constitutional text that, in the brief period of expulsion of the Portuguese government from Pernambuco, structured a local government with separation of powers, provision of rights and certain guarantees—such as freedom of the press and the immovability of magistrates) and definition of how power would be exercised (see Marcelo Labanca Corrêa de Araújo and Edilisse Maria de Almeida Rodrigues, 'O ideal federalista na revolução pernambucana de 1817 e a construção do constitucionalismo brasileiro' in César Caula, Marcelo Casseb Continentino, Paulo Rosenblatt and Walber de Moura Agra (eds), *Bicentenário da Lei Orgânica da Revolução de 1817: um marco na história constitucional brasileira* (Editora Forum 2018) 277).

called the 'General Council of the Province' which was composed of elected members and was vested with constitutional powers (art. 71). A few years later, Law no. 16 (12 August 1834), also known as the Additional Act to the Constitution, changed the name of the Provincial Councils to 'Legislative Assemblies' (the term that is still used today under the federal constitution), expanding the legislative powers of the subnational entities. In fact, art. 10 and 11 of the Law no. 16 established several topics within the competence of the legislative assemblies of the provinces, such as civil, judicial and ecclesiastical division of the respective province, roads and navigation within the respective province, subnational taxes, public aid houses, convents and any political or religious associations (but not totally free of central government control (arts. 16 e 20).[5]

The first Brazilian Constitution of 1824, even though it was unitary and imperial in form, did not disregard the administrative-territorial divisions that had been established since colonial times. However, this does not mean that Brazil was a decentralized country with subnational entities vested with political autonomy, not least because decentralization and autonomy have different meanings. From the beginning of its political formation in the 1500s, the imperial and unitary characteristics of the system were supplemented by a subnational organization that was gradually consolidated into what would eventually become the Brazilian states. In fact, the constitutional structure of the unitary state provided for provinces, subnational Legislative Assemblies and, from the central level, also a bicameral legislative branch where the Senate was formed from provincial elections (art. 40). In this way, the Brazilian Imperial Constitution assumed a federal characteristic on the legislative branch: at the central level, two chambers— one for Deputies, another for Senators;[6] and, at the subnational level, Legislative Assemblies with a constitutional role and competencies.

Despite the constitutional option for territorial decentralization, it was only with the fall of the Empire, on 15 November 1889, that Brazil officially became a Federative Republic. The proclamation of the Republic was part of a military coup led by Marshal Deodoro da Fonseca, who ousted the Emperor Dom Pedro II, instituting a provisional government, decreeing the end of the Empire and the beginning of a Federative Republic. On 24 February 1891, almost a year and a half after the fall of the Empire, Brazil's first federative constitution was established, with the former provinces finally becoming states.[7] So, there was no 'coming-together' context in the

---

5 <http://www.planalto.gov.br/ccivil_03/leis/lim/LIM16.htm> accessed 26 September 2020.
6 'Art. 14. The General Assembly is made up of two Chambers: Chamber of Deputies, and Chamber of Senators, or Senate' (free translation).
7 It should be clarified that the text of the first Brazilian federal constitution had its validity before its publication. It is curious, but the provisional government issued Decree 510, on 22 June 1890, with the text of the Constitution that should be analysed by Parliament but which was already in force: 'Considering the supreme urgency to accelerate the definitive organization of the Republic and deliver, as soon as possible, the government of itself, decided to formulate, under the broadest democratic and liberal bases, according to the lessons of experience, our needs and principles that inspired the November 15 revolution, the current origin of all our public law, the Constitution of the United States of Brazil, which is published with this act in order to be submitted to the country's representation in its next meeting, coming immediately into force on the points specified below' (free translation) (available at <http://legis.senado.leg.br/norma/388004/publicacao/15722625> consulted on 12 December 2019). Subsequently, Decree 914-A, of October 23, 1890 republished the constitutional text with amendments <https://www2.camara.leg.br/legin/fed/decret/1824-1899/decreto-914-a-23-outubro-1890-517812-publicacaooriginal-1-pe.html> accessed 20 January 2020. But it is correct to affirm that the first Brazilian federative constitution appeared, in fact, in 1891, when the texts of the Decrees were approved by the Parliament, emphasizing that there was no subsequent ratification process before states (contrary to what happened with the American constitution).

formation process of the Brazilian federation, but, on the contrary, there was an imperial unitary country that decomposed itself into a mononational federal state.[8]

There were several reasons for the fall of the Empire. Problems related to taxation and excessive central interference in provincial politics caused the Emperor to lose support. There were also calls for greater political autonomy for the provinces and opposition to the Emperor's centralizing decisions. The Brazilian federation was therefore inaugurated not as a way of preserving cultural, linguistic or social diversities, but in order to respond to claims for more political autonomy on the part of territorially decentralized entities that had been integrated into the imperial single state. The name of the country was accordingly changed to the 'United States of Brazil',[9] with a strong inspiration from the North American model.

In the formation of the Brazilian federalism, it is not possible to affirm that there was a single political bloc that disintegrated itself into several states, since there were non-autonomous structures during the colonial period. However, because there were hereditary captaincies there is a sense in which the construction of the federation endorsed a previous existing territorial division. But this does not mean that there was a federal aggregation or 'coming-together' of previously independent states. Rather, from a legal point of view, the state institutions were set up by the federal constitution. According to Riker's theory, examined by Alfred Stepan, a coming-together federation must have previously sovereign units with a capacity to make 'federal bargains'. These bargains can occur because there are individual polities that have strong identities and possess sovereignty, also perceiving that they would better face external threats if they agree to pool their sovereignty towards making a federation. This did not exist in the beginning of the Brazilian federal state. Although Stepan proposes that Brazil is a coming-together federation that is farther from the 'ideal type',[10] the Brazilian case is actually more like a holding-together federation, that is, an apolitical system with strong unitary features which 'holds together' subnational entities when becoming a federation and devolving powers to them.

8 On the difference between multinational and non-multinational states and where Brazil fits, see Alfred Stepan: 'Democratic federations that may be multicultural, and that may have significant indigenous populations, but that are not multinational as I have defined the term, are Austria, Australia, the United States, Germany, Argentina, and Brazil. (…) If we employ the definitions I have just advanced, we can create, for analytic purposes, a dichotomy between multinational states and mononational states.' Alfred Stepan, 'Toward a New Comparative Politics of Federalism, Multinationalism, and Democracy: Beyond Rikerian Federalism' in Edward L. Gibson (ed.), *Federalism and Democracy in Latin America* (Johns Hopkins University Press 2004) 29, at 39–40.
9 Art. 2 of Decree 01, 1889, which instituted the Federation in Brazil, thus declared: 'Art. 2nd—The Provinces of Brazil, brought together by the Federation, are constituting the United States of Brazil' (free translation) A similar normative content can be seen in art. 1st of the first Brazilian federative Constitution, of 1891.
10 See Stepan (n 9), at 33, and 36, figure/table 2.1.

In fact, according to the provisional federal government of 1889,[11] for the cycle to be complete,[12] each state of the federation should create its own state constitution. It was in this context that the establishment of state constitutions was inaugurated. The formation of state constitutions was not a 'bottom-up' process, but was a determination of the central government, directed to the states, as a prerequisite to the formation of the federal constitution. In accordance with these requirements, the first Brazilian state constitutions were thus established concurrently with the federal constitution of 1891. But because the state constitutions were subsequent to the federal constitution, naturally they could not contradict the Federal Charter.

Since 1891, Brazil has had a succession of federal constitutions (in the years 1934, 1937, 1946 and 1967) prior to the establishment of the current federal constitution in 1988. This practice of establishing state constitutions *after* the establishment of the federal constitution was maintained in all such cases, including in the current 1988 Constitution. In the latter case, art. 11 of the transitional Constitutional Provisions Act expressly required states to promulgate their own constitutions within one year from October 1988 and that they would have to comply with federal constitutional principles. Each of the Brazilian states accordingly drew up its respective state constitution within that time frame. Each such constitution determines the basic institutional structures of the state and provides some protections of fundamental rights at the state level.

As a result, constitutional law in Brazil has two aspects, premised on the distinct establishment of the federal constitution and several state constitutions. However, as the state constitutions were drafted after the federal constitution, their content and scope are controlled by federal rules that must be complied with. If eventually a rule of a state constitution were to be contrary to a rule of the federal constitution, the federal constitution will necessarily prevail.

The establishment of the state constitutions after the federal constitution is consistent with the origin of the Brazilian federation generally: as a 'holding-together' rather than a 'coming-together' federation. In the remainder of this chapter, we will explain the role played by Brazilian state constitutions and why the development of state constitutionalism has been very limited, principally due to the many limitations imposed on the state constitutions by federal constitutional rules. Moreover, the Brazilian state constitutions do not offer spaces for accommodation of non-political diversities in Brazilian society, since the system of political-territorial decentralization was not established to protect cultural, ethnic, religious or linguistic differences, but to enable territorial inhabitants to exercise a degree of self-government.

11 The Decree no. 001 of 15 November 1889 installed a provisional government and established the United States of Brazil as a Federative Republic: <http://www.planalto.gov.br/ccivil_03/decreto/1851-1899/D0001.htm#:~:text=DECRETO%20N%C2%BA%201%2C%20DE%2015,devem%20reger%20os%20Estados%20Federais.> accessed 29 September 2020.
12 This expression was used by the Federal Decree no. 802, 1890, asserting that the constitutional organization of the states is necessary to 'close the cycle' of federal formation in Brazil. Therefore, there was an express federal determination for state governors to convene Legislative Assemblies to approve their state constitutions that would be prepared by the state governors themselves: 'Art. 3: The current Governors will promulgate, in each State, their constitution, pending the subsequent approval of the respective legislative assembly, but put into effect immediately as to the composition of that assembly and its constituent functions' (free translation). <https://www2.camara.leg.br/legin/fed/decret/1824-1899/decreto-802-4-outubro-1890-517470-publicacaooriginal-1-pe.html> accessed 20 January 2020.

7.2 Autonomy

7.2.1 Scope

As explained, for each state of the Brazilian federation there is a state constitution. This does not mean, however, that there is a relevance of subnational constitutionalism as an important space for constitutional self-determination or that state constitutions are considered relevant normative instruments for the standardization of state structures. To explain why, it is necessary to understand the extent of subnational constituent autonomy by examining the limitations imposed by the federal constitution and the central authority, including an identification of which constitutional matters can be regulated by the subnational entities and under what conditions.

The Brazilian federal constitution is long and detailed. The very bulk and extent of the constitution leaves relatively little space for the state constitutions to operate. The federal constitution adopts different techniques to restrict the field of state constitutions, sometimes establishing explicit rules directed at the states, sometimes establishing rules for the central sphere which end up regulating the state sphere as well. There are four types of norms present in the federal constitution that act as limits to the autonomy of states when drafting their state constitutions. These are: a) norms of foreordination; b) sensitive norms; c) established norms; and d) the principle of symmetry.[13]

The foreordination norms found in the federal constitution regulate aspects of the states' political organization. For an example, article 27 establishes the number of state deputies per Legislative Assembly, art. 28 establishes the procedure for the election of State Governors and art. 75 fixes the number of advisers to the State Court of Accounts. These are rules that pre-structure state institutions and powers.

The sensitive norms in the federal constitution are rules that must be observed by the states under penalty of federal intervention. This is the case with art. 34, VII, which states that the Federal government can intervene in the states to ensure, for example, the democratic, republican form, the representative nature of the regime and respect of human rights.

The established norms in the federal constitution are residual in character. They consist of mandatory rules that regulate matters at the federal level, such as norms which define fundamental rights or division of powers between the federal government and the states. Although primarily directed to federal institutions, these norms must also be respected by the states when drafting their constitutions.

The principle of symmetry concerns federal constitutional rules that were drafted so as to apply to the federal government but, by interpretive extension, are also applied to states. This is the case, for example, with article 66, which confers a power of veto on the federal president over proposed legislation. The article refers expressly to the 'President of the Republic', but, by the principle of symmetry, this rule has been interpreted to apply also to state governors. Consequently, a state constitution cannot remove from the governor the veto power, although the rule applies formally only to the president. The principle of symmetry is widely used by the Brazilian Supreme Court to say what rules or provisions can and cannot be contained in the state constitutions. Another example is that because the Federal constitution requires that the

---

13 For this typical Brazilian debate, see Leo Ferreira Leoncy, *O Controle de Constitucionalidade Estadual* (Saraiva 2007). See also Marcelo Labanca Corrêa de Araújo, *Jurisdição Constitucional e Federação: o princípio da simetria na jurisprudência do STF* (Elsevier 2009).

President of the Republic must obtain authorization from the National Congress in order to be absent from the country for more than 15 days, it has been held that the state constitutions cannot establish shorter periods in respect of absences by their respective state governors. It is in this sense that, according to the Brazilian Supreme Court, there must be symmetry between federal and state frameworks.[14]

The degree of autonomy enjoyed by the states with respect to their own constitutions is a complex matter. The federal constitutional text affirms that the states can create their own constitutions, but expressly determines that the principles of the federal constitution must always be respected (art. 25). However, the precise parameters of what should be respected is not clearly determined, which gives judges significant interpretive power. For an example, the Brazilian system at the federal level is presidential. Therefore, a state constitution cannot establish a parliamentary system for the state. However, this rule is not written; it is the result of interpretation of the constitution based on the symmetrical application of the separation of powers principle.[15] This is why the degree of constitutional autonomy enjoyed by the states is significantly reduced, due to a centralizing interpretation of the federal constitution by the Supreme Court.

In view of these limitations, the question then arises: what are the matters that can be freely addressed by the state constitutions within their reduced field of action? The answer is two-fold. First, all the norms referring to the organic structuring of state powers which do not conflict with the principles and norms of the federal constitution on the same subject, are within state power, as this derives from the state's capacity for self-organization. What happens in practice, however, is that the Brazilian state constitutions end up copying the rules already legislated by the federal constitution to discipline the powers of the states, reproducing them in the state constitutional text.[16] Secondly, fundamental rights are also within state competence, as long as they respect the rules of the federal division of competences. In this respect, Brazil adopts two competence-sharing systems. Under the dual aspect the competencies of the central government are expressly stated while the state powers are residual, while under the cooperative aspect the competencies are shared.[17]

There is a debate in Brazil about the level of generality or specificity that a norm must have in order for it to be in the constitution or in ordinary law. Matters are generally addressed in the

14 Direct Process of Unconstitutionality ADI 821, Rio Grande do Sul. The Court judged articles 238 and 239 of the Constitution of the State of Rio Grande do Sul to be unconstitutional insofar as it established rules for the body of the administrative structure. The argument used by the Court was that, at the federal level, it is up to the president to propose the creation, structuring and attributions of public administration bodies. So, at the state level, the state constitution could not address this issue, because doing so would violate the competence of the governors. <https://jurisprudencia.stf.jus.br/pages/search/sjur330964/false> accessed 7 July 2020.
15 Federal Supreme Court, Representação Interventiva n. 94. The Court said that the Constitution of the State of Rio Grande do Sul was unconstitutional insofar as it dealt with the governor's secretaries with a parliamentary bias. If the federal government is not parliamentary, then state governments cannot be either (the principle of separation of powers must be maintained symmetrically). Samantha Ribeiro Meyer-Pflug, *Memória jurisprudencial: Ministro Castro Nunes* (Supremo Tribunal Federal 2007) 41.
16 In this sense, a very interesting study was carried out by Claudio Couto, who, using a computer program that identifies plagiarism, diagnosed several similarities between the Brazilian state constitutions among themselves and also between the state constitutions and the federal constitution. See Cláudio Gonçalves Couto and Gabriel Luan Absher-Bellon, 'Imitation or coercion? State constitutions and federative centralization' (2018) 52(2) *Brazilian Journal of Public Administration* 321, also available at <http://bibliotecadigital.fgv.br/ojs/index.php/rap/article/view/74665/pdf_187> accessed 12 May 2020.
17 See Marcelo Labanca Correa de Araújo, *Teoria da Repartição de Competências Legislativas* (Fasa 2009).

federal constitution to protect them from changes by ordinary legislation.[18] The federal constitution has more than 300 articles and the state constitutions follow the same model.

7.2.2 Procedure

In addition to the scope of the state constitutions, there is also an issue related to the procedural steps for making and changing them.

Regarding the constitution-making process, as noted, the Brazilian state constitutions were always constructed *after* each new federal constitution. Brazil has, so far, had seven such constitutions: 1824, 1891, 1934, 1937, 1946, 1967 (extensively amended in 69) and, finally, 1988. Thus, with each appearance of a new federal constitution, new state constitutions also appeared, uniformly, as a federal imposition on the states.[19] With the sole exception of the 1824 Imperial Constitution, the Brazilian federal constitutions always included in their text a temporal rule that obliged the Legislative Assemblies of the states to create state constitutions within a specific period.[20] There is no need of approval from the homeland citizen.

Under the current constitutional regime, once a state constitution has been created it is possible to propose amendments through a parliamentary legislative process that involves two essential stages: a) initiation of an amendment proposal; and b) deliberation and approval within the state Legislative Assembly. The amendment processes do not require approval by the citizens of the state.

The Brazilian Supreme Court has developed a jurisprudence which applies the principle of symmetry to these two steps in the process. This means that the states must adopt, in their constitutions, the same procedural steps as are provided for the federal constitution for its amendment. At the federal level, the President of the Republic and federal parliamentarians (at the request of at least one third of the congressmen) are entitled to propose a constitutional amendment. Accordingly, parliamentarians cannot individually initiate constitutional changes: the proposal must be signed by a third of the members of any one of the two chambers. Under the principle of symmetry, this process is transferred to the states. A state constitution can only be amended pursuant to a proposal submitted by one-third of state parliamentarians or by the state governor, on the same basis as is required at a federal level.[21] Also regarding the approval process, the number of members who must approve of the proposed change must be respected. In this sense, considering that the approval of an amendment to the federal constitution must be approved by three-fifths of the federal Parliament, an eventual amendment to the state

---

18 See the Constitution of the State of Pernambuco, article 216, which prohibits the installation of atomic power plants in the state territory.

19 This Brazilian logic, with the states creating their constitutions at the same time, is very different from the United States, as highlighted by TARR: 'The federal constitution was adopted 222 years ago and has been amended only 27 times. In contrast, states change their constitutions regularly, amending them frequently and even replacing them periodically. Only 19 states retain their original constitutions, and most states have had three or more'. G. Alan Tarr, 'State constitutional Design and State Constitutional Interpretation' (2011) 72 *Montana Law Review* 7, 14–15.

20 Regarding the 1891 Constitution, this was regulated in the aforementioned Decree 802 above. For the others: from 1934, art. 3rd. Transitional Provisions; 1937, art. 181; 1946, § 9 of art. 11; 1967, art. 188 and, finally, 1988, art. 11 of the Transitional Provisions. All of these federal constitutional provisions have stipulated an obligation on member states to prepare their state constitutions within a period fixed by federal rule.

21 As more than a half of the state legislative branches can also propose, together, federal amendments, the same rule is applied to the legislative branch of the municipalities within the states: they can propose state amendments.

constitution must also have the same three-fifths approval by the state Parliament, due to symmetry. No more, no less.[22]

The procedure for creating and altering state constitutions in Brazil does not include any provision for monitoring, authorization, veto or approval by federal government authorities. In this sense, the constitutional autonomy of the states is ensured. The only federal control is exercised through judicial review, which can control or limit possible constitutional changes if the Supreme Court considers that some rules of a state constitution conflict with the federal constitution. Formally, the states are autonomous in the process of drafting their constitutions, subject to the requirement that the state constitutions must respect the norms contained in the federal constitution.

In summary, several observations can be made. First, Brazilian subnational constitutionalism is present not only in the state constitutions, since there are several rules at the federal constitution that deal with relevant state matters. Second, federal constitutional rules are not only used for the regulation of federal arrangements; there are federal rules that must be reproduced in, and are often simply copied by, the state constitutions. Third, it is possible to identify norms in the federal constitution that impose limits on subnational constituent autonomy. Fourth, the Supreme Court plays an important role in delimiting subnational constituent autonomy and, consequently, in defining the space for subnational constitutionalism.[23] Fifth, due to these constraints, the state's constitutional autonomy is only partial. State constitutions may regulate issues such as state political organization and state powers, as well as matters of fundamental rights at the state level, on the condition that they respect the division of legislative powers established in the federal constitution. This reduced autonomy can be explained by two factors. On one hand, the federal constitution pre-exists the state constitutions and the federal constitution is lengthy and detailed and addresses matters that could otherwise have been left to the state constitutions. On the other hand, the Brazilian state constitutions were created by the state Legislative Assemblies on terms ultimately determined by the federal constitution, which established a deadline for them to be created. Sixth, there is no requirement of popular ratification for the amendment of the state constitutions. Seventh, the rules for the amendment of the state constitutions cannot be freely established by states because they must follow the same process required at a federal level. Eighth, despite all these constraints, the making or changing of state constitutions does not depend on the approval of any central entity, either during the deliberation process or after its adoption at a state level.

22 The Brazilian Federal Supreme Court analysed the constitutionality of the Constitution of the State of Santa Catarina, in southern Brazil, which had established a different quorum, of four-fifths, for the approval of a state constitutional amendment. The rule of the Santa Catarina State Constitution was declared unconstitutional for offending the principle of symmetry (an interpretive construction of the Court), although there is no specific rule in the federal constitution determining any quorum for the approval of state amendments (only for federal amendments). Direct Process of Unconstitutionality ADI 486–7, Distrito Federal. <http://redir.stf.jus.br/paginadorpub/paginador.jsp?docTP=AC&docID=390648> accessed 3 October 2019. There was one time when the Supreme Court understood it in a differently way, validating the citizen proposal amendment to the state constitution of Amapá (although there is not the same provision on the federal level). Federal Supreme Court, available at <http://www.stf.jus.br/portal/cms/verNoticiaDetalhe.asp?idConteudo=393827> accessed 3 October 2019.
23 As Robert Williams says, 'Subnational constitutional space might also be accordion-like, expanding and contracting over the years through changes to the national constitution or judicial interpretation of it'. (Robert F. Williams, 'Teaching and Researching Comparative Subnational Constitutional Law' (2011) 115 *Penn State Law Review* 1109, at 1113 <http://www.pennstatelawreview.org/115/4/115%20Penn%20St.%20L.%20Rev.%201109.pdf> accessed 26 January 2020).

7.3 Position of the subnational constitution within the subnational entity

The technique of elaborating/creating and changing/modifying the Brazilian state constitutions thus follows the model adopted by the federal constitution. The federal constitution is codified in a single document and amendments to the constitution change the original text and become part of it.[24] There is a single exception to this: the international human rights treaties that are approved by the National Congress (with a quorum similar to that of constitutional amendments) have a constitutional status, even though they are not contained in the federal constitution.[25] In the case of state constitutions, the approach is the same: there is a single document enacted by the Legislative Assemblies setting out the organization of the state and the protection of human rights. When amendments to the state constitutions are made these become integral parts the constitutional text.

Since the state constitutions are derived from and subject to the federal constitution, the states do not have the constituent power to elaborate norms that contradict any provision of the federal constitution. This makes it possible for an 'unconstitutional' rule to be contained in a state constitution.

At the internal level of the state itself, the state constitution is hierarchically superior to ordinary laws enacted by the state legislature. When drafting state laws, the state parliament must therefore be careful not to create situations that may generate conflicts between state law and the state constitutional rule.

It is necessary, however, to note that the legislative capacity of the Brazilian states (which do not differ from each other) can be manifested in state constitutions (including their amendments) or in state infra-constitutional laws. The federal constitution confirms the legislative competence of states (art. 24 and 25), but (with a very few exceptions) does not discriminate between which matters should be addressed at a constitutional level or those which should be addressed in ordinary laws.[26] It follows that the Brazilian states have taken advantage of their capacity, which they could exercise as part of their residual legislative power, to develop unique constitutional approaches to specific issues. Rather, they almost invariably reproduce the rules contained in the federal constitution. This is largely due to the strong influence of the centralized jurisprudence of the Federal Supreme Court, with the result that the state constitutions are not politically visible and their potential is not realized by state political actors.

This gives rise to another important point that must be highlighted, namely that political parties do not construct narratives around the state constitutions as a means of advancing or defending their agendas. Considering that the political parties in Brazil are all national (art. 17, I—there are no regionalized parties), their agendas are largely shaped by and focused on central government policies and are not oriented to state constitutional issues.

In summary, the Brazilian state constitutions are codified in a single document; are in a lower hierarchical relationship in relation to the federal constitution while higher in relation to

---

24 It is rare to find constitutional norms of federal constitutional amendments that are not incorporated into the text of the Constitution. An example that can be cited is Article 2nd of Constitutional Amendment 32, 2011, which was not incorporated into the text of the 1988 Constitution and remains in force as a separated rule.

25 Article 5th of the federal constitution of 1988.

26 Among the exceptions is the definition of the salary of state courts judges (art. 37, § 12); minimum retirement age (art. 40, III); rules on Courts of Accounts (art. 75) and jurisdiction of the State Court (art. 125, § 1); Those subjects must be within state constitutions, remaining prohibitive to be treated by state law. Other than that, there is no rule stating that certain matters within the competence of states must necessarily be exercised by state constitutions, and not by state laws.

ordinary state laws; and have only minimal political visibility and their use by social and political actors in constitutional debates is highly limited, not least because political parties do not make political use of state constitutions, since in Brazil the parties are national, not regionalized.

7.4 Content

As explained, the 1988 Constitution established a system for allocating legislative powers that combines the dual and cooperative federalism models.[27] In this context, what are the subjects dealt with in the state constitutions and by state governing institutions?

7.4.1 *Identity*

All 26 of the Brazilian state constitutions have a very similar structure: a preamble, fundamental principles, provision of rights, rules on political and administrative frameworks, separation of powers and other rules dealing with matters such as the social-economic order and state administration.

Most state constitutions entrench three symbolic elements for the state: a state flag, a state anthem and a state coat of arms. However, there is no discussion, at a state level, of state citizenship or anything resembling this. This reflects the unnecessary promotion of separatist movements in the country.

As explained earlier, Brazilian society is a composition of at least three different ethnic groups, but these are not expressed in territorial terms and have not given rise to strong regional identities. Brazil is not a divided multinational state, in the sense that there are groups that link their claims to territorialities due to ethnic or linguistic criteria, for example. This is significant because multinational and mononational federalisms give rise to different kinds and degrees of constitutional asymmetry. In mononational federalism, asymmetry is usually related to the size, economic power and political influence of particular states. In such countries, the differences are more a matter of 'degree' than 'kind'. In multinational federations, on the other hand, asymmetries are usually based on competing definitions of the political identity of the entire community and its conception of the 'good life', with the result that the federal structure needs to 'hold together' a diverse collection of political units that contain a diversity of languages, cultures, religions or national identities.[28]

If there are cultural differences among the inhabitants of the Brazilian states, those differences do not generate identities capable of giving rise to the existence of state constitutions which seek to support or advance the particularities of each state. The Brazilian states do exhibit a degree of asymmetry in terms of their *de facto* arrangements (in relation to matters such as population, culture and economic activities). But the states in Brazil all have an essentially similar relationship to the central government with the same legal framework and with the same power and competences as compared to each other.

For this reason, it cannot be said, in the Brazilian case, that the state constitutions are fields for recognition of specific identities linked to territory. Naturally, there are feelings of belonging

---

27 On the specific issue of the municipality in Brazil, according to the 1988 Constitution, municipalities have constitutional stature, endowed with political autonomy. Therefore, it is said that Brazil would have a three-dimensional federalism, a combination of federal government, states and municipalities.

28 See Ferran Requejo and Miquel Caminal Badia, *Federalism, Plurinationality and Democratic Constitutionalism: Theory and Cases* (Routledge 2012).

felt by the citizens of each state, but this is not significant enough to support the use of state constitutions as a means of demanding sovereignty, rather than autonomy.

7.4.2 *Organization of powers*

The Brazilian federal constitution provides that: 'The states are organized and governed by the Constitutions and laws they may adopt, in accordance with the principles of this Constitution' (art. 25).[29] The last part of this rule has been understood by the Supreme Court to require the states to reproduce in their state constitutions the principles and organizational models as those established at the federal level. Thus, the separation of powers that is required at the federal level must be used as a model for structuring the organization of powers at the state level.

All state constitutions have articles that address the organization of powers. As at the federal level, we can see the same three state powers: the executive branch, with its chief (the governor of the state); the legislative branch (called the Legislative Assembly) and the judicial branch (the state Court of Justice—*Tribunal de Justiça*). However, in these respects the state constitutions reproduce the provisions of the federal constitution without adding anything of substance, except in relation to the jurisdiction of the State Court.[30] Thus, the states do not have the decision-making power to change the arrangement of the organization of powers defined at the federal level. There is a very strong jurisprudence, consolidated by the Supreme Federal Court, which, pursuant to the principle of symmetry, reduces the space of acting at state level very significantly.[31]

There are many examples. Historically, the Brazilian federation has almost always been presidential. So, if at the federal level we have a single head of government (the federal president), there must be a singular head of government also at a state level (each state governor). There was only one time when the Brazilian federation experimented with a parliamentarian system, in 1961.[32] At that time, article 4 (as amended) required the states to adopt the same parliamentarian model as recently implemented at a federal level.[33] It follows that if in the future the federal government were to become parliamentary once again, state governments would also have to become parliamentary. This is the logic of Brazilian federalism.

This is well illustrated by the recent statement of the Federal Supreme Court that

> the principle of separation and independence of the Powers does not have a universal *a priori* and complete formula: therefore, when erected, in the Brazilian system, in a constitutional dogma of compulsory observance by the states, what they must impose as a standard are not abstract conceptions or concrete experiences from other

---

29 Available at <https://www2.senado.leg.br/bdsf/bitstream/handle/id/243334/Constitution_2013.pdf?sequence=11&isAllowed=y> accessed 22 October 2019.

30 This aspect was expressly delivered, by the federal constitution, to the state constituent, in accordance with art. 125.

31 See Leonam Liziero, 'A simetria que não é princípio: análise e crítica do princípio da simetria de acordo com o sentido de federalismo no Brasil' (2019) 11(2) *Revista Direito da Cidade* 392. As the author says, the symmetry principle is a panacea to legitimize or centralize the federal government (406).

32 Brazilian parliamentarism lasted from constitutional amendment 4 of September 1961 until constitutional amendment 6, January 1963, returning to presidentialism.

33 Available at <http://www.planalto.gov.br/ccivil_03/Constituicao/Emendas/Emc_anterior1988/emc04-61.htm#art11> accessed 20 February 2020.

countries, but the current Brazilian model of separation and independence of the Powers, as conceived and developed in the Constitution of the Republic.[34]

Thus, although there are several state constitutional rules dealing with the organization of powers, the states do not have the power to innovate on this topic, but must adhere to what has already been predetermined by the federal constitution.

7.4.3 *Fundamental rights*

Among the matters the state constitutions can regulate, it is the protection of fundamental rights that perhaps offers the greatest potential.

At present, there are some minor asymmetries between the states. These mostly concern the ability of the states to enact different legislation on fundamental rights, albeit always within the narrow field of legislative competence granted to them by the federal constitution. The states are also able to enact laws that are part of cooperative legislative arrangements between the central government and state governments directed towards reducing regional inequalities.[35]

The most promising opportunity for independent development of the state constitutions on the subject of fundamental rights derives from the combined effect of two constitutional articles. The first is art. 24, which establishes the concurrent competencies of the federation and the states. Within the topics of state power defined by art. 24, a state can enact fundamental rights legislation and include these rights in the state constitution. These provisions could address issues such as minority rights, equal rights, social rights and the protection of people with disabilities, for example. Using these powers, it would be open to the states to develop a state-based rights jurisprudence that went beyond the federal catalogue of rights. The second avenue is through art. 25 of the federal constitution, which grants states the capacity to regulate topics that fall within its residual powers, to the extent they are not matters assigned by the constitution to the federal level. Depending on the willingness of the states to explore these possibilities, they will be able to regulate an array of subject matters that are not within the jurisdiction of the federal government.[36]

Some Brazilian state constitutions already innovate in the area of protection of rights. The state constitution of Pará forbade, even before the federal constitution, acts of discrimination on the basis of sexual orientation (art. 3 and the Rio de Janeiro constitution established a set of prisoners' rights (art. 27).

---

34 Direct Process of Unconstitutionality ADI 98, Mato Grosso, available at <https://jurisprudencia.stf.jus.br/pages/search/sjur104427/false> accessed 2 February 2020.
35 See Ricardo Victalino de Oliveira, *A configuração Assimétrica do Federalismo Brasileiro* (Master Thesis, Faculdade de Direito da Universidade de São Paulo 2010), available at <https://www.teses.usp.br/teses/disponiveis/2/2134/tde-08092011-093940/publico/Dissertacao_Ricardo_Victalino_de_Oliveira.pdf>. See also Dircêo Torrecillas Ramos, pointing out that 'many federal constitutions determine some degree of de jure symmetry in state constitutions to ensure the compatibility of the whole federal system' (free translation) ('O Federalismo Assimétrico: Unidade na Diversidade' in Dircêo Torrecillas Ramos (ed.), *O Federalista Atual: Teoria do Federalismo* (Arraes 2013) 121, at 133).
36 For the Brazilian case of state rights, see Luís Fernando Sgarbossa and Laura Cabrelli Bittencourt, 'Os 30 anos das constituições estaduais no Brasil e os direitos fundamentais estaduais', available at <https://faculdadeslondrina.com.br/ojs/index.php/revistaidcc/article/view/37> accessed 20 February 2020.

7.4.4 Policy principles

The often-ideological nature of policy principles in relation to issues such as the structuring of the social and economic order is addressed in the federal constitution, which stipulates that Brazil is a social state. The state constitutions do likewise. The Brazilian state constitutions accordingly address an array of 'policy principles', including private and public property rules, health policy or budgetary discipline, water, public education, shelter for homeless people and social assistance.

In relation to the policy principles that are established in the state constitutions, rules are included which structure the administrative arrangements within the state appears, particularly in relation to the powers attributed to administrative bodies for the development of these policy principles.[37] According to Couto and Absher-Bellon, there is some room for state autonomy in this area, 'not so much in terms of long-range legislative innovations, but mostly in terms of the drafting and implementation by the state of policies whose broad guidelines are established centrally'.[38] Some of the areas indicated by the authors are healthcare and education.

The following conclusions can be drawn concerning the degree of autonomy exercisable by the states in respect of the content of their constitutions. Firstly, state constitutions are not used as a way to enhance questions of identity, largely due to mononational nature of Brazilian federalism; secondly, although state constitutions contain rules dealing with the organization of powers, these rules are mostly derived from the rules operating at a federal level; thirdly, however, state constitutions have the potential to explore and provide for new fundamental rights; and fourthly, it is common for Brazilian state constitutions to contain policy principles.

7.5 Multilevel constitutionalism

Brazil contains and is part of a multilevel constitutional system particularly in relation to the protection of fundamental rights at an international, inter-American, federal and state level. This gives rise to complex issues in relation to the relationship of the particular layers at which this occurs and the particular institutions charged with promoting and protecting human rights. What happens, for example, when the same fundamental right is provided for in the federal and state constitutions? More generally, is there any participation by subnational entities in the central decision-making arenas that create federal constitutional rules? And does international human rights protection have any impact on the Brazilian state constitutions?

In the Brazilian case, the double provision of rights in the federal and state constitutions does not generate negative conflict. The issue must be considered not only in terms of the enactment of rights, but also in the ability of political and administrative institutions to provide them with protection. Let us take the example of the right to inclusion for people with disabilities, which is a topic shared between the central and state governments (art. 24). The concurrent distribution of this power gives rise to the development of relevant public policies at both levels. When

---

37 See, for example, art. 176 and 179 of the Constitution of the State of Pernambuco, which establishes the public education policy, or, still, art. 197, on access to culture. Also art. 170 to 178 of the Amazonas State Constitution, regulating public fisheries, agrarian and mining policies and articles 249 to 251: public policies relating to forest peoples.

38 See Couto and Absher-Bellon (n 16).

the issue proves problematic, the Supreme Federal Court resolves the issue by interpretation, determining which level is able to provide the best protection of the right.[39]

However, the existence of rights at different levels (state and federal) does not imply that these government spheres engage in dialogue for the joint construction of these rights. Subnational entities only participate in the central decision-making arena indirectly through the federal Senate, which is composed of parliamentarians representing the people of the states, not the governments of the states. The state governments do not have any legal powers they can use to intervene directly into the federal decision-making process. However, politically the federal parliamentarians who are part of the support base of the state governors are, in practice, influenced by the states and express this influence in their votes within the National Congress.

While there is little if any inter-governmental engagement in the drafting of federal norms, there is a degree of interaction between governments in the application of those norms, including those which result from the implementation of international treaties. As noted, international human rights treaties must be approved by the Brazilian parliament through a legislative process identical to that required for constitutional amendments. In this respect, the treaties will be treated as norms having the status of federal constitutional rules which therefore prevail over state constitutional provisions, unless the international standard offends the immutable federalism constitutional clause, protected against changes. In that case, the international treaty will not prevail.

In summary:

1. the presence of the same right in more than one level or normative sphere does not, in principle, create difficulties for its protection;
2. legally, there is no participation of subnational entities in the process of creating or reforming the federal constitution, except for the existence of the Senate;
3. international human rights treaties can be approved by the same process as constitutional amendments and are hierarchical superior to state constitutions.

7.6 Constitutional review

The Brazilian system of judicial review centres on a Supreme Court, rather than a Constitutional Court, that has constitutional jurisdiction to examine, in an abstract and a concentrated manner, the unconstitutionality of any law, as well of federal or state normative act (art. 102, I, a). There are also state courts, the so-called 'Courts of Justice' in each state that also exercise judicial review over state constitutional amendments and state laws.[40]

As a consequence, there are two layers of courts (federal and state) that have jurisdiction to enforce the state constitutions through the exercise of judicial review. Let us imagine that a certain federal rule is made by the National Congress and that its normative content is in conflict with the state constitution. The Federal Supreme Court may decide to uphold the state constitution over the federal rule, basing this determination on the system of distribution of

---

39 This interpretation was recently given by the Federal Supreme Court, on the occasion of the disagreement between central government and state governments on the best policy to combat the coronavirus pandemic. The Court understood by legitimizing the action of the states, more protective than the federal legislation, available at <https://portal.stf.jus.br/noticias/verNoticiaDetalhe.asp?idConteudo=441075&ori=1> accessed 21 April 2020.
40 About State Judicial Review in Brazil, see Leo Ferreira Leoncy (n 13).

legislative powers between the federal government and the states. In this way the Federal Supreme Court can act as the protector of the state constitution.

Likewise, state Courts of Justice can also exercise judicial review to declare state laws unconstitutional on the basis of the state constitution. The difference is that the federal court will use the federal constitution as the ultimate basis of its decision,[41] while the state court will use the state constitution as providing the constitutional standard to be applied.

However, because the procedures for the creation of state constitutional rules are defined in the federal constitution, then if the state constitution itself has violated them, the state constitution may be subject to constitutional review.

In conclusion:

1. the federal Supreme Court and the state courts can exercise judicial review to protect the state constitution;
2. the procedural requirements for state constitutional amendments can also be subject to judicial review, making it possible for the subnational constitution itself to be revised if it is inconsistent with the limits established in the federal constitution.

7.7 Conclusions

The following conclusions can be stated concerning the strength of subnational constitutionalism in Brazil from the template definition for subnational constitutions:

> basic documents for given subnational entities which lay down entrenched basic rules on (a) subnational identity, (b) representative structures, (c) organization of powers, (d) fundamental rights and/or policy principles, and (e) require the approval of the people or representatives of the subnational entity.

The question (a) regarding the content 'identities' is controversial in Brazil, as well explained. There are formally individualized states, each one with its own constitution. However, their structures and societies are quite similar to each other.

Regarding representative structures (b), the state constitutions establish the representative structures within the states. These consist of state Legislative Assemblies, state deputies and state governors. In addition, the federal Senate indirectly represents state interests.

Regarding the organization of powers (c) in the state constitutions, we cannot say that is an expression of state autonomy because the state rules on this topic reproduce those established at the federal level. Even though basic rules on the separation of powers exist in the state constitutions, these are essentially reproductions of the federal constitution.

It is also possible to identify fundamental rights and policy principles (d) in the state constitutions but, regarding fundamental rights, it has a limited number of minor issues since the state legislative branch has a space of action compressed by constitutional federal legislative powers. The number of subjects left by the federal constitution to the states effectively reduces the capacity of the state constitutions to establish and protect fundamental rights.

Lastly (e), there is no provision at a state constitutional level for the approval by the people in the establishment or amendment of state constitutional provisions. This approval occurs only

---

41 See Julio Canello, *Judicializando a Federação? O Supremo Tribunal Federal e os atos normativos estaduais* (PhD thesis, IESP-UERJ 2016).

through representatives within the state legislature, although it also occurs without interference from the federal level.

Accordingly, particularly in relation to the content of the state constitutions, Brazil is a borderline case. At best, it is an example of weak subnational constitutionalism; there are only two ways in which the states have a degree of autonomous control over their state constitutions.

In relation to the procedures that govern the establishment and amendment of constitutional norms, although the original establishment of the Brazilian state constitutions was required by the federal constitution, there is no interference by federal institutions in the deliberative process, voting and subsequent approval of the state constitutions or their amendment. In this latter respect, the autonomy Brazilian state constitutions can be classified as strong.

8

SUBNATIONAL CONSTITUTIONALISM IN CANADA

A hysteretic approach to distinctive constitutional identities

Benjamen Franklen Gussen

8.1 Context

Shortly after the end of the American Civil War (1861–65), the remaining British colonies in North America were united through a system more centralized than that seen in the United States.[1] The union was created through a number of British statutes, starting with the British North America Act 1867.[2] The last United Kingdom statute constituting Canada was the Canada Act 1982.[3] Schedule B of this statute contains the Constitution Act 1982, which defines the Constitution of Canada (see below). Today, Canada is composed of 13 subnational entities: ten provinces and three territories. Each unit has its own statute-making powers. The provinces, however, have more autonomy from the federal government than the territories.[4]

Canadian subnational constitutionalism is the product of Canada's status as the first independent realm (Dominion) within the British Empire—a status influenced by managing the risks

---

1 Peter B. Waite, *The Life and Times of Confederation, 1864–1867* (University of Toronto Press 1962) 37–8, footnote 6. Note that an earlier unification occurred in 1840. The Union Act, 1840 (UK), RSC 1985, Appendix II, No. 4 united the provinces of Ontario and Quebec. This union lasted until Confederation in 1867.
2 The Constitution Act 1867 (30 & 31 Vict c 3), reproduced in RSC 1985, Appendix II, No. 5. This Act was previously known as the British North America Act 1867. It received the royal assent on 29 March 1867.
3 Canada Act 1982, c. 11 (UK).
4 Given that the territories have no jurisdiction other than that devolved to them by the federal Parliament, the analysis in this chapter will focus on the provinces.

DOI: 10.4324/9781003052111-8

of a new confrontation with the revolutionary neighbour to the south.[5] The Preamble to the Constitution Act 1867 also explains the nature of the envisaged union:[6] '... to be federally united into One Dominion ... with a Constitution similar in Principle to that of the United Kingdom'.[7] Today, the 1867 Act is part of the *Constitution of Canada*, a system of interdependent constitutions, as defined in section 52(2) of the Constitution Act 1982. The instruments in section 52(2)(b) include 30 Acts and orders listed in the schedule to the Act. This is where we find subnational constitutional instruments such as the Alberta Act 1905 and the Saskatchewan Act 1905.[8] The list is not exhaustive and expands through judicial implication.[9]

Canadian provinces have adopted weak constitutions. The provinces do not have written constitutions — bar one. They continue to be governed by statutes passed by the British Parliament in the nineteenth century, or in the case of the territories, by the federal government.

However, Canadian provinces have powers to adopt their own constitutions.[10] What is truly distinctive about Canadian federalism is that they continue to refrain from doing so.

8.1.1 Type of the multi-tier system

(i) *Hybrid (coming together and holding together)*. The Constitution Act 1867 unified three colonies, the United Province of Canada, Nova Scotia and New Brunswick, while providing the framework for admission of all the other colonies and territories in British North America.

(ii) *Multinational*. The 1867 Act also split the United Province of Canada into English- and French-speaking provinces, resembling the historical division into the provinces of lower

---

5 There were other driving forces behind Canadian federalism, including the Industrial Revolution, and the unification taking place in Europe. See, for example, Garth Stevenson, *Unfulfilled Union: Canadian Federalism and National Identity* (5th edn, McGill–Queen's University Press 2009) 20–1. However, the Dominion was mainly a response to potential military confrontations with the United States. The defeat of the Confederacy only strengthened the 'manifest destiny' theory promulgated by the United States in the nineteenth century, which prophesized the expansion of the United States across the rest of North America. See Robert Walter Johannsen, *Manifest Destiny and Empire: American Antebellum Expansionism* (Texas A&M University Press 1997) 18–19. A similar support comes from the theory of 'continentalism'. The claim stands notwithstanding that these theories were dominated by calls for peaceful expansion, such as the Alaska purchase (on 18 October 1867). See generally, Mark Joy, *American Expansionism, 1783–1860: A Manifest Destiny* (Routledge 2014); Charles Vevier, 'American Continentalism: An Idea of Expansion, 1845–1910' (1960) 65(2) *The American Historical Review* 323; Nikolay N Bolkhovitinov, 'The Crimean War and the Emergence of Proposals for the Sale of Russian America, 1853–1861' (1990) 59(1) *Pacific Historical Review* 15; Mary Alice Cook, 'Manifest Opportunity: The Alaska Purchase as a Bridge Between United States Expansion and Imperialism' (2011) 26(1) *Alaska History* 1.
6 The use of the term 'dominion' in the 1867 Act should not be confused with 'dominion status', which was not recognized until after World War I, when several former colonies were recognized as having dominion status—see Balfour Declaration 1926. The word in the 1867 Act comes from Psalms 72:8 and was suggested by Sir Leonard Tilley in 1866 as a compromise between the use of 'the Kingdom of Canada', which was seen as unacceptable to the United States, and the use of 'colony', which was unacceptable to Canadians. See W. Stewart Wallace (ed.), *The Encyclopedia of Canada* (University Associates of Canada 1948) vol 2, 223.
7 The other British Dominions were recognized only after the Balfour Declaration of 1926, and their status was finally confirmed through the Status of Westminster 1931, c 4. The same military rationale underlines these instruments in the context of World War I and World War II.
8 The Alberta Act 1905 (4–5 Edw 7 c 42); The Saskatchewan Act 1905 (4–5 Edw 7 c 42).
9 For example, the existence of unwritten constitutional components was affirmed in 1998 by the Supreme Court of Canada (SCC). See *Reference re Secession of Quebec* [1998] 2 SCR 217 [148].
10 In the case of the territories, their jurisdiction continues to be defined by the federal Parliament.

and upper Canada.[11] This concession to (sub)national identity also influenced the creation of the Northern Territories (1870), Yukon (1898) and Nunavut (1999).[12]

(iii) *Triadic.* The federation was created to help diffuse the tensions between English-speaking Ontario and French-speaking Quebec. More powers continue to devolve to First Nations in the territories.

(iv) *Overlap.* Both federal and provincial legislatures have enumerated exclusive legislative powers in the *Canadian Constitution*.[13] In practice, however, the courts used the doctrine of 'double aspect' to enlarge the concurrent or overlapping powers between the central and provincial legislatures.[14]

(v) *Symmetric.* Notwithstanding the largely uniform subnational constitutional space, there are special rights enjoyed by Quebec.[15] Divergence continues to evolve along linguist lines.

8.1.2 Pre-existence of subnational constitutions

Some provincial constitutions existed in Canada before federation.[16] The first type was based on the royal prerogative, through letters patent, for example, the constitutions of the Maritime colonies. The second was statutory, for example, the statute establishing the colony of British Columbia.[17] These constitutional instruments continued to have effect after Confederation;[18] they are still part of the *Constitution of Canada*.[19]

Other provincial constitutions, such as the constitutions of the prairie provinces (Alberta, Saskatchewan and Manitoba) derive from the Constitution Act 1867.[20] The constitutions of the three territories were by Imperial orders-in-council: Northwest Territories was admitted in 1870, Yukon in 1898 and Nunavut in 1999.

However, much of the constitutional space enjoyed by the provinces has been absorbed under the Constitution Act 1982, including electoral boundaries, legislative terms and commercial signage.[21]

---

11 See Milton J. Esman, 'The Politics of Official Bilingualism in Canada' (1982) 97(2) *Political Science Quarterly* 233.

12 Identity concerns are most relevant when it comes to Nunavut. See André Légaré, 'Inuit identity and regionalization in the Canadian Central and Eastern Arctic: a survey of writings about Nunavut' (2008) 31(3–4) *Polar Geography* 99.

13 As defined in section 52(2) of the Constitution Act 1982.

14 See *Hodge v The Queen* (1883) 9 App Cas 117.

15 For example, ss 93, 93A, 98, and 133 of the Constitution Act 1867, and Quebec's representation in the Senate.

16 J.E. Read, 'The Early Provincial Constitutions' (1948) 26(4) *Canadian Bar Review* 626.

17 British Columbia Government Act 1858 (21–2 Vic c 99).

18 See for example, sections 64 and 88 of the Constitution Act 1867. Similar saving provisions can be found in the instruments admitting the other provinces into Canada.

19 Although some suggest that the 1867 Act was a break away from the pre-Confederation constitutional development. See Peter Price, 'Provincializing Constitutions: History, Narrative, and the Disappearance of Canada's Provincial Constitutions' (2017) 9(3) *Perspectives on Federalism* E31.

20 The Manitoba Act 1870 (33 Vic c 3), the Alberta Act 1905 (4–5 Edw 7 c 3), the Saskatchewan Act 1905 (4–5 Edw 7 c 42).

21 Nelson Wiseman, 'Clarifying Provincial Constitutions' (1996) 6 *National Journal of Constitutional Law* 269.

8.1.3 *The principal arguments in the debate on subnational constitutionalism*

Debates on subnational constitutionalism are largely absent from Canadian political discussion.[22] With the exception of Quebec,[23] and more recently Alberta,[24] there are no political or popular agendas to reform subnational constitutions. There are three main reasons for this lacuna. First, given the difficulty of defining the content of the prerogative subnational constitutions in Canada, the role of provincial constitutions eventually weakened, both in the practice and the theory of Canadian politics.[25] Second, Canadian constitutional policymaking continues to be largely decided by subnational executives rather than legislatures.[26] Third, there is an interconnectedness between provincial and federal constitutions that became more significant after the Constitution Act 1982. This interconnectedness shifted the debate from one focused on subnational constitutionalism, to one focused on the *Constitution of Canada*.[27]

8.2 Constitutional autonomy

Subnational governance in Canada is legitimized and constrained by the *Constitution of Canada*, ordinary federal and provincial legislation, and constitutional conventions. However, Canadian (national and subnational) constitutionalism is also one of executive federalism.[28] The guiding principle is political flexibility rather than (legal) conceptions of autonomy.[29]

8.2.1 *Subnational constitutionalism*

In addition to political limitations, there were three main legal limitations on the provincial constitutions that existed prior to 1867.[30] First, the Crown had the unrestrained power to amend or revoke any colonial constitution and annex the territory of that colony to another colony or veto any colonial legislation. Second, parliamentary sovereignty meant that colonial laws were inoperative if they were repugnant to any legislation of the British Parliament applicable to the colony.[31] Third, provincial laws enacted under the provincial constitutions had no extra-territorial operation.

---

22 F.L. Morton, 'Provincial Constitutions in Canada' (Paper presented at the Federalism and Sub-national Constitutions: Design and Reform, Bellagio, Italy, March 22–26, 2004).

23 The distinctive regional identity in Quebec is driven mainly by social grievances. Wiseman (n 21), at 270.

24 More recent attempts toward constitutional reform can be seen in Alberta, mainly due to economic grievances. See Morton (n 22); Richard Albert, 'Secession and Constitution in Alberta' in Jack M Mintz, Ted Morton and Tom Flanagan (eds), *Moment of Truth: How to Think About Alberta's Future* (Sutherland House 2020).

25 Morton (n 22).

26 See Gerald Baier, 'Canada: Federal and Sub-national Constitutional Practices' in Michael Burgess and G. Alan Tarr (eds), *Constitutional Dynamics in Federal Systems: Sub-national Perspectives* (McGill–Queen's University Press 2012) 174, at 182. For a critical evaluation of 'executive federalism' see Clement Akwasi Botchway, 'The Need for Executive Federalism in Federal-Provincial Relations: The Canadian Example' (2017) 9(5) *Journal of Public Administration and Policy Research* 68.

27 Wiseman (n 21), at 282.

28 Baier (n 26). See also Martha A Field, 'The Differing Federalisms of Canada and the United States' (1992) 55(1) *Law and Contemporary Problems* 107, at 118.

29 Ronald L. Watts, *Executive Federalism: A Comparative Analysis* (Queen's University Press 1989) 3.

30 Read (n 16), at 623.

31 Sections 2 and 3 the Colonial Laws Validity Act 1865 (28 & 29 Vic c 63).

Today, the *Constitution of Canada* plays a role not very different from the royal prerogative model that existed before 1867.[32] First, the *Constitution* creates an agency relationship between the provincial governments and the federal government.[33] Second, it defines the constitutional space within which the provinces can operate.[34] Third, it provides the federal government with powers to intervene directly in areas of provincial government competence.[35] Fourth, it expressly states that the position of the lieutenant governor is a national position, and hence cannot be amended by the provinces.[36] Fifth, the *Constitution*, through the Canadian Charter of Rights and Freedoms, provides the Supreme Court of Canada with further controls on the conduct of provincial governments.[37] Last, the *Constitution* requires the provinces to have freely elected representative legislative bodies.[38]

As to the territories (Northwest Territories, Nunavut and Yukon), unlike the provinces, they obtain their legislative authority from ordinary federal legislation. Their constitutions can be amended only by the federal Parliament. The federal government, however, continues to delegate decision-making powers to the territories, including authority over local governments, and over the provision of public goods such as health and education.[39] These powers continue to expand and now 'approximate' those of the provinces.[40] For example, the Preamble of the Yukon Act,[41] which replaced the 1898 Yukon Act,[42] explains that 'Yukon is a territory that has a system of responsible government that is similar in principle to that of Canada'.

32 See Campbell Sharman, 'The Strange Case of a Provincial Constitution: The British Constitution Act' (1984) 17(1) *Canadian Journal of Political Science* 87, at 88–91.

33 This agency is created through Part V of the Constitution Act 1867. Section 58 in Part V refers to 'Lieutenant' Governors. The general meaning of this word suggests a deputy acting for a superior. Compare this designation with s 110 of clause 9 of the Commonwealth of Australia Constitution Act 1900 (Cth).

34 See Mark E. Oppe, *The Utilization of Constitutional Space to Maximize Sub-National Autonomy in Federations* (Master's Thesis, University of Alaska, 2009) 112.

35 See Donald Creighton, *Canada's First Century* (Macmillan of Canada 1970) 65. Note, however, that the powers of disallowance and reservation have been used only sparingly. See Claude Bélanger, 'The Powers of Disallowance and Reservation in Canadian Federalism' *Studies on the Canadian Constitution and Canadian Federalism* (2001); Eugene Forsey, 'Disallowance of Provincial Acts, Reservation of Provincial Bills, and Refusal of Assent by Lieutenant-Governors since 1867' (1938) 4(1) *Canadian Journal of Economics and Political Science* 47.

36 Section 92(1) of the Constitution Act 1867 (repealed), and section 41 of the Constitution Act 1982. The Lieutenant Governor position itself defines some of the machinery of provincial government and entrenches these processes beyond any unilateral amendment by the provinces.

37 See Oppe (n 34), at 68 and Wiseman (n 21). See also the discussion under section 4.3.

38 For case law on this point, see Sharman (n 32), at 88–91, footnote 7. Also see Christopher D. Bredt and Markus F. Kremer, 'Section 3 of the Charter: Democratic Rights at the Supreme Court of Canada' (2004/2005) 17 National Journal of Constitutional Law, suppl. Constitutional Update 2004, 19.

39 G Dacks (ed.), *Devolution and Constitutional Development in the Canadian North* (McGill–Queen's University Press 1990).

40 See Jeremy Webber, *The Constitution of Canada: A Contextual Analysis* (Hart Publishing 2015) 134, footnote 2. On the trend of expanding the power of the territories, see Adam P. MacDonald, 'Expanding the Federation? The Ongoing Process of Devolution in the Yukon Territory' (2008) Federalism-e 47.

41 SC 2002 c 7.

42 61 Vic c 6.

8.2.2 Self-constituent capacity[43]

The provincial colonial constitutions continued to exist after the colonies were admitted to the Canadian union, subject to the provisions of the Constitution Act 1867.[44] However, there has been change in the way the executive head was appointed,[45] and a curtailment of the legislative powers of the provincial assemblies through the vertical division of powers between the federal and provincial governments.[46]

Generally, Canadian provinces have a wide scope in their subnational constitutional space. Matters over which they exercise autonomous powers include elections, composition and functioning of parliament and the government.[47] Subject to the constraints in the Constitution Act 1982,[48] the provinces have the power to draft and amend their own constitutions.[49] The provinces can supersede sections of the Constitution Act 1867 without the need for formally amending the Act. The provinces can introduce functional amendments to the federal constitution; hence, when Quebec abolished its upper chamber, this amendment rendered spent sections of the *Constitution of Canada*.[50]

In terms of government goals and the ability to define protected rights, Canadian provinces enjoy a wide scope, although, again, there are federal limits, for example, in terms of the exploration of natural resources, or the protection of French as an official language (to the exclusion of English).[51] Fewer limits can be discerned when it comes to the power to structure the governmental institutions, to define the process for enacting provincial law, and the power to divide powers among governmental institutions.[52]

8.3 Position of the subnational constitutions within the subnational entity

8.3.1 Form of subnational constitutions

Provincial constitutions include ten broad rubrics:[53] General Constitutional Acts, Intergovernmental Relations, Executive Power, Legislative Power, Judicial Power, Fundamental

---

43 Self-constituent capacity refers to both the power to adopt constitutions and the involvement in federal constitutional amendments. See G. Alan Tarr, 'Subnational Constitutions and Minority Rights: A Perspective on Canadian Provincial Constitutionalism' (2008) 2 *Revue Québécoise de Droit Constitutionnel* 174, at 177; G. Alan Tarr, 'Explaining Subnational Constitutional Space' (2011) 115 *Pennsylvania State Law Review* 1133, at 1134.

44 Section 88 of the 1867 Act extends the pre-Union constitutions of Nova Scotia and Brunswick into the post-Confederation era.

45 Under section 58 of the Constitution Act 1867, the Lieutenant-Governor is appointed by Governor General.

46 As detailed in sections 91 and 92 of the Constitution Act 1867.

47 See Patricia Popelier, 'The Need for Sub-National Constitutions in Federal Theory and Practice' (2012) 4(2) *Perspectives on Federalism* E36, at E40.

48 Part V of the Constitution Act 1982 (ss 38 to 49). Section 45 of the Constitution Act 1982 authorizes legislatures to make laws amending the constitution of the province. Sections 38, 41, 42 and 43 of that Act authorize legislative assemblies to give their approval by resolution to certain other amendments to the Constitution of Canada.

49 Sections 58–90 of the 1867 Act. Section 92 of the 1867 Act, which was repealed and replaced by section 45 of Constitution Act 1982. Sections 38, 41, 42 and 43 give the provincial legislatures the power to approve certain amendments to the *Constitution of Canada*. See also J.E.C. Munro, *The Constitution of Canada* (Cambridge University Press 1889) 231.

50 Sections 72 to 79 of the Constitution Act 1867.

51 See Price (n 19).

52 See Morton (n 22), Baier (n 26), at 179.

53 See generally Christian L. Wiktor and Guy Tanguay (eds), *Constitutions of Canada: Federal and Provincial* (Oceana Publishers, 1987) vol 2.

Rights, Language Rights, Native Rights, Emergency Measures, and Miscellaneous. To these instruments should also be added Orders-in-Council, the Standing Orders of Legislatures, and Constitutional Conventions (such as responsible government).[54] Other elements can be found in ordinary provincial statutes, such as electoral acts. There are also elements of the provincial constitutions in the Constitution Acts of 1867 and 1982, especially in the Charter of Rights and Freedoms.[55]

8.3.2 Use of subnational constitutions

Today, provincial constitutions are occulted. They play a marginal role in Canadian scholarship on constitutionalism.[56] From the late nineteenth century to the mid-twentieth century constitutional scholarship was dominated by a dualist narrative with focus on both provincial and federal constitutions. Later, however, especially after the 1982 patriation,[57] there was a shift to a monist narrative with the federal constitution as the only foundation of Canadian constitutionalism.[58]

One reason for the discounted symbolic value of provincial constitutions is their inextricable link to the federal constitution, both in public consciousness and in jurisprudence.[59]

Another reason is the opaque nature of these constitutions. They are simply what the provincial legislatures say they are. They cannot be found in one document, and a significant part of these constitutions is unwritten.[60]

8.4 Content of the subnational constitutions

With the exception of British Columbia, Canadian provinces have chosen to have 'flexible', unwritten constitutions. As stated earlier, each of these constitutions is found in a usually unspecified, long list of statutes, orders-in-council, parliamentary standing orders and constitutional conventions. For example, the constitution of Quebec includes the provisions of the Constitution Act 1867 pertaining to the provinces of Canada in general and Quebec in particular (for example, section 63 in relation to the appointment of Executive Officers for Ontario and Quebec); organic provisions relating to the distribution of powers and individual rights (for example, the Act respecting the National Assembly,[61] the Executive Power Act,[62] the Election Act,[63] the Referendum Act,[64] the Charter of human rights and freedoms,[65] the Charter of the French language[66] (in total around 15 Acts); the constitutional conventions applicable to the

---

54 Wiseman (n 21), at 280.
55 Constitution Act 1982 c 11 sch B pt 1 ('*Canadian Charter of Rights and Freedoms*').
56 Wiseman (n 21), at 270.
57 Morton (n 22).
58 Price (n 19).
59 See, for example, David Schneiderman, 'Unwritten Constitutional Principles in Canada: Genuine or Strategic?' in Rosalind Dixon and Adrienne Stone (ed.), *The Invisible Constitution in Comparative Perspective* (Cambridge University Press 2018) 517; Sujit Choudhry, 'Unwritten Constitutionalism in Canada: Where Do Things Stand?' (2001) 35 *Canadian Business Law Journal* 113.
60 See Wiktor and Tanguay (n 53) vol 2, O79.
61 CQLR c A-23.1.
62 CQLR c E-18.
63 CQLR c E-3.3.
64 CQLR c C-64.1.
65 CQLR c C-12.
66 CQLR c C-11.

Crown, the Executive and the Parliament; the common law rules on the royal prerogative exercised by the Lieutenant Governor of Quebec; and the constitutional case law of the courts of Quebec and the federal courts of Canada.[67]

The other provinces have similar constitutional instruments. For example, the Manitoba Act 1870,[68] which created the province of Manitoba, is part of the *Constitution of Canada*, and is listed as a constitutional document in the appendix to the Constitution Act 1982.

Some Acts are commonly considered as part of provincial constitutions. For example, provincial electoral Acts, although they are not part of the Schedule to the Constitution Act, 1982, are commonly considered to be part of their respective provincial constitutions.[69]

8.4.1 Subnational identity

Relative to the constitutions of the other two Anglo-American federations, the *Constitution of Canada* pays little attention to the symbolism of nationhood.[70] There is no mention of Canada as a nation in the Preamble of the Constitution Act 1867, while the Preamble to the Constitution Act 1982 makes only a functional reference to 'Canada'. The occultation of subnational constitutionalism in Canada (see 3.2 above) is therefore an extrapolation of this hysteretic attitude towards nationhood. Notwithstanding, Canadian provinces adopted symbols of subnational identity. For example, the coat of arms of Quebec have been approved and authorized by a provincial order-in-council on 9 December 1939. The flag was adopted by order-in-council on 21 January 1948, and by An Act Respecting the Flag and Emblems of Quebec.[71] The same constitutional embroidery exists in all other provinces in Canada.[72]

The provinces have no constitutional right to decide on matters of nationhood and citizenship.[73] For example, while Quebec has successfully changed the name of its legislative assembly to the National Assembly (Assemblée nationale du Québec), this symbolic gesture does not affect the recognition of its independence, at least not unilaterally. Hence, in *Reference re Secession of Quebec*,[74] the Supreme Court of Canada (SCC) made it clear that under the *Constitution of Canada*, unilateral secession was not legal. Only through negotiations can the independence of Quebec, and by extension the independence of other Canadian subnational entities, be consummated.[75]

---

67 Jacques-Yvan Morin and José Woehrling, *Les constitutions du Canada et du Québec: du régime français à nos jours* (Études 1992) 141.

68 SC 1870 c 3.

69 In the *Patriation Reference* (1981), the SCC considered provincial electoral Acts as part of the written federal constitution. See *Manitoba (Attorney General) v Canada (Attorney General)* [1981] 1 SCR 753, 876.

70 See Benjamen Gussen, 'On the Hardingian renovation of legal transplants' in Vito Breda (ed.), *Legal Transplants in East Asia and Oceania* (Cambridge University Press 2019) 84–108; Benjamen Gussen, 'Reflections on La Fata Morgana: Watsonian "Prestige" and Bagehotian "Efficiency"' (2017) 12(1) *The Journal of Comparative Law* 80.

71 CQLR c D-12.1.

72 See Wiktor and Tanguay (n 53).

73 The existence of nationhood should not be conflated with its (legal) recognition by the Canadian House of Commons. A distinctive status in the constitutional order, or a right to secession flow from recognition not existence. Quebec, Alberta and the other Provinces and Territories, may lay claims to nationhood, and hence reveal aspirations for independence from the rest of Canada, but doing so does not create any constitutional rights.

74 (1998) 161 DLR (4th) 385.

75 Ibid. paras 151–2.

Similarly, in relation to issues pertaining to the status of languages in the provinces, the constitutional space is limited. For example, the Quebec Charter of the French Language was passed by the National Assembly, and granted Royal Assent on 26 August 1977.[76] In 1979, some Articles were rendered inoperative by a ruling of the SCC.[77] The SCC put limits on the constituent powers of Quebec by determining that fundamental terms or conditions of Confederation such as language provisions are outside unilateral amendment powers.

8.4.2 *Organization of powers*

The structure of the provincial executive, legislative and judicial branches of government is regulated by the *Constitution of Canada*.[78] However, the functional aspects of these branches are regulated by provincial instruments.

8.4.2.1 *The exercise of competencies*

There is no 'a priori' position on the scope of provincial constitutions.[79] Both federal and provincial governments have enumerated powers in the *Constitution of Canada*, in total 48 enumerated powers. Of these 30 are assigned to the central government,[80] 16 are assigned to the provinces[81] and two are concurrent.[82] Residual powers are assigned to the federal Parliament.[83] While the matters that can be regulated by the provinces are enumerated in the Constitution Act 1867, the actual scope of the provincial constitutions remains unspecified.

Provincial constitutions can 'cast a relatively wide net'.[84] Constitutional matters are context-dependent, and other constitutional matters also come under the competencies of the provinces. The scope of provincial constitutions continues to evolve through the jurisprudence of provincial and federal courts.[85] A provincial statute is considered an amendment to the provincial constitution when the former operates on provincial government institutions, or when it relates to the federal principle.[86] The SCC, however, also points to a significant limitation on the power of provinces to amend their constitutions in that it does not allow for the introduction of political institutions foreign and incompatible with the Canadian system.[87]

8.4.2.2 *The parliaments*

The federal Parliament is made up of the Queen, represented by the Governor General, and two chambers, a non-elected upper house (the Senate), and an elected lower house (the House of

---

76 CQLR c C-11.
77 *Quebec (Attorney General) v Blaikie (No 1)* [1979] 2 SCR 1016.
78 Recall, however, that the *Constitution of Canada* does not have a 'unitary' character. See Wiktor and Tanguay (n 53) vol 2, G6. See also Peter Russell, *The Judiciary in Canada: The Third Branch of Government* (McGraw-Hill Ryerson 1987).
79 Wiseman (n 21), at 288.
80 Sections 91 and 92(10) of the Constitution Act 1867.
81 Sections 92, 92A and 93 of the Constitution Act 1867.
82 Sections 94A and 95 of the Constitution Act 1867.
83 Section 91 of the Constitution Act 1867.
84 Wiseman (n 21), at 285.
85 See Benjamen Gussen, *Axial Shift* (Palgrave Macmillan 2019) 402.
86 See the SCC ruling on the extent of provincial constitutions in *OPSEU v Ontario (Attorney General)* [1987] 2 SCR 2. See also Wiseman (n 21) 285.
87 Wiseman (n 21), at 285.

Commons).[88] In contrast, each provincial legislature is made up of a Lieutenant-Governor, and one elected chamber usually called the Legislative Assembly.[89] While the delegation of legislative powers between these levels is prohibited,[90] the delegation of administrative powers is possible.[91] The territories have elected unicameral legislative assemblies that create and amend the law in each territory.[92]

Five of the ten provinces once had upper chambers or Legislative Councils. All upper chambers were eliminated between 1876 (Manitoba) and 1968 (Quebec). Provinces can also change the name of their legislative assembly as did Quebec in 1968, which is now called the National Assembly,[93] even though it is still referred to as the 'legislative assembly' in section 59(2) of the Constitution Act 1982.

In addition, although the Constitution Act 1867 sets the duration of provincial parliaments to four years,[94] the provinces extended their period to five years. The legislatures of Saskatchewan (1943) and Ontario (in 1918 and 1942) went even further and 'prolonged their own, rather than future legislatures'.[95] In 1943, the Ontario Court of Appeals accepted that the legislature can extend its term as an amendment to the provincial constitution.[96] The 'only constitutional means of checking such power was the reserve power of the Lieutenant General and Ottawa'.[97]

In exercising their functions, provincial Legislative Assemblies have to follow the division of legislative powers between the federal and provincial governments as set out in the Constitution Act 1867,[98] the constitutional principles relating to the parliamentary system, and the form of responsible government which prevails in Canada. Members of the Legislative Assembly have to be elected pursuant to existing provincial legislation relating to representation.[99] The Lieutenant Governor, the chief executive officer of the province, also exercises some legislative functions.

8.4.2.3 The government

For the ten provinces, executive power derives from provincial statutes as well as the *Constitution of Canada*. The concepts of representative and responsible government require that this power is exercised under particular conditions. Representative government is instituted in the form of a bicameral legislature, with an elected House of Assembly and a nominated Legislative Council. Responsible government is reflected in an appointed Executive Council.[100] The Executive

---

88 Sections 17 to 57 of the Constitution Act 1867.

89 See Wiktor and Tanguay (n 53) vol 2, F5.

90 See *AG Nova Scotia v AG Canada* [1951] SCR 31.

91 *PEI Potato Marketing Board v HB Willis Inc* [1962] 2 SCR 392; *Coughlin v Ontario Highway Transport Board* [1968] SCR 569; *R v Smith* [1972] SCR 359.

92 See Gary Ley and Graham White, *Provincial and Territorial Legislatures in Canada* (University of Toronto Press 1989); Charles Cecil Lingard, *Territorial Government in Canada* (University of Toronto Press 1946); Bruce Alden Cox (ed.), *Native People, Native Lands: Canadian Indians, Inuit and Metis* (McGill–Queen's University Press 2002).

93 An Act Respecting the National Assembly, CQLR c A-23.1.

94 Section 85 of the Constitution Act 1867.

95 See Wiseman (n 21), at 281. Note that Newfoundland's first House of Assembly had done the same in 1836, but it was dissolved before the extension took effect. See also GE Gunn, *The Political History of Newfoundland, 1832–1864* (University of Toronto Press 1966) 31–2.

96 *R ex rel Tolfree v Clark* [1943] OR 501 (CA).

97 Eugene Forsey, *Freedom and Order: Collected Essays* (McClelland & Stewart 1974) 216.

98 Especially in sections 91 to 95 of the Constitution Act 1867.

99 See Wiktor and Tanguay (n 53).

100 To be clear, the Executive Council could continue to exist as a matter of law even if responsible government did not operate in Canada. See Earl of Durham, *Report on the Affairs of British North America* (1839).

Council consists of the Premier of the province and Cabinet of Ministers and plays an advisory role similar to the Queen's Privy Council for Canada on the federal level (in advising the province's Lieutenant Governor).

The executive power is vested in the Lieutenant Governor advised by the Executive Council.[101] The functions and powers of the Lieutenant Governor and the Cabinet of Ministers are similar to those of the components of the federal executive power.[102] The Premier and the Cabinet, according to constitutional conventions, exercise the executive power. They 'advise' the Lieutenant Governor and the Lieutenant Governor ordinarily acts on that advice. The Lieutenant Governor remains the nominal head of the provincial executive.

Similarly, the executive power in the three territories is vested in an Executive Council which consists of the Commissioner, the Premier and the Cabinet of Ministers. These Councils advise the Commissioner similar to the way the Executive Councils in the provinces advise the Lieutenant Governor.[103]

8.4.3 *Protection of fundamental rights*

Fundamental rights in Canada are grouped into five broad categories:[104] political, legal, economic, egalitarian and language rights. These rights are protected by both common and statutory law. Canada adopted the Charter of Rights and Freedoms in 1982,[105] which has paramountcy over provincial constitutions.[106]

Some of the provisions protecting human rights can be found in the Constitution Act 1867.[107] Other fundamental rights are provided for in ordinary federal and provincial statutes. Federal statutes include the Canadian Bill of Rights,[108] the Canadian Human Rights Act,[109] Official Languages Act,[110] Criminal Code,[111] and the Personal Information Protection and Electronic Documents Act.[112] The rights of native peoples in Canada are protected by the Indian Act.[113]

An example of provincial legislation that complements the federal Charter of Rights and Freedoms is Quebec's Charter of Human Rights and Freedoms,[114] An Act Respecting Access to Documents Held in Public Bodies and the Protection of Personal Information,[115] and the Freedom of Worship Act.[116] There is also An Act Respecting the Constitution Act 1982,[117] which excepted the statutes of Quebec from the application of certain section of the federal

---

101 See Wiktor and Tanguay (n 53).

102 As described in sections 9 to 16 of the Constitution Act 1867.

103 See R.G. Robertson, 'The Evolution of Territorial Government in Canada' in J.H. Aitchison, *The Political Process in Canada: Essays in Honour of R MacGregor Dawson* (University of Toronto Press 1963) 136–52; C. Cecil Lingard, *Territorial Government in Canada* (University of Toronto Press 1946).

104 Wiktor and Tanguay (n 53) vol 2, H5.

105 Constitution Act, 1982 c 11, sch B pt 1 ('*Canadian Charter of Rights and Freedoms*').

106 See, for example, *Dixon v British Columbia (Attorney General)* (1986), 7 BCLR (2d) 174, 186.

107 For example, section 93 protecting denominational schools, or section 133 concerning language rights.

108 SC 1960 c 44.

109 RSC 1985, c H-6.

110 RSC 1985, c 31 (4th Supp).

111 RSC 1985 c C-46.

112 SC 2000 c 5.

113 RSC 1985 c I-5.

114 CQLR c C-12.

115 CQLR c A-2.1.

116 CQLR c L-2.

117 CQLR c L-4.2.

Charter of Rights and Freedoms. In addition, Quebec has legislation protecting native rights.[118] The status of French as the official language in Quebec is also protected by the Charter of the French Language.[119]

8.4.4 *Enunciation of policy principles*

Canadian policymaking continues to be determined by subnational executives, with little input from legislatures.[120] A disciplined version of the two-party system has resulted in 'party government' rather than 'parliamentarian government'.[121] This defining feature of the constitutional arrangement in Canada, what came to be known as 'executive federalism', relies on a deliberate exclusion of the public from policymaking.[122] This arrangement, therefore, leaves only a symbolic role for enunciations of policy principles.

One can find such policy principles in the *Constitution of Canada*. For example, the Preamble to the Constitution Act 1867 states as a grand principle that the 'Union would conduce to the Welfare of the Provinces and promote the Interest of the British Empire'. Similarly, the Preamble to the Constitution Act 1982 states that 'Canada is founded upon principles that recognize the supremacy of God and the rule of law'. In addition, section 36 of the Constitution Act 1982 states that 'Parliament and the legislatures, together with the government of Canada and the provincial governments are committed to (a) promoting equal opportunities for the well-being of Canadians; (b) furthering economic development to reduce disparity in opportunities; and (c) providing essential public services of reasonable quality to all Canadians'.

The signalling function of these statements is most noticeable in the subnational constitutional space. The quintessential example comes from policies of the Quebec government; in particular, Bill 21, which bans the use of religious symbols.[123] Section 1 of the Bill declares Quebec a 'lay State' and enunciates three policy principles delineating Quebec's laicity. These principles are: equality of all citizens, freedom of conscience, freedom of religion. In addition, section 4 provides a fourth principle in the form of a right to lay institutions. While those framing social change as the objective of this law represent the majority, some have also seen the

---

118 For example, An Act Respecting the Cree Nation Government, CQLR c G-1.031; An Act Respecting Cree and Inuit Native Persons CQLR c A-33.1; and An Act to Establish the James Bay Regional Zone Council CQLR c C-59.1.

119 CQLR c C-11. See *Quebec Association of Protestant School Boards et al v Attorney General of Quebec* (1984) 54 National Reporter 196.

120 It seems that in the case of British Columbia, the written constitution places more power in the hands of the executive. See Baier (n 26), at 182, 183.

121 The legislatures play a policy-making role through their committees, especially when enactment of legislation is required. See Patrick Malcolmson and Richard Myers, *The Canadian Regime: An Introduction to Parliamentary Government in Canada* (4th edn, University of Toronto Press 2009) 192. See also Anthony M. Sayers and Andrew C. Banfield, 'The Evolution of Federalism and Executive Power in Canada and Australia' in Arthur Benz and Jörg Broschek (eds), *Federal Dynamics: Continuity, Change, and the Varieties of Federalism* (Oxford University Press 2013).

122 See David Cameron and Richard Simeon, 'Intergovernmental Relations in Canada: The Emergence of Collaborative Federalism' (2002) 32(2) *Publius: The Journal of Federalism* 49.

123 An Act Respecting the Laicity of the State, CQLR c L-0.3. See Phil Lord, 'What is the True Purpose of Quebec's Bill 21?' (2020) 9(3) *Directions* 1.

'symbolic and constitutive' function of this law.[124] Another example of this symbolism can be gleaned from Quebec's migration policy.[125]

8.5 Multilevel constitutionalism

8.5.1 *The relationship between the federal and subnational constitutions*

The federal and provincial constitutions form a constitutional system due to their interdependence. For example, when the provinces revise part of their electoral Acts, they are also amending the *Constitution of Canada*.[126] Moreover, no part of the *Constitution of Canada*[127] is paramount over any other part. Each provision (federal or provincial) must be read in light of the other provisions.[128]

The provinces were involved in the constitutional negotiations leading up to the adoption of the Constitution Act 1982.[129] In addition, under Part 5 of the Constitution Act 1982, most provisions require the approval of seven provinces containing at least 50 per cent of Canada's population.[130]

8.5.2 *The impact of international and European law on subnational constitutionalism in Canada*

The federal government can enter into treaties under the Crown prerogative powers.[131] The provinces can also enter into treaties with other countries, although only after review and upon approval by the federal government.[132] However, Quebec has claimed the right to conclude treaties on matters within its jurisdiction without such approval,[133] arguing that the power of the

---

124 Lord (n 123).
125 See Darryl Leroux, 'Québec Nationalism and the Production of Difference: The Bouchard-Taylor Commission, the Hérouxville Code of Conduct, and Québec's Immigrant Integration Policy' (2010) 49 *Quebec Studies* 107.
126 Wiseman (n 21), at 281.
127 As defined by section 52 of the Constitution Act 1982,
128 *Reference re Roman Catholic Separate High Schools Funding* (1986), 25 DLR (4th) 1, 54; 13 OAC 241, aff'd [1987] 1 SCR 1148.
129 See *Reference Re Resolution to amend the Constitution* [1981] 1 SCR 753.
130 See, for example, Richard Albert, 'The Difficulty of Constitutional Amendment in Canada' (2015) 39 *Alberta Law Review* 85.
131 See, for example, *Turp v Canada* (2012) 415 FTR 192 (FC).
132 France Morrissette, 'Provincial Involvement in International Treaty Making: The European Union as a Possible Model' (2012) 37(2) *Queen's Law Journal* 577, at 582 (footnote 26). See also Hugo Cyr and Armand de Mestral, 'International Treaty-Making and Treaty Implementation' in Peter Oliver, Patrick Macklem, and Nathalie Des Rosiers (eds), *The Oxford Handbook of the Canadian Constitution* (Oxford University Press 2017).
133 See Morrissette (n 132), citing 'Documents sur la position du Québec en matière de conclusion et de mise en œuvre d'accords internationaux' in Jacques-Yvan Morin, Francis Rigaldies and Daniel Turp (eds), *Droit international public: notes et documents*, t 2 (Éditions Thémis 1997) 127–46; Jacques-Yvan Morin, 'La personnalité internationale du Québec' (1984) 1 *Revue Québécoise de Droit International* 163, at 251, 260, 262; Canada, Department of Foreign Affairs and International Trade, News Release no 170, 'Axworthy Eager to Assist Quebec Government in Concluding a Legal Cooperation Arrangement with France' (22 October 1997); Henri Brun, Guy Tremblay and Eugénie Brouillet, *Droit Constitutionnel* (5th edn, Yvon Blais 2008) 45–8; Hugo Cyr, *Canadian Federalism and Treaty Powers: Organic Constitutionalism at Work* (PIE Peter Lang 2009) 186–96.

provinces to enter into treaties comes from the division of executive powers in the Constitution Act 1867, which allows all elected governments to exercise the royal prerogative. In practice, however, 'the right to conclude treaties is exercised exclusively by the Governor General in Council, regardless of the subject matter'.[134]

When the subject matter of a treaty involves provincial jurisdiction, the federal government must negotiate treaties with the provinces; although, historically, formal consultation mechanisms 'have been at best moderately successful'.[135] In comparison with EU member states, Canadian subnational units (both provinces and territories) do not have a 'continual presence during negotiations'.[136]

Treaties entered into by Canada are binding only at international law, until transformed into domestic law through legislation or judge-made law (dualist approach).[137] However, the protection of human rights has a stronger nexus with international and European instruments. Hence, the *International Covenant on Civil and Political Rights*[138] and customary (non-treaty) international law[139] can inform the interpretation of the Canadian Charter of Rights, given the rule that a constitution should be interpreted as much as possible in conformity with international law.[140] The *European Convention on Human Rights* also informs the interpretation of the Canadian Charter.[141]

8.6 Constitutional review

Given the constitutional occultation of the provinces, it is not surprising that only a 'few provinces have even explored the idea of conducting any kind of comprehensive constitutional review or thinking'.[142] The provincial legislatures are simply content with the constitutional *status quo*, one that ensures 'executive federalism' continues to dominate decision making on the federal and provincial levels.

The two types of courts in Canada,[143] federal[144] and provincial,[145] have therefore been more influential in reviewing constitutional matters. The provincial courts have judges that are either

---

134 Morrissette (n 132), at 582. See also A.E. Gotlieb, *Canadian Treaty-Making* (Butterworths 1968).
135 Morrissette (n 132), at 577 and 604–6.
136 Ibid. 577.
137 Peter W. Hogg, *Constitutional Law of Canada* (Thomson Reuters 2017) [36.9(c)].
138 *International Covenant on Civil and Political Rights*, opened for signature 16 December 1966, 999 UNTS 171 (entered into force 23 March 1976).
139 See *R v Hape* [2007] 2 SCR 292 [40] (per LeBel J).
140 For relevant Canadian case law, see Hogg (n 137), at [36.9(c)], footnote 185.
141 *European Convention on Human Rights*, as amended by Protocols Nos 11 and 14, 4 November 1950, ETS 5. See also G. Zellick, 'The European Convention on Human Rights: Its Significance for Charter Litigation' in Robert J. Sharpe (ed.), *Charter Litigation* (1987) Ch 5; Errol P. Mendes, 'Interpreting the Canadian Charter of Rights and Freedoms Applying International and European Jurisprudence on the Law and Practice of Fundamental Rights' (1982) 20 *Atlanta Law Review* 383; Berend Hovius, 'The Limitation Clauses of the European Convention on Human Rights: A Guide for the Application of Section 1 of the Charter' (1985) 17 *Ottawa Law Review* 213.
142 Baier (n 26), at 186.
143 See generally Wiktor and Tanguay (n 53).
144 Create by section 101 of the Constitution Act 1867. See also Supreme Court Act (SCA) RSC 1985 c S-26.
145 Wiktor and Tanguay (n 53).

appointed by the federal[146] or the provincial government.[147] The provincial superior courts are the Court of Appeal, which is the highest court; and the first instance court, known as the Supreme (or Superior) Court, which has a general jurisdiction.[148] The other provincial courts are the district and county courts, who have limited jurisdiction and territorial power;[149] and inferior courts such as magistrate's courts.

The federal and provincial governments have explicitly conferred the power upon the SCC on the one hand, and their appeal or superior courts on the other, to render upon request advisory opinions on constitutional (or any other) matters.[150] This advisory procedure accounts for roughly one-third of all decisions rendered on constitutional matters.[151] Perhaps the SCC decision on Quebec's 1998 secession question is the classic example of this 'executive federalism' approach.[152] The 'executive' qualifier is due to opinions being given independent of any factual determination, and also due to the fact that the executive initiates the proceeding.[153] The approach is a natural extension of the 'executive federalism' that can be gleaned from the occultation of provincial constitutions in favour of a model more aligned with the historical letters patent model.[154]

The First Ministers' conference, which is the annual (and *ad hoc*) federal-provincial Prime Minister's meeting, and the Council of the Federation, which is the bi-annual congress of the premiers of the ten provinces and three territories, are therefore seen as the primary mechanism for resolving constitutional conflicts.[155]

8.7 Conclusion

Canadian subnational constitutionalism is embedded in a federal constitutional system where provincial constitutional space is defined by provisions in the *Constitution of Canada*, in provincial statutes and by constitutional conventions. This federal system can be described as hybrid, multinational, triadic, overlapping and largely symmetric. The system gives primacy to an executive strand of federalism, where subnational entities expand their constitutional space through negotiations with the federal government, rather than through legal challenges or legislative

---

146 Per sections 96 and 100 of the Constitution Act 1867.

147 Per section 92(14) of the Constitution Act 1867. However, the 1867 Act provides that judges of the superior, district and county courts in each province are appointed by the Governor General (section 96), and that their salaries are fixed and provided for by the Parliament of Canada (section 100). In addition, section 91(27) reserves the power to legislate in matters of criminal law and procedure to the Parliament of Canada.

148 These courts are considered superior based on sections 96, 99 and 100 of the Constitution Act 1867.

149 These courts do not exist in Quebec.

150 Wiktor and Tanguay (n 53) vol 2, G7.

151 Ibid.

152 *Reference re Secession of Quebec* [1998] 2 SCR 217. Other decisions that reflect judicial policymaking as part of constitutional review include *Reference Re: Offshore Mineral Rights* [1967] SCR 792, and *Forest v Manitoba (Attorney General)* [1979] 2 SCR 1016.

153 See section 53 SCA, RSC 1985 c S-26.

154 Compare this constitutional culture with that in the United States and Australia, where the states have 'filled' the constitutional space available to them by adopting written constitutions.

155 Edward McWhinney, 'Constitutional Review in Canada and the Commonwealth Countries' (1974) 35 *Ohio State Law Journal* 900, at 908. See also Herman Bakvis, Gerald Baier, Douglas Brown, *Contested Federalism: Certainty and Ambiguity in the Canadian Federation* (Oxford University Press 2009).

intervention.[156] This approach is unique, even compared to the other two great Anglo-American federations, namely the United States and Australia.

Canadian provinces have a relatively wide constitutional space. Their ability to adopt their own constitutions continued after becoming part of the Canadian federation, although, with the exception of British Columbia, they opted for flexible, unwritten, constitutions, not very different from the letters patent that marked the origins of their constitutionalism. More critically, their consent is a prerequisite when modulating their constitutional space, even if by amendments to the *Constitution of Canada*. Within limits enshrined in the Constitution Act 1867 and Constitution Act 1982, their competencies include amending their constitutions, legislating protections of rights, including language rights, and adopting symbols of nationhood (such as coats of arms, flags and anthems).

Subnational constitutions continue to be linked to the *Constitution of Canada*, in a way not very different from the top-down system created by the royal prerogative constitutions that existed pre-Confederation, and not very different from the dependence of the colonies on the British government. Today, the federal government plays the same role in their capacity as the Crown in right of Canada. The same constituent power before Confederation, namely the Crown, continued its role after Confederation, even after the repatriation of the Canadian Constitution in 1982.[157]

As to the territories, their constitutions derive from federal legislation rather than directly from the *Canadian Constitution*. Notwithstanding, their relationship to the federal government continues to evolve in a way that emulates the relation between the federal government and the provinces.

Relative to the United States and Australia, Canadian subnational constitutions have weaker content. However, the procedures by which such constitutions are established are comparable to the other two Anglo-American federations. The resilience of Canadian subnational constitutions comes from the *Constitution of Canada* that continues to influence their constitutional space.

---

156 Notwithstanding, there was litigation surrounding patriation in 1981–82 (several cases, especially the *Quebec Veto Reference* [1982] 2 SCR 793 and *Patriation Reference* [1981] 1 SCR 753), *Reference re Remuneration of Judges of the Provincial Court* (PEI) [1997] 3 SCR 3, *Reference Re Secession of Quebec* [1998] 2 SCR 217 and even *Reference re Authority of Parliament in relation to the Upper House* [1980] 1 SCR 54 and *Reference re Senate Reform* [2014] 1 SCR 704. Also, litigation challenging Provincial Electoral Boundaries 1991: *Reference Re Provincial Electoral Boundaries (Sask)* [1991] 2 SCR 158. Notwithstanding, expanding the subnational constitutional space is largely through negotiation.

157 This setup is similar to 'multilevel constitutionalism' in relation to the parallel existence of the supranational European constitution with the constitutions of the Member States. See Ingolf Pernice, 'Multilevel constitutionalism in the European Union' (2002) 27(5) *European Law Review* 511, at 513.

9

SUBNATIONAL CONSTITUTIONALISM IN ETHIOPIA

Constitutional *déjà vu*

Yonatan Tesfaye Fessha

Subnational constitutionalism in Ethiopia, to put it bluntly, is marginal. But this is not because the states that make up the Ethiopian federation do not have the power to adopt state constitutions. In fact, all nine states have adopted, and at some point amended, their respective constitutions. It is marginal because state constitutions are not regarded as an important part of constitutional governance. The state constitutions do not feature in constitutional and policy debates. Neither do they generate interest among the public. This lack of interest in state constitutions is not limited to the general public, who are often oblivious to their existence, but extends to the leaders and politicians of the subnational units. In short, state constitutions are not taken seriously.

This chapter offers a concise account of the nature, scope and relevance of state constitutions in Ethiopia. The intention is not to provide a detailed discussion of each of the nine state constitutions, but rather to indicate their general features and trends in their development. This is made easier by the fact that the nine state constitutions are hardly different from one another, leaving one with an experience of *déjà vu* when reading one state constitution after another. This, the chapter argues, is attributed to the fact that the federation operates within a dominant party state in which a single party controls both the federal and all nine state governments.

The chapter begins by describing the context within which the state constitutions operate. The focus here is on the nature of the federal arrangement that the country has adopted in 1995. This is followed by a section that discusses the nature of the autonomy the federal constitution grants to the states and, in particular, focuses on the constitution-making power of the state governments. This is about the constitutional space that is made available to the states. It also briefly discusses the procedure that the states must follow when amending their respective constitutions. The paper then moves to discuss the forms and uses of state constitutions. This is about the political relevance of state constitutions. The content of state constitutions forms the object of the next section. The focus is on how the constitutions define the identity of their respective states, organize the structures of state government and protect fundamental rights. Their link

   DOI: 10.4324/9781003052111-9

with the federal constitution and their reviewability forms the object of the two sections that follow before the article concludes by making few general remarks.[1]

9.1 Context

Like many African countries, Ethiopia is a kaleidoscope of diversity. It was in the last quarter of the nineteenth century that the largely Christian and bi-ethnic kingdom, located in what is today the northern part of Ethiopia, transformed itself into a multi-ethnic and multi-religious Empire, expanding five times its original size, first under the leadership of King Menelik (1889–1913) and then Emperor Haile Selassie (1930–74). More than 80 ethnic groups inhabit the country. Both Christianity and Islam have a very long history in the country. Although religion has not served as a basis for political mobilization, ethnicity has. The attempt of successive leaders, including Emperor Haile Selassie and the military regime that replaced him (1974–91), to build a nation did not sit well with members of some of the ethnic communities. They saw the decision of the state to build a nation with a single language as an attempt to destroy their cultural and political identity. This has provoked violent responses from some ethnic groups. In response to successive state policies that sought to modernize the country by introducing a public sphere in which the language of one ethnic group is spoken, several communities were engaged in protracted armed struggle against the state. The major armed forces that challenged state policy were the Eritrean liberation fronts that launched armed struggle when Emperor Haile Selassie dissolved the United Nations-sponsored federation with Eritrea and incorporated the latter as one of its other deconcentrated provinces. The political and armed movements in Eritrea inspired other groups within Ethiopia that also sought to engage in counter-nationalism. Some of the political formations that claim to represent the Oromo, the largest ethnic group in the country, also framed their struggle in terms of decolonization. Others, like the political movement in the Tigray region, sought more autonomy from the national government.

Both the government of Haile Selassie and the military junta that overthrew the monarchy in 1974 and ruled the country for 17 years used military force to maintain unity, but without long-term success. In 1991, the combined efforts of the ethnic-based armed forces of northern Ethiopia brought down the military government, paving the way to the establishment of a transitional government that was dominated by ethnic based rebel forces and other political organizations that were organized along ethnic lines. At this time efforts to redefine the Ethiopian state also started in earnest. The traditional view of Ethiopians as sharing a common nationhood was replaced by a vision of Ethiopia as a house of many nations and ethnicities. This was evident in the Transitional Charter, the constitutive document of the transitional government, which organized the subnational entities along ethnic lines. This view of the Ethiopian state was codified in the 1995 Constitution, which eschewed the commonly used opening words, 'we the people of…', and instead opted for 'we the nations, nationalities and peoples of Ethiopia'.

Some argue that the Constitution, given its presentation of Ethiopia as a country of 'nations, nationalities and peoples', defines the federation as a multinational federation, although nowhere in the Constitution is the term actually used. Many observers, however, consider the Constitution to be based on, or establish, a system of ethnic federalism. Ethnicity is not only the organizing principle of the federation, but ethnic communities are transformed, by a mere constitutional fiat, into constituent nations. Irrespective of the designation used to describe the federation, the new dispensation

---

1 Given that the nine state constitutions provide for a similar content, often using the same words, a decision is made not to cite the relevant clauses of the nine constitutions in a footnote. A citation is provided only when a state constitution provides for content that is different from the other constitutions.

represents a major departure from a past that claimed, or sought to construct, a common nationhood and in which the political expression of ethnicity was discouraged and suppressed.

The outcome is a federation that is composed of nine states that are by and large demarcated along ethnic lines. Five of the nine states are predominantly inhabited by a single ethnic group and are designated by the name of that ethnic group. Although there are several ethnic groups in the remaining four states, their internal organization reveals that ethnicity is taken seriously. The logic of guaranteeing a homeland for each ethnic group is pursued vigorously. If ethnic groups do not acquire their own state, they are given their own local government, in one form or another. This idea of giving ethnic groups a homeland flies, however, in the face of a demographic reality that betrays homogeneity almost at every level of territorial organization. Although the state of Oromia is defined as the homeland of the Oromo, more than three million inhabitants of the state belong to other ethnic groups. The same is true with the other states. Some might be more diverse than others, but ethnic diversity characterizes the population of all nine states.

The nine subnational entities that constitute the federation are asymmetrical in many respects.[2] There is huge variation among the states in terms of population and size, ranging between the state of Harari which hosts 0.23 per cent of the Ethiopian population to the state of Oromia which is inhabited by 36 per cent of the population. The variation in terms of the size of their respective territorial areas is equally startling. The micro subnational unit of Harari is territorially 1,200 times smaller than the largest state of Oromia. Disparities in socioeconomic development are also visible. Despite these and other asymmetries that characterize the subnational entities, Article 47(4) of the constitution acknowledges and guarantees the 'equal rights and powers' to the nine states. The subnational units may be socially, economically and demographically asymmetric, but the constitution affirms their constitutional equality in terms of their constitutional rights and privileges. The subnational entities are equal members of the federation.

9.2 Autonomy

The federal constitution allows each state to adopt and execute its own constitution.[3] Based on this, all nine states have adopted and, at some point, revised, their respective constitutions. The majority of states adopted their constitutions in 1995, with Benshangul/Gumuz and Gambela following suit in 1996 and the state of Afar finally joining the bandwagon only in 1998.[4] Between 2001 and 2002, all of the states, with the exception of the state of Harari, revised their constitutions. The state of Harari amended its constitution in 2004. As the paragraphs that follow reveal, the state constitutions have ample subnational constitutional space to structure their respective political life as they deem fit.

9.2.1 Scope

The federal constitution, according to article 9 of the Constitution, is the supreme law of the land. Any law, including a law enacted by state governments, that is incompatible with the federal constitution is rendered ineffective. More specifically, the state constitutions, according to

---

2 Yonatan Fessha and Biniyam Bezabih, 'Federation among unequals: A country study of constitutional asymmetry in Ethiopia' in Patricia Popelier and Maja Sahadzic (eds) *Constitutional Asymmetry in Multinational Federalism: Managing multinationalism in multi-tiered systems* (Brill 2019) 137.

3 Constitution of the Federal Democratic Republic of Ethiopia, Art. 50(5) & Art. 52(2) (b).

4 Christophe Van der Beken, 'Sub-national constitutional autonomy and institutional innovation in Ethiopia' (2015) 2 *Ethiopian Journal of Federal Studies* 2.

Article 50(5) of the federal constitution, must be consistent with the provisions of the federal constitution. However, unlike some constitutions that extensively regulate the composition and functioning of subnational institutions, the Ethiopian Constitution says little about how the states should structure their political life.[5] This is true, for example, with respect to the structure of state governments. Article 52 (2) of the Constitution leaves it to each state to establish 'a state administration that best advances self-government, a democratic order based on the rule of law; to protect and defend the Federal Constitution'. The federal constitution does not, therefore, establish a national system of political structures at the level of the subnational entities. This permits the states wide leeway for institutional innovation and experimentation. This is so both in terms of the form and system of government that the state constitutions can establish.

To begin with, the absence of a national system of subnational political structures means that state constitutions can provide for an electoral system that is different from the national one. Each state can adopt legislative and executive structures that are distinct from the federal government and also from the other states. Each state is free to determine the size of its state legislature. This even seems to imply that the states are not necessarily obliged to follow the federal government and establish parliamentary systems of government at a state level.[6]

In terms of the composition and organization of local government, the federal constitution also leaves a lot of room for the states. The determination of the structure of government units below the state administration is left to the states. Local governments are under the jurisdiction of the states. Although the Constitution allows them to establish 'administrative levels' of government as they deem 'necessary', in line with the spirit of federalism, the Constitution also obliges the states to provide adequate powers to the lowest units of governments to enable the people to participate directly in the administration of such units.[7] This suggests that the states must provide for democratically responsible local governments, rather than merely deconcentrated local administrations pursuant to which decisions are made at state level and local administrations simply serves as implementing agents. Arguably, the self-determination rights the constitution provides to ethnic communities also imposes a limitation on the form of local government the states can create. The constitution provides ethnic communities the right to establish units of self-government in the territory they inhabit, which could be a state or a local government.[8] This arguably requires the state constitutions to acknowledge and accommodate the self-governance rights of ethnic communities through forms of ethnic-based local autonomy.[9]

In practice, eight of the state constitutions have established three-tiered systems of local government. The exception is the state of Harari, which on account of its very small size provides

---

5 Perhaps the only exceptions in this regard are the provisions of the federal constitution that regulate the structure and jurisdiction of state courts as well as the appointment and removal of state court judges.

6 Article 45 of the federal constitution states that 'The Federal Democratic Republic of Ethiopia shall have a parliamentarian form of government'. Based on this, Ayele argues that the states are required to establish a parliamentary system of government. He bases his argument on the fact that Article 45 of the federal constitution refers not to the federal government but to 'the Federal Democratic Republic of Ethiopia', which, according to Article 50 of the Constitution, 'is made up of both the states and the federal government'. For more, see Zemelak Ayele, 'Subnational constitutions in the Ethiopian federal system in light of the demos, the federalists and deliberative democracy models of subnational constitutionalism' *Journal of Ethiopian Law* (forthcoming 2020).

7 Constitution of the Federal Democratic Republic of Ethiopia, Art. 50(4).

8 Constitution of the Federal Democratic Republic of Ethiopia, Art. 39(3).

9 For more on this, see Zemelak Ayele and Yonatan Fessha, 'Local government in federal systems: The case of Ethiopia' (2012) 58(4) *Africa Today* 88.

only for a single tier of local government.[10] At the bottom of the other state local government systems is a *Kebele* administration that is directly elected by the people. On top of the *Kebele* administration is a *Woreda* administration comprised of a number of *Kebeles* and which is also directly elected by residents. Serving as an intermediary between the *Woreda* and the state government is a *Zone* administration that is also directly elected. In addition to these regular local government structures, many state constitutions provide for the establishment of special local government structures. These are ethnic-based local administrations established to make an ethnic group a majority in an area it inhabits.[11] These special local government structures are established, depending on population size, either as a *Special Woreda* or a *Nationality Zone*. Consistent with the purpose for which they are established, these local government administrations, in addition to being responsible for discharging the usual functions of local government, are responsible for determining the working language of the administration as well as promoting the language, education and culture of the ethnic groups that inhabit the area.[12]

The latest round of revision of constitutions of some of the states have undermined the autonomy of local governments. This is particularly the case in the states of Somali and Oromia. In 2005, the state of Oromia amended its constitution to allow the president of the state 'to dissolve any *woreda* council which it believes has endangered the region's constitution'.[13] Similarly, the 2003 amendment of the constitution of the state of Somali gave the president the power to 'assign and transfer the *woreda* chairman where found necessary for the wellbeing of the public of the region'.[14]

Arguably, a decision of a federal government to regulate the structure of the state governments would require a constitutional amendment given that the Constitution has left such matters to the states. This raises the question whether some of the current practices are in line with the Constitution. One could, for example, question the constitutionality of the federal law that requires elections of the state parliaments to be held simultaneously with election of the federal parliament. The power of the state governments to establish a state administration arguably includes the power to set dates of election for the state parliament even if these are different from those for federal parliament. This is important because a separate date for the election of state parliaments allows state electoral campaign and debates to focus on subnational issues. It is widely established that when national and subnational elections are held simultaneously, it is more likely that the process and outcome of the election will be determined by national politics.

9.2.2 Procedure

The states do not only have ample constitutional space to draft their own constitutions, but also amend them. Yet, the leeway they enjoy in drafting the contents of their respective constitutions is restricted when it comes to amending some aspects of their constitutions. This is not, however, a result of a limitation placed by the federal constitution as it is due to a self-imposed constraint. This particularly relates to the amendment of the chapters on fundamental rights and freedoms.

---

10 Constitution of the state of Harari, Article 75.
11 The states that have established ethnic local governments include the states of Amhara, Gambella, Afar, Benishangul-Gumuz and the state of the Southern Nations, Nationalities and Peoples (hereinafter SNNP).
12 For more on this, see Zemelak Ayele, 'The politics of local government and subnational constitution' (2014) 6(2) *Perspective on Federalism* 89.
13 Constitution of the state of Oromia, Art. 57(3) (h).
14 Constitution of the state of Somali, Art. 84(2).

Aspects of the state constitutions dealing with fundamental rights are more difficult to amend than other sections of state constitutions. This is not because of any especially high threshold required to amend those provisions. It is because the state constitutions have effectively left the amendment of fundamental rights and freedoms in the hands of the federal government. According to the constitutions of the states of Amhara, Afar, Southern Nations, Nationalities and Peoples' Region (SNNP), Benshangul/Gumuz, Harari, Somali and Gambella, the rights and freedoms provided in their respective constitutions will only be amended when the same rights and freedoms are amended in the federal constitution. In the case of some of these states, additional voting at the level of state parliament is also required to complete the act of amending fundamental rights and freedoms provided in the constitution. In Benshangul/Gumuz, for example, the federal amendment will come into effect only if it is supported by more than half of the local government councils within the state by a majority vote, as well as by a three-fourths vote of the state parliament.[15]

The state constitutions place a higher threshold for amending the rest of the provisions of their respective constitutions by requiring a majority or three-fourths vote of the state parliament and support from either half or two-thirds of the local government councils by a majority vote or, in some of the states, by two-thirds majority votes.[16] In states that provide for ethnic-based local governments, the approval of at least half of those councils is required. It is only the Constitution of Somali that leaves the amendment of the Constitution to the state parliament alone, which must none the less support constitutional amendment by a two-thirds majority before it is adopted.[17] In the states of the SNNP and Harari, both of which have bicameral parliaments, amending the constitution requires the approval of both houses of parliament by a two-thirds majority vote, either through a joint session, separate sitting or both.[18]

From the foregoing, it is clear that the state constitutions, like the federal constitution, require stringent procedures to be followed for their amendment. At the same time, the states have a wide discretion concerning the amendment of their respective constitutions. The federal constitution does not require the states to follow any rules or fulfil any conditions when amending their constitutions. In this context, it appears somewhat odd that the state constitutions have made constitutional amendment of fundamental rights subject to the amendment of the same rights in the federal constitution. One explanation is that the fundamental rights and freedoms provided by the state constitutions must not be in conflict with those provided by the federal constitution. The system is also consistent with the proposition that the rights and freedom provided by state constitutions must not fall below the minimum floor set by federal constitution. However, this would not mean that the state constitutions cannot provide for a more favourable regime of fundamental rights. By denying the state electorate and their representatives the power to amend their own constitutions in relation to freedoms and rights, they have relinquished the capacity of their state constitutions to adopt higher standards of rights protection.

It is noteworthy that the amendment procedures in almost all states (except for the state of Somali) follow the federal system. The power to amend state constitutions is not limited to the state parliaments, but also involves the local government councils, including councils of both

---

15 Constitution of the state of Benshangul Gumuz, Art. 119.
16 In the case of the SNNP, the support of the legislative assemblies of two-thirds of the local councils (zones and special *wereda*) by majority votes is also required.
17 Constitution of the state of Somali, Art. 109.
18 Constitution of the state of Harari, Art. 79.

regular and ethnic-based local governments.[19] It is also important to note that, unlike many federations where state constitutions need to be ratified by citizens through a referendum,[20] the state constitutions in Ethiopia, like the federal constitution, do not provide for popular ratification, both in the making and amendment of the constitutions.

9.3 Position of the subnational constitution within the SNE

The ample constitutional space that the states inhabit promises an environment in which the state constitutions are dynamic and relevant. That is, however, far from the reality. State constitutions are not given attention. One can confidently suppose that a random survey of the state electorate would reveal that an overwhelming majority of them would not even be aware of the existence of state constitutions. State constitutions are not the subject of extensive scholarly investigation. The few journal articles focusing on state constitutions are either poor quality or outdated.[21] The only major work on subnational constitutionalism is a book by Christophe van der Beken that provides a thorough examination of the state constitutions.[22] For reasons that will become clear later, the state constitutions have not been the subject of court litigation. Even subnational politicians rarely if ever invoke them when engaging in public debate. A study of the use of the state constitution in the state of Oromia found out that successive presidents of the state failed entirely to mention the state constitution in the numerous speeches they made.[23] Leaders of the state governments are more likely to rely on or invoke the federal constitution than their own state constitutions.

The fact that all state constitutions have been subject to revisions, at least once, might be taken to suggest that they possess at least some level of relevance. Yet the amendment of the state constitutions were not the result of local initiatives or motivated by a need to respond to local needs. Rather, they have been the result of political wrangling taking place at the national level. More importantly for our purpose, the fact that all state parliaments amended their constitutions around the same time and in relation to similar sections of their respective constitutions suggests that the state governments were simply implementing decisions made elsewhere, either at the level of the ruling political party that controls all state governments or the federal government.[24] The ruling party, which controls the federal government and all nine state governments, operates based on the principle of democratic centralism that requires federal and state officials to toe

19 In practice, none of the states have complied with the constitution-making and amendment procedure. The state constitutions were drafted, adopted and subsequently revised without the involvement of the local government councils. The drafts and revisions of state constitutions were prepared and submitted for adoption to the state council by the state executive. For more on this, see Tsegaye Regassa, 'Sub-national constitutions in Ethiopia: Towards entrenching constitutionalism at state level' (2009) 3(1) *Mizan Law Review* 33.

20 John Dinan, 'Patterns and developments in subnational constitutional amendment processes' (2008) 39 *Rutgers Law Journal* 837.

21 An earlier work by Tsegaye Regassa and more recent few articles by Christophe Van der Beken and Zemelak Ayele are some of the few important works that focus on subnational constitutions.

22 Christophe Van der Beken, *Completing the constitutional architecture: A comparative analysis of sub-national constitutions in Ethiopia* (Addis Ababa University Press 2017) 242.

23 Getachew Dissasa, 'The Role and Relevance of Subnational Constitutions in the Ethiopian Federal System in Promoting Effective Self-rule and Regional Autonomy: The case of Oromia Regional State's Constitution' (2008, Unpublished MA thesis: Centre for Federalism and Governance Studies, Addis Ababa University).

24 Ayele (n 6), at 14 notes that the state constitutions 'were adopted in 1995 and revised in the early 2000s in a rushed, centrally driven, and politically motivated drafting and adoption processes which did not involve the public that the state constitutions are supposed to govern'.

the lines of the central decision-making body. In short, the amendments were not the work of state governments themselves.

9.4 Content

The ample constitutional space available to states would also suggest the mushrooming of institutional innovation and experimentation with respect to how to structure political life. One important purpose of a subnational constitution is to enable a political community to define itself constitutionally and determine how it wants to be governed.[25] This section examines how the state constitutions have defined their respective political communities and structured state governments.

9.4.1 Identity

The decision of the Ethiopian constitution to redefine the Ethiopian state in federal terms is evident in the opening paragraphs of the preamble of the Constitution. As mentioned earlier, the preamble eschews the usual opening that projects an image of a single people or nation, 'We the people'. Instead, the preamble presents the country as an ensemble of 'nations, nationalities and peoples'. It is these groups of communities, and not the people of Ethiopia, that are regarded as the custodian of sovereignty.[26] In as much as this represents the recognition of ethnic diversity that characterizes the country, it is also criticized for promoting a fragmented image of the Ethiopian population.

In line with the spirit of the federal constitution, the state constitutions have not also shied away from defining the identity of the state they seek to regulate. Some of the state constitutions expressly identify with a particular ethnic group or groups. The preamble to the Constitution of the state of Oromia begins with 'We the Oromo people' and not with the 'We the people of the state of Oromia'. Article 8 of the same Constitution vests sovereignty not in the people of the state but in the 'people of the Oromo nation', indicating again the Oromo as the owners of the state. This distinguishes it from the constitutions of the state of Amhara, which vests sovereignty in the 'peoples of the Amhara Region'.[27] Article 2 of the Constitution of the Benshnagul Gumuz identifies four ethnic groups as owners of the state. Berta, Shinasha, Gumuz, Mao and Como are declared as the constituent communities of the state. Inhabitants of the state that belong to other ethnic groups, who account for almost half of the state population, are reduced to guests whose presence is simply acknowledged by the Constitution.

Other state constitutions may not have picked ethnic groups as owners of the state or custodians of state sovereignty but nevertheless indicate, in one way or another, the special place that some ethnic communities are assumed to have in the state. This is done, for example, by singling out and mentioning particular ethnic groups in the preamble of the state constitution. The Constitution of the state of Gambella opens with 'We the nations, nationalities and people of Gambella', suggesting the state as the home of a diverse population. But midway through, the preamble suddenly switches to 'We the Agnwa, Nuer, Mezenger, Opo and Como nationalities', singling out the five ethnic communities that are regarded as indigenous to the state, with no mention of almost half of the state population that is identified with other nationalities or ethnicities. The Constitution of Harari similarly commences with the inclusive words, 'We the

25 Jonathan L. Marshfield, 'Models of subnational constitutionalism' (2011)115 *Penn State Law Review* 1151.
26 Constitution of the Federal Democratic Republic of Ethiopia, Art. 8.
27 Constitution of the State of Amhara, Art. 8 (1).

nations, nationalities and peoples of the state of Harari', but then singles out and focuses on the history of self-rule of 'the people of Harari' and their conquest in 1886, ignoring the more than two-thirds of the population of the state that belong to other ethnic groups.[28]

These formulations reinforce the widely held view that the states are identified with particular ethnic groups, providing a constitutional basis for the view that the states are the homelands of particular ethnic groups. These are, of course, extensions of the nature of the federal arrangement that the country has adopted.

9.4.2 *Organization of powers*

The Ethiopian dual model of federalism divides powers between the federal and state governments with little concurrent powers. The states are not only allowed to have their own parliament and executive branches of government but also a judiciary. The Constitution says little about the structure and form of the state governments. It leaves the matter to the state constitutions.

9.4.3 *The state governments*

Like the federal constitution, each of the state constitutions has established a parliamentary system. The party or a coalition of parties with the majority of seats in the state legislature ordinarily form a government under the leadership of a chief executive commonly referred to as the state president. The president, who is the highest executive power of the state, is elected by the state parliament from among its members.[29] The only exception in this regard is the Constitution of Harari, which reserves the power to nominate the state president to the second chamber, a body which, as explained below, is fully controlled by individuals belonging to one ethnic group, the Harari.[30] The nomination must, however, be accepted by a two-thirds majority vote in a joint session of the two houses.[31] The two-thirds majority requirement for the selection of the president seems to set a high threshold. However, considering that members of the Harari community control half the Harari State Council, the two-thirds majority requirement seems appropriate in order to ensure that the Harari, who account for 10 per cent of the population of the state, do not 'impose their candidate for regional presidency'.[32]

---

28 The preambles of almost all state constitutions begin by recounting past injustices. When doing so, however, they do not simply refer to the injustice suffered by the population of the state. They refer to the injustice suffered by the particular ethnic community or communities that are deemed to be either owners or indigenes of the state and then mention others, almost in passing.

29 It must be mentioned that the state constitutions do not use the title president to refer to the head of government. They refer to the head of government as the chief executive. In practice, however, they are referred to as presidents. It must be noted that the practice of electing the president is not really in line with the process that a parliamentarian form of government dictates. The real decision of appointing a president does not lie with the state parliament. It is the party that decides the person who assumes the highest executive authority of the state in question. More disturbingly, it is not also a matter left to subnational politicians. The long arm of the national bosses of the ruling party is evident in the selection of the person who becomes the head of government. For more, see Yonathan Fessha, 'A federation without federal credentials: The story of federalism in a dominant party state' in Nico Steytler and Charles Fombad (eds) *Decentralization and constitutionalism in Africa* (Oxford University Press 2019).

30 Constitution of State of Harari, Art. 59(4).

31 Constitution of State of Harari, Art. 51 (2) (d).

32 Van Der Beken (n 4), at 26.

Unlike the federal constitution that separates between the offices of the head of state and head of government, the state constitutions vest both offices in one person. Typical of a parliamentary form of government, however, there are no term limits imposed on the president, which is also the case with the prime minister of the federal government. Once elected, state presidents can serve the whole legislative period, which is five years. The president nominates members of the executive council, the cabinet as it is referred to by state constitutions, which must be approved by the state council. There are also no limits on the number and type of minsters that a president can appoint, including those who can be appointed from outside the state parliament. The only requirement is that the deputy president must be selected by the state parliament from among its members.

The president and the executive council are collectively responsible to the state parliament for the exercise of their powers and the performance of their functions.[33] The executive council is responsible for drawing the state budget and formulating economic and social policies and strategies, both of which must be approved by the state council. The council is also responsible for coordinating the state administration and its various institutes. In this regard, state governments enjoy wide discretion in controlling their own civil service. The only requirement is that they ensure that 'educational, training and experience requirements for any job, title or position approximate national standards'.[34]

Despite the accountability of the executive to the state parliament, the state constitutions, with the exception of the Constitution of the SNNP,[35] do not provide for circumstances under which a state government can resign or be removed. It is not clear if the parliament can, by a vote of no confidence, cause the removal of a president and his or her government. The constitutions do not also provide for the 'impeachment' of a president for committing serious violation of the constitution or for not being able to perform the functions of the office of a president. Given the parliamentarian form of state governments, however, one can reasonably argue that the executives must always retain the confidence of parliament in order to stay in power.

9.4.4 The parliaments

The federal constitution says nothing about the composition and functioning of state parliaments. This is a matter left entirely to the state constitutions. This suggests that each state can decide on an electoral system and determine the size and composition of its legislature. This again makes room for institutional diversity at the subnational level.

However, most of the states have adopted a unicameral parliament whose members are directly elected by the residents of the state in a first past the post system, with the candidate receiving the plurality of vote (largest vote) representing a constituency. Unlike the federal constitution that limits the number of members of the House of Peoples' Representatives to 550, the state constitutions, except for the Constitution of the state of Harari,[36] do not regulate the size of their respective legislatures. Members are elected for a term of five years. They are protected from any prosecution or administrative action attacking them for the votes they cast and the opinions they express in the councils. A member may not be subject to arrest or prosecution

33 Individual responsibility of members of the executive council is not mentioned in any of the state constitutions. But it is a practice that the head of bureaus, the ministers of state governments as they are called in Ethiopia, provide the legislature with regular reports on matters that fall under their respective portfolios.
34 Constitution of the Federal Democratic Republic of Ethiopia, Art. 52(2) (f).
35 Constitution of the SNNP, Art. 57(2).
36 Constitution of the State of Harari, Art. 48.

without the permission of the relevant council, 'except in the case of flagrante delicto'. It is important to note that the councils are not full-time bodies as they are only required to hold at least two sessions annually.

Although most of the state constitutions provide for a unicameral parliament, two state constitutions establish a bicameral parliament. The first is the Constitution of the SNNP, a state that is home to more than 50 ethnic groups.[37] Established after the 2001 amendment of the state constitution, the second chamber of the SNNP, the Council of Nationalities, like its federal counterpart, the House of Federation, is composed of representatives of ethnic groups that inhabit the state. Each ethnic group is represented by one member, with each group receiving an additional representative for each one million of its population. The members are not directly elected but drawn from the members of the councils of the largely ethnic-based local governments. Like the House of Federation, the council can hardly be regarded as a second chamber as it is not involved in the legislative process, which is largely left to the lower house. The approval of the Council is not a requirement for the passing of a law. The closest that the Council comes to the legislative process is when it exercises its power to participate in the process of initiation and amendment of the state constitution.

The powers of the Council of Nationalities mirrors that of the House of Federation.[38] It is largely empowered to deal with matters of ethnic relations. For example, it has the power to decide issues relating to the rights of ethnic communities to establish systems of self-government in a form of ethnic-based local government. It is tasked with the duty 'to promote and consolidate the unity and equality of the peoples of the state'. It has also the power to resolve disputes that may arise between different administrative hierarchies. Its involvement extends to disputes with neighbouring states and 'questions of border delimitation', although its role with respect to such disputes is limited to studying and submitting them to the House of Federation and following up on their implementation. Following the federal constitution, which has unusually allocated the power of constitutional interpretation to the second chamber of the federal parliament, the SNNP Constitution also reserves the power to interpret the state constitution to the Council of Nationalities. The Council discharges this task with the help of a Council of Constitutional Inquiry, an advisory body that is largely composed of legal experts.

The other state constitution that provides for a bicameral parliament is the Constitution of Harari. The second chamber, the Harari National Assembly, is unique both in terms of composition and the power it exercises.[39] The 14 representatives that constitute the Assembly must belong to the Harari ethnic group.[40] Unusual for a state parliament, membership is not limited to individuals who reside within the state but rather extends to individuals who belong to the community but happen to reside in other parts of Ethiopia. This makes the Assembly more like the cultural councils that are common in countries that provide for non-territorial autonomy. This is also suggested by the powers the Assembly exercises and the functions it performs, which

---

37 Constitution of the State of the SNNP, Art. 58.

38 Constitution of the State of the SNNP, Art. 59. See also Proclamation No. 60/2003, 'The consolidation of the House of the Council of Nationalities and definition of its powers and responsibilities', Debub Negarit Gazeta 29 June 2003.

39 The lower chamber, the People's Representative Assembly (PRA), is composed of 22 directly elected representatives, and together with the 14 people Harari National Assembly, constitute the Harari State Council.

40 Constitution of the State of Harari, Art. 49. In addition, the state constitution reserves 4 of the 22 seats of the lower chamber to representatives elected from an electoral constituency (i.e. Jegol) where the Harari account for the overwhelming majority of the inhabitants, offering 'a de facto guaranteed representation to the Harari' (Van der Beken (n 4), at 23). This, in effect, allows 10 per cent of the population of the state to control half of the seats in the state parliament.

are largely focused on identity-related matters.[41] The Assembly is, for example, responsible for adopting laws and policies pertaining to the language and culture of the Harari community. It is responsible for issuing directives pertaining to the recognition and preservation of historical and cultural sites, including artefacts, shrines, mosques and monasteries. It is also responsible for the implementation of the right to self-determination as provided in Article 39 of the state constitution. It also selects the individuals that represent the Harari nationality in the House of Federation. What seems to be unusual for a cultural council is the power of the Assembly to nominate the president of the state. The decision to give this power to the council appears to reflect the views that the Harari are a minority entitled not only to cultural protection but also political empowerment. It seems to be based on the premise that important positions of appointment must be reserved to the Harari. This should not be surprising given that the Harari are regarded, as the designation of the state itself suggests, as the owners of the state, even though they merely account for 10 per cent of the state population.

Finally, following the national example, most of the state constitutions provide for the reservation of seats for representatives of minorities. However, the state constitutions leave the details of these special representations to be determined by law.[42] The only two constitutions that do not provide for reserved seats are those of Tigray and Afar. Perhaps this is made unnecessary by the fact that the two states guarantee the representation of their respective minorities through the creation of special electoral constituencies. Typical of majority-minority electoral districts, the electoral constituencies are drawn in such a way that the minorities account for the majority of the constituents and, as a result, are in a good position to elect their representatives.[43]

9.4.5 *Fundamental rights*

Chapter 3 of the federal constitution provides for fundamental rights and freedoms. Divided into human rights and democratic rights, the chapter provides a wide array of protections. Furthermore, it requires the rights to be 'interpreted in a manner conforming to the principles of the Universal Declaration of Human Rights, the International Covenants on Human Rights and other international instruments adopted by Ethiopia'.[44] The Constitution obliges all branches of the state governments at all levels to 'respect and enforce the fundamental rights and freedoms provided in Chapter 3.[45] This raises the question about the relevance of state constitutions that include a catalogue of rights and freedoms.

The utility of incorporating a list of fundamental rights in state constitutions becomes more questionable when one notices that almost all state constitutions have simply copied the federal constitution and provide for an almost identical catalogue of rights and freedoms.[46] Further, all state constitutions, as mentioned earlier, subject the amendment of rights and freedoms they provide to the amendment of the same rights and freedoms in the federal constitution. In other words, the state constitution effectively denies the state electorate and their parliament the right to amend these aspects of their own constitution. The Constitution of the state of Oromia takes

41 Constitution of the State of Harari, Art. 59.
42 To date, none of the states have adopted such a law.
43 Christophe Van der Beken, *Unity in Diversity—federalism as a mechanism to accommodate ethnic diversity: The case of Ethiopia* (LIT Verlag 2012) 246.
44 Constitution of the Federal Democratic Republic of Ethiopia, Art. 13(2).
45 Constitution of the Federal Democratic Republic of Ethiopia, Art. 13 (1).
46 Perhaps the only variation is that some of the state constitutions have enhanced the status of the right to life by making it a right that cannot be derogated from even during a state of emergency. See Constitution of the state of Amhara, Art. 114(4); Constitution of the state of Afar, Art. 106(4)).

this further by requiring the interpretation of rights provided in the state constitution must conform with the interpretation that the House of Federation offers 'with respect to a similar provision in the federal constitution'.[47]

As argued earlier, it is problematic that state constitutions deny themselves the option of going beyond the minimum set of rights provided by the federal constitution. Enhanced protection to individual rights through the provision of additional rights is, after all, one of the of the objectives of subnational constitutions.[48] The position of the state constitutions on the amendment of fundamental rights removes from the states the opportunity to provide for rights and freedoms that respond to their specific context and the needs and preferences of their electorate. This is a missed opportunity especially given the fact that the states in Ethiopia have, in principle, their own institutions that can enhance the protection of individual rights by enforcing those same rights.

9.4.6 *Policy principles*

Chapter 10 of the federal constitution provides for 'national policy principles and objectives'.[49] The chapter sets forth political, social, economic, cultural, and environmental objectives. It also provides for principles regulating foreign relations and national defence. The Constitution expects both federal and state governments to be guided by those principles and objectives when implementing the Constitution as well as other laws and policies.

Following the national example, the state constitutions provide for policy objectives and principles in almost the same words. The only difference is that the state constitutions do not include principles regulating foreign relations and national defences, and understandably so, as these are matters that fall under the jurisdiction of the federal government. Here again the states miss an opportunity to formulate and emphasize policies that address the needs and preferences of their respective population. Arguably, the states that are predominantly inhabited by pastoral communities could have different economic and environmental objectives than those dominated by communities that are characterized by a sedentary lifestyle.[50]

9.5 Multilevel constitutionalism

9.5.1 *The relation between the federal and subnational constitutions*

As is clear from the foregoing, the federal constitution leaves the organization, powers and functions of subnational institutions to be regulated by the state constitutions. It does not also require state constitutions to comply with a set of specific principles or criteria when establishing subnational institutions. Article (52(2) (a)) of the Constitution simply requires states to 'establish a State administration that best advances self-government, a democratic order based on the rule of law; to protect and defend the Federal Constitution'. A similarly broad framework is provided in

---

47 Christophe van Der Beken, 'Sub-national constitutional autonomy in Ethiopia: On the road to distinctive regional constitutions', paper submitted to workshop 2: Sub-national constitutions in federal and quasi federal constitutional states World Congress of Constitutional Law, Oslo (16–20 June 2014) 13.
48 Marshfield (n 25).
49 Constitution of the Federal Democratic Republic of Ethiopia, Arts. 85–92.
50 One instance where a state constitution appears to respond to local needs is in the decision of the drafters of the Constitution of the state of Afar to impose on the executive branch of the state a duty to 'create a conducive environment to improve the living standard of the pastoralists' (Constitution of the state of Afar, Art. 56(8)).

Article 88 of the Constitution, which sets out the political objectives that must guide the implementation of laws and policies by federal and state governments, and which expects state government to promote and support the self-rule of all Ethiopian peoples at all levels. As will be discussed shortly, the federal constitution regulates state courts to a limited extent. The only two other respects in which the constitution explicitly constrains the constitutional powers of the subnational entities concern fundamental rights and policy principles, which must be respected and enforced both by federal and state governments, and subnational civil service, which must generally comply with federal standards.[51]

Clearly, the states in Ethiopia are left with broad constitutional space. The federal constitution gives ample room for states to determine their state structures. Although the fact that the federal constitution does not establish a national system of subnational political structures opens a room for the adoption of tailor-made design, this, as it is clear by now, has not materialized. There is hardly any variation among the political structures established by the state constitutions. The only variation that has not been mentioned earlier is that the Constitutions of Somali and Benishangul recognize the role of traditional institutions and leaders through provision for the establishment of a council of elders and clan leaders.[52] Yet the constitutions do not go beyond mandating the establishment of these traditional institutions. Neither the two constitutions nor a subsequent law has provided for the establishment, composition and functioning of such traditional bodies. As a result, the institutional variations that the state constitutions have produced, if any, are simply marginal.

On the other hand, the states are in a much better position to affect the contents of the federal constitution. This is because the states are extensively involved in the amendment of the federal constitution. In fact, unlike other federations, where subnational entities' participation is limited to involvement through representatives in second chambers, the states in Ethiopia must directly decide on proposed amendments. For example, a proposal to amend fundamental rights and freedoms provided in the Constitution and the two articles dealing with the amendment of the Constitution must be supported by the legislative assemblies of all states by a majority vote. This is in addition to their indirect involvement through the House of Federation, which must also support such proposal by a two-thirds majority vote. The blessing of the states is also required to amend any of the remaining articles of the constitution. Those constitutional amendments require the support of the legislative assemblies of two-thirds of the state parliaments by majority votes.

9.6 Constitutional review

Ethiopia has opted for a dual court system, with the state courts exercising jurisdiction over state matters alongside federal courts. Unlike the executive and legislative branches of state governments whose particular structure is left to be determined by the state constitutions, the judicial branch is, to some extent, regulated by the federal constitution. The federal constitution requires each state to establish first instance, high and supreme courts,[53] which they have done. The federal constitution also allows the states to recognize customary and religious courts.[54] Until recently all state supreme and high courts were also functioning as federal, high and first instance

---

51 Constitution of the Federal Democratic Republic of Ethiopia, Art. 52 (2) (f).
52 Constitution of the state of Afar, Art. 63; Constitution of the state of Somali, Art. 56.
53 Constitution of the Federal Democratic Republic of Ethiopia, Art. 78 (3).
54 Constitution of the Federal Democratic Republic of Ethiopia, Art. 78(5). Article 73 of the Constitution of the SNNP provides for the same.

courts respectively. This is because the federal constitution delegates the jurisdiction of federal high and first instance courts to the state courts until the House of Peoples' Representatives, by two-thirds majority vote, establishes nationwide federal high and first instance courts as it deems necessary.[55] The federal government has now established federal high courts in five of the nine states.[56]

The state supreme courts have the final say on state matters. This power is, however, undermined by the power of the Cassation Division of the Federal Supreme Court to review any final court decision that contains a basic error of law.[57] This has led to a situation where the Federal Supreme Court has not only reviewed matters that were decided by state courts using federal law but also state law. This has given the federal supreme court the final say on the meaning of state law. This suggests that the court system is not completely dual in nature.

In line with the federal constitution that prevents federal courts from reviewing the constitution,[58] the state constitutions do not provide for judicial review. State courts cannot determine the constitutionality of laws and actions of state governments. In most of the states, that is left to a constitutional interpretation commission. Although the composition of these political bodies varies from one state to another, most of them are composed of members of local government councils. In some of the states, representation in the commission is limited to representatives of communities that are regarded as 'owners' or 'founders' of the state. The only exception is the constitution of the state of SNNP which, as mentioned earlier, gives the power of constitutional review to its second chamber, the Council of Nationalities.

Like the House of Federation, the constitutional interpretation commissions and, in the case of the SNNP, the Council of Nationalities, are assisted by an expert body, a Constitutional Inquiry Council. Often composed of the president and deputy president of a state supreme court, lawyers nominated by the president and appointed by state parliament and three members of the state parliament, the role of the expert body is limited to examining constitutional disputes and submitting its recommendation to a constitutional interpretation commission or, in the case of the SNNP, to the Council of Nationalities for final and binding decision. This means that the politicians that sit in the constitutional interpretation commissions and the Council of Nationalities are the ultimate interpreters of state constitutions. This subjects the model of constitutional review adopted by the states to the same criticism that is directed against the House of Federation, the political body that, as mentioned earlier, is tasked with interpreting the federal constitution. It leaves matters of constitutional interpretation in the hands of politicians that are neither competent nor impartial when interpreting constitutions and dealing with constitutional disputes.[59]

9.7 Conclusion

If you have seen one, you have seen them all. That largely applies to the constitutions of the nine states that make up the federal Ethiopia. There might be slight differences in how the states

---

55 Constitution of the Federal Democratic Republic of Ethiopia, Art. 80.

56 Federal High Court Establishment Proclamation No 322/2003.

57 Constitution of the Federal Democratic Republic of Ethiopia, Art. 80(3) (a).

58 The federal constitution leaves the power to interpret the Constitution and determine constitution disputes to the House of Federation, the second chamber of the federal parliament. See Constitution of the Federal Democratic Republic of Ethiopia, Arts. 62(1) and 83(1).

59 For more on the Ethiopian model of constitutional review, see Yonatan T. Fessha 'Judicial review and democracy: A normative discourse on the (Novel) Ethiopian approach to constitutional review' (2006) 14(1) *African Journal of International and Comparative Law* 53.

define themselves. They are, however, similar in the structures of state governments they establish and in their decision to simply transplant the rights and freedoms incorporated in the federal constitution. The same is true in their decision to exclude courts from constitutional adjudication and task a political body to determine the constitutionality of laws.

The identical nature of the state constitutions is linked to the fact that a single political party controls the federal government and all nine state governments. As argued elsewhere, however, this fact alone does not explain the total lack of constitutional appetite among the subnational entities.[60] A ruling party that is committed to the principle of federalism might provide for an internal structure that allows ample room for institutional innovation and experiment. The problem is that the ruling party functions in a centralized manner, and as a result, the state governments are reduced to implementing agents of the federal government. The ruling party functions in a manner that is indifferent to the federal system.

With the election of Abiy Ahmed to power in April 2018 and the series of political reforms introduced since then, however, the political landscape is changing rapidly. The subnational political space is being increasingly occupied by state governments that are asserting their autonomy more aggressively. Just recently, the state of Tigray used its constitution to declare a state of emergency over the Covid-19 pandemic, though the federal government was yet to declare a national state of emergency.[61] This suggests that the use of subnational constitutions to extend autonomy or shield the state from the actions and laws of the federal government might become more common. Subnational politics could then give rise to dynamic and vibrant subnational constitutionalism. Only then, perhaps, will we start to see states effectively making use of their ample constitutional space.

---

60 Fessha (n 29).

61 Addis Standard (26 March 2020) Tigray region declares state of emergency, available at https://addisstandard.com/news-alert-tigray-region-declares-state-of-emergency-to-prevent-spread-of-covid19/. accessed 31 March 2020.

10

SUBNATIONAL CONSTITUTIONALISM IN GERMANY

Constitutional autonomy, unitarian federalism and intertwined policymaking

Werner Reutter[1]

10.1 Context

For many the German national constitution, the Basic Law (BL), is far more than just a legal document establishing a political order, guaranteeing fundamental rights and prescribing national objectives.[2] It also is the focus of what has been coined 'constitutional patriotism' (Verfassungspatriotismus) that needs citizens to identify themselves with the basic values, institutions and procedures of the German republic. In this ambitious conceptualization of the German nation, the BL is a necessary pillar, but to my knowledge, none of the scholars taking part in the debate on 'constitutional patriotism' ever mentioned subnational constitutions in this context. As Gardner has pointed out, subnational constitutions can, but do not have to, become 'charters for living', i.e. charters 'of self-governance self-consciously adopted by subnational populations for the purpose of achieving a good life by effectively ordering subnational governmental power and by protecting the liberties of subnational citizens'.[3] Subnational constitutions can also just 'formalize the administrative subordination of the subnational to the national government'.[4] German *Land* constitutions fall between these two types. On the one hand, they grant

1 This work was supported by the Deutsche Forschungsgemeinschaft under Grant RE 1376/4-1; AOBJ 64495. I use the terms 'state', 'subnational unit' and 'Land' interchangeably. When quoting constitutions, I use officially translated texts. The article very much profited from the introduction to this volume and Patricia Popelier's chapter on 'Subnational constitutionalism in Belgium' whose structure I took as a template. I am also grateful to all three editors and an anonymous reviewer for their helpful comments on an earlier draft of the paper. The usual disclaimer applies, of course.
2 Dolf Sternberger, 'Verfassungspatriotismus' [1979] in Dolf Sternberger, *Verfassungspatriotismus. Schriften Band X* (Insel 2010) 13; Jürgen Habermas, *Eine Art Schadensabwicklung. Kleine politische Schriften* (Suhrkamp 1987); Jürgen Habermas, 'Staatsbürgerschaft und nationale Identität' [1990], in Jürgen Habermas, *Faktizität und Geltung* (Suhrkamp 1992) 632.
3 James A. Gardner, *In Search of Sub-National Constitutionalism.* Paper prepared for the Seventh World Congress of the International Association of Constitutional Law. Athens, Greece, June 11–15, 2007. University at Buffalo Law School. Baldy Center for Law & Social Policy. Legal Studies Research Paper Series. Paper No. 2007-016, available at: http://ssrn.com/abstract=1017239; cf. also James A. Gardner, 'The Failed Discourse of State Constitutionalism' (1992) 90 *Michigan Law Review* 761.
4 Gardner, *In Search of Sub-National Constitutionalism* (n 3), at 7.

DOI: 10.4324/9781003052111-10

subnational governments a 'significant role in the direct or indirect protection of the liberty of subnational citizens'.[5] Simply put, they make self-rule possible in the German *Länder*. On the other hand, there is no 'underlying popular ideology' that would allow to qualify German *Land* constitutions as 'charters for living' in the sense described by Gardner. At least, according to a 2008 poll, just one of ten respondents identified himself or herself with the *Land* he or she lived in. In the same poll, 32 per cent of the respondents identified themselves with the federal level and 29 per cent with the local community.[6] Overall, the findings of this and similar polls suggest 'that to a large extent Germans do not view the Länder as an independent political level'.[7]

Yet, this theoretical qualification does not tell us much about the contribution *Land* constitutions make to the functioning and the stability of democracy in Germany.[8] In Germany—as in many other countries—we can observe a trend towards decentralization and regionalization. Notably, since unification, economic discrepancies, cultural differences and political cleavages between the *Länder* triggered several major reforms of the federal system and put the widespread view into question that *Land* constitutions are at best of secondary importance and under the shadow of the Basic Law.[9] As one scholar noted, *Land* constitutions and *Land* constitutional courts are 'in' and show specific profiles.[10] Notwithstanding the varying conceptions on the functions and the importance of German *Land* constitutions, it should be obvious that we can only fully understand German constitutional democracy if we give subnational constitutions their due credit. This also brings a discrepancy to the fore. Historically and constitutionally, Germany represents a coming-together federation. Compared to other countries, its society can be regarded as homogenous even though increasing economic, political and cultural differences between *Länder* or groups of *Länder* (East/West; North/South) underscore tendencies of fragmentation. Moreover, the *Länder* have either preceded, created or joined the Federation, and they enjoy full constitutional autonomy.

5 Gardner, *In Search of Sub-National Constitutionalism* (n 3), at 6.

6 Thieß Petersen, Henrik Scheller and Ole Wintermann. 'Public Attitudes towards German Federalism: A Point of Departure for a Reform of German (Fiscal) Federalism? Differences between Public Opinion and the Political Debate' (2008), 17 *German Politics* 559, at 566.

7 Petersen, Scheller and Wintermann (n 6), at 582; see also: Renate Köcher, 'Föderalismus im Spiegel der Demoskopie' in Ines Härtel (ed.), *Handbuch Föderalismus—Föderalismus als demokratische Rechtsordnung und Rechtskultur in Deutschland, Europa und der Welt. Band III: Entfaltungsbereiche des Föderalismus* (Springer-Verlag 2012) 749.

8 Others understand *Land* constitutions as manifestations of territorially defined values, interests, and identities or picture an 'East German constitutionalism' on the horizon. See, e.g., Eckhard Jesse, Thomas Schubert and Tom Thieme, *Politik in Sachsen* (Springer VS 2014) 53–5; Hans Vorländer, 'Verfassungstheorie und demokratischer Transitionsprozess. Der (ost-) deutsche Konstitutionalismus' in Astrid Lorenz (ed.), *Ostdeutschland und die Sozialwissenschaften. Bilanz und Perspektiven 20 Jahre nach der Wiedervereinigung* (Verlag Barbara Budrich 2011) 245; Astrid Lorenz, 'Die ostdeutschen Landesverfassungen als dynamische Integrationsstifter' in Astrid Lorenz (ed.), *Ostdeutschland und die Sozialwissenschaften. Bilanz und Perspektiven 20 Jahre nach der Wiedervereinigung* (Verlag Barbara Budrich 2011) 75.

9 See, e.g., Christian Pestalozza, 'Einführung' in *Verfassungen der deutschen BundesLänder mit dem Grundgesetz*, 10th edition (C.H. Beck 2014) XVII; Andrea Stiens, *Chancen und Grenzen der Landesverfassungen im deutschen Bundesstaat der Gegenwart* (Duncker & Humblot 1997); Werner Reutter, *Verfassungspolitik in Bundesländern. Vielfalt in der Einheit* (Springer VS 2018).

10 Matthias Dombert, '§ 27 Landesverfassungen und Landesverfassungsgerichte in ihrer Bedeutung für den Föderalismus' in Ines Härtel (ed.), *Handbuch Föderalismus. Band II: Probleme, Reformen, Perspektiven des deutschen Föderalismus* (Springer-Verlag 2012) 19, at 20.

According to Art. 20(1) BL federalism is a crucial pillar of constitutional democracy in Germany. It also impacts upon the role *Land* constitutions play in this system and is governed by five principles: the eternity clause (i), the dual state structure (ii), intertwined policymaking and the tendency towards unitarian policies (iii), the homogeneity principle (iv), and the principle of federal or respectively *Land*-friendly behaviour (v).[11]

(i) *Eternity clause*: According to the eternity clause of Art. 79 (3) BL, an amendment to the Basic Law 'affecting the division of the Federation into *Länder*, the participation on principle in the legislative process or the principles laid down in Articles 1 and 20 shall be inadmissible'. In other words, as long as the Basic Law applies, Germany will be a federal democracy. We find similar clauses in some of the *Land* constitutions.[12] Yet, the eternity clause only stipulates that there has to be an upper state and at least two *Länder*. In addition, there must be a venue for the *Länder* to participate in national lawmaking. Currently, the '*Länder* shall participate through the Bundesrat in the legislation and administration of the Federation and in matters concerning the European Union'.[13] This includes all *Länder* having a say in decisions on territorial reforms. Oddly enough, this is a competency of the federation because Art. 29 (2) BL stipulates that revisions 'of the existing division into *Länder* shall be effected by a federal law, which must be confirmed by referendum'. That is the constitutional principle. In reality, the merger of the three *Länder*—Württemberg-Baden, Baden and Württemberg-Hohenzollern—into Baden-Württemberg in 1952 and the failed merger of Berlin and Brandenburg in 1996 have been put into practice without reference to the provisions of Art. 29 BL.[14] In both cases the Basic Law had to be amended in order to realize the territorial reforms. In conclusion, any future territorial reform is only feasible if the *Länder* and the people affected agree.

(ii) *Dual state structure*: A second important principle is the dual structure of the federal state, which grants both the Federation and the *Länder* equal status. Both enjoy state quality and both are entitled to maintain the institutions necessary for exercising public powers. In addition, the *Länder* must manage sufficient competencies and resources. It is common knowledge that the Federation does not allot these privileges to the *Länder*.[15] On the contrary, the Federation and the *Länder* have to be legitimized separately and independently from each other. In this respect and from a constitutional point of view, the *Länder* are on par with the Federation.[16]

---

11 Hans-Jochen Vogel, 'Die bundesstaatliche Ordnung des Grundgesetzes' in Ernst Benda, Werner Maihofer and Hans-Jochen Vogel (eds), *Handbuch des Verfassungsrechts. Studienausgabe Teil 2*, 2nd edition (de Gruyter 1983) 1041; Heinz Laufer and Ursula Münch, *Das föderale System der Bundesrepublik Deutschland*, 8th edition (Bayerische Landeszentrale für politische Bildungsarbeit 2010) 91–102; Sven Leunig, *Die Regierungssysteme der deutschen Länder im Vergleich*, 2nd edition (Springer VS 2012); Sven Leunig and Werner Reutter, '*Länder* und Landesparlamente im föderalen System der Bundesrepublik Deutschland' in Ines Härtel (ed.), *Handbuch Föderalismus—interdisziplinär. Föderalismus als demokratische Rechtsordnung und Rechtskultur in Deutschland, Europa und der Welt* (Springer Verlag 2012) 743; Donald P. Kommers and Russell A. Miller, *The Constitutional Jurisprudence of the Federal Republic of Germany*, 3rd. edition (Duke University Press 2012) 79–151; Werner Reutter, *Die deutschen Länder. Eine Einführung* (Springer VS 2020) 37-52.
12 E.g. Art. 56(3) Bavarian Constitution, Art. 20(1) Bremen Constitution. These clauses do, of course, not mention federalism as this is exclusively regulated in the Basic Law.
13 Art. 50 BL.
14 Art. 118 and 118a BL; BVerfGE 1, 14; Kommers and Miller (n 11), at 80–7.
15 But see also Pestalozza (n 9), at recital 87–92 and 153–82.
16 BVerfGE 13, 54 ('Hessen-Urteil'), 60, 175 (209); 64, 301 (317), 34, 9 (20).

(iii) *Intertwined policymaking and unitarianism*: The third constitutional principle in question rules on the separation of powers between the Federation and the *Länder*. According to Art. 30 BL, the 'exercise of state powers' and the 'discharge of state functions [...] is a matter for the *Länder*'. However, this subsidiarity clause shows an important limitation, as it applies only as far as the Basic Law does not provide 'otherwise'. As it turns out, the exception, the 'otherwise', is far more important than the general rule of subsidiarity. The Basic Law confers a whole range of legislative powers to the Federation, while the *Länder* mostly have to execute federal laws—if the Basic Law 'does not otherwise provide or permit'.[17] This distribution of tasks based on state functions makes intertwined policymaking and cooperation between the *Länder* and the Federation obligatory. The separation of tasks causes a 'network-like system of interlocking politics' in which each participant enjoys 'veto power of considerable strength'.[18] These structures seemingly promote cooperation among *Land* executives and bargaining as a major mode of conflict resolution. At the same time, they privilege unitarian policies.[19]

(iv) *Homogeneity clause*: The constitutional orders in the *Länder* must 'conform to the principles of a republican, democratic and social state governed by the rule of law within the meaning of this Basic Law.'[20] Furthermore, the Federation has to 'guarantee that the constitutional order of the *Länder* conforms to the basic rights and to the provisions' just mentioned.[21] The term 'conform' does not mean that *Land* constitutions have to be 'identical' to the Basic Law. On the contrary, *Land* constitutions can deviate more or less from the principles mentioned in Art. 28(1) BL. Notably the principle of democracy can take different forms, and it remains to be seen how the *Länder* put this principle into practice.

(v) *Federal/Land friendly behaviour*: The fifth principle is unwritten constitutional law and results from judgments of the Federal Constitutional Court.[22] According to this principle, the Federation and the *Länder* enter into a 'mutual trust relationship'. The federal government must act in a *Land*-friendly manner and the *Länder* must act in a Federation-friendly manner.[23] This not only entails an obligation to show consideration for each other, but the principle of federal-friendly behaviour also means that the *Länder* support each other (financially) or that public administrations cooperate. Moreover, the principle of federal-friendly behaviour makes it impossible for a *Land* to quit the Federation. An 'exit' of a *Land* from the Federal Republic of Germany is impossible.

With regard to *Land* constitutions, these principles have two important implications. One is constitutional, the other one political.

---

17 Art. 83 BL.

18 Manfred G. Schmidt, 'Germany. The Grand Coalition State' in Josep M. Colomer (ed.), *Comparative European Politics*, 3rd edition (Routledge 2008) 58, at 80–1.

19 Laufer and Münch (n 11), at 181–200; Sabine Kropp, *Kooperativer Föderalismus und Politikverflechtung* (VS Verlag für Sozialwissenschaften 2010); Gerhard Lehmbruch, *Parteienwettbewerb im Bundesstaat. Regelsysteme und Spannungslagen im politischen System der Bundesrepublik Deutschland*, 3rd edition (Westdeutscher Verlag 2000); Fritz W. Scharpf, Bernd Reissert and Fritz Schnabel, *Politikverflechtung. Theorie und Empirie des kooperativen Föderalismus in der Bundesrepublik* (Scriptor 1976).

20 Art. 28(1) BL.

21 Art. 28(3) BL.

22 BVerfGE 12, 205 (254), 34 9 (44); 81, 310 (337).

23 Laufer and Münch (n 11), at 101–2; Vogel (n 11), at 1061–3.

- Constitutionally, the five principles just outlined create an ambiguous status of *Land* constitutions. On the one hand, *Land* constitutions are supposed to respect the provisions laid down in Art. 28(1) BL.[24] In addition, Art. 31 BL gives federal law precedence over *Land* law.[25] On the other hand, the *Länder* are free to adopt and change their constitutions at their own discretion. The Basic Law neither prescribes specific contents nor is the Federation entitled to interfere with the adoption or the change of constitutions in the *Länder*. The *Länder* are autonomous in this respect because they possess state quality.[26] If a *Land* constitution includes an article in conflict with the national law, this article is just not applicable. For example, six *Land* constitutions that came into effect in 1946 and 1947 included clauses that made capital punishment possible. After the Basic Law had been put into force, these constitutional provisions remained unchanged. Hesse was the last *Land* that repealed the clause on the death penalty from its constitution (as late as 2018).[27]
- Politically, the prerogatives of the people in the *Länder* are circumscribed as well. Ideas travel easily among the German *Länder*. Pestalozza claims that *Land* executives and parliaments consult each other or imitate constitutional provisions. These political processes lead to more or less standardized subnational constitutions.[28] Many scholars see subnational constitutions, therefore, not only shaped by the national level but also by processes of adaptation and homogenization, which could eventually even jeopardize a crucial precondition of federalism, namely diversity. Furthermore, intertwined policymaking, strong unitarian tendencies and the parties confine the room for manoeuvre available to the *Länder*.

It goes without saying that the combination of 'self-rule' and 'shared rule',[29] of autonomy and hierarchy, of dual state structure and homogeneity, trigger tensions and sometimes even conflicts between the Federation and the *Länder*. It also impacts on subnational constitutionalism in Germany.

10.2 Autonomy

10.2.1 Scope

Due to their state quality the German *Länder* enjoy autonomy with regard to the content of their constitutions and the way they adopt and change these legal documents. *Länder* can even choose to have no constitution at all. For example, Lower Saxony qualified its first constitution of 1951 as preliminary (Vorläufige Niedersächsische Verfassung), and in 1950 Schleswig-Holstein adopted a derivative constitution called *Land* statute (Landessatzung). At the same time, both constitutional levels have to fit with each other in order to ensure constitutional congruence and integrate the subnational entities into the overarching federal democracy. These requirements make it necessary to give the Basic Law precedence over *Land* law (Art. 31 BL). In consequence, both the Basic Law and the *Land* constitutions shape the structure and the functioning

---

24 BVerfGE 123, 267–437 ('Lissabon-Vertrag').

25 See also Art. 71, 72 and 74 BL; Vogel (n 11), at 1053–65; Konrad Hesse, *Grundzüge des Verfassungsrechts der Bundesrepublik Deutschland*, 19th edition (C.F. Müller 1993) 89–109; Martin Möstl, 'Landesverfassungsrecht— zum Schattendasein verurteilt? Eine Positionsbestimmung im bundesstaatlichen und supranationalen Verfassungsverbund' (2005) 130 *Archiv des öffentlichen Rechts* 350; Pestalozza (n 9), at recital 172–83.

26 BVerfGE 36, 342 (360f.); Pestalozza (n 9), at recital 174.

27 In 2018 Art. 21 and 109 of the Constitution of Hesse have been repealed; cf. also Fabian Wittreck, 'Die Todesstrafe in den deutschen Landesverfassungen' (2001) 49 *Jahrbuch des öffentlichen Rechts (N.F.)* 157–214.

28 Pestalozza (n 9), 174–81.

29 That is the seminal definition of federalism from Daniel J. Elazar, *Exploring Federalism* (University of Alabama Press 1987).

of the political order in the German *Länder*. While the Basic Law is mostly concerned with maintaining the republican principle, the social state, and the rule of law (including the recognition of fundamental rights), the *Land* constitutions structure the *Land* polities and may grant social or basic rights going beyond federal provisions. In consequence, *Land* constitutions differ not only from each other but also from the Basic Law. We may distinguish three types of *Land* constitutions: pre-Basic-Law constitutions, post-Basic Law constitutions, and post-unification constitutions (Table 10.1).[30]

Table 10.1 Structure and content of German *Land* constitutions

	Articles on							No. of articles (year of adoption)
	Basic principles[a]		State organs [b]		State functions[c]		Other matters	
	# of articles	(%)	# of articles	(%)	# of articles	(%)	# of articles	%	# of articles
Land constitutions passed before the Basic Law								
Hesse	65	(43.0)	41	(27.2)	35	(23.1)	10	(6.6)	151 (1946)
Bavaria	93	(49.2)	47	(24.9)	38	(20.1)	11	(5.8)	189 (1946)
Bremen	69	(44.2)	53	(34.0)	28	(17.9)	6	(3.8)	156 (1947)
Saarland	65	(48.5)	33	(24.6)	31	(23.1)	5	(3.7)	134 (1947)
Rhineland-Palatinate	77	(53.1)	28	(19.3)	32	(22.1)	8	(5.5)	145 (1946)
Land constitutions passed after the Basic Law								
Schleswig-Holstein	9	(15.0)	27	(45.0)	21	(35.0)	3	(5.0)	60 (1950)
North Rhine-Westphalia	30	(32.3)	35	(37.8)	24	(25.8)	4	(4.3)	93 (1950)
Berlin	38	(37.3)	21	(20.6)	37	(36.3)	6	(5.9)	102 (1950)
Lower Saxony	6	(7.7)	34	(43.6)	31	(39.7)	7	(9.0)	78 (1951)
Baden-Württemberg	27	(28.4)	31	(32.6)	27	(28.4)	10	(10.5)	95 (1953)
Hamburg	6	(7.8)	42	(54.5)	25	(32.5)	4	(5.2)	77 (1952)
Land constitutions passed after unification								
Brandenburg	55	(46.6)	34	(28.8)	25	(21.2)	4	(3.4)	118 (1992)
Mecklenburg-West Pomerania	20	(24.7)	32	(39.5)	26	(32.1)	3	(3.7)	81 (1993)
Saxony	51	(41.5)	31	(25.2)	31	(25.2)	10	(8.1)	123 (1992)
Saxony-Anhalt	41	(40.2)	33	(32.4)	26	(25.5)	2	(2.0)	102 (1992)
Thuringia	48	(44.9)	31	(29.0)	25	(23.4)	3	(2.8)	107 (1993/4)

a) Basic rights and duties, social life, basic principles; b) government, parliament; c) legislative, executive (including finances) and legal branch; d) conclusion and transitional provisions.
Source: Astrid Lorenz and Werner Reutter, 'Subconstitutionalism in a Multilayered System. A Comparative Analysis of Constitutional Politics in the German Länder' (2012) *IV Perspectives on Federalism*, 153, available at http://www.on-federalism.eu/attachments/141_download.pdf (accessed 3 January 2014).

30 I ignore constitutions which are not operative any more (from Württemberg-Baden, Württemberg-Hohenzollern and Baden); that includes the constitutions of the five *Länder* in the former Soviet Occupied Zone; they became invalid in 1952.

- Five constitutions were put into force before the Basic Law came into being in 1949. On average, they include far more articles than the ones passed in the early 1950s or after unification (155 vs 84 or, respectively, 106). These differences are mostly due to stipulations on basic principles and fundamental rights. While the five pre-Basic Law constitutions possess on average 74 articles regulating fundamental rights and basic principles, the other 11 constitutions have on average 30 articles on the same issues. These differences are due to the fact that the five pre-Basic Law constitutions had to fill the constitutional void that existed in Germany between the end of World War II and the adoption of the Basic Law. They had to set up political orders in a comprehensive fashion and serve as full-fledged constitutions.
- In contrast, the six *Land* constitutions that came into being in the early 1950s were significantly shorter and less detailed as far as basic principles were concerned. As already mentioned, the constitutions of Lower Saxony and Schleswig-Holstein even abnegated their status as constitutions. One was called a 'statute', the other was marked as preliminary. The constitution of Hamburg contains not a single fundamental right. The six post-Basic Law constitutions had on average 84 articles, of which 19 regulated basic principles, fundamental rights and duties.
- The five constitutions passed after unification demonstrate that the content of a *Land* constitution is shaped by local political choices and need not merely mimic its national counterpart. Most constitutions of the five new *Länder* partly reiterate the fundamental rights of the BL, but they also add a long list of social rights and state goals. In addition, they contain the usual provisions relating to the structure of the polities and the functions of the state.

Overall, we see that the *Länder* are autonomous with regard to their constitutions, but this autonomy is politically and constitutionally embedded. The Basic Law and the homogeneity clause frame the constitutional space that the *Länder* can fill. At the same time, the dual state hypothesis provides the *Länder* with the leeway to fill this space, as they like.

10.2.2 Procedure

Neither the adoption nor the change of German Land constitutions follow a common pattern.[31] The German Basic Law does not rule on these matters. The German *Länder* autonomously decide whether a constitution has to be put before the people in order to come into effect or whether a vote of the *Land* parliament suffices to adopt an amendment. In effect, we find both forms in the *Länder*. Nine *Land* constitutions required a vote both from the *Land* parliament and from the people in order to come into force; in seven *Länder* only the parliament decided. Only in Thuringia more than 50 per cent of all eligible voters approved the constitution in a referendum. In seven *Länder* a referendum on the constitution was not required. In eight *Länder* half of all eligible voters approved the constitution; in Rhineland-Palatinate, just 35 per cent of all eligible voters supported the constitution, which came into being nonetheless because only a simple majority of the votes cast was required.

31 See: Pestalozza (n 9), at recital 31–74; Reutter (n 9), at 53–65 and 215–27; Werner Reutter, 'The changeableness of subnational constitutions: A qualitative comparative analysis' (2019) 54 *Government and Opposition* 75–97; Martina Flick, 'Landesverfassungen und ihre Veränderbarkeit' in Markus Freitag and Adrian Vatter (eds), *Die Demokratien der deutschen Bundesländer. Politische Institutionen im Vergleich* (Budrich 2008) 221; Sven Hölscheidt, 'Die Praxis der Verfassungsverabschiedung und der Verfassungsänderung in der Bundesrepublik' (1995) 26 *Zeitschrift für Parlamentsfragen* 58.

All *Land* constitutions prescribe that an amendment has to take the form of a law approved by a higher majority in the *Land* parliament than a normal bill. Apart from that, we find significant differences between the *Länder* with regard to the required majority, the parliamentary procedure and the people's role.

(i) *Required majority*: The *Land* constitutions prescribe the majority required for an amendment. In 13 *Länder* a two-thirds majority in parliament is necessary. In Hesse and Bavaria any constitutional change has to be accepted in a referendum by a simple majority of the votes cast. In Baden-Württemberg, a two-thirds majority of the votes cast in parliament suffices to change the constitution if this majority represents at least fifty percent of all members of parliament.

(ii) *Parliamentary process*: In principle, the process of amending a constitution follows the usual steps of parliamentary lawmaking. The same institutions that submit normal bills to a parliament can also submit bills that aim at changing the constitution. Yet, according to the constitutional stipulations in combination with the varying parliamentary rules of procedure, in some *Länder* a single member of parliament enjoys this prerogative, while in other *Länder* only parliamentary parties or a specified number of MPs can start the legislative process. In 15 *Länder* the people can initiate such a legislative process as well. In some *Länder* an amendment to a constitution just needs two readings in parliament, while in others three readings are mandatory. Furthermore, in two *Länder* a referendum has to sanction the decision made by the parliament, while in others it is optional to ask for a popular vote depending on a decision by the parliament and/or the government. Once again, these differences highlight the autonomy of the *Länder*.

(iii) *Participation of the people*: Contrary to the federal level, where the people have no say in these matters, in the *Länder* the people—i.e. the eligible voters—can participate in constitutional politics in three ways. First, the people can submit a proposal to the parliament,[32] which is possible in all *Länder* except for Hesse.[33] However, only the Bavarian people have used this option, and have done so several times. Second, in 14 *Länder* if the parliament rejects the proposal the people can overrule this decision and adopt the amendment in a popular vote. This has only happened twice, again in Bavaria. Finally, in Bavaria and Hesse the people have to approve any constitutional change in a referendum; in the other *Länder* the parliament can decide these issues without the people being involved.

The differences just described underline the autonomy the *Länder* enjoy in constitutional politics. Thus, it is hardly surprising that the number of constitutional amendments vary significantly. Berlin has changed its constitution 1.6 times per year, while Saxony has done so just once since its constitution came into effect in 1993 (i.e. 0.04 amendments per year). In contrast, the BL has been changed more frequently than *Land* constitutions even though the national constitution is more difficult to amend than *Land* constitutions.

---

32 At the federal level only parliamentary parties (or at least 5 per cent of the members of the Federal Diet), the federal government and the federal council enjoy the prerogative to initiative a legislative process by submitting a bill to the parliament. The people (whoever that is) are deprived of this privilege. Needless to say, interest groups or other political actors can draft a bill and send it to the parliament as a petition but that does not start the legislative process.

33 See Pestalozza (n 9), at recital 43.

10.3 Position of the subnational constitution within the *Länder*

Land constitutions are superior legal documents. They fulfil the usual functions ascribed to constitutions. They set up polities and shape the relation between the state and its people. Also in a formal sense, these legal documents qualify as constitutions. Their change requires a greater majority than normal parliamentary acts. Moreover, in all 16 *Länder* there is a constitutional court that has the obligation to interpret the constitution and put it effectively into practice. In addition, civil movements started to use provisions in *Land* constitutions in order to pursue their goals. For example, in Berlin and Bavaria there are two initiatives aimed at socializing real estate companies in order to curb rising rents. Finally, *Land* constitutions have been laboratories for the constitutionalization of post-materialist issues such as gender equality and environmental protection. In these ways the *Länder* possess full-fledged constitutional powers and their constitutions impact on political life within the *Länder*.[34]

10.4 Content

In the German legal tradition, a constitution should address two aspects: the structure and the functioning of the political system on the one hand, and the rights of citizens on the other.[35] The German *Land* constitutions follow this trajectory—more or less. Most *Land* constitutions include chapters on fundamental rights (e.g. protection of human dignity, personal freedom). Some of these rights repeat federal provisions even in matters in which the *Land* has no legislative competency[36] or which are in conflict with federal law.[37] For example, Art. 18 of the Brandenburg Constitution grants the 'right of asylum', which is a right that the *Land* can neither give nor take away. Some constitutions also define duties[38] and obligations or include state goals.[39]

10.4.1 Identity

After 1945 the Allied military governments created most German *Länder* more or less from scratch. Nonetheless, all German *Länder* refer to their pre-war historical tradition and claim to be specific and different.[40] In order to reinforce their regional identity *Länder* also use symbols of sovereign nation-states. They constitutionally define their flags, their anthems, their coat of arms or collective holidays. For example, Art. 4 of the Constitution of Brandenburg determines the *Land* colours (red and white) and the coat of arms (red eagle on a white background). We find similar stipulations in most of the other constitutions. In addition, preambles appeal to

---

34 See Reutter (n 9); Werner Reutter and Astrid Lorenz, 'Explaining the frequency of constitutional change in the German *Länder*' (2016) 46 *Publius: The Journal of Federalism* 103.

35 See Pestalozza (n 9), at recital 92–150.

36 For example, Art. 7, 9, and 17 Brandenburg Constitution.

37 For example, Art. 29 Constitution of Hesse grants trade unions the right to strike and prohibits employers to lock out workers which contradicts federal regulations.

38 For example, Art. 126(1) Bavarian Constitution makes the upbringing of children a duty for the parents; according to Art. 29(1) Brandenburg Constitution it is the duty of all persons 'to protect nature'.

39 For example, Art. 128–41 Bavarian Constitution; Art. 39–51 Brandenburg Constitution; Art. 11 and 12 Bremen Constitution.

40 Andreas Anter and Astrid Lorenz, 'Der "Brandenburger Weg"—Ein Mythos?' in Astrid Lorenz, Andreas Anter and Werner Reutter, *Politik und Regieren in Brandenburg* (Springer VS 2016) 247; Jesse, Schubert and Thieme (n 8), at 331–7.

moral values like Christian tradition, human dignity, the rule of law or liberalism.[41] In addition, 11 *Land* constitutions also contain chapters on Basic Principles that are supposed to govern the constitution (like the democratic principle, the rule of law and separation of powers).[42]

The *Land* constitutions are embedded in two ways. On the one hand *Land* constitutions remain under the shadow of the Basic Law. Federal law not only has precedence over *Land* law but the Basic Law also rules on crucial issues such as human rights, the welfare state, the rule of law and the federal system. These subjects support social integration. As pointed out, there are some inroads in these issues at the *Länder* level, which are, however, far from challenging the supremacy of the national constitution. On the other hand, politics and policies in Germany are nation-centric. With few exceptions (e.g. education, police) the Federation manages the competencies for all crucial policies. Even more important, it disposes of financial resources and can thus politically interfere on the subnational level.

10.4.2 Organization of powers

Except for Hamburg and Hesse, all German *Land* constitutions include provisions on how state organs execute state functions based on the principle of democracy.[43] For example, Art. 2 of the Constitution of Brandenburg reads: 'All state authority shall be derived from the people' (par 2) and 'Legislation shall be exercised through referenda and the Landtag. Executive power shall lie in the hands of the *Land* government, administrative bodies and self-governing bodies. The dispensation of justice shall be entrusted to independent judges.' (par 4) In consequence, each *Land* has a parliament, a government, and a constitutional court. In addition, as explained below, in all *Länder* the people can act as legislator.[44]

10.4.2.1 German Land parliaments

The 16 subnational constitutions determine the composition, functioning and basic tasks of the *Land* parliaments.[45] The Basic Law just requires the people of each *Land* to be represented by a 'body chosen in general, direct, free, equal and secret elections'.[46] Within these general constraints, the *Länder* constitutions determine the detailed features of the Land parliaments in considerably diverse ways.

---

41 See, e.g., the preamble of the Brandenburg Constitution: 'We, the citizens of the Land of Brandenburg, have given ourselves this Constitution in free self-determination, in the spirit of the traditions of law, tolerance and solidarity in the Mark Brandenburg, based on the peaceful changes in the autumn of 1989, imbued with the will to safeguard human dignity and freedom, to organize community life based on social justice, to promote the well-being of all, to preserve and protect nature and the environment, and determined to fashion the Land of Brandenburg as a living member of the Federal Republic of Germany in a uniting Europe and in the One World'.

42 For example, Art. 1–9 Constitution of Schleswig-Holstein, Art. 1–4 Brandenburg Constitution, Art. 1–6b Constitution of Lower Saxony.

43 For example, Art. 4 Bavarian Constitution, Art. 3(1) Berlin Constitution, or Art. 47 Constitution of Thuringia.

44 Since 1946 only 26 laws have been adopted in a referendum by the people of the Länder.

45 For the following see Leunig (n 11), at 60–158; Werner Reutter, *Föderalismus, Parlamentarismus und Demokratie* (Verlag Barbara Budrich 2008).

46 Art. 28 (1) BL.

- *Elections*: Each *Land* has its own law on elections.[47] In consequence, the *Länder* display various combinations of electoral aspects. For example, Bremen and Saarland have pure proportionality systems; the other *Länder* mimic the federal example and have systems of personalized proportionality. The latter is a mixed electoral system in which voters cast (at least) two votes, one for a representative in a single-seat constituency, and the other one for a party. Before 1970, a term length of five years existed only in the Saarland; all other *Land* parliaments were elected for four years. Now, only Bremen has a term length of four years; all other *Länder* have changed the term length to five years. In 12 *Länder*, the voters have two votes (one for a candidate in a constituency and one for a party); in two *Länder* the voters have just one vote, in Bremen they have five votes and in Hamburg they have ten. In addition, the parties representing minorities in Brandenburg (Sorbs) and Schleswig-Holstein (Danes) enter parliament even if they receive less than 5 per cent of the votes and remain below the electoral threshold that exist in both *Länder*. In four *Länder*, parties can enter parliament either by overcoming the electoral threshold (five per cent hurdle) or if a party candidate succeeds in at least one constituency.
- *Parliaments*: The *Länder* regulate all matters pertaining to the composition, the size, and the functioning of parliaments through provisions contained in their constitutions, ordinary legislation or rules of procedure (Geschäftsordnung). For example, the Bavarian *Landtag* itemizes 16 laws, rules of procedure and implementation rules addressing aspects of parliamentary affairs.[48] *Land* constitutions establish Land parliaments as state organs, describe their tasks, and provide basic rules concerning their structure and functioning. For example, the Constitution of Brandenburg grants the members of parliament a free mandate (Art. 56), indemnity (Art. 57), immunity (Art. 58), the right of refusal to give evidence (Art. 59) and the right to financial compensation (Art. 60). The Brandenburg Constitution also addresses certain basic procedural and structural issues such as the status of parliamentary groups (Art. 67) and parliamentary committees (Art. 70). In addition, the constitution defines the majority needed for an effective decision (Art. 65). Other matters (such as the level of compensation, the size of the parliaments, the functioning of parliamentary groups) are regulated in statutes or in rules of procedures adopted by the parliament.[49]

Thus, everything pertaining to the election, composition and functioning of the *Land* parliaments is regulated by the *Länder*. Indeed, the *Länder* could, if they wanted to, adopt a presidential form of government. Bearing this in mind, the apparently substantial differences between the *Länder* may seem less important because all *Länder* picked a parliamentary form of government. The *Länder* also deviate from their federal counterpart in several important respects. All *Land* parliaments are smaller, consist of only one chamber[50] and convene less frequently. In addition,

---

47 Reutter (n 45), at 69–98; Matthias Trefs, 'Die Wahlsysteme der *Länder*' in Achim Hildebrandt and Frieder Wolf (eds), *Die Politik der BundesLänder. Staatstätigkeit im Vergleich* (Springer VS 2008) 331; Christina Eder and Rafael Magin, 'Wahlsysteme', in Freitag and Vatter (n 31) 33.

48 See the homepage of the Bavarian parliament: https://www.bayern.landtag.de/dokumente/rechtsgrundlagen/.

49 Reutter (n 45); Leunig (n 11); Werner Reutter, 'Zur Größe von Landesparlamenten. Kriterien für eine sachliche Diskussion' (2019) 50 *Zeitschrift für Parlamentsfragen* 263.

50 The only second chamber in the German *Länder*, the Bavarian Senate, was a corporatist institution in which all major interest groups were represented (trade unions, business, churches, etc.). It had hardly any competences at all and was abolished in 1999.

they can dissolve themselves,[51] and the people can also adopt laws by referendum which is not possible at the national level. It should be noted, however, that *Länder* cannot pass laws in relation to political parties. It is the Federal Diet that made all decisions affecting the status, structure and funding of parties (with the approval of the Federal Council and very often following rulings of the Federal Constitutional Court).

10.4.2.2 The people as legislators

In contrast to the national level, all *Land* constitutions grant the people the prerogative to decide on bills.[52] In some *Länder* the people can also dissolve parliament.[53] This competency is an inherent part of the state quality of the *Länder*. Yet, except for Bavaria—and to a lesser degree the Saarland—this privilege was hardly used before 1990. In the aftermath of the East German revolution and the ensuing constitutional debates in the five new *Länder*, direct democracy became popular in western Germany as well. However, it is not a must to include provisions on direct democracy into a *Land* constitution. Hamburg changed its constitution and made its people into potential legislators only in 1996.

Hence, since 1996 the people of all *Länder* can become legislator. However, there are substantial differences between the *Länder* with regard both to the formal procedures and the practical use to which the power is put. Following Rohner, we can distinguish three models: a two-tier-model consisting of Volksbegehren (petition for a referendum) and Volksentscheid (referendum), a three-tier model in which a parliamentary debate precedes the referendum, and a hybrid model combining elements of the other two models.[54] In some *Länder* only normal bills can be put before the people; other *Länder* also permit popular initiatives and referendums on constitutional amendments. Furthermore, if a petition for a referendum is admitted we find varying regulations concerning the number of signatures that are necessary to initiate the procedure (between 7 and 20 per cent of all eligible voters), and the period in which the signatures have to be collected (between two weeks and four months). In order to pass a bill in a final referendum, between 15 and 25 per cent of all eligible voters have to support the proposal, as well as the majority of the votes cast. In three *Länder* (Bavaria, Hesse, Saxony) no quorum exists at this stage. If the referendum is to amend the constitution, the quorum ranges between 25 and 50 per cent of all eligible voters; in addition, in seven *Länder* at least two-thirds of the votes cast have to be in favour of the amendment. According to Rohner, only 4 per cent of all petitions to a referendum have been successful; another 1.6 percent were partly successful.[55]

---

51 Since 1946 17 parliaments have been dissolved. See Leunig (n 11), at 108–22; Reutter (n 45), at 222–30; Leunig and Reutter (n 11), at 12–13.

52 See Andreas Rohner, *Direct Democracy in the German* Länder: *History, Institutions, and (Mal)Functions.* C2D Working Paper Series 38/2011 (Centre for Research on Direct Democracy 2011), available at: https://www.zora.uzh.ch/id/eprint/94811/1/C2D_WP38.pdf (accessed 11 November 2019); Frank Rehmet, *Volksbegehrensbericht 2019. Direkte Demokratie in den deutschen BundesLändern 1946 bis 2018 von Mehr Demokratie e.V.* (Mehr Demokratie e.V. 2018), available at: https://www.mehr-demokratie.de/fileadmin/pdf/Volksbegehrensbericht_2019.pdf (accessed 11 November 2019); Hermann K. Heußner and Otmar Jung (eds), *Mehr direkte Demokratie wagen. Volksbegehren und Volksentscheid: Geschichte—Praxis—Vorschläge* (Olzog 1999); Andreas Kost (ed.), *Direkte Demokratie in den deutschen Ländern. Eine Einführung* (Verlag für Sozialwissenschaften 2005).

53 Rohner (n 52), at 18–19; Leunig (n 11), at 122–5.

54 See Rohner (n 52), at 9–14.

55 Rohner (n 52), at 17; see also Rehmet (n 52), at 24.

10.4.2.3 German Land *governments*[56]

Each *Land* constitution contains a chapter on the *Land* government which defines the status, composition and functions of the executive. Notwithstanding many differences, all *Länder* have a parliamentary form of government in which the executive branch depends on the parliament.

- *Status*: In all *Länder*, the governments are organs of the state (Staats-/Verfassungsorgane). The constitution establishes how a government comes into being, requires that the government run its own budget, and is empowered to issue a standing order (Geschäftsordnung) that is passed by the government and that rules on how the cabinet should work.
- *Composition*: In all *Länder* the parliament must elect the head of government. In most cases this used to be a comparatively smooth and straightforward process. As a rule, popular elections provide one or more parties with the necessary majority, namely more than half of the seats in parliament. If need be, two or more parties enter a coalition. The strongest parliamentary party nominates his or her frontrunner in the popular election as head of government to be elected by the *Land* parliament. The then-installed head of government selects his or her members of the cabinet. The constitutions define the composition of the government, which normally consists of a prime minister (called First Mayor in Bremen and Hamburg and Governing Mayor in Berlin) and members of a cabinet. In Hamburg and Bremen a member of the government cannot be a member of parliament, while in North Rhine-Westphalia the prime minister has to be a member of parliament.[57] In most *Länder*, the constitution also includes basic principles concerning the way the government is supposed to work. In most cases the government can only act as collective body (Kabinettsprinzip) in which the prime minister determines policy guidelines (Richtlinienkompetenz) while the ministers run their departments independently (Ressortprinzip). In Bremen the Mayor is merely the first among equals. He or she has no *Richtlinienkompetenz*. Needless to say, we find numerous variations on how to form a government. For example, in 11 *Länder* (e.g. Thuringia) a minority government is possible, while in five *Länder* the parliament can only install a government with an absolute majority. Or, in some *Länder* the ministers or the cabinet as a collective body are subject to confirmation by the parliament, while in others it is at the prime minister's discretion to select and appoint the members of his or her cabinet. Moreover, in most *Länder* the parliament can only bring down a government with a constructive of no confidence (i.e. by electing a new head of government). But in some *Länder* (e.g. Berlin) the government can be ousted from office by a simple vote of no confidence. The rise of the right-wing extremist or populist AfD (Alternative für Deutschland) that succeeded in entering all *Land* parliaments made coalition formation extremely difficult. It led to minority governments in Thuringia in 2020 or to coalitions composed of parties that do not have much in common, as in Saxony-Anhalt (2018).
- *Function*: All *Land* constitutions vest the executive power in the government. It has to put laws into practice and manage the public administration.

---

56 Leunig (n. 11), at 158–69.
57 Art. 108 Bremen Constitution; Art. 39 Hamburg Constitution; Art. 52 Constitution of North Rhine-Westphalia. If the mayor of Bremen and Hamburg is member of the *Land* parliament, his or her mandate is dormant.

10.4.2.4 *Constitutional courts in the German* Länder

Since 2008 all German *Länder* have a constitutional court.[58] These courts are established by the *Länder* in their respective *Land* constitutions. The *Land* constitutions are the legal benchmarks used in the adjudication of political and legal issues in the *Länder*. Thus, the constitutional courts in the German *Länder* are manifestations of self-rule in subnational units. They apply and interpret subnational laws and subnational constitutions. The differences between these courts are quite remarkable. The number of judges ranges from 8 to 38, the number of staff from 0 to 6, the budgets range from 24,500 to 843,700 euros (in the year 2016), and their workload from 1 case to 180 cases per year.[59]

Land constitutional courts are supposed to ensure that *Land* constitutions are effectively put into practice. In order to fulfil this mandate, the courts can act as 'arbitrators of disputes', when they decide on conflicts between state organs;[60] as 'negative legislators', when they invalidate laws passed by the *Land* parliament; or as 'courts of last resort' when they are called upon by citizens who claim that their fundamental rights have been infringed.[61]

10.4.3 *Fundamental rights*

The German Basic Law starts with the provision that '[h]uman dignity shall be inviolable' (Art. 1(1) BL), followed by a list of fundamental rights. In addition, Germany has ratified the European Convention of Human Rights and other human rights treaties that are directly applicable as domestic law.[62] The Federal Constitutional Court connects them to the rights included in the Basic Law. These provisions also apply in the *Länder*. Yet, there is a scholarly debate if and on how far *Länder* can adopt fundamental rights because 'provisions of *Land* constitutions shall also remain in force insofar as they guarantee basic rights in conformity with Articles 1 to 18 of this Basic Law'.[63] Even though this provision originally referred to *Land* constitutions predating the Basic Law, the general understanding of this clause is that the *Länder* can enact new fundamental rights other than those included in the Basic Law. As noted earlier, some *Land* constitutions also contain provisions on social rights, state objectives, or reiterate and strengthen rights included in the Basic Law.[64]

---

58 Before setting up a constitutional court in 2008, Schleswig-Holstein had invoked the Federal Constitutional Court to resolve constitutional disputes according to Art. 99 BL. In these cases the Federal Constitutional Court acted as a *Land* constitutional court; its judgments applied to Schleswig-Holstein only.

59 Werner Reutter, 'Zum Status der Landesverfassungsgerichte als Verfassungsorgane' in Werner Reutter (ed.), *Verfassungsgerichtsbarkeit in Bundesländern. Theoretische Perspektiven, methodische Überlegungen und empirische Befunde* (Springer VS 2020) 155.

60 Martina Flick, *Organstreitverfahren vor den Landesverfassungsgerichten. Eine politikwissenschaftliche Untersuchung* (Peter Lang 2011); Franziska Carstensen, 'Parlamentsrechtliche Entscheidungen von Landesverfassungsgerichten in Organstreitverfahren' in Reutter (n 59) 239.

61 Werner Reutter, 'Landesverfassungsgerichte: "Föderaler Zopf" oder "Vollendung des Rechtsstaates"?' (2018) 54 *Recht und Politik* 204; Oliver W. Lembcke and Michael Güpner, 'Analyse der Landesverfassungsgerichtsbarkeit in vergleichender Absicht. Ein Beitrag zur Typologisierung und Quantifizierung' (2018) *ZLVR—Zeitschrift für Landesverfassungsrecht und Landesverwaltungsrecht* 94, available at: https://www.zlvr.de/archiv/ (accessed 15 August 2019).

62 In Germany, international treaties have the same status as simple federal laws. The executive and the judicial branches of government are bound by these laws (Art. 20 (3) BL).

63 Art. 142 BL.

64 For example, the Berlin Constitution contains clauses on due process (Art. 8(2)), on gender equality and non-discrimination due to sexual orientation (Art. 10(2 and 3)), on the right to equal treatment (Art. 11), on the freedom of information (Art. 14), on the right to work (Art. 18), on expropriation (Art. 23) or on the right to adequate housing (Art. 28).

10.4.4 *Policy principles*

The German Basic Law includes a limited number of policy principles or state goals, which have been partly created and shaped by the Federal Constitutional Court. For example, Art. 3(2) BL stipulates that the 'state shall promote the actual implementation of equal rights for women and men and take steps to eliminate disadvantages that now exist'. Art. 20a contains the following: 'Mindful also of its responsibility toward future generations, the state shall protect the natural foundations of life and animals'.[65] The Federal Constitutional Court ruled on existing human rights laid down in the BL. Moreover, on numerous occasions it also showed a 'remarkable display of judicial activism'.[66]

10.5 Multilevel constitutionalism

10.5.1 *The Basic Law and* Land *constitutions*

The preamble to the Basic Law defines the *Länder* as the constituent units that 'have achieved the unity and freedom of Germany in free self-determination'. Obviously, the *Länder* can only play this role if they enjoy the power to 'self-rule'. The state quality of the *Länder*, the prerogative to adopt constitutions and set up a democratic order are manifestations of this understanding. Most *Land* constitutions recognize that the *Länder* are part of the Federation.[67] Some constitutions even explicitly acknowledge the supremacy of federal law even though Art. 31 BL already determines that this is the case.[68]

At the same time, the *Land* constitutions have to conform to the homogeneity principle and the *Länder* participate in federal lawmaking and unitarian policymaking. To facilitate this, there are numerous committees and institutions which coordinate policymaking between the *Länder* and the Federation. The *Länder* participate in federal lawmaking via the Federal Council and are entitled to permanent representation with the federal government. The Federal Council must approve by two-thirds majority any proposed amendment to the Basic Law and in relation to about 40 per cent of legislative topics falling within federal competence it must approve federal bills by an absolute majority of votes. In these ways the *Land* governments enjoy substantial veto power on crucial issues. Overall this means that German federalism is based on 'self-rule' and 'shared rule' at both levels.

10.5.2 *The impact of the international and European legal space on subnational constitutionalism in Germany*

Germany is a Member State of the European Union. It is constitutionally obliged to establish 'a united Europe'[69] and to participate in the development of the European Union. The European Union does not know *Länder*—it only recognizes what are called 'regions' within the Member States—whereas it is the Federation which has competency in relation to the implementation

---

65 Art. 20a BL.

66 Kommers and Miller (n 11), at 408. The quote refers to the ruling of the Federal Constitutional Court on the Federal Census Act of 1983. With this decision, the court invented the 'right to informational self-determination'.

67 For the following see Pestalozza (n 9), at recital 87–91; Art. 23(2) Constitution of Baden-Württemberg, Art. 1(2) Berlin Constitution.

68 For example, Art. 152 Bremen Constitution.

69 Art. 23 par.1 BL.

of European law. However, this does not rule out the possibility that in the future European integration may impact upon the constitutional development in the German *Länder*.

Even though the European Union and the *Länder* are supposed to operate within distinct constitutional spaces ('Verfassungsräume'), the constitutions of Baden-Württemberg, Bavaria, Brandenburg, Mecklenburg-West Pomerania, Lower Saxony and Saxony include commitments to Europe. Furthermore, some *Länder* have concluded accords with neighbouring regions in France, the Czech Republic and Poland. More importantly, the *Länder* can veto any transfer of competencies to the European Union if these competencies affect their legislative or executive powers. Like Belgium, in matters that concern competencies of the *Länder*, ministers of the *Länder* and/or the Federation represent Germany at the European level.[70] Just as they have in Berlin in relation to the federal government, all German *Länder* have installed offices in Brussels to coordinate their policies and represent their interests in the EU independently of the federation. In addition, *Land* parliaments have established committees on European affairs, the *Länder* can initiate a process of subsidiarity control based on the Early Warning System,[71] and they participate in the European Committee of the Regions.

10.6 Judicial review

In contrast to the cooperative character of federalism, judicial review is based on a dual understanding of the relationship between the federation and the *Länder*. Both the Federal Constitutional Court and the 16 *Land* constitutional courts operate autonomously. They manage their own jurisdictions in which they rule independently from each other.[72] Yet, this dual character of judicial federalism is not unlimited as judgments of the Federal Constitutional Court enjoy precedence over rulings of its subnational counterparts if these rulings are inconsistent with national law. This interplay between autonomy and hierarchy in the system of judicial federalism sometimes triggers tensions and conflicts.[73]

---

70 Art. 16(2) of the European Union reads as follows: 'The [European] Council shall consist of a representative of each Member State at ministerial level, who may commit the government of the Member State in question and cast its vote'.

71 According to Article 6 of Protocol No. 2 on the Application of the Principles of Subsidiarity and Proportionality *of the Lisbon Treaty national* **parliaments** *are entitled to carry out subsidiarity checks on draft EU legislative acts. Within eight weeks from the date of transmission, they can submit a 'reasoned opinion' stating why the parliament considers the draft in question does not comply with the subsidiarity principle. Each national Parliament may consult regional parliaments with legislative powers*; I adjusted this summary from: https://portal.cor.europa.eu/subsidiarity/regpex/Pages/Early-Warning-System.aspx; see also: Werner Reutter, 'The Quandary of Representation in Multilevel Systems and German Land Parliaments' in Gabriele Abels and Annegret Eppler (eds), *Subnational Parliaments in an EU-Multi-level Parliamentary System: Taking Stock of the Post-Lisbon Era* (Studienverlag 2016) 207.

72 Andreas Voßkuhle, 'Die Landesverfassungsgerichtsbarkeit im föderalen und europäischen Verfassungsgerichtsverbund' (2011) 59 *Jahrbuch des öffentlichen Rechts der Gegenwart* 215; Werner Reutter, 'Landesverfassungsgerichte in der Bundesrepublik Deutschland. Eine Bestandaufnahme' in Werner Reutter (ed.), *Landesverfassungsgerichte. Entwicklung, Aufbau, Funktionen* (Springer VS 2017) 1.

73 See, for example, rulings on the right to wear headscarves as civil servants from the Federal Constitutional Court and the Bavarian Constitutional Court; BVerfGE 138, 296; BayVerfGH, Az. Vf. 11-VII-05; BayVerfGHE 60, 1; BayVerfGH, Az: Vf. 3-VII-18; Sascha Kneip, 'Verfassungsgerichte und Demokratie in Bund und Ländern' in Reutter (n 59).

10.7 Conclusion

Without doubt, from a comparative perspective the German *Länder* have strong constitutional powers. They enjoy constitutional autonomy and invoke the prerogative to adopt and change their constitutions at their own discretion, both procedurally and content-wise. The Federation has no say in these matters. Nonetheless, German *Land* constitutions seem foremost legal documents shaping the political order in the German *Länder* and thus contributing to German constitutional democracy. So far, they failed to turn into 'charters for living' that would help the people to pursue happiness or strive for a good life. The *Länder* and their constitutions are also not paramount for the 'protection of liberty' by creating institutions 'capable of protecting popular liberty against incursions by government'.[74] In Germany, this is the job of the Basic Law. The national constitution is the focus of national identity and the basis for what has been coined 'constitutional patriotism'. It also established the Federal Constitutional Court whose major task is to protect 'popular liberty against incursions by government'.

This does not rule out the fact that *Land* constitutions are significant and substantial documents. In fact, they establish a political order in the *Länder* and thus organize democracy at the subnational level. The discrepancy between constitutional prerogatives and symbolic/political importance finds its cause in the fact that the constitutional autonomy of the *Länder* is politically embedded and circumscribed in three ways. First, the party systems in the *Länder* and in the Federation show similar structures and thus transcend the constitutional borders of the *Länder*. Second, we find processes of policy-learning and harmonization among the *Länder* which promote unitarian tendencies. Finally, the Federation manages the competencies in most crucial policies, thus undermining the role of subnational constitutions in Germany. In essence that means that constitutional autonomy of the *Länder* does not fit with German cooperative federalism. In other words, we find contradictory principles ruling on the same issue. The dualist principle makes constitutions possible, while cooperative federalism and unitarian tendencies make constitutionalism in the *Länder* impossible.

---

74 J Gardner, *In Search of Sub-National Constitutionalism* (n 3), at 3.

11

SUBNATIONAL CONSTITUTIONALISM AND ASYMMETRICAL FEDERALISM IN INDIA

Subnational constitutionalism or constitution within the Constitution?

M.P. Singh and Rekha Saxena

Subnational constitutionalism, broadly conceived, is much more widely prevalent in the universe of comparative federalism than is commonly known in the run-of-the-mill political science literature. It exists in one form or another in territorial and multinational federations as well as territorially and ethnically decentralized devolutionary states, including supranational confederal unions like the European Union.[1] India also reluctantly adopted this mechanism at the time of making its postcolonial Constitution (1950), specifically in relation to the state of Jammu and Kashmir by granting it the special right to adopt a subnational Constitution (Article 370). However, this right has been whittled down over the decades since the 1950s, and was finally de-operationalized on 5 August 5 2019 on the basis that it was conducive to separatism and terrorism and was hampering the economic development of the state.

In India, subnational constitutionalism manifests as a deeper variant of asymmetrical federalism, particularly when it is compared with weaker forms of asymmetry such as the conferral of special status or autonomy on certain territorial communities through certain parts of the national constitution itself, which are often referred to as 'constitutions within the Constitution' in the Indian context. This kind of asymmetrical federalism is illustrated by the 5th and the 6th Schedules and Articles 371 and 371A to 371J series of the Indian Constitution. While the 5th and 6th Schedules are parts of the original Constitution, the Article 371 series was inserted by subsequent amendments between 1956 and 2012.

This paper discusses India's aborted experiment with subnational constitutionalism as well as its continuing engagement with asymmetrical federalism through its composite national Constitution. Section 1 explains the context and background that necessitated a combination of symmetrical and asymmetrical treatment of the various states in the national Constitution as well as a solitary experiment with subnational constitutionalism in the exceptional case of the

---

1 See Michael Burgess and G. Alan Tarr (eds), *Constitutional Dynamics in Federal Systems: Subnational Perspectives* (McGill-Queen's University Press 2012).

DOI: 10.4324/9781003052111-11

state of Jammu and Kashmir. Section 2A discusses the extent of autonomy of the symmetrical as well as asymmetrical states in the Indian national Constitution. Section 2B addresses the extent of autonomy enjoyed by the state of Jammu and Kashmir particularly through its subnational constitutional capacity. Section 3 discusses the status and content of the Jammu and Kashmir subnational Constitution within the Indian Constitution as a whole and offers an account of its eventual failure and abrogation. Section 4 examines the relationship between subnational units and the national Constitution and the processes of amendment for both the national and subnational constitutions. Section 5 discusses whether federal judicial review applies to the subnational Constitution. Finally, Section 6 presents an appraisal of India's experience with asymmetrical federalism and subnational constitutionalism, the former of which may be regarded as relatively successful, while the latter, in the case of Jammu and Kashmir, proved ultimately unsuccessful and was de-operationalized.

11.1 Context

The pre-independence seeds of subnational constitutionalism in India were encapsulated by two documents of the British Raj: (i) the Government of India Act, 1935, a British statute which embodied the first federal Constitution in India, a document which sought to unite British Indian provinces and princely Indian states; and (ii) the Cabinet Mission Plan, 1946, a last-ditch effort of the British imperial state to avert the partition of India on the eve of the transfer of power to India under a confederal Union of the Hindu-majority provinces and the Muslim-majority provinces. At both these moments, apart from the imperial power, the principal Indian protagonists were the British Indian provinces under the direct rule of the Crown-in-Parliament in London and the princely Indian states under the suzerainty of the British Crown (via a series of subsidiary alliances between the British Raj and the Indian states). For a variety of reasons, neither of these succeeded in warding off the fracturing of the country along subnational or national lines. The failure of the confederal union under the Cabinet Mission Plan led to the partition of India and the birth of a separate nation of Pakistan. The attempt to unify the princely states into an Indian Union in 1935 also failed at that time due to the reluctance of the princes to play ball. But at the moment of India's independence with partition in 1947, it partly succeeded.

Around the time of independence, there was an interlude during which the princely states were integrated into the Indian constitutional structure, a task largely accomplished by the Constituent Assembly. At the start of the Assembly's work, the princely states were entirely outside of the framework of the Indian Union, as the Independence of India Act, 1947 gave them the option of remaining independent or joining either India or Pakistan. Shortly thereafter most of them became loosely (confederally) attached to the Union of India, a link secured through the vigorous diplomacy of the Deputy Prime Minister and Home Minister Sardar Ballabhbhai Patel, though some preferred to remain fully independent. Kashmir with a Hindu Maharaja and predominantly Muslim subjects wished to remain independent, but finally signed an Instrument of Accession with the Dominion government of India on 26 October 1947, in the context of Pakistan-sponsored aggression. India intervened militarily in defence of Kashmir, and simultaneously appealed to the United Nations. The UN Security Council proclaimed a ceasefire before the Pakistan-supported forces were entirely driven out, and proposed a plebiscite after withdrawal of the Pakistan-sponsored aggressors and reduction of Indian security forces to a bare minimum. However, this never happened, delaying the signing of Kashmir's instrument of merger. This created an anomaly in that, while the representatives of all other princely states to the Constituent Assembly had already been nominated by their rulers, Kashmir's representatives were missing. Nonetheless, the Constituent Assembly deliberated on the issue and decided in favour of allotting four seats to Kashmir (now renamed the state of Jammu and Kashmir) and requesting the Maharaja to nominate the representatives, as advised by his premier Sheikh M. Abdullah, the leader of the largest political party in the state, within the Jammu and Kashmir National Conference.

Article 1 of the Indian Constitution named Jammu and Kashmir as a constituent state of the Indian Union. Article 370 was included in the Constitution of India, as a 'temporary provision', granting special status to the state of Jammu and Kashmir and allowing it to frame its own Constitution. However, this was subject to amendment or de-opartionalization by an order issued by the president of India with the consent of the state government and endorsement of the Constituent Assembly of the state of Jammu and Kashmir.

The amendment or repeal of Article 370 was kept apart from the general amending provision of the Indian Constitution under Article 368, and applies exclusively to Jammu and Kashmir. The Constituent Assembly of Jammu and Kashmir was elected in 1951, which unanimously ratified the state's accession to India. It then completed the process of making the state's Constitution in 1956, which came into force on 26 January 1957.

There are three other provisions of the Indian Constitution granting special status to certain other territories of India under the 5th and 6th Schedules and Article 371 series. These are often referred as 'Constitutions within the Constitution'. The purpose of these Schedules is to facilitate the integration of tribal tracts and communities with the Indian nation, which during the British rule in India were kept separate from the general administration of the provinces within which they happened to lie. These tribal communities and areas were largely concentrated in the province of Assam in the northeast but were also scattered among other provinces throughout the colony. Large areas in the northeast were predominantly tribal, whereas the inland tribal tracts were smaller in size. The former were called 'excluded', and the latter 'partially excluded' tracts under the Government of India Act, 1935. The finer details of special provisions for tribal people and territories/states in these two Schedules and their working will be discussed in section 2A below.

As noted, the Article 371 series of the Constitution makes asymmetrical 'special provisions' for 11 states of the Indian Union, including six states of the northeast of India, namely Assam, Nagaland, Manipur, Sikkim, Mizoram and Arunachal Pradesh. The inclusion of these six states became necessary due to the reorganization of previously existing states, creation of new Union territories, granting of statehood to previous Union territories, and acquisition of new territories by accession of a previously independent state (Sikkim) (see Articles 13 and 368). Notably, whereas Article 370 in relation to the state of Jammu and Kashmir was a part of the Constitution from the time of its commencement on 26 January 1950, Articles 371 and 371A to 371J were substituted or inserted into the text of the Constitution by way of later amendments. These special provisions relate to states or parts of states for reasons of cultural autonomy as well as backwardness or special disadvantages. These areas are spread across almost all major regions of the country.

From the foregoing discussion, it can be seen that only the state of Jammu and Kashmir had a separate existence in British India under the suzerainty of the British Crown. It was reluctantly granted a separate subnational Constitution largely conforming to the pattern of the national Constitution of India and the legislative, executive and judicial powers of the state dovetailed with the national institutions.

The position of the tribal tracts under the 5th and the 6th Schedules of the Constitution of India were not comparable to the standing of Kashmir during the British Raj as they were not separate states with either sovereign or suzerain status. Rather, they were 'partially excluded areas' or 'excluded areas' within the provinces in which they fell under the Government of India Act, 1935.

11.2 2A: Extent of autonomy of states in the national Constitution

In this section, we first discuss the mainline symmetrical aspects of the national Constitution, followed by the provision for asymmetrical states and substate regions of states within the Constitutions of India.

11.2.1 *Symmetrical part*

The national Constitution of India is a blueprint for a highly centralized cooperative federalism, which some may even call coercive federalism. It is a two-in-one constitutional text in the sense that the Constituent Assembly designed it to function as a federal system, except that during national, state or financial emergencies it can be transformed into a unitary system subject to parliamentary approval, review and extension for the duration of the emergency (Articles 352, 356 and 360).

The extent of the autonomy of the states in normal times under the mainline symmetrical part of the Constitution is limited. The Constitution is highly centralized in relation to legislative, executive and administrative, financial, external relations, and judicial powers. This is also true of Union and state elections (excepting local government polls) as well as of the process of amending the Constitution.

11.2.2 *Asymmetrical part: Tribal tracts/communities*

The Constituent Assembly's solution to the integration of tribal tracts/communities through the granting of autonomy to what were called 'partially excluded' and 'excluded' areas and communities from the general administration under the British Raj Government of India Act, 1935, took the form of the 5th and 6th Schedules of the Constitution, respectively. The former, captioned 'Provisions as to the Administration and Control of Scheduled Tribes', is related to Article 244 (1) of the Constitution and concerns 'Scheduled Areas' and 'Tribal Areas in any state of the Union other the states of Assam, Meghalaya, Tripura and Mizoram in the Northeast'. The latter, captioned 'Provisions as to the Administration of Tribal Areas in the States of Assam, Meghalaya, Tripura and Mizoram', is related to Articles 244(2) and 275(1). Article 275(1) relates only to the 6th Schedule states (i.e. Assam, Meghalaya, Tripura and Mizoram) and provides for annual grants-in-aid to these states in the form of differential, need-based assistance to meet the costs of such schemes of development as may be undertaken by the states with the approval of the government of India for the welfare of the Scheduled Tribes of the state concerned or for raising the level of administration of the Scheduled Areas therein to the level at par with the rest of the areas of that state. It is this special treatment that leads to the 5th and 6th Schedules being dubbed 'constitutions within the Constitution', including by a former Chief Justice of India, M. Hidayatullah.[2]

11.2.3 *Fifth schedule*

Under the 5th Schedule the administration of Scheduled Areas and Scheduled Tribes is the responsibility of the president of India/Union executive and kept out of the majoritarian control of the government of the state where they are located. The governor of the state appointed

---

2 See Nayakara Veeresha, 'Fifth Schedule: a critique', *The Deccan Herald*, 1 January 2018, <www.deccanherald.com/content/651307/> accessed 2 May 2020.

by the president of the Indian Union in these affairs is not bound by the advice of the chief minister and the Council of Ministers of the state, and acts directly under the president and the Union executive. The key constitutional body in these affairs is the Tribal Advisory Council (TAC). It consists of not more than 20 members of whom nearly three-quarters must be representatives of the Scheduled Tribes in the Legislature Assembly of the state. The governor is responsible for determining the mode of appointment of the member and the chairman of the TAC and its rules of business and procedures in general. It is the duty of the TAC to advise on such matters pertaining to the welfare and advancement of the Scheduled Tribes as may be referred by the governor. The governor is also empowered to direct by public notification that any law of the Union Parliament or state legislature shall not apply to a Scheduled Area or shall apply with certain exceptions or modifications in a state. Scheduled Areas in a state are declared in the first place by the president/Union executive under the 5th Schedule. The 5th Schedule also empowers the governor to 'make a regulation for the peace and good government of any area in a State which is for the time being a Scheduled Area'. In making all these regulations the governor must consult the Tribal Advisory Council, if it exists, and submit the regulations for the 'assent' of the president of India/Union executive.

The 5th Schedule of the Constitution also requires the governor of a state having Scheduled Areas therein to send an annual report to the president of India regarding the administration of such areas or whenever required by the president. The executive power of the Union extends to giving directions to the state government as to the administration of such areas. Overall, the governors and the president were generally not very true to their constitutional obligations and generally left things in the hands of the chief minister and the majoritarian government of the day in the state.[3]

11.2.4 Sixth schedule

The autonomy of 6th Schedule Tribal Areas in the states of Assam, Meghalaya, Tripura and Mizoram are far greater than those of the 5th Schedule Tribal Areas both in theory and practice. Meghalaya and Mizoram are predominantly tribal Christian in population with English as the official language of their governments. Historically, all these four states were fully 'excluded' areas under the Government of India Act, 1935.

The constitutionally recognized areas under the 6th Schedule are Autonomous Districts and Autonomous Regions and the key constitutional bodies corresponding to these areas are the District Councils and the subdistrict Regional Councils. The District Council consists of not more than 30 members of whom not more than four persons are nominated by the governor and for different Scheduled Tribes in an Autonomous District, the governor may by public notification create Autonomous Regions for each of them, whose administration shall be vested in a Sub-district Regional Council as delegated to it by the District Council. The District Council's jurisdiction extends to all areas within a district except those which are under the authority of a Regional Council within the district.

The District Councils and Regional Councils enjoy extensive legislative powers relating to: (1) allotment, occupation and use of land excepting the state's reserved forests so declared by the government, and compulsory acquisition of land for public purposes; (2) management of local community forests not reserved by the state; (3) use of water for agriculture; (4) regulation of *jhum* (slash and burn farming) or other forms of cultivation; (5) use of village or town councils

---

3 See Nayakara Veeresha, 'Governance of the Fifth Schedule Areas: Role of Governor' (2017) 63 *Indian Journal of Public Administration* 444.

and their powers; (6) local administration and police, public health and sanitation; (7) appointment or succession of tribal chief or headman; (8) laws relating to property, family and social custom. All the above laws are subject to submission to and assent by the governor which is generally granted.

Autonomous District and Autonomous Regional Councils also enjoy considerable autonomy in the realm of administration of civil justice as per customary or statutory laws. In addition, the District Council can establish primary schools and with the previous approval of the governor, make regulations and control as to the language and manner in which primary education shall be imparted in the primary schools of the district.

Autonomous District Councils and Autonomous Regional Councils in the states of Assam, Meghalaya, Tripura and Mizoram are granted immunity in the exercise of their legislative powers from the legislative powers of their respective state legislatures and those of the Union Parliament unless they themselves desire to be governed by them with certain exceptions and modifications. The Governor of the respective states give notice concerning their applicability and can do so with certain exceptions and modifications.

The governors of these four states can also appoint a commission to inquire into and report on the administration of Autonomous Districts and Autonomous Regions. The governors of these states can annul or suspend acts or resolutions of the Autonomous District Councils and Autonomous Regional Councils if they are 'likely to endanger the safety of India' or are 'likely to be prejudicial to public order'. These actions of the governors of these states are subjects to the approval of the state legislatures concerned. The governors of these states may also dissolve the District or Regional Councils on the recommendation of the commission of inquiry mentioned above and order a fresh general election immediately, or take over their administration themselves with the previous approval of the state legislature or may place the administration of the area under the commission of inquiry appointed by the governor with the approval of the state legislature. Such emergency measures may not exceed a period of six months.

In view of the reserved or special autonomous legislative, executive and judicial powers exercised by the autonomous District and Regional Councils in the four 6th Schedule states, these areas do not form part of any reserved constituency for election to the state Assemblies. Instead, they are parts of the general constituencies delimited for the Assemblies of these states. The remainder of the 6th Schedule proceeds to specify Tribal Areas in the four states where Autonomous Districts and Regions may be delineated. Specific provisions about each of these states are also mentioned in the Constitution.

The power to amend these two Schedules of the Constitution of India is vested in the Parliament of India alone by simple legislative process. This process is not deemed to be an amendment of the Constitution for purposes of the general amending provision in the Constitution in Article 368. (See Fifth Schedule Section 7(1) and (2); and Sixth Schedule, Section 21(1) and (2).) Following the reorganization of Assam and upgrading of Union territories to statehood during the 1970s, all these states also came to be covered by the Article 371 series with state-level autonomies as discussed below, which now supersedes District- and sub-District-Region-level autonomies. Amendment to the Article 371 series is subject to Article 368(2) relating to federal provisions requiring majority of the total membership of each house of the Parliament and a majority of not less than two-thirds majority of members of each house present and voting as well as ratification by not less than one-half of the state legislatures. Thus the Article 370 series is more strongly entrenched in the Constitution than the 5th and 6th Schedules.

11.2.5 Article 371 series

The Article 371 series of the Constitution makes special provision for 11 states of the Indian Union, including six states of Northeast India. Articles 371 and 371A to 371J were substituted or inserted into the text of the Constitution by way of later amendments. Five of them relate to the various parts of the mainland states, namely Maharashtra and Gujarat, Andhra Pradesh, Telangana, Karnataka and Goa. These make special provision obliging the Union and/or state governments to set up separate development boards for backward regions, allocate funds for backward regions, make adequate arrangement for opportunities for education and employment and reservation of seats and posts for these purposes for the people of backward regions, provide for the establishment of a central university in a backward region of a state, and guarantee a minimum number of seats in a state's Legislative Assembly (i.e. for the state of Goa).

Six of these special provisions under the Article 371 series relate to the states of Northeast India having partly or predominantly tribal populations, namely Assam, Nagaland, Manipur, Sikkim, Mizoram and Arunachal Pradesh. 'Unlike Assam, most of [the] hill tribes did not possess the [historical] experience of state formation and continued to be governed by their own, established tribal organisation'.[4] Excepting Assam, which originally included the rest of these states, the remaining five were subsequently carved out of it, beginning with Nagaland, created as a state in 1962, and the others first created as Union territories and subsequently elevated as states within the Indian Union over the 1970s and 1980s to deal with their tribal identities for statehood, which happened to be both federative or even independent, although the latter has not been conceded.

Nagaland: The Nagaland is a predominantly tribal Christian state with English as its official language. Despite 17 Naga sub-tribes, a miniscule Naga middle class formed the Naga National Council, which remained active from the late 1940s to the early 1950s, and sought to forge a common Naga tribal identity. Naga political activity subsequently veered to insurgency, the oldest in the Northeast region.

The Indian state of Nagaland was created after a 16-point agreement between the government of India and the Naga rebels in 1960, and Article 371A was incorporated into the Indian Constitution by the 13th Constitutional Amendment (1962). According to this Article, the Union Parliament cannot legislate in matters of Naga religion or social practices, Naga customary law and procedure, administration of civil and criminal justice, and ownership and transfer of land without concurrence of the state Assembly. However, the Article also particularly empowers the centrally appointed governor of the state to overrule the decision of the chief minister and the Council of Ministers of the state on law and order situation in the state. This special power of the Governor extends to allocation and utilization of federal fiscal transfers to the state and formation of a Regional Council for the Tuensang District within the Nagaland state. These special powers of the governor can be transferred to the Council of Ministers if the president of India on a report by the governor or otherwise is satisfied that it is no longer necessary for the governor to have these special powers. In 1992, Governor M.M. Thomas dissolved the Nagaland Legislative Assembly on the advice of the then chief minister under Article 172(2) (b), appointing him as the caretaker CM and ordering a fresh election. This action displeased the Indian government and it imposed presidential rule in the state and dismissed the governor. A framework agreement between the government of India (Prime Minister Narendra Modi) and the National Socialist Council of Nagaland (Isaac-Muivah Group) on 3 August 2015 has come

---

4 Udayon Misra, *The Periphery Strikes Back: Challenges to Nation-State in Assam and Nagaland* (2nd edition, Indian Institute of Advancesd Study 2013) 9.

after more than six and a half decades of marginalized Naga militancy. It marks a shift from exclusive sovereignty of Nagas to shared sovereignty of Nagas within the Union of India.[5] However, a turnaround occurred in August 2020 when Muivah asserted that the Naga flag and a Constitution were non-negotiable. He also said that the Naga Framework Agreement, 2015, included the idea of unification of all Naga-inhabited areas across Assam, Arunachal Pradesh and Manipur without, however, dividing these three states or fractions of them being added to a 'Greater Nagalim'.[6] These developments are reminiscent of a combination of territorial federalism with communitarian federalism of a kind resembling the Belgian system. The government of India had been silent, however, about the idea of a subnational Constitution or a communitarian federal union of Nagas across the four states of Nagaland, Assam, Arunachal Pradesh and Manipur.

Mizoram: A somewhat similar degree of asymmetrical federal autonomy was granted to the state of Mizoram. Following the memorandum of settlement (Mizoram Accord) between the government of India and the insurgent Mizo National Front on 30 June 30 1986,[7] the 53th Amendment to the Indian Constitution conferred statehood on the erstwhile Union territory of Mizoram under Article 371G of the Constitution. Under this Article, no Act of Parliament of India in respect of the subjects of Mizo customary religious, personal and family laws, property matters, administration of civil and criminal justice will apply to the state unless the Legislative Assembly of the state so decides by a resolution. It was also agreed that the state's Assembly was to consist of no fewer than 40 members. Following these changes, the insurgency has ceased in Mizoram. However, Mizos have tended to push non-Mizo tribes out of the state, forcing them to take refuge in neighbouring states.

Assam: Article 371B of the Indian Constitution provides for the creation of a committee of the Legislative Assembly of Assam by the president/governor consisting of members of that Assembly elected from tribal areas of the state specified in Part I of the Table appended to paragraph 20 of the 6th Schedule, namely the North Cachar Hill District and the Karbi Anglong District and such number of other members of that Assembly as may be specified in the order and for modifications to be made in the Assembly's rules of procedure for proper functioning of the said committee [22nd Constitutional Amendment, 1969, and North-Eastern Areas (Reorganisation) Act, 1971].

Manipur: Article 371C provides for creation of a committee of the Legislative Assembly of Manipur by the president/governor consisting of those elected from the hill areas of the state and entailing modifications in the rules of procedure of the said Assembly and for the responsibility of the governor in order to secure proper functioning of the committee. The governor of the state shall also send regular reports to the president regarding the administration of the hill areas in the state. The Hill Areas of Manipur are mainly inhabited by tribes which are either Nagas or Kukis—two different conglomerates of Manipur tribes from the other tribes and Hindu population in the plains. Unlike those in the other northeastern states, the District Councils in Manipur are newer and outside the scope of the 6th Schedule of the Constitution. Regular elections to these councils were held between 1973 and 1984. Later, due to the demand for inclusion in the 6th Schedule by the tribes, especially the Nagas, and non-acceptance of it by the government of India, the elections remained suspended for almost two decades. The state government of Manipur amended the Manipur (Hill Areas) District Councils Act, 1971, in

---

5 P.S. Dutta, *Ethnic Peace Accords in India* (Vikas Publishing House 1995).

6 *The Indian Express* (Chandigarh, 15 August 2020), pp. 1–2.

7 Mizoram Accord 1986, The South Asia Terrorism Portal, <peacemaker.un.org/sites/peacemaker.un.org/files/IN_860630_Mizoram%20Accord.pdf> accessed 18 April 2020.

2008, increasing the membership and powers of these councils and held elections in 2010 and 2015. These elections significantly marked a shift 'from opposition to acquiescence' on the part of the tribes.[8]

Sikkim: Article 371F contains special provisions with respect to the state of Sikkim, which, following a referendum in 1975, joined the Union of India. The king of Sikkim at the time of accession belonged to the Lepcha tribe practising Mahayana Buddhism, the other tribes being the Bhotia and Limbu, also Buddhist. Three-fourths of the state's population are Nepalese Hindu and speak a Nepalese dialect called Gorkhali. The structure of the government of Sikkim and all laws immediately before the state's joining the Indian Union were incorporated into the Constitution of India by the 36th Amendment, 1975, subject to transition of some of Sikkim's traditional political institutions and practices. The Legislative Assembly was guaranteed to consist of not less than 30 members. The Parliament of India, in order to protect the rights and interests of different sections of the population of Sikkim, may determine the number of seats in the Assembly to be allocated to particular sectors of the population and delimit the constituencies thereof. The governor is charged with 'special responsibility for peace and an equitable arrangement for ensuring the social and economic advancement of different sections of the population of Sikkim'. In discharge of these special responsibilities, the governor must, under the occasional presidential directions, act in his personal discretion and is not bound by ministerial advice (36th Constitutional Amendment, 1975). Sikkim is by now an island of peace and unity in the Indian federal Union, yet this special gubernatorial power is retained due the historical connexions of Lepcha kings of Sikkim with Tibet and Chinese annexation of Tibet.[9]

Arunachal Pradesh: Special provisions with respect of the state of Arunachal Pradesh under Article 371H provide that the Legislative Assembly of the state shall consist of not less than 30 members. The governor of the state is charged with 'special responsibility with respect of law and order in the state', which he must discharge after consulting the Council of Ministers but in doing so exercise his individual judgement. If the governor reports to the president that his (the governor's) special responsibility is no longer necessary, it can be de-operationalized (55th Constitutional Amendment, 1986). Arunachal Pradesh is a part of the Indo-China border or territorial dispute.

11.3 2B: Subnational constitutionalism in Jammu and Kashmir—autonomy

The preamble of the subnational Constitution of Jammu and Kashmir began by speaking in the name of 'We, the people of Jammu & Kashmir'.[10] Article 3 then proclaimed that the state 'shall be an integral part of the Union of India', whose territories 'shall comprise all the territories which on the fifteenth day of August, 1947, were under the sovereignty or suzerainty of the Ruler of the State'. This means that the state laid claim to territories presently occupied by Pakistan and China. Article 5 stated that: 'The executive and legislative power of the State extends to all matters except those with respect to which Parliament has power to make laws for the State under the provisions of the Constitution of India'. The state's Constitution broadly followed the model of the parliamentary-federal Constitution of India. The state legislature was

---

8 Kham Khan Suan Hausing, 'From Opposition to Acquiescence: The 2015 District Council Elections in Manipur' (2015) 50(46–7) *Economics & Political Weekly* 79.
9 Mahendra Prasad Singh's telephone conversation with a former Governor of Sikkim, Shir B.P. Singh, on 5 May 2020.
10 Available at <jklaw.nic.in/the_constitution_of_jammu_and_kashmir_1956.pdf > accessed 20 April 2020.

left with exclusive jurisdiction on the State List of legislative subjects, while the Union Parliament's jurisdiction was limited to the matters in the Union and Concurrent Lists of the Seventh Schedule of the Indian Constitution, 'which, in consultation with the State are declared by the President [of India] to correspond to matters specified in the Instrument of Accession' with the Dominion of India, namely defence, external affairs and communication. However, Article 370(3) of the Constitution of India empowered the president of India to declare by public notification whether the special status of the state emanating from the Instrument of Accession as mentioned in Article 370 'shall cease to be operative or shall be operative only with such exceptions and modifications and from such date as he may specify' with 'the recommendation of the Constituent Assembly of the state'.

Every government since Prime Minister Nehru's kept extending various parts of the Indian Constitution with the consent of the state government and Legislative Assembly of the state as the legatee of the Constituent Assembly of the state under Article 370(3), either under a chief minister's government or under the president's/governor's rule, until the bulk of the national and subnational Constitutions had become virtually overlapping. Yet the presence of Article 370 remained a matter of psychological and symbolic value at least to the Muslim majority in the Kashmir valley, if not also to the two other regions of the state—the Hindu-majority Jammu and non-Muslim majority Ladakh (Muslims 46 per cent, Buddhist 40 per cent, Hindus 12 per cent, others 2 per cent). The latter two, in fact, welcomed this trend. The Muslim majority in the state as a whole only harped on federal autonomy from New Delhi, giving short shrift to intra-state regional autonomy and federalism in the state.

The Bhartiya Janata Party (BJP) had always been strongly opposed to Articles 370 and 35A of the Indian Constitution. The former has already been discussed above. The latter empowered the legislature of the state to define 'permanent residents' of the state for enjoyment of certain rights pertaining to employment and owning certain properties in the state. The BJP election manifestos promised to abrogate these constitutional provisions. However, neither the BJP-led National Democratic Alliance (NDA) government at the Union government headed by Atal Bihari Vajapayee in the late 1990s nor Narendra Modi during 2014–19 the People's Democratic Party (PDP)-BJP government could implement this agenda due to the susceptibilities of coalition partners who had different views on this issue.

The Modi government early in its second term (2019–present) abrogated both Articles 370 and 35A by a presidential order and parliamentary ratification on 5 August 2019.[11] This was done using Clause (3) of Article 370 itself, which stipulated that 'Notwithstanding anything in the foregoing provisions of this article, the president may, by public notification, declare that 'this article shall cease to be operative or shall be operative only with such exceptions and modifications and from such date as he may specify', on 'the recommendation of the Constituent Assembly of the State'. The government argued that since the Constituent Assembly of the state dissolved itself in 1957, its role under the Constitution could be performed by the state legislature. However, since the state was under governor's rule under Section 92 of the Constitution of Jammu and Kashmir (cf. Article 356 of the Constitution of India) at the time, state legislatures' powers were exercisable by the Union Parliament.

Simultaneously, the Union government reorganized the State of Jammu and Kashmir under Article 3 of the Indian Constitution into the two Union Territories—Jammu and Kashmir and Ladakh, the former with an Assembly and the latter without one. Home Minister Amit Shah said in the Rajya Sabha that full state status would be restored to Jammu and Kashmir (but not

---

11 Ministry of Law and Justice (Legislative Department), Notification, New Delhi, 5 August 2019, The Constitution (Application to Jammu and Kashmir) Order, 2019.

Ladakh) at an appropriate time.[12] The Union government's case for these moves was that they would help to deal with terrorism in the state, curb corruption, end discriminatory laws against 'non-permanent residents' and Kashmiri women, end electoral malfeasance by the locally dominant and undemocratic political parties, create conditions for economic investment and development in the state, etc. Simultaneously with these fundamental constitutional changes, a large number of regional political leaders were put under detention and a lockdown on communication systems was imposed indefinitely. A series of petitions were filed in constitutional courts against all these moves. Their hearings in the High Court and the Supreme Court are still underway and their outcomes are keenly awaited. Early in January 2020, the Supreme Court directed the Jammu and Kashmir administration to review within a week all orders imposing curbs in the said Union territories; and it considered that access to internet is a fundamental right under Article 19 of the Indian Constitution (*The Times of India*, 10 January 2020). Eminent jurist Harish Salve considers this action to be consistent with the Constitutions of India and Jammu and Kashmir and the laws of the land.[13] A five-judge bench of the Supreme Court is seized with pleas challenging the constitutional validity of the 5 August 2019 decisions of the Union government abrogating provisions of Article 370 and reorganizing the state into two Union territories.

Among a handful of past cases related to Jammu and Kashmir, *Sampat Prakash v. State of Jammu & Kashmir* (Supreme Court 1968) appears to have the most direct bearing on the current issues. The court affirmed that (i) Article 368, the general amending provision in the Indian Constitution, is replaced by Article 370 in the case of Jammu and Kashmir; and (ii) the president of India, in extending provisions of the Indian Constitution to Jammu and Kashmir, must first consult the 'government of the state'. Arguably, the abrogation of the state's special status by the decision of 5 August would have been more consistent with constitutional morality if it had not been done at a time when the governor's powers were exercisable by the president due to the declaration of an emergency within the state. A.G. Noorani takes an extreme legal position on extending the Indian Constitution to the state under governor's/ president's rule as a 'fraud on the Constitution'.[14]

11.4 Status and content of the subnational Constitution

There was an explicit subnational constitutionalism in the Indian case only in the state of Jammu and Kashmir from January 1950 to August 2019. Yet it was a restrained and constrained right from the start as Article 370 was incorporated in Part XXI of the Indian Constitution captioned 'Temporary, Transitional and Special Provisions'.

By presidential orders, beginning with the Constitution (Application to Jammu and Kashmir) Order, 1954, the bulk of the Indian Constitution was incrementally applied to Jammu and Kashmir.[15]

Like the national Constitution of India, the subnational Constitution of Jammu and Kashmir opened with a preamble that replicated verbatim the preamble of the national Constitution of India, only substituting the words 'We, the people of India …' with 'We, the people of the State Jammu and Kashmir …'.

---

12 *LiveMint*, 5 August 2019, available at <www.livemint.com/news/india> accessed 12 April 2020.
13 Harish Salve, 'Harish Salve on Why the Supreme Court is Unlikely to Void Article 370 Move', available at <thewire.in/law/harish-salve-supreme-court-article-370-kashmir> accessed 6 May 2020.
14 See A.G. Noorani, *Article 370: A Constitutional History of Jammu and Kashmir* (Oxford University Press 2011).
15 P.M. Bakshi, *The Constitution of India* (15th edition, Universal Law Publishing 2018) Appendix: 471–83.

The subnational Constitution, like the national Constitution, provided for a parliamentary form of government with an executive comprising the governor to be appointed by the President of India as the constitutionally nominal head of the state and a chief minister and his Council of Ministers collectively responsible to the directly elected Legislative Assembly of the bicameral legislature, the upper house being a Legislative Council consisting of members partly elected by the members of the Legislative Assembly from among persons distributed among the various regions of the state, partly by an electoral college of rural and urban local self-governing bodies, and partly nominated by the governor from among socially and economically backward classes and persons having special knowledge and practical experience in areas such as literature, science, art, cooperative movement and social service. The judicial powers and institutions of the subordinate courts and High Court in the subnational Constitution of the state and the Supreme Court in New Delhi also conformed to the general patterns in the national Constitution. This was likewise true of state civil services and All India Services and the Public Service Commission in the state. State elections, like national parliamentary elections, were also conducted by the Election Commission of India, leaving only the local panchayat and municipal elections in the hands of the state government, as in other states of the Indian Union.

Patterns of fiscal federalism in Jammu and Kashmir are not different from the ten other sub-Himalayan states spread from the northwest to northeast India. Given their relatively smaller resources and productive base these states are more dependent on federal fiscal transfers than other states of the mainland states of the North and the South regions.

The subnational Constitution provided for a flag of the state in addition to the national flag of India. It adopted Urdu and English as the co-official languages of government of the state. This is in line with other states of the Indian Union which adopt a regional language and/or English as the official language of the state government.

11.5 Multilevel federal constitutionalism and subnational constitutionalism

It would be more accurate to talk about multilevel governance rather than multilevel subnational constitutionalism and multilevel federal constitutionalism in the case of India. Subnational constitutionalism in Jammu and Kashmir now stands abrogated. The national Constitution covers the structures and functions and powers of the Union as well as all state governments.

India has only a two-level federal structure. The third-tier local governments in India—the rural and urban—are devolutionary or delegational rather than federal. The panchayats and municipal councils are governed by state legislations, local government being a state subject in the 7th Schedule of the Constitution. This state of affairs remains unchanged even after the 73rd and 74th Amendments (1993) to the Constitution of India relating to rural and urban local governments, respectively.

As discussed above, some tribal communities and states and backward districts in some states can be said to have been given multicultural asymmetrical treatment within the national Constitution itself, i.e. under the 5th and 6th Schedules and the Article 371 series of the Constitution. But these communities and states have been given no role in amending the Constitution.

The erstwhile subnational Constitution of Jammu and Kashmir could be amended by the bicameral state legislature by not less than a two-thirds majority of the total membership of each house separately and the grant of assent by the federally appointed governor. However, no bill seeking to amend the procedure of amendment, the relationship of the state with the Union of India, or the extent of executive and legislative power of the state could be initiated in either house of the state legislature (Section 147). Thus the subnational Constitution could be amended by the state legislature but the relationship of the state with the Union of India was unamendable.

11.6 Constitutional review

The centralized federal system of India features strong judicial review under the Constitution, and this included the subnational Constitution of Jammu and Kashmir when it existed. The constitutional courts—state High Courts and the Supreme Court—can review executive actions and parliamentary Acts in areas of fundamental and statutory and customary rights, federal division of powers, tripartite separation of powers and principles of natural justice. Judicial review has been further made stronger in constitutional law, particularly since the landmark judgments of the Supreme Court in *Keshavananda Bharati v. State of Kerala*, AIR 1973 SC 1461; *Minerva Mills Ltd. v. Union of India*, AIR SC 1789; *S.R. Bommai v. Union of India*, AIR 1994 SC 1918; and *I.R. Coelho v. State of Tamil Nadu*, AIR 2007 CSC 861, which invented and reiterated the judicial doctrine of the unamendability of the basic structure of the Constitution, going beyond the express provisions of the Constitution.

11.7 Appraisal

Unlike the USA, Canada, Australia and Germany, India has a single, integrated Constitution for the national as well as state governments, with the solitary exception of the Indian state of Jammu and Kashmir, the subnational Constitution of which was abrogated in 2019. The Indian Constitution also continues to have some asymmetrical features for tribal states and some tribal communities and some other backward states and regions within some states. Subnational constitutionalism and asymmetrical federalism, both not favoured in South Asia, generally for being suspected to be halfway houses for separatism, were reluctantly embraced by the Indian Constitution in pursuit of federal and national integration in the context of India's uniquely complex social, cultural and regional diversities. These complexities have been discussed critically in the theoretical literature on comparative government and politics.[16] However, in more recent literature, both subnational constitutionalism and asymmetrical federalism have come to be seen more positively, as an increasingly common means of securing unity where this would otherwise be very difficult or impossible to achieve.[17]

The Indian constitutional design and experience suggest that both subnational constitutionalism and asymmetrical federalism were very helpful in weaving together the deep diversities in the rimland regions and states, beyond the mainlands of the northern plains and the southern

---

16 See Charles D. Tarlton, 'Symmetry and Asymmetry as Elements of Federalism: A Theoretical Speculation' (1965) 27 *The Journal of Politics* 861.

17 See Burgess and Tarr (n 1); Jonathan L. Marshfield, 'Models of Subnational Constitutionalism' (2011) 115 *Penn. State Law Review* 1152; John McGarry, 'Asymmetry in Federations, Federacies and Unitary States' (2007) 6 *Ethnopolitics* 105; Will Kymlicka, 'Federalism and Nationalism in Canada: A Comparative Perspective' in Rekha Saxena (ed.), *Mapping Canadian Federalism for India* (Konark 2002) 80; Charles Taylor, 'The Politics of Recognition' in Amy Gutmann (ed.), *Multiculturalism: Examining the Politics of Recognition* (Princeton University Press 1994) 25; Alain-G. Gagnon, *The Case for Multinational Federalism: Beyond All-Encompassing Nation* (Routledge 2010); M.P. Singh and Rekha Saxena, *Federalizing India in the Age of Globalization* (Primus Books 2013); Rekha Saxena, 'Asymmetrical Federalism in India: Promoting Secession or Accommodating Diversity?' in Alain-G. Gagnon and Michael Burgess (eds), *Revisiting Unity and Diversity in Federal Countries: Changing Concepts, Reform Proposals and New Institutional Realities* (Brill Nijhoff 2018) 362.

peninsula. The Northeast and Northwest regions are marked by especially deep diversities of culture, languages, religions and tribes. The two mainlands are predominantly Hindu and speakers of languages belonging to the two largest linguistic families: Indo-Aryan in the North and Dravidian in the South.

The Northeast region also experienced insurgency since the 1960s but the Indian Union has successfully employed various constitutional devices like reorganization of the composite state of Assam into Union territories carved out of it and subsequently raised them to the status of statehood, coupled with the 6th Schedule asymmetrical federal autonomy. Persistence of insurgencies have been sought to be dealt with by proclamation of constitutional emergencies and the use of security forces to restore constitutional order.

Geopolitically, the most extremely vulnerable regions of India—the Northeast and Northwest—also happen to be riddled with the deepest diversities and complexities. Both Pakistan and China, as factors in both the west and the east, to say nothing of the north, have posed serious threats to the security and national integrity of India. All the major wars so far have been with these powers. With the 1971 breakup of Pakistan and the liberation of Bangladesh, the eastern threat from Pakistan has disappeared but terrorist infiltration from Pakistan and homegrown terrorist activities and Islamic radicalization in Kashmir has intensified. These factors have significantly contributed to the failure of subnational constitutionalism in the Indian state of Jammu and Kashmir. Belatedly, the idea of a subnational Constitution has been put forward by the Naga rebels in course of negotiating a Framework Naga Agreement with the government of India as mentioned above. It is highly improbable that the government of India will agree to it.

11.8 Authors of this paper/chapter

M.P. Singh, a former Professor of Political Science at University of Delhi, is presently a National Fellow at Indian Institute of Advanced Study, Shimla. India, for two years working on Indian Federalism in a Comparative Perspective. Rekha Saxena is Professor at the Department of Political Science, University of Delhi, Delhi, India, Honorary Senior Advisor, Forum of Federations, Canada and Vice-Chairperson, Centre for Multilevel Federalism, India.

SUBNATIONAL CONSTITUTIONALISM IN ITALY

Unfulfilled expectations?

Giacomo Delledonne, Matteo Monti and Giuseppe Martinico[1]

12.1 Context

For decades, Italy has been classified as an archetypical example of a regional state that resulted from a top-down federalizing process.[2] The Constitution of the Italian Republic, enacted on 27 December 1947, clearly departed from the unitary, strongly centralized model of territorial organization that had been in force since the establishment of the Kingdom of Italy in 1861. The centralizing features of that system had been confirmed and even strengthened under the Fascist regime. After the downfall of the regime, the promotion of sub-state autonomy was part of the effort to enhance pluralism—be it social, religious or territorial—in order to break with an authoritarian past. For this purpose, the Constituent Assembly opted for the establishment of regions, an entirely new intermediate layer of government between the state and local government authorities (provinces and municipalities). In so doing, the constituent fathers and mothers embraced proposals that had been made by some streams of political thought in the *Risorgimento* as well as by Luigi Sturzo's Italian People's Party.[3]

The Constitution thus established regions provided with legislative, administrative and financial autonomy. Regional autonomy includes the power to adopt a *statuto*, that is, a fundamental charter containing the basic norms of regional organization. Unlike Spain, the Italian regions were enumerated in the text of the Constitution from the beginning. There were 19 original regions, but in 1963, some years before the actual launch of the regional governments, Article 131(1) was amended to create Molise. The extension of regional legislative, administrative and financial autonomy is defined in Articles 117 to 119 of the Constitution.

---

1 This chapter is the result of joint reflections. However, Sections 12.2.1, 12.3, 12.4.2 and 12.4.3 have been written by Giacomo Delledonne, Sections 12.1, 12.2.2, 12.4.4 and 12.5.1 by Matteo Monti, and Sections 12.4.1, 12.5.2 and 12.6 by Giuseppe Martinico. Section 12.7 has been jointly written by the three authors.
2 See discussion by Francesco Palermo and Karl Kössler, *Comparative Federalism: Constitutional Arrangements and Case Law* (Hart 2017) 50–5.
3 See Alessandro Candido, 'Sul regionalismo italiano dal Risorgimento a Sturzo. Prime note' (2010) *Le Carte e la Storia* 151.

The Constitution makes a crucial distinction among the regions. Five regions—that is, Friuli-Venezia Giulia, Sardinia, Sicily, Trentino-Alto Adige/South Tyrol and Valle d'Aosta/Vallée d'Aoste— 'have special forms and conditions of autonomy pursuant to the special *statuti* adopted by constitutional law' (Article 116(1) of the Constitution). The origin of the five special regions makes it necessary to add some shades to the idea of a purely top-down federalizing process.[4] By the time the Constituent Assembly was discussing the draft text of the Constitution, some of these regions had already adopted their own *statuti di autonomia*.

After the downfall of Fascism and the end of World War II, secessionist and autonomist movements arose in the territories of Sicily, Sardinia, Valle d'Aosta/Vallée d'Aoste, Trentino and Alto Adige/South Tyrol. The secessionist impulses in some of these areas were indirectly enhanced by the aggressive policy that had been pursued by the Fascist regime, which had tried to assimilate the traditional linguistic minorities of Valle d'Aosta/Vallée d'Aoste and Alto Adige/South Tyrol. In this respect, the Italian regional system was built with the aim to keep together the new post-fascist state. The special status granted to four of these regions was designed specifically to avoid secession and civil unrest. To a certain extent, secessionist claims in Valle d'Aosta/ Vallée d'Aoste and Alto Adige/South Tyrol were encouraged by the French and Austrian governments respectively. A special status was also accorded to Friuli-Venezia Giulia, a region that had a situation complicated by the unsettled border dispute with Yugoslavia. For the purposes of this chapter, it is worth highlighting that, in order to contain pro-independence claims in those regions, pre-constitutional autonomy regimes were granted in Sicily and Valle d'Aosta/Vallée d'Aoste. The Sicilian *statuto* was drafted by a *Consulta regionale* before the war ended and was finally enacted by royal law decree no. 455/1946. In Valle d'Aosta/Vallée d'Aoste, the Italian Provisional Government set the basis for special regional autonomy by enacting two laws concerning autonomy (laws no. 545 and 546 of 1945), starting with the creation of a regional council. Since the *statuti* of Sicily and Valle d'Aosta/ Vallée d'Aoste both predate the Constitution, the Constituent Assembly had to take this into account when discussing the regime of the regions.[5] These regional charters, most of all the Sicilian *statuto*, had to be coordinated with the Constitution of the Republic. However, some of the members of the Assembly elected in those regions struggled to keep the *statuti* unchanged; in their speeches, they echoed, more or less consciously, familiar compact-like theories.[6] In sum, the Italian federalizing process has mostly followed a top-down pattern, but the very existence of the special regions testifies to the relevance of quite different concerns. Constituent fathers like Gaspare Ambrosini were conscious that regions, as an entirely novel government entity, would allow the consideration of distinctive territorial peculiarities.[7] Institutional diversity among regions was not perceived as an accidental feature but as an integral part of the model.

Although the Eighth Transitional and Final Provision of the Constitution provided for the election of the regional councils, as the regional legislatures are called, 'within one year of the

---

4 See Giacomo Delledonne and Matteo Monti, 'Secessionist Impulses and the Italian Legal System: The (Non) Influence of the Secession Reference' in Giacomo Delledonne and Giuseppe Martinico (eds), *The Canadian Contribution to a Comparative Law of Secession: Legacies of the Quebec Secession Reference* (Palgrave 2019) 185, at 187–96.

5 See, among others, Giovanni Tarli Barbieri, 'Il regionalismo prima della Costituzione repubblicana: la sofferta genesi dello statuto siciliano' in Nicola Antonetti and Ugo De Siervo (eds), *Ambrosini e Sturzo. La nascita delle Regioni* (il Mulino 1998) 195; Giovanni Tarli Barbieri, 'La crisi politico-istituzionale valdostana nella crisi del regionalismo italiano', *Consulta OnLine*, 10 April 2020 <www.giurcost.org> accessed 3 May 2020.

6 See Gaetano Silvestri, 'Le Regioni speciali tra limiti di modello e limiti di sistema' (2004) *le Regioni* 1119, at 1120–1.

7 See Agatino Cariola and Francesca Leotta, 'Art. 116' in Raffaele Bifulco, Alfonso Celotto and Marco Olivetti (eds), *Commentario alla Costituzione* (Utet 2006) 2178, at 2180.

entry into force of the Constitution' itself, the process went differently. The establishment of regional governments was considerably slowed down because of the so-called constitutional freezing; that is, the parliamentary majority at the time was not particularly interested in a quick, effective implementation of the main innovations introduced by the Constitution. Only in 1970 were the regional legislatures elected in the 15 ordinary regions.

At the beginning of the twenty-first century, the regions were granted greater legislative, administrative and financial autonomy. A comprehensive reform of Title V of the Second Part of the Constitution, containing norms for the sub-state units of the Republic, was intended to pave the way for a comprehensive reshaping of the Italian regional model.

12.2 Autonomy

12.2.1 Scope

Most of the relevant constitutional norms are to be found in Article 123 of the Constitution. This provision states that each ordinary region has its own charter (*statuto*) and regulates its contents as well as the limits on regional *statuti*-making autonomy. Article 123 was significantly amended in 1999 as part of a reform process that was supposed to transform the Italian model of 'regional state' into a 'federal' or 'quasi-federal' one. The current wording of Article 123 should be assessed in the light of the previous state of affairs in order to grasp the underlying rationale of the 1999 reform.

In its early wording, Article 123(1) made clear that the *statuti* would play a very different role from that of fully fledged regional constitutions; their purpose was to lay down norms concerning the 'internal organisation' of each region 'in harmony with the Constitution and the laws of the Republic'. In its current wording, which has been in force since 1999, Article 123(1) provides a wider scope for the *statuti*; now they are supposed to contain norms concerning 'the form of government and basic principles for the organisation of the region and the conduct of its business'. Furthermore, *statuti* 'shall regulate the right to initiate legislation and promote referenda on the laws and administrative measures of the region as well as the publication of laws and regional regulations'. Even the limits on the regional *statuto*-making power were modified; it is now required that the contents of the *statuti* be 'in harmony with the Constitution'.

In 2001, constitutional law no. 3/2001 further amended Article 123 by adding a fourth paragraph. Among the indefectible contents of the *statuti*, another element is the regulation of the (regional) Council of Local Government Authorities (*Consiglio delle autonomie locali*, CAL). The main tasks of the CAL are to represent the institutional viewpoint of local government authorities and to contribute to the ordinary lawmaking process by submitting non-binding advisory opinions. More generally, the CAL acts as a forum in which the regional government and local governments engage in dialogue. Indeed, one of the main goals of constitutional and legislative reforms in the 1990s was to promote a closer cooperation between regional and local governments than had been the case.[8]

Article 123(1), as amended in 1999, seems to set less stringent limits on the regional *statuti* than in the past. However, the Constitutional Court frustrated such expectations. According to the Court, the mention of 'harmony', 'far from defusing it, strengthens the need for scrupulous respect of all the provisions of the Constitution, as it aims … to avert the danger of a *statuto* that formally respects the Constitution but ultimately eludes its spirit'.[9] A related risk is that the very

---

8 See Paolo Carrozza, 'Per un diritto costituzionale delle autonomie locali' (2007) *Rivista di diritto costituzionale* 219.
9 Constitutional Court, judgment no. 304/2002; see also judgment no. 196/2003 (mentioning 'harmony with all the precepts and principles derived from the Constitution'). All the judgments of the Court are available at <www.cortecostituzionale.it>.

notion of the spirit of the Constitution proves to be too vague to guide and limit the *statuti*-making processes. One scholar has suggested that the spirit of the Constitution should be identified with its fundamental principles, that is, its axiological core.[10]

The *statuti* play quite a different role in each of the five special regions. According to Article 116(1) of the Constitution, the *statuti* lay down the 'special forms and conditions of autonomy' of each region. The *statuti* of the special regions do not, therefore, only contain provisions on the form of government, the basic organizational principles and the system of local sources. They also lay down the terms of the legislative, administrative and financial autonomy of each of these regions, including the distribution of the related competences. As one scholar phrased it, Title V of the Second Part of the Constitution and the individual special *statuti* 'constitute distinct systems'.[11] The special *statuti* were enacted between the late 1940s and the early 1960s. The current *statuto* of Trentino-Alto Adige/South Tyrol dates to 1972; the *statuto*, based on the Package Agreement for South Tyrol concluded by Italy and Austria, devolved strong autonomy to the two constitutive provinces of the region, which were to be known as *autonomous provinces*.

12.2.2 Procedure

It is necessary to distinguish between ordinary and special regions to get a proper understanding of how the regional *statuti* are enacted. With regard to the former, the relevant provision is Article 123(2) and (3) of the Constitution, under which the *statuti*-making and *statuti*-amending procedures are regulated. In 1999, this procedure was significantly modified. The regional *statuti* now take the form of a regional law for which a special procedure is mandated.[12] In some respects, the procedure laid down in Article 123 resembles the constitution-amending procedure regulated by Article 138 of the Constitution.[13]

The *statuti*-making procedure is based on three procedural steps. First is the adoption of the *statuto* by the Regional Council, that is, the regional legislature. The *statuto* has to be approved by a majority of the members of the Regional Council 'with two subsequent deliberations at an interval of no less than two months' (Article 123(2) of the Constitution). A higher majority threshold is thus required for adopting a *statuto* than for ordinary regional laws. This, alongside the double deliberation requirement, makes it possible to draw a parallel with the constitution-amending procedure.[14]

The *statuto* is then published in the regional official bulletin. No approval of the central Government is required; however, the central Government *may* refer the issue of the constitutionality of the *statuto* to the Constitutional Court within 30 days of its publication. Moreover, the *statuto* must be submitted to popular referendum 'if one-fiftieth of the voters in the region or one-fifth of the members of the Regional Council so request within three months from its

---

10 See Monica Rosini, *Statuti regionali e armonia con la Costituzione* (Giappichelli 2016) 86–7.

11 Omar Chessa, 'La specialità regionale tra leggi di revisione della Costituzione e altre leggi costituzionali' (2009) *le Regioni* 297, at 299.

12 Before 1999, *statuti* were approved by the regional legislature but took the form of a 'law of the Republic'.

13 As noted by Rolando Tarchi and Demis Bessi, 'Art. 123', in Bifulco, Celotto and Olivetti (n 7), 2451, at 2473.

14 Under Article 138 of the Constitution, constitutional amendments 'shall be adopted by each house after two successive debates at intervals of not less than three months, and shall be approved by an absolute majority of the members of each house in the second voting. Said laws are submitted to a popular referendum when, within three months of their publication, such request is made by one-fifth of the members of a house or five hundred thousand voters or five regional legislatures. The law submitted to referendum shall not be promulgated if not approved by a majority of valid votes. A referendum shall not be held if the law has been approved in the second voting by each of the houses by a majority of two-thirds of the members.'

publication' (Article 123(3) of the Constitution). Although the wording of this provision is not straightforward, the Constitutional Court has suggested that judicial review should have precedence over the regional referendum in order to avoid 'a vote concerning an act whose validity might be denied, in whole or in part, by the Constitutional Court'.[15]

One point deserves mention: after 1999, some of the regions were remarkably slow in enacting their *statuti*. It took more than ten years for the legislatures of Basilicata, Molise and Veneto to adopt new *statuti*. Quite surprisingly, the process went on for quite a long time both in Lombardy and Veneto, the two northern regions that have been at the forefront of the movement for greater autonomy in the last three decades, including fiscal autonomy and a differentiated status. This seems to suggest that the adoption of a new *statuto* was not seen as instrumental in promoting the claims for greater regional autonomy. This feeling was strengthened by the first judgments that the Constitutional Court rendered with regard to the *statuti*. As will be shown later in greater detail (Section 12.4), there is a gap between the early expectations, including the emergence of some kind of *constitutions in all but name* at the regional level,[16] and the subsequent developments.

None of the *statuti* of the 15 ordinary regions were submitted to referendum. This means that the *statuti* were not particularly controversial in the political debates at the regional level. Neither opposition lawmakers nor groups of voters embarked on referendum campaigns that would probably have struggled to trigger the public's interest. By contrast, some of the *statuti* were referred to the Constitutional Court by the government. Most of the time, and with some relevant exceptions, this happened against the background of a political conflict between a conservative state executive and centre-left regional administrations.[17] Therefore, the Court rendered judgments on the constitutionality of the *statuti* of Calabria, Tuscany, Umbria, Emilia-Romagna, Abruzzo and Molise.[18]

Different rules apply to the five special regions. According to Article 116(1) of the Constitution, their *statuti* take the form of a constitutional law. Therefore, the special *statuti* are adopted by the Italian Parliament pursuant to the procedure laid down in Article 138 of the Constitution. As mentioned previously (Section 12.1), the *statuto* of Sicily and a draft *statuto* of Valle d'Aosta/Vallée d'Aoste had been adopted by the regional assemblies ahead of the entry into force of the Constitution of the Italian Republic. Shortly before the end of the term of the Constituent Assembly, these *statuti* were converted into constitutional laws with limited room for amendments.[19] Right now, the legal regime of the special *statuti* is a frequent object of criticism. This primarily has to do with the fact that, properly speaking, these *statuti* are not regional acts discussed and adopted by the regional legislatures. Quite to the contrary, the autonomy of the special regions does not include the power to adopt their own *statuti*. This might not have been the case when the Sicilian and Valdostan governments were established; however, the power to amend the *statuti* currently in force lies in the hands of the national Parliament.[20] As part of the comprehensive reform of Title V of the Second Part of the Constitution, constitutional law

---

15 Constitutional Court, judgment no. 304/200. See also Elena Malfatti, Saulle Panizza and Roberto Romboli, *Giustizia costituzionale* (5th edn, Giappichelli 2016) 157–60.

16 See discussion by Marco Olivetti, *Nuovi statuti e forma di governo delle regioni. Verso le Costituzioni regionali?* (il Mulino 2002).

17 See Giacomo Delledonne and Giuseppe Martinico, 'Handle with Care! The Regional Charters and Italian Constitutionalism's "Grey Zone"' (2009) *European Constitutional Law Review* 218, at 223.

18 Constitutional Court, judgments no. 2/2004, 372/2004, 378/2004, 379/2004, 12/2006, and 63/2012.

19 See Delledonne and Monti (n 4).

20 See A. Saitta, 'L'autonomia siciliana alla prova della riforma costituzionale' (2015) 6(4) *Rivista AIC* 1, at 9 <www.rivistaaic.it> accessed 3 May 2020.

no. 2/2001 modified some aspects of the procedure for amending the special *statuti*. First, although these *statuti* take the form of a constitutional law, they cannot be subject to a national referendum, as it is the case with the constitutional laws that are not approved by a supermajority in both houses (Article 138(2) of the Constitution). Second, the regional legislatures are more actively involved in the procedure, as they are required to submit an advisory opinion on the draft amendments.[21]

12.3 Position of the *statuti* within the regions

The Constitution identifies the *statuto* as the regional act that regulates the basic elements of the regional institutional system (see Section 12.2.2). Although the *statuto* is a regional law, it is the result of a special procedure. A regional legislature cannot resort to an ordinary law to regulate issues that are reserved for the *statuto* under Article 123 of the Constitution.[22] After 1999, regional legislatures in the 15 ordinary regions were supposed to replace the first-generation *statuti* that mostly dated back to the early 1970s with new charters. A question arose: could regional legislatures exercise their *statuto*-making power on the basis of a step-by-step approach? The Constitutional Court answered affirmatively, as regional autonomy also includes the power to determine how and when the *statuti* should be enacted. Consequently, a gradual revision and replacement of the older *statuti* is not incompatible with Article 123 of the Constitution. The idea that this practice would 'create confusion among the voting public ... because it would make the global reform project uncertain and precarious' is ill-founded.[23]

Because a *statuto* must have specific *content* and be enacted pursuant to a specific *procedure*, regional legislatures often resort to the enactment of *leggi statutarie* that regulate *statuto*-related issues but are not formally part of the *statuto* themselves.[24] Borrowing from Richard Albert's classification of models of constitutional amendment, a *statuto* 'is codified in a text that is amendable by a special procedure authorizing the alteration of its text and it is amendable also by the adoption of separately codified' *leggi statutarie*.[25]

Among regional laws, the electoral law, referred to in Article 122 of the Constitution, plays a crucial role. As the Constitutional Court made clear, a regional legislature should adopt the new *statuto* before passing a new electoral law under Article 123 of the Constitution. According to the Court, the electoral law should not contradict the basic aspects of the regional form of government as regulated in the *statuto*.[26]

As for the *statuti* of the five special regions, constitutional law no. 2/2001 enabled their legislatures to adopt *leggi statutarie regionali* that would modify their forms of government and electoral laws in the wake of the global reform of Italian regionalism in 2001. The special *statuti*, which take the form of (state) constitutional laws (see Section 12.2.2), have thus been complemented by fully regional *leggi statutarie*.

Due to a number of reasons, related to Italy's political culture and to the case law of the Constitutional Court (see Sections 12.2 and 12.4), the relevance of the regional *statuti* in the Italian legal and political debates is limited. However, their contents testify to a certain willingness to experiment with differentiation among the regions.

---

21 See L. Cappuccio, 'Il procedimento di revisione degli statuti speciali introdotto dalla legge costituzionale n. 2 del 2001. Una nuova ipotesi di rottura costituzionale?' (2003) *le Regioni* 399.
22 Constitutional Court, judgment no. 196/2003.
23 Constitutional Court, judgment no. 304/2002.
24 See Beniamino Caravita di Toritto, 'L'autonomia statutaria' (2004) *le Regioni* 304, at 311–12.
25 Richard Albert, *Constitutional Amendments: Making, Braking, and Changing Constitutions* (OUP 2019) 235.
26 Constitutional Court, judgment no. 45/2011.

12.4 Content

12.4.1 Identity

After Article 123 of the Constitution was amended in 1999, and another even more ambitious constitutional reform was enacted into law in 2001, a number of enthusiastic legislators and commentators saw the *statuti* as a kind of regional constitution, defining the identity of each region in a state that is becoming more and more complex and plural. This is why most of the *statuti* that have come into force since the early 2000s contain provisions, sometimes included in a preamble, in which the founding principles of each region and the fundamental rights of its inhabitants are catalogued.[27] The possibility of codifying regional bills of rights will be discussed in detail in Section 12.4.3; however, many *statuti* also include statements that aim to summarize the identity of their respective regions. The following provisions from Latium's *statuto* are a good example of such legislative policies:

> The region shall promote national unity as well as European integration … as fundamental values of its identity …
>
> The region shall contribute to the promotion of Rome as the capital of the Republic and symbol of Italian unity, the centre of Catholicism and religious dialogue, a meeting place for different cultures and a universal historical and cultural heritage …
>
> The region recognises the principles derived from the Universal Declaration of Human Rights.

Emilia-Romagna, according to the preamble to its *statuto* of 2005, is founded on the 'values of the Resistance against Nazism and Fascism and the ideals of liberty and national unity of the *Risorgimento*, and is based on the principles and rights recognized by the Italian Constitution and the European Union'.

Most of the time, these identity-related statements have not had significant practical effect. This is primarily due to the fact that Italian political debates are not strongly shaped by territorial cleavages, except for two of the special regions in the north. In addition, the main political parties have a deeply centralized structure. In the last two decades, the most visible exception has been Veneto. The Venetian *statuto* of 2012 puts strong emphasis on the 'self-government of the Venetian people', which is supposeed to be in accordance with 'the characters and traditions of its history' (Article 2(1) of the *statuto*).[28] The regional legislature actively promoted the recognition of the Venetian people as a national minority under the Framework Convention for the Protection of National Minorities, asked to call for a referendum on secession and adopted a law granting special status to the regional flag. These moves have all been declared unconstitutional by the Constitutional Court.[29] They have been criticized in their attempt to entrench the position of Veneto as a separated community, to the detriment of the principles of unity and indivisibility of the Republic (Article 5 of the Constitution).[30]

The five special *statuti*, which were enacted between the late 1940s and the early 1970s, do not generally contain any identity-related statements. An attempt to entrench some references

27 See critical analysis by Emanuele Rossi, 'Principi e diritti nei nuovi Statuti regionali' (2005) *Rivista di diritto costituzionale* 51.
28 See Andrea Morrone, 'Avanti popolo … regionale' (2012) *Quaderni costituzionali* 615.
29 Constitutional Court, judgments no. 118/2015, 81/2018, and 183/2018.
30 See Giovanni Tarli Barbieri, 'Regione Veneto o "Repubblica di San Marco"? Riflessioni sparse a partire dalla sent. 183/2018 della Corte costituzionale' (2019) *le Regioni* 186.

to subnational identities in the special *statuti* can be found in three proposals for amending the *statuto* of Valle d'Aosta/Vallée d'Aoste that were discussed by the local Regional Council. The same happened when civic participation processes, also known as the *Convenzione/Konvent*, were organized in the Autonomous Province of Bolzano/South Tyrol in order to submit proposals for amending the *statuto* of Trentino-Alto Adige/South Tyrol. The *Convenzione/Konvent*, in which pro-independence extremist groups actively took part, also suggested that a right to self-determination be entrenched in the *statuto*.[31] The *statuto*-amending process is currently frozen; consequently, these claims have not been pursued further.

12.4.2 Organization of powers

Since 1999, the organization of powers in the regions has been based on a quasi-parliamentary model that makes the Italian system unique among European federal and regional states. Retracing the legal foundations of this peculiar model highlights the inherent limits of the regional *statuto*-making power. As mentioned earlier (Section 12.2.1), the *statuti* are supposed to regulate 'the form of government and basic principles for the organization of the region and the conduct of its business'.

However, the Constitution favours, more or less implicitly, a specific model. Based on a joint reading of Articles 122(5) and 126(3) of the Constitution, amended in 1999, unless the *statuto* provides otherwise, both the president of the region and the Regional Council are directly elected. If the Regional Council passes a motion of no confidence, the president has to resign *and the legislature is dissolved too*. The same happens if the president is removed, dies or resigns voluntarily: a snap election is called to elect a new president and the Regional Council. Furthermore, a directly elected president has the power to appoint and to revoke the members of the *Giunta*, as the regional executive is known (Article 121(4) of the Constitution). As stated by the Constitutional Court, the '"normal" form of government' is based on a strong president; the effect is a 'radical simplification of the regional political system and a unification of the majority around the President'.[32]

The Constitution does not mandate the adoption of such a model; however, it is quite difficult for regional lawmakers to depart from it. By the time the regional legislatures started discussing the new *statuti*, the direct election system had already been applied in 2000 pursuant to a transitional rule. Furthermore, the system seems to have enhanced the visibility and institutional strength of the regional governments. Restoring a system based on the election of the president by the Regional Council, as had been the case since 1970, was not perceived as a viable option.[33]

Aside from the relationship between the president and the Regional Council, the Constitution also sets explicit limits on the scope of the regional *statuto*-making power. According to Article 121(1) of the Constitution, the institutional system of the regions is based on three organs: the president, the executive (*Giunta*) and the Regional Council. No *statuto* can do without these organs, which are indefectible.[34] Neither can regional councils be renamed parliaments due to

---

31 See Matteo Cosulich, 'Parallele divergenti? Modello, metodo e merito nei lavori della Convenzione bolzanina e della Consulta trentina' (2018) *Osservatorio AIC* 6(3) 153 <www.osservatorioaic.it> accessed 3 May 2020.

32 Constitutional Court, judgment no. 2/2004.

33 See Andrea Pertici, 'Art. 122' in Bifulco, Celotto and Olivetti (n 7), 2424, at 2435.

34 See Lino Panzeri, 'Organi "non necessari" e forma di governo regionale: brevi note sul tema in riferimento ai nuovi statuti' (2006) *Giurisprudenza costituzionale* 4739.

the unique status of the Parliament within Italy's constitutional order.[35] However, there is some room for institutional differentiation. Many *statuti* have established bodies in charge of monitoring compliance of regional draft laws with the *statuto* itself (see Section 12.6). Other *statuti* have tried to counterbalance the institutional pre-eminence of the president by strengthening the rights of the political minorities. In this vein, the *statuto* of Tuscany introduced an opposition spokesperson (*portavoce dell'opposizione*) in the Regional Council. Although this innovation was not particularly successful, the Tuscan model is quite unique in that the regulation of opposition groups has long been an unfinished business in Italy.[36]

As mentioned in Section 12.3, the electoral system and the cases of ineligibility and incompatibility of the president, the other members of the executive and the regional councillors are not regulated in the *statuto* but in a regional law. The content of the regional electoral laws has to be 'in accordance with the fundamental principles established by a law of the Republic that also establishes the term of elective offices' (Article 122(1) of the Constitution). Strong homogeneity requirements between the electoral laws for the regional councils and the electoral law for the Italian Parliament—for instance, the adoption of proportional representation—have never been entrenched, even before 1999.[37] Since the amendment of the Constitution in that year, increasing diversity among the electoral laws of the 15 ordinary regions has been the rule rather than the exception.

Slightly greater institutional diversity can be found in the five special *statuti*.[38] After the adoption of constitutional law no. 2/2001 (see Section 12.3), Sicily, Sardinia, Friuli-Venezia Giulia[39] and the Autonomous Province of Trento opted for the direct election model. In turn, Valle d'Aosta/Vallée d'Aoste and the Autonomous Province of Bolzano/South Tyrol did not depart from the indirect election system. This choice was clearly related to the presence of linguistic minorities and ethno-regionalist parties and the need to avoid an excessive simplification of the political process. With respect to Valle d'Aosta/Vallée d'Aoste, the persistence of the indirect election model is also due to the significant partisan fragmentation resulting from the proportional voting system that has been in force since 1962.[40] In the Autonomous Province of Bolzano, the indirect election model is related to the consociational democratic model in which the three linguistic groups (Italians, Germans and Ladins) have been involved.[41] Additionally, since 2003, the presidents of the Autonomous Province of Trento and the Autonomous Province of Bolzano/South Tyrol have rotated in the post of president of Trentino-Alto Adige/South Tyrol every two and a half years.

---

35 Constitutional Court, judgment no. 106/2002.

36 See Pier Luigi Petrillo, 'Nuovi statuti regionali e opposizione' (2005) *le Regioni* 829, at 842–4.

37 Under the previous wording of Article 122 of the Constitution, the electoral system for the regional councils was regulated 'by a law of the Republic'. See also Alessio Rauti, 'Il sistema di elezione dei Consigli regionali fra antiche e nuove questioni di "topografia costituzionale"' (2015) *le Regioni* 567, at 573–80.

38 As mentioned earlier (Section 12.2.1), the *statuto* of Trentino-Alto Adige/South Tyrol contains provisions that apply to the regional government, the Autonomous Province of Trento, and the Autonomous Province of Bolzano.

39 In Friuli-Venezia Giulia, an attempt to stick to the indirect election model was defeated in a referendum in September 2002.

40 See Valerio Onida, 'Aspetti dell'autonomia della Regione Valle d'Aosta' (1971) *Rivista trimestrale di diritto pubblico* 261.

41 See Günther Pallaver, 'South Tyrol's Consociational Democracy: Between Political Claim and Social Reality' in Jens Woelk, Francesco Palermo and Joseph Marko (eds), *Tolerance through Law: Self Governance and Group Rights in South Tyrol* (Brill 2008) 303; Guido Panzano, 'Power-sharing Executives in Northern Ireland and South Tyrol: Theories, Structures, Practices and Political Stability' (2018) 1(2) *Rivista di Diritti comparati* 136 <www.dirritticomparati.it> accessed 3 May 2020.

The extent of the power of the *statuti* to regulate the regional form of government was significantly shaped—and, in fact, undermined—by the emergency decrees adopted in the early 2010s when the economic and financial crisis was at its highest. Decree-law no. 138/2011 mandated all 20 regions and the autonomous provinces to reduce the size of their regional councils and executives. These emergency measures, which were adopted amidst growing discontent with the regional system, were challenged before the Constitutional Court. The Court found them to be unconstitutional insofar as they applied to the special regions and the autonomous provinces of Trento and Bolzano. As the special *statuti* have the form of constitutional laws, a decree-law cannot trigger their modification. By contrast, the Court upheld the challenged provision insofar as it applied to the 15 ordinary regions. The Court did not deny that it is for the *statuti* to regulate the regional form of government and, consequently, to determine the size of the regional organs. However, the principle of equal representation, derived from the right to equal suffrage referred to in Article 48 of the Constitution, would be contradicted if the size of regional councils were to vary too much. Therefore, a measure adopted 'in the framework of the general purpose of limiting public expenditure' was found to implement a principle of equal representation of constitutional significance and to be compatible with the *statuto*-making power of the ordinary regions.[42]

12.4.3 Fundamental rights

As mentioned previously in Section 12.4.1, the short-lived enthusiasm for second-generation *statuti* led a number of regional legislatures to codify regional bills of rights in the text of the new *statuti*. This practice was questioned, however, when the Italian state government challenged the *statuti* of Tuscany, Emilia-Romagna and Umbria before the Constitutional Court. Some provisions in these charters recognized certain domestic partnerships, including sex-same partnerships. The central government claimed that such recognition clashed with the value, entrenched in the Constitution of the Italian Republic, of the family based on marriage (Article 29 of the Constitution). For example, under their *statuti* the legislatures of these regions would have been allowed to consider, as far as housing policies were concerned, not only married couples but also unmarried ones. Since regional legislatures were previously not supposed to rule on such issues under the heading of either 'form of government', 'organisation' or '[regional] business', provisions concerning these subjects were not within their competence. In this way, a seemingly abstract dispute on regional law had significant in repercussions for controversial questions concerning relationships, marriage and family law. These cases could be regarded as the expression of a conflict between a conservative government and three centre-left regional governments. However, they also reflected a clash as to what the new *statuti* would stand for, whether basic charters regulating the institutional systems of the regions or something resembling regional constitutions with significant substantive content.

In judgments 372/2004, 378/2004 and 379/2004, the Constitutional Court avoided the difficult issues involved. It did not declare the provisions in the *statuti* unlawful, but it interpreted them in a way that greatly diminished their meaning, as a way of avoiding taking sides in the debate over the recognition of domestic partnerships. The Court theorized the existence of a new kind of propositions that could be contained in the *statuti*. It defined these as 'an expression of the various political convictions in the regional community'. Their function, the Court said,

---

42 Constitutional Court, judgment no. 198/2012. See also Giovanni Tarli Barbieri, 'La potestà legislative regionale in materia elettorale alla luce delle più recenti novità legislative e giurisprudenziali' (2013) *le Regioni* 97, at 109–12.

is to express those convictions at the highest legal level of the region. However, since their significance does not affect the legal system—they just make clear the dominant feelings in that particular region—they have no legal force, their function being properly (and only) 'political' and 'cultural'. The Court distinguished these cultural statements from 'programmatic norms', a doctrinal category which enjoyed great popularity between the time when the Constitution came into force in 1948 and the beginning of the Court's activity in 1956.[43]

In its judgments of 2004, the Italian Constitutional Court held that, since the *statuti* are not regional constitutions, their provisions could not be considered to be programmatic norms. Whereas the Constitution of 1948 is the highest source of law in the Italian legal system—not only in hierarchical but also in interpretive terms—the *statuti* are sub-constitutional sources whose scope is determined by the Constitution itself. Their non-prescriptive norms are neither able to give direction to the legislature nor to influence interpretation; in short, *statuti* are not regional constitutions.[44] If regional legislatures were to implement them, they would violate the national Constitution. As stated by the Court, such provisions, when contained in regional charters, have 'no legal effect', 'a regional law pretending to implement them would be illegitimate'.[45]

Not all provisions concerning rights and principles may be regarded as merely cultural statements. In a subsequent judgment, no. 365/2007, the Constitutional Court scrutinized a regional ordinary law of Sardinia which set up a regional assembly entrusted with writing a draft for the new *statuto* (*Consulta per il nuovo statuto di autonomia e sovranità del popolo sardo*). According to that law, this *Consulta* had to take into account 'the principles and characters of regional identity … autonomy and sovereignty; … to promote the rights of Sardinian citizens with regard to the specific traits of the island … to define autonomy and regional sovereignty'. The Italian government questioned the constitutionality of the law before the Court. In the government's view, these provisions would clash both with the principle of equality and with the constitutional definition of the Republic as 'one and indivisible' (Article 5 of the Constitution). Faced with such strong arguments, the Sardinian defence claimed that the legislation in question could be interpreted as a collection of merely political statements, thus making it 'basically harmless' and not illegitimate. The Court firmly rejected the analogy, since the law on which it rendered its judgment was aimed at setting up a procedure to revise the regional *statuto*—that was not the same as the cultural statements inserted among the general principles in a regional charter.[46]

12.4.4 Policy principles

Provisions in the second-generation *statuti* often refer to policy principles. In many respects, these provisions have followed the same path as the regional bills of rights.

Distinct arguments apply to the five special *statuti*. The scope of application of these *statuti* has often been extended due to the work of the *commissioni paritetiche*, which are mixed committees composed of representatives of the central government and representatives of the regional government in equal parts. The *commissioni paritetiche* are in charge of the elaboration of the draft implementing decrees of the special *statuti*. In practice, they have played an important role in implementing specific provisions of the *statuti*, including detailed regulation of regional financial

---

43 See John Clarke Adams and Paolo Barile, 'The Implementation of the Italian Constitution' (1953) 47 *The American Political Science Review* 61, at 63.
44 See Tarchi and Bessi (n 13), at 2465.
45 Constitutional Court, judgment no. 365/2007.
46 Constitutional Court, judgment no. 365/2007.

autonomy and some specific policies. This is particularly true of the Autonomous Province of Bolzano/South Tyrol.[47]

12.5 Multilevel constitutionalism

12.5.1 *The relation between the Constitution and the* statuti

As stated previously (see Sections 12.2.1 and 12.4.3), the scope of the *statuto*-making power is limited. Fundamental rights protection is mostly reserved to the Constitution, which also has a friendly attitude towards international law, including European Union law. Article 117(2), which regulates the distribution of legislative competences between the state and the ordinary regions, confers on the Italian Parliament the exclusive power to determine the basic standards of protection of civil and social rights throughout the national territory (including, under certain conditions, the five special regions).[48]

A long-standing flaw in the Italian model of regional state is that the regions, at least at first glance, are excluded from state lawmaking and policymaking. Although the Constitution defines the Senate as a representative assembly 'elected on a regional basis' (Article 57(1)), the only significant implication of this provision is that the constituencies for electing the Senate must coincide with the regions. Meanwhile, an executive-centred system of bilateral conferences has gradually developed.[49] The regions are also not involved in constitution-amending procedures, although five regions may trigger a constitutional referendum if the two chambers adopt a draft constitutional amendment (Article 138(2) of the Constitution). As regards the five special regions and the autonomous provinces, their *statuti* give their presidents a right to participate in the meetings of the state government with voice but without vote.[50]

12.5.2 *The impact of the international and European legal space on subnational constitutionalism in Italy*

Italy's membership in the European Union (EU) has affected the constitutional distribution of powers and competences. This is one of the effects of the well-known territorial blindness of the European Union.[51] Under EU law, each Member State is the only entity responsible to comply with EU law requirements. On several occasions, the Court of Justice of the European Union has ignored domestic power divisions when dealing with cases of non-compliance. This has forced Italian actors to modify the original distribution of powers enshrined in the Constitution

47 See Francesco Palermo, 'Ruolo e natura delle commissioni paritetiche e delle norme di attuazione' in Joseph Marko, Sergio Ortino and Francesco Palermo, *L'ordinamento speciale della Provincia autonoma di Bolzano* (Cedam 2001) 826; Roberto Bin, 'L'autonomia e i rapporti tra esecutivo, legislativo e le commissioni paritetiche' in Andrea Di Michele, Francesco Palermo and Günther Pallaver (eds), *1992. Fine di un conflitto. Dieci anni dalla chiusura della questione sudtirolese* (il Mulino 2003) 205.
48 See Cesare Pinelli, 'Sui "livelli essenziali delle prestazioni concernenti i diritti civili e sociali" (art. 117, co. 2, lett. m, Cost.)' (2002) *Diritto pubblico* 881, at 893.
49 See Ilenia Ruggiu, *Contro la Camera delle Regioni. Istituzioni e prassi della rappresentanza territoriale* (Jovene 2006).
50 See Article 21(3) of the *statuto* of Sicily, Article 47(2) of the *statuto* of Sardinia, Article 44(3) of the *statuto* of Valle d'Aosta/Vallée d'Aoste, Article 44 of the *statuto* of Friuli-Venezia Giulia and Articles 40(2) and 52(4) of the *statuto* of Trentino-Alto Adige/South Tyrol.
51 See comprehensive analysis by Giuseppe Martinico, 'The Impact of "Regional Blindness" on the Italian Regional State' in Elke Cloots, Geert De Baere and Stefan Sottiaux (eds), *Federalism in the European Union* (Hart 2012) 362.

in order to avoid EU penalties.[52] The Constitutional Court has generally been lenient towards adaptations to the list of legislative competences set forth in Article 117 of the Constitution. This, in turn, has contributed to strengthening long-standing centralizing trends. The Court seemed to allow for the possibility that EU law requirements may lead to a shift in the original distribution of competences.[53] At the same time, however, the Court stressed the need to comply with the fundamental, unamendable principles of the Italian constitutional system, the so-called 'counter-limits'. Accordingly, the implementation of EU law must take the Member States' internal structure (be it centralized, decentralized or federal) into account.[54] In 2001, the substitution power of the state, a key tool for ensuring effective implementation of supranational law, was entrenched in Article 120(2) of the Constitution.

Discussion about the power of the regions to develop international relations surfaced as early as the 1970s. In the absence of a clear constitutional and legislative framework, the regions engaged in direct contacts with subnational units in other states. The international activities of the regions could be systematized thanks to the case law of the Constitutional Court. Article 117(9) of the Constitution, which was part of the 2001 amendment, formally entrenched the power of the regions to conclude agreements with states (*accordi*) and subnational units of other states (*intese*): such power can be exercised 'in the areas falling within their responsibilities ... in the cases and according to the forms laid down by state legislation'.[55]

Finally, law no. 234/2012 has enabled the legislatures of the regions and the autonomous provinces to take part in the Early Warning System under the Protocol on the Role of National Parliaments in the European Union. Regional legislatures can send their remarks to the Italian Parliament for the purposes of the subsidiarity control mechanism.

12.6 Judicial review

In the Italian legal system, regional *statuti* have the status of ordinary laws. However, regional laws containing provisions incompatible with the *statuti* can be found to violate Article 123 of the Constitution and, consequently, be struck down by the Constitutional Court. As the Court stated, if a regional law violates the *statuto*, 'it indirectly violates Article 123 of the Constitution'.[56] The case law of the Constitutional Court related to such controversies is not particularly rich.[57] In its judgments, the Court either described the *statuti* as hierarchically superior to the other regional laws or held that the discipline of specific objects, for instance, the regional 'form of government', is reserved for them.[58]

When the new regional *statuti* were being elaborated, the problem of ensuring compliance with their provisions immediately arose. All but one of the new *statuti* in the ordinary regions[59] have provided for the establishment of a new body of control, usually called a *Consulta statutaria*

52 See, for instance, Paola Bilancia, Francesco Palermo and Ornella Porchia, 'The European Fitness of Italian Regions' (2010) 2(2) *Perspectives on Federalism* 122 <www.on-federalism.eu> accessed 3 May 2020.
53 Constitutional Court, judgments no. 399/1987 and 224/1994.
54 Constitutional Court, judgment no. 126/1996.
55 See Paolo Caretti, 'Potere estero e ruolo "comunitario" delle Regioni nel nuovo Titolo V della Costituzione' (2003) *le Regioni* 555, at 556–9.
56 Constitutional Court, judgment no. 119/2006. See also judgments no. 48/1983, 993/1998, 119/2006, 68/2010 and 188/2011.
57 See Roberto Romboli, 'Articolo 57' in Paolo Caretti, Massimo Carli and Emanuele Rossi (eds), *Statuto della Regione Toscana. Commentario* (Giappichelli 2005) 283, at 284.
58 See Francesca Bailo, 'La Consulta statutaria' in Pasquale Costanzo (ed.), *Lineamenti di diritto costituzionale della Regione Liguria* (Giappichelli 2011) 418, at 418–19.
59 The exception being the *statuto* of Marche.

or *Commissione di garanzia statutaria*, which is charged with the task of giving advice on possible conflicts between regional laws and the *statuti*.[60] When one of these bodies issues a negative opinion on a draft law, an obligation arises for the Regional Council to review the regional law at stake, which can then be adopted a second time. The task of these control bodies is to issue non-binding advisory opinions during the lawmaking process.[61] This is because regions lack the authority to establish regional constitutional courts. The Constitutional Court is the only organ that can perform judicial review of legislation and strike down laws. In the earliest stage of Italian regionalism, a High Court for Sicily (*Alta Corte per la Regione siciliana*) operated by virtue of Articles 24 to 26 of the special Sicilian *statuto*. However, soon after the Constitutional Court started its activity, its existence was deemed to be incompatible with the centralized system of constitutional adjudication regulated by the Constitution.[62]

A distinct question is how the consultative bodies should deal with the fundamental principles of the *statuti* (see Section 12.4.3) when scrutinizing the consistency of regional laws with the *statuti*. There is no norm of constitutional law that prevents them from doing so. The possibility of reviewing the regional laws and of expressing negative advice in relation of them in the light of what the Constitutional Court has labelled as 'cultural statements' could signal that the general provisions of the *statuti* are not completely devoid of legal effect. It could also represent an example of real—although indirect—conflict between the Constitution and the fundamental regional provisions, as they cause a potential obstacle for the legislative function entrusted to the regional legislatures by the national Constitution.

On the whole, the legislative implementation of the provisions in the *statuti* has not fully measured up to early expectations. In four regions, the legislature has never established the body of control. In Calabria and Liguria, bodies of control were established only to be later suppressed. Furthermore, regional lawmakers have generally been reluctant to turn to the bodies of control for advice.[63]

12.7 Conclusion

The regional *statuti* are hardly irrelevant: they lay the foundations of the institutional system in the regions and occasionally reveal a certain willingness to experimenting with innovative solutions. In procedural terms, they result from discussion and deliberation in the Regional Council, and a possible subsequent step is a regional referendum on the draft *statuto*.[64] However, the *statuti* suffer from limited visibility in both political and legal discourse. In the aftermath of constitutional reforms in 1999 and 2001, there were expectations that the drafting of second-generation *statuti* in the 15 ordinary regions would play a key role in the transition of Italy from regionalism to (quasi-) federalism. Some leading judgments of the Constitutional Court in the following years showed that such expectations were based, at least to some extent, on mistaken assumptions. The *statuti* are not regional constitutions, and their objects are inherently limited. They contain provisions concerning the regional institutions, civic participation, and the system of legal sources, but they hardly qualify as constitutions in the sense of the Introduction to this book. This does not mean that the *statuti* cannot contribute to the improvement of regional

---

60 See, for example, Article 57 of the *statuto* of Tuscany, Article 69 of the *statuto* of Emilia-Romagna, and Article 57 of the *statuto* of Campania.
61 See judgment no. 378/2004 of the Constitutional Court.
62 Constitutional Court, judgments no. 38/1957 and 6/1970.
63 See Paolo Caretti, 'Gli organi di garanzia statutaria a un bivio: o riforma o progressiva scomparsa per desuetudine' (2017) *Istituzioni del federalismo* 909, at 915–17.
64 This is not true of the five special *statuti* (see Section 12.2.2).

governance. For example, bearing in mind the strong position of the president, from which it is quite difficult to depart, the *statuti* can strengthen the powers of the legislature and possibly the rights of political minorities. They can also focus on the relationship between the regional government and local government authorities, a constant concern in Italy.

These distinctive traits of the Italian case can be seen to be related to a deeply ingrained logic of post-war European multi-tiered systems.[65] The Italian constitutional system is based on a centralized model of constitutional adjudication. This is of the greatest relevance for a constitutional analysis of the regional *statuti*: the existence of one centralized Constitutional Court is no less relevant than the fact that the *statuti* are not regional constitutions. In this respect, the controversy regarding the regional bodies of control, is particularly revealing.[66]

The wavering attitude of the regional political elites also deserves attention in order to understand the evolution of the *statuti*. Due to the great popularity of federalism and decentralization in the 1990s and 2000s (with limited awareness of the differences between them), it is beyond doubt that in some of the Italian regions there were plans and expectations that could have given rise to a kind of subnational constitutionalism. However, the role that the *statuti* would play in this regard was not entirely clear. The *statuti* often open with magniloquent preambles, whose practical implications have not been considered carefully. Moreover, the occasional attempts to exploit regional identities have been inspired, more often than not, by the pursuit of other claims, for instance, in order to negotiate for greater autonomy, most notably financial autonomy.

In subsequent years, the lack of a strong consensus on what the Italian regional model stands for has become more and more evident.[67] 'Federalist' enthusiasm in the 2000s was followed by a strong anti-regional backlash in the wake of the economic and financial crisis, as the case of the reduction of the size of the regional legislatures reveals (see Section 12.4.2). In the last two years, the debate has been marked by a strong push towards asymmetric regionalism, but the difficult handling of the coronavirus crisis may well be a prelude to another shift in public opinion. This uncertainty obviously impacts the position of the *statuti* within the regions and, more generally, within the Italian constitutional order.

A distinctive strand of subnational constitutionalism might be emerging in two special regions, Valle d'Aosta/Vallée d'Aoste and Trentino-Alto Adige/South Tyrol. This has to do, among other things, with the presence of linguistic minorities and of political parties that bring together such minorities, such as the Union Valdôtaine and the Südtiroler Volkspartei. The mutual influence between the regional autonomous regime—including intergovernmental fiscal relations and the protection of linguistic minorities—and the local political system has been described as a 'double-sided multiplying effect'.[68] However, due to the specific features of the special *statuti*, this peculiar constitutional environment is not properly reflected in the fundamental charters of Valle d'Aosta/Vallée d'Aoste and Trentino-Alto Adige/South Tyrol (see Sections 12.2.2 and 12.4.1).

---

65 Differences with the United States are striking: see Tom Ginsburg and Eric A. Posner, 'Subconstitutionalism' (2010) 62 *Stanford Law Review* 1583, at 1584.

66 See Andrea Cardone, 'Gli organi di garanzia statutaria tra suggestioni del diritto comparato, "paletti" della Corte costituzionale ed apodittiche ricostruzioni del sistema delle fonti', in Massimo Carli, Guido Carpani and Arturo Siniscalchi (eds), *I nuovi statuti delle regioni ordinarie* (il Mulino 2006) 277.

67 See Alessandro Morelli and Annamaria Poggi, 'Le Regioni per differenziare, lo Stato per unire. A ciascuno il suo' (2020) 5(1) *Diritti regionali* <www.dirittiregionali.it> accessed 3 May 2020.

68 See Paolo Carrozza, 'Nazione', *Digesto delle discipline pubblicistiche*, vol. 10 (Utet 1995) 126, at 156.

13

SUBNATIONAL CONSTITUTIONALISM IN MALAYSIA

Weak states in a strong federation

Richard Foo and Hoong Phun ('HP') Lee

13.1 Context

Malaysia presents the conundrum of 13 states which are faced with a strong central government in a federation that is also complicated by a significant asymmetry of powers between 11 original states and two later states with greater autonomy. The centralization of power is such that the federation often appears to function like a unitary state. In such a system, the state constitutions—while clearly established and accepted—play only a limited role. The imperative for a highly centralized federation also means that the states have very little freedom or 'constitutional space'[1] to design their own constitutional arrangements.

13.1.1 General country information

The federation comprises 13 states and three federal territories located on two separate landmasses.

Eleven states—Perlis, Kedah, Penang, Perak, Selangor, Negeri Sembilan, Melaka, Johor, Pahang, Terengganu and Kelantan—are located in 'Peninsular Malaysia' (or 'Malaya'), as are the federal territories of Kuala Lumpur (the national capital) and Putrajaya (the federal administrative centre). Two other 'Borneo states'—Sabah and Sarawak—are located in 'East Malaysia', with the federal territory of Labuan situated offshore from Sabah.

The country was created in two steps during the British decolonization process after the Second World War. In 1957, the Peninsular states became an independent nation as the Federation of Malaya. Then, in 1963, the Borneo states simultaneously gained independence and combined with the Peninsular states to form an expanded federation renamed Malaysia.[2]

---

1 Robert F. Williams and G. Alan Tarr, 'Subnational Constitutional Space: A View from the States, Provinces, Regions, Lander and Cantons' in G. Alan Tarr, Robert F. Williams and Josef Marko (eds), *Federalism, Subnational Constitutions, and Minority Rights* (Praeger 2004) 3.
2 Singapore also joined Malaysia but separated in 1965: text to n 31.

 DOI: 10.4324/9781003052111-13

The federation is not large in terms of territory and population. Its area is about 330,800 km²
and its population includes some 29 million citizens.[3] Most of the population (80 per cent)
resides in Peninsular Malaysia. With 11 of 13 states and the main population, political and economic centres all located in Peninsular Malaysia, the federation is 'Malaya-centric'.

13.1.2 Territory-based, multicultural and multinational federation

The federation is primarily a territory-based federation. It was not intentionally established
along ethno-cultural lines. The Malaysian citizenry consists of four major ethnic groups: the
Malays (56 per cent); the Chinese (23 per cent); the Indians (7 per cent); and the 'native' people
groups from Sabah and Sarawak (13 per cent).[4] The populations in all states are more or less
mixed.

Nonetheless, different groups predominate in Peninsular Malaysia and in East Malaysia.

The dominant group in Peninsular Malaysia are the Malays, who are collectively Muslims.
Historically, Peninsular Malaysia is known as the Malay Peninsula. Nine states (the 'Malay
States')[5] still have traditional Malay-Islamic monarchs (the 'Malay Rulers') included within their
modern constitutions.

In East Malaysia, the natives constitute the majority. The different groups in Sabah and
Sarawak have their own languages, culture and religions. Many natives are Christians. Insofar as
the federation recognizes the ethno-cultural and political uniqueness posed by these states, each
may be regarded as a distinct 'nation' within the federation.

While Malaysian citizenship is common to all groups, the Malays and the natives are regarded
as the country's indigenous peoples. They have a 'special position' within the constitutional system which gives them certain privileges. This feature resulted from a so-called 'social contract'
negotiated between the Malay and the non-Malay communities before Malaya's independence
in 1957, and it later included the natives when Malaysia was formed.

13.1.3 Consociational politics and government

Malaysian politics is mainly race-based. Political parties, however, tend to form coalitions which
offer consociational government to accommodate the interests of all groups.

A single coalition continuously governed the country during the first six decades. From 1957
to 2018, the Barisan Nasional ('BN' or National Front) held power both as the federal government and as the state government in most of the states for most of the time.[6] However, in the
pivotal 14th general election held in 2018, BN finally lost power and the Pakatan Harapan
('Harapan' or Hope Alliance) and their allies formed government at the centre and in eight
states.

During the BN era, same-party rule at both federal and state levels had a constricting effect
on federalism, especially as the federal government also became more authoritarian. Harapan
promised to 'revive the true spirit of federalism'[7] but, in February 2020, the Harapan

---

3 Mohd Uzir Mahidin, 'Current Population Estimates, Malaysia, 2018–2019' (Department of Statistics Malaysia,
    15 July 2019) <https://www.dosm.gov.my/v1/index.php?r=column/cthemeByCat&cat=155&bul_id=aW
    JZRkJ4UEdKcUZpT2tVT090Snpydz09&menu_id=L0pheU43NWJwRWVSZklWdzQ4TlhUUT09>
    accessed 28 November 2019.
4 Ibid.
5 States other than Penang and Melaka.
6 BN began as the Alliance (1952–73).
7 *Buku Harapan* (Pakatan Harapan 2018) 58.

government collapsed when defectors realigned with BN and other parties to form a new federal government. Implications for federalism currently remain fluid.

13.1.4 *Highly centralized, asymmetric federation*

The federal system is governed by 14 documents: the Federal Constitution and 13 state constitutions.

The Federal Constitution determines the federal-state distribution of powers. Schedule 9 prescribes three detailed legislative lists: the 'Federal List' for exclusive federal powers, the 'State List' for exclusive state powers and the 'Concurrent List' for shared powers. Sabah and Sarawak have extra powers under the lists. The states hold the residual power but the lists are already comprehensive.[8] As expected, the federation holds more, and the more important, powers, although the states also have significant powers over land, agriculture, forestry, local government, and Islamic law and native law matters.[9] However, other provisions in the Federal Constitution (including those establishing the intergovernmental councils)[10] may dictate whether or how the states exercise some powers. Uniform federal law may also override some state powers.[11] In fiscal terms, the federation collects about 90 per cent of all government revenue before intergovernmental transfers and maintains roughly 85 per cent of expenditures.[12]

The highly centralized federation originated from a plan to govern pre-independence Malaya as a unitary state. When that project failed for political reasons, the next best arrangement was a highly centralized federal system and, later, a similar federation. This evolution occurred over four constitutional stages, undergoing processes of both aggregation and devolution.

In 1946, the British aggregated the 11 political units in Malaya to form the Malayan Union.[13] However, the Malays opposed this arrangement because it ended the prior legal fiction that each Malay State was a sovereign state (in reality, a colonial 'adviser' governed the state) and ceded full sovereignty to the British. They also contended that wider citizenship for the non-Malays threatened the Malay 'proprietorship' of Malaya.

Hence, in 1948, the Federation of Malaya ('the 1948 Federation') replaced the Malayan Union.[14] With Malay State sovereignty reinstated, a federal system accommodated the nine states. However, this 'federation' was 'almost as unitary as the Malayan Union'.[15] The notional distribution of powers gave the colonial central government near-complete powers, and essentially left each Malay State with only powers over parochial matters of Islam and Malay custom.[16] The inter-communal issues were separately resolved by guaranteeing the Malays a 'special position' while safeguarding 'the legitimate interests of other communities'.[17]

The transition to a democratic independent Federation of Malaya ('the 1957 Federation') forced the creation of a 'true' federation. Prior events predetermined the preservation of the

---

8 Colonial Office, *Report of the Federation of Malaya Constitutional Commission* (1957) para 121 (Reid Report).
9 Text to nn 115, 117.
10 National Land Council, National Council for Local Government and National Finance Council: Federal Constitution arts 91, 95A, 108.
11 Federal Constitution art 76.
12 George Anderson, *Fiscal Federalism: A Comparative Introduction* (Oxford University Press 2010) 17, 21.
13 *Malayan Union and Singapore: Statement of Policy on Future Constitution* (Cmd 6724, 1946). Previously, Penang, Melaka and Singapore formed the Straits Settlements.
14 Federation of Malaya Agreement 1948 (FMA).
15 Ronald L. Watts, *New Federations: Experiments in the Commonwealth* (Oxford University Press 1966) 25.
16 Reid Report paras 23–7.
17 FMA cl 19(1).

nine Malay States. However, a federation 'based on Parliamentary democracy' required not only turning the Rulers into Westminster-style constitutional monarchs but also giving the states 'a measure of autonomy',[18] since politically dissimilar governments might be elected at the two levels of the system. Thus, the new constitution devolved some real powers to the states. All states acquired the same degree of autonomy. Nonetheless, state autonomy was restricted because 'a strong central government' remained 'essential' to the country's economic development.[19] The constitution also reinforced the Malay identity based on 'race, religion and royalty'. Besides the elements of the Rulers and the 'special position',[20] Malay became the national language[21] and Islam the established 'religion of the Federation'.[22]

Another aggregation in 1963 admitted Sabah and Sarawak (and Singapore) for the formation of Malaysia,[23] and the federation finally accommodated an asymmetry of powers between the original and the new states. Singapore, already self-governing and prosperous, retained greater autonomy especially over its revenue and free port and accepted having fewer seats in the federal legislature than was proportionate to its population.[24] However, resource-rich Sabah and Sarawak were underdeveloped and lacked democratic self-government. To protect their interests, these states insisted on special conditions, the so-called 'Eighteen/Twenty Points'. The natives too were guaranteed the 'special position'. The states acquired: certain freedoms from Islam as the established religion and Malay as the official language; power to exercise immigration controls; greater autonomy over local matters;[25] and a disproportionately higher representation in the federal legislature.[26] Together, Sabah, Sarawak and Singapore were allocated more than one-third of all lower house seats, enabling them to block constitutional amendments.[27] Certain amendments also required the states' agreement.[28] A separate High Court for Sabah and Sarawak would provide judicial protection.[29] Malaya, Singapore, Sabah and Sarawak signed the 'Malaysia Agreement',[30] and the revised constitution, incorporating those conditions, became the Federal Constitution.

In 1965, Singapore was expelled from the federation after it would not accommodate itself to 'the basic political and constitutional structure of Malaya'.[31] The central government soon also regarded the guarantees of autonomy to Sabah and Sarawak as inimical to nation-building,[32] but

---

18 Reid Report para 3(i).
19 Reid Report paras 15.
20 Federal Constitution art 153.
21 Federal Constitution art 152.
22 Federal Constitution art 3.
23 Poh-Ling Tan, 'From Malaya To Malaysia' in Andrew Harding and H.P. Lee (eds), *Constitutional Landmarks in Malaysia* (LexisNexis 2007) 25.
24 Gordon P. Means, *Malaysian Politics* (2nd edn, Hodder & Stoughton 1976) 297.
25 For details, see Tan (n 23).
26 Means (n 24), at 301.
27 Nicholas Fung Ngit Chung, 'The Constitutional Position of Sabah' in Francis A. Trindade and H.P. Lee (eds), *The Constitution of Malaysia: Further Perspectives and Developments* (Oxford University Press 1986) 92, at 109.
28 Federal Constitution Part XIIA.
29 Text to n 157.
30 Agreement concluded between the United Kingdom of Great Britain and Northern Ireland, the Federation of Malaya, North Borneo, Sarawak and Singapore (Cmnd 2094, 1963) (Malaysia Agreement or MA63).
31 Means (n 24), at 366.
32 Ibid. 380.

was able through political means to both circumvent the guarantees and keep those states within the federation.[33]

13.1.5 'Federation' and 'states'

Malaysia exhibits the essential features of a federation.[34] However, the strong centralization—in both constitutional law and 'operational reality'[35]—has led some commentators to question whether the states have any genuine autonomy for the system to be called a federation. Actually, the states do have their defined autonomy but the system demands 'close co-operation' between the federal and the state spheres of autonomy to facilitate national development.[36] Harding, who earlier called Malaysia 'a quasi-federation',[37] accepts that the states are 'only just able to maintain their measure of autonomy'.[38] Means concluded that 'the states have retained substantial powers and remained vigorous and autonomous components of the political system'.[39]

The federation has only two types of subnational units: the states and the federal territories. The latter have no constituent power and are not discussed here. The Federal Constitution designates the 13 states as 'States'.[40]

In terms of type, Sabah and Sarawak, despite their greater autonomy, are no different from a Peninsular state. However, a misconception exists that each is a sort of greater 'region' that is 'equal' to Peninsular Malaysia as a whole. Originally, reflecting the states' different origins leading to the Malaysia Agreement, Federal Constitution art 1(2) listed '[t]he States of the Federation' in three categories: '(a) the States of Malaya, namely [the eleven states]; (b) the Borneo States, namely, Sabah and Sarawak; and (c) the State of Singapore'. Four parties had agreed to create Malaysia, but they agreed that the three new states 'shall be federated with the existing *States* of the Federation of Malaya'.[41] After an amendment in 1976 streamlined art 1(2) by naming all 13 states in one alphabetical list, Sabah and Sarawak contended that this 'downgraded' them to 'mere states'. The Harapan government's attempt in 2019 to restore art 1(2) to its original form (without Singapore) failed to materialize; ironically, because opposition legislators from Sarawak refused to cooperate.[42] Political rhetoric continues to describe Sabah and Sarawak as 'equal partners' of Peninsular Malaysia.[43]

13.1.6 Contestations

Present-day contestations concerning federalism in Malaysia obviously are not about striving to establish the states as constitutional subnational entities, since they are already recognized as such

---

33 Ibid. 433; James Chin, 'Exporting the BN/UMNO model: Politics in Sabah and Sarawak' in Meredith L. Weiss (ed.), *Routledge Handbook of Contemporary Malaysia* (Routledge 2018) 83.
34 Ronald L. Watts, *Comparing Federal Systems* (2nd edn, McGill–Queen's University Press 1999) 7, 28.
35 Ibid. 14.
36 Reid Report para 83.
37 Andrew Harding, *Law, Government and the Constitution in Malaysia* (Kluwer 1996) 182.
38 Andrew Harding, *The Constitution of Malaysia: A Contextual Analysis* (Hart 2012) 159.
39 Gordon P. Means, *Malaysian Politics: The Second Generation* (Oxford University Press 1991) 296.
40 Federal Constitution art 1(2).
41 Malaysia Agreement art 1 (emphasis added).
42 Sharon Ling, 'Sarawak wants comprehensive constitutional amendments to safeguard state rights' (*The Star*, 30 April 2019) <https://www.thestar.com.my/news/nation/2019/04/30/sarawak-wants-comprehensive-constitutional-amendments-to-safeguard-state-rights> accessed 25 November 2019.
43 'In Kuching, PM raises failed "equal partner" constitutional amendment' (*Malaysiakini*, 17 September 2019) <https://www.malaysiakini.com/news/492167> accessed 25 November 2019.

within the system. With the central government politically weakened since 2008, debates have focused on decentralizing powers, whether by fulfilling existing state rights or by devolving more powers to the states.[44] Sabah and Sarawak are particularly aggrieved that their autonomy has been disregarded. Notwithstanding the federal government's recent ameliorations,[45] 'buyer's remorse' for having joined Malaysia and secessionist pressures are now apparent in those states.[46]

Yet, the contestations are mainly about enlarging the states' legislative-executive space, not their 'constitutional space'. Reflecting the relative unimportance of state constitutions to state autonomy in the Malaysian system, the states have not demanded greater freedom to decide their own constitutional arrangements.[47]

13.2 Autonomy

13.2.1 Content

The states' 'constitutional space' is governed by a framework set by the Federal Constitution. The Federal Constitution—which is 'the supreme law of the Federation'[48]—is very comprehensive in prescribing the political institutions and processes for both the federal and the state levels, and dictates the system's entire 'constitutional architecture'.[49] It sets the electoral system, with a single Election Commission that conducts both federal and state elections according to federal law.[50] It contains a bill of fundamental rights that states too must observe.[51] Part VI specifically deals with federal-state relations. The Schedule 9 federal-state distribution of powers gives the states a power to legislate on the 'Machinery of the State Government'.[52] However, state law is always subordinate to the Federal Constitution and to federal law. Any state law that is inconsistent with the Federal Constitution would be void and federal law prevails over any conflicting state law.[53] In fact, the states' power to enact their 'machinery of government' is subject to a basic model that the Federal Constitution prescribes for the states, which mirrors what it also provides for the federal level.

The federal-level arrangement consists of a constitutional monarchy, Westminster-model parliamentary government and a judicial system. The national King is elected quinquennially from among the Malay Rulers. The federal legislature is Parliament, comprising the lower house (the House of Representatives) and the upper house (the Senate). General elections to the fully

44 Tricia Yeoh, 'Reviving the Spirit of Federalism: Decentralisation Policy Options for a New Malaysia' (*IDEAS*, April 2019) <http://www.ideas.org.my/wp-content/uploads/2019/04/PI59-Reviving-the-Spirit-of-Federalism.pdf > accessed 25 November 2019.
45 'MA63: Seven issues resolved, 14 need further discussion, says PM's Office' (*Malay Mail*, 19 August 2019) <https://www.malaymail.com/news/malaysia/2019/08/19/ma63-seven-issues-resolved-14-need-further-discussion-says-pms-office/1782156> accessed 25 November 2019.
46 James Chin, 'The ghost of Borneo, talk of secession are back to haunt Malaysia' (*CNA*, 10 April 2019) <https://www.channelnewsasia.com/news/commentary/sarawak-sabah-malaysia-bill-secession-ma63-sar-exit-11428822> accessed 25 November 2019.
47 See, e.g., Ling (n 42).
48 Federal Constitution art 4(1).
49 Michael Burgess and G. Alan Tarr, 'Introduction: Sub-national Constitutionalism and Constitutional Development' in Michael Burgess and G. Alan Tarr (eds), *Constitutional Dynamics in Federal Systems: Sub-national Perspectives* (McGill–Queen's University Press 2012) 3.
50 Federal Constitution art 113(1).
51 Federal Constitution Part II.
52 Federal Constitution Sch 9 State List item 7.
53 Federal Constitution arts 4(1), 75.

elected lower house must be held every five years.[54] The political party that obtains the 'confidence' of the majority of lower house members forms the federal executive government: the federal cabinet comprising the prime minister and other ministers.[55] Notwithstanding the federal system, the Federal Constitution establishes a single system of federal law courts that exercises a general jurisdiction over all federal and state matters,[56] except Islamic law and native law matters that are handled by specialized state courts.[57]

The Federal Constitution prescribes an analogous state-level arrangement by dictating the basic contents of state constitutions. Schedule 8 prescribes a set of 'essential provisions' that all state constitutions must contain and, in reality, state constitutions replicate those provisions almost verbatim within their contents. Section 13.4 below will discuss those contents.

Besides prescribing a constitutional arrangement for the states, the Federal Constitution also gives the federation two 'policing' powers over the states. First, Parliament may enforce a state constitution's compliance with Schedule 8. If at any time a state constitution does not contain the Schedule 8 'essential provisions' or contains other inconsistent provisions, then Parliament may enact federal law to remedy the non-compliance.[58] Second, Parliament may enforce constitutional government and the observance of constitutionalism in a state. If Parliament considers that any provision of the Federal Constitution or the state constitution is being 'habitually disregarded' in a state, then Parliament may enact federal law 'for securing compliance' with the provision.[59] Conceivably, federal actions to restore constitutional government may include dissolving the state legislature, forcibly removing the state government or persons governing the state unconstitutionally and imposing temporary federal rule in a state.[60] Parliament may exercise these two powers regardless of other provisions in the Federal Constitution. So far, these powers have not been used.[61]

If the above 'prescribe and police' scheme is not already comprehensive, Parliament may be able to amend the Federal Constitution to strengthen the federal framework controlling state constitutional autonomy. The Schedule 8 'essential provisions' are not necessarily static. If Parliament alters any 'essential provision', then each state must also bring its constitution into line with the alteration.[62] Parliament may also amend other provisions in the Federal Constitution, e.g. the Schedule 9 federal-state distribution of powers.[63]

Parliament's main method for amending the Federal Constitution is a federal law, enacted for that purpose, passed by a special majority of not less than two-thirds of all members (not simply members present and voting) in each house of Parliament.[64] If the federal ruling party holds those majorities, then Parliament may easily amend the Federal Constitution. Until 2008, that was in fact the case and the BN-controlled Parliament routinely amended the Federal Constitution.[65] Except for certain matters concerning Sabah and Sarawak,[66] amendments do

---

54 For the Senate's composition, see text to n 137.

55 Federal Constitution art 43.

56 Text to n 147.

57 Text to nn 115, 117.

58 Federal Constitution art 71(4).

59 Federal Constitution art 71(3).

60 Reid Report paras 187–8.

61 Compare 'emergency powers': text to n 69.

62 See, e.g., Constitution (Amendment) Act 1993 (Act A848).

63 See, e.g., Constitution (Amendment) Act 2005 (Act A1239).

64 Federal Constitution art 159.

65 H.P. Lee, Richard Foo and Amber Tan, 'Constitutional Change in Malaysia' (2019) 14 *Journal of Comparative Law* 119.

66 Federal Constitution Part XIIA.

not require the states' agreement and, as will be seen, the states have very little ability to oppose constitutional amendments by Parliament or influence the constitutional arrangements that the federation may apply to them.[67]

The federal courts, however, may limit Parliament's power to amend the Federal Constitution. Previously, Malaysian judicial jurisprudence held that, as long as Parliament followed the pre-scribed procedure, Parliament could amend the Federal Constitution as it thought fit and the courts disclaimed any power to review the substantive effect of amendments. However, with their recent adoption of a 'basic structure doctrine', the courts will now invalidate any amend-ment by Parliament that in substance is inconsistent with the Federal Constitution's 'basic structure'.[68] Just how this new approach might now limit the federation's ability to change the federal framework that controls state constitutional autonomy remains untested.

Besides the above, the Federal Constitution also enables the federation to override state autonomy by using 'emergency powers'. The federal government may invoke such powers if any 'grave emergency' arises in the federation or any part thereof.[69] A proclamation of a state of emergency triggers a separate regime within the Federal Constitution that extends federal power to the states and severely restricts judicial review of the federation's actions. Historically, the use of such supposedly exceptional powers has been commonplace in Malaysia. Five differ-ent states of emergencies have existed (the last ones only revoked in 2011). Two of those directly overturned state constitutional autonomy.[70] Given those precedents, the federation's emergency powers are always a potential factor against state autonomy during any crisis.

The states have very weak autonomy in terms of deciding the content of their constitutions. While, in theory, they have some discretion to introduce other provisions not inconsistent with the Schedule 8 'essential provisions', for innovations to the basic model of government pre-scribed for them, that discretion is limited. In reality, states have not actively sought to use such discretion. Constitutional reform hardly features in state agendas, and state constitutional amend-ments have largely followed the federation's lead with changes to the federal framework.

13.2.2 Procedure

Each state constitution apparently empowers the state to initiate and make its own constitutional amendments without federal approval. However, those provisions are also prescribed by the Schedule 8 'essential provisions'. In doing so, Schedule 8 distinguishes between two types of provisions contained in state constitutions.

In relation to the constitutions of the Malay States, which contain provisions concerning the Malay monarchy ('monarchy provisions'), Schedule 8 stipulates that state legislatures have no power to amend 'provisions affecting succession to the throne and the position of the ... Malay customary dignitaries'.[71] Instead, those constitutions typically provide that the Ruler (alone or together with some royal council) may decide any amendments to those provisions.[72] This is because, while the Rulers are state figures, their acceptance within the overall system is

---

67 Text to n 136.

68 *Semenyih Jaya Sdn Bhd v PTD Hulu Langat* [2017] 3 MLJ 561 (FC).

69 Federal Constitution art 150.

70 See H.P. Lee, 'The Ningkan Saga: A Chief Minister in the Eye of a Storm' in Andrew Harding and H.P. Lee (eds.), *Constitutional Landmarks in Malaysia* (LexisNexis 2007) 77; Khairil Azmin Bin Mokhtar, 'The Emergency Powers (Kelantan) Act 1977' in Andrew Harding and H.P. Lee (eds), *Constitutional Landmarks in Malaysia* (LexisNexis 2007) 135.

71 Federal Constitution Sch 8 s 19(2).

72 See, e.g., Selangor Constitution art 98(2).

determined by the Federal Constitution. Subject to the modern constitutional system it establishes, the Federal Constitution preserves the Rulers' traditional position and powers.[73] Specifically, the federation guarantees a Ruler's right 'to succeed and to hold, enjoy and exercise the constitutional rights and privileges of Ruler … in accordance with the [state constitution]';[74] federal law makes it a criminal offence to 'question' a Ruler's position and powers;[75] and these provisions cannot be changed without the Rulers' consent.[76] Thus, concurrently, the states have no democratic freedom to determine those provisions concerning the succession and the monarchical institutions. As things stand, neither Parliament nor a state legislature may advocate any abolition of the monarchical systems.[77]

Apart from that situation, the Schedule 8 'essential provisions' stipulate that, in all states, the state legislature may amend all other provisions in the state constitution. Those provisions are of course mainly (although not exclusively) the 'machinery of government' provisions that Schedule 8 has stipulated for the states. For these provisions, Schedule 8 prescribes two different methods of amendment.

As a basic rule, state constitutions are ostensibly just as entrenched as the Federal Constitution: any amendment requires a state law, enacted for that purpose, passed by a special majority of not less than two-thirds of all members of the (unicameral) state legislature.[78]

However, three types of amendments require only an ordinary state law passed by a simple majority of votes. These amendments reflect matters already determined by the federation, i.e.: (a) amendments to bring a state constitution 'into accord' with Schedule 8 'essential provisions'; (b) amendments to alter the state legislature's total membership (which follows the number of state constituencies fixed by Parliament); and (c) amendments to redefine a state's territory following any federal law altering state boundaries.[79] These exceptions mean that, in fact, most amendments do not require the special majority.

In prescribing the above procedures, Schedule 8 also stipulates that the state constitutions 'may not be amended by any other means'.[80] Thus, the procedural framework prescribed for state constitutional amendments is both comprehensive and exclusive.

13.3 Position of the state constitutions

The state constitutions are well established within both the federal system and each state. All states have apparently self-sufficient, single-document written constitutions. All the Malay States possessed such constitutions by the time the 1948 Federation commenced,[81] Penang and Melaka acquired their constitutions with the inception of the 1957 Federation, and Sabah and Sarawak acquired theirs upon joining Malaysia.

Especially at the latter two stages, the process of drafting or revising the Federal Constitution had deliberately included designing matching state constitutions in order to complete the federal system. The primary role of state constitutions is to complement the Federal Constitution

---

73 Federal Constitution art 181.
74 Federal Constitution art 71(1).
75 Sedition Act 1948 (Act 15) s 3(1)(f).
76 Federal Constitution art 159(5).
77 Federal Constitution arts 63(5), 72(5).
78 Federal Constitution Sch 8 s 19(4).
79 Federal Constitution Sch 8 s 19(5).
80 Federal Constitution Sch 8 s 19(3).
81 Johor's constitution dates from 1895 and Terengganu's from 1911. The other constitutions were written for the 1948 Federation: Reid Report para 177.

by providing the states with a 'machinery of government' that the Federal Constitution itself prescribes but otherwise the state constitutions have limited purpose and use.[82] Consequently, state constitutions have very low visibility in public discourse. Generally, they only attract attention, and their application becomes important, when contests occur over the formation or survival of a state government[83] or when internal disputes affect a Malay monarchy.[84]

Even Sabah and Sarawak rely on the Eighteen/Twenty Points, the Malaysia Agreement or the Federal Constitution rather than on their state constitutions to assert their state rights.[85]

13.4 Content

As indicated above, the state constitutions may contain two types of content. The constitutions of Penang, Melaka, Sabah and Sarawak contain 'machinery of government' provisions but not 'monarchy provisions'. The Malay State constitutions have both types of provisions and are typically divided into two such parts; and they contain 'monarchy provisions' besides those prescribed by Schedule 8.

13.4.1 Subnational identity

Subnational identity is perhaps most strongly asserted by the Malay State constitutions. They depict Malay-Islamic sultanates alongside their democratic systems and, in reality, the Rulers remain powerful figures of Malay rights, religion and even politics.[86] Some Malay heartland states especially identify as model 'Islamic states'.[87] Each constitution establishes Islam as the state religion and the Ruler as 'Head of the Religion' with the authority attached to that position as recognized by the Federal Constitution.[88] The constitutions maintain the elaborate monarchical structures, with provisions for the monarch; the consort; succession to the throne; regencies and abdications; titled chiefs and royal councils; heraldic symbols; and the state honours system. These constitutions expressly provide that both the state's chief minister and the top public servant must be a Malay-Muslim,[89] although they also provide that ultimately, under the Westminster model, any non-Malay who commands the state legislature's majority support should be appointed chief minister.[90] Following the Federal Constitution, these constitutions reinforce the Malay 'special position' by authorizing the reservation of quotas for Malays in the public services, in education and in trade within the state.[91]

The constitutions of Penang and Melaka originally did not establish any state religion, although the Federal Constitution required these constitutions to establish the national King as

82 See Section 13.4 below.
83 See, e.g., *Mohammad Nizar v Zambry* [2010] 2 MLJ 285 (FC).
84 See, e.g., *Sultan Ismail Petra v Tengku Muhammad Faris Petra* [2011] 1 MLJ 1 (FC).
85 See, e.g., Stephanie Lee, 'Sabah wants MA63 implemented before next GE' (*The Star*, 19 November 2019) <https://www.thestar.com.my/news/nation/2019/11/19/sabah-wants-ma63-implemented-before-next-ge> accessed 26 November 2019.
86 See, e.g., 'Malaysian PM Mahathir addresses recent tensions with Malay rulers and their constitutional role' (*The Straits Times*, 8 June 2018) <https://www.straitstimes.com/asia/se-asia/pm-mahathir-addresses-recent-tensions-with-malay-rulers-and-their-constitutional-role> accessed 25 November 2019.
87 Jan Stark, 'Constructing an Islamic Model in Two Malaysian States: PAS Rule in Kelantan and Terengganu' (2004) 19 *Sojourn: Journal of Social Issues in Southeast Asia* 51.
88 Federal Constitution art 3(2).
89 See, e.g., Selangor Constitution arts 51–3.
90 Text to nn 105, 112.
91 See, e.g., Selangor Constitution art 91.

the 'Head' of Islam for the Muslim community within each state (since, in theory, the appointed state titular head need not be a Muslim).[92] However, after the federal government initiated a national 'Islamization' policy in the 1980s (when BN federal-state same-party rule prevailed),[93] the state legislatures introduced provisions establishing Islam as the state religion.[94] Nonetheless, these states appear more secular and egalitarian, and socially less conservative, than the Malay States. The state community may decide Islamic and other issues without any Ruler's authoritative influence and the constitutions do not provide for the Malay 'special position' at the state level. In Penang, a non-Malay chief minister has always headed the government.

Similarly, the constitutions of Sabah and Sarawak originally did not establish any state religion and, until 1976, these states were not even required to establish any 'Head' of Islam.[95] Today, Sabah has established Islam as the state religion,[96] but Sarawak continues to avoid any establishment clause.[97] These states of course promote their 'native' identity, with provisions to safeguard the 'special position' of the natives, not the Malays,[98] but the states nonetheless proudly identify as having greater racial and religious tolerance and harmony than the Peninsular states.[99] The constitutions enable the use of English or native languages in the state legislatures.[100] The Sabah Constitution also specifies the state flag and crest.[101] Apart from these features, these constitutions do not specially assert distinctive identities for the Borneo states within the federation.

13.4.2 *Representative structures and organization of powers*

As prescribed by the Schedule 8 'essential provisions', the state-level governmental arrangement is a 'simplified version'[102] of the federal-level arrangement. It similarly incorporates a state titular head, parliamentary government and state law courts. Only the first two elements are addressed within the state constitutions, by the 'machinery of government' provisions. The courts are separately established by ordinary state law.

The titular head is the Malay Ruler (in a Malay State) or an appointed head (in the other states).[103] All state constitutions provide that the titular head must generally act in accordance with the state government's advice.[104] A titular head may exercise a personal discretion in appointing the state chief minister or in considering a chief minister's request for a dissolution of the state legislature to hold a general election;[105] but, in theory, such discretion is limited to determining whether any person sufficiently commands the 'confidence' of a majority within the legislature in order to form the state government or avoid an early dissolution of the legislature.

---

92 Federal Constitution art 3(3).
93 Hoong Phun Lee, 'The Islamisation Phenomenon and the Rule of Law in Malaysia' in Guiguo Wang and Fan Yang (eds), *The Rule of Law: A Comparative Perspective* (City University of Hong Kong Press 2013) 139.
94 Penang Constitution art 5; Melaka Constitution art 5.
95 Federal Constitution art 3(3).
96 Sabah Constitution art 5A.
97 Sarawak Constitution art 4A.
98 Sabah Constitution art 41; Sarawak Constitution art 39.
99 'Keep peninsula hate speeches, issues out of Sarawak—STAR' *The Borneo Post* (Kuching, 19 August 2019) 6.
100 Sabah Constitution art 24(8); Sarawak Constitution art 24(8).
101 Sabah Constitution art 42A.
102 Reid Report para 179.
103 Federal Constitution Sch 8 ss 22–3.
104 Federal Constitution Sch 8 s 1.
105 Federal Constitution Sch 8 s 2(2).

The state constitution authorizes the state legislature to exercise state legislative power.[106] All state legislatures are unicameral.[107] General elections to the legislature must be held every five years.[108] The constitution may fix the total membership of the legislature or authorize state law to do so.[109] However, since states do not regulate their own electoral systems,[110] that number must necessarily follow the number of state electoral constituencies fixed by Parliament. In practice, state general elections are held concurrently with federal general elections.[111] Other contents in the state constitutions concerning the legislature include detailed provisions regarding: eligibility for membership in the legislature; casual vacancies; the presiding 'speaker'; the regulation of proceedings; the enactment of state law, including the titular head's duty to assent to legislation; state taxation and finances; and amendments to the state constitution (discussed earlier).

The state constitutions formally vest executive authority in the titular head but such authority is exercisable by the state government and other entities authorized by state law.[112] The state government is also a cabinet form of government, comprising the chief minister and state ministers who are members of the party commanding the 'confidence' of the majority within the state legislature. Thus, the government may direct the business and legislative agenda of the legislature while being collectively accountable to it.[113]

The state courts, although not mentioned in the state constitutions, may be established by ordinary state law because the states' legislative competence is defined by the Federal Constitution, particularly the Schedule 9 State List. Thus, state law establishing the courts is based on those provisions. As noted earlier,[114] there are two possible state court systems with specific jurisdictions. All states may legislate to apply aspects of Islamic law (mainly matters concerning family law, estate succession and religious offences) to Muslims within the state and, accordingly, each state may establish a system of 'syariah [ie, sharia] courts'.[115] Federal law, however, limits the syariah courts' criminal jurisdiction,[116] and states may not invest syariah courts with powers beyond such limits. In addition, Sabah and Sarawak may apply similar aspects of 'native law' to natives in their states and each state has a separate 'native courts' system.[117] Constitutionally, the state courts are inferior to the federal courts which have judicial review powers to ensure that all governmental organs operate within their legal limits.[118]

Since the states' legislative competence is defined by the Federal Constitution, theoretically states may be able to find 'constitutional' powers outside their constitutions that they may possess under the Federal Constitution or federal law, which do not conflict with the Schedule 8 'essential provisions' or other federal powers. Even from this perspective, the states' 'constitutional space' has proved very restricted.

---

106 Federal Constitution Sch 8 s 11.
107 Federal Constitution Sch 8 s 3.
108 Federal Constitution Sch 8 s 9.
109 See, e.g., Perak Constitution Part I art 29; Selangor Constitution art 62.
110 Text to n 50.
111 Except in Sarawak.
112 See, e.g., Selangor Constitution art 50.
113 Federal Constitution Sch 8 s 2(5).
114 Text to n 57.
115 Federal Constitution Sch 9 State List item 1.
116 Syariah Courts (Criminal Jurisdiction) Act 1965 (Act 355).
117 Federal Constitution Sch 9 State List item 13.
118 *Indira Gandhi v Pengarah Jabatan Agama Islam Perak* [2018] 1 MLJ 545 (FC).

The 'freedom of information' laws introduced by Penang and Selangor in 2011 for more transparent state governance—'a significant step for Malaysian democracy'[119] because no such laws existed at the federal level or in other states—are still impeded by a federal law which prohibits disclosure of important state information;[120] although, following those breakthroughs, the Harapan government had considered reforms at the federal level.[121]

Penang was unable to reintroduce elections to local government councils within the state for democratic accountability at this third tier of government. Although states may legislate for 'local government elections',[122] for the Peninsular states, this power is subject to policies set by the National Council for Local Government and federal laws 'ensuring uniformity of laws and policy',[123] and a federal law precludes such elections.[124]

Penang also could not create a community-policing agency within its government to complement the national police in the state. While a lower court accepted the organization was 'an organ or a machinery of the state government lawfully established pursuant to its powers conferred by the Federal Constitution',[125] the top court ruled the matter was outside the state's powers and contravened federal law. The court took a minimalist view of the state's 'constitutional space', saying the activity was 'not part of what is needed to keep the government of the state functioning'.[126]

These cases highlight the states' inability to shape their governmental arrangements, even at the fringes of the basic model imposed by the Schedule 8 'essential provisions'.

13.4.3 Fundamental rights

The Federal Constitution Part II contains an extensive bill of rights guaranteeing fundamental liberties, including: the right to life and personal liberty; freedom from slavery and forced labour; equality in law; protection against retrospective criminal laws and 'double jeopardy' trials; freedoms of movement, speech, assembly, association and religion; and rights to property. Certain rights are subject to limitations or exceptions that Parliament may enact in federal law. The scope and contents of rights are authoritatively determined by the federal courts.[127] Thus, rights protection and contestations are based almost exclusively on the Federal Constitution and play out as national rather than state issues.

State constitutions do contain one rights guarantee that prohibits racial discrimination within the state public services. However, this is not a guarantee initiated by state constitutions. It is yet another provision prescribed by the Schedule 8 'essential provisions',[128] which essentially compels states to apply the federal 'equality' right to that state scenario. Other apparent rights

---

119 'Malaysia: International Focus' (*The Constitution Unit*, undated) <https://www.ucl.ac.uk/constitution-unit/research/research-archive/foi-archive/international-focus/malaysia> accessed 25 November 2019.
120 Official Secrets Act 1972 (Act 88).
121 Hashini Kavishtri Kannan and Veena Babulal, 'Govt to draft Freedom of Information Act to replace Official Secrets Act' (*New Straits Times*, 18 July 2019) <https://www.nst.com.my/news/nation/2019/07/505404/govt-draft-freedom-information-act-replace-official-secrets-act> accessed 25 November 2019.
122 Federal Constitution Sch 9 State List item 4(a).
123 Text to nn 10, 11.
124 *Government State of Penang v Government of Malaysia* [2014] 6 MLJ 322 (FC).
125 *Government of the State of Penang v Minister of Home Affairs* [2017] 4 MLJ 770 (CA), [41].
126 See Jocelyn Ann Dragon, 'Federal Court rules Penang has no power to set up PPS' (*Malaysiakini*, 14 May 2019) <https://www.malaysiakini.com/news/476119> accessed 25 November 2019.
127 *Lee Kwan Woh v PP* [2009] 5 MLJ 301 (FC).
128 Federal Constitution Sch 8 s 18.

provisions in state constitutions also do not customize or elaborate on the fundamental rights for any state contexts, beyond what the federal bill of rights already covers.[129]

The Federal Constitution already requires the states to observe fundamental rights without the state constitutions pledging rights protection. In reality, the challenge is to ensure that states respect those rights protected by the Federal Constitution.[130]

13.4.4 Policy principles

The state constitutions do not declare any mandatory or aspirational policy principles for state governance. The Federal Constitution (unlike the Indian Constitution) does not express any 'directive principles of state policy'.[131] However, the Federal Constitution incorporates certain underlying concepts commonly associated with Westminster-model written constitutions, such as liberal democracy, the rule of law, separation of powers and individual liberty under the law. Just as these concepts should guide federal governmental actions, the same concepts as appropriate to the state constitutions should guide state governmental actions.

Given that context, the establishment clauses for Islam in the constitutions have become very controversial. The clause in the Federal Constitution was originally intended not to undermine the operation of secular liberal democratic government,[132] but following the national Islamization project,[133] the Malay-Muslim majority now claims that the clause subjects the entire constitutional system to Islamic norms and that Malaysia is constitutionally an 'Islamic state'.[134] The claims are highly contested, but similar claims in relation to the establishment clauses in state constitutions, especially in the Malay States, would demand that the states too should be governed according to Islamic principles.

13.5 Multilevel constitutionalism

13.5.1 Relationship between federal and state constitutions

The Federal Constitution and the state constitutions are interconnected because the former determines the latter's role in providing states with a system of government. Beyond performing that task, the state constitutions have little capacity to function as communicating vessels between the two levels of government or to check central power, simply because the Federal Constitution is so comprehensive and prescriptive, and state autonomy so limited.

The states also have very little 'self-constituent capacity' to influence the constitutional arrangements that the federation may apply to them. Not only may Parliament amend the Federal Constitution without the states' approval,[135] but the states are also only weakly represented within Parliament itself.

Originally, the upper house of Parliament (the Senate) acted primarily as a 'states' house' but this is no longer the case. The Senate comprises members appointed by the federal government

129 See, e.g., Perak Constitution Part I art 7; Johor Constitution First Part art 58.
130 See, e.g., *State Government of Negeri Sembilan v Muhamad Juzaili* [2015] 6 MLJ 736 (FC).
131 *Phang Chin Hock v PP* [1980] 1 MLJ 70 (FC).
132 *Che Omar v PP* [1988] 2 MLJ 55 (SC).
133 Text to n 93.
134 Nadirah H Rodzi, 'Malay group Ikatan Muslimin Malaysia wants Malaysia declared an "Islamic state"' (*The Straits Times*, 29 December 2018) <https://www.straitstimes.com/asia/se-asia/malay-group-wants-malaysia-declared-an-islamic-state> accessed 25 November 2019.
135 Text to n 66.

('federal senators') and members elected by the state legislatures (two per state) ('state senators'). Amendments having reversed the original ratio that provided for a majority of state senators, today federal senators far outnumber state senators (44 to 26, only three short of a two-thirds majority).[136] Furthermore, Parliament's 'weak bicameralism' concentrates power in the fully elected lower house. As a 'house of review', the Senate has much weaker powers and may normally only delay but not veto legislation from the lower house. The Senate may veto constitutional amendments (since those require its approval by a two-thirds special majority)[137] but a ruling party controlling the lower house and more than one state would already possess that majority. During the BN era, the Senate invariably 'rubber-stamped' bills from the lower house.[138]

Representation of state interests in the lower house is also limited. Theoretically, lower house members may support state issues, particularly since members of a state legislature (including state ministers) may be separately elected to the lower house as federal members of Parliament. However, state interests are likely to be marginalized if the ruling party commands a strong majority in the house and same-party rule exists in the states. After Singapore's expulsion, Sabah and Sarawak also no longer hold sufficient lower house seats to be able to block constitutional amendments in Parliament.[139] Exceptionally, however, state intentions might prevail if the federal government is compelled to rely on the support of members from opposition-held states. For example, the constitutional amendment in 1976 that 'downgraded' Sabah and Sarawak[140] was supported by BN members from those states,[141] but the attempted reversal in 2019 failed because the Harapan federal government lacked the required two-thirds majority in the house without the support of opposition members from Sarawak.

13.5.2 *Malaysia and ASEAN*

Malaysia is a founding member of, and the only federation within, the Association of South East Asian Nations (ASEAN). The ASEAN Charter 2008 aims to initiate an 'ASEAN Community' for political-security, economic and socio-cultural cooperation.

While the Charter made ASEAN a legal entity and established an institutional framework, it avoided creating any supranational body, and ASEAN remains an intergovernmental organization based on principles of national sovereignty, non-interference in member state internal affairs and consensus-based decision-making. The Charter is not a legally-binding supranational constitution.[142]

Accordingly, it does not change the federal-state relationship within Malaysia. Participation in ASEAN and domestic implementation of ASEAN decisions are exclusively federal decisions.[143] For such implementation, Parliament may enact federal laws extending even to exclusive state matters (except Islamic law and native law matters). The states need only be 'consulted' before any such law is enacted and have no veto power.[144]

---

136 Lee, Foo and Tan (n 65) 126.
137 Text to n 64.
138 Text to n 65.
139 Text to n 27. But see text to n 28.
140 Text to n 42.
141 Wong Chin Huat, 'Sabah and Sarawak downgraded by their MPs in 1976' (*Malaysiakini*, 8 April 2019) <https://www.malaysiakini.com/news/471345> accessed 25 November 2019.
142 Walter Woon, 'The ASEAN Charter: Ten Years On' (2017) 39 *Contemporary Southeast Asia* 245, at 250.
143 Federal Constitution Sch 9 Federal List item 1(d).
144 Federal Constitution art 76.

13.6 Constitutional review

The powers of constitutional review to uphold state constitutionalism are located entirely at the federal level.

As discussed above, Parliament possesses two powers to ensure that states incorporate the Schedule 8 'essential provisions' and practise constitutionalism.[145]

The Federal Constitution Part IX also establishes the federal courts as an independent third branch of government to uphold constitutional supremacy within the federal system. Since these courts are the national judicature,[146] their constitution, organization and powers are determined at the federal level.[147] The states have no powers in this respect.[148]

The superior courts—the two High Courts (one designated for 'Malaya', the other for 'Sabah and Sarawak'), the Court of Appeal and the apex Federal Court—function as constitutional courts as well as ordinary courts for other matters. These courts authoritatively interpret the Federal Constitution and state constitutions, and decide all constitutional issues. In particular, the Federal Court exclusively decides all federal-state disputes and any dispute involving federal or state legislative competence.[149] The Court also has an exclusive 'advisory jurisdiction' to rule on the federal government's questions arising out of the Federal Constitution (including issues concerning the states).[150]

In performing judicial review, the courts may invalidate: (a) unlawful federal or state governmental actions; (b) unconstitutional federal or state laws; and (c) 'unconstitutional constitutional amendments'. As with amendments to the Federal Constitution,[151] the courts may review state constitutional amendments for procedural compliance[152] and for substantive compliance, since state constitutions must conform to the Schedule 8 'essential provisions' and must never be inconsistent with the Federal Constitution as a whole.

Given their task to ensure state compliance with the Federal Constitution's restrictive provisions, the courts have shown little capacity to promote state constitutional autonomy. They have generally defended state legislative-executive powers from federal encroachment.[153] However, where cases involved enhancing state *constitutional* autonomy, they have acted more conservatively. One crucial decision during Malaysia's formation ruled that the Peninsular states had no autonomy in the federal decision to admit new states to the federation, although that event fundamentally changed the federation's composition and character.[154] Current decisions maintain a minimalist attitude to the states' 'constitutional space'.[155]

For Sabah and Sarawak, the separate High Court is now seen as inadequate to protect their rights.[156] Although the Court is a federal court, its chief judge is appointed in consultation with

145 Text to nn 58, 59.
146 Text to n 56.
147 Federal Constitution Sch 9 Federal List item 4.
148 But see text to nn 158, 159.
149 Federal Constitution art 128.
150 Federal Constitution art 130.
151 Text to n 68.
152 Text to nn 78, 79.
153 *Government of Malaysia v Government of the State of Kelantan* [1968] 1 MLJ 129 (FC); *Mamat v Government of Malaysia* [1988] 1 MLJ 119 (SC).
154 *Government of the State of Kelantan v Government of the Federation of Malaya* [1963] 1 MLJ 355.
155 Text to n 127.
156 See, e.g., Ruben Sario, 'Final appeals for Borneonisation policy thrown out' (*The Star*, 21 August 2015) <https://www.thestar.com.my/news/nation/2015/08/21/final-appeals-for-borneonisation-policy-thrown-out> accessed 25 November 2019.

the states,[157] and a court comprising local judges nominated by the chief judge is considered necessary for the local circumstances. Changes to the Court's constitution, jurisdiction and judicial tenure also require the states' consent.[158] However, Parliament amended the Federal Constitution in 1994, abolishing the states' ability to appoint one category of 'entry level' judges to the Court and, today, after further reforms, all judicial appointments are federally decided.[159] Important decisions on local issues are also seen as negated by insufficiently informed decisions in the appellate courts dominated by judges from the Peninsular states.[160]

13.7 Conclusion

While the states in Malaysia appear to be 'full-fledged' constitutional entities within the federal system, closer examination of the system shows that those states have very weak constitutional autonomy. The 'constitutional architecture' determined by the Federal Constitution leaves negligible 'constitutional space' for the states. The constitutions of the Malay States strongly project their identity as Malay-Islamic sultanates but the federal entrenchment of this historical legacy does not at the same time allow much potential for other democratic constitutional narratives. The federal framework also does not enable state constitutions to have sufficient significance as vehicles for the expression of fundamental rights or principles of state policy.

The state constitutions are not seen as important for those purposes because, ultimately, they serve a very limited utilitarian purpose of providing states with a 'machinery of government', in the sense that they simply lay down the mechanical parts and processes of government. Even these are dictated by the Federal Constitution's ability to regulate both the contents of state constitutions and the states' constitution-making power, with the states lacking constitutional participation in the federal system to influence the Federal Constitution.

The state constitutions have provided stable constitutionalism for the states. However, even as issues of state autonomy become more dynamic in public discourse, stronger state constitutional autonomy remains unlikely to emerge soon in the highly centralized federation.

---

157 Federal Constitution art 122B(3).
158 Federal Constitution art 161E(2)(b).
159 *Robert Linggi v Government of Malaysia* [2011] 2 MLJ 741 (HC).
160 Kristy Inus, 'Sabah Law Society wants more judges with "Bornean experience" to hear cases from Sabah, S'wak' (*The Star*, 16 September 2019) <https://www.thestar.com.my/news/nation/2019/09/16/sabah-law-society-wants-more-judges-with-039bornean-experience039-to-hear-cases-from-sabah-s039wak> accessed 25 November 2019.

14

SUBNATIONAL CONSTITUTIONALISM IN MEXICO

Medium state autonomy in a centralized federation

José Ma. Serna de la Garza

14.1 Context

According to Nettie Lee Benson, there are three factors that explain the establishment of federalism in Mexico: a) the administrative reform implemented in New Spain by Charles III of Bourbon in the late eighteenth century (which divided the colony into 12 territorial jurisdictions called *intendencias*);[1] b) the regime of the Spanish Constitution of Cádiz (1812) that established 'diputaciones provinciales' in New Spain (which were local representative bodies);[2] and c) the political-economic development of relevant regions of the country that were far away from the capital (Mexico City) and were to some extent self-sufficient.[3] These processes created local political groups scattered around the country that soon started to claim increased political autonomy within their regions. Subsequently these claims were transformed into a demand for the adoption of the federal form.

Under these conditions, after Mexico declared its independence from Spain in 1821, political groups discussed whether the new state should adopt a unitary or a federal organization. The decisive moment of this discussion took place in the constituent assembly that was elected in 1824 to approve Mexico's first constitution. Within that assembly, the main defender of the unitary form was Fray Servando Teresa de Mier, under the following arguments:[4] 1. Mexico (formerly New Spain) had always had a centralized form of government, so Mexicans were not used to the provinces having their own governments; 2. in Mexico a federation was being proposed as an illogical imitation of the US federal system, however, conditions and circumstances in Mexico were very different from those that existed in the US; and 3. if in the US federalism had served to unite what was disunited, in Mexico, it would serve to disunite what had always been united.

---

1 What today is Mexico was a colony of Spain between 1521 and 1821. During those years, the colony was called 'New Spain'.

2 The Spanish Constitution of Cadiz, approved in 1812, applied in the territory of Spain and in all its colonial possessions. In 1812, what today is Mexico was still a colony of Spain.

3 Nettie Lee Benson, *The Provincial Deputation in Mexico* (University of Texas Press 1992).

4 A historial review of this debate can be found in Jorge Carpizo, *La Constitución Mexicana de 1917* (Porrúa 1983) 242–5; and in Mario de la Cueva, *La Constitución de 5 de Febrero de 1857* (UNAM 2007) 23.

DOI: 10.4324/9781003052111-14

For his part, the main spokesman for the adoption of the federal form of state, Miguel Ramos Arizpe, argued differently:[5] 1. it was true that Mexico (formerly New Spain) had been governed under centralized formulas, but it was also true that at the end of the colonial period and through the institution of the 'diputaciones provinciales', the provinces had begun to exercise an autonomous government of their own, and had become accustomed to it; 2. moreover, Ramos Arizpe recalled that during 1823–24, as the first Mexican national constitution was being discussed, the 'diputaciones provinciales' of Jalisco, Oaxaca, Yucatán and other provinces sent a clear message through a series of pronouncements, stating that a condition to remain united was the adoption of a federal form of political organization; and 3. Ramos Arizpe concluded that in Mexico federalism would serve to unite what was at risk of becoming disunited.

In this context, the Constituent Congress that was writing and would approve the first Mexican national constitution issued on 31 January 1824 a pre-constitutional text, the so-called 'Constitutive Act of the Mexican Federation'. The Constitutive Act was intended to calm the political pressure coming from the provinces.[6] It did so by assuring them that the Constitution that would be approved soon would establish a federal form of state. Indeed, this is precisely what happened, when the 'Federal Constitution of the Mexican United States' was approved on 4 October 1824.[7]

The first subnational constitutions in Mexico were drafted after the approval of this national constitution.[8] The first of them, the constitution of the state of Jalisco, was approved in the city of Guadalajara on 18 November 1824. Many others followed between 1825 and 1827. In all these cases, state constitutions were approved by constituent assemblies popularly elected in each of the states.

After this period, there were several 'waves' of subnational constitutionalism, mostly associated with the approval of a new constitution at a federal level, as occurred in 1857 and 1917.[9] The 1917 events are especially significant for a number of reasons. Firstly, they led to the approval of the constitution that still today is in force in Mexico: the federal constitution of 5 February 1917.[10] Secondly, this constitution was the result of the Mexican Revolution which was a major social movement that started in 1910, and which shaped contemporary Mexico. Thirdly, and in connection with subnational constitutions, it is important to notice that the commander in chief of the revolutionary forces, Venustiano Carranza, who was then in charge of the federal executive power, issued a decree on 22 March 1917,[11] ordering provisional governors in every state to call for elections in order to re-establish the constitutional order in each state. The decree also required that the state legislatures thus elected assume 'constituent power'[12] for the purpose of

---

5 See Ibid.
6 Article 6 of the Constitutive Act of the Mexican Federation stated that states 'are independent, free states, and sovereign, in what exclusively refers to their administration and internal government, as detailed in this Act and in the general Constitution'.
7 On 1 June 1823, the governing 'Junta' in Oaxaca declared that this state had become 'free and sovereign', independent from the central government. On 16 June 1823, the provisional government of Jalisco did exactly the same.
8 Article 24 of the Constitutive Act of the Mexican Federation established that 'State constitutions cannot oppose this Act nor whatever is established in the general constitution: therefore, they cannot be approved until the publication of the latter'.
9 Between 1824 and 1917 Mexico had eight documents that count as 'constitutional texts'. These documents affected subnational constitutions in different ways. In the extreme, the 'Seven Constitutional Laws' of 1836 established a unitary state in which states and their subnational constitutions were abolished.
10 This constitution was the result of the Mexican Revolution which started in 1910.
11 Decree Number 13, of 22 March 1917, issued by Venustiano Carranza.
12 This concept is actually the one used in Article 4 of Carranza's Decree Number 13.

adapting state (subnational) constitutions to the new rules and principles of the recently approved national constitution.

In spite of these developments and of the constitutional consolidation of the federal principle, 'living federalism' in Mexico has not been effective, especially in the absence of a true constitutional government and rule of law, both under the military dictatorship of general Porfirio Díaz (1877–1910) and during the period of the so called 'hegemonic party system'[13] that emerged in Mexico after the Mexican Revolution and which lasted until 2000.

Today, in the context of Mexico's centralized federal system, subnational constitutionalism is to an important extent subordinated to developments that take place at the level of the national constitution. The antecedents of such centralization can be found in the already mentioned hegemonic party system that existed in Mexico between 1929 and 2000: an omnipotent president of the Republic who was the true leader of the political party that controlled most political positions both at the national and subnational levels was able to subordinate all state and municipal authorities, and to introduce in the design of Mexico's federal arrangement a logic of centralization (i.e. in the formula for the allocation of powers and in the formula of fiscal federalism). Even today, as Mexico has a multi-party and competitive system, this logic prevails in the institutional and normative design of its federal system. Not even Mexico City, which has a different constitutional status when compared with that of the states, and in spite of its economic and political weight in the country as a whole, is able to escape from this centralizing trend.

14.2 Autonomy

14.2.1 Scope

To describe the scope of autonomy of subnational constitutions in Mexico, I will use the distinction between *complete* and *incomplete* national constitutions developed by Donald Lutz,[14] who has argued that the national constitution of the United States of America (US) is an *incomplete* constitution, which depends for its operation on subnational constitutions to *complete* it. In this way, Lutz argues, subnational constitutions are part of the national constitution.[15]

Based on the aforementioned distinction, it is possible to identify federal states in which the national constitution is very 'incomplete', as is the case of the US, which opens a quite broad subnational constitutional space (or scope); while in other cases, the national constitution is 'complete', leaving a relatively narrow space for the development of subnational constitutionalism.

Using this conceptual distinction, we can say that the Mexican Constitution of 1917 is 'complete' in the sense that it specifies a series of structural and substantive elements of subnational governments that must necessarily be included in the subnational constitutions. Therefore, the subnational constitutional space is not wide in scope.

---

13 By 'hegemonic party system' I mean one in which in spite of the existence of several political parties, one of them is clearly predominant and political-electoral competition is unequal and unfair, which in turns prevents the possibility of rotation in government. See Giovanni Sartori, *Parties and Party Systems: A Framework for Analysis*, vol. I (Cambridge University Press 1976).

14 Donald S. Lutz, 'The United States Constitution as an Incomplete Text' (1988) 496 *Annals of the Academy of Political and Social Science* 23.

15 Robert Williams and Alan Tarr have also used the concept of complete/incomplete constitution, and have applied it to describe the degrees to which the US constitution can be seen as complete or incomplete in connection with subnational constitutions. Robert F. Williams and G. Alan Tarr, 'Subnational Constitutional Space: A View from the States, Provinces, Regions, Länder, and Cantons' in G. Alan Tarr et al. (eds), *Federalism, Subnational Constitutions, and Minority Rights* (Praeger Publishers 2004) 3.

Specifically, Article 116 of the national constitution establishes an extensive list of items that must be incorporated in and developed by subnational constitutions. For instance, the first paragraph of this article states that:

> Public power of a state shall be divided into three branches: executive, legislative and judicial. Two or more of these powers cannot be united in one single person or corporation, nor shall the legislative branch be vested in one single person.

Moreover, the second paragraph of Article 116 states that public powers of a state 'shall be subjected to the state constitution, according to the following provisions', and what follows is a large list of rules and principles that must be followed by subnational constitutions in the organization of the executive, legislative and judicial branches of government at the state level, as well as concerning the organization of local elections and other local public authorities.

In this way, Mexico's national constitution provides a complete constitutional architecture of the federal system in the subnational level, and this circumstance has led to significant homogeneity among the state constitutions. However, Article 116 has evolved over time. The 13 reforms that have been made to the article since 1917 have even further increased the prescriptiveness of the national constitution at the expense of the subnational constitutional space. These reforms that Article 116 have established rules on are: a) the strengthening of local judicial powers (judicial guarantees); b) the organization of local electoral processes (in fact, this is a recurring theme of the reforms to 116); c) the creation of oversight bodies in the states; d) the duty to follow the rules on remuneration of local public servants and to include within their budget projects the disaggregated tabulations of the compensation proposed by their public servants; e) the duty of the state legislatures to foresee the way that citizens can present initiatives of law; f) the duty to establish autonomous bodies in the local constitutions to guarantee the right of access to public information and protection of personal data at the level of the states; and g) the duty of state constitutions to allow the re-election of state legislators (which was forbidden before the national Constitution was amended in 2014).

The capacity of Mexico City to establish its own constitution is established in Article 122 of the national constitution. This article is as extensive as Article 116. It provides very detailed rules on how the Constitution of Mexico City must organize the executive, legislative and judicial branches of government; and how it must design different kinds of agencies, for example autonomous constitutional agencies in charge of guaranteeing the right to transparency and access to public information; or in charge of protecting human rights. Moreover, some provisions of Article 116 also apply to Mexico City. For instance, Article 122.A.IX of the national constitution states that the Constitution and statutes of Mexico City shall comply with the rules in Article 116.IV of the national constitution and the corresponding federal laws in electoral matters.

14.2.2 Procedure

All subnational constitutions in Mexico provide for a mechanism of reform, but this mechanism varies from one state to another. In general terms, the amendment procedures of subnational constitutions are less rigid than the one that corresponds to the national constitution, considering that states do not have senates or second chambers.[16] In some states, a constitutional reform

---

16 Amending the national constitution requires a two-thirds vote in both the Chamber of Deputies and the Senate, plus ratification by the majority of state legislatures.

requires a favourable vote of a qualified majority of the state legislature: in some states, two-thirds of the total number of state legislators; in other states, two-thirds of the legislators present; in one state, 70 per cent of the total number of state legislators (Guanajuato). In other states, in addition to this requirement, the amendment procedure also requires the approval of either a majority or an absolute majority of the municipal councils ('*Ayuntamientos*').

Some subnational constitutions establish a time limit within which municipal councils have to vote on the reform proposal, in the understanding that if they do not discuss and vote on the proposal within that time frame, they will be considered to have accepted the proposed reform.[17]

14.3 Position of the subnational constitution

The subnational constitutions of each state are concentrated in one document. That is to say, they are 'codified'. Moreover, they are supreme in what concerns the 'internal regime' of each state. The supremacy of subnational constitutions derives from Articles 40 and 41 of Mexico's national constitution:

> Article 40. It is the will of the Mexican people to become a representative, democratic, secular and federal Republic, composed of free and sovereign states in everything concerning their internal regime, and of Mexico City, united in a federation established according to the principles of this fundamental law.'
>
> Article 41. The people exercise their sovereignty through the Powers of the Union, within their areas of competence, and by those of the States and Mexico City, with regard to their internal regimes, in the terms respectively, established by this Federal Constitution and by the Constitution of each State and of Mexico City, which in no case may contravene the provisions of the Federal Pact.

From the text of these two articles, it is possible to see that the supremacy at the subnational level is conditioned by the allocation of competences defined in the national constitution. However, some subnational constitutions expressly establish their own supremacy, as is the case for the Constitutions of Chiapas (Article 78.I), Chihuahua (Article 88Bis.I) and Veracruz (Article 56.I). In connection with the supremacy of subnational constitutions, a recent trend can be identified in a number of states, characterized by the emergence of systems for guaranteeing that supremacy. Under the hegemonic party system (1929–2000), subnational constitutionalism was almost entirely subordinated to national constitutionalism. Constitutional change in the states occurred as a consequence—as a reflex reaction—to changes in the federal constitution. In contrast, by the late 1990s and under a multi-party and increasingly competitive political system, new room for manoeuvre was created, allowing state political actors to shape their subnational constitution in original and sometimes creative ways, trying to respond to local needs and demands.

This trend was inaugurated by the state of Veracruz in 2000, whose congress reformed its constitution in order to include a Chapter on Human Rights that includes rights not included in the federal constitution and a clause that incorporates at the state level rights established in international treaties signed by Mexico. In addition, the reform created procedural mechanisms for the protection of the state constitution: a) the procedure for the protection of human rights (analogous to the federal writ of *amparo*); b) an action of constitutional controversy (to resolve

---

17 In the state of Aguascalientes, this time limit is 15 days (Article 94.II); in the state of Colima, 30 days; in the state of Jalisco, one month (Article 117).

disputes of competences between state branches of government, between the latter and munici-pal governments, or between municipal governments); c) an action of unconstitutionality (as an abstract mechanism of constitutional review at the Veracruz state level); and d) an action against legislative omissions (that seeks to force the state congress to pass a piece of legislation whose omission thus far affects mandates of the Constitution of Veracruz). The court with jurisdiction over these actions is the so called 'Constitutional Chamber' (*Sala Constitucional*), formed with three magistrates, and which forms part of the Superior Court of the state of Veracruz.

Interestingly, this reform of the Constitution of Veracruz was challenged through an action of constitutional controversy filed at the federal level by several municipalities of Veracruz (con-trolled by a political party different from that of the governor and of the majority of the state congress). The Supreme Court decided that it did not breach the federal constitution because the new mechanisms of constitutional review established at the subnational level were intended to guarantee only the additional rights contained in the state constitution and therefore had no effect on the rights contained in the federal constitution.[18]

This decision encouraged other states to follow the same path. However, after a period of intense debate, and efforts to redesign institutions and enact new provisions, the trend lost momentum. The all-absorbing federal writ of *amparo*, by which state courts' decisions derived from the new procedures, started to be reviewed by federal courts. Why should plaintiffs resort to state judicial review procedures, if the decisions rendered at this level could be later reviewed by federal courts through the writ of *amparo*, and additionally having the option of using the federal *amparo* instead of subnational judicial mechanisms of constitutional control?

In spite of this, today the constitutions of 21 states (out of 31), establish diverse mechanisms of subnational constitutional control (similar to those established by the Constitution of Veracruz). Those states are: Campeche, Chiapas, Coahuila, Colima, Durango, Estado de México, Guanajuato, Guerrero, Hidalgo, Morelos, Nayarit, Nuevo León, Oaxaca, Queretaro, Quintana Roo, Sinaloa, Tabasco, Tlaxcala, Veracruz, Yucatán and Zacatecas. In addition, the Constitution of Mexico City also establishes mechanisms of this kind.

It is also important to note that subnational constitutions can be modified as a result of suc-cessful challenges at the national level, through judgments of federal courts in proceedings such as the writ of *amparo*, constitutional controversies or actions of unconstitutionality. This has hap-pened with particular intensity in relation to the standards that the national constitution estab-lishes to organize elections at the level of states. In 1996, Article 116.IV of the national constitution was amended to introduce a series of standards that subnational constitutions and electoral laws must follow. In addition, the constitutional reform of 1996 made it possible to use the action of unconstitutionality to challenge subnational constitutions and electoral laws that contradict those standards. Political parties officially registered either before the national or the subnational electoral authorities have successfully challenged subnational constitutional-elec-toral norms, thus forcing amendments and adaptations in subnational constitutions.

The Supreme Court of Mexico has stated that subnational constitutions can establish mecha-nisms to control legislative omissions by subnational legislatures.[19] The Court has said:

> There is no [national] constitutional provision preventing State Constitutions from
> establishing, as part of their mechanisms of constitutional control, a mechanism to

18 SCJ, Constitutional controversy 16/2000, *Semanario Judicial de la Federación y su Gaceta*, Ninth Epoch, Plenary session, XVI, August 2002, p. 903. Published in the Official Gazette of the Federation on 21 June 2000. Thesis: P.XXXIII/2002.
19 Mexico's national constitution does not foresee an action against legislative omissions.

supervise and order that legislative or regulatory omissions be remedied, and to make effective and judicially enforceable the terms and requirements set forth in the laws and decrees of the [state] Legislative Power, when it is foreseen in them the emission or reform of other normative bodies in order to give full effectiveness to the Constitution or to the laws of each federative entity.[20]

There are also mechanisms in the national constitution intended to protect the subnational constitutional space.[21]

To the extent that certain subject-matters fall within the exclusive jurisdiction of subnational governments, subnational constitutions can become very visible in civil society. For example, the organization of metropolitan zones that exist within one state only is a matter that pertains exclusively to state law. Discussion of changes in the existing scheme of metropolitan governance that require the amendment of the subnational constitution can become very visible. This has happened recently, for example, in the state of Nuevo León, where a controversial constitutional reform proposal has been discussed for months, concerning the norms and institutions for governing the metropolitan zone of Monterrey.[22]

In cases of 'political trial'[23] against state governors or other public officials, subnational constitutions also become quite visible. For example, in 1998, the Congress of the state of Morelos filed an accusation against the governor of that state, Jorge Carrillo Olea, alleging that he was liable for causing serious harm to fundamental public interests as a consequence of his failure to comply with his constitutional duties to fight organized crime and for having allowed the operation of criminal groups related to drug trafficking and several cases of kidnapping. As required by the state constitution, the state legislature filed a petition to the Superior Tribunal of the state seeking the governor's removal and disqualification as a public servant for the maximum period allowed by state law, as well as an order prohibiting him from leaving the state territory. In this case,[24] a conflict eventually developed between the state's judicial and legislative power on the interpretation of the subnational constitution concerning the impeachment procedure. Summarizing: the Superior Court of the state of Morelos dismissed the petition of the state congress, alleging that the Constitution of Morelos did not expressly subject the governor to the possibility of a 'political trial'. Against this decision, the Congress of Morelos filed a constitutional controversy (21/99) to Mexico's Supreme Court, reasoning that the national constitution did subject all governors to the possibility of being subject to a political trial. In the end, the Supreme Court decided in favour of the Congress of Morelos, stating that Article 137 of Morelos' Constitution had to be interpreted in a systematic way, in connection with Article 135

20 SCJN, Action of unconstitutionality 8/2010. General Attorney of the Republic. Tenth Epoch, Plenary Session, Semanario Judicial de la Federación y su Gaceta, XIII, October 2012, vol. 1, p. 287. Thesis: P./J. 24/2012 (10a).

21 For example, the so-called 'federal guarantee', originally provided for in Article 122 of the Constitution, and now located in the first paragraph of Article 119 of the Constitution: 'The Powers of the Union have the duty to protect the federal entities against foreign invasion or violence. In the event of uprising or internal social unrest, the Powers of the Union must protect the federal entity, as long as they are called by the local legislature, or by the governor if legislature is not in session'.

22 The proposal was controversial because it sought to create new agencies (a 'Council for the development of the Metropolitan zone of Monterrey' and 'Commissions of Metropolitan Development') that would assume competences that under the existing circumstances belong to municipal councils, related to urban planning and to the provision of a number of public services.

23 This is the Mexican version of the impeachment procedure under American constitutional law.

24 I have referred in detail to this case in José María Serna de la Garza, *The Constitution of Mexico: A Contextual Analysis* (Hart Publishing 2013).

of that constitution which stated that the governor and other public servants of Morelos shall be responsible in terms of Title Four of the national constitution (which establishes general rules on political, administrative and criminal responsibility applicable to all federal, state and municipal public servants).[25]

14.4 Content

14.4.1 Identity

According to the national constitution, the source of all powers in Mexico is the 'People'. Moreover, the core principles that form the identity of Mexico's political organization as a state can be found in Article 40 of the national constitution: Mexico shall be governed by the principles of representative democracy, secularity, federalism and republicanism and its political organization shall be 'made up by free and sovereign States in everything related to its domestic regime, and by Mexico City, united in a federation established according to the principles of this fundamental law'.

These principles are also part of the identity of the subnational constitutions because the first paragraph of Article 115 of the national constitution mandates that the states comprising the United Mexican States shall adopt a republican, representative, democratic, secular and popular form of government for their own organization (and shall be divided into municipalities, which shall be the basis of the political and administrative organization).

From a sociological perspective, Mexico is relatively homogenous in terms of ethnic origin, language and religion. Of the 120 million Mexicans that were reported in the most recent population census (2010), the majority were persons of combined European and Indigenous American descent ('mestizos'), who are Catholics[26] and speak Spanish;[27] 25.7 million Mexicans consider themselves as members of the indigenous population (21.5 per cent of the total population),[28] while 1.4 million Mexicans consider themselves Afro-descendants (1.2 per cent of the total population).[29] In addition, the percentage of Mexico's population born in a different country amounted in 2010 to around 0.9 per cent of the population.[30] Moreover, as shown by the most recent population census in Mexico, 77.8 per cent of Mexicans live in urban areas, while 22.2 per cent live in rural areas.[31]

In spite of these numbers, the dispersion of the population in a country of almost 2 million square kilometres, with a huge geographic diversity, has caused the emergence of important regional differences in terms of cultural and political identities. However, these differences have not compelled any subnational political community to claim recognition as a 'nation within the nation' (as for example has happened with Cataluña in its relationship with Spain); nor is there any secession claim of any component of the Union.

---

25 Serna de la Garza (n 24), at 70.
26 In the most recent population census in Mexico, made in 2010, showed that 89.3 per cent considered themselves Catholics, while 8 per cent are Protestants and Evangelists. INEGI, *Censo de Población y Vivienda*, México, 2010.
27 7,328,000 over three years old speak a Native-American language. Of this number, 12 out of every 100 do not speak Spanish. Gobierno de México, *Numeraila Indígena* 2015.
28 Gobierno de México, *Numeraila Indígena* 2015.
29 INEGI, Principales resultados de la *Encuesta Intercensal 2015 Estados Unidos Mexicanos*, México, 2015, 77 (available at: http://internet.contenidos.inegi.org.mx/contenidos/productos/prod_serv/contenidos/espanol/bvinegi/productos/nueva_estruc/702825078966.pdf).
30 INEGI, *Censo de Población y Vivienda*, México, 2010.
31 INEGI, *Volumen y Crecimiento. Población total según tamaño de la localidad para cada entidad federativa*, México, 2010.

It is true that states have subnational emblems and, in some cases, even state anthems and flags. However, national symbols (flag, anthem and emblem) are predominant in public places and civic ceremonies. National flag ceremonies and the duties that the authorities of the three orders of government have in this respect (federal, state and municipal authorities) are regulated in detail in the Law on the Emblem, Flag and Anthem.

14.4.2 *Organization of powers*

As mentioned before, the national constitution prescribes in several of its articles (particularly Article 116) how the institutions and political processes of the federative entities should be designed normatively. It therefore provides a relatively complete constitutional architecture for the federal system at the subnational level. This has led to significant homogeneity among subnational constitutions. In particular, the national constitution contains detailed rules on the organization of powers at the subnational level. Among many other topics, these rules refer to: the principle of separation of powers; basic rules on the election and period of government of states executives; the systems and formulas for the election of state legislators; the definition of remunerations of state public servants and of state systems of public accountancy; the mechanism by which citizens can propose legislative reforms; the organization of state judicial powers; the guarantees of judicial independence; the requisites to be appointed as state judge; the term of office and remunerations of state judges; the organization of state elections for governors, legislators and municipal authorities; the establishment of public entities in charge of organizing state elections and for solving disputes derived from state elections; public financing of political parties at state level; and the establishment of state administrative courts and of public entities in charge of guaranteeing the right to have access to public information. However, states are not prevented from creating public entities and agencies different from those established in article 116 of the national constitution. They can establish the public entities they deem necessary to meet the specific needs and demands of their societies, without interfering in the competences and powers of the federal government and in the field of powers that corresponds to and is proper to the public authorities established in Article 116 of the national constitution.[32] Indeed, states do have some margin of constitutional creativity, as can be shown with a series of institutions that have firstly appeared at the subnational constitutional level, before reaching the national level, among others: ballotage (state of San Luis Potosí); non-partisan candidacies (states of Yucatan and Sonora); plebiscite (state of Chihuahua); and referendum (state of Chihuahua and others).[33] This demonstrates how subnational constitutions, despite their narrow scope, serve as laboratories for institutional innovation.

The basic formula for allocating competences between the federal and state governments is the residual clause established in Article 124 of the national constitution: the powers not expressly attributed to the federal authorities are reserved to the states and to Mexico City. The national constitution also imposes a series of prohibitions on the exercise of certain powers by the states. Some of those prohibitions are absolute in character (in no circumstances can states exercise the powers listed in Article 117 of the national constitution) and others are relative (states can exercise the powers listed in Article 118 of the national constitution, but only with the authorization of the federal Congress). In addition, Article 115 of the national constitution allocates

32 Elisur Arteaga Nava, *Derecho constitucional estatal* (Porrúa 1988) 4.
33 Javier Hurtado, 'El Federalismo en México: mitos, realidades y posibilidades' (2019) 335 *Este País* 7.

competences and powers that belong to municipal governments.[34] A significant proportion of the topics addressed in the national constitution are shared or concurrent between the national and state governments. This enables responsibilities to be shared among the levels of government. Public policies concerning such matters are implemented according to a distribution of competences defined by the federal legislature.[35]

A recent and interesting development has to do with the Constitution of Mexico City, which was approved on 31 January 2017.[36] This constitution has two distinguishing features. Firstly, it creates several institutions that do not have a basis in the national constitution. Secondly, it contains a very broad catalogue of human rights.

To illustrate the first point, Mexico City's constitution established, among other things, the possibility of revoking the mandate of certain public officials; it established a public defender's office as an 'autonomous constitutional agency'; and it created a mechanism for the appointment of Mexico City judges in which citizens play a role. None of these features has a basis in Article 122 of the national constitution (which is the article that defines the constitutional status of Mexico City's government).

This constitution was challenged on different grounds. One of the plaintiffs' most important arguments was that Mexico City's constituent assembly created and designed several public agencies that did not have any basis in the national constitution. However, in its judgment of 6 September 2018, Mexico's Supreme Court decided against the plaintiffs on the basis that: a) Mexico's federal system allows for its 'political subunits' to establish institutions of self-government 'according to the principles and rules of our federal pact'[37]; b) the fact that the national constitution recognizes that member states may have a 'constitution', and not an 'organic law' nor a 'Statute of Government', has important political and legal consequences; c) the concept of a 'constitution' has historic, symbolic and substantive implications, since it denotes not only the fact that they are higher norms, but it also entails that these normative instruments are a manifestation of the people's sovereignty and of the social pact that is the basis of self-government of each subnational entity. The Supreme Court also stated that the diversity allowed by the federal system is reflected in the ability each subnational entity has to structure in a different way its own government and public policies. The Court concluded that 'Mexico City and the rest of the federated entities are free to create mechanisms, arrangements and innovative provisions which, as long as they do not contradict or are not incompatible with the content of the Federal Constitution, human rights and the criteria of this Supreme Court, can detach

---

34 For example, municipal governments have the power to pass rulings related to the public services that fall under their exclusive jurisdiction, such as potable water, cemeteries, markets, parks, public security and transport, among others; however, this competence has to be exercised according to the bases outlined by the legislature of the state to which they belong. See Serna de la Garza (n 24), at 142–3.

35 Under Mexican constitutional law, the notion of 'concurrent powers' refer to the possibility of sharing responsibilities among the different levels of government in the design and implementation of public policies on the same subject matter, according to a distribution of competences defined by the federal legislature. This happens, for example, in policy areas such as education, health, environmental protection and urban planning; the federal Congress can pass a statute which allocates competences and responsibilities between the two (or three) levels of government (to do this, Congress must have an express authorization in the national constitution).

36 Historically, Mexico City does not have the constitutional status of a 'state', nor has it had a constitution. Today, still, Mexico City is not a 'state', but it has a constitution of its own.

37 Judgment issued by the SCJ in Plenary session, in connection with the Action of Unconstitutionality 15/2017, published in the Official Gazette of the Federation on 25 April 2019, paragraphs 478–88.

themselves—totally or partially—from the systems of government' that exist in other federated entities and at the federal level. [38]

14.4.3 *Fundamental rights and policy principles*

All subnational constitutions in Mexico contain a section on fundamental rights. However, the manner in which these rights are incorporated varies from one state to another. Some subnational constitutions include a general clause recognizing that the inhabitants of the state shall enjoy the rights provided in the national constitution and in international treaties on human rights signed by Mexico. Other subnational constitutions reproduce all or a large part of the catalogue of rights provided in the national constitution and in some human rights treaties.[39]

Some subnational constitutions also establish specific rights that reflect local concerns. For instance: the right to marry and to form a family (Baja California Sur); the right to use of renewable energy sources and the right to medical care charged to state funds of anyone deprived of his/her liberty in the context of a criminal accusation (Chihuahua); the right to an indemnity for damages caused by the state government (Colima); the right to funerary services for indigent persons and the right of distinguished students to have access to scholarships (Durango); the right to honour and prestige (Hidalgo); the right to live with dignity (Michoacán); the right to know personal genetic information (Nayarit); the right to artistic education (Oaxaca); the right to family life (Puebla); the right to free scientific research (Sinaloa); the right to donate tissues and cells and to receive transplants (Tlaxcala); the right of persons older than 64 years of age to a monthly payment to support themselves (Chiapas); social rights of the Mayan people (Yucatán); the right to identity related to gender and to 'disorders of sexual differentiation in all stages of human development'; and the right to self-determination and autonomy of Afro-Mexican peoples and communities (Guerrero). In addition, the Constitution of Zacatecas establishes the duty of the state government to 'combat the causes of migration that harm human dignity'.[40]

Cases of constitutions adopting innovative rights that later on are incorporated into the constitutions of other states and even in the national constitution (legal transplants) are not infrequent. That was the case, for example, of the right to the protection of health, which first appeared in the Constitution of Baja California (1975) and then in the Constitutions of Hidalgo (1979), Morelos (1980) and in the national constitution (1983). Another example is the right to have access to culture, which was originally introduced into the Constitution of Michoacán (1970), and was subsequently adopted by the Constitutions of Baja California Sur (1975), Oaxaca (1990), Querétaro (2008) and by the national constitution (2009).

Following the tradition of a policy-oriented constitution that exists at the national level, subnational constitutions also establish detailed guidelines on policy that all authorities, including state legislatures, must follow. As examples, I can mention the cases of Hidalgo, whose constitution states in the fourth paragraph of its Article 5, that the principle of the best interest of the child 'should guide the design, execution, monitoring and evaluation of public policies aimed at children'. Or the second paragraph of Article 2 of the Constitution of Querétaro, which mandates that 'The State will promote norms, policies and actions to achieve equality

---

38 Ibid.
39 Jorge Ulises Carmona Tinoco, 'La problemática de incorporación y la eficacia de los derechos humanos en el constitucionalismo local' in David Cienfuegos (ed.), *Constitucionalismo local* (Porrúa 2005) 111.
40 In Spanish: 'El Estado combatirá en sus causas la migración que lesiona la dignidad humana'. A detailed discussion on these rights contained in subnational constitutions can be found in CésarAstudillo, *El Bloque y el Parámetro de Constitucionalidad en México*, (Tirant lo Blanch 2014) 104–11.

between men and women, in all areas'. And in the extreme, the case of the Constitution of Chiapas, whose Article 77 establishes that:

> To eradicate extreme poverty, raise the human development index and the quality of life of the inhabitants of the State and the municipalities that comprise it, the Powers of the State and the Municipalities, in the sphere of their competence, shall establish and implement public policies in order to achieve the Millennium Development Goals of the United Nations Development Programme.

Interestingly, Mexico's Supreme Court has established that state legislatures, when legislating on the indigenous peoples' rights and institutions, must do so under the understanding that the rights of those peoples granted by the national constitution are 'minimum rights' that must be respected, but that can be extended by state congresses according to the specific characteristics of the indigenous peoples of each state, provided that such expansion is made without violating the standards established by the national constitution.[41]

An important development is the controversy around the reform passed by the legislature of Mexico City in May of 2007, which de-criminalized the voluntary termination of pregnancy within the period of 12 weeks after conception. This reform was challenged through two actions of unconstitutionality (146/2007 and 147/2007) by the federal Attorney General[42] and by the president of the Commission on Human Rights (Mexico's federal ombudsman), alleging that it was contrary to the right to life of the product of conception granted by the Mexican Constitution, as well as by a series of international instruments ratified by Mexico. The Supreme Court decided that the reform was within the constitutional sphere of competence of Mexico City's legislature. In its turn, the Catholic Church organized a campaign throughout the entire country, promoting reforms to subnational constitutions establishing the principle that life shall be protected from the moment of conception. In a tour de force that showed the Church's political muscle, between 2008 and 2011, 18 out of the 31 states of Mexico reformed their constitutions to this effect.

Finally, a distinguishing feature of Mexico City's constitution is that it contains a very broad catalogue of human rights. For example, and apart from the 'classical' civil, political, economic, social, cultural and environmental rights, Mexico City's constitution recognizes, among many other things: the 'right to a free development of one's personality'; the right to a dignified life and to a dignified death; the right to the 'recognition of one's identity'; the recognition of all forms of family community (all of which shall be equally protected by the law); the right to sexuality and to decide with whom to share it; reproductive rights; the right to 'good public administration'; the right to have access to and to develop science and technology; the right to a sustainable development; the rights of LGBT persons; the rights of homeless people; and the rights of afro-descendant people.

---

41 SCJ, Ninth Epoch, Second Chamber, Semanario Judicial de la Federación y su Gaceta, XVI, November of 2002, page 446. Thesis: 2ª. CXXXIX/2002. Amparo directo en revisión 123/2002. Indigenous community of Zirahuén, Municipality of Salvador Escalante, State of Michoacán.
42 The Attorney General formed part of the PAN government of President Felipe Calderón. The PAN is the political party more closely identified with the interests of the Catholic Church in Mexico.

Several of these rights provisions in Mexico City's constitution have been challenged.[43] One of the most important arguments of plaintiffs was that Mexico City's constituent assembly could not expand the content of rights contained in the national constitution, nor could it create rights that were not recognized by the national constitution. However, in its judgment cited above, the Supreme Court decided against the plaintiffs stating that Mexico City, 'as well as the rest of the States of the Republic, can recognize, conceptualize, qualify, expand, develop and even create human rights', so long as they do not contradict the national constitution.[44]

14.5 Multilevel constitutionalism

14.5.1 *The relation between the national and subnational constitutions*

National and subnational provisions in Mexico are linked in different ways. Firstly, in Articles 116 and 115, the national constitution regulates the basic profile that subnational constitutions must have, mostly concerning the organization of state and municipal governments. But this does not mean that states are not allowed to go beyond the national constitutional framework.

Secondly, state legislatures participate in the amending procedure of the national constitution. According to Article 135 of the national constitution, this procedure requires the vote of two-thirds of the present members of each house of the Congress of the Union, plus the approval by the majority of state and Mexico City's legislatures. In theory, this might seem to be a 'rigid' procedure. And indeed, formally speaking it is. However, in practice Mexico's national constitution is very 'flexible', in the sense that it is reformed quite frequently. What happens in practice is that, when at the national level political parties with representation in Congress reach a consensus on a constitutional amendment (which happens very often), state legislatures join the proposal and approve it almost immediately. The explanation of this is the system of strong, disciplined and centralized political parties that exist in Mexico, which has created a culture of partisan consensus when it comes to reforming the national constitution.

14.5.2 *The impact of the Inter-American system for the protection of human rights on judicial federalism*

Two relatively recent developments have started to change the terms of the debate about judicial federalism in Mexico. The first of these is a series of judgments of the Inter-American Court of Human Rights and specifically its doctrine of 'control of conventionality'. The second is the constitutional reform of 10 June 2011 on human rights and the understanding of Mexico's Supreme Court of Justice of the country's incorporation into the Inter-American system on human rights. These developments have meant that all courts in the land, federal and from the states, have the power to 'disapply' statutes they deem contrary to human rights established in the Constitution or in international treaties signed by Mexico. This is an important step away

---

43 On February 5, 2017, the Decree issuing the Constitution of Mexico City was published in the Official Gazette of the Federation and in the Official Gazette of Mexico City, which established that it would enter into force on 17 September 2018. Soon afterwards, various government actors, political parties, and autonomous agencies filed seven constitutional proceedings before the Supreme Court of Justice of the Nation: four actions of unconstitutionality and three constitutional controversies.

44 Judgment issued by the SCJ in Plenary session, in connection with the Action of Unconstitutionality 15/2017, published in the Official Gazette of the Federation on April 25, 2019, paragraph 146.

from the traditional 'centralized' system of judicial review (control of constitutionality), towards a 'diffuse' system of constitutional justice.

My reference to the doctrine of 'control of conventionality' deserves an additional explanation. This doctrine derives from several judgments of the Inter-American Court on Human Rights (IACHR). In one of those judgments in which Mexico was found responsible for a series of human rights violations, the IACHR defined said doctrine as follows:

> 339. With regard to judicial practices, this Tribunal has established, in its jurisprudence, that it is aware that the domestic judges and tribunals are subject to the rule of law and that, therefore, they are compelled to apply the regulations in force within the legal system. But once a State has ratified an international treaty such as the American Convention, its judges, as part of the State's apparatus, are also submitted to it, which compels them to make sure that the provisions of the Convention are not affected by the application of laws contrary to its object and purpose, and that they do not lack legal effects from their creation. In other words, the Judiciary shall exercise a 'control of conventionality' ex officio between domestic regulations and the American Convention, evidently within the framework of its respective competences and the corresponding procedural regulations. Within this task, the Judiciary shall take into consideration not only the treaty but also the interpretation the Inter-American Court, final interpreter of the American Convention, has made of it.[45]

For its part, Mexico's Supreme Court of Justice discussed the implications of this judgment for Mexico's judicial system in the 'Expediente Varios 912/2010', stating as a conclusion that as a consequence of the 2011 constitutional reform on human rights, the rights contained in the Constitution must be interpreted in accordance with international treaties on the same matter, in such a way that they better protect the person (pro persona principle); and that all Mexican courts, both federal and from the states, have the duty to verify that the laws they apply are in accordance with the Constitution and with international human rights treaties (and their interpretation by the IACHR). For the Supreme Court, all judges may decide on the non-application in the specific case of rules that they consider contrary to the Constitution or to international human rights treaties.[46]

14.6 Constitutional review

In 2000 the state of Veracruz approved an 'integral' reform of its subnational constitution. This reform was challenged by the city council of the municipality of Córdoba on various grounds (i.e. invasion of competences of municipal governments that derive from the national constitution; the municipality of Córdoba also alleged that the reform had not been really a reform to the existing subnational constitution, but a new constitution, which would have required the election of a constituent assembly among others). In its decision, the Supreme Court of Mexico expressed its vision of the margin that subnational institutions have to reform their constitutions, by saying that Article 116 of the national constitution establishes the 'minimal questions' that subnational constitutions should express in their texts. This is because the national constitution

---

45 Inter-American Human Rights, *Radilla Pacheco v United Mexican States*, Judgment of November 23, 2009.

46 This statement contradicts the traditional view of Mexico's Supreme Court, according to which only the federal court could disapply statutes for being contrary to the Constitution. See 'Expediente Varios 912/2010', published in the Official Gazette of the Federation on 4 October 2011.

itself does not impose any express limits on the ability of the states to carry out reforms of their subnational constitutions. The Supreme Court pointed out that the national constitution does not prohibit or even restrict the power of state congresses to modify the texts of their subnational constitution; it only points out the principles that must be respected in order to achieve harmony with the fundamental principles of the national constitution and prevent any contradiction with it.[47]

The Supreme Court of Mexico has made it clear, however, that subnational constitutions can be reviewed through the so-called action of unconstitutionality, which is an abstract mechanism for controlling the constitutionality of 'general norms' which are contrary to the national constitution (subnational constitutions, federal and state statutes and international treaties qualify as 'general norms'). The Supreme Court has said:

> to consider that the Constitutions of the States of the Republic cannot be analyzed in this way [through the action of unconstitutionality], would imply that these local norms could escape the abstract control of their subordination with respect to the Federal Constitution, which is inadmissible, since according to the content of Articles 40, 41 and 133 of the Political Constitution of the United Mexican States, this order is the Supreme Law of the entire Union and although the States are free and sovereign in everything concerning their internal regime, their Constitutions in no way are allowed to contravene the provisions of the Federal Pact.[48]

Concerning the power of subnational courts as guardians of subnational constitutions by reviewing state legislation against the latter, I must say that their role has been very limited. For instance, during the four years of its existence (2002–07), the Superior Chamber of Chiapas' Superior Tribunal heard and solved one subnational constitutional case only. Moreover, the picture offered in 2009 by one of the few scholars who has done empirical research on the activities of subnational constitutional courts is still quite valid: as reported by Julio Bustillo, between 2000 and 2009, of the total constitutional judicial proceedings filed at state level, only 40 per cent were resolved on their merits. The rest were dismissed on formal and procedural grounds.[49]

The perception that subnational constitutional courts do not play a relevant role has led to proposals in favour of their disappearance. This has already happened in the State of Chihuahua;[50] and it has been proposed in the States of Chiapas[51] and Veracruz.[52]

14.7 Conclusion

There has been little theoretical reflection about state constitutionalism in Mexico. One reason has to do with the centralized character of Mexico's federal system and political process.

---

47 SCJN, Constitutional controversy 16/2000. Ayuntamiento del Municipio de Córdoba, *Semanario Judicial de la Federación y su Gaceta*, Ninth Epoch, Plenary Session, XVI, August 2002, p. 901. Thesis: P./J. 33/2002.
48 SCJN, Action of unconstitutionality 9/2001. Deputies of the LVII Legislature of the state of Tabasco. Ninth Epoch, Plenary session, *Semanario Judicial de la Federación y su Gaceta*, XIII, March 2001, p. 447. Thesis: P./J. 16/2001.
49 Julio Bustillos, 'La realidad de la justicia constitucional mexicana en el siglo XXI (a través de sus resoluciones definitivas' (2009) 21 *Cuestiones Constitucionales. Revista Mexicana de Derecho Constitucional* 64.
50 Amendment to the Constitution of Chihuahua of 29 April 2017.
51 Proposal of the Governor of Chiapas, Rutilio Escandón. Diario *El Universal*, 16 December 2019.
52 Proposal of a group of state legislators, published in the Parliamentary Gazette of Veracruz, No. 44, 8 June 2017.

Constitutional scholars have accordingly tended to focus on the national constitution alone. One of the few authors who has discussed state constitutionalism, Diego Valadés, considers the state constitutions to be 'derived' from the general constitution; the 'derived' normative order of the states is therefore able to move within the margins, which can be wider or narrower, that are allowed by the 'originary' constitutionalism.[53] The extent of this margin of flexibility is determined by the residual powers clause of Article 124 of the federal constitution, the prohibitions to the states that the latter defines in its Articles 117 and 118, and the rules and standards that subnational constitutions have to follow in the organization of state and municipal political and administrative structures (found in Articles 116 and 115 of the federal constitution, respectively).

This means that in Mexico there is less 'subnational constitutional space' than in many other federal states. Mexico's national constitution is more 'complete' than many other federal constitutions. Indeed, Mexico's federal constitution mandates that many provisions and matters must be contained in the state constitutions.

Mexico's states do not have full constitutional autonomy. They are limited both normatively and politically speaking—normatively, because the national constitution establishes a very extensive and detailed list of rules and principles that subnational constitutions must follow; and politically, because in spite of the fact that, formally speaking, states have the capacity to impact on the national constitution's provisions that determine their status and organization, this does not happen in the actual political process: when participating in the procedure of amending the national constitution, state legislators clearly tend to follow the impulses coming from the national party authorities, rather than those coming from their state constituencies.

In general terms, subnational constitutions in Mexico are similar to each other. Under the hegemonic party system (1929–2000), subnational constitutionalism was subordinated to national constitutionalism, and constitutional change in the states occurred as a consequence— that is, as a reflex reaction—to changes in the federal constitution. This in turn led to significant uniformity among the state constitutions. However, the new room for manoeuvre created with the emergence of a multi-party and competitive political system, at least since the year 2000, has enabled state political actors to shape their subnational constitution in original and creative ways, leading to some degree of differentiation. This trend may be further encouraged by the decision of the Supreme Court in connection with the challenges against Mexico City's constitution of 2017,[54] in which it sent a clear message: the states are free to create institutions of government, mechanisms, arrangements and innovative provisions, and can recognize, conceptualize, qualify, expand, develop and even create human rights, so long as they do not contradict or are not incompatible with the national constitution.

---

53 Diego Valadés, *Constitución y Política* (UNAM, Instituto de Investigaciones Jurídicas, 1987) 80–1.
54 Judgment issued by the SCJ in Plenary session, in connection with the Action of Unconstitutionality 15/2017, published in the Official Gazette of the Federation on 25 April 2019.

15

SUBNATIONAL CONSTITUTIONALISM IN SOUTH AFRICA

An empty promise

Nico Steytler[1]

The Western Cape's provincial constitution of 1997 re-emerged from obscurity in 2019 when a provision relating to the position of a Commissioner for Environment was sought to be removed. It made news again in 2020 when, after a lapse of 23 years, the first Commissioner for Children was appointed to this constitutional office. Until these two events, the provincial constitution was invisible, and more or less moribund in practice. Furthermore, it has remained the only provincial constitution in the country ever since the Constitutional Court trashed the KwaZulu-Natal provincial legislature's outrageous attempt in 1996. This state of affairs raises a number of questions: why was the provincial competence of adopting a provincial constitution included in the national Constitution? Why has this competence been exercised by only two provinces, and when one did so successfully, why did it prove to be of such limited value?

It is argued, first, that the inclusion of the competence was one of the measures of holding together the new democratic South Africa in face of a race and ethnic-based conflict. Second, as the ruling African National Congress (ANC) was opposed to federalism, none of the provinces under its control sought to exercise this 'federal' measure. Third, as this competence provides little scope for a provincial voice, the two attempts by opposition-held provinces could hardly express a provincial identity. Fourth, the small impact the Western Cape provincial constitution has had illustrates the emptiness of the constitutional promise of provincial constituent power.

15.1 Context

The provincial competence to adopt a provincial constitution formed part and parcel of the negotiations (1993–94) to establish a hybrid-federal system of government within a new constitutional democracy. One of the key disputed issues between the two main negotiating parties—the African National Congress (ANC) representing the black majority and the National Party (NP) representing the white minority government—was federalism. The NP and its initial

1 The support of the South African Research Chairs Initiatives of the Department of Science and Technology, and the National Research Foundation, through the South African Chair in Multilevel Government, Law and Development, is gratefully acknowledged.

DOI: 10.4324/9781003052111-15

alliance partners in some of the ethnic-based homeland governments, notably the Inkatha Freedom Party (IFP) of Mangosuthu Buthelezi, with a strong Zulu-nationalist orientation, argued for a federal system principally for two reasons: first, the homeland leaders sought to retain some of the power and patronage they enjoyed under the NP's apartheid policy. Indeed, in 1991 the legislature of the KwaZulu homeland adopted a 'provincial constitution' which was confederal in nature, including its own military force, a high level of self-governance, as well as the right to secession.[2] The whites, on the other hand, could not gain much from an ethnic-based federation because they were dispersed across the 87 per cent of the land mass they owned or controlled.[3] The NP's interest was a weakened central government, controlled by the ANC, and strong provinces, some of which they may capture in alliance with local ethnic black elites.

The ANC would have none of this. Their liberation movement was based on non-racialism and non-ethnicity. Ethnicity was equated to tribalism, used by the NP in its pernicious strategy of dividing and ruling the black majority. The ANC sought to protect language and culture interests but through individualized rights in a Bill of Rights. What the ANC wanted was a unified, unitary state, with a strong centralized government to undo the ravages of apartheid—the legacy of structural inequality caused by racial oppression. Federalism, so the argument went, would simply perpetuate apartheid.

A compromise was eventually reached in 1993 between the ANC and the NP on non-centralism, assiduously avoiding the word 'federalism'. The interim Constitution, a negotiated instrument, provided for weak provinces having only concurrent powers with the national government, but with a qualified override clause. The structures and procedures of provincial legislatures and executives were also fully set out. It also contained the provincial competency for the adoption of a provincial constitution which could not be inconsistent with the national Constitution. The reasoning for including such a straightjacketed provincial constituent power could only have been symbolic, a sop to the federalists. It imitated the subnational constitutions of the United States, Australia, India, Germany and Brazil, but without allowing any room for their own identity.

This interim Constitution, adopted in December 1993 by the apartheid Parliament, paved the way for the first democratic elections to be held on 27 April 1994. The weakness of the 1993 Constitution was that the IFP had withdrawn from the negotiating process as it perceived that it was not regarded as the third negotiating party of equal status to that of the ANC and the NP. It also was opposed to the interim Constitution because of its weak federal provisions, and thus refused to participate in the April elections. The IFP had the capacity to spoil a peaceful transition to majority rule, as at that time an intense civil war was raging in the province of Natal between the Zulu nationalists (clandestinely supported by the white government) and the ANC. In attempts to lure the IFP to participate in the elections, amendments to the interim Constitution were effected in which the provisions relating to provincial constitutions were of significance.

In an effort to entice the IFP into participating in the elections, a strengthening of the provincial powers were included in the first amendment of the interim Constitution of 3 March 1994, but without securing the buy-in of the IFP beforehand.[4] First, provinces could devise 'legislative and executive structures and procedures *different* from those provided in the

---

2 Stephan Ellman 'Federalism Gone Awry: The Structure of Government in the KwaZulu/Natal Constitution' (1993) 9 *South African Journal on Human Rights* 165.

3 The right-wing Afrikaner nationalist sought such a 'volkstaat', but in the end failed to locate such a promised land. See Nico Steytler 'The Withering away of Politically Salient Territorial Cleavages in South Africa and the Emergence of Watermark Ethnic Federalism' in George Anderson and Sujit Choudhry (eds) *Territory and Power in Constitutional Transitions* (Oxford University Press 2019) 219.

4 This section is taken from Steytler (n 3).

Constitution'.[5] Second, a number of functional areas were added to the provincial concurrent list: airports, consumer protection, provincial sport, soil conservation and 'indigenous law and customary law'.[6] The inclusion of 'indigenous law and customary law' was significant because for the first time the link between ethnicity and provinces was made. Third, a further Constitutional Principle was added: in the final Constitution, provincial powers and functions 'shall not be substantially less than or inferior to those provided in [the interim] Constitution',[7] thus affirming the permanent nature of the concessions. Finally, in an amendment aimed specifically at the IFP, there was a name change: Natal, the colonial name, became 'KwaZulu/Natal'.[8] This symbolic move for the first time assigned an ethnic label to a province, breaching the non-ethnic principle in the naming of all provinces.

The IFP was not seduced by these new powers and the conflict in the province continued. A week before election day the IFP stepped back from the brink, agreeing to participate in the election, gaining an ostensibly insignificant amendment to the Constitution: a provincial constitution could provide for 'the institution, role authority and status of a traditional monarch in the province', and in the case of KwaZulu-Natal, there must be a provision for the 'Zulu monarch'.[9] The recognition of a traditional monarch, lying at the apex of black ethnicity, would give those provinces with a majority ethnic group, a distinct ethnic identity. In the case of KwaZulu-Natal, the reference to the Zulu monarch made that province unashamedly Zulu. Moreover, this was not a transitional arrangement; the provision in a provincial constitution relating to 'the institution, role authority and status of a traditional monarch' was cemented in the Constitutional Principles.[10] Thus, two days before the election day of 27 April, the second amendment to the Constitution was adopted by the apartheid Parliament. The contours of provincial constitutions were thus forged in the killing fields of KwaZulu-Natal; it opened a small window for provincial constitutions to reflect an ethnic identity.

The 1994 national elections swept the ANC into power with 62.6 per cent of the vote, the National Party garnered 20.4 per cent, and the IFP 10.5 per cent. In the Western Cape, the National Party achieved a majority of 53.2 per cent, while in KwaZulu-Natal, the IFP's majority was 50.3 per cent,[11] allowing both opposition parties the taste of provincial power, albeit in governments of provincial unity.

The elected national Parliament doubled up as the Constitutional Assembly (CA), charged with the task of drafting within two years a 'final' constitution which complied with a set of Constitutional Principles, which included safeguards for provincial autonomy. This constitution-making structure thus provided the IFP an opportunity to enhance its federal claims. However, the IFP withdrew from the CA, because of alleged outstanding issues linked to their participation in the elections (including the need for international mediation), although Buthelezi took up his ministerial seat in the Government of National Unity to which he was entitled.[12] In the end the CA adopted a constitution in which the status and powers of provinces were reduced

---

5 Act 2 of 1994, s 7 (emphasis added).
6 Act 2 of 1994, s 14.
7 Constitutional Principle XVIII(2), added by Act 2 of 1994, s 13.
8 Act 2 of 1994, s 1. In the final Constitution the name became hyphenated—'KwaZulu-Natal'—indicating a joining together of two parts. This name construction is used in the rest of the chapter.
9 Constitution of the Republic of South Africa Second Amendment Act, Act 3 of 1994, s 1, assented to on 26 April 1994.
10 Act 3 of 1994, s 2, amending Constitutional Principle XIII.
11 On the fairness of the balloting process in KwaZulu/Natal, see Peter Harris, *Birth—the Conspiracy to Stop the '94 Election* (Umuzi 2010); David Welsh, *The Rise and Fall of Apartheid* (Jonathan Ball Publishers 2009) 556.
12 Any party obtaining 5 per cent of the national vote was entitled to a cabinet position.

compared to the interim Constitution, but the provisions relating to provincial constitutions remained essentially the same.

With the IFP in the driving seat in KwaZulu-Natal, the provincial legislature commenced with a provincial constitution-making process in 1995. With the concurrence of the ANC and other minority parties, the legislature adopted a draft provincial constitution in that year that sought to establish a federal system which the IFP could not secure through the CA. However, the Constitutional Court had little hesitation in rejecting the draft constitution as being wholly inconsistent with the 1993 Constitution. Following this decision, the Western Cape, also in opposition hands, sought to draft a provincial constitution, this time under the 1996 Constitution, but with the explicit aim of achieving Constitutional Court approval, which it eventually achieved in 1997. Since then, no other province has adopted a provincial constitution.

15.2 Autonomy to draft a provincial constitution

15.2.1 Scope

The 1996 national Constitution (NC) sets very restricted parameters in terms of which a provincial legislature can adopt a provincial constitution (PC), and the scope for variations from the NC has been narrowed down further by the Constitutional Court.

The scope of a PC commences on a prohibitory note: 'A provincial constitution, or constitutional amendment, must not be inconsistent with this [national] Constitution'.[13] This consistency principle entails that a PC must be in conformity with the entire NC, and in particular with Chapter 6 dealing with provinces, which provides comprehensively for the structures and processes of the legislature and the executive.

The consistency principle is softened by two permissive exceptions. First, a PC 'may provide for provincial legislative and executive structures and procedures that differ from those provided in this Chapter 6'.[14] The second exception, and seemingly in the alternative, is that a PC may provide for 'the institution, role, authority and status of a traditional monarch, where applicable'.[15] The two permissive exceptions are themselves constrained by a consistency principle in two respects. First, any different legislative or executive structure or procedure must comply with two foundational values of the new constitutional dispensation: the founding values contained in Section 15.1 and the principles of cooperative government entrenched in Chapter 3.

Section 15.1 contains a set of broad-ranging values, reflecting their repression during the apartheid years. It is stated that the Republic of South Africa is one, sovereign, democratic state founded on the following values:

(a) Human dignity, the achievement of equality and the advancement of human rights and freedoms.
(b) Non-racialism and non-sexism.
(c) Supremacy of the constitution and the rule of law.
(d) Universal adult suffrage, a national common voters roll, regular elections and a multi-party system of democratic government, to ensure accountability, responsiveness and openness.

---

13 Constitution 1996 (NC), s 143(1).
14 Ibid., s 143(1)(a).
15 Ibid., s 143(1)(b).

The key object of Chapter 3 on Cooperative Government was to establish, in the words of the Constitutional Court, a 'new philosophy' of cooperative government,[16] and not one of competitive federalism. Such cooperative government is predicated on a common loyalty to the NC, 'the Republic and its people'.[17]

The second principle entails that a PC may not give a province powers and functions other than those given by the NC.[18] This reiterates one of the principles of executive cooperative government in Chapter 3: organs of state 'must not assume any power or function except those conferred on them in terms of the Constitution'.[19]

Perhaps the most important restriction lies in a financial disincentive; a province must provide for itself any resources that it requires for anything additional to what the Constitution envisages.[20] With no direct taxing powers, and little access to any own source revenue,[21] provinces have very little operational room to finance any new constitutional structures or procedures.

15.2.2 Procedure

Aligned to the NC amendment process, a special majority of at least two-thirds in provincial legislature is required for the adoption or amendment of a provincial constitution.[22] No public participation or approval through a mandatory referendum is required. However, a review by the Constitutional Court is mandatory, the only instance where an abstract review of any legislation—national or provincial—is compulsory. The Constitutional Court must positively certify that a provincial constitution is consistent with the provisions relating to provincial constitutions.[23] This mandatory step also applies when a PC is amended. Only once the Constitutional Court has certified such compliance may the Premier of a province assent to the PC for it to become law.[24]

Once a provincial constitution has passed the test of consistency with the NC, the issue of conflict between it and national legislation remains. The conflict resolution rules accord no specific status to a provincial constitution and follow the general conflict resolution mechanisms when there is a conflict between national and provincial legislation:[25] first, on a matter which the NC specifically requires or envisages the enactment of national legislation, that national law prevails over any conflicting provision in a PC; second, a valid national legislative intervention in the exclusive provincial legislative jurisdiction[26] prevails over a conflicting PC provision; and, third, in the case of national legislation in the field of a concurrent functional area, the general (qualified) override clause applies.[27]

---

16 *Certification* judgment para 468.
17 NC, s 41(1)(d).
18 NC, s 143(2).
19 NC, s 41(1)(f).
20 Constitution, s 227(4).
21 Provinces raise between 3 and 5 per cent of their revenue; the rest comes from transfers. Bongani Khumalo, Jugal Mahabir and Ghalieb Dawood, 'South Africa's intergovernmental fiscal relations system' in Nico Steytler and Yash Pal Ghai (eds) *Kenya-South Africa Dialogue on Devolution* (Juta 2015) 201.
22 NC, s 142.
23 NC, s 144(1).
24 NC, s 145.
25 NC, s 147.
26 NC, sch 5.
27 NC, s 146.

The strictures of the general framework have been tested by the provincial legislatures of KwaZulu-Natal and the Western Cape, to which we now turn.

15.3 Position of the subnational constitutions

As will be seen in the subsequent section, the only provincial constitution that survived Constitutional Court scrutiny was that of the Western Cape. The form of the constitution, which came into operation in 1997, is that of a unified document; it is the only legal instrument imbued with constitutional status. However, as will be explained below, the Constitution contains many of the provisions of the NC and only a sprinkling of new or original provisions. The PC is quite emphatic about its status vis-à-vis other provincial laws: 'Subject to the national Constitution, it is the highest law in the Western Cape'.[28] Any law or action inconsistent with the WC PC is thus void. How the WC PC was used, symbolically and in practice, or why a political attempt was made in KZN to draft a provincial constitution, is best discussed after detailing the two very different scenarios below.

15.4 Content

15.4.1 Judicial definitions of provinces' constitution-making powers

The ANC, who controlled seven of the nine provinces,[29] was in principle against the expansion of the provincial system, and, moreover, saw no necessity in drafting PCs;[30] as the Constitutional Court later observed, the NC provided 'a complete blueprint for the regulation of government within provinces which provides adequately for the establishment and functioning of provincial legislatures and executives'.[31] In the two provinces where the ANC did not have a majority—KwaZulu-Natal and the Western Cape—the incumbent ruling parties, the IFP and the NNP respectively, sought to adopt provincial constitutions in an attempt to craft some sort of provincial identity.[32] In the mandatory review process of the draft PCs, the Constitutional Court gave a definitive interpretation of the parameters of provinces' constitution-making powers.

15.4.2 Draft KwaZulu-Natal provincial constitution, 1996

While the Constitutional Assembly commenced its deliberation in February 1995 on the new constitution, the IFP, which withdrew from that process soon afterwards, threw its efforts into shaping the federal arrangements from below in KZN.[33] The IFP had a bare majority of seats in

---

28 Western Cape Provincial Constitution (WC PC), s 4.
29 In 2004 the ANC controlled all the provinces, and since 2009 only the Western Cape remain in the hands of the main opposition party, the Democratic Alliance.
30 See Stuart Woolman 'Provincial constitutions' in Stuart Woolman and Michael Bishop (eds) *Constitutional Law of South Africa* (2nd edn, Juta 2005) 21–4.
31 Certification of the Constitution of the Western Cape, 1997 [1997] ZACC 8 ('Certification WC judgment') para 15.
32 Christina Murray 'Provincial constitution-making in South Africa: the (non)example of the Western Cape (2001) Neue Folge Band 49 *Jahrbuch des öffentlichen Rechts* 481 (also available at <http://www.publiclaw.uct.ac.za/usr/public_law/staff/Murray%20Provincial%20Constitutions%20in%20South%20Africa%20-%20the%20non-example%20of%20the%20Western%20Cape%202001.pdf>, to which page references are made) 14; Woolman (n 30).
33 Veronica Federico, 'South African quasi-federalism' in Hugh Corder, Veronica Federico and Romano Orrù (eds) *The Quest for Constitutionalism: South Africa since 1994* (Routledge 2014) 15.

the 81-seat provincial legislature (41 seats), and would thus require for a two-thirds majority the support of the minority parties (NP, Democratic Party, Minority Party and African Christian Democratic Party), excluding the ANC with 32 per cent of the seats and the Pan African Congress with one seat. In the end all the parties voted unanimously for the PC, because, as some commentators noted, in the context of the lingering KZN civil war, a unanimous vote was a symbolic gesture towards peace building and reconciliation in that province.[34] Once the gesture of goodwill was made, the ANC in the province and the ANC-controlled national government strenuously attacked the obvious unconstitutionality of the KZN PC before the Constitutional Court.[35] Not only did the Constitutional Court view the unanimous support in the provincial legislature as irrelevant to its judicial task, but it was also puzzled by the ANC's switching of opinion.[36] On the IFP's part, it may have viewed the PC as no more than a cynical political statement showing the limits of federal arrangements in the interim Constitution, and perforce in the final constitution.

The KZN PC manifestly fell outside the parameters of the available constitutional space the interim Constitution allowed; it sought to create a federal system which was not provided for. First, it defined KZN as 'self-governing'[37] and based on the 'principle of federal partnership'.[38] Second, it included a Bill of Rights with rights relating to fair trials, labour and states of emergency. Third, it established a provincial constitutional court and a provincial police force. To save the Bill's obviously unconstitutional provisions, two legal techniques were employed: first, through a consistency clause, only provisions consistent with the national Constitution would be valid, and, second, through a suspensive clause—provisions in conflict with the national Constitution did not apply until such time that the province has been empowered by national Constitution to enact them.

No special place for the Zulu monarch, King Goodwill Zwelithini, was provided for because by that time, the ANC breached the political relationship between the monarch and Buthelezi by winning over the King to their camp.[39]

The Constitutional Court had to review the KZN PC in terms of the then operative interim Constitution. At the very same time it was also reviewing the draft text of the 'final' Constitution adopted in May 1996.[40] It delivered its judgment in both cases on the same day (6 September) and the two should thus be read jointly. As the provisions in the 'final' Constitution on provincial constitutions were regarded as 'substantially the same' as in the interim Constitution,[41] the *Certification KZN* judgment remains good law.

The Court asserted first and foremost the most basic principle of provincial constitution-making: it has to be done foursquare within the interim Constitution. In the *Certification NC* judgment, the Court emphasized the limited scope for a PC: it 'is not a provincial constitution suitable to an independent or confederal state but one dealing with the governance of a province

---

34 See George Devenish 'The making and significance of the Draft KwaZulu-Natal Constitution' (1995) 9 *Yearbook of South African Law* 3, referred to in Woolman (n 30) ch 21 15 n 5; Murray (n 32), at 13.

35 *Certification KZN* judgment para 12.

36 *Certification KZN* judgment para 12.

37 Draft KwaZulu-Natal Provincial Constitution (KZN PC), cl 1(1).

38 KZN PC, cl 1(5).

39 It took another ten years before the KZN Legislature, now under the ANC control, passed the Traditional Leadership and Governance Act in 2005, setting out the role and status of the Zulu monarch. See Woolman (n 30) 4.

40 The hearing of the KZN PC took place from 25 to 27 June, while that for the NC took place the following week—1 to 5, and 8 to 11 July 1996.

41 *Certification NC* judgment, para 343.

whose powers are derived from the [NC]'.[42] A province could thus not give itself powers that it did not have: 'a province cannot by means of the bootstraps of its own constitution confer on its legislature greater powers than those granted it by the interim Constitution'.[43] In the *Certification NC* judgment the Court, referring to its judgment in the *Certification KZN* case, reiterated the principle: 'a provincial legislature manifestly does not have the power, through adopting a constitution, to alter the power relationship between itself and the national level of government, or to usurp powers which are not vested in it'.[44] The Court found that the KZN PC transgressed this basic rule. It thus chided the KZN Legislature because the KZN PC 'would appear to have been passed by the KZN Legislature under a misapprehension that it enjoyed a relationship of co-supremacy with the national Legislature and even the Constitutional Assembly'.[45]

Second, the KZN PC repeated numerous provisions found in the interim Constitution as if the PC was the basis of them and not the interim Constitution, displaying yet another example of the usurpation of powers.[46]

Third, the two provisions seeking to save the constitution from invalidity—the consistency and suspensive clauses—could not immunize the Bill from the Court's scrutiny; the Court must be able to certify that each and every provision was compliant with the national Constitution.

Fourth, a province could have a Bill of Rights, restraining the provincial government even more than the national Bill of Rights, but only in areas of provincial competence. It thus could not include fair trial rights as the province had no competence over the courts or the police.

The Court thus refused to certify the draft PC on these grounds, although there were many more inconsistencies. Because the KZN PC was so at odds with the constitutional framework, the judgment set out only broad principles. A more detailed interpretation of the scope of provincial constitution-making had to wait for the next opposition-held province, the Western Cape, to venture down this path.

15.4.3 Western Cape provincial constitution

In the Western Cape Provincial Legislature the National Party, now after a cosmetic makeover calling itself the New National Party (NNP), was in a more or less similar situation as the IFP in KZN; with 23 seats in the 42-seat chamber, it had 55 per cent of the vote, while the ANC's 14 seats gave it exactly 33.3 per cent. The NNP needed the other minor opposition parties, the Democratic Party (3 seats), the Freedom Front (1 seat) and the African Christian Democratic Party (1 seat) to muster the requisite two-thirds majority—66.6 per cent exactly. The political divide had some demographic basis; the majority of population were so-called Coloureds (54.2 per cent), followed by Africans (20.9 per cent) and then whites (20.8 per cent).[47] While the majority of Coloureds and white Afrikaans-speakers sided with the NNP and the white English-speakers supported the more liberal Democratic Party, Africans overwhelmingly voted for the ANC, as did a large section of the coloured community.

The NNP's appetite for a provincial constitution stemmed from the desire to give an identity to the province,[48] and the party commenced the drafting process during 1996 with a clear intent, in light of the Constitutional Court's certification judgments on the KZN PC and NC,

---

42 *Certification NC* judgment, para 349.
43 *Certification KZN* judgment, para 8.
44 *Certification NC* judgment, para 348.
45 *Certification KZN* judgment, para 15.
46 *Certification KZN* judgment, para 24.
47 Statistics South Africa, *The People of South Africa Population Census, 1996* (Statistics South Africa 1998) table 2.6.
48 Murray (n 32).

to seek a positive certification outcome. A public consultation process was followed which included holding hearings across the province and receiving submissions.[49] The Western Cape (WC) PC was eventually passed by a two-thirds majority, with the ANC voting against it. The latter then continued their opposition before the Constitutional Court in the certification hearing. Although its challenges covered most of the text, the Court faulted the WC PC on three grounds only. In the process, the Court gave clear guidance on the future scope of provincial constitution-making.

15.4.3.1 *Completing an incomplete provincial 'constitution'*

If the PC sought to capture the essence of a provincial government—'the fundamental identifying marks of the state, the organization of public authority, the relations of public bodies with individuals, and the determination of some basic policy principles'[50]—there was precious little to be added to the NC. If the filling in of only bits and pieces was permitted by the NC, the PC would not look much like a constitution. Included in the WC PC were thus also those provisions in the NC which empower provinces, which in toto amounted to 39 of the 84 provisions.[51] The difficulty was, of course, that the PC could not give itself those powers as if it was the source of those powers, and thus conflict directly with the *Certification KZN* judgment. Aimed at completeness, WC PC thus includes a repetition of provisions of the NC with the following safeguard: 'The legislative and executive powers and functions of the Western Cape recorded in this Constitution emanate exclusively from the national Constitution'.[52] The Court thus had no objection to this provision as the PC subservience is clear; there was no usurpation of powers. It did, however, create the problem that when the NC's provisions concerning provinces were later amended, they made the copied PC provisions inconsistent with the NC and thus invalid.

The Court objected, however, to two pieces of 'filling in': who does the swearing in of the Premier and the cabinet and what is the meaning of 'paid work' that members of the provincial executive may not do?

In terms of the NC, the Chief Justice of the Constitutional Court, or a judge designated by him or her, must apply the prescribed oath or solemn affirmation to the premiers and members of the executive councils before they may assume office.[53] In practice the Chief Justice, sitting in Johannesburg, 1,400 km away, designates the most senior judge of the Western Cape High Court, who is a mere 100 m away from the Premier's office, in the building next door, to do the ceremonial honours. In replacing constitutional principle with pragmatism, the PC allocated the duty to the Judge President next door. The Constitutional Court correctly found that this provision usurped a function of the Chief Justice, making this error one of the three grounds in refusing certification.

The Court also rejected the PC provision giving the provincial legislature the power to statutorily define the meaning of 'paid work' which members of the executive may not do. Here the reasoning is less convincing. The NC provides that a member of a provincial executive council, being a full-time position, may not 'undertake any other paid work'.[54] The meaning of 'paid

49 See Dirk Brand, 'Western Cape Constitution' (1999) 31 *Rutgers Law Journal* 961.
50 Chapter 1 Introduction.
51 Murray (n 32), at 4.
52 WC PC, cl 3(2).
53 NC, ss 129, 131, 135 read with schedule 2 item 5.
54 NC, s 136(2)(b).

work' is obviously not a neatly defined concept, but rather calls for interpretation, a task the Court arrogated to itself, thereby preventing the provincial legislature from doing so. But how, commentators asked, would the Court do so if there were no legislative instrument that it could review?[55] The task of the Court would then be, appropriately, to test the legislation against its own interpretation of the concept. This ground for withholding certification shows a stingy interpretation that disallows any variation between provinces, where circumstances may well differ.

15.4.3.2 In search of an identity?

As noted above, due to the racial demographics unique in South Africa, where Africans formed a minority in the Western Cape, the quest for a Western Cape identity along linguistic or cultural lines would be highly problematic in the new South Africa of the rainbow nation. Neither the preamble nor any other measure directly sought to push such a line, but the possibilities were there.

The preamble, devoid of any localized sentiment, declares loyalty to the NC, and strives for the development of the province. The ANC found objectionable the opening phrase—'In humble submission to the Almighty God'—both because it was the opening line of the old apartheid constitution and that it was at odds with a secular state. The Court found, however, that the preamble could not impose any type of religion on the province; besides, the NC's preamble itself ends with the religious invocation: 'May God protect our people'.

The ANC was also wary of the provision that '[a] provincial Act may provide for (a) provincial symbols; [and] (b) conferral of provincial honours'.[56] They feared that waving a provincial flag would invoke a separate identity, coming so soon after the establishment of the new South Africa where common loyalty to the new flag and national symbols was yet to be cemented. The legal argument that this provision would impinge on the president's power to bestow honours did not carry much weight with the Court, which found nothing objectionable in these provisions. In any event, the province did not design its own flag, but along with all the other provinces, sported its own coat of arms, with quintessentially Western Cape symbols, such as an anchor featuring its maritime history, a bunch of grapes showcasing its wine industry, and two antelopes—the extinct quagga and the endemic bontebok. The motto of 'Spes Bona' harks back to an earlier nomenclature of the Cape of Good Hope.

15.4.3.3 Stepping out: Different legislative and executive structures and procedures

The main opportunity for some sort of provincial uniqueness would be the establishment of legislative and executive structures and procedures that differed from the NC. The WC PC's attempt ranged from the negligible (the name of the legislature) to the more profound (a separate electoral system).

The Court viewed the constitutionally permitted exception as going only to the form and not the substance of legislative and executive structures and procedures.[57] Although not contested on this ground, the self-aggrandisement of naming of provincial legislature a 'Provincial

---

55 Woolman (n 30) ch 21 17.
56 WC PC, cl 6(1).
57 *Certification WC* judgment, para 16.

Parliament' and the Members of the Executive Council (MECs) as 'Ministers' was accepted by the Court as merely a matter of form, not substance.[58]

Determining the size of the provincial parliament required direct reliance on the exception of a different legislative structure. In terms of the interim Constitution, the size of the provincial legislature was 42 members, which the PC repeated. However, the NC provided that the size is determined by the Electoral Commission in terms of a formula. The Court found that this was indeed a change of form which is legitimately permitted. The real test came with regard to a unique electoral system for the Western Cape. The NC provides for a provincial electoral system as 'prescribed by national legislation' which 'results, in general, in proportional representation'.[59] At that time the NC provided for a closed party-list system of proportional representation.[60] Given the lack of accountability such a PR system facilitates (elected representatives are not responsive or accountable to any geographical constituencies), a combination of both a PR and constituency-based system was proposed.[61] Copying section 46 of the NC, the WC PC added the clause that the electoral system should be 'based predominantly on the representation of geographic multi-member constituencies; and results, in general, in proportional representation'.[62] The question was thus whether introducing a constituency element could be brought under the umbrella of a 'legislative structure or procedure'. The Court baulked. For it the provision went beyond 'form' to the 'substance' of the legislative structure; the former entailed 'no more than a difference regarding the nature and the number of the elements constituting the legislative structure'.[63] The reasoning, described as 'opaque',[64] is skimpy as well; the Court stated that the test is not 'whether the regulation of that matter can have some bearing on the representation in a legislative structure, but whether it bears on the structure itself'.[65] This test would, of course, not help the Court much should the PC have included a second house, necessitating an electoral system.[66] Murray suggests that the real reasoning lies in the politics of transition. She speculates that the ANC and the Court may have feared that the NNP would have exploited racially divided districts, following the contours of the deeply entrenched spatial geography of apartheid.[67]

15.4.3.4 Innovative measures

The WC PC had some innovative structures not related to the legislature or executive: Commissioners for the Environment and for Children and cultural councils. It further contained a list of Directive Principles of Provincial Policy. Only the cultural councils were challenged.

The Commissioner for the Environment was a desirable institution, justified in part by the unique natural habitat of the province. It is not part of the provincial executive, but is independent and subject only to the NC, the PC and legislation, and must perform the allocated functions

---

58 *Certification WC* judgment, para 39.
59 NC, s 105(1) (a) and (d)
60 NC, schedule 6 item 11.
61 On the contemporary debates on the demerits of the PR system, see Jacques de Ville and Nico Steytler (eds) *Voting in 1999: Choosing an Electoral System* (Butterworths 1996).
62 WC PC, cl 14.
63 *Certification WC* judgment, para 49.
64 Woolman (n 30) ch 22 11.
65 *Certification WC* judgment, para 49.
66 Murray (n 32), at 4.
67 Murray (n 32), at 4.

impartially without 'fear, favour or prejudice'.[68] Not only must an appointment be approved by the provincial parliament with a supporting vote of at least 60 per cent, but a removal is premised on the ground of 'misconduct, incapacity or incompetence', approved by at least a two-thirds majority in the legislature.[69] It has no executive powers, but must monitor urban and rural development that may impact the environment, investigate complaints, and make recommendations to provincial organs of state.[70] The Commissioner for Children is very different; it is not established explicitly as an independent institution; the incumbent is appointed and removed by the Premier on the recommendation of the provincial parliament by a simple majority.[71] Its mandate is, then, also to 'assist the Western Cape government in protecting and promoting the interests of children' in the province, by monitoring, investigating, researching, educating, lobbying, advising and reporting on matters affecting children.[72] As both the functional areas of environment and social development fall with the list of concurrent national and provincial competences,[73] no objections were raised against these institutions.

More contentious was the mandatory establishment and funding of 'cultural councils' 'for a community or communities in the Western Cape, sharing a common cultural and language heritage'.[74] This provision has its origins in the NC; the constitutionally established Commission for the Promotion and Protection of the Rights of Cultural, Religious and Linguistic Communities has as one of its functions the recommendation for the establishment or recognition 'in accordance to national legislation', of 'a cultural or other council or councils for a community or communities in South Africa'.[75] This was a sop for Afrikaner nationalists who feared for their language and culture.[76] The Court had no objection to this provision as cultural matters fall both within the provinces' concurrent and exclusive powers. The underlying concern of the ANC, who objected to the provision, was, according to Murray, that it would be restricted to cultural councils based only on language and culture, and that institutions promoting harmony across language and culture would fall outside the funding range.[77] She was also sceptical of the motives of the NNP: it may reflect 'the New National Party's on-going interest in group rights and its emphasis on protecting Afrikaner identity rather than on healing past wounds'.[78]

What Murray regarded as the 'most imaginative move' in the WC PC were the 'Directive Principles of Provincial Policy'; they are a combination of restating as guidelines rights in the NC (such as promotion on non-racialism, affirmative action, and respect for the rights of cultural, religious and linguistic communities, realising the rights of access to housing, health care, food and water, and social security, etc.) with some policy-laden text (such as 'the creation of job opportunities, the promotion of a work ethic, [and] the promotion of a market orientated economy'.[79] Particularly loathsome to the ANC and its South African Communist Party alliance partner was the latter, as they argued that economic policy was a national matter.[80] For the

---

68 WC PC, cl 71(3).
69 WC PC, cls 75 and 77.
70 WC PC, cl 72(1).
71 WC PC, cl 80.
72 WC PC, cl 79(1).
73 NC, sch 4.
74 WC PC, cl 70.
75 NC, s 185(1)(c).
76 Nico Steytler and Johann Mettler, 'Federal arrangements as a peacemaking device during South Africa's transition to democracy' (2001) 31(4) *Publius: The Journal of Federalism* 93.
77 Murray (n 32), at 8.
78 Murray (n 32), at 9.
79 WC PC, cl 81(e)–(g).
80 Murray (n 32), at 10.

Court, noting that India, Ireland and Namibia all have such legally unenforceable directive principles, the only question was whether their scope falls within the province's competences. As many functional areas with an economic impact fall in the province's concurrent competence, there could not be objections per se, and, should a conflict arise, it would be resolved in terms of the dispute resolution mechanism of the NC.

15.4.3.5 *The use and usefulness of the Western Cape provincial constitution*

After the rejection of the WC PC, the provincial legislature removed the three offending clauses and resubmitted the new draft to the Constitutional Court, which gave it its stamp of approval.[81] The WC PC was signed into law on in January 1998 and came into force in that year. What has been its significance since then? Not much. Already in 2001, Murray remarked: 'The most strik-ing feature of the new Western Cape Constitution is how little it changes'.[82] In the next two decades, even the 'little changes' proved to be a charitable assessment.

The only significant impact the WC PC has was on the size of the WC provincial parliament. In preparation for the 1999 provincial election, the Electoral Commission determined in terms of a nationally legislated formula that the Western Cape was entitled to a 39-member legislature. This was duly contested and the Constitutional Court came down firmly in favour of the 42-member provincial legislature as determined in the WC PC.[83]

And then the PC went into a slumber for the next 20 years. It was not used in practice as the *vade mecum* of provincial officials and no litigation seeking to assert its supremacy status followed. Although it was arguably mandatory to do so, neither a Commissioner for the Environment nor a Commissioner for Children was appointed. No doubt, the province was constrained by the requirement that it should, from its meagre own revenue, fund these new structures. What did happen was, however, that some of the provisions copied from the NC became invalid because of amendments to the NC, for example, calling dates for election, Money Bills, intervention in municipalities, taxes and loans.

In 2018 amendments to the WC PC were first raised; the object was to subtract burdensome provisions rather than explore new avenues. The reasons advanced were first, as noted above, that in a number of areas the WC PC now conflicted with the amended NC, and second, that there was no need for a Commissioner for the Environment as there was sufficient national legislation to cover the field adequately (and an appointment would 'consume scarce state resources').[84] By 2020 no amendment Bill was adopted to be forwarded to the Constitutional Court for certifica-tion, but the Premier could proudly announce the first appointment of a person to the position of Commissioner for Children, taking up the position on 1 June 2020, 22 years after the post was first established.[85]

Although a Commissioner for the Environment would 'consume scarce resources', that is seemingly not a consideration for a new 2020 proposed amendment that would see the provincial parliament increase its membership from 42 to 52 or 54. The proposal, which the

81 Certification of the Amended Text of the Constitution of the Western Cape, 1997 [1997] ZACC 15.
82 Murray (n 32), at 15.
83 Premier of the Province of the Western Cape v Electoral Commission 1999 (11) BCLR 1209 (CC).
84 Constitution of the Western Cape First Amendment Bill: briefing 29 January 2019, https://pmg.org.za/committee-meeting/27797/, accessed 19 May 2020.
85 <https://iafrica.com/western-cape-childrens-commissioner-to-take-office-from-1st-june/> accessed 19 May 2020.

ANC is buying into [86] (because they are sure to capture the province after the recent implosion of the ruling Democratic Alliance), is based on the argument that because the population of the province grew from 4 million to 6 million in the intervening 25 years, they need more MPLs to serve the communities. This is, of course, an empty fob; there are no 'constituencies' to serve in the strict party-based PR system. There is only an informal system through which political parties deploy their MPLs to geographical areas, serving not as community representatives, but as party apparatchiks. As it is the wont of political parties, they will push to further open the window for more patronage, each party believing it stands to benefit from an enlarged legislature at the next election in 2024.

The only other flickering of interest in a provincial constitution was again in KZN, this time after the ANC in 2004 gained an absolute majority in the provincial legislature. The process was initiated by the ANC to give some kind of recognition to the Zulu monarch with whom it had close political ties.[87] Although each of the major parties—ANC, IFP and Democratic Alliance—submitted a draft, the process fizzled out as no agreement could be reached. As the same objective could be achieved through the passing of a provincial law, the role and function of the Zulu monarch was secured through ordinary provincial legislation.[88]

15.4.4 Constitutional Court's jurisprudence

In the three certification judgments, the Constitutional Court set the parameters of provincial constitution-making. In reviewing the KZN PC the Court faced the ugly side of such constitution-making: wayward and totally contrary to the project of building a new united South Africa. The scope of constitutional differences with regard to 'legislative and executive structures and procedures' was thus confined to form rather than substance, a refrain repeated in the *Certification FC* judgment. When it came to the WC PC, a parsimonious application of the exception was given, which in effect suffocated the little life there may have been in provincial constitutions. It is thus difficult not to agree with Woolman's conclusion that the Constitution does 'not create a meaningfully independent basis for the exercise of power by the provinces'[89] and that, unless the Constitutional Court reverses its stance on provinces, 'provincial constitutions will never amount to anything more than window dressing'.[90]

In the Court's jurisprudence of the next two decades on provincial matters the same parsimonious approach has largely been followed. I have argued elsewhere that the Constitutional Court has consistently not found in favour of provinces for broad socio-political reasons.[91] In the very fragile years after the commencement of the new constitutional democracy, the Court sought to emphasize the unity of the country in the KZN case, and any regurgitation of old apartheid habits in the Western Cape. In other decisions on provincial powers, when confronted with poor provincial governance, it voted for order under the benign hand of the national

86 Lester Kiewit, 'ANC agrees to discuss more seats in Western Cape' 7 Feb 2020 *Mail & Guardian*, <https://mg.co.za/article/2020-02-07-anc-agrees-to-discuss-more-seats-in-western-cape/>.
87 Woolman (n 30) 21–4 n 3.
88 KwaZulu-Natal Traditional Leadership and Governance Act 5 of 2005.
89 Woolman (n 30) 21–2.
90 Woolman (n 30) 21–2.
91 Nico Steytler 'Judicial neutrality in the face of ineptitude: The Constitutional Court and multi-level government in South Africa' in Hans-Peter Schneider, Jutta Kramer and Beniamino Caravita di Toritto (eds), *Judge Made Federalism* (Nomos Verlag 2009) **27**; Nico Steytler 'The Constitutional Court in South Africa: Reinforcing an Hourglass System of Multi-Level Government' in Nicholas Aroney and John Kincaid (eds) *Courts in Federal Countries: Federalists or Unitarists?* (University of Toronto Press 2017) 328.

government. However, in the face of a failing national government, and some provinces—Gauteng and the Western Cape—showing elements of good governance, the Court may well change its tune.

15.5 Multilevel constitutionalism in South Africa

The dominance of the NC over a PC is more or less complete; as the NC provides 'a complete blueprint' for provincial governments,[92] a PC would not be plugging any gaps. With the parsimonious reading the Constitutional Court has given of a province's constitution-making powers, and its abstract review prior to the enactment of a PC, overlaps and conflicts will not readily arise between the two texts. The more likely conflicts arising between a PC and national legislation are dealt with in terms of the paramountcy clause in the NC which favours national legislation.[93]

Given the very limited scope of provincial constitution-making, do provinces nevertheless play a part in shaping the NC? Through their participation in the National Council of Provinces (NCOP), each of the nine provinces, having one vote each, has an important say in amendments to the NC. First, any amendment on matters affecting provinces requires two-thirds support from both the National Assembly and the National Council of Provinces (NCOP) (six of the nine provinces).[94] As the Constitutional Court has given a broad interpretation to matters affecting provinces,[95] it serves as a blocking device against the shrinking of provincial constitutional space. In case of changes to the foundational values in Section 15.1, three-quarters support in the National Assembly is required, but only a two-thirds majority is required in the NCOP. Amendments to the Bill of Rights require only a two-thirds majority in the National Assembly, and six provincial votes in the NCOP.[96] In the case of amendments to any other provisions, the NCOP plays no role. It needs to be emphasized that the delegation, composed of six permanent members elected by the provincial legislatures and four members of the executive, votes in accordance to a mandate given by the provincial legislatures. Thus, the provinces can play an important role in safeguarding its interests in the NC.

15.6 Constitutional review

A provincial constitution serves the same function as the national constitution; it binds the provincial legislature and executive to its strictures.[97] As with the national Constitution,[98] the provincial constitution is thus the supreme law pertaining to provincial legislation and executive actions; any law or action inconsistent with it is invalid. Constitutional review is thus also available under a provincial constitution. Apart from the conflict between the WC PC and a regulation by the Electoral Commission about the size of the provincial parliament,[99] no other court case has been brought under the PC. The explanation is obvious; as most of the PC is copied

---

92 *Certification WC* judgment, para 15.
93 NC, s 147.
94 NC, s 74(3).
95 Tongoane and Others v National Minister for Agriculture and Land Affairs and Others 2010 (8) BCLR 741 (CC).
96 NC, s 74(1) and (2).
97 NC, ss 104(3) and 125(6)(b).
98 NC, s 2.
99 Premier of the Province of the Western Cape v Electoral Commission 1999 (11) BCLR 1209 (CC).

from the national constitution, a review would rather take place in terms of the NC than the derivative PC.

15.7 Evaluation

The weak constitution-making capacity of provinces emerged from South Africa's own brand of centralized multilevel government. The new constitutional democracy of 1994 brought together black and white and ethnic-based Bantustans, some of which where nominally 'independent', but this very act of bringing together militated against any disaggregation through provinces that could be based on the odious principles of race and ethnicity. In line with the compromise of allowing only a limited degree of non-centralism in the form of provinces and local government, their self-constituting space was equally constrained.

In a country divided on the basis of race and ethnicity, the ANC feared that the unity so hard fought for may be undermined by giving provinces a free hand to shape their own identity which may preserve historic ethnic divisions. Thus, at first, only nominal constitutional-making space was on offer; however, through the continued conflict in KZN a window of opportunity was slightly opened in the interim Constitution for differences in legislative and executive structures and procedures. This window, preserved in the NC the Constitutional Court closed firmly.

Because of the negligible constitution-making space, the only provincial constitution managing to jump through the exacting hoops of the NC had little vibrancy. Not even the two innovative structures—the Commissioners for the Environment and for Children—were implemented from the start due to constitutionally imposed financial constraints. Its invisibility thus comes as no surprise. As the WC PC was precluded from basing any provincial identity based on race or ethnicity in a deeply divided country and province, it served no symbolic purpose as a marker of identity.

As a provincial constitution can mainly impose restrictions on power additional to those of the NC,[100] and provinces have no own revenue resources available for new institutions and experimentation, there has been scant appetite for this form of legal ordering. But where a provincial constitution can serve the interests of politicians, which the proposed increase in the size of the Western Cape Parliament does, it may evoke some interest.

Although on the face of it 'different legislative and executive structures and procedures' were to be tolerated, the Constitutional Court's narrow interpretation of this competence resulted in the WC PC being a mirror image of the NC's 'blueprint' of provincial government. Amendments to the PC follow a similar process to that of the NC, but with the additional requirement of prior scrutiny by the Constitutional Court before it may be enacted.

Although a PC can embroider on the national Bill of Rights as long as further experimentation falls within a province's substantive functional areas, there was little incentive in the WC for that. As the national Bill of Rights is already expansive and comprehensive, a provincial Bill of Rights would have served only as a further restraint on a provincial government—not an attractive proposition for any politician. Moreover, the two institutions—the Commissioners for the Environment and for Children—which could have played an important role in realizing the socioeconomic rights enshrined in the NC pertinent to the environment[101] and children,[102] became dead letters due to cost implications and sufficient national protective legislation.

---

100 Woolman (n 30) 21–2 n 2.
101 NC, s 24.
102 NC, s 28.

In WC PC's Directive Principles of Provincial Policy, the only identity advanced was not one of regional identity, but that of party political ideology; the advancement of a market economy was a national policy of the NPP (representing mostly the propertied class), which was distinct from the ANC's strong socialist instincts seeking state-driven economic development.

Perhaps because of the limited scope for provincial constitution-making, provinces play, through the National Council of Provinces, a significant role in national constitution-making. The NCOP is part of the constitutional amendment process but only as far as matters concerning provincial interest and the foundational values of Section 15.1 and cooperative government. This role is mainly protective of the status quo, requiring the two-thirds majority of the nine provinces for any such amendment; on a strict reading of the text, it may not introduce constitutional amendments advancing the position of provinces.[103] In any event, as the NCOP functions along party lines, the support of the ruling party in both chambers would be required.

The prospect of constitutional review is, of course, also the litmus test of whether a provincial constitution meets a central tenet of constitutionalism. This, however, begs the question whether a provincial constitution has added any provisions that may elicit a constitutional challenge. The little added by the WC PC has not provided any. After a successful defence of the size of the provincial parliament, no litigation arose from it in the next two decades. Should any of the actions of the province be challenged, the NC would be the suitable legal measurement. This, in a sense, sums up the constituent power of provinces; it's too thin to serve any of the usual purposes of a constitution. It is an empty promise.

103 NC, s 73(3).

16

SUBNATIONAL CONSTITUTIONALISM IN SPAIN

Confluence of wills in a basic institutional norm

Gonzalo Gabriel Carranza

16.1 Context

The precise nature of the territorial form of state in Spain is not defined in the Constitution (SC). Title VIII, called 'on the territorial organization of the State' (where presumably we could find an indication of the type of power-sharing adopted in Spain) does not indicate in any way whether our country is a federal, confederal, regional or unitary one, as other Constitutions do (*v. gr.* Article 20 Basic Law of Germany, Article 2 Constitution of Austria or Article 6 Constitution of Portugal). Article 2 SC states that the Constitution:

> is based on the indissoluble unity of the Spanish nation, the common and indivisible homeland of all Spaniards, and recognizes and guarantees the right to autonomy of the nationalities and regions of which it is formed and the solidarity between them.

Despite this omission, both the Constitutional Court and scholars affirm that Spain is a multi-tiered system, territorially defined as 'autonomous state' *(Estado autonómico)*, with a distinctive reference to territorial autonomy.

The current territorial form of the State is the result of a long and complex construction process[1] in which the model of the 2nd republic and other European regional and federal systems was taken as a reference. From 1939 to 1975, this country lived under a dictatorship until the death of General Franco. During this period, the regions lacked autonomy and centralism prevailed. From 1975 on, the complex process of transition to a democracy began, and discussions about the territorial form of State were particularly relevant. In December 1978 the current Constitution was finally approved, and the nationalities and regions had the chance to access to different grades of autonomy throughout a new territorial form: the Autonomous Communities

---

1 Manuel Aragón Reyes, 'La Construcción del Estado Autonómico' in Manuel Aragón Reyes, *Estudios de Derecho Constitucional* (CEPC 2013) 823.

(ACs, or *Comunidades Autónomas*) which are properly 'territories with autonomy' but they are not 'States', because Spain is only one State, the national.[2]

The Constitution does not indicate which ACs form part of the Spanish territory. Rather, the option to create them was left to: 'the bordering provinces with common historical, cultural and economic characteristics, the island territories and the provinces with a historical regional entity' (Article 143 SC).

It would be each one of the 50 provinces that should decide whether to be part of an AC, thus accessing their self-government throughout their own Statute of Autonomy (SA—in Spanish *Estatuto de Autonomía*—as the equivalent to the 'subnational Constitutions'—SNC). This option means that the landscape at that time was not entirely clear as the resulting map could have consisted of territories both with and without autonomy; moreover, the ACs could have organized themselves in a way that they considered appropriate, assuming powers that were believed appropriate and leaving aside those that were not.[3] This possibility allowed by the constitutional system, finally materialized in the choices made, has been defined by scholars as a 'dispositive principle' or 'principle of voluntariness' which, as rightly pointed out, is the characteristic feature of the SC[4] since it allows that the provincial territories make a decision among the different possibilities that the Constitution itself offers. In short, the 17 ACs that finally resulted from the 'territorial option' are (in terms of federal theory) the result of a territorial disintegration process, rather than a strictly integrative process.

The resulting ACs reflect the territorial and socio-cultural diversity of Spain, where different historical and regional nationalities are combined into a single Spanish nation. Their integration, which until the beginning of this century was more or less fruitful,[5] has continued to battle the latent desire of certain radical nationalists to become independent. This trend has deepened during recent years through what has popularly been referred to as the 'Catalan issue', a strong independence movement led by the Catalan Government and Parliament over several years, with growing intensity since the attempt to independence in 2017. That attempt led to the application of the State's coercion instrument by the central Government for the first time in history (Article 155 SC, inspired by Article 37 of the Bonn Basic Law). Since then, relations between the Spanish State and Catalonia have been marked by constant political conflict.

The Catalan conflict is not the only nationalist challenge in Spain. There is also the remarkable strength of Basque nationalism, which challenged the central State at the beginning of this century, especially through the so-called 'Ibarretxe Plan', devised by the Basque *Lehendakari* (as the president of the AC). That project aimed to modify its own SA, turning the AC into a sort of 'associated free State'. However, the covertly secessionist initiative in the Basque Country was unsuccessful, as were its demands.

As previously referred, the legal form assumed by SNC in Spain are 'Statutes of Autonomy', although it must be noted that these are not, strictly speaking, 'Constitutions' as those are typically understood in federal States and specifically in the introduction of this book. Furthermore, the SAs are post-constitutional instruments far from the idea of pre-constitutional sovereignty contained within the Constitutions of some member states of a federal country. Such a clarification

---

2 Even before a provisional system of 'pre-autonomies' was implemented trying to 'test' this method of transferring powers to the regions and nationalities, especially to Catalonia and the Basque Country, which were at the forefront of agitations for regional self-governance. From this system practically emerged the current map of territorial distribution: Eliseo Aja, *Estado autonómico y reforma federal* (Alianza 2014) 36.
3 César Aguado Renedo, 'El principio dispositivo y su virtualidad actual en relación con la estructura territorial del Estado' (1997) 98 *Revista de Estudios Políticos* (Nueva Época) 137, at 138.
4 Ignacio de Otto, *Derecho constitucional. Sistema de fuentes* (Ariel, 2010, 1st edition, 12th reprint) 256.
5 Juan José Solozábal Echavarría, 'El Estado federal como Estado compuesto' (2001) 6 *Historia y Política* 121, at 132.

is necessary since the SNC do not *formally* exist in Spain, because the SA strictly constitute Organic Laws of the State (Article 81.1 SC), so their 'approval, modification or repeal will require an absolute majority of the Congress, in a final vote on the project as a whole' (Article 81.2 SC). However, it should be noted that the process for the approval and modification of the Statutes is promoted by the ACs themselves and not by the State's central organs. Statutes *materially* exercise the function of 'fundamental rule' of the ACs, establishing their internal organization, the method of their reform and, since the reform process started about 20 years ago, they also have a rights catalogue recognized within its boundaries. In general, the majority doctrine (to which we adhere) refers to the SAs as 'agreed laws', since their adoption or reform implies a 'complex act' in which two wills converge, that of the ACs and the State (in this specific case, that of Congress), which is the one that finally determines whether or not the legal instrument has been approved.

Beyond the theoretical debate, there are two generations of SAs in Spain. The first is composed of those Statutes which were initially approved, defining the internal limits of each AC and through which these subnational entities (SNE) gradually assumed the competences allowed by Article 148 SC. The second generation is made up of all those that have been reformed during this century by many ACs to 'update' their basic rules, although it ended up meaning the 'replacement' of some old SAs by new ones.[6] In most of them, there are clear demands for self-government, guided by nationalist and regionalist identity declarations, together with formulas to 'shield' their own competences to prevent any possible central State intrusion into their autonomy. It should be highlighted that this process took place in times of economic prosperity, before the outbreak of the financial crisis affecting Spain and many other countries from 2008 on, and furthermore, that this process has been especially addressed by the Constitutional Court, which in 2010 resolved Judgment 31 (of 28 June) on some contents of the Statue of Catalonia that had been challenged by several members of Congress who considered that this AC had exceeded its competences. Finally, much of its content was declared constitutional thanks to an interpretation in accordance with the Constitution.

In short, the territorial power distribution system in Spain is defined by the primacy of the dispositive principle and the territorial autonomy, and a constant desire for greater self-governance within SNEs in a context where some of them have deeply nationalist identities. Thus, the SA became the rule that entrenches the Communities in their own powers *vis-à-vis* the central State.

16.2 Autonomy

16.2.1 Scope

The 1978 Constitution established that there would be two ways for territories to become self-governing, which would also be reflected in certain requirements concerning the content of their SAs. On the one hand, a group of ACs would have access to the maximum possible autonomy if they met a series of substantive and formal requirements demanded by Article 151 SC. The territories that did so (Catalonia, Basque Country, Galicia and Andalusia), accessed a 'fast track' to the maximum number of possible competences without the need for revision after five years (Article 148.2 SC), but they could do that only after a negotiation process with the central State, which must be followed by a referendum and a final ratification by the national Parliament (Article 151.2 SC). For these ACs, the Constitution established, in Article 152.1, a basic institutional organization which formally the other ACs would lack: a Legislative

---

6 Pedro Cruz Villalón, 'La reforma del Estado de las Autonomías' (2006) 2 *Revista d'estudis autonòmics y federals* 77, at 78.

Assembly, a Governing Council and a High Court of Justice, which is the final step in the judicial organization in its territorial scope, without prejudice to the corresponding jurisdiction to the Supreme Court of Spain. On the other hand, the other ACs approved their Statutes under the general provisions, following the guidelines of Article 146 SC, although initially without the requirement for a process of negotiation and without the need of a referendum. Notwithstanding these particularities, the text of all SAs must be passed as Organic Laws by the national Parliament.

The SA is frequently not referenced specifically within the Constitution. Nevertheless, the few references help us to understand its dynamics. Article 147.1 SC is the most relevant, as it states that: 'the Statutes shall be the basic institutional norm of each Autonomous Community and the State shall recognize and protect them as an integral part of its legal system'.

The second paragraph of the same article indicates what each Statute must necessarily contain:

a) The name of the Community that best corresponds to its historical identity. b) The delimitation of its territory. c) The name, organization, and headquarters of its autonomous institutions. d) The powers assumed within the framework established by the Constitution and the bases for the transfer of the services corresponding to them.

All these provisions are fulfilled in the 17 SAs, which from the beginning included them in their texts.

As noted, since the beginning of this century a wave of reforms sought to 'extend' the content of the Statutes. This resulted in significant changes to the autonomic system,[7] particularly through the inclusion of a catalogue of declarations, rights and duties; the regulation and creation of institutions such as the Ombudsman's Office or advisory councils; the extension (or rather the specification) of their competences; and—among other particularities—the inclusion of specific references to the international relations of the SNEs. They also regulate collaboration with other ACs and with the State and they contain historical statements intended to advance nationalist identity claims; indeed, this has occurred even in territories where nationalism has not been historically significant (for example, Aragon or Andalusia). What particularly attracted the attention of scholars was the inclusion of a catalogue of rights, because most of them are already included in the Constitution or in the European laws, and its reiteration in the Statutes was not needed.[8]

After the reforms, many of the SAs fulfil practically the same functions and have the same characteristics as the Constitutions of the members of the federal States, beyond the fact that, formally, as we have seen, they are not expressions of constituent power. They have even been referred to as quasi-constitutional rules.[9] Therefore, a real modification of the material constitutional system took place, even though this happened without the alteration of a single comma in the SC itself. Moreover, in the famous Judgment of the Constitutional Court 31/2010 an important issue was reaffirmed: the Statutes can modulate the territorial model, but its limits are always in the Constitution, whose core characteristics remain unchanged.[10]

---

7 José Tudela Aranda, *El fracasado éxito del Estado autonómico* (Marcial Pons 2016) 144. In this respect, there had already been talk of a 'change of model': Miguel Ángel Aparicio Pérez, 'Proceso de reforma estatutaria. Una introducción' in Josep Maria Castellà Andreu and Marco Olivetti (eds), *Nuevos Estatutos y reforma del Estado* (Atelier 2009) 21, at 32–3.
8 Since the Constitution, although it does not indicate that the SA cannot contain rights, does not prohibit them.
9 Juan José Solozábal Echavarría, 'Los derechos y libertades en los nuevos Estatutos de Autonomía' in VV.AA., *La carta canadiense de derechos y libertades, los primeros 25 años* (Fundación Manuel Giménez Abad 2007) 6.
10 Tudela Aranda (n 7), at 149.

16.2.2 Procedure

We have already seen how the SAs were approved. Regarding their reform, Article 147.3 SC provides that, as a general principle: 'The reform of the Statutes will follow the procedure established in them and will require, in any case, the approval of the national Parliament, using an Organic Law'.

Article 152.2 SC makes specific provision for ACs that have acceded to the fullness of competences via the 'fast track' process: it requires that once a reform is approved by the national Parliament, the SA must be submitted to a referendum among voters registered in their census (Article 151 SC).

We need to pay attention to the reference established in Article 147.3 SC as it refers directly to the regulation of each of the SAs, which opens the stage to manifold specific rules.[11] There are two processes that must be followed: first, the AC must approve the proposal of reform in its autonomous Parliament, and then reforms must be implemented through an Organic Law passed by an absolute majority of the national Parliament. The meeting of both wills (the State and the AC) has led to talk about the 'rigidity' of the process. Thus, the traditional procedure of reform of any subnational Constitution is 'doubly assured' in Spain through a mechanism of constitutional protection of the autonomy of the SNEs against possible unilateral action of either the central constituted powers or the autonomous powers.[12]

It is also important to consider SAs' general contents. Most of them require that the reform initiative finds approval by the absolute majority of the autonomous Parliament. If the national Parliament wishes to alter the reform proposal, a 'dialogue' mechanism is established between both representative bodies. As a consequence, the process can be paralyzed or blocked at any time by the AC, preventing final approval by the central Parliament. Some of SAs' preconditions are that the reforms should be approved by two-thirds of the Parliament's members,[13] in others the absolute majority,[14] and in others a positive vote of three-fifths is required.[15] Finally, many of the Statutes reformed at the beginning of this century incorporated the need for approval of the reforms by SNE referendum in their texts.[16]

16.3 Position of the subnational Constitutions within the SNE

The SAs constitute a single document in which the competences assumed by SNEs are listed. However, Article 150 SC qualifies the distribution of powers affected by the SAs. The first paragraph of that article empowers the national Parliament to enact 'framework laws' *(leyes marco)*.

---

11 Many of these rules are not characterized by clarity and are difficult to interpret and apply: Antonio Gutiérrez Llamas, *Los procedimientos para la reforma de los Estatutos de Autonomía de las Comunidades Autónomas* (Civitas 1991) 28.

12 Josep Maria Castellà Andreu and Esther Martín Núñez, 'Estatuto de Autonomía y sistema de fuentes autonómico' in Castellà Andreu and Olivetti (n 7), 47, at 52.

13 Article 222.1.b) of the Statute of Catalonia; Article 248.1.b) of the Statute of Andalusia; Article 58.1.b) of the Statute of Cantabria; Article 91.2 of the Statute of Castile and Leon; Article 139.2 of the Statute of the Balearic Islands; Article 56.1.b) of the Statute of Galicia; Article 91.2.a) of the Statute of Extremadura; Article 58.2 of the Statute of La Rioja; Article 64.1 of the Statute of Madrid.

14 Article 46.1 of the Basque Country Statute; Article 54.1.b) of the Statute of Castilla-La Mancha.

15 Article 115.1 of the Statute of Aragon; Article 56.2 of the Statute of the Principality of Asturias; Article 200.2 of the Statute of the Canary Islands; Article 81.1 of the Statute of Valencia; Article 55.2 of the Statute of Murcia.

16 Article 115.7 of the Statute of Aragon; Article 200.2 of the Statute of the Canary Islands; Article 81.5 of the Statute of Valencia; Article 91.2.e) of the Statute of Extremadura.

This enables the Parliament to grant some or all SNEs particular powers to enact laws that comply with the framework of principles contained in the national law. Yet, the influence of the Parliament over the content of such autonomous legislative norms is potentially subject to judicial review by ordinary courts and the Constitutional Court. This kind of law, however, has not often been used.[17]

The second paragraph of Article 150 refers to the 'laws of transfer and delegation' (*leyes de transferencia y delegación*). These are Organic Laws that have been used on more than one occasion.[18] Through them, the central State can transfer or delegate to the ACs different powers corresponding to matters of State which, by their very nature, are susceptible to being transferred or delegated. In such cases, the laws must provide for the consequent transfer of financial means and mechanisms of control by the State.

The third paragraph of Article 150 SC provides:

> The State may enact laws establishing the principles necessary to harmonize the regulatory provisions of the Autonomous Communities, even in the case of matters falling within their competence, when the general interest so requires. It is for the national Parliament, by an absolute majority of each Chamber, to assess this need.

Laws of this kind, which are not Organic Laws and are enacted by the State, are intended to standardize the system preserving the unity of the legal order. They are exceptional rules that imply a certain control by the State of the exclusive legislative power of the AC.[19] Only one attempt was made to use this rule, after the 1981 and 1992 autonomic pacts, through the 'organic law of harmonization of the autonomic process' (commonly known as LOAPA).[20]

The SA is understood as the 'basic institutional rule' of each AC (Article 147.1 SC). In this sense, it is fully consolidated by the social and political community as the 'constitutional' legal instrument of the SNE, since the internal institutional organizational rules are condensed within it and, following the reforms, in many of them there is also an accumulation of declarations and

---

17 José Antonio Montilla Martos, 'Artículo 150' in Miguel Rodríguez-Piñero, Bravo Ferrer and María Emilia Casas Baamonde (eds), *Comentarios a la Constitución española*, Tomo II (BOE, Ministerio de Justicia, Fundación Wolters Kluwer y Tribunal Constitucional 2018) 1540, at 1554.

18 LOTRACA; LOTRAVA; Organic Law 5/1987 of 30 July 1987 on the delegation of State powers to the Autonomous Communities about road and cable transport (amended by Organic Law 5/2013 of 14 July 1993); Organic Law 9/1992 of 23 December 1992 on the transfer of powers to Autonomous Communities which have become autonomous by Article 143 of the Constitution; Organic Law 16/1995 of 27 December 1995 on the transfer of powers to the Galician Autonomous Community; Organic Law 6/1997 of 15 December 1997 on the transfer of executive powers concerning the traffic and circulation of motor vehicles to the Autonomous Community of Catalonia; Organic Law 6/1999 of 6 April 1999 on the transfer of powers to the Autonomous Community of Galicia. From this set of laws, it is possible to preach two major paths followed by the organic legislator to carry out the transfer of competences. The first, where the list of powers to be transferred or delegated is not directly contained in the law but is obtained by reference to another of equal rank, as happens, for example, with LOTRACA and LOTRAVA. On the other hand, there is a second way, by which a wide list of matters and functions that are transferred to different Communities is indicated, as it is reported through the Organic Laws 5/1987, of 30 July and 9/1992, of 23 December. It should be noted that no further assumptions of the same nature have been made until the time of writing.

19 In Spain, the reference to the 'exclusivity' of the powers of the ACs has been understood as 'relative' by the Constitutional Court which has qualified its meaning according to the context (*v. gr.* Judgments of the Constitutional Court 37/1981 of 16 November; 1/1982, of 28 January; or 5/1982, of 8 February).

20 Judgment of the Constitutional Court 76/1983 of 5 August. The attempt was abandoned after the Constitutional Court determined that such a law could not be promulgated as an Organic Law or as a harmonizing law and it also pointed out the unconstitutionality of many of its articles.

rights. Moreover, as the SA is the rule that clarifies the Communities' autonomy, the autonomous political authorities have defended their content at all costs. This is particularly clear in the attempts to reform the Basque Country's Statute and the effective reform of the Catalan Statute; in both cases, the main objective of the SNEs was to 'shield' their competences so that no central authority could have an influence on their exercise.[21] Nationalist parties have played key roles in the constitutional controversies that have developed in both Catalonia and in the Basque Country.[22]

16.4 Content

16.4.1 Identity

References to identity within the SAs are prevalent in those ACs that have strong nationalist identities (Catalonia and Basque Country). But since the Statute's reform era, there has been a kind of 'emulation' of these identity claims even in ACs where this issue had not previously been politically evident, such as Andalusia, Cantabria, Murcia, La Rioja and Aragon, among others. The premise is that if one Community has something, the others must have it also.

Statements of identity appear not only in the Preambles to the Statutes but also in the guiding principles prescribed for the actions of public authorities. Likewise, in the SAs, there are several references to so-called 'historical rights' that are the basis of certain political asymmetries concerning the particular rights of specific ACs, such as the identification of the local language as an official language or the entitlement of the SNEs to have their own civil or special law.

Several SAs also contain regulations of important symbols. Some of them have a long list of such symbols (for example, Article 8 of the Statute of Catalonia), including the flag of the region, the day of the regional festival (normally linked to some transcendental historical event of the Community or some religious festivity) and even an anthem or a hymn.

16.4.2 Organization of powers

Although the fact that the SC had anticipated a special 'fast track' category of ACs, this model was followed by all the other SNEs. Thus, in each AC there is a president who heads a Government in which executive power is vested (corresponding to the 'cabinet' of the Community), the members of which are responsible for the execution of the particular competences assumed by the AC. The SNEs also have their own Parliaments, which enact autonomous laws and have the powers conferred on them by the SAs. The judicial powers, however, are not vested in each AC, but rather in the central State. While there is no 'Autonomous Judicial Power', the SNEs do have competence in relation to the 'administration of justice', allowing them to regulate some of the organizational and budgetary aspects of the judicial system such as the office hours, selective processes of the personnel assisting the judges, collection of judicial fees, etc.

In the SAs a series of institutions have been created which are a mirror image of central institutions (*v. gr.* the autonomous Ombudsman or advisory councils). In fact, the degree of similarity is such that many times it has been said that the ACs have simply duplicated them

---

21 Regarding the 'Ibarretxe Plan', see Roberto L. Blanco Valdés, *El laberinto territorial español* (Alianza 2014) 264–94. Regarding the Catalan Statute, see Josep Maria Castellà Andreu, *Estado autonómico: pluralismo e integración constitucional* (Marcial Pons 2018) 69.

22 Juan José Solozábal Echavarría, 'Partidos nacionalistas y partidos nacionales en el Estado autonómico', *Revista de Libros* (Madrid, 1 September 2002) <https://www.revistadelibros.com/articulos/estado-autonom-ico-partidos-nacionalistas-y-partidos-nacionales> accessed 21 February 2020.

unnecessarily.[23] The purpose of many of these institutions is to relegate the State to a marginal position, depriving it of actions or coordination of activities within the framework of the AC.[24] It must be noted that after the economic crisis many of them were finally removed.

16.4.2.1 *The exercise of competences*

The distribution of competences in Spain is not clear: it is not only the constitutional regulation that must be taken into account, but also the varying degree of powers assumed by the SAs, the laws of Article 150 SC and the interpretation given to each area by the Constitutional Court. This peculiarity of the system, which has been defined as an 'anomaly' from a comparative point of view, entails numerous problems because it is structurally complex and unsatisfactory.[25]

There is not full agreement on the categories within the competence distribution scheme, since even those that initially could be called 'exclusive' may not be.[26] In any case, it should be brought to mind that all the competencies assumed by the SA are limited by the principles of 'prevalence' and 'supplementarity'. Under the first, the rules of the State 'shall, in the event of conflict, prevail over those of the Autonomous Communities in all matters not falling within the exclusive competence of the latter'. Under the second, State law is supplementary to the law of the ACs 'in any case' (Article 149.3 SC).

16.4.2.2 *The Parliaments*

As has been pointed out, the existence of autonomous Parliaments is linked to the autonomy of the SNEs. Motivated by the democratic expression they represent, all the ACs have decided through their SAs to have their own Parliament, although the SC does not expressly require them to do so.

Unlike in the case of the national Parliament (with two chambers, one for Congress of Deputies and one for the Senate), the autonomous regions have only one chamber. All the SAs recognize the Parliament (or Assembly, as the case may be) as an institution in which Community power is vested. Due to their own autonomy, each SA has extensively regulated their composition, internal functioning, the conditions of eligibility of its members, as well as its constitution and dissolution, among many other issues. Furthermore, they reflect the threefold autonomy enjoyed by the national Parliament: regulatory, budgetary and staff autonomy. In respect of the latter, it has been specified that this power of self-organization has been effective in terms of its exercise, but not very original in terms of its design, because the SAs have followed practically the same regulations established by the State Parliament in a sort of 'institutional mimicry'.[27]

The regulation of these Parliaments has been practically homogeneous in all the SAs, which has helped to consolidate an autonomous parliamentary culture.[28] As for the regulation of the

---

23 Santiago Muñoz Machado, *Informe sobre España* (Crítica 2012) 182.
24 Castellà Andreu (n 21), at 66.
25 Antonio Arroyo Gil, *Distribución y delimitación de competencias* (Marcial Pons 2019) 103.
26 Judgment of the Constitutional Court 1/1982, of 28 January.
27 Beatriz S. Tomás Mallén, 'Potestad de autoorganización y reglamento parlamentario' in Pablo Oñate (ed.), *Organización y funcionamiento de los parlamentos autonómicos* (Tirant Lo Blanch 2006) 9, at 16.
28 José Tudela Aranda. 'El Parlamento autonómico y la calidad de la democracia' in José Tudela Aranda, *Los Parlamentos autonómicos en tiempos de crisis* (Fundación Manuel Giménez Abad 2015) 15, at 21.

electoral regime, the premise has been the emulation of the general electoral law (applicable to the elections of the State) in the autonomous territories.[29]

16.4.2.3 The Government

In Spain, we speak of the 'Executive' of the AC since, as with the State, there are two figures that make it up: the President of the Community and the Government. Once again, the regulation of the executive has been virtually a copy of the constitutional regulations established for the president of the central government and the Central Government Council.

16.4.3 Fundamental rights

In the reform of SAs that took place two decades ago, a catalogue of rights with very broad content was incorporated into their text. There are two common elements in the recognized rights: on the one hand, their predominant nature as social utility rights (and, subordinately, as participation rights) and, on the other hand, their nature as subjective public rights. At the same time, they are not directly enforceable and cannot be legally altered by the ACs.[30] Nevertheless, the aim that has been pursued by incorporating such catalogues of rights into the SAs is to give them a certain visibility or constitutional vocation,[31] which ultimately makes them similar to the Constitutions of the member States of a federal State, not only limiting their content to the institutional organization of the AC.

The rights contained in the SAs are heterogeneous; some contain more content than others, and in some a certain concept may have the legal nature of a right and in others it may simply be a guiding principle of public policy.[32]

16.4.4 Policy principles

The SAs also incorporated an extensive list of guiding principles that guide public policy in their territory, which include reaffirmations of the regional or nationalist identity itself. They are expressed in generally broad terms. They concern such matters as: promotion of the social, political, cultural or economic order and the full exercise of rights; fostering identity values; actively promoting territorial equity and internal social cohesion; promoting consultation and dialogue with various institutions; adopting employment policies; stimulating scientific and technical research; pursuing sustainable development; promoting European integration through participation in its institutions among many other things, ranging from the rational use of water to the promotion of youth policies. In short, the aim of these principles is to guide the political action of the SNE in order to strengthen its autonomy.

---

29 Carlos Fernández Esquer, 'Algunos problemas en la articulación jurídica de los sistemas electorales autonómicos' (2016) 97–9 *Revista de las Cortes Generales* 327, at 329.

30 Mercè Barceló i Serramalera, 'Las Declaraciones de Derechos y Deberes Estatutarias. Especial referencia al Estatuto de Autonomía de Cataluña' in Castellà Andreu and Olivetti (n 7), 135, at 136–7.

31 Enriqueta Expósito and Miguel Ángel Cabellos Espiérrez, 'Conclusiones generales. Derechos y principios en los Estatutos de Autonomía' in Miguel Ángel Aparicio (ed.), Josep Maria Castellà Andreu and Enriqueta Expósito (coord.), *Derechos y principios rectores en los Estatutos de Autonomía* (Atelier 2008) 345, at 353.

32 Expósito and Cabellos Espiérrez (n 31), at 360.

16.5 Multilevel constitutionalism

16.5.1 *The relation between the federal and subnational Constitutions*

Three aspects of the relation between the central and subnational Constitutions need to be addressed: the question of rights, the participation of subnational authorities in the appointment of national authorities and the participation of the ACs in constitutional reform.

Even though the SAs include a specific list of rights, the SNEs do not have the competence to specify their detailed content, so their specific defence must always follow the regulations established both in the Constitution and in the State laws that develop them, which will be organic if they are fundamental. The Constitutional Court has explained that, in the case of the rights set out in the SAs, there is a substantive difference: on the one hand, there are rights linked to the powers of institutional organization, and, on the other, there are rights which are linked to the competences of the ACs. Whilst the former are subjective rights, the latter do not constitute 'rights' as such, but are rather the expression of a guideline, an objective or a mandate to the public authorities.[33] In either case, however, when there is a dispute over the scope of a given statutory right, it will be the Constitutional Court that will resolve the dispute through its interpretation.

With regard to participation of SNEs in the appointment of a State's bodies, it should be noted that there are constitutional and legal provisions which consider this, some of which have also been developed within the SAs themselves. All of them manifest the participation and intervention of the ACs in the decisions and functioning of the State. Firstly, Article 69.5 SC provides that the autonomous Parliaments shall appoint at least one senator and one other for every million inhabitants, ensuring, in all cases, adequate proportional representation.[34] This Article also indicates that the regulation *in extenso* of its procedure is found in each of the 17 SAs. Secondly, the ACs participate in the election of the judges that make up the Constitutional Court, because the Organic Law of the Constitutional Court requires this (Article 16.1). In particular, it means that judges elected by the Senate must come from among the candidates presented by the autonomous Parliaments, in the terms determined by the Regulations of the Chamber (Article 184 of the Regulations of the Senate). This was not the case initially, but was the result of a 2007 amendment challenged before the Constitutional Court, which resolved the issue in Judgments 49/2008 of 9 April and 101/2018 of 24 July. The Court determined that the Senate is not completely bound to the proposals for judges presented by the autonomous Parliaments, so if their proposals are not approved, the Senate could take into consideration its own preferred candidates.[35] In practice, most of the judges appointed by the Senate come from the proposals of the autonomous Parliaments.

Finally, SNEs can participate in the constitutional reform process due to the authorization given to them by Article 166 SC (in relation to Article 87.1 and 2 SC). In particular, subnational Parliaments have the right to initiate constitutional reform, something that was the subject of

33 Judgment of the Constitutional Court 247/2007, of 12 December, FJ 15.
34 Here we are referring only to the participation of SNEs in the appointment of State bodies. It should be noted that most of the senators are not appointed by the autonomous Parliaments but directly elected by the people. Regarding the Senate itself, this chamber is one of the greatest deficiencies of the Spanish constitutional system, since the ACs are not adequately represented and its functioning as a second chamber is very limited, since the bicameralism in Spain is absolutely imperfect, with the Congress of Deputies predominating over the majority of the decisions made by the Senate. See Carlos Garrido López, *El Senado ante el enigma de la representación territorial* (Marcial Pons 2019).
35 Manuel Aragón Reyes, 'La reforma de la Ley Orgánica del Tribunal Constitucional' (2009) 89 *Revista Española de Derecho Constitucional* 11, at 12.

intense debate in 1978 because it was an atypical right in federal States.[36] Nevertheless, this was defended on the basis that the ACs need to be integrated into the system as subjects participating in the condition of State.[37] References to this in the SAs are generally limited to confirming that this power granted by the Constitution falls within the competences of the Parliaments.

16.5.2 The impact of the international and European legal space on subnational constitutionalism in Spain

Spain is a member of both the European Union and the European Convention on Human Rights. As it has a constitutionally extensive catalogue of rights to which European provisions are added, the presence of a specific catalogue of rights in the SAs is argued by some to be 'unnecessary', as it does not provide any added value and generate legal inequalities among the ACs[38]—although others see them as 'additional rights' that allow an integrative and multilevel vision of recognition and protection of human rights.[39]

The problem that the Spanish State often faces is that, in accordance with the distribution of competences, in those matters that affect the exclusive competences of the ACs and that are discussed within the EU institutions, the SNEs do not have the capacity to make their voice heard in an express manner, nor do they have the legitimacy to assert their position before the EU.[40] If necessary, they can only indirectly challenge the validity of Community acts through the Committee of the Regions.

Another facet that arises from the same problem is that cases are brought against Spain for non-compliance by the ACs with European legislation. This issue has been the subject of numerous cases in which the country has been condemned for failing to guarantee Spain's compliance with its obligations at the European level.[41]

Finally, it should be noted that SNEs do not have veto power over international matters, even when their regulation affects their own competences. When it happens, they must go before the Constitutional Court to control them.

16.6 Constitutional review

In this area, we will only analyse the regulations of the Constitutional Court. It should be noted that its Organic Law expressly provides in Article 27.2.a) and e) that both the SA and the laws, acts and regulations with the force of the law in the AC are liable to be declared unconstitutional. The president of the central Government, the Ombudsman, 50 deputies or even

---

36 Fernando Santaolalla López, 'Artículo 166' in Fernando Garrido Falla (ed.), *Comentario a la Constitución* (Civitas 2001) 2717, at 2719.

37 Juan Luis Requejo Pagés, 'Artículo 166' in Rodríguez-Piñero y Bravo Ferrer and Casas Baamonde (n 17), 1865, at 1868.

38 Raúl Canosa Usera, 'La declaración de derechos en los nuevos Estatutos de Autonomía' (2007) 20 *Teoría y Realidad Constitucional* 61, at 112.

39 Enriqueta Expósito, 'La regulación de los derechos en los nuevos Estatutos de Autonomía' (2007) 5 *Revista d'estudis autonòmics i federals* 147, at 153.

40 Manuel Cienfuegos Mateo, 'Comunidades Autónomas, Tribunales de la Unión Europea y responsabilidad por el incumplimiento autonómico del Derecho comunitario. Reflexiones a partir de la práctica reciente' (2007) 5 *Revista d'estudis autonòmics i federals* 39, at 41. In this regard, some cases in which the lack of legitimacy became apparent are Comunidad Autónoma de Valencia—Generalidad Valenciana / Comisión (T-357/05) o Comunidad Autónoma de Madrid/Comisión (T-148/05).

41 Among others: in an infringement by Galicia, Commission v Spain, C-323/03; in one by Valencia, Commission v Spain, C-332/04; in one by Castilla y León, Commission v Spain, C-221/04.

50 senators have the right to request this. Likewise, the Court has full power to analyse positive competence conflicts (Articles 62 to 67) that arise between the State and the ACs or between two ACs, whether the conflict arises from the SC, the SA, organic or ordinary laws, or acts or provisions enacted to delimit the areas proper to the State and the Communities (Article 59.1). The competence, in this case, will be of the central Government (Article 62) or the Communities' Government (Article 63.1). The same Organic Law regulates the negative conflict of competence when two entities declare themselves incompetent in a matter (Articles 68 to 72).

The Organic Law also establishes that the unconstitutionality of draft reform SAs may be reviewed *ex ante* (Article 79). This article was incorporated in 2015 after the experience of the statutory reforms and the challenges to them that were subsequently made, and which were resolved by the Constitutional Court in the Judgment of the Catalan Statute 31/2010.

Finally, Article 161.2 of the Organic Law establishes a procedure that allows the central Government to challenge regulatory provisions without the force of law and resolutions issued by any body of the ACs. This procedure has been widely used in recent years against resolutions of the Parliament or Government of Catalonia promoting their independence.

As it is noted, the Constitutional Court can control the constitutionality of the rules and the content of the SAs, but there is no specific procedure to control the adaptation of the laws and government acts of the ACs to their own SAs, which is reserved for ordinary judicial control.

Regarding the powers of the SNEs, the Constitutional Court has fulfilled a task of clarifying the distribution of powers between the State and the ACs. From the analysis of its judgments, it cannot be said that it has been inclined to restrict the autonomous powers more than the State powers, but rather to reconcile the interpretation of the powers according to who has the capacity to legislate and who has the capacity to execute.

16.7 Conclusions

The peculiarities that we saw concerning the SA lead us to the conclusion that these are essential legal instruments in the Spanish territorial system. They constitute the very expression of its autonomy and the instrument through which its self-government is ensured.

Regarding the determination of the content of the SAs, the power of the SNEs is medium. Although initially they have a wide freedom of regulation, this is restricted by the possibility of submitting their content to an *ex ante* constitutionality control and also by the possible modifications of the content that the national Parliament is allowed.

About the process of approval and reform of the SAs, the power of SNEs is weak, since the necessary approval of the central Parliament is required. The will of the SNE is therefore limited.

17

SUBNATIONAL CONSTITUTIONALISM IN SWITZERLAND

A Sleeping Beauty waiting to be kissed

Eva Maria Belser[1]

17.1 Context

Subnational constitutionalism is significantly older than national constitutionalism in Switzerland. When the then 25 cantons came together in 1848 and transformed the old Confederation into a modern federation, they all had and maintained their own written cantonal constitutions. The new federal constitution simply added a new tier of government empowered to produce over-riding law in enumerated fields. The cantons aggregating into one state had no intention to give up their various constitutional regimes or any other differences which were not inconsistent with the minimal standards of conformity necessary to cooperate militarily and economically.[2]

This understanding of Swiss federalism has never fundamentally changed. Despite two total revisions of the federal constitution (in 1874 and 1999) and hundreds of partial revisions, many of them extending the list of federal competencies, the cantons continue to enjoy far-reaching autonomy and ability to determine their constitutional fate. Their constitutions still matter—or so it would seem.

But they don't. Notwithstanding its dignified age and impressive reach, subnational constitu-tionalism in Switzerland today is significantly less important than national constitutionalism. Cantonal constitutions turned into Sleeping Beauties a very long time ago. Few Swiss people know about the constitution of their cantons, and parliaments, governments, courts and scholars rarely refer to them. Researchers have described this as a paradox: while cantonal law is highly significant, cantonal constitutions are politically and legally insignificant.[3]

Something that looked like a renaissance of subnational constitutionalism occurred in the 1960s when numerous cantons totally revised their constitutions, and a second at the turn of the millennium when another group of cantons chose to rewrite their basic laws. However, the most

---

1 The author is most grateful to MLaw Sandra Egli and BLaw Liliya Tseytlina for their valuable support by the drafting of this chapter.
2 See Preamble, Federal Constitution of the Swiss Confederation of 18 April 1999 (Swiss Federal Constitution, SFC).
3 Andreas Auer, 'Les constitutions cantonales: une source négligée du droit constitutionnel suisse' (1990) 91 *Schweizerisches Zentralblatt für Staats- und Verwaltungsrecht* 14.

 DOI: 10.4324/9781003052111-17

obvious effect of the cantonal revisions has been an increase in the diversity of age and length of the cantonal constitutions, not an augmented interest in what they say. Currently, three categories of cantonal constitutions can be distinguished:

- Old and deeply Sleeping Beauties: three cantonal constitutions are as old as they are brief, two still date from the nineteenth century (Appenzell Innerrhoden and Zug) and one (Valais/Wallis) from 1907 (but is currently under total revision).
- Middle-aged and slumbering: 12 constitutions have been rewritten during the last decades of the twentieth century and are more detailed.
- Young and snoozing: 11 constitutions are younger than the current federal constitution which entered into force in 2000 and are often longer than it.

The oldest constitution of Appenzell Innerrhoden (1872) is the shortest (only 48 provisions), the youngest constitution of Genève (2012) is the longest (237 provisions). It is hard to say whether the more recent constitutions are more relevant or whether the cantonal constitution-makers have simply become more garrulous. As we will see, some of the new constitutions contain treasures of constitutional innovation, in particular those drafted by constitutional assemblies[4], but most of them still wait to be brought back to life by a kiss, to be discovered by legal scholarship and to be put into practice by cantonal authorities.

Swiss subnational constitutionalism can be situated within the broader context of *an aged and symmetric coming-together federation* characterized by *territorial stability*, *linguistic diversity*, and a less noted but more relevant *urban-rural divide*:

(i) *An aged coming-together federation*: to pay tribute to former independence, the Swiss cantons are still considered 'sovereign except to the extent that their sovereignty is limited by the Federal Constitution'.[5] They are listed by their names in the constitution and enjoy a guarantee of existence.[6]

(ii) *A high level of self and shared rule*: the cantons exercise all rights not delegated to the Confederation by the federal constitution[7] and enjoy considerable lawmaking powers in fields such as education and culture, health and social assistance, policing, planning, infrastructure, transport and public services, relations between the state and churches, and environment protection. They also have a voice in the making of shared rules on the federal level which cannot be overheard.[8]

(iii) *Symmetry*: all cantons enjoy equal autonomy and participation rights and carry the same burdens and responsibilities. The only exception to federal symmetry relates to the former half-cantons, Obwalden and Nidwalden, the two Basel (Stadt and Landschaft), and the two Appenzell (Ausserrhoden and Innerrhoden). These cantons solved internal conflicts by dividing into two before the making of the federation in 1948 and were not allowed a 'double voice'. The current constitution of 1999 no longer uses the diminutive label 'half-canton', but maintains the exceptions to symmetry: the former half-cantons each elect only one representative to the second chamber, the Council of States, while all other cantons

4 Pascal Mahon, 'La constitution vaudoise dans le contexte du mouvement constitutionnel suisse du dernier quart de siècle in Pierre Moor (ed.), *La Constitution vaudoise du 14 avril 2003* (Stämpfli 2004) 1, at 12–13.
5 Art. 3 SFC; Giovanni Biaggini in *Basler Kommentar* (BSK), Art. 3 BV N 78.
6 Art. 1 and 53 para. 1 SFC.
7 Art. 3 SFC.
8 See Art. 45 and 55 SFC.

elect two; and whenever referenda require a double majority of the people and the cantons, the former half-cantons each have half a cantonal vote.[9] Their upgrading into cantons with full voting rights has been considered from time to time but discarded for good reasons—upgrading the mostly small and exclusively German-speaking cantons would have noticeable effects on the overall federal equilibrium.[10]

(iv) *Territorial stability*: the Swiss federation was originally formed by 19 full and six half-cantons. These historic units are very unequal in size, population, geography, economy, language, religion and culture, and some are unreasonably small when it comes to serving an increasingly mobile population. Despite this, the territorial structure of the country has proved stable and has only been changed once. The number of cantons was raised to 26 when the new canton of Jura was carved out of the territory of the canton of Bern in 1979.[11] Amalgamations of cantons are considered now and then—Basel Stadt and Basel Landschaft in 1948, 1969 und 2014, Genève and Vaud in 2012—but all attempts failed in popular votes.[12] Cantonal identities have remained strong enough to prevent major territorial adjustments.

(v) *Religious and political divides*: historically, the religious divides have been salient and the cause of violent clashes. After the short confessional war of 1847 between opposing Catholic and Protestant cantons, an 'agreement not to agree' on religious matters was a crucial element of the peace-making process resulting in the federal constitution. The regulation of the relationship between the church and the state was to remain a responsibility of the cantons which opted for a variety of approaches. This variety still exists but is no longer a source of controversy. Political debate is today more focused on political, economic and social issues, with the Latin regions tending to be more favourable to state involvement and internationalization, while the German-speaking regions are more sceptical towards both.

(vi) *Linguistic diversity*: while German, French, Italian and Romansh are national languages, most cantons are monolingual.[13] Fortunately, linguistic, religious and political divides are cross-cutting. The minority of Italian speakers have traditionally cooperated with Catholics in other cantons, and protestant French cantons have found allies in protestant cantons on the other side of the linguistic border (the famous 'Röstigraben'). This fortunate coincidence is among the reasons why linguistic diversity has always been an important characteristic of the Swiss Confederation but not a deep dividing line.

(vii) *Urban-rural divide*: at the time of the making of the Swiss federation, religious, political and economic cleavages, and not language, were the dominant features of conflict. Federalism was adopted to accommodate the small, conservative and dominantly Catholic cantons of central Switzerland which had lost the Sonderbund War of 1847. All of them were German-speaking and feared being dominated by the large, liberal and dominantly Protestant cantons of the same linguistic community. The urban-rural cleavage seems to

---

9 Art. 142 para. 2 and 150 para. 2 SFC.

10 See Eva Maria Belser, 'The Swiss Ständerat: a Model of Perfect Bicameralism' (2018) 10(2) *Perspectives on Federalism* 158.

11 In 1975 three of six mostly French-speaking districts decides to enter the new canton of Jura, three decided to stay in the canton of Bern. The controversy of some Bernese territories joining Jura is a still unresolved issue (Liliane Denise Minder and Simon Mazidi, 'The Case of Jura in Switzerland' (2019) 19 *Fédéralisme*, 'Exploring Self-determination Referenda in Europe' 1.

12 Eva Maria Belser, Bernhard Waldmann and René Wiederkehr, *Staatsorganisationsrecht* (Schulthess Verlag 2017) N 18.

13 Art. 4 and 70 para. 1 and 2 SFC.

be the deepest as it divides the country when it comes to formulating social and ecological policies or defining its relationship to the European Union and the wider world. Today, urban centres such as Zürich (German-speaking) and Genève (French-speaking) often have more interests in common than they have with rural cantons of the same linguistic family.

17.2 Autonomy

The fact that the cantons have their own constitutional systems and can amend them at will has been neglected but not challenged. The cantons' broad autonomy in all matters, including constitutional ones, is unquestioned. From a comparative perspective, their powers undoubtedly qualify as strong.[14]

17.2.1 Scope

The scope of cantonal autonomy is traditionally divided in four aspects:

(i) *Autonomy of organization*: the cantons are free to organize themselves. They autonomously decide on their institutions, the competences, elections, sizes and tasks of their parliaments, governments, court systems and civil services. Overall, there is considerable homogeneity between the organization of cantons which have been inspired by the federal constitution, the revised constitutions of other cantons and international trends. Nevertheless, there are also interesting differences between the cantonal systems referring to cantonal popular rights, elections systems, institutional checks and balances, or rules on party financing.

(ii) *Autonomy of tasks*: while the Confederation must fulfil the duties, which are assigned to it by the federal constitution, the cantons freely decide on the duties they fulfil within the scope of their powers.[15] Some cantons use their constitutions to list these tasks, other leave legislative space to cantonal parliaments and peoples. The system chosen by each canton often determines whether residual competences are left to the communes or not. The cantons also freely decide whether they want to fulfil their tasks on their own or in cooperation with other cantons based on inter-cantonal cooperation, inter-cantonal treaties and inter-cantonal organizations.[16] Swiss subnational units also have the right to conclude international treaties within the scope of their areas of jurisdiction and frequently do so.[17]

(iii) *Financial autonomy*: the cantons, just like the Confederation, levy direct taxes on individuals and legal entities. The Confederation has a mandate to harmonize direct taxes but matters such as tax scales, tax rates and tax allowances are excluded from harmonization.[18] Additionally, cantons freely decide about spending and debts and all have established their own debt brakes. As the financial system follows the principle of fiscal equivalence, the central government cannot use the power of the purse to rule beyond its competences.

---

14 Giovanni Biaggini in BSK, Art. 3 BV N 79; Francesco Palermo and Karl Kössler, *Comparative Federalism— Constitutional Arrangements and Case Law* (Hart Publishing 2017) 79; Ronald L. Watts, *Comparing Federal Systems* (3rd edn, McGill-Queen's University Press 2008) 31.
15 Art. 41 and 42 SFC.
16 Art. 48.
17 Art. 54 SFC, for a comparative perspective see Palermo and Kössler (n 13), at 444.
18 Art. 129 SFC.

(iv) *Autonomy in the implementation of federal laws*: as an integrated federation, the Swiss federal tier only rarely implements its laws but relies on the cantons to do so. While the cantons are obliged to implement federal law—and to carry the financial burdens related to this—they enjoy a considerable margin of discretion when doing so.[19] In consequence, most Swiss law is harmonized rather than unified and different cantonal approaches and priorities persist in all legal fields.

17.2.2 Procedure

Only one provision of the federal constitution limits the constitutional powers of the cantons. Cantons must adopt a democratic constitution which does not contradict federal law. The procedure to adopt and revise cantonal constitutions, is composed of a cantonal and federal phase.

17.2.2.1 The Cantonal Adoption

In general, the cantons are free to determine their own constitution-making processes. However, they have to comply with the federal requirement of adopting 'a democratic constitution' which requires 'the approval of the People' and the ability to revise the constitution 'if the majority of those eligible to vote so request'.[20] Scholars still ponder about the exact meaning of these requirements[21] but their practical application was only an issue when the Confederation was established, and not since. In 1850, the federal parliament did not allow Uri to introduce a waiting period of six years and instead obliged the canton to permit constitutional amendments 'at any time'—just like the federal constitution;[22] in 1852, Schaffhausen was prevented from establishing a two-thirds quorum for popular votes on constitutional matters, and Graubünden from requiring a double majority of the population and the districts.[23] Since then, there has never been a claim that a cantonal constitution was not 'democratic'. Consequently, the scholarly opinion that the cantons are not allowed to introduce a bicameral parliament has never been challenged. Despite the boldness of the statement—a bicameral parliament as it exists on the federal level is not 'democratic' enough to be introduced at the cantonal level—the debate has not reached the ear of any of the Sleeping Beauties.

It is interesting to note that only the recent total revisions of Valais have been initiated by the people; for all others, the cantonal parliaments and governments have been the driving forces. With the exception of Ticino, all cantons first carried out a popular referendum on the question of whether or not the cantonal people approve the project of a total revision before the final draft was put to a second vote. Generally, there has been quite an enthusiasm for total revisions—with typically more than two-thirds of the populations voting in favour. However, this has not led to a lasting interest in cantonal constitutionalism. In a number of cantons, the vote on total revision was combined with the question whether a constitutional assembly or the cantonal parliament should be in charge of preparing the draft. The cantonal populations opted for a constitutional assembly in some cantons (e.g. Basel Stadt, Fribourg, Vaud, Valais) and for cantonal

---

19 Art. 46 SFC.
20 Art. 51 para. 1 SFC.
21 See Andreas Auer, *Staatsrecht der schweizerischen Kantone* (Stämpfli 2016) N 587; Alexander Ruch in *St. Galler Kommentar* (SGK), Art. 51 N 13 f.
22 Art. 192 para. 1 SFC. See Art. 77 Cantonal Constitution (CC) UR 1850 (Alexander Ruch in SGK, Art. 51 N 14).
23 Pierre Tschannen, *Staatsrecht der Schweizerischen Eidgenossenschaft* (2nd edn, Stämpfli 2016) §18 N 15.

parliaments in others (Aargau, Bern, Neuchâtel, St. Gallen, Schaffhausen, Genève).[24] Some cantonal constitutions provided an answer to this question (in Genève an elected constitutional assembly is required, while in Graubünden and Schwyz a parliamentary process is mandated). A last group of cantons used a total revision referendum to simultaneously amend the constitutional amendments rules.[25] Cantons opting for a parliamentary procedure typically establish special committees which regularly include external members, and all drafting actors make considerable efforts to enable public participation, sometimes including special consultation of the youth or resident foreigners.[26]

Most revisions of cantonal constitutions are not total but partial. In all cantons, partial revisions can be initiated by the executive, the legislative or the people. Usually, the cantonal constitutions define the number of signatures necessary to request a partial revision which varies from several thousands[27] to several hundreds[28] and is not necessarily proportionate to the size of the respective population.[29] No canton, however, asks for more than 10 per cent of those eligible to vote.[30] The time allocated for the collection of the signatures also differs significantly between the cantons.[31]

Popular initiatives must comply with overriding law. In most cantons, it is up to parliaments, not courts, to review initiatives and declare them invalid in case of a violation of national or international law. In Genève and Vaud, the governments are competent for this preventive control.[32] Vaud is the only canton in which the validity control takes place before the signature collection starts;[33] in all the others, the authorities decide when the popular initiative has been handed in. The validity or non-validity decision of the cantonal authority can be challenged before the Federal Supreme Court for violation of democratic rights.[34]

17.2.2.2 *The federal approval*

Cantonal constitutions must comply with the federal minimum requirement of being 'democratic' and of not being 'contrary to federal law'.[35] In order to guarantee this, all cantonal constitutions need the approval of the Confederation. From a comparative perspective, the mandatory approval may seem far-reaching as every single amendment of a cantonal constitution must be submitted to the Confederation. Such preventive tests require conformity with all

---

24 See Bernhard Ehrenzeller and Roger Nobs, 'Gemeinsamkeiten und Unterschiede der totalrevidierten Verfassungen' (2009) 110 *Schweizerisches Zentralblatt für Staats- und Verwaltungsrecht* 1, at 7–8.

25 Zürich hence opted for a constitutional assembly even though the cantonal constitution originally mandated parliament and Luzern adopted an amendment providing for a change in the other direction.

26 Ehrenzeller and Nobs (n 23), at 8; for the procedure in Appenzell Ausserrhoden: Hans-Jürg Schär, 'Die neue Ausserrhoder Kantonsverfassung' (1996) 97 *Schweizerisches Zentralblatt für Staats- und Verwaltungsrecht* 337, at 341 ff. and in Vaud: Francine Crettaz, 'Chronique d'une révision accomplie' in Moor (n 3) 39, at 40 ff.

27 15,000 in Bern (Art. 58 para. 2 CC BE), 12000 in Vaud (Art. 79 CC VD), 10000 in Ticino (Art. 85 para. 2 CC TI). In Genève the threshold is at three percent of those eligible to vote (Art. 56 para. 1 CC GE)).

28 300 in Appenzell Ausserrhoden (Art. 51 para. 2 CC AR), 500 in Nidwalden (Art. 54 para. 4 lit. Ziff. 2 CC NW), 600 in Uri (Art. 38 para. 2 CC UR).

29 The demographically smaller Ticino asks for more signatures (10,000, Art. 85 para 2 CC TI) than the densely populated Zürich (6,000, Art. 24 lit. a CC ZH).

30 Tschannen (n 22), at §18 N 17.

31 In most of the cantons, the duration is between four to six months but it is 18 months in Basel-Stadt (Art. 47 para. 4 CC BS) and 90 days in Fribourg (Art. 42 para. 2 CC FR).

32 Art. 60 para 1 CC GE.

33 Art. 80 para. 1 CC VD.

34 See, e.g., BGE 143 I 129; BGE 144 I 281.

35 Art. 51 para. 1 and 2 SFC.

national and international law, and therefore seem to have the potential to limit the scope of cantonal autonomy in significant ways. However, they do not. Cantons in fact enjoy a very large constitutional autonomy. This is mostly due to the fact that competence for preventive review is not attributed to the Federal Supreme Court but to the bicameral Federal Assembly and members of parliament are hesitant to declare cantonal constitutional provisions null and void which have been accepted by the canton.[36]

Most legal scholars criticize the political rather than legal character of the federal approval.[37] While it makes sense to allow a federal parliament to decide whether cantonal constitution-making procedures have been 'democratic' enough to comply with minimal federal requirements, it is problematic to entrust a political body with the power to preventively control compliance of the cantonal constitutions with all overriding law. Such a comprehensive review is highly demanding and should be based on the exchange of legal arguments assessed by a neutral body. In practice, this does not occur. The cantons submit their new or revised constitutions to the Federal Council which presents a very brief message drafted by the federal administration to the Federal Assembly. Parliament, then, typically without further ado, decides to guarantee the cantonal constitution or their new or amended norms. If conformity is controversial, the Federal Assembly prefers to refer to the doubtful principle 'in dubio pro populo'—and to refrain from questioning a norm which has been approved by a cantonal majority.

Since 1848, the Federal Assembly approved all total revisions of cantonal constitutions and most of the thousands of partial revisions. In only very few cases, preventive control resulted in a non-conformity decision, motivated by political rather than legal arguments:

(i)   In 1948, the Federal Assembly refused to guarantee norms of the constitutions of the Canton of Basel Stadt and Basel Landschaft providing for a process of reunification, as it considered this was a violation of the federal obligation to protect 'the existence and territory of the Cantons'.[38] In 1960, however, the parliament changed its mind and approved the new constitutional attempts of the two Basel cantons to prepare for amalgamation.[39]

(ii) When the Federal Assembly in 1977 reviewed the constitution of the newly established constitution of Jura, it declared invalid a norm providing for the future inclusion of French-speaking territories of Bern into Jura. The cantonal norm allowed an extension of the cantonal territory only in case the Bernese Jurassic territories would secede from Bern respecting 'federal law and the law of the respective canton'[40]. The federal parliament still referred to the broad principle of federal loyalty to withhold a guarantee. After Bern had accepted the carving out of three of its districts, it seemed politically unwise to confront it with a cantonal norm signalling that Jura was hungry for more.

---

36 Art. 172 para. 2 SFC.
37 See, e.g., Auer (n 20), at N 571; Giovanni Biaggini in *Orell Füssli Kommentar* (OFK), Art. 51 BV N 26; Ralph David Doleschal, *Die abstrakte Normenkontrolle in den Kantonen* (Schulthess 2019) 650; Guillaume Lammers, *La démocratie directe et le droit international—prise en compte des obligations internationales de la confédération et participation populaire à la politique extérieure* (Stämpfli 2015) 113.
38 Federal Decree of 8 October 1947 (AS 1948 219).
39 Message of 20 November 1959 on guaranteeing the constitutions of Basel-Stadt and Basel-Landschaft, BBl 1959 II 1355 and of 22 June 1960, BBl 1960 II 221.
40 Message of 20 April 1977 on guaranteeing the constitution of the future canton Jura, BBl 1977 II 264.

(iii) In 2007, a constitutional norm of Genève limited access to the Court of Auditors to persons above the age of 27 and of secular status for violation of the principle of equality and religious freedom.[41]

(iv) In 2013, the National Council (but not the Council of States) twice refused to approve a constitutional norm of Schwyz providing for an electoral system violating—according to the Federal Supreme Court's case law—the principle of equal voting power.[42]

17.3 Relevance

All 26 cantonal constitutions are codified in a single document carrying the title constitution (Verfassung/constitution/costituzione/constituziun). Most cantonal constitutions are comprehensive when it comes to establishing and framing institutions and guaranteeing individual rights and freedoms but the formal documents do not necessarily contain all provisions substantially qualifying as constitutional law. Often, laws on political rights, naturalization, equality or data protection comprise norms which are fundamental enough to be part of the constitution. But if they are included in a statute, they are not technically part of the constitution. As different procedures apply to the making and revision of constitutional and statutory law, the distinction between the two is formal: a norm is constitutional when it is formally part of the document called the constitution, and sub-constitutional when it is not—whatever its content and (symbolic) value.[43]

In the legal hierarchy of norms, cantonal constitutions are on top of the pyramid. They enjoy primacy over all other cantonal norms which must be interpreted in conformity with the respective constitution and invalidated if this is not possible. As cantonal constitutions are subnational, they must, however, give way to all national and international law. More controversially, this rule also applies to inter-cantonal treaties and the law produced by inter-cantonal bodies. As the federal constitution obliges the cantons to comply with inter-cantonal law,[44] the roughly 800 inter-cantonal concordats and the numerous international organizations executing them raise similar concerns about democratic deficits as international law does. Cantons publish their constitutions in their respective legal databases and print them as booklets freely available at cantonal chancelleries. In addition, the federal legal database consisting of all federal and international law includes cantonal constitutions. This is an exception to the rule that each tier of government publishes only its own laws.[45] The federal law on publications thus treats the cantonal constitutions as special: unlike all other cantonal laws, they are guaranteed by the Confederation and therefore must be officially compiled with other federal laws.

Little is known about the use of cantonal constitutions. Obviously, they determine important matters starting from the official name of the canton, its institutions, procedures and tasks, its linguistic and religious regime, and its relations to its communes as well as its neighbours. Cantonal administrations thus necessarily refer to cantonal constitutions when organizing elections and referenda, drafting subordinate law and executing it; cantonal courts must have them in mind when adjudicating certain matters and cantonal governments and parliaments

41 Message of 18 October 2006 on guaranteeing the constitution of Geneva, BBl 2206 8785.
42 Message of 15 August 2012 on guaranteeing the constitution of Schwyz, BBl 2012 7913.
43 Alexander Ruch in SGK, Art. 51 N 4.
44 Art. 48 para. 5 SFC.
45 Art. 11 Federal Act on the Compilations of Federal Legislation and the Federal Gazette (PublG).

quote them when initiating or rejecting plans or drafts, at least occasionally. But that probably is about it.

Cantonal constitutional law is not regularly taught at any of the ten Swiss law faculties, and only few faculties offer optional (and irregular) courses on the topic. All Swiss law faculties attract students from several or all cantons, a fact that partially explains their hesitance to teach cantonal law. Consequently, young lawyers only discover cantonal law once they start practising law in one of the cantons. For similar reasons, there is a scarcity of legal research in the field of cantonal constitutional law. Some scholars have published books on the constitutional and administrative law of their cantons (but this only applies to cantons big enough to constitute a market)[46] and two have endeavoured to comprehensively present the constitutional law of the cantons.[47] In legal journals, cantonal constitutional law is virtually absent.[48] It probably is just not attractive enough to write and publish on issues which, in the case of the smaller cantons, only matter for a few tens of thousands of people. Because scholars rarely write about cantonal constitutions, few people read about them and take note of innovations and shortcomings. As a consequence of the lack of scholarly interest, civil society actors, including political parties, rarely refer to cantonal constitutions. Newspapers report on cantonal constitutional initiatives and revisions—nationwide if the matter is innovative or controversial (foreigners or minors voting rights, fundamental rights for primates)—but fall silent once the norm has been accepted or rejected in a referendum. The fact that so many political parties and civil societies make the effort of starting a cantonal constitutional initiative seems to be either to use this as a tool in an (electoral) campaign or to test a political idea first (and with little financial and other burden) on the cantonal ground before raising it nationally. The initiatives prohibiting the burka seem to have followed this strategy. Right-wing parties first successfully launched an initiative in Ticino (where hardly any burka or niqab have been seen), before starting to collect signatures for a federal initiative.[49]

17.4 Content

It is a challenging task to discuss the content of 26 cantonal constitutions which are of very different age, length and style. If we leave aside the oldest constitutions which are often modernized through constitutional practice, we can, however, note that the others follow a surprisingly similar structure. They are all conceived as full-blown constitutions in their own right, not as

---

46 Tobias Jaag, Markus Rüssli, *Staats- und Verwaltungsrecht des Kantons Zürich* (5th edn, Schulthess 2019); Kurt Nuspliger and Jana Mäder, *Bernisches Staatsrecht und Grundzüge des Verfassungsrechts der Kantone* (4th edn, Stämpfli 2012); Giovanni Biaggini, Alex Achermann, Stephan Mathis and Lukas Ott, *Staats- und Verwaltungsrecht des Kantons Basel-Landschaft II* (Verlag des Kantons Basel-Landschaft 2005); Denise Buser, *Neues Handbuch des Staats- und Verwaltungsrechts des Kantons Basel-Stadt* (Helbing Lichtenhahn 2008); Isabelle Häner, Markus Rüssli and Evi Schwarzenbach Evi (eds) *Kommentar zur Zürcher Kantonsverfassung* (Schulthess 2007); Mahon (n 3).

47 Auer (n 20); Denise Buser, *Kantonales Staatsrecht. Eine Einführung für Studium und Praxis* (2nd edn, Helbing Lichtenhahn 2011).

48 For a few exceptions to the rule: Andreas Auer, 'Les constitutions cantonales: une source négligée du droit constitutionnel suisse' (1990) 91 *Schweizerisches Zentralblatt für Staats- und Verwaltungsrecht* 14; Marcel Bolz, 'Die Verfassung des Kantons Aargau—Was hat sich bewährt? Wo besteht Handlungsbedarf?' (1999) 100 *Schweizerisches Zentralblatt für Staats- und Verwaltungsrecht* 571; Ehrenzeller and Nobs (n 23); Bernhard Ehrenzeller, '10 Jahre solothurnische Kantonsverfassung—Was hat sie uns gebracht? Ein Rück- und Ausblick' (1999) 100 *Schweizerisches Zentralblatt für Staats- und Verwaltungsrecht* 553; Schär (n 25).

49 Left-wing parties followed the same strategy when they launched cantonal initiatives for the transparency of campaign and party financings (two of them were accepted in Schwyz and Fribourg in 2018).

minimal constitutions or mere organizational statutes, and include a preamble, general principles, a human rights catalogue, political rights, institutional arrangements, rules on decentralization, tasks, finances and amendment rules.

17.4.1 Identity

In the federal constitution, references to national symbols are strikingly absent; there is no mention of the flag, the emblems, the currency, the national anthem or even the capital.[50] The same is true for the cantonal constitutions which generally are taciturn when it comes to their own flags and emblems. Cantonal constitutions clarify the name of the subnational unit—formally called a canton, Stand, republic, state or member state—while the federal constitution refers to all units as cantons. All cantonal constitutions (with the exception of Appenzell Innerrhoden, Thurgau and Zug) start with a preamble, the newer ones clearly inspired by the federal preamble. Only the preamble of the constitution of Jura, born out of an internal secession process, stands out, as it refers to the French Human Rights Declaration of 1789 and the UN Declaration of 1848 and proclaims a need to re-establish the sovereignty of the Jurassic people and to implement the right to self-determination.

The majority of constitutions are adapted in the name of the people of the respective canton (e.g. 'we, the people of Obwalden …'). As all the subnational units are unitary entities and do not replicate the federal structure internally, they abstain from referring to a dual constitution-maker (as the federal constitution does by mentioning 'the Swiss People and the Cantons').

The majority of the cantonal constitutional preambles are adopted 'in the name of God' (as the federal constitution is) but Genève, Neuchâtel and Ticino are not. Uri, as an exception, identifies the people of Uri as a population which predominantly follows the Christian faith, and Fribourg refers to a population which believes in God or follows values from other sources. But as the relation between the state and the church is a cantonal competence, differences relating to religion reach much deeper. While some cantons entertain privileged relationships with the official churches and recognize them as public institutions (e.g. Valais[51], Nidwalden[52]), others have opted for strict separation (e.g. Genève[53]). More recently, some cantons have used their competence to accommodate an increasingly diverse population and provide for special relationships with non-Christian religious communities.[54]

While German, French, Italian and Romansh are national languages, most cantons, free to choose their own official language, are monolingual.[55] Seventeen cantons are German-speaking, four are French-speaking, one is Italian-speaking (Ticino), three are bilingual (Bern/Berne, Fribourg/Freiburg, Valais/Wallis[56]), and one is trilingual (Graubünden/Grischun/Grigioni). Monolingualism is also the choice of Ticino despite the fact that the small commune of Bosco Gurin traditionally is German-speaking. According to the constitution, Ticino is 'of Italian culture and language'[57]. Bern is the only canton reserving seats in parliament and government for the linguistic minorities of the French-speakers.[58] Graubünden declares German, Romansh and

50 Giovanni Biaggini in BSK, Art. 3 BV N 5.
51 Art. 2 para. 4 CC VS.
52 Art. 34 para 1 and 35 CC NW.
53 Art. 3 para. 2 CC GE.
54 See, e.g., Art. 131 CC ZH, Art. 171 CC VD and Art. 133 CC BS.
55 Art. 4 and 70 para. 1 and 2 SFC.
56 Art. 6 para. 1 CC BE, Art. 6 para. 1 CC FR and Art. 12 para. 1 CC VS.
57 Art. 1 para. 1 CC TI.
58 Art. 73 para. 3 and Art. 84 para. 1 CC BE.

Italian to be cantonal and official languages with equal status, refers to the aim of promoting cultural diversity, and provides for special protective measures in favour of Romansh speakers.[59]

17.4.2 Organization of powers

As the federal constitution requires only that the cantons adopt a 'democratic' constitution, the political organization of the cantons varies significantly. While some variations are mostly symbolic, others are practically significant.

(i) *Cantonal Executives*: all cantons have opted for directly elected collegial governments although an indirect election by parliament (like at the federal level) would be considered sufficiently 'democratic'.[60] The cantonal governments consist of five or seven members and are, except for Zug and Ticino, elected by majority vote. There is variation in the degree of professionalization,[61] election periods[62] and incompatibility rules,[63] but overall cantons solve matters related to their governments in similar ways.

(ii) *Cantonal Parliaments*: when it comes to the cantonal legislature, the differences are more striking. All cantons have elected parliaments, but Appenzell Innerrhoden and Glarus still preserve popular assemblies where decisions are taken by the people present raising their hands. The two remaining historic exceptions, deeply rooted in Swiss traditions of direct democracy, oblige Switzerland to make a reservation to Art. 25 lit. b of the UN International Covenant on Civil and Political Rights as in popular assemblies the right to secret balloting cannot be guaranteed.[64]

While there is a tendency to reduce the size of cantonal parliaments, the largest cantonal parliament of Zürich still consists of 180 members, the smallest of Appenzell Innerrhoden only has 50 members. All cantonal parliaments are unicameral. Except for Appenzell Innerrhoden and Graubünden which opt for a majority vote, and Zug which uses a mixed system, all cantonal parliaments are elected by proportional vote. Recently, the Federal Supreme Court has interfered with cantonal election systems based on arguments that small election districts unfairly disadvantage smaller parties and violate the right to equal voting.[65] The court cases have been very controversially received and triggered cantonal initiatives to more strongly entrench cantonal election autonomy in the federal constitution. As these initiatives have not been pursued, the federal case law is binding on cantons and obliges them to establish larger constituencies and, if these remain small for cultural reasons, to provide for alternative mechanisms (such as the association of constituencies or the use of the double Pukelsheim election method).[66] While special quotas for minorities (as provided for the French-speakers in Bern) have been accepted by the Federal Assembly, a cantonal attempt to introduce high and inflexible gender quotas has been declared unconstitutional by the Federal Supreme Court.[67]

---

59 Preamble, Art. 3 para. 1 CC GR.
60 Eva Maria Belser and Nina Massüger in BSK, Art. 51 BV N 35.
61 The members of the government of Appenzell Innerrhoden work part time.
62 Four years in general, but five years in Fribourg and Jura (Art. 106 CC FR; 65 CC JU).
63 Vaud does not allow members of the cantonal government to be elected to the Federal Assembly.
64 BGE 121 I 138.
65 BGE 136 I 352.
66 See Klara Grossenbacher, *Das grosse Ringen um die kantonalen Parlamentswahlsystem*, Newsletter IFF 2/2018, at 6.
67 BGE 131 II 361; BGE 123 I 152.

(iii) *Direct Democratic Right*: all cantons provide for a panoply of popular initiative and veto rights which go far beyond the direct democratic rights at the federal level. In addition to the constitutional initiatives, which are mandatory, all cantons allow for legislative initiatives as well as popular veto rights in the form of mandatory and facultative referendums against cantonal laws, finance and administrative decisions.[68] The extent of these rights and the conditions for their exercise (e.g. the number of signatures to be collected to trigger a popular vote) vary greatly. In addition, some cantons experiment with supplementary direct democratic rights and allow for a constructive referendum (enabling the initiative committee to propose its own alternative to the vetoed law),[69] popular motions (allowing to impact on the parliamentary agenda),[70] popular debates (permitting non-elected people to defend their cause in parliament)[71] and global budget initiatives (offering the opportunity to submit a cantonal budget).[72]

Within the limits of federal law, cantons autonomously define voting rights. While some cantons were less slow than the Confederation to introduce female voting, most did so at the same time (in 1971) or slightly later. The men of Appenzell Ausserrhoden waited until 1989 to introduce equal voting rights and Appenzell Innerrhoden notoriously had to be forced to do so by the Federal Supreme Court in 1990.[73] When it comes to voting rights for foreigners, some (French-speaking) cantons might again pave the way for the Confederation. Jura and Neuchâtel have introduced active voting rights for foreigners on the cantonal and active and passive voting on the communal level, others did so on the communal level only, still others allow communes to make their own choices. In Glarus, voting age in cantonal matters has been reduced to the age of 16,[74] but the cantonal attempt to rejuvenate the democratic body has not been followed by other cantons.

(iv) *Cantonal Judiciary*: the organization of the judiciary is largely a cantonal competence and differences in the cantonal court systems are substantive. Smaller cantons tend to have a straightforward structure with district and cantonal courts, larger cantons have often established special labour, commercial and family courts. It is in the field of the judiciary that the ratification of the European Convention on Human Rights (ECHR) in 1974 has most affected subnational constitutionalism: the case law of the European Court of Human Rights soon made it clear that numerous cantonal practices were not in line with Article 5 and 6 ECHR and that some of the reservations and explanatory statements "Switzerland had issued at the time of ratification" were invalid. While these supranational standards have effectively harmonized the Swiss judiciary, the most obvious diversity in the field relates to judicial review. Jura and Genève, for instance, have established cantonal constitutional courts mandated to review cantonal laws,[75] in Vaud, the constitutional court constitutes a chamber of the highest cantonal court,[76] and in Nidwalden and Graubünden, the cantonal administrative court is mandated to adjudicate constitutional matters and review laws.[77] Other

---

68 See, e.g., Auer (n 20), at N 1004 ff.
69 Art. 63 para. 3 CC BE.
70 Art. 41 CC NE, Art. 47 CC FR, Art. 31 CC SH, Art. 34 CC SO, Art. 61 para. 2 CC OW.
71 Art. 56 para. 1 lit. a CC AR.
72 Art. 33a CC SO.
73 BGE 116 Ia 359 E. 7.
74 See https://www.ch.ch/de/demokratie/abstimmungen/wer-ist-stimmberechtigt/.
75 Art. 104 para. 1 CC JU, Art. 124 lit. a CC GE.
76 Art. 136 para. 2 CC VD.
77 Art. 69 para. 2 CC NW.

cantons do not allow for abstract review of cantonal laws or only under special circumstances or foresee it only for other acts than laws.[78]

(v) *Decentralization*: As in most old federations, the Swiss federal system relies on two tiers only and treats communes as creatures of the cantons. It is true that the federal Constitution of 1999 includes a norm on communes but it guarantees their autonomy merely 'in accordance with cantonal law'.[79] Cantons thus continue to determine the level of internal decentralization, can de- or re-centralize at will and can provide for forced local amalgamations. In contrast to cantons, communes have no guaranteed right of existence[80] and their number is decreasing rapidly, mostly through voluntary (but incentivized) amalgamations. As a rule, French-speaking cantons tend to be more centralized than German-speaking cantons, which guarantee far-reaching local autonomy, including in financial matters.[81]

17.5 Multilevel constitutionalism

While the relationship between the cantons and their constitutions is one of equality, there is a clear hierarchy when it comes to federal and international law. Communication between the different tiers of constitutionalism is intense and numerous feedback loops exist to allow top-down as well as bottom-up interaction.

17.5.1 *The relation between federal and the cantonal constitutions*

All amendments of the federal constitution must be based on the approval of the Swiss people *and* the cantons.[82] Hence, the majority of the cantons (but not individual cantons) can veto any constitutional change, including transfers of power from the cantonal to the federal tier. If the majority of cantons, however, strongly oppose a constitutional amendment, it is usually not pursued, but as a rule, cantons do not oppose tailor-made harmonization steps as they are deeply interconnected—and their populations organize their life and work across cantonal borders.

Cantons have numerous other means of participation at the federal level. As the delegates of the cantons sitting in the second chamber, the Council of State, vote without instructions,[83] other mechanisms are more effective. Cantons can use cantonal initiatives to place an issue on the agenda of the Federal Assembly,[84] participate in consultation processes,[85] and have a constitutionally guaranteed right to be informed comprehensively and in a timely manner on all matters of interest, and a right to be heard and consulted.[86] If several cantons oppose a federal proposal or parts of it, their concerns will usually be considered. This is supported by the fact

---

78 See, e.g., Art. 116 CC BS; Art. 79 para. 2 CC ZH; Art. 51 Administrative Justice Act Schaffhausen; Art. 68 ff. Administrative Justice Act Aargau; Art. 55 para. 2 CC GR.

79 Art. 50 para. 1 SFC.

80 See BGE 131 I 91 E. 2.

81 Laetitia Mathis and Nicolas Keuffer, 'La refonte du fédéralisme suisse: impacts sur les autonomies cantonale et communale' (2015) 16 *Fédéralisme* 37.

82 Art. 140 para. 1 lit. a SFC.

83 Art. 161 para 1 SFC.

84 Art. 160 para. 1 SFC; Art. 115 Federal Act on the Federal Assembly (ParlG); Daniela Thurnheer in BSK, Art. 160 BV N 1.

85 Art. 45, 55 and 147 SFC and Art. 2 para 1 Federal Act on the Consultation Procedure (VlG).

86 Martin Graf in SGK, Art. 160 N 8.

that eight cantons can call for an optional referendum and request that federal acts and important international treaties are submitted to a vote of the people.[87] The referendum right of the
cantons has only once been used (to successfully oppose a federal tax law in 2003) but this
incident has strengthened the voice of cantons even more. To more forcefully communicate
with the federal tier, the cantons coordinate their actions in inter-cantonal conferences domi-
ciled in the House of Cantons and often speak with one voice.

Communication between the different constitutional tiers is intense. Historically, the federal
constitution has taken inspiration from the cantons, and the federal and cantonal constitutions
all have been and are harmonized by international (human) rights law. More recently, the structure and numerous provisions of the federal constitution are copied at the cantonal level.
Interaction between constitutions of different tiers has been most pertinent in the field of
human rights. When the federal human rights catalogue was still in an embryonic state, the cantonal fundamental rights played a crucial role. During a period of judicial activism in the 1960s
and 1970s the Federal Supreme Court recognized unwritten constitutional human rights and,
by doing so, filled the gaps of the written federal constitution.[88] One of the conditions for
recognizing basic rights and freedoms at the federal level was that cantonal guarantees existed
and there was an (evolving) federal consensus that such right or freedom should exist.[89] Cantonal
constitutions then were important drivers of human rights innovation, and will hopefully play
this role again in the future.

When the unwritten constitutional guarantees were codified in the federal constitution of
1999, cantonal fundamental rights no longer seemed to matter.[90] There was some hope for a
renaissance of cantonal constitutionalism when numerous cantons completely revised their constitutions and often drafted sumptuous human rights catalogues sometimes going beyond the
international and federal guarantees. However, for the time being, these complementary cantonal guarantees, such as the right to a healthy environment,[91] day-care,[92] a minimum salary,[93]
educational assistance,[94] emergency housing,[95] maternity protection[96] or the protection of all
forms of family life,[97] have not yet changed the Swiss human rights landscape.[98] The same is true
for the unconditioned right to access official documents[99] or the right to receive a timely answer

---

87 Art. 141 SFC.
88 Ulrich Häfelin, Walter Haller, Helen Keller and Daniela Thurnheer, *Schweizerisches Bundesstaatsrecht* (9th
     edn, Schulthess 2016) N 14.
89 For example, BGE 121 I 367, S. 370 E. 2a; BGE 115 Ia 234, S. 268 E. 10a; Eva Maria Belser, Bernhard
     Waldmann and Eva Molinari, *Grundrechte I* (Schulthess 2012) 59 N 7; Tschannen (n 22), at §7 N 17.
90 See Eva Maria Belser, 'Kantonale Grundrechte und ihre Bedeutung für die Verwirklichung der
     Menschenrechte im mehrstufigen Staat' in Samantha Besson and Eva Maria Belser (eds.), *La Convention euro-
     péenne des droits de l'homme et les cantons/Die Europäische Menschenrechtskonvention und die Kantone* (Schulthess
     2014) 67.
91 Art. 19 CC GE.
92 Art. 11 para. 2 lit. a CC BS.
93 Art. 13 para. 3 CC TI.
94 Art. 3 para. 1 lit. b CC SG.
95 Art. 33 CC VD.
96 Art. 35 CC VD und 35 CC FR.
97 Art. 12 Abs.1 lit. c CC SH.
98 Giovanni Biaggini in OFK, Art. 189 BV N 6. See for a contemporary attempt to claim an unwritten fed-
     eral right to social aid based on a cantonal consensus on the matter: Eva Maria Belser and Thea Bächler,
     'Das Grundrecht auf Sozialhilfe—Von der Notwendigkeit, ein ungeschriebenes Grundrecht anzuerkennen,
     das über das Recht auf Hilfe in Notlagen hinausgeht' (2020) 121 *Schweizerisches Zentralblatt für Staats- und
     Verwaltungsrecht* 463.
99 Art. 18 CC NE; Art. 19 para. 2 CC VD; Art. 19 para.2, CC FR.

to petitions.[100] Diligent lawyers, in addition to international and national guarantees, quote cantonal constitutions in their appeals but the Federal Supreme Court usually replies with a text block copied from one case to the next: 'the appeal does not demonstrate that the cantonal right goes beyond the international and national guarantees which is why the court will not refer to it'.[101]

17.5.2 *The impact of international and European law*

The ratification of the European Convention of Human Rights (ECHR) in 1974 significantly impacted the federal and cantonal constitutions and was a catalyst for substantive harmonization. The case law of the European Court of Human Rights initiated profound changes in cantonal constitutionalism, especially in the field of criminal and administrative law, and one of the objectives of the Federal Constitution of 1999 was to codify (European) human rights law within Switzerland.[102] At the same time, cantonal competences have often been mentioned as reasons for the Swiss reluctance to ratify additional protocols to the ECHR (such as protocol 1 guaranteeing a right to education or protocol 12 guaranteeing a general prohibition of discrimination) and UN human rights treaties, as well as a general tendency to register reservations to the application of international standards and deny the justiciability of international human rights guarantees.

The fear of endangering federalism and direct democratic rights was crucial for the Swiss population and the cantons when deciding to refuse membership of the European Economic Area in 1992. For similar reasons, bilateral negotiations between Switzerland and the European Union were critically received in many cantons. As the Confederation has a comprehensive mandate in the field of international relations, cantonal authorities feared that international treaties relating to matters within their competence (such as education and research, health, police) would compromise their autonomy. To compensate for reduced self-rule, they pushed for more shared rule in international relations, and successfully so.[103] Today, most international delegations and negotiation teams—in Brussels, Genève as well as New York—include representatives of the cantons and international relations are slowly evolving from an exclusive federal into a concurrent competence.

17.6 Constitutional review

Implementing the cantonal constitutions and bringing them to life is primarily the task of the cantonal authorities. In some cantons, cantonal parliaments, governments and administrations are the central actors; in others, the judiciary is more strongly involved. As the last complaint authority, the Federal Supreme Court hears disputes concerning the violations of cantonal constitutional rights.[104] There are, however, hardly any cases as these cantonal rights are largely considered co-substantial with national and international guarantees.

The Federal Constitution notoriously does not provide for full constitutional review of federal acts. As a consequence, it implicitly allows the federal parliament to violate the

---

100 Art. 20 para. 2 CC NE; Art. 2 w CC SG; Art. 19 para. 2 CC SH; Art 25 para. 2 CC FR.
101 For example, BGE 138 I 331 E. 5.1; BGE 100 Ia 392 E. 4a.
102 Message of 20 November 1996 on the new Federal Constitution, BBl 1997 I, p. 62.
103 Art 55 SFC and Art. 1 ff. Federal Act on the participation of the cantons in federal foreign policy (BGMK).
104 Art. 189 para. 1 lit. d SFC.

constitution—but fortunately no longer international human rights law.[105] In contrast, the Federal Supreme Court has an unlimited mandate to review cantonal acts and cantonal decisions and to provide for abstract and concrete review.[106] There is, however, an important exception to constitutional review as a result of the preventive conformity control of all cantonal constitutions by the Federal Assembly described above: the parliamentary decision is final and cannot be challenged before the Federal Supreme Court.[107] While there is abstract review of cantonal norms by the judiciary, this is not the case when the controversial norm is a constitutional norm and has been approved by federal parliament.

In addition, the parliamentary guarantee also hinders concrete review of cantonal constitutional law. The Federal Supreme Court consistently rules that cantonal constitutional norms are immunized by the act of parliament and can only be reviewed when overriding national and international law has changed in the meantime and raises new conformity questions.[108] This case law was the reason why it took the Federal Supreme Court so incredibly long to impose female suffrage in Appenzell Innerrhoden. The constitutional norm limiting cantonal political rights to men had been approved by the Federal Assembly after the federal tier had introduced equal voting rights in 1971, which was late enough as it was. It was only in 1990 that the Federal Supreme Court reviewed the cantonal constitution based on later amendments of overriding law (such as the reinforcement of gender equality in the federal constitution and the ratification of the ECHR).[109]

The self-restraint of the Federal Supreme Court represents a real challenge for the implementation and protection of human rights in Switzerland. Once the Federal Assembly has approved a cantonal norm—typically based on rudimentary legal considerations and without an adversary exchange of arguments—the judiciary considers reviewing the norm as a taboo. Consequently, old and new norms of cantonal constitutions raising human rights questions are unlikely ever to be reviewed by a Swiss court.

17.7 Conclusion

This case study on Swiss subnational constitutionalism confirms most of the hypotheses under investigation in this volume. The Swiss cantons have very strong powers to adapt and revise their subnational constitutions. Their far-reaching powers are undoubtedly linked to the fact that all cantons already had their codified constitutions as members of the old Confederation. These constitutions were hardly affected by the making of the Swiss federation in 1848. Despite its linguistic, religious and cultural diversity, Switzerland is not a divided multinational federation. The internal tensions are probably more intense than most observers assume and the language cleavages are real. But the cantons are not national units claiming rights to self-determination. Rather, they share numerous commonalities across borders. Jura constitutes an interesting example. As the youngest of all, it is the only canton that refers to the right of the Jurassic people to self-determination and engages in more effort to celebrate its constitutional identity.

As Swiss cantons enjoy comprehensive legislative, executive and financial autonomy, their cantonal constitutions matter. Their symbolic value is, however, very limited. When cantonal constitutions are revised, the process generally receives considerable but short-lived attention. Overall, cantonal constitutions fulfil the important task of establishing and constraining cantonal

105 BGE 125 II 417; Yvo Hangartner and Martin E. Looser in SGK, Art. 190 N 7 and N 40.
106 Art. 82 Federal Act on the Federal Supreme Court; Tschannen (n 22), at § 22 N 29.
107 Art. 189 para. 4 SFC.
108 BGE 111 Ia 239, E. 3; Andreas Stöckli in BSK, Art. 172 BV N 17.
109 BGE 116 Ia 359.

power, defining cantonal tasks, designing decentralization and guaranteeing rights and freedoms—but do so in a sober way.

The Swiss case study only partially confirms the hypothesis that subnational constitutions organize powers in the same way as the federal constitution. Like the federation, all 26 cantons maintain a unique system of a collegial government which is neither parliamentarian nor presidential. While the federal government is elected indirectly, all cantons have, however, opted for direct elections. Other differences stem from the fact that the federal constitution organizes a federation while cantonal constitutions a decentralized unit with no bicameralism, no qualified majorities, and—for most cantons—no guarantee of the existence and territories of the communes.

Subnational constitutions serve as constitutional laboratories. Historically, the federal institutional arrangements and fundamental rights were inspired by the cantonal constitutions. For decades, the Federal Supreme Court operated similarly to the ECHR and dynamically developed guarantees by referring to a consensus on the lower tier. Since the adaption of a comprehensive federal fundamental rights catalogue in 1999, the relevance of cantonal constitutions decreased. However, as the federal constitution comes of age, bottom-up constitutional innovation is likely to gain importance again. Recently, there are some interesting learning and feedback loops at the crossroads of institutional and human rights matters (e.g. round tables, comprehensive action plans, ombudspersons).

The Swiss case also reveals that strong representation can exist simultaneously with strong constitutional autonomy. As Swiss cantons have always enjoyed both, strong subnational representation cannot be reduced to a merely compensatory mechanism. It is, however, true that the ongoing centralization process has shifted attention from autonomy to representation, consultation and joint decision-making procedures. Cantonal delegates participate more and more effectively at the federal level, with significant influence on federal decisions before proposals reach the Federal Assembly. In addition to formal representation, informal contacts such as federal dialogues, mixed working groups, etc., are flourishing. As participation is most effective when cantons speak with one voice, horizontal intergovernmental cooperation has become a very important feature of Swiss federalism.

When it comes to constitutional review, Switzerland is an outsider. Conflicts between democracy and the rule of law are generally solved by giving preference to the former. Cantonal constitutions undergo a preventive conformity control by the Federal Assembly which generally rubberstamps cantonal constitutional norms accepted by the people of the respective cantons ('in dubio pro populo'). Parliamentary constitutional review is final and cannot be challenged before the Federal Supreme Court. The latter is constitutionally prevented from receiving an abstract review request and has decided to abstain from concrete review as well. As a result, norms of cantonal constitution can only be challenged when overriding law, such as national and international law, has been adapted later than parliamentary review and raises conformity issues which did not exist at the time the parliament decided. This practice results in limitations on human rights enforcement. Some cantonal norms, such as the privileges of churches, the prohibition of the burka, the control of party financing or the language regime, are unlikely ever to be reviewed by the federal judiciary as overriding law is unlikely to raise new questions. The best hope for full human rights reviews therefore comes from the European Court of Human Rights which could potentially find a violation of the right to an effective remedy (Art. 13 ECHR).

18

SUBNATIONAL CONSTITUTIONALISM IN THE UNITED KINGDOM

Constitutional statutes within the context of an uncodified constitution

Nikos Skoutaris

18.1 Context

The United Kingdom is a union of four nations: England, Wales, Scotland and Northern Ireland. The principality of Wales 'has been closely integrated with England for the purposes of law and administration since the late Middle Ages'.[1] England completed the conquest of Wales between 1272 and 1307 under Edward I. Through the Law in Wales Acts 1535 and 1542, Wales was legally annexed to the Kingdom of England, the legal system of England was extended to Wales and the norms of English administration were introduced to the principality.

'Edward I and other English kings failed in their attempts to overwhelm Scotland by force'.[2] Still, the thrones of Scotland and England were united when James VI of Scotland succeeded Elizabeth I as James I of England. A formal political union, however, between the British nations that had been ruled by the same monarchs since 1603, was only forged a century later. By virtue of the Treaty of Union, the Union with Scotland Act 1706 passed by Westminster and the Union with England Act 1707 passed by the Parliament of Scotland, Scotland was united with England 'into One Kingdom by the Name of Great Britain'.[3] Under those constituent documents,[4] a parliament of Great Britain, the Crown of Great Britain and the Government of Great Britain were created. Within this new UK Parliament, Scottish representation was secured.[5] Notwithstanding the dissolution of the Scottish Parliament, Scotland retained its own legal system and different system of education and religious establishment throughout this time. In fact, the Treaty of the Union provided for the preservation of a number of distinctive Scottish institutions including the Court of Session and the High Court of Judiciary 'in all time coming'.[6]

---

1 Peter Leyland, *The Constitution of the United Kingdom: A Contextual Analysis* (2nd edn, Hart Publishing 2012) 253.
2 Leyland (n 1), at 23.
3 Treaty of Union 1706, Art I.
4 See Elizabeth Wicks, 'A New Constitution for a New State? The 1707 Union of England and Scotland' (2001) 117 *Law Quarterly Review* 109.
5 Treaty of Union 1706, Art XXII.
6 Treaty of Union 1706, Art XIX.

DOI: 10.4324/9781003052111-18

The relationship between Great Britain and Ireland has been complex and often turbulent. Following resolutions by the parliaments in Dublin and London, Ireland was united with Great Britain by the Acts of Union 1800. In response to the clear discontent of the Irish nationalists with the prevailing arrangements, the Liberal Party attempted to introduce a considerable degree of self-government on the island of Ireland. However, the Home Rule Bills of 1886, 1893 and 1912 failed to achieve a majority in Westminster. To accommodate deep-seated differences between unionists and nationalists in Ireland, the Government of Ireland Act 1920 'was based on partition between the six counties in the North, comprising Northern Ireland with a Parliament in Belfast, and the remainder of Ireland with a Parliament in Dublin'.[7] The Irish resistance, however, during the Irish War of Independence led the United Kingdom to sign the Anglo-Irish Treaty with representatives of the Irish Republic. The treaty provided for the establishment of the Irish Free State and gave the right to Northern Ireland to opt out of the nascent self-governing dominion.[8] Indeed, Northern Ireland exercised this right and a parliamentary system of devolved government was established in the region while the rest of the island eventually achieved its independence. Having failed to effectively address the needs of the nationalist/republican/Irish/Catholic community, Westminster suspended the devolution arrangements in the North in March 1972. During an era of political violence known as 'The Troubles', Northern Ireland was directly governed by London.

While there was considerable centralization of power with regard to Northern Ireland, during the 1970s, there was also an attempt to devolve power to Scotland and Wales. The original devolution legislation, however, did not attract the required popular support in the relevant referendums in 1979. The plans for the establishment of a Welsh Assembly were defeated by a majority of 4:1. In Scotland, 51.6 per cent of those who voted supported the proposal for the creation of a Scottish Parliament. But with a turnout of 64 per cent, this represented less than a third of the electorate. According to the relevant legislation, the devolution act were to be repealed if less than 40 per cent of the total electorate approved it.

In 1997, however, the Labour Party achieved a landslide electoral win with a manifesto commitment to introduce devolution for Scotland and Wales. This time, the electorate approved the plans in the respective referendums. In Scotland, three out of four voters supported the establishment of a Scottish Parliament, while in Wales, devolution was approved with 50.3 per cent.[9] The Scottish Parliament and the Scottish Government in their modern form were established by the Scotland Act 1998 while the Welsh system of governance was introduced by the Government of Wales Act 1998. Both acts have been amended a number of times. The most important changes can be found in Scotland Acts 2012 and 2016 and the Government of Wales Act 2006 and Wales Acts 2014 and 2017, respectively.

Unlike Scotland and Wales, the devolution in Northern Ireland was not a free-standing policy coming out of a political party's manifesto. It is one facet of the Belfast/Good Friday Agreement (hereafter GFA), which put an end to the sectarian violence that had plagued Northern Ireland for decades. The Agreement was signed on 10 April 1998, after many years of complex talks and negotiations. It is comprised of two interrelated documents: a multi-party agreement by most of Northern Ireland's political parties (the Multi-Party Agreement); and a

---

7 Leyland (n 1), at 21; for a brief historic account of how the partition on the island of Ireland was established, see Diarmaid Ferriter, *The Border: The Legacy of a Century of Anglo-Irish Politics* (Profile Books 2019).

8 The conflictual nature of events that led to the establishment of the Irish Free State gave rise to competing interpretations of the nature of the of the Constitution of the Irish Free State (1922). *Cf. State (Ryan) v Lennon* [1935] IR 170 and *Moore n Attorney-General for the Irish Free State* [1935] AC 484.

9 Following a successful referendum, Tony Blair's administration also managed to pass The Greater London Authority Act 1999 which established the office of an elected mayor and a separately elected assembly for the capital of the UK.

legally binding international agreement between the British and the Irish Governments registered with the Secretariat of the UN (the British-Irish Agreement). It highlighted that Northern Ireland was an integral part of the United Kingdom but established its constitutionally recognized right to secede.[10] Such a unique constitutional status was 'accompanied by unusual multilevel governance'.[11] Accordingly, a power-sharing arrangement for the governance of the province was established (Strand 1) alongside north/south institutions that regulate the relationship between Northern Ireland and the Republic of Ireland (Strand 2) and East/West institutions that facilitate the relationship between the UK and the Republic (Strand 3). Like the devolution arrangements in Scotland and Wales, the Northern Ireland system of governance has been amended.[12] Because of the consociational and power-sharing character of this post-conflict settlement, however, such amendments have traditionally been the by-products of arduous negotiations and painful compromises between the two ethno-religious communities.

The succession of amendments to the devolution acts illustrates one of the important characteristics of the modern version of the UK territorial constitution, namely that devolution is 'a process not an event'.[13] The system has developed over time in response to the needs and demands of three very different political communities. This piecemeal approach reflects the idiosyncratic nature of the UK constitution. But it does not mean that the symbiosis of those different legal and political orders in the UK is without its problems, tensions and challenges.

18.2 The extent of the subnational constituent autonomy

18.2.1 Content

The UK constitution has gradually evolved over centuries without having ever been codified in one single document. The UK constitutional arrangement has developed over time 'through a combination of statutes, events, conventions, academic writings and judicial decisions'.[14] It consists of 'the set of laws, rules and practices that create the basic institutions of the State, and its component and related parts, and stipulate the powers of those institutions and the relationship between the different institutions and between those institutions and the individual'.[15]

Within this fluid constitutional landscape, parliamentary sovereignty has traditionally been regarded as the foundational principle of this legal order. In Dicey's words, the UK Parliament has 'the right to make or unmake any law whatsoever'.[16] This means that the Crown in Parliament comprised of the House of Commons, the House of Lords and the Sovereign is omnipotent with regard to its lawmaking power.[17]

---

10 Northern Ireland Act 1998, s. 1. See Section 18.4.1 of the chapter.
11 Katy Hayward, '"Specific Solutions" & "Distinct Arrangements": More of the Same for Post-Brexit NI?' *Slugger O' Toole*, 11 December 2017 <https://sluggerotoole.com/2017/12/11/specific-solutions-distinct-arrangements-more-of-the-same-for-post-brexit-ni/> accessed 1 August 2020.
12 See, for example, Northern Ireland (St Andrews Agreement) Act 2006.
13 Ron Davies MP, HC Debs, vol.304, col. 1108 (21 January 1998).
14 *R (on the application of Miller and another) v Secretary of State for Exiting the European Union* [2017] UKSC 5, at para 40.
15 House of Lords Constitutional Committee, <www.publications.parliament.uk/pa/ld200102/ldselect/ldconst/11/1103.htm> accessed 1 August 2020.
16 Albert V. Dicey, *An Introduction to the Study of the Law of the Constitution*, (10th edn, Macmillan 1959) 40.
17 The UK Parliament has the power to pass or repeal any law: relating to the Parliament itself (Septennial Act 1716); with 'extra-territorial' effect (War Crimes Act 1991); with retrospective effect (Indemnity Act 1920); that is, in (alleged) breach of international law and UK's international obligations (*Mortensen v Peters* (1906) 8 F(J) 93), which is even considered immoral (*Madzimbamuto v Lardner-Burke* [1969] 1 AC 645,723).

Interestingly, in Scotland, such Diceyan orthodoxy has been questioned. Lord Cooper in *MacCormick v Lord Advocate* noted that

> [t]he principle of the unlimited sovereignty of parliament is a distinctively English principle which has no counterpart in Scottish constitutional law.... Considering that the Union legislation extinguished the parliaments of Scotland and England and replaced them by a new parliament, I have difficulty seeing why it should have been supposed that the new parliament of Great Britain must inherit all the peculiar characteristics of the English parliament but none of the Scottish parliament, as if all that happened in 1707 was that Scottish representatives were admitted to the parliament of England.[18]

Be that as it may, given the fundamental role that the Crown in Parliament and the primary legislation promulgated by it possess within the UK constitutional order, it is rather unsurprising that the three UK devolved systems of governance are based on a series of Acts of the UK Parliament. These legislative acts occupy a special place within the UK constitutional order. It has been authoritatively said that they belong to the category of 'constitutional statutes' that cannot be impliedly repealed.[19] Still, they are legislative acts that have received the royal assent after going through the relevant legislative process. As such it is the British Parliament—and not the devolved nations—that is the authoritative source of the devolution statutes (with the possible exception of the Northern Ireland Act which is a by-product of an international agreement). Although there is no UK codified constitution establishing the British Parliament and the other governing institutions of the UK, the devolution acts positively establish and empower the devolved institutions.[20]

Within this context, the devolution statutes play a pivotal role with regard to the vertical separation of powers.[21] Generally speaking, the devolved parliaments may legislate in those areas that are not exclusively reserved to the UK Parliament and include *inter alia* foreign affairs, defence and the Constitution itself.[22] This does not mean of course that Westminster is prevented from legislating with regard to those regions. To the contrary, its continuing power to legislate for Wales, Scotland and Northern Ireland is explicitly affirmed.[23] However, pursuant to the Sewel Convention, Westminster does 'not normally legislate with regard to devolved matters except with the agreement of the [relevant] devolved legislature'.[24] Recently, this convention has been codified with regard to Scotland and Wales.[25]

---

18 *MacCormick v Lord Advocate* 1953 SC 396.
19 See Section 18.5 of the chapter.
20 See Section 18.4.2 of the chapter.
21 See Section 18.4.3 of the chapter.
22 See Scotland Act 1998, s.29; Northern Ireland Act 1998, s.6; Government of Wales Act 2006, s. 108A.
23 Scotland Act 1998, s. 28(7); Northern Ireland Act 1998, s. 5(6); Government of Wales Act 2006, s. 107(5).
24 Memorandum of Understanding and Supplementary Agreements Between the United Kingdom Government, the Scottish Ministers, the Welsh Ministers, and the Northern Ireland Executive Committee (October 2020), para. 14 <https://assets.publishing.service.gov.uk/government/uploads/system/uploads/attachment_data/file/316157/MoU_between_the_UK_and_the_Devolved_Administrations.pdf> accessed 1 August 2020; see also Devolution Guidance Note 8: Post-Devolution Legislation Affecting Northern Ireland <https://assets.publishing.service.gov.uk/government/uploads/system/uploads/attachment_data/file/60983/post-devolution-primary-ni.pdf> accessed 1 August 2020.
25 See Scotland Act 2016, s. 2 amending Scotland Act 1998, s. 28; Wales Act 2017, s. 2 amending Government of Wales Act 2006, s.106.

Since its inception,

> the scope of the convention has evolved so as to require the consent of the [devolved parliaments] not only where the UK Parliament seeks to legislate in devolved policy areas, but beyond that where a UK bill seeks to vary the legislative competence of the [devolved parliaments] or the executive competence of the [devolved] Ministers.[26]

This means that when Westminster wishes to alter the level of constituent autonomy of a devolved nation, they have to seek the consent of the respective regional legislature. To the extent that the consent mechanism is followed and respected, the regional legislatures may have a determinative say over such amendments.[27]

Having said that, amendments to the devolution acts have to be enacted by Westminster 'save to the extent that a devolved legislature has been granted power to amend them directly'.[28] To give but an example of the latter, Section 3 and 4 of Scotland Act 2016 and Section 5 of Wales Act 2017 transferred to the regional institutions the competence to take control of their electoral arrangement.[29] Other examples of where the devolved institutions may amend the content of the devolution acts relate to the appointment of certain office holders, their remuneration, etc.[30]

Interestingly, with regard to Northern Ireland, a special mechanism for the enhancement of its subnational constituent autonomy is provided. This flexibility mechanism has allowed the devolved arrangement to adapt to the dynamic processes of the peace settlement. Schedule 3 of the Northern Ireland Act provides for a list of 'reserved matters' that may be transferred to the Northern Ireland Assembly if cross-party support is secured. As a consequence, those competences may be devolved only if the political parties in Northern Ireland demonstrate they can cooperate. For instance, the restoration of devolution in the aftermath of the 2006 Saint Andrews Agreement led to further transfer of powers to Stormont with regard to the very sensitive 'reserved powers' of policing, prisons and criminal law. Despite the unstable and conflictual character of the Northern Irish political system, a further Stormont Agreement in December 2014 on conflict-related legacy issues paved the way for 'legislation to devolve the power to set the rate of corporation tax in Northern Ireland'[31] in accordance with the Corporation Tax (Northern Ireland) Act 2015.

---

26 Chris McCorkindale, 'Echo Chamber: The 2015 General Election at Holyrood—a Word on Sewel', *Scottish Constitutional Futures Forum*, 13 May 2015 <https://www.scottishconstitutionalfutures.org/OpinionandAnalysis/ViewBlogPost/tabid/1767/articleType/ArticleView/articleId/5594/Chris-McCorkindale-Echo-Chamber-the-2015-General-Election-at-Holyrood-a-word-on-Sewel.aspx> accessed 1 August 2020.

27 On Sewel Convention, see Akash Paun and Kelly Shuttleworth, 'Legislating by consent: How to revive the Sewel Convention' *Institute for Government Insight*, September 2018 <https://www.instituteforgovernment.org.uk/sites/default/files/publications/legislating-by-consent-sewel-convention.pdf> accessed 1 August 2020.

28 Nicholas Aroney, 'Devolutionary Federalism within a Westminster-Derived Context' in Aileen McHarg et al. (eds), *The Scottish Independence Referendum: Constitutional and Political Implications* (Oxford University Press 2016) 295, at 303; See Scotland Act 1998, Schedule 4, para. 4 and Government of Wales Act 2006 Schedule 7B, para. 7.

29 See, for example, the Scottish Elections (Reform) Act 2020 that regulates a wide range of issues associated with reform of Scottish Parliament and local government elections in Scotland.

30 Ibid.

31 Bingham Centre for the Rule of Law, *A Constitutional Crossroads: Ways Forward for the United Kingdom* (British Institute of International and Comparative Law 2015) 7.

18.2.2 *Procedure*

As mentioned before, the initial devolution acts and their amendments have been approved by Westminster. In the case of Northern Ireland, because of the post-conflict nature of the arrangement, any amendment has to respect the UK's international obligations stemming from the GFA. In addition, amendments to its constituent autonomy traditionally have to receive the explicit approval of the two ethno-religious communities. This is why such consensus is a necessary condition for the successful triggering of the flexibility mechanism enshrined in Schedule 3. With regard to the other two devolved arrangements, it is important to point out that the political elites of Scotland and Wales have gradually become more involved in the process of amending those acts, not least because of the functioning of the Sewel Convention.

The Scotland Act 1998 founded the modern version of the Scottish devolved institutions. Unlike the Spanish case, where the regions had a very significant role in the drafting of the Statutes of Autonomy, this Act has been the product of a more top-down constitutional process. It is true that 'Scottish devolution was fomented by local agitation, led by organisations such as the Scots National League, Scottish Nationalist Party, Scottish Covenant Association, Campaign for a Scottish Assembly, and Scottish Constitutional Convention' and in that sense there was significant de facto Scottish input.[32] The drafting of the initial devolution act, however, was formally at least largely the result of Westminster-based process influenced by the UK Government's White Paper on the topic: *Scotland's Parliament*.[33]

Gradually, however, the input of the Scottish political community in the drafting of the amendments to the Scotland Act has increased. For instance, Westminster took into account the suggestions of the Commission on Scottish Devolution, also referred to as the Calman Commission, when it adopted the Scotland Act 2012. The Commission had 15 members, including nominees of the three Unionist parties (Labour, Conservatives and Liberal Democrats) but not of the ruling Scottish National Party. One of the main conclusions of the Commission was that 'a big enough part of [the] budget [of the Scottish Parliament should] come from devolved taxation for it to be genuinely accountable'.[34] To this effect, a new Section 80C was introduced into the Scotland Act 1998, 'which would allow [the Scottish Parliament] to set a "Scottish rate" of income tax which, above a minimum level necessary to pay for UK-wide expenditure administered by central government would not be tied to the UK rates'.[35]

Equally, in the wake of the Scottish independence referendum of 2014, the then UK Prime Minister David Cameron announced the establishment of the Smith Commission. The Commission was part of the process of fulfilling 'The Vow' made by the three main unionist parties promising more powers for Scotland in the event of a No vote.[36] Following the rejection of independence, the Smith Commission, comprised of representatives of all five parties represented in the Scottish Parliament, was asked to produce recommendations for further

---

32 Aroney (n 28), at 306.
33 UK Government, White Paper *Scotland's Parliament* (Cm 3658) <https://commonslibrary.parliament.uk/research-briefings/rp98-1/> accessed 1 August 2020.
34 Commission on Scottish Devolution, *Serving Scotland Better: Scotland and the United Kingdom in the 21st Century* (2009) <https://commonslibrary.parliament.uk/research-briefings/sn04744/> accessed 1 August 2020, at p. 9.
35 Roger Masterman and Colin Murray, *Exploring Constitutional and Administrative Law* (Pearson 2014) 348.
36 The Vow <https://www.dailyrecord.co.uk/news/politics/david-cameron-ed-miliband-nick-4265992> accessed 1 August 2020.

devolution, which were published in November 2014.[37] Most of the recommendations of the Commission have been adopted in the Scotland Act 2016, underlining the fact that the revision of the Scottish constitutional act (Scotland Act 1998) is less of a top-down process any more.

What is more interesting is that before the enactment of both the Scotland Acts 2012 and 2016, the Scottish Parliament approved those amendments by passing legislative consent motions. This was in agreement with the so-called 'Sewel Convention'. The consent motion concerning the passage of the Scotland Bill in 2011 was 'worded in *conditional* terms, inviting the UK Government first to consider the amendments and proposals made by the Scotland Bill Committee at Holyrood and then later to return with an amended bill for further debate in a second legislative consent motion'.[38] The result was a new bill which sought conciliation between the two positions and which led to the successful grant of a consent motion.

With regard to Wales, the drafting of the Government of Wales Act 1998 was also largely a top-down process. The little demand for significant political autonomy was reflected in the very limited competences of this devolved legislature as we shall later see. Four years after the creation of the National Assembly of Wales, the then First Minister Ivor Richard created a Commission to consider whether the powers of the Assembly were adequate to the people of Wales. The Richard Commission was partly comprised of independent Commissioners and partly of appointees from the four elected parties to the Assembly. Westminster took into account the report of the Commission when it decided to enhance the Assembly's powers by enacting the Government of Wales Act 2006. In order for the Assembly to obtain an enhanced level of autonomy, two-thirds of its members had to pass a resolution requesting that primary lawmaking powers be transferred to it. In addition, this proposal had to gain the support of the Welsh voters in a referendum.[39] In February 2010 the Assembly passed such a resolution and one year later the Welsh voters supported the initiative by 63.5 per cent.

A few years later, the coalition government of Conservatives–Liberal Democrats suggested the establishment of yet another Commission, which would look at the case for devolution of fiscal powers to the Welsh institutions and whether there was support for further modifications to the then constitutional arrangements. The Silk Commission, much like the Smith Commission in Scotland, were comprised of representatives of the elected parties to the National Assembly. It produced two reports: one on finance published in November 2012 and one on legislative matters published in March 2014. The former led to the adoption of Wales Act 2014, which contains very similar provisions to the Scotland Act 2012. The latter led to the St David's Day process and the Wales Act 2017.

18.2.3 Asymmetry

In the previous two sub-sections, we noted the increase of the subconstitutional space of the devolved entities. The gradual increase in subnational constituent autonomy took place within the context of the deep asymmetry that characterizes the UK constitutional order.

There are two kinds of asymmetry between sub-state entities that may affect the operation of the relevant state. The first might be described as political asymmetry.[40] It 'arises from the

---

37 Smith Commission, *Report of the Smith Commission for further devolution of powers to the Scottish Parliament* <https://webarchive.nationalarchives.gov.uk/20151202171029/http://www.smith-commission.scot/wp-content/uploads/2014/11/The_Smith_Commission_Report-1.pdf> accessed 1 August 2020.
38 Ibid.
39 Government of Wales Act 2006, ss 103–6.
40 Charles D. Tarlton, 'Symmetry and Asymmetry as Elements of Federalism: A Theoretical Speculation' (1965) 27 *Journal of Politics* 861.

impact of cultural, economic, social and political conditions affecting the relative power, influence and relations of different regional units with each other and with the federal government'.[41] In the case of the UK, England possesses 85 per cent of the population and more than 80 per cent of seats in the House of Commons (533 out of 650). At the same time, there is a lack of robust mechanisms for the collegiate representation of the regional tier. The House of Lords is by no means a territorial chamber. This has meant that England dominates Westminster politics while the very different historical trajectories of the other three UK constituent nations have led them to very different political aspirations.

Devolution reflects all the aforementioned political asymmetries that exist within that Union State by allowing for a second type of asymmetry: constitutional asymmetry.[42] This refers 'specifically to the degree to which powers assigned to regional units by the constitution are not uniform'.[43] England, despite its size, does not have a regional legislature while the very different political realities that led to each devolved arrangement are reflected in the drafting process and content of the devolution acts. The Northern Ireland Act is part of a peace settlement plan that was negotiated between the political parties of the two main ethno-religious segments, the UK and the Republic of Ireland. The initial devolution acts for Scotland and Wales were a political by-product of the landslide victory of New Labour. But even between the latter two constitutional arrangements there were important differences. The Scotland Act 1998 provided, as we shall see in Section 18.4, for a much higher level of autonomy than the Government of Wales Acts 1998 and 2006.

More importantly, devolution has created an issue of asymmetrical political representation often referred to as the 'West Lothian question'.[44] The Members of the House of Commons representing the 59 constituencies in Scotland, 40 in Wales and 18 in Northern Ireland can vote on bills about England only. At the same time, the 533 Members of Parliament representing English constituencies have little or minimal say over devolved issues as law-making power has been transferred to the regional institutions. This:

> raises serious questions about the role of MPs as members of the UK parliament, and about the nature of the Union itself. The Union has traditionally been built on an equality whereby all members can vote on all matters, regardless of territorial extent of their application, as members of a single parliamentary body.[45]

In March 2013, the McKay Commission, an expert committee set up by the UK Government to consider how the House of Commons might deal with legislation which affects only part of

---

41 Ronald L. Watts, *Comparing Federal Systems* (3rd edn, McGill-Queen's University Press 2008) 125.

42 On constitutional asymmetry in the UK, see Brice Dickson, 'Work in Progress. A Country Study of Constitutional Asymmetry in the United Kingdom' in Patricia Popelier and Maja Sahadzic (eds), *Constitutional Asymmetry in Multinational Federalism: Managing Multinationalism in Multi-tiered Systems* (Palgrave Macmillan 2019) 461.

43 Ibid.

44 Tom Dalyell, the Westminster MP representing the Scottish constituency of West Lothian first raised it as a question in a debate in the House of Commons: 'For how long will English constituencies and English Honourable members tolerate … at least 119 Honourable Members from Scotland, Wales and Northern Ireland exercising an important, and probably often decisive, effect on English politics while they themselves have no say in the same matters in Scotland, Wales and Northern Ireland?' HC Deb, 13 November 1977, col 123.

45 Meg Russell and Guy Lodge 'The Government of England by Westminster' in Robert Hazell (ed.), *The English Question* (Manchester University Press 2005), 64, at 87.

the United Kingdom published its report.[46] There, it recommended that 'decisions at the United Kingdom level with a separate and distinct effect for England (or for England-and-Wales) should normally be taken only with the consent of a majority of MPs for constituencies in England (or England-and-Wales)'.[47] This position was endorsed by the then UK Government. In fact, the morning after the 2014 Scottish independence referendum, the then Prime Minister David Cameron suggested that 'a crucial part missing from this national discussion [on UK's territorial constitution] is England'.[48] He emphasized that '[t]he question of English votes for English laws—the so-called West Lothian question—requires a decisive answer'.[49] On 22 October 2015, the 'English Votes for English Laws' system was implemented by introducing changes to the House of Commons Standing Orders. According to it, whenever the Speaker of the House certifies that a certain bill (or parts of a bill) relates only to England (or England-and-Wales), an additional committee stage is added to the legislative process in the House of Commons. There, a Grand Committee comprised only of Members of Parliament representing English (and Welsh) constituencies debates the bill. The committee has the power to accept the bill, in which case it will proceed through the rest of the legislative process. But it can also veto, preventing it from being adopted.

18.3 Position of the UK devolution acts within the UK constituent nations

As Acts of the sovereign UK Parliament, the legal status of the devolution acts is different from the acts produced by the devolved legislatures. As we shall see in Section 18.6, the doctrine of parliamentary sovereignty dictates that the UK courts do not have the power to judicially review primary legislation approved by the UK Parliament, including the devolution acts. Still, they can review the acts of the devolved legislatures. In fact, the courts use the devolution acts that describe the vertical division of competences between London and the devolved nations to review whether a certain act of a devolved legislature is *ultra vires*.

Given that they provide for the institutional framework and the competences that the devolved regions can exercise, they could be considered as their constitutional charters. However, such characterization is only informal in the cases of Scotland and Wales. An amendment proposed by the SNP to formally recognize the Scotland Act 1998 as 'The Written Constitution of Scotland' was rejected.[50]

UK courts have also refused to endorse the idea that the Scotland Act is the constitution of the region. The Inner House of the Scottish Court of Session made clear in *Imperial Tobacco* that '[t]he Scotland Act is not a constitution but an Act of Parliament'.[51] To reach this conclusion, the court referred to the fact that there was 'no authority for the Scotland Act to be interpreted any

---

46 The McKay Commission, *Report of the Commission on the consequences of devolution for the House of Commons* <https://webarchive.nationalarchives.gov.uk/20130403030728/http://tmc.independent.gov.uk/wp-content/uploads/2013/03/The-McKay-Commission_Main-Report_25-March-20131.pdf> accessed 1 August 2020.

47 Ibid., at pp. 8–9.

48 David Cameron statement on the UK's future <https://www.bbc.co.uk/news/uk-politics-29271765> accessed 1 August 2020.

49 Ibid.

50 Scotland Bill 2015, New Clause 6; United Kingdom, *Parliamentary Debates*, House of Commons, H C Deb, Vol. 597, 15 June 2015, col. 26.

51 *Imperial Tobacco v Lord Advocate* [2012] CSIH 9 at para.71.

more generously or purposively than any other statute'.[52] Unlike the Northern Ireland Act, which is based on the GFA, there was no international agreement underlying the Scotland Act.

It is precisely this unique and historic role to put an end to an intractable conflict that has led the UK courts to recognize the particular constitutional significance of the Northern Ireland Act 1998. In *Robinson* v *Secretary of State for Northern Ireland*, Lord Bingham recognized that the 1998 Act:

> was passed to implement the Belfast Agreement … in an attempt to end decades of bloodshed and centuries of antagonism. The solution was seen to lie in participation by the unionist and nationalist communities in shared political institutions, without precluding … a popular decision at some time in the future on the ultimate political status of Northern Ireland.[53]

He described the 1998 Act as 'in effect a constitution'.[54] Lord Hoffmann added that it was 'a constitution for Northern Ireland framed to create a continuing form of government against the background of the history of the territory and the principles agreed in Belfast'.[55]

18.4 Content

18.4.1 Identity (nationhood and citizenship)

In accordance with the pragmatic character of the UK constitution, the devolution acts do not engage in questions related with identity, nationhood and citizenship. In any case, Westminster enjoys an exclusive competence to regulate issues concerning British nationality.[56] Having said that, in the aftermath of the UK's withdrawal from the EU, the Scottish Government favoured the transfer to Scotland of the competence to set immigration policy. First Minister Nicola Sturgeon argued that '[d]evolving immigration powers by introducing a Scottish Visa would allow Scotland to attract and retain people with the skills and attributes we need for our communities and economy to flourish'.[57] Unsurprisingly, the UK Government rejected such a Quebec-like arrangement.[58]

Because of its consociational characteristics, the Northern Ireland arrangement provides for an exception in this area as well. According to the Declaration of Support, the signatories to the GFA:

> recognise the birthright of all the people of Northern Ireland to identify themselves and be accepted as Irish or British, or both, as they may so choose, and accordingly confirm that their right to hold both British and Irish citizenship is accepted by both Governments and would not be affected by any future change in the status of Northern Ireland.[59]

---

52 Adam Tomkins, 'Confusion and Retreat: The Supreme Court on Devolution', *British Government and the Devolution*, 17 February 2015 <https://britgovcon.wordpress.com/2015/02/17/confusion-and-retreat-the-supreme-court-on-devolution/> accessed 1 August 2020.

53 *Robinson* v *Secretary of State for Northern Ireland* [2002] UKHL 32, para. 10.

54 Ibid., para. 11.

55 Ibid., para. 33.

56 Scotland Act 1998, Schedule 5, s. B6; Government of Wales Act 2006, Schedule 7A, s. B2; Northern Ireland Act 1998, Schedule 2, s. 2.

57 <https://www.gov.scot/news/plan-for-scottish-visa/ > accessed 1 August 2020.

58 Gina Davidson, 'Nicola Sturgeon's Scottish immigration visa plan refused by UK Government' *The Scotsman*, 27 January 2020 <https://www.scotsman.com/news/scottish-news/nicola-sturgeons-scottish-immigration-visa-plan-refused-uk-government-1395997> accessed 1 August 2020.

59 GFA, Declaration of Support, point 1.vi.

In the recent case *De Souza*, an Irish citizen born in Northern Ireland who had never held a British passport claimed that the scope of the aforementioned provision was to provide a right to choose one's citizenship. The Upper Tribunal (Immigration and Asylum Chamber) rejected the claim. Instead, it held that this section of the GFA provides for a right to identity alone. The people of Northern Ireland therefore remain British citizens even if they identify as Irish, unless they revoke their British nationality.[60] Notwithstanding this decision, a few months later the Home Office announced that family members of British or dual British-Irish citizens from Northern Ireland would be able to apply for the EU settlement scheme as if they were family members of an EU citizen residing in the UK.[61] Although the Home Office denied that the decision had any link with *De Souza*, it in fact recognized the special status of the people of Northern Ireland and their right to identify as either British or Irish, or both.

More interestingly, 'Westminster has formally conceded that Northern Ireland can secede from the United Kingdom to join a united Ireland, if its people, and the people of the Irish Republic, voting separately, agree to this'.[62] Article 1 of the legally binding British-Irish Agreement recognizes this right in no uncertain terms. In particular, the UK and the Republic of Ireland:

(i) recognise the legitimacy of whatever choice is freely exercised by a majority of the people of Northern Ireland with regard to its status, whether they prefer to continue to support the Union with Great Britain or a sovereign united Ireland;

(ii) recognise that it is for the people of the island of Ireland alone, [...] to exercise their right of self-determination on the basis of consent, freely and concurrently given, North and South, to bring about a united Ireland, if that is their wish, accepting that this right must be achieved and exercised with and subject to the agreement and consent of a majority of the people of Northern Ireland;

(iii) acknowledge that while a substantial section of the people in Northern Ireland share the legitimate wish of a majority of the people of the island of Ireland for a united Ireland, the present wish of a majority of the people of Northern Ireland, freely exercised and legitimate, is to maintain the Union and, accordingly, that Northern Ireland's status as part of the United Kingdom reflects and relies upon that wish; and that it would be wrong to make any change in the status of Northern Ireland save with the consent of a majority of its people;

(iv) affirm that if, in the future, the people of the island of Ireland exercise their right of self-determination on the basis set out in sections (i) and (ii) above to bring about a united Ireland, it will be a binding obligation on both Governments to introduce and support in their respective Parliaments legislation to give effect to that wish.

Those international legal obligations concerning the status of Northern Ireland have also been enshrined in UK legislation. Section 1 of the Northern Ireland Act 1998 is a rare example of a provision of a constitutional statute explicitly recognizing the right of secession of a region.

---

60 *The Secretary of State for the Home Department v De Souza*, Upper Tribunal (Immigration and Asylum Chamber), Appeal Number: EA/06667/2016, decision of 14 October 2019.

61 Jayne McCormack, 'Emma De Souza: Home Office 'concession' over NI immigration rules' *BBC*, 14 May 2020 <https://www.bbc.com/news/uk-northern-ireland-52660737> accessed 1 August 2020.

62 John McGarry, 'Asymmetrical Autonomy in the United Kingdom' in Marc Weller and Katherine Nobbs (eds), *Asymmetric Autonomy and the Settlement of Ethnic Conflicts* (University of Pennsylvania Press 2010) 148, at 156.

Schedule 1 of the Northern Ireland Act describes under which circumstances a referendum for the reunification of Ireland can and should be called by the UK Secretary of State. Recently, in *Re McCord*, the High Court of Justice in Northern Ireland discussed and clarified the afore-mentioned Northern Ireland Act provisions.[63] It held that the Secretary of State has:

> a discretionary power to order a border poll under Schedule 1 paragraph 1 even where she is not of the view that it is likely that the majority of voters would vote for Northern Ireland to cease to be part of the United Kingdom and to become part of a united Ireland.[64]

However, if it appears to her that a majority would be likely to vote for a united Ireland, then, she is under a duty to call a poll.

> It is necessarily implied in this provision that the Secretary of State must honestly reflect on the evidence available to her to see whether it leads her to the conclusion that the majority would be likely to vote in favour of a united Ireland. Evidence of election results and opinion polls may form part of the evidential context in which to exercise the judgment whether it appears to the Secretary of State that there is likely to be a majority for a united Ireland.[65]

A similar statutory duty for calling a referendum does not exist with regard to the secession of Scotland from the UK. As already mentioned, the Scottish Parliament has residual powers over the legislative competences that are not explicitly allocated to Westminster. The latter include the constitution of which 'the Union of the Kingdoms of Scotland and England' is part. This means that '[a]s a matter of UK law, the Scottish Parliament cannot pass a declaration of independence'.[66] However, referendums are not listed as a reserved matter in Schedule 5. Therefore, there is a question to be asked whether Holyrood can lawfully 'hold a referendum about whether another constitutional institution should do so'.[67] To put it differently, the constitutional right of the Scottish legislature to organize another independence referendum is at least disputed. This is why the declared aim of the Scottish Government remains to this day the same. They want to achieve a similar political agreement to the one that led to the 2014 independence referendum.[68]

In December 2019, a week after the UK Parliament elections, the Scottish Government published its case for a second independence referendum: *Scotland's Right to Choose: Putting Scotland's Future in Scotland's Hands.* [69] Their case is based on three claims: first, that the Scottish people have the sovereign right to determine their own constitutional future; second, that Brexit

---

63 *Re Raymond McCord* [2016] NIQB 106.

64 Ibid., at para. 18.

65 Ibid., at para. 20.

66 Evan Smith and Alison Young, 'That's how it worked in 2014, and how it would have to work again' *UK Constitutional Law Association Blog*, 15 March 2017 <https://ukconstitutionallaw.org/2017/03/15/ewan-smith-and-alison-young-thats-how-it-worked-in-2014-and-how-it-would-have-to-work-again/> accessed 1 August 2020.

67 Ibid.

68 See the *Edinburgh Agreement* with which the 'two Governments of Scotland' agreed to hold an independence referendum <http://www.number10.gov.uk/wp-content/uploads/2012/10/Agreement-final-for-signing.pdf> accessed 1 August 2020.

69 <https://www.gov.scot/publications/scotlands-right-choose-putting-scotlands-future-scotlands-hands/> accessed 1 August 2020.

consists of a material change of circumstances that justifies a second independence referendum; third, that the electoral wins of the Scottish National Party in the 2016 Holyrood elections and the 2017 and 2019 Westminster elections provide for a mandate to the Scottish Government to organize such referendum.

In Annex B of this blueprint, the Scottish Government goes a step further by putting forward a number of suggested amendments to the devolution act. They propose that the Scotland Act should legally recognize the right of self-determination of the Scottish people. As a result of that, the Scottish Parliament should assume the competence to organize an independence referendum permanently. And if the people in Scotland vote in favour of independence, the UK and Scottish Governments should be under a statutory duty to cooperate in securing the transition to independence. The current UK Government has already ruled out the possibility of a second independence referendum.

To sum up, unlike Scotland, there is a clear and well-founded constitutional pathway for the secession of Northern Ireland from the United Kingdom and the unification of the island of Ireland. This does not mean that such event is necessarily more politically feasible than Scottish independence. Theresa Villiers, the former Northern Ireland Secretary, has made clear that, according to her, 'there is nothing to indicate that there is majority support for a poll'.[70] To this effect, one has to bear in mind that there does not seem to be agreement among the Northern Irish political elites concerning the need to organize such a referendum and that the ethno-religious segment that would be more willing to support the reunification of Ireland, i.e. the Irish/nationalist/republican/Catholic one, is—at the moment and until the political demographics change—in the minority.

18.4.2 Representative structures

The Scottish and the Welsh systems of governance are based on a parliamentary model. The unicameral legislatures of Scotland and Wales are comprised of 129 and 60 members respectively. They are democratically elected under the additional member system. This means that 73 Members of the Scottish Parliament and 40 members of its Welsh counterpart represent individual geographical constituencies elected on the basis of a plurality ('first-past-the-post') system of voting. The remaining members are returned from eight Scottish and five Welsh electoral regions using the D'Hondt method of proportional representation.[71] The aim of the electoral system is to make the overall results more proportional, countering any distortions in the constituency results. Elections for those regional legislatures take place every five years. Following an election, a government is formed after the respective legislative body has nominated a First Minister. After a nomination has been accepted, the First Minister is empowered to appoint ministers from the members of the regional parliament to form the government.[72]

The consociational character of the Northern Ireland arrangement is primarily evident in the power-sharing elements of the GFA. The Northern Ireland Assembly is a democratic body consisting of 90 members who are elected every four years by single transferable vote from 18 five-member constituencies.[73] At the centre of the Northern Irish system of governance lies the principle of consent. First of all, the region 'shall not cease' in its entirety to be part of the UK

70 Available at www.theguardian.com/uk-news/2016/jun/24/arlene-foster-northern-ireland-martin-mcguinness-border-poll-wont-happen.
71 See, generally, Scotland Act 1998, Part 1 and Government of Wales Act 2006, Part 1.
72 Scotland Act 1998, ss. 44–7; Government of Wales Act 2006, ss. 45–8.
73 Northern Ireland Act 1998, Part IV.

'without the consent of a majority of the people of Northern Ireland voting in a poll held for the purposes'.[74] Secondly, the governance of the region is based on the consent of both ethno-religious communities. The Belfast/Good Friday Agreement provides for a 'system of compulsory power-sharing at every level of decision-making to ensure joint-participation by both communities in the process of government'.[75] According to section 16 of the Northern Ireland Act 1998, 'the largest political party of the largest political designation shall nominate [...] the First Minister' while 'the largest political party of the second largest political designation shall nominate [...] the deputy First Minister'. At the moment and until the political demographics change, this provision means that the First Minister is from a unionist/loyalist party while the Deputy is from a nationalist/republican one. However, the ministers are not chosen by this dyarchy. Instead, section 18 of the Northern Ireland Act provides that the ministerial posts are allocated to all of those parties with significant representation in the Assembly. The number of posts to which each party is entitled is determined according to the D'Hondt method of proportional representation. The actual posts are chosen by the parties in the order the seats were awarded. This does not mean that apart from the two largest parties, the other parties are required to enter the executive. They can choose to go into opposition if they wish. However, until now all Northern Irish cabinets have been comprised of at least four parties. Finally, consent is often required when it comes to voting in the Northern Ireland Assembly.

> 'According to the requirement for "parallel consent", a majority from each group of [members of the Assembly] designated as unionist and as nationalist is required to approve important legislation (e.g. on financial matters) and decisions (e.g. the appointment of the Speaker)'.[76]

18.4.3 *Organization of powers*

The horizontal separation of powers in the devolved systems of governance follows the pattern of the vast majority of parliamentary systems around the world. The regional governments exercise executive power while the parliaments legislate. Concerning the judicial system, however, the UK never had a single unified legal system. Scotland and Northern Ireland retained their own separate legal/judicial systems while England and Wales shared another one. There are exceptions to this rule. For instance, in immigration law, the Asylum and Immigration Tribunal's jurisdiction covers the whole of the United Kingdom, while in employment law there is a single system of employment tribunals for England, Wales and Scotland but not Northern Ireland. In addition, the UK Supreme Court has general appellate jurisdiction from courts of all four constituent nations.

Concerning the vertical separation of powers, because there is no codified constitution, the allocation of powers to Northern Ireland, Scotland and Wales can be found in the respective constitutive acts. The Scottish Parliament has had the power to enact primary legislation from the very beginning. Its powers are defined negatively. According to Section 29 of Scotland Act 1998, it may legislate on any area that is not considered a 'reserved' competence of Westminster.

74 Northern Ireland Act 1998, s. 1.
75 Leyland, (n 1) at p. 258.
76 Katy Hayward and David Phinnemore, 'Breached or Protected? The "Principle" of Consent in Northern Ireland and the UK Government's Brexit Proposals', *EUROPP*, 11 January 2019 <https://blogs.lse.ac.uk/europpblog/2019/01/11/breached-or-protected-the-principle-of-consent-in-northern-ireland-and-the-uk-governments-brexit-proposals/> accessed 1 August 2020.

A list of the latter is provided by Schedule 5 of Scotland Act 1998. They include international relations, energy, and aspects of road, rail and marine transport. Scotland, on the other hand, has residual powers over the competences that are not explicitly allocated to Westminster including education, health and policing among else and as of recently some tax-raising powers.[77]

'Devolution in Wales has been in a constant flux since 1998.'[78] Initially, the Welsh Assembly was not a lawmaking body equivalent to the Scottish Parliament. Unlike its counterpart in Scotland whose competences have been defined negatively, Schedule 2 of the Government of Wales Act 1998 enumerated the very limited powers of the Assembly. The Assembly could not pass primary legislation, but only subordinate legislation of specific relevance to Wales.[79] This changed eight years later. The Government of Wales Act 2006 'granted the Welsh Assembly Government the power to request permission from the UK Government (by Order in Council) to enact primary legislation within specified fields of devolved competence, known as "Assembly Measures"'.[80] The 2006 Act, however, did not only allow for a modest extension to the competences of the National Assembly. It also provided for a procedure according to which the Assembly could assume wider powers to make primary legislation in certain enumerated areas.[81] According to this procedure, following a resolution passed by the Assembly requesting primary lawmaking powers to be devolved to Wales, the proposal had to receive the support of the electorate in a referendum. The Assembly passed such a resolution and the majority of the Welsh voters approved the proposal in 2011. As a result, the Welsh Parliament was able to pass laws without first obtaining the approval of the UK Parliament. This was not the last amendment, however. As mentioned earlier, several of the recommendations of the Silk Commission were adopted in the Wales Act 2014 and some of them in the Wales Act 2017. In particular, the changes made to the former parallel the tax provisions of the Scotland Act 2012, while the latter changes implemented a 'reserved powers model'.[82] This has led to the significant narrowing of the asymmetry between the Welsh and the Scottish arrangements.

The Northern Ireland Act 1998 is one facet of a plan for a peace transition. In that sense, the competences devolved to Stormont reflect the tentative nature of devolution. Section 6 of the Act provides that the Assembly has power to pass primary legislation in all matters that are not expressly excluded from its powers. In this way, the devolution act implements an arrangement similar to the Scottish and Welsh ones according to which the Assembly possesses residual powers. However, while Schedule 2 enlists those 'excepted matters' that are reserved as central state powers, in the case of Northern Ireland there is also the aforementioned Schedule 3 that provides for a list of 'reserved matters' that may be transferred to its Assembly if cross-party support is evident. The category of 'reserved matters' thus encapsulates the idea of devolution as a 'process not an event'. As we saw above, such transfer took place for the first time in the aftermath of the St Andrews Agreement in 2006.

---

77 For the tax-raising powers of the Scottish Parliament, see Scotland Act 1998, Part 4A.
78 Ibid.
79 Government of Wales Act 1998, s 22(1).
80 Masterman and Murray (n 35), at 355 citing Government of Wales Act 2006, ss. 93–102.
81 Government of Wales Act 2006, ss. 103–16.
82 Wales Act 2017, s. 3 amending Government of Wales Act 2006, s. 108A.

18.4.4 Fundamental rights

Despite the fact that there is clear reference in the GFA to a Bill of Rights for Northern Ireland, such a bill was never drafted.[83] The same applies to the other two devolved nations. There are no regional Bills of Rights created by or for the devolved regions and their institutions. However, the devolution acts provide that the devolved entities are legally bound by the European Convention of Human Rights (ECHR hereafter). The sub-state legislatures and executives in Northern Ireland, Scotland and Wales are therefore required to comply with 'Convention rights'. A legislative act passed by a regional parliament that is incompatible with the ECHR is considered *ultra vires*.[84] The same applies with regard to secondary legislation enacted by the regional executives.[85] The aforementioned provisions are compatible with section 6(1) of the Human Rights Act 1998. The latter imposes a horizontal duty on all UK public authorities including the devolved institutions to act compatibly with Convention rights.

The critical importance of the ECHR within the legal orders both of the devolved nations and the UK is self-evident. However, there have been a number of suggestions for radical reform of the Human Rights Act and the relationship of the UK with the Convention more generally. The 2015 Conservative Party manifesto committed five times to 'scrap' the Human Rights Act and to replace it with a British Bill of Rights.[86] The then Home Secretary Theresa May argued in favour of the UK quitting the ECHR.[87] The more recent 2019 Conservative manifesto contains a much more modest and nebulous pledge to 'update' the 1998 Act, without specifying what it would entail.

Although the intentions of Prime Minister Johnson with regard to the Convention are not entirely clear, it is important to highlight some of the problems that a radical reform would raise with regard to devolution. First of all, a possible withdrawal of the UK from the ECHR or a 'scrapping' of the Human Rights Act would breach the UK's international obligations stemming from the GFA. Under that agreement the UK Government committed to 'complete incorporation into Northern Ireland law of the European Convention on Human Rights (ECHR), with direct access to the courts, and remedies for breach of the Convention'.[88] Related to that, Article 2 of the Protocol on Ireland/Northern Ireland that is attached to the Agreement on UK's Withdrawal from the EU provides that the UK should ensure that 'no diminution of rights, safeguards or equality of opportunity, as set out in that part of [GFA] entitled Rights, Safeguards and Equality of Opportunity results from its withdrawal from the Union'.[89] As pointed out, the GFA requires the UK to enshrine the ECHR in the law of Northern Ireland. Given that such

---

83 See GFA, Strand One at points 5, 11, 26. On this unimplemented element of GFA, see Anne Smith and Colin Harvey, 'Continuing the Conversation about a Bill of Rights for Northern Ireland' *UK Constitutional Law Association Blog*, 21 July 2017 <https://ukconstitutionallaw.org/2017/07/21/anne-smith-and-colin-harvey-continuing-the-conversation-about-a-bill-of-rights-for-northern-ireland/> accessed 1 August 2020.

84 Scotland Act 1998 s. 29(2)(d); Northern Ireland Act 1998 s. 6(2)(c); Government of Wales Act 2006 ss. 94(6)(c) and 108A(2)(e).

85 Scotland Act 1998 s. 57(2); Northern Ireland Act 1998 s 24(1)(a); Government of Wales Act 2006 s 81(1).

86 <http://ucrel.lancs.ac.uk/wmatrix/ukmanifestos2015/localpdf/Conservatives.pdf> accessed 1 August 2020.

87 Laura Kuenssberg 'Theresa May: UK should quit European Convention on Human Rights' *BBC*, 25 April 2016 <https://www.bbc.com/news/uk-politics-eu-referendum-36128318> accessed 1 August 2020.

88 GFA, Rights, Safeguards and Equality of Opportunity, point 2.

89 Agreement on the Withdrawal of the United Kingdom of Great Britain and Northern Ireland from the European Union and the European Atomic Energy Community, Protocol, Protocol on Ireland/Northern Ireland [2020] OJ L29/1.

a move would amend the competences of the devolved entities, their consent seems necessary in accordance with the Sewel Convention.[90] In the current political context, such consent should not be taken for granted.

18.4.5 *Policy principles*

Similarly to what we have noted with regard to identity, the devolution acts do not contain specific policy principles that the devolved institutions should respect and promote. The only exception is with respect to Northern Ireland. Given the region's turbulent past (a time characterized by violence, segregation and discrimination), the GFA introduced an equality agenda as an integral part of the post-conflict transition. There, the UK Government pledged:

> to create a statutory obligation on public authorities in Northern Ireland to carry out all their functions with due regard to the need to promote equality of opportunity in relation to religion and political opinion; gender; race; disability; age; marital status; dependants; and sexual orientation.[91]

Accordingly, section 75 of the Northern Ireland Act incorporated within the regional legal order such statutory duty on the subnational institutions. The public sector equality duty was a critical 'confidence building' measure that gave nationalist/republican political elites the necessary political space to buy into the other elements of the power-sharing agreement.[92] Its importance is also highlighted by the fact that the aforementioned Article 2 of the Protocol on Ireland/Northern Ireland not only makes an explicit reference to the Equality of Opportunity provisions of the GFA but also provides that a number of EU legislative instruments concerning protection against discrimination will continue to be legally binding in Northern Ireland even after Brexit.[93]

18.5 Multilevel constitutionalism

18.5.1 *Relation between the UK devolution acts and other Acts of Parliament*

Given that the Parliament enjoys supreme lawmaking power, 'if two inconsistent Acts be passed at different times, the last must be obeyed'.[94] In other words, provisions in a more recent statute will always prevail over those in an older statute notwithstanding the potential constitutional significance of the latter. At face value, such a rule threatens the subnational constituent autonomy of the devolved regions as more recent laws passed from Westminster might curtail their subconstitutional space or even impliedly repeal parts of the devolution acts.

During recent decades, however, this Diceyan orthodoxy has been partly challenged. Lord Wilberforce was one of the first to express some doubts as to whether the so-called doctrine of implied repeal applies to statutes of constitutional significance.[95] But it was Laws LJ in *Thoburn*

90 McCorkindale (n 26).
91 GFA, Rights, Safeguards and Equality of Opportunity, point 3.
92 Christopher McCrudden, Equality and the Good Friday Agreement: Fifteen Years On' *UK Constitutional Law Association Blog*, 29 March 2013 <https://ukconstitutionallaw.org/2013/03/29/christopher-mccrudden-equality-and-the-good-friday-agreement-fifteen-years-on/> accessed 1 August 2020.
93 For a list of those instruments, see Protocol on Ireland/Northern Ireland (n 89), Annex 1.
94 *Dean of Ely v Bliss* (1842) 5 Beav 574, 582.
95 In *Earl of Antrim's Petition* [1967] 1 AC 691, 724 he held that '[i]n strict law there may be no difference in status [...] as between one Act of Parliament and another, but I confess to some reluctance to holding that an Act of such constitutional significance as the Union with Ireland Act is subject to the doctrine of implied repeal'.

that clarified that constitutional statutes including the devolution acts may only be expressly and not impliedly repealed.[96] According to him:

> a constitutional statute is one which (a) conditions the legal relationship between citizen and state in some general, overarching manner, or (b) enlarges or diminishes the scope of what we would now regard as fundamental constitutional rights.[97]

The special status of constitutional statutes within the UK legal order has been reaffirmed by the Supreme Court in *HS2*.[98] There, the highest court of the land accepted that '[t]he United Kingdom has no written constitution, but [it has] a number of constitutional instruments'. More importantly for the purposes of this chapter, the devolution acts are recognized as constitutional statutes.[99] In *H v. Lord Advocate*, the UK Supreme Court made clear that the Scotland Act 1998, as a 'constitutional statute', cannot be impliedly but only expressly repealed.[100]

The judiciary has thus recognized the special constitutional status of the devolution acts within the idiosyncratic UK constitution. However, because of parliamentary sovereignty, the Parliament cannot bind its successors and thus 'enact unchangeable enactments'.[101] 'A sovereign power cannot, while retaining its sovereign character, restrict its own powers by any parliamentary enactment.'[102] This means that—in theory at least—Westminster has the power to expressly repeal the devolution acts and abolish the devolved systems of governance. This is very important, if one takes into account that less than 20 per cent of the members of the Parliament represent constituencies of the three devolved regions. So their direct political influence over such a decision would be rather limited.

With regard to Northern Ireland, such a move—albeit legal under UK law—would equate to a breach of the UK's international obligations stemming from the GFA. In the case of Scotland and Wales, it is worth highlighting Section 1 of Scotland Act 2016 and Wales Act 2017. Those provisions enshrined in UK law the concept that the respective systems of devolved government 'are a permanent part of the United Kingdom's constitutional arrangements'.[103] With those, the UK Government undertook the commitment not to abolish those devolved systems 'except on the basis of the people of Scotland [and Wales] voting in a referendum'.[104]

The uneasy co-existence of devolution with the principle of parliamentary sovereignty is further illustrated in the delineation between the legislative competence of Westminster and the devolved legislatures. As we already mentioned, sections 29 of the Scotland Act 1998, 6 of the Northern Ireland Act 1998 and 108A of the Government of Wales Act 2006 provide that the regional legislatures enjoy the residual power to legislate with regard to areas that are not reserved to Westminster. However, this 'does not affect the power of the Parliament of the United Kingdom to make laws' for those devolved regions.[105] The latter provision is compatible with the idea that Westminster is omnipotent with regard to its law-making power. At the same

---

96 *Thoburn v Sunderland City Council* [2003] Q.B. 151, at paras. 62–3.

97 Ibid., at para. 62.

98 *R (Buckinghamshire County Council) v Secretary of State for Transport* [2014] 1 WLR 324.

99 Ibid. at paras. 206–7. This finding has also been upheld in *R (on the application of Miller and another) v Secretary of State for Exiting the European Union* [2017] UKSC 5, at para 67.

100 *H v Lord Advocate* [2012] UKSC 24.

101 Dicey (n 16), at 60.

102 Ibid.

103 See Scotland Act 1998, s. 63A; Government of Wales Act 2006, s. A1.

104 Ibid.

105 Scotland Act 1998, s. 28(7); Northern Ireland Act 1998, s. 5(6); Government of Wales Act 2006, s. 107(5).

time, according to the Sewel Convention, 'the UK Parliament [will] not normally legislate with regard to devolved matters except with the agreement of the devolved legislature'.[106] This convention aims to create the necessary constitutional space for the devolved institutions to exercise their autonomy. In fact, with regard to Scotland and Wales, the most recent devolution acts set this convention into statutory footing.[107]

Such codification raised the question whether Westminster had become constitutionally bound to ask for the consent of the Scottish Parliament when they intend to encroach on or amend the competences of the regional legislatures. The 11 judges of the UK Supreme Court unanimously decided in *Miller* that the statutory footing of the convention does not transform it into judicially enforceable 'law'. It merely entrenches it as a political convention.[108] As such, judges 'cannot give rulings on its operation or scope, because those matters are determined within the political world'.[109]

A recent decision of the Supreme Court further underlines this somewhat paradoxical relationship. In the *Scottish Continuity Bill* case, the Court describes the Scottish Parliament as 'a legislature of unlimited legislative competence subject to the limitation in sections 28 and 29 of the Scotland Act'.[110] Such pronouncement encapsulates the recognition of the breadth of the powers of the devolved legislatures within a system dominated by the principle of parliamentary sovereignty.[111]

18.5.2 *The impact of the international and European legal space on subnational constitutionalism in the UK*

On 31 January 2020, the United Kingdom officially withdrew from the EU. Brexit marked the first time that a Member State had decided to bring to an abrupt end the federalist 'Sonderweg' of 'an ever closer union'. The withdrawal of the UK from the EU constitutional order of states was always expected to pose a number of questions and challenges, including issues related to devolution.

Before the Brexit referendum took place, the Scottish First Minister argued for an amendment to the relevant law that would require that 'for the UK to leave the EU, each of the four constituent nations—England, Scotland, Wales and Northern Ireland—would have to vote to do

---

106 Memorandum of Understanding and Supplementary Agreements Between the United Kingdom Government, the Scottish Ministers, the Welsh Ministers, and the Northern Ireland Executive Committee, (October 2020), para. 14 <https://assets.publishing.service.gov.uk/government/uploads/system/uploads/attachment_data/file/316157/MoU_between_the_UK_and_the_Devolved_Administrations.pdf> accessed 1 August 2020.

107 Scotland Act 1998, s. 28(8); Government of Wales Act 2006 s. 107(6).

108 *R (on the application of Miller and another) v Secretary of State for Exiting the European Union* [2017] UKSC 5, para. 149.

109 Ibid., at para. 146.

110 *The UK Withdrawal from the European Union (Legal Continuity) (Scotland) Bill—a reference by the Attorney General and the Advocate General for Scotland* [2018] UKSC 64 at para. 25.

111 On the *Scottish Continuity Bill* case see Chris McCorkindale and Aileen McHarg, 'Continuity and Confusion: Towards Clarity?—The Supreme Court and the Scottish Continuity Bill', *UK Constitutional Law Association Blog*, 20 December 2018 <https://ukconstitutionallaw.org/2018/12/20/chris-mccorkindale-and-aileen-mcharg-continuity-and-confusion-towards-clarity-the-supreme-court-and-the-scottish-continuity-bill/> accessed 1 August 2020; Mark Elliott, 'The Supreme Court's judgment in the *Scottish Continuity Bill* case' *Public Law for Everyone Blog*, 14 December 2018 <https://publiclawforeveryone.com/2018/12/14/the-supreme-courts-judgment-in-the-scottish-continuity-bill-case> accessed 1 August 2020.

so, not just the UK as a whole'.[112] By making this argument, Scottish First Minister Nicola Sturgeon was trying to avoid a situation where Scotland or another constituent nation would be taken out of EU without its expressed will.

On 23 June 2016, 52 per cent of voters that participated in the Brexit referendum voted to leave the EU, while Scotland and Northern Ireland voted to remain.[113] As a result, the following morning Nicola Sturgeon made clear that she intended to 'take all possible steps and explore all options to give effect to how people in Scotland voted—in other words, to secure [their] continuing place in the EU and in the single market in particular'.[114] The reason for this was that 'Scotland faces the prospect of being taken out of the EU against [its] will'.[115] At the same time, Sinn Féin called for a referendum for the unification of Ireland and thus for Northern Ireland to remain in the EU.[116] Unsurprisingly, the UK Government was not amenable to the idea separate referendums being held in the constituent nations of the UK.

In the aftermath of the Brexit referendum, the regional institutions sought to engage with the UK Government on the terms of the UK's departure from the EU. There were two main forums through which they tried to achieve this aim: the Joint Ministerial Committee on EU Negotiations (JMC hereafter), and the Ministerial Forum. The JMC on EU Negotiations was established to provide a means for the devolved administrations to be fully engaged in determining the UK's approach to Brexit. The Ministerial Forum was created to complement engagement at the JMC, specifically in relation to UK positions for the EU–UK Future Relationship. Despite the fact that there were around 30 meetings of those two bodies, the regional governments often expressed concerns over the effectiveness of those institutions and especially about whether they were suited to developing a joint position.[117]

The devolved governments had very different views about Brexit to those of the central government. For instance, the Scottish Government argued in favour of a differentiated Brexit that would have entailed Scotland remaining in a much closer relationship with the EU via an EEA membership.[118] Unsurprisingly, the UK Government rejected this proposal. However, it agreed with the proposal that there would be a differentiated Brexit with regard to Northern Ireland. In order to keep the Irish territorial border between the Republic of Ireland and Northern Ireland frictionless, the relevant Protocol attached to the UK's Withdrawal Agreement provides for a rather imaginative solution. The Protocol recognizes that *de jure* Northern Ireland remains within the UK customs union,[119] but EU customs legislation applies to the region even

112 Tom Freeman, 'Sturgeon: Give UK nations veto in EU exit referendum' *Holyrood*, 29 October 2014 <https://www.holyrood.com/news/view,sturgeon-give-uk-nations-veto-in-eu-exit-referendum_13903. htm> accessed 1 August 2020.

113 In Scotland, 62 per cent voted to remain in the EU, while 56 per cent in Northern Ireland. In England, 53 per cent voted to leave while 52.5 per cent voted to leave in Wales.

114 Sturgeon's speech after the referendum result <stv.tv/news/politics/1358534-nicola-sturgeon-speech-in-full-after-eu-referendum-result/> accessed 1 February 2019.

115 Ibid.

116 <www.businesspost.ie/sinn-fein-seeks-irish-reunification-vote-as-britain-votes-for-brexit/> accessed 1 February 2019.

117 Richard G. Whitman 'Devolved External Affairs: The Impact of Brexit' *Chatham House Research Paper* <https://www.debrige.de/wp-content/uploads/brexit/Richard-Whitman-Devolved-External-Affairs-paper.pdf> accessed 1 August 2020.

118 See Scottish Government, *Scotland's Place in Europe* <http://www.gov.scot/Publications/2016/12/9234> accessed 1 August 2020. For a discussion of the idea of differentiated Brexit see Nikos Skoutaris 'Territorial Differentiation in EU law: Can Scotland and Northern Ireland Remain in the EU and/or the Single Market?' (2017) 19 *Cambridge Yearbook of European Legal Studies* 287.

119 Protocol on Ireland/Northern Ireland (n 89), Art. 4.

after the end of the transition period on 31 January 2020.[120] Similarly, a significant part of the EU *acquis* on the free movement of goods enjoys extraterritorial application[121] with regard to Northern Ireland,[122] as is the case for EU law provisions concerning VAT and excise.[123] This means that Northern Ireland has a much closer relationship with the EU than the rest of the UK, adding an extra dimension to the special status of this devolved entity within the UK constitutional order. It also means that trade between the two sides of the Irish Sea is not frictionless any more. The extent of the friction in the intra-UK trade depends on the future UK–EU relationship. The more distant it is, the less frictionless the trade is between Northern Ireland and its metropolitan state.

A final issue with regard to Brexit and devolution is the repatriation of powers. At the end of the transition period, a number of competences that were exercised at the EU level returned to the UK. The obvious question is: at which level? Which tier 'took back control' of those repatriated powers?

According to the devolution acts, the devolved institutions cannot legislate in breach of EU law.[124] However, by and large EU law is not binding on the UK after the end of the transition period. This had the potential to create significant legal vacuums in a number of areas such as environmental law, consumer protection and workers' rights, where EU law has been the dominant regulatory authority. In order to avoid such an outcome, it was of utmost importance that the UK Government and Parliament found a way to bridge those gaps without clogging up the parliamentary timetable for years to come. This is why the European Union (Withdrawal) Act 2018 preserves and carries over into UK law the full body of EU law even after Brexit takes place as provided in Sections 2, 3 and 4.

UK statutes enacted after Brexit can amend this body of 'retained EU law' and, in principle, the devolved institutions have a similar power over areas of their own competences. The regional institutions are able to exercise this power, unless a minister of the British Government freezes the devolved powers in the areas that EU law used to regulate.[125] Such power of the UK executive to issue statutory instruments curtailing the legislative autonomy of the regional legislatures will expire two years after the end of the transition period.[126] Statutory instruments freezing the powers of the devolved parliaments can last up to five years.[127] Unsurprisingly, the Scottish Parliament refused to consent to this provision, arguing that its consent was required by the Sewel Convention. Nevertheless, Westminster passed the law. This led the Scottish Government to declare that '[t]he UK Government has effectively suspended the established legislative consent process in relation to legislation concerning EU withdrawal'.[128]

More importantly, the Scottish Parliament enacted a bill providing 'for continuity of EU law in Scotland after Brexit'.[129] In April 2018, the Supreme Court was asked to rule on the legality of this bill that was passed from Holyrood before the European Union (Withdrawal) Act 2018

---

120 Ibid., Art. 5(3).
121 Ibid., Art. 5(5).
122 Ibid., Art. 5(4).
123 Ibid., Art. 8.
124 Scotland Act 1998, s. 29; Northern Ireland Act 1998, s. 6; Government of Wales Act 2006, s. 108A.
125 The EU (Withdrawal) Act 2018, s. 12.
126 Ibid.
127 Ibid.
128 Scottish Government, 'Legislative Consent Memorandum: Agriculture Bill', Scottish Parliamentary Corporate Body, 29 October 2018 <www.parliament.scot/S5ChamberOffice/SPLCM-S05-19.pdf> accessed 1 August 2020.
129 Paun and Shuttleworth, (n 27).

was passed by Westminster.[130] In fact, its enactment was delayed as it was referred to the Supreme Court under section 33(1) of the Scotland Act 1998. The latter provides that the Advocate General, the Lord Advocate or the Attorney General 'may refer the question of whether a Bill or any provision of a Bill would be within the legislative competence of the Parliament to the Supreme Court for decision'. The court ruled that the Scottish bill had been almost entirely within devolved competence at the time it had been passed. However, the subsequent passage of the Withdrawal Act rendered it *ultra vires*. In light of that judgment, the Scottish parliament decided not to proceed with the bill. So, this piece of devolved legislation did not become law because of the subsequent passing of an Act of the UK Parliament that never received the consent of Holyrood. Instead, the Scottish Government introduced a second Continuity Bill that provides for 'keeping the pace power'. Accordingly, Section 1 of the bill allows Scottish Ministers to make regulations to align Scottish law with EU law.

The aforementioned episode was not the last one that revealed the effect of Brexit on UK intergovernmental relationships. Eighteen months later, the UK Government asked Parliament to pass the European Union (Withdrawal Agreement) Bill (2019–20) with which they wished to implement the Withdrawal Agreement into domestic law. The UK Government did not dispute that the bill fell within the scope of the Sewel Convention. However, for the first time in UK constitutional politics, all three devolved legislatures refused to provide their consent to the bill. Nevertheless, the UK Government passed the bill. A cabinet minister explained the Government's position as follows:

> We recognise that taking the Bill to Royal Assent without the consent of the devolved legislatures is a significant decision and it is one that we have not taken lightly. However, it is in line with the Sewel convention. [...] The Sewel convention—to which the Government remain committed—states that the UK Parliament 'will not normally legislate with regard to devolved matters without the consent' of the relevant devolved legislatures. The circumstances of our departure from the EU, following the 2016 referendum, are not normal; they are unique.[131]

Be that as it may, the aforementioned arrangements that curtail the legislative autonomy of the devolved institutions over 'retained EU law' have an expiry date. Once this passes, the devolved governments will no longer be obliged to conform to (retained) EU law or to statutory instruments freezing their power to amend. This will make it possible for greater policy divergence to develop, potentially disrupting the UK's internal trade. To guard against that possibility the UK Government proposed a Market Access commitment in Internal Market Bill.[132] According to this, Westminster recently introduced in primary legislation both a principle of mutual recognition and a principle of non-discrimination to guarantee the continued right of all UK companies to trade unhindered in every part of the UK.[133]

---

130 *Scottish Continuity Bill* case (n 114).
131 Michael Gove, HC Deb, 23 January 2020, col 17WS.
132 https://services.parliament.uk/Bills/2019-21/unitedkingdominternalmarket/documents.html> accessed 1 August 2020.
133 Ibid., at p. 11.

18.6 Judicial review

According to Dicey, there is 'no person or body recognised by the law of England as having a right to override or set aside the legislation of Parliament'.[134] This means that there is no other body or institution including the judiciary that has the authority and/or the power to challenge and review the validity of laws that have received the royal assent after following the relevant legislative procedure, including the devolution acts. Article 9 of the Bill of Rights of 1689 provides that 'proceedings in Parliament ought not to be impeached or questioned in any court or place out of Parliament'. The UK judiciary has not challenged 'the simple rule that the duty of the court is to obey and apply every Act of Parliament, and that the court cannot hold any such Act to be ultra vires'.[135] This is of crucial importance given that '[t]he rule of judicial obedience [to Parliament] … is the ultimate political fact upon which the whole system of legislation hangs'.[136]

Such immunity from judicial review is only afforded to Acts of the Westminster Parliament. Acts passed by the devolved institutions can be judicially reviewed. In fact, the job of policing the boundaries of the devolution legislation is entrusted to the UK judiciary. They have to ensure that devolved institutions do not legislate on areas where they do not enjoy competence.[137] The Supreme Court has gone a step further, holding that the devolution acts do not provide an exhaustive list of the grounds of review. The regional legislatures are also prevented from violating common law principles of constitutional significance such as the rule of law.[138]

Having said that, when UK courts review the legality of an act of a regional legislature, they are under a duty to read the relevant legislation 'as narrowly as is required for it to be within competence if such reading is possible'.[139] Indeed, the UK judiciary have exhibited remarkable self-restraint to avoid encroaching on the subnational constituent autonomy. The judges have accepted that the provisions of the devolution acts 'should, consistently with the language used, be interpreted generously and purposively, bearing in mind the values which the constitutional provisions are intended to embody'.[140] In order to do that, the courts often engage in granular analysis, so as to determine whether any particular provision of an act of the regional parliament is *ultra vires*.[141]

Generally speaking, the very limited number of cases during the last 20 years of the devolution and the rather cautious approach of the UK courts underline the political nature of the UK territorial constitution and the reluctance of the judiciary to become an active umpire in the disputes between the different tiers.

18.7 Conclusion

'[F]ederalism provisions of constitutions are often peculiarly the product of political compromise in historically situated moments, generally designed as a practical rather than a principled accommodation of competing interests.'[142] This is even more so in the case of states like the UK,

---

134 Dicey (n 16), at 40.
135 *Manuel v Attorney General* [1982] 3 All ER 822.
136 William Wade 'The Basis of Legal Sovereignty' (1955) *Cambridge Law Journal* 172.
137 Scotland Act 1998, s. 29; Northern Ireland Act 1998, s. 6; Government of Wales Act 2006, s. 108A.
138 *AXA General Insurance Limited and Others* [2011] UKSC 46, para. 153.
139 Scotland Act 1998, s. 101. See also Northern Ireland Act 1998, s. 83; Government of Wales Act 2006, s. 154.
140 *Robinson v Secretary of State for Northern Ireland* [2002] UKHL 32, para. 11.
141 For an example of such analysis, see the *Scottish Continuity Bill* case (n 114).
142 Vicki C. Jackson, 'Narratives of Federalism: Of Continuities and Comparative Constitutional Experience' (2001) 51 *Duke Law Journal* 223, 273–4.

which have not adopted a fully federal model but have opted for a system of asymmetrical devolution. The pragmatic constitutional solutions that characterize the UK system represent an attempt to reconcile calls for regional autonomy with a desire to retain the borders of the State and the effectiveness of the central government. In order to find the balance between those aims, the UK constitutional order has used the instrument of (sub-)constitutional documents to allow for some 'site-specific' decentralization/devolution. Each and every one of the UK devolution acts is a by-product of the very different set of political and historical conditions that led to its adoption. At the same time, those statutes can be also read as an attempt to accommodate the different aspirations of their regions.

Given the idiosyncratic character of the uncodified UK constitution, there is no constitutional text that the devolution acts have to comply with as such. If one follows a traditional Diceyan view of parliamentary sovereignty, then one might say that—in theory at least—Westminster can intervene in all areas and even abolish the devolved institutions. However, the democratic legitimacy with which the devolution arrangements have been endowed makes their abolition politically unthinkable while the international and municipal law commitments that the UK Government has undertaken makes their preservation necessary. In that sense, they can be seen as 'significant cracks in what has traditionally been a monolithic acceptance [...] of Westminster's untrammeled legislative power'.[143] One may wonder whether their mere existence sits somehow uncomfortably with the traditional Diceyan view expressed by the Supreme Court according to which '[s]overeignty remains with the United Kingdom Parliament'.[144]

---

143 Stephen Tierney, 'Quiet Devolution: Sub-State Autonomy and the Gradual Reconstitution of the United Kingdom' in George A. Tarr and Michael Burgess (eds) *Constitutional Dynamics in Federal Systems: Sub-National Perspectives* (McGill-Queen's University Press 2012) 195, at 205.

144 *AXA General Insurance Limited and Others* [2011] UKSC 46, para. 46.

19

SUBNATIONAL CONSTITUTIONALISM IN THE UNITED STATES

Powerful states in a powerful federation

James A. Gardner

The United States has an extremely robust network of subnational constitutions. It is one of the few federations in the world in which subnational entities are understood to be fully competent polities with virtually complete constituent powers of self-organization and self-authorization. The authority to adopt a subnational constitution is consequently understood to be an incident of subnational sovereignty, a concept in turn derived from a conception of the basic federal order itself as highly decentralized.

Within this order, subnational powers of self-governance are understood to be plenary except as limited either permanently by the federal constitution, or temporarily by the exercise of national power that supersedes state law under the US Constitution's Supremacy Clause. Thus, the dominant constitutional issue within the US federal system has never concerned the scope of power or authorization of the states, but rather the scope and authorization of the national government, and its consequent authority to occupy policy domains and to enact laws that constrain the authority of states to pursue their own preferred forms and paths of self-governance. On that issue, there is a longstanding, bitter dispute, going all the way back to the founding, of such profundity that, even today, to make any assertion about the nature of the US federation is necessarily to enter into a deeply political debate.

19.1 Context: Nature of the federation

Foreign observers routinely characterize the United States as a classic example of a coming-together federation.[1] Its constituent units were independent before the nation was founded, and each unit governed itself fully under its own constitution. Within US legal and political discourse, however, the nature of the founding was ambiguous from the start. On one hand, the American colonies were founded at different times, for different purposes, in different circumstances—to secure religious liberty, for example, or for purposes of commercial exploitation.

---

1 Thomas O. Hueglin and Alan Fenna, *Comparative Federalism: A Systematic Inquiry* (University of Toronto Press 2015) 100; Francesco Palermo and Karl Kössler, *Comparative Federalism: Constitutional Arrangements and Case Law* (Hart Publishing 2017) 42–3.

DOI: 10.4324/9781003052111-19

These differences were reflected in the colonies' initial governing instruments, royal charters granted by the British Crown. Moreover, the colonies over time developed different forms of economic organization, which in turn interacted with demographic patterns such that the North became more urban, industrial, egalitarian and wealthier, and the South more rural, agrarian and poorer, with greater inequality.

On the other hand, with the significant exception of an enslaved African population in the South—which, of course, was unable to express itself politically—the populations of the colonies were neither ethnically nor linguistically diverse, the great majority being of British descent. All 13 colonies had a common colonial master throughout their existence, and all thus received the same legal, social and linguistic inheritances. The Revolution itself (1776–83) was conducted collaboratively and simultaneously, with no colony attempting to remain allied with the mother country. The colonies governed themselves collectively before they achieved independence, first through the pre-revolutionary Continental Congress, and after 1781 under the Articles of Confederation, a confederal constitution that endured until ratification of the US Constitution in 1789.

Thus, the founding period provides some evidence to support three different conceptions of the United States federation. One is that it was formed through voluntary agreement by 13 distinct political societies. A second is that the founding states were throughout their history fundamentally a single populace that had been governed for administrative reasons in a decentralized fashion, and which acquired self-sovereignty collectively following independence. A third view is that the original relationship of the thirteen colonies is irrelevant because it was completely superseded by the adoption of the United States Constitution. This view, which draws heavily on the contractarian premises of the brand of constitutionalism to which the American founders adhered, conceives the adoption of a constitution as a kind of singularity in which a new order not only replaces but destroys all traces of the previous one.[2]

None of this would be a matter of great importance but for the original curse of the nation's founding—slavery—which made the nature of the federation politically salient from the start. Southerners, perpetually fearful that disapproving northerners would use control of the national government to undermine slavery, almost immediately began to develop an account of the US federation according to which the states possessed the plenary sovereignty of independent nations; the United States possessed only so much authority as the states chose to delegate (which, on this account, was minimal); and the constitutional mechanism of federalism existed to protect the states against the slightest national intervention in their internal organization and policy choices.[3]

By the 1850s, during the run-up to the US Civil War (1860–65), southern intellectuals had developed a thicker account of the founding that supplemented this legal account with an ethnographic one. According to this account, southerners and northerners were descended from distinct British sub-populations and were thus ethnically distinct, and lived within societies characterized by fundamentally distinct and deeply incompatible cultures.[4] The better view,

---

2 Jacob T. Levy, 'Not So Novus an Ordo: Constitutions without Social Contracts' (2008) 37 *Political Theory* 191, at 195.

3 John C. Calhoun, *A Discourse on the Constitution and Government of the United States* in John C. Calhoun, *A Disquisition on Government and Selections from the* Discourse (Bobbs-Merrill 1953).

4 William R. Taylor, *Cavalier and Yankee: The Old South and American National Character* (George Braziller 1961) 15; Emory M. Thomas, *The Confederate Nation, 1861–1865* (Harper & Row 1979) 9; David M. Potter, *The Impending Crisis, 1848–1861* (Harper & Row 1976).

however, is that this account was little more than political propaganda intended to strengthen the South's case for secession.[5]

In the North, public opinion was divided. Some accepted the southern account of the nature of American federalism, but others, motivated by anti-slavery sentiment, began to develop a competing account of the union in which the nation was conceived as a single, unified polity; its interests were superior to the necessarily parochial interests of any state; national power was consequently great; and the national government had significant authority to take steps to eradicate the evil of slavery.[6]

These disputes were of course settled militarily and constitutionally by the Civil War. Even so, disagreement about the nature of the federation remained unsettled socially and politically. Following its defeat, the South grudgingly retired its formal, *de jure* system of slavery, but replaced it with an almost equally brutal, informal regime of 'Jim Crow' racial segregation and white political domination.[7] At the same time, southern propaganda about southern distinctiveness and the highly decentralized nature of the federation actually grew more intense,[8] and for a full century following the end of the Civil War the southern states maintained successfully, both in Congress and in the courts, that federalism insulated them from national power to impair the illiberal Jim Crow regime.[9]

To this day, an essentially multinational account of US federalism, influenced by this long record of southern propaganda, can still be found, not only in the academic literature,[10] but even occasionally in decisions of state courts, an issue treated below in Section 19.6. The long and continuing history of this dispute, however, means that to enter into this debate is necessarily to take a position in contemporary US politics. To claim that the United States is a coming-together federation formed by previously distinct sovereigns that retained their original sovereignty is, to some extent, to ally oneself with southern secessionism and Jim Crow segregationism;[11] while to maintain that the United States is a single, unified polity that has merely decentralized itself for purposes of self-governance and the protection of liberty[12] is inevitably to take the side of unionism, antislavery and the twentieth-century civil rights movement.

5 John Hope Franklin, 'As for Our History' in Charles Grier Sellers (ed.), *The Southerner as American* (University of North Carolina Press 1960); Drew Gilpin Faust, *The Creation of Confederate Nationalism: Ideology and Identity in the Civil War South* (Louisiana State University Press 1988); James A. Gardner, 'Southern Character, Confederate Nationalism, and the Interpretation of State Constitutions: A Case Study in Constitutional Argument' (1998) 76 *Texas Law Review* 1219.

6 Paul C. Nagel, *One Nation Indivisible: The Union in American Thought, 1776–1861* (Greenwood Press 1964).

7 C. Vann Woodward, *The Strange Career of Jim Crow* (Oxford University Press 1955).

8 James A. Gardner, 'Southern Character, Confederate Nationalism, and the Interpretation of State Constitutions: A Case Study in Constitutional Argument' (1998) 76 *Texas Law Review* 1219, at 1232–3.

9 Edward L. Gibson, *Boundary Control: Subnational Authoritarianism in Federal Democracies* (Cambridge University Press 2012) ch. 3; Robert Mickey, *Paths Out of Dixie: The Democratization of Authoritarian Enclaves in America's Deep South, 1944–1972* (Princeton University Press 2015).

10 For example, Frederick Jackson Turner, *The Significance of Sections in American History* (Henry Holt and Co. 1932); David Hackett Fischer, *Albion's Seed: Four British Folkways in America* (Oxford University Press 1989); Daniel J. Elazar, 'The Principles and Traditions Underlying State Constitutions' (1982) 12 *Publius* 11; Ernest A. Young, 'The Volk of New Jersey? State Identity, Distinctiveness, and Political Culture in the American Federal System' (2015) Duke Law School Public Law & Legal Theory Series No. 2015–11. For a critique, see James A. Gardner, *Interpreting State Constitutions: A Jurisprudence of Function in a Federal System* (University of Chicago Press 2005) ch. 2.

11 William H. Riker, *Federalism: Origin, Operation, Significance* (Little, Brown 1964) 153–5.

12 James A. Madison, 'The Federalist, Nos. 46–51' in Clinton Rossiter (ed.), *The Federalist Papers* (Mentor 1961) (orig. ed. 1787–88).

None of this, however, diminishes the basic agreement in the United States that the states possess a great degree of power; that American states are fully competent polities for purposes of subnational self-government; and that state self-governance through subnational constitutions is normal and desirable. The dominant debate within American federalism—and consequently within American subnational constitutionalism—has, to the contrary, concerned the scope of *national* power, with the nature of the federation vigorously contested because of the difference it makes in the degree to which the federal constitution, or laws enacted by the national government, are capable of constraining the otherwise plenary scope of subnational authority. Notwithstanding this dispute, national power has greatly increased since the founding (*infra* Section 19.2.2), and the United States has become much more centralized than contemplated by the original constitutional plan.

19.2 Autonomy

19.2.1 *Symmetry of subnational autonomy*

Among US subnational entities, all 50 US states enjoy perfect symmetry in their powers and autonomy. Of course, there is significant asymmetry among the states in their resources and endowments—California, for example, has nearly 70 times the population of Wyoming, and its economic output is nearly 90 times that of Vermont. These informal asymmetries influence the functional power and importance of the states in many institutional settings, including the US House of Representatives, where state polities are represented in proportion to their populations. In the Senate, however, where each state has equal representation (Art. I, § 3), resource and population asymmetries have no significant impact.

Although all states enjoy symmetrical formal status and power, other subnational entities in the United States do not. The District of Columbia, the capital city (population 633,000), is unrepresented in Congress, though its residents may vote for president and vice-president.[13] The US also maintains several 'territories' or 'possessions' that it acquired during periods of colonial expansion, which enjoy far less autonomy than the states. These include Puerto Rico, the US Virgin Islands, Guam and American Samoa. These territories are not represented in Congress, and their populations are ineligible to vote for any federal office.

19.2.2 *Scope of state autonomy*

As indicated above, the scope of state autonomy in the United States is presumed to be plenary except as limited by the US Constitution. These limitations are, on their face, minimal. The residual clause of the US Constitution provides: 'The powers not delegated to the United States by the Constitution, nor prohibited by it to the States, are reserved to the States respectively, or to the people'.[14] By operation of this provision, as well as by inference from the structure of the US Constitution,[15] the states are presumed to possess all powers of which they are not by the Constitution affirmatively dispossessed. Article I, § 10 of the US Constitution provides a short list of powers that the states are specifically denied. These include the powers to make treaties, coin money, enact ex post facto laws, grant titles of nobility or, without congressional consent, levy import or export taxes, or maintain a peacetime army or navy. A potentially more

---

13 US Const., amend. XXIII (1961).
14 US Const., amend. X (1791).
15 McCulloch v. Maryland, 17 US 316 (1819).

significant express limit on state power is the Guarantee Clause, which requires states to maintain a 'republican' form of government (Art. IV, § 4), meaning a representative democracy. However, the US Supreme Court has held this provision to be judicially unenforceable, meaning its enforcement is left to Congress, which has thus far never invoked it to intervene in state political affairs.[16]

Over time, however, the US Supreme Court has recognized other, more significant limitations on subnational power that it has found to be implicit in the federal constitutional scheme. The most significant is a doctrine of implied limitation on the scope of state economic regulation known as the 'dormant Commerce Clause'. Under this doctrine, states are forbidden to regulate their own economies in ways that (1) 'discriminate' against commerce originating in or flowing to other states, i.e., amount to economic protectionism; or (2) impose an excessive 'burden' on interstate commerce.[17] This doctrine is designed to preserve and encourage the growth of a national economic market.[18] Another implicit limitation on state power is a prohibition on adopting and conducting foreign policy.[19] Yet another is the requirement that subnational power be deployed consistent with human rights guaranteed at the national level.

In practical terms, however, the most significant limitations on state power are not standing constitutional limits on the scope of state autonomy, but contingent limitations imposed by the enactment of national laws and policies. The Supremacy Clause of the US Constitution provides: 'The Constitution, and the Laws of the United States which shall be made in Pursuance thereof; and all Treaties made … under the Authority of the United States, shall be the supreme Law of the Land'.[20] The US Supreme Court has given this provision a rather broad interpretation so that state law is 'preempted', or invalidated, not only when it directly conflicts with federal law, but also when it impedes or frustrates the achievement of federal objectives, or when the federal regulatory scheme is so 'pervasive' as to 'fully occupy' a regulatory domain, thereby leaving no room at all for state regulation, even when the state law in question might be consistent with the federal scheme.[21]

The significance of the Supremacy Clause for state autonomy lies in the enormous growth of the national regulatory state since the 1930s. Nearly all the most extensive US programmes of social welfare, environmental protection, consumer protection, transportation policy, labour relations and old-age and pension policy have been enacted at the national level, greatly narrowing the ability of states to regulate in domains of significant economic and social interest that would otherwise be available to them. Moreover, the federal government has often deployed its power to spend money in a way that imposes practical limitations on state autonomy by conditioning the receipt of federal funds on compliance with federal programmatic and regulatory requirements.[22] Thus, the main battle lines between national and subnational power in the United States are typically defined by state efforts to preserve their autonomy by attempting

---

16 Luther v. Borden, 48 US 1 (1849). The inactivity of the US Congress under this clause thus contrasts greatly with that of the Argentine central government, which has invoked a nearly identical clause on roughly 170 occasions to intervene in provincial affairs. Mario D. Serrafero, 'La intervención federal en Argentina: Experiencia y jurisprudencia' (n.d.) <http://www.forumfed.org/libdocs/Misc/Arg8_Serrafero%20paper%20 Esp.pdf>.
17 South Carolina State Highway Dept. v. Barnwell Bros., Inc., 303 US 177 (1938); Philadelphia v. New Jersey, 437 US 617 (1978).
18 H.P. Hood & Sons, Inc. v. DuMond, 336 US 525 (1949).
19 Zschernig v. Miller, 389 US 429 (1968); Crosby v. National Foreign Trade Council, 530 US 363 (2000).
20 US Const. art. VI, cl. 2.
21 Gade v. National Solid Wastes Management Ass'n, 505 US 88 (1992).
22 South Dakota v. Dole, 483 US 203 (1987); National Federation of Independent Business v. Sibelius, 567 US 519 (2012).

through political means to confine the reach of national legislation, or by negotiating state opt-out provisions, efforts that have generally achieved only occasional success.[23]

19.2.3 Procedures

19.2.3.1 Federal oversight

The US Constitution makes no mention at all of subnational constitutions; the power of states to adopt such constitutions was not only well established by 1789, but was viewed as inherent in the sovereignty possessed by the original states. As a result, the procedures for adoption and amendment of state constitutions are regulated entirely by the states themselves in their own constitutions.

19.2.3.2 Procedural variations

All states distinguish between adoption and amendment of state constitutions. New constitutions typically must be adopted by convention—that is, by exercise of the people's constituent power through the election of representatives to a constitutional convention specifically authorized to draft and to submit for popular approval a new constitution. At one time, such conventions were relatively common.[24] Of the 233 constitutional conventions held by American states, 143 were held during the nineteenth century. However, no state has held a full-scale convention since 1986,[25] meaning that amendment has become the preferred, and essentially the exclusive, procedure for making formal changes to state constitutions.

 Procedures for amending state constitutions differ somewhat from state to state. Delaware is unique in permitting amendment of the state constitution by a two-thirds vote of the state legislature without any requirement of popular ratification.[26] All other states utilize one or both of two procedures.

 The first is legislative enactment of a proposed amendment which is then submitted to the voters for approval. Legislative approval requirements range from a simple majority of both houses (ten states), to a two-thirds majority of both houses (16 states). Fifteen states additionally require legislative approval in two consecutive legislative sessions before referral to the voters.[27]

 The second procedure for constitutional amendment is direct popular proposal and approval of an amendment by initiative, a procedure available in 18 states, mainly in the west. Initiative amendment typically requires the collection of signatures, in some cases from registered voters and in others from citizens, on a petition demanding a vote on the proposed amendment. Signature thresholds vary between 3 and 15 per cent of the number of votes cast in the most recent election for statewide or national offices. Most initiative states require approval only of a simple majority of voters; a few require a supermajority.[28]

 A frequently self-imposed procedural limitation on initiative amendments is the 'single subject rule', which requires initiative measures to confine themselves to one subject matter at a

23 Gardner (n 10), at 94–8.
24 John J. Dinan, *The American State Constitutional Tradition* (University Press of Kansas 2006) 8–9.
25 John Dinan, *State Constitutional Politics: Governing by Amendment in the American States* (University of Chicago Press 2018) 30–1.
26 Del. Const. art. XVI, § 2.
27 Dinan (n 25), at 14.
28 Dinan (n 25), at 16–19.

time.[29] The restriction appears rooted in an idealized conception of the legislative process that disapproves of logrolling and vote-trading as undesirable deviations from ideal lawmaking behaviour, which requires individualized consideration of every proposal on its merits.

19.3 Position of state constitutions within the states

The position of subnational constitutions within the state legal systems is equivalent to the role of national constitutions within national legal systems. First, they are entrenched, in the sense that they cannot be altered or repealed through ordinary legislative processes. Second, they provide the fundamental law of the subnational units that adopt them: all ordinary state legislation and state governmental actions must comport with the state constitution. Moreover, US subnational constitutions are both unified and comprehensive—everything that is of 'constitutional' rank within the state legal system is to be found within the four corners of the state constitution and its amendments; the US legal system does not at any level recognize the existence of 'constitutional laws' of the type found in Austria or Italy, for example.

As described below in Section 19.4, the main functions of American state constitutions are to organize subnational power and to entrench certain policy commitments. However, state constitutions also may be, and from time to time are, used as vehicles for the expression of subnational resistance to national power and policies.[30] For example, California added the so-called Victims' Bill of Rights to its constitution in 1982. This provision eliminated from the California Constitution the so-called 'exclusionary rule', which excludes from consideration by courts in criminal cases evidence of guilt that was acquired by the police in contravention of constitutional limits on government authority to search for and to seize inculpatory evidence. In so doing, the people of California expressed strong disapproval of the scope of the federal exclusionary rule, which at the time had been given a broad construction by the US Supreme Court, causing the prevention or invalidation of many convictions in which evidence of the defendant's guilt was clear, but had been acquired by unconstitutional means.[31] In many instances, discussed further in Section 19.6, state supreme courts have construed state constitutions to provide more robust protection for human rights than the US Constitution, and have often done so in ways that express criticism of the US Supreme Court's construction of the federal document.

More commonly, however, US state constitutions tend to lack symbolic value to the state populace, and even to lack political salience within their states. In fact, state constitutions tend to be poorly known or understood by state polities.[32] In contrast, Americans tend to know much more about the US Constitution, and are much more likely to orient themselves toward national constitutional principles than toward state ones.[33]

In general, American political parties do not, even at the state level, adopt commitments to the reform of state constitutions. To the extent parties concern themselves with constitutional reform, they tend to focus on the federal constitution. There are no regional political parties in the United States that mobilize around ethnic, religious or linguistic distinctions with implications for the content of subnational constitutions. Thus, in the United States, there are no parties

29 Robert F. Williams, *The Law of American State Constitutions* (Oxford University Press 2009) 405–8.

30 James A. Gardner, 'State Constitutional Rights as Resistance to National Power: Toward a Functional Theory of State Constitutions' (2003) 91 *Georgetown Law Journal* 1003.

31 Gardner (n 10), at 166–7.

32 G. Alan Tarr, *Understanding State Constitutions* (Princeton University Press 1998) 1–2.

33 David N. Schleicher, 'Federalism and State Democracy' (2017) 95 *Texas Law Review* 763; James A. Gardner, 'The Myth of State Autonomy: Federalism, Political Parties, and the National Colonization of State Politics' (2013) 29 *Journal of Law & Politics* 1.

equivalent to, say, Scottish or Catalan nationalist parties that advocate either secession or amendment of national or subnational constitutions in ways that would change the role of the subnational unit within the national polity.

19.4 Content of US subnational constitutions

19.4.1 Identity

The practice of using subnational constitutions as vehicles for the assertion of a distinctive subnational identity is essentially non-existent in the United States. Although virtually all US state constitutions begin with a preamble declaring them to have been made by 'the people' of the state, such references are understood in context to refer merely to the state population as a civic sub-community of the nation rather than as a socially or culturally distinctive group with an enhanced or historically grounded claim to self-determination. Moreover, states have no authority to define or condition subnational citizenship: the Fourteenth Amendment of the US Constitution provides: 'All persons born or naturalized in the United States … are citizens of the United States and of the state wherein they reside'. Under this provision, any person with US citizenship automatically becomes a citizen of any state in which he or she chooses to settle, and state citizenship changes with every subsequent interstate change of residence.

Furthermore, state constitutions almost never include any description of the state polity in ethnic, religious or linguistic terms. The one exception is provisions in some states declaring English to be the official language of the state.[34] Such provisions generally express a fear that some kind of implicit state ethnic or linguistic identity is endangered by settlement within the state of native Spanish speakers. Official language provisions generally have only symbolic value, and when they do go further and attempt to direct official behaviour, they risk invalidation under federal constitutional principles of freedom of speech and equal protection.[35]

The rarity with which US subnational constitutions make claims about subnational identity has several causes. First, identity in the US has been understood historically more in civic than ethnic terms; to be an American has generally meant to subscribe to a certain set of liberal principles and ideals rather than to belong to any particular ethnic, religious or linguistic group.[36] Second, subnational identities in the United States are in fact not distinctive.[37] Although the US population is extremely diverse racially, ethnically, religiously and linguistically, that diversity does not align with state boundaries. Indeed, the boundaries of US states have been aptly described as 'highly arbitrary and … represent nothing but cartographers' and Congressmen's convenience'.[38] Third, as discussed above, state constitutions—perhaps for the reasons just described—have low political salience and so are unlikely to recommend themselves to state polities as vehicles for the expression of a distinctive identity, even if such identities existed.

---

34 For example, Alabama Constitution, amend. 509 (1990); Arizona Constitution, art. 28 1–6 (2006); Colorado Constitution art. I, § 30a (1989); Florida Constitution art. II, § 9 (1988).
35 Ruiz v. Hull, 957 P.2d 984 (Ariz. 1998).
36 Gardner (n 8), at 1285–6.
37 Gardner (n 8), *passim*.
38 Russell Kirk, 'The Prospects for Territorial Democracy in America' in Robert A. Goldwin (ed.), *A Nation of States: Essays on the American Federal System* (Rand McNally 1963) 42.

19.4.2 *Organization of powers*

US states have virtually plenary powers of self-organization, subject only to the minimal federal constitutional restrictions that the form of government be 'republican' and not monarchical or aristocratic.[39] Within this framework, every state constitution divides the state government into three branches, legislative, executive and judicial. Forty-nine of the 50 states have additionally chosen to follow the federal model of a bicameral legislature (Nebraska, with a unicameral legislature, is the one exception). However, in many states the legislature is conceived as essentially a part-time and largely amateur assembly that draws citizens to the capital temporarily for business and then returns them as quickly as possible to their customary place in civil society. This is accomplished by constitutional provisions that limit the frequency and duration of legislative sessions, impose short terms of office (typically no more than two years) and establish restrictive limits on the number of terms a legislator can serve (often no more than four or six years). For example, the Montana Constitution provides: 'The legislature shall meet each odd-numbered year in regular session of not more than 90 legislative days'.[40]

The intention of these provisions is benign and democratic: they seek to align the interests of legislators and citizens by ensuring that legislators are drawn from the general citizenry rather than a distinct political class, and that they remain in close touch with their constituents. However, the actual effect of these provisions appears to be to reduce the power of the legislature, thereby transferring power to the governor and the executive branch bureaucracy, which are permanent, full-time, professional and well funded.[41]

On the executive side, all states have adopted a presidential rather than parliamentary structure of governance, with an independently elected governor serving as chief executive of the state. However, unlike the US Constitution, which creates a unitary executive branch under the direction of a single chief executive, most state constitutions provide for independent popular election not only of the governor, but also of lower executive branch officials such as the state's attorney general or chief financial officer, and many provide for popular election to numerous other cabinet-level executive offices. In North Carolina and North Dakota, for example, ten executive branch officials are separately elected, including the Commissioners of Education, Agriculture, Labor and Insurance.

In addition, unlike the US Constitution, the constitutions of 38 states provide for popular election of all or nearly all state judges. In some states, judges are elected in ordinary partisan elections in which they campaign on partisan ballot lines, though subject to professional rules of self-restraint that tend to dampen the intensity of campaigning by judicial candidates.[42] Such rules do not apply, however, to parties or advocacy groups, which have increasingly been spending large sums on judicial races.[43] In some states, judicial elections are nonpartisan. In others, judges initially run for election and then stand periodically for 'retention' in uncontested

39 US Const. art. I, § 9, art. IV, § 4.
40 Mont. Const. art. V, § 6.
41 John. M. Carey, et al., 'The Effects of Term Limits on State Legislatures: A New Survey of the 50 States' (2006) 31 *Legislative Quarterly* 105; Thad Kousser, *Term Limits and the Dismantling of Legislative Professionalism* (Cambridge University Press 2005).
42 See, e.g., Williams-Yulee v. Florida Bar, 135 S.Ct. 1656 (2015).
43 Brennan Center for Justice, *Who Pays for Judicial Elections? The Politics of Judicial Elections 2015–16* (New York: New York University 2017) <https://www.brennancenter.org/sites/default/files/publications/Politics_of_Judicial_Elections_Final.pdf>.

elections where the question put to the voters is whether the judge should be retained for another term.[44]

The theory behind judicial elections is that they increase the democratic accountability of judicial officials. Although this is acknowledged to diminish their independence, in states that employ judicial elections the tradeoff of independence for accountability is deemed worthwhile.[45]

19.4.3 Human rights

Every US state constitution contains its own bill of rights. Following the model of the English Civil Rights Act of 1689, the original states generally included a bill of rights in their constitutions immediately following independence, and when the US Constitution was amended in 1791 to add a federal bill of rights, its drafters looked for guidance primarily to existing state constitutions.[46] As a result, the US constitutional system contains two distinct levels of rights protection. Although the interaction of these two levels of protection can be complex, generally speaking, federal rights protections establish a minimum level of respect for human rights, or 'floor', below which states are prohibited to go. However, states are free (1) to establish greater, more expansive protection for federally protected rights above the federal floor; and (2) to offer protection for rights given no protection at the federal level.

19.4.3.1 Duplicative rights

Most of the rights contained in state constitutions duplicate to some degree, or overlap significantly with, rights protected at the federal level. Thus, most state constitutions contain specific protection for rights of speech, religion, due process and equality, and prohibit unreasonable searches and seizures, self-incrimination, double jeopardy, and cruel punishments, all of which are protected independently at the federal level.

Why state constitutions tend so frequently to duplicate federal rights protections presents something of a puzzle. One possibility, of course, is to offer greater protection for such rights than is provided by the federal bill of rights. This does occur from time to time. For example, the New York Constitution provides greater protection for free speech than the federal constitution, and several states provide greater protection against unreasonable searches than the federal constitution.[47] Most often, however, state constitutional rights are construed to provide a level of protection that is exactly or substantially identical to that provided by their federal counterparts, a phenomenon often referred to as 'lockstep' interpretation.[48] The interpretation of state rights protection to match protections provided independently at the federal level suggests that many human rights provisions in state constitutions are included mainly for symbolic reasons, to express the state polity's commitment to various kinds of individual liberty.

---

44 Melinda Gann Hall, 'State Supreme Courts in American Democracy: Probing the Myths of Judicial Reform' (2001) 95 *American Political Science Review* 315; G. Alan Tarr, *Without Fear or Favor: Judicial Independence and Judicial Accountability in the States* (Stanford University Press 2012) ch. 3.

45 Chris W. Bonneau and Melinda Gann Hall, *In Defense of Judicial Elections* (Routledge 2009).

46 Hans A. Linde, 'First Things First: Rediscovering the States' Bills of Rights' (1980) 9 *Baltimore Law Review* 379, at 382.

47 William J. Brennan, 'State Constitutions and the Protection of Individual Rights' (1977) 90 *Harvard Law Review* 489.

48 Williams (n 29), ch. 7.

Another possible explanation for rights duplication is to provide backup protection for state citizens should the federal government fail to offer adequate protection for the rights concerned. However, if that is indeed the aim, the strategy is not likely to be effective as a practical matter. State constitutional rights are capable of constraining the behaviour only of state government officials, not of federal ones. Thus, if federal officials are failing to observe or enforce rights guaranteed by the federal constitution, the existence of state constitutional protections cannot protect the state populace against abuses originating at the federal level.

However, 'dialogic' models of federalism offer a different view. These models conceive of the intergovernmental exchange of ideas as a mechanism by which federal and other decentralized systems collectively work out normatively desirable or best-practice solutions to common problems. On this view, state divergence from federal approaches to the same basic human right can precipitate system-wide rethinking of the underlying issues, and has in at least some notable instances caused changes in the behaviour of federal courts.[49]

19.4.3.2 *Unique state rights*

Many state constitutions also contain individual rights provisions that have no federal counterpart. The most prominent of these is the right to an education, recognized in varying degrees by the constitutions of most states.[50] Another is the right to a remedy, available in 39 states, which, broadly speaking, prohibits the state from depriving individuals of access to judicially crafted remedies for injuries of types that have traditionally been available under the common law. The main impact of this right is to constrain the discretion of the legislature to alter traditional remedies in the field of tort law.[51]

Although virtually all rights contained in American constitutions are negative rights that restrain the state, a few state constitutions also contain positive rights, which require for their effectuation affirmative state action. For example, a provision of the New York Constitution adopted in 1938, during the Great Depression, provides: 'The aid, care and support of the needy are public concerns and shall be provided by the state …'.[52] Similarly, the Montana Constitution provides: 'The legislature shall provide such economic assistance and social and rehabilitative services as may be necessary for those inhabitants who, by reasons of age, infirmities, or misfortune may have need for the aid of society'.[53] Some state constitutions also contain positive rights provisions requiring the state to protect the environment. For example, the Illinois Constitution provides: 'Each person has the right to a healthful environment. Each person may enforce this right against any party, governmental or private, through appropriate legal proceedings …'.[54] For the most part, however, state courts have not construed positive rights provisions of state constitutions to impose much of an obligation on state governments.[55]

---

49 Gardner (n 30); Lawrence Friedman, 'The Constitutional Value of Dialogue and the New Judicial Federalism' (2000) 28 *Hastings Constitutional Law Quarterly* 93.
50 The US Supreme Court ruled that the US Constitution does not recognize such a right in San Antonio Indep. School Dist. v. Rodriguez, 411 US 1 (1973).
51 David Schuman, 'The Right to a Remedy' (1992) 65 *Temple Law Review* 1197.
52 N.Y. Const. art. XVII, § 1.
53 Mont. Const. art. XII, § 3(3).
54 Ill. Const. art. XI, § 2.
55 Helen Hershkoff, 'Positive Rights and State Constitutions: The Limits of Federal Rationality Review' (1999) 112 *Harvard Law Review* 1131; José L. Fernandez, 'State Constitutions, Environmental Rights Provisions, and the Doctrine of Self-Execution: A Political Question?' (1993) 17 *Harvard Environmental Law Review* 333.

19.4.4 Policy principles

Among the world's constitutions, the US Constitution is unusually short and terse, confining itself almost exclusively to laying out the structure of the national government and allocating powers among the various actors. US state constitutions are very different: most are considerably longer—on average more than three times longer than the national constitution[56]—and the principal reason is that they not only devote considerable space to substantive policy commitments, but often go into great detail on the subjects they regulate. Indeed, American state constitutions are often criticized for being excessively 'legislative' in character—that is, setting out regulated matters with such particularity as to risk undermining the gravity and dignity of the constitution.[57] This degree of detail is, in turn, often attributed to the relative ease with which state constitutions can be amended, but the phenomenon also seems to reflect an attitude toward state constitutions that conceives of them as entitled to considerably less reverence than is typically accorded the federal constitution.[58]

Some policy domains commonly regulated extensively by state constitutions include:

- transportation policy, including the construction and funding of canals and railroads;
- corporations, including the conditions for granting corporate charters;
- natural resources, including river levees, water allocation and usage, parks and recreational areas, mining and resource extraction, and environmental protection;
- state and municipal finance, including taxation, borrowing, debt and budgets;
- education policy, including methods of finance and governance.[59]

In addition, numerous state constitutions contain more isolated provisions dealing with issues as disparate as lotteries, alcoholic beverages, racial preferences in university admissions, stem-cell research and animal welfare.[60]

19.4.5 Self-imposed limits on state autonomy

Given the very broad autonomy that US states possess to decide upon the structure and content of subnational principles of constitutional self-governance, one might expect US state constitutions to differ significantly from one another and from the federal constitution. In fact, however, the federal and state constitutions tend to bear very strong resemblances, and in many cases to recognize and establish identical constitutional norms, often using very similar or even identical language.

This was not always the case. The earliest state constitutions diverged from one another significantly in structure and content, but by the 1830s or 1840s, US state constitutions had substantially converged on a common set of institutions and constitutional practices of self-governance.[61] Although it is difficult to discern the precise causes for this constitutional

---

56 Albert L. Sturm, 'The Development of American State Constitutions' (1982) 12 *Publius* 57.

57 Note, 'California's Constitutional Amendomania' (1949) 1 *Stanford Law Review* 279; William F. Swindler, 'State Constitutions for the 20th Century' (1971) 50 *Nebraska Law Review* 477; James A. Gardner, 'The Failed Discourse of State Constitutionalism' (1992) 90 *Michigan Law Review* 761, at 818–22.

58 Gardner (n 10), at 26–7.

59 Tarr (n 32); Dinan (n 24), Dinan (n 25).

60 Dinan (n 25).

61 James A. Gardner, 'Autonomy and Isomorphism: The Unfulfilled Promise of Structural Autonomy in American State Constitutions' (2014) 61 *Wayne Law Review* 31.

isomorphism, likely explanations for this kind of policy diffusion include a perception of prestige surrounding the US Constitution, cross-borrowing and imitation in constitutional drafting processes; the belief that certain kinds of provisions have enjoyed success over time; and professional convergence on certain models as normatively superior.[62]

19.5 Multilevel constitutionalism

19.5.1 Resolution of conflicts

Under the Supremacy Clause of the US Constitution, provisions of the federal constitution are 'the supreme law of the land', and state constitutional provisions may not conflict with federal ones. Any such conflicts are resolved in favour of the federal document, and conflicting state constitutional provisions are considered invalid. In the case of provisions protecting human rights, as indicated in Section 19.4.3, where national and subnational provisions both protect the same right, the national provision sets the minimum level of protection, or 'floor', and state constitutions are free to provide a more generous level of protection for the right in question. In principle, state constitutions may also provide a lower level of protection,[63] but by operation of the Supremacy Clause, state courts are obliged in such cases to enforce the higher level of protection offered by the US Constitution. States are free to protect rights which receive no federal protection at any level they choose.

19.5.2 Participation of subnational units in revision of national constitution

Under Article V, no change may be made to the US Constitution without the approval of three-quarters of the states. That approval may be provided either by state legislatures, meeting in the ordinary course of business; or by special ratifying conventions convened for that purpose. The mode of state approval is determined by Congress when referring proposed amendments to the states for their consideration (Article V).

19.5.3 Interaction with treaty law

The US Constitution specifically provides that treaties between the United States and other countries are supreme law to which all state constitutions must conform. As a practical matter, however, the impact of treaty law on state constitutions (and other forms of state law) is limited, for three reasons. First, the power to make treaties is reserved under the federal constitution exclusively to the federal government, so unlike subnational units in some European countries, such as Austria or Belgium, states have no opportunity to bind themselves individually to treaty obligations (Art. I, § 10). Second, the United States government has historically been reluctant to constrain its own policy discretion through binding treaty commitments, and that latitude is therefore enjoyed derivatively by the states. Third, the US Supreme Court has taken a narrow view of the conditions in which treaty norms may be considered to bind the states, holding that unless a treaty obligation is clearly self-executing, it must be operationalized through congressional implementing legislation,[64] of which there is very little.

---

62 Ibid.
63 Jeffrey S. Sutton, *51 Imperfect Solutions: States and the Making of American Constitutional Law* (Oxford University Press 2018) 183–4.
64 Medellin v. Texas, 552 US 491 (2008).

19.6 Constitutional review

19.6.1 *Jurisdiction of courts*

In the US federation, each level of government, state and national, has its own judicial system. As a result, state courts bear principal responsibility for policing state and local government compliance with the state constitution. Such decisions are not subject to further review by federal courts.[65]

Claims arising under the state constitution may be heard by federal courts in two circumstances. One is when it is alleged that a provision of the state constitution violates the federal constitution. The other circumstance is when a claim concerning the meaning of the state constitution is brought initially in federal court under the federal system's 'diversity' jurisdiction, which allows federal courts to adjudicate state law claims when brought by citizens of one state against citizens of another state.[66] However, because it is extremely rare for a federal court to adjudicate a case concerning the state constitution under its diversity jurisdiction, the great majority of cases adjudicating issues of state constitutional law are handled in the state court system, and those decisions are final and unreviewable.

19.6.2 *Complications of dual constitutional protection of human rights*

Judicial review by state courts of state constitutions has at times produced controversy in the United States, particularly in the area of human rights. As described in Section 19.4.3, in the US federal system both levels of government have independent authority to provide constitutional protection for individual rights. Where state constitutional rights lack a federal counterpart, judicial elaboration and enforcement of those rights has generally been uncontroversial. However, where state and federal constitutional protections for rights are duplicative, state judicial rulings giving broad constructions to the rights in question have occasionally provoked controversy.

The most common approach by state courts to state constitutional rights provisions that duplicate federally protected rights is to interpret them to have precisely the same reach and application as the federal version of the right—that is, in 'lockstep' with the federal right.[67] Rulings by state courts that construe state constitutional rights more broadly and generously than the equivalent federal right have at times caused considerable political controversy. Although within the legal profession, the precise grounds of the controversy have concerned technical issues of interpretational methodology, the relevant methodological disagreements are actually rooted in still unsettled disagreements, described in Section 19.1, about the nature of the US federation.

From the legal point of view, the focus of dispute concerns the circumstances in which a state court is methodologically justified in construing a rights provision of a state constitution to grant a higher level of protection to an individual right than is provided by the counterpart provision of the federal constitution.[68] As a matter of formal law, there is no question that state polities have the authority to set higher levels of protection for rights in their own subnational constitutions than the national polity has established in the national constitution.[69] The question,

---

65 Michigan v. Long, 463 US 1032 (1983).
66 Under the US Const. amend. XIV, people acquire state citizenship automatically upon taking up residence in the state.
67 Gardner (n 10), at 45–7.
68 Gardner (n 10).
69 Brennan (n 47); Williams (n 29).

however, concerns what ought to count as evidence that state polities have exercised this theoretical authority.

Distinctive constitutional language, controlling precedent or clear legislative history are all possible indicators that a state constitutional right is broader in scope than its federal counterpart,[70] but these decisive indicators almost never exist.[71] This has led some state courts to turn to other interpretive aids, including inferences from what courts take to be the distinctive 'character' of the state polity. For example, in an opinion holding that the Oregon Constitution's protection of free speech extends, unlike the federal First Amendment, to obscene expression, the Oregon Supreme Court rested its ruling partly on the contention that Oregon's founders 'were rugged and robust individuals dedicated to founding a free society unfettered by the governmental imposition of some people's views of morality on the free expression of others'.[72] The Texas Supreme Court, in another free speech case, held that the Texas Constitution provides greater protection than the federal Constitution against the issuance of gag orders by trial courts.[73] The court argued that the Texas Constitution must be understood to 'reflect Texas' values, customs, and traditions',[74] and supported its divergent reading of the Texas free speech provision by reference to the different 'experiences and philosophies' of the state's founders, whose views were shaped by 'years of rugged experience on the frontier'.[75]

The plausibility of such rulings depends entirely on the plausibility of the underlying belief that the polities of the various states—or at least of some states—hold values or possess social or cultural characteristics that are sufficiently distinct and deep-seated to be reflected in decisions concerning fundamental aspects of constitutional self-governance.[76] As indicated in Section 19.1, such contentions are dubious on the merits,[77] and appear to have been influenced by a lengthy, politically motivated propaganda campaign by southern states undertaken to justify first the institution of slavery, and then federal non-interference in informal practices of racial domination.

However, another possible motivation for state courts to construe duplicative state constitutional rights more broadly than their federal counterparts—and one more consistent with the premises and operation of federalism—is simple disagreement with parallel decisions of the US Supreme Court construing the federal constitution.[78] Federal systems are designed not to resolve and end disagreements within a society, which is not a feasible goal, but instead to channel disagreements that do arise into the mould of national-subnational contestation. Thus, if in a federation internal disagreement emerges over highly contestable issues such as the meaning of societal commitments to free speech or the appropriate treatment of those accused of crimes, it would be natural and predictable for those disagreements to find expression in competing rulings of state and national courts adjudicating the contested subject matter.

In the United States, such conflicts between state and national courts have emerged concerning, for example, the meaning of constitutional protections against 'unreasonable' searches and 'cruel and unusual' punishments, and concerning the scope of constitutional protection for individual autonomy in intimate relations, in particular regarding gay sex and marriage.[79] In all

---

70 Hans A. Linde, 'E Pluribus—Constitutional Theory and State Courts' (1984) 18 *Georgia Law Review* 165.
71 Gardner (n 57).
72 State v. Henry, 732 P.2d 9, 16 (Or. 1987).
73 Davenport v. Garcia, 834 S.W.2d 4 (Tex. 1992).
74 Ibid., 16, *quoting* LeCroy v. Hanlon, 713 S.W.2d 335, 339 (Tex. 1986).
75 Ibid., quoting James C. Harrington, The Texas Bill of Rights (1987) 41.
76 Philip Bobbitt, *Constitutional Fate: Theory of the Constitution* (Oxford University Press 1982) 94.
77 Gardner (n 10).
78 Ibid.
79 Gardner (n 10), at 100–8.

these cases, at least some state courts have construed state constitutional rights protections to provide greater protection to the right in question than is provided by the counterpart federal right.

Such decisions, however, have from time to time provoked not only a public outcry against the rulings, but in many cases political punishment of the courts involved, an outcome facilitated in most states by the electoral accountability of judges. For example, in 2010 three justices of the Iowa Supreme Court were defeated in a retention election after conservative groups mounted a campaign against them based on their votes in a ruling that recognized a right to same-sex marriage under the Iowa Constitution.

Political and electoral punishment of state judges for disagreeing publicly with the US Supreme Court casts strong doubt on the theory of state cultural distinctiveness. It suggests, to the contrary, that all Americans share fundamentally similar views on the proper reach and application of human rights, and at the very least it suggests dominance in the public mind of national institutions as the appropriate forums in which to work out the meaning of collective values. Thus, the autonomy of states to choose their own level of protection for human rights may be more theoretical than real.

20

CONCLUSION

Nine hypotheses to explain variation in subnational constitutional autonomy

Patricia Popelier, Nicholas Aroney and Giacomo Delledonne[1]

20.1 Measuring subnational constitutional autonomy

In the introduction to this edited volume, we defined subnational/state constitutions as 'basic documents for given subnational or state entities which lay down entrenched fundamental rules addressing key matters in one or more of the following categories: subnational identity, representative structures, organization of powers, fundamental rights and policy principles, which are adopted by the people of the subnational entity or their representatives'. Applying this definition, the subnational or state entities (SNEs) of many but not all of the 18 jurisdictions covered by this volume have, at least to some extent, a degree of constitutional autonomy. However, in two jurisdictions, India and the UK, regular SNEs do not enjoy substantial subnational autonomy at all, even though India is commonly regarded as a genuine (though centralized) federal system. In other federal systems, such as Belgium, subnational constitutional autonomy is relatively weak. This undermines the assertion, often put forward,[2] that subnational constitutional autonomy is an inherent or essential feature of federal systems of all kinds, even though it is clearly an important feature of many such systems. More subtle distinctions therefore need to be made.

The introduction proposed that the strength of subnational constituent power can be measured by reference to both the content of subnational constitutions and the procedures by which such constitutions are established and changed. The jurisdictions examined in this volume display different combinations of these two elements. The first indicator refers to the power of SNEs to determine the substantive content of the SNE constitution with respect to the key matters described above (i.e. subnational identity, representative structures, organization of powers, fundamental rights and policy principles). As explained in Index 1 in Appendix 1 to this concluding chapter, we assessed the subnational content autonomy in each country on a 5–0-point

---

1 We are grateful to Laura Martens (University of Antwerp) for statistical support.
2 For example, Anna Gamper, 'A "global theory of federalism"? The nature and challenges of a Federal State' (2005) 6 *German Law Journal* 1297, at 1305–6, 1312; James A. Gardner, 'In Search of Sub-National Constitutionalism' (2008) 4 *Eu. Const. L. Rev.* 325; Werner Heun, *The Constitution of Germany. A Contextual Analysis* (Hart 2011) 50, 80. See also Cristina Fasone, 'What Role for Regional Assemblies in Regional States? Italy, Spain and the United Kingdom in Comparative Perspective' (2012) 4 *Perspectives on Federalism* 171, at 175–6.

scale, ranging from countries where SNEs can make substantial arrangements in respect of all of these key matters (5, very strong) to countries where SNEs have no such capacity whatsoever (0). We then converted this to a value between 0 and 1. Table 20.1 shows that according to this measure, eleven of the countries examined in this volume—Argentina, Australia, Bosnia and Herzegovina, Brazil, Canada, Ethiopia, Germany, Italy, Spain, Switzerland and the US—have 'very strong' or 'strong' subnational constitutional autonomy in relation to content. In four others—Belgium, Malaysia, India and UK—we classify these powers as 'very weak' or 'weak', whereas in Austria, Mexico and South Africa, federal blueprints and/or jurisdictional interference restricts them to a level which we classify as 'moderate'.

In the UK, the question remains whether the devolution acts are subnational constitutional acts or central acts which establish the constitutional arrangements for the devolved entities. In his country report, Skoutaris emphasizes: 'the uneasy co-existence of devolution with the principle of parliamentary sovereignty'. Leaving aside the Northern Ireland Act, which is a special case due to the international obligations that surround it, one could argue both ways. On the one hand, it is arguable that they are subnational constitutional acts, because they are specific to each devolved entity separately and involve the entities by political convention. On the other hand, they are recognized by the Supreme Court as Acts of the sovereign Parliament, which means that amendments have to be enacted by the Parliament, but only with the consent of the devolved parliaments. As Skoutaris puts it: If Westminster wishes to alter the level of constituent autonomy of a devolved nation, the regional legislatures have a determinative say, but only 'to the extent that the consent mechanism is followed and respected'. This emphasizes the difference between the legal framework, and what happens in practice, discussed below. For this reason, we have classified the devolution acts as central constitutional acts. Nevertheless, the UK chapter points out that the devolved entities have the competence to amend the content of the devolution acts with regard to specific matters. To that extent, the entities have constitutional power of their own, even if this only comes down to a few non-substantial arrangements. One might argue that they are so few that it comes down to no constitutional autonomy at all. In Table 20.1, we have adopted the most optimistic reading. Westminster, however, can still overrule the subnational acts, which amounts to a discretionary veto power by the central authority (see Index 1 in Appendix 1).

The second criterion is whether SNEs are able to adopt or make changes to their constitutions on their own initiative using their own procedures and without central interference. Here, the case studies reveal a wide set of procedural factors, ranging from discretionary central veto powers, through *ex ante* legality tests, to exclusive subnational control according to a procedure determined at the subnational or perhaps central level. As explained in Index 1 in Appendix 1, we assessed the subnational procedural autonomy in each country on a 5-0-point scale,[3] ranging from countries where SNEs can adopt their own constitutions without central interference according to a procedure adopted by the SNE itself (5) to countries where the SNEs have no power to adopt or influence the content of their own constitutions whatsoever (0). Appendix 2 explains the results. Again, we converted this to a value between 0 and 1. Table 20.1 shows that procedural autonomy is strong in most of the examined countries that have strong content autonomy, with Italy, Spain and Switzerland as outliers. Moderate content autonomy is paired with strong procedural autonomy (Austria, Brazil and Mexico). Weak content autonomy is sometimes paired with strong procedural autonomy (Belgium, Malaysia), at other times with moderate (South Africa) or weak (India, UK) procedural autonomy. While the picture is mixed,

3 Table 3.2. in Patricia Popelier, *Dynamic Federalism* (Routledge 2021) 104.

there is a significant correlation between content autonomy and procedural autonomy, [4] particularly due to the cases in which both are strong.

We then combined the values for content and procedural autonomy, as a measure of overall constitutional autonomy which gives equal weight to content and procedure. This aggregate value shows that the SNEs in most countries (13 out of 18) have strong or very strong powers to adopt their own constitutions. The question arises whether in the five remaining countries (Belgium, India, Malaysia, South Africa and the UK) this is compensated by the involvement of the SNEs in the central constitution. Therefore, we measured this involvement, using a scale that we applied to each country in consultation with the authors.[5] Index 2 in Appendix 1 shows the scale, and Appendix 3 explains the results. We return to this question below, in our discussion of hypothesis 8. For now, Table 20.1 shows the aggregate score for self-constituent capacity. Here, 12 out of 18 countries are qualified as having strong or very strong self-constituent capacity. To calculate this score, we have not given equal weight to both aspects (subnational constitutions and involvement in the central constitution) because the latter always implies negotiations with

Table 20.1 Self-constituent capacity

Country	Subnational constitutions			Involvement in central constitution-making	Self-constituent capacity
	Value content	*Value procedure*	*Aggr. value*	*Value*	*Aggr. value*
Argentina	1	1	1	0.44	0.81
Australia	1	1	1	0.56	0.85
Austria	0.40	1	0.70	0.44	0.61
*Belgium**	0.20	0.80	0.50	0.67	0.56
B&H	1	1	1	0.78	0.93
Brazil	0.60	0.80	0.70	0.56	0.65
Canada	0.80	1	0.90	1	0.93
Ethiopia	1	1	1	0.67	0.89
Germany	1	1	1	0.67	0.89
India	0	0	0	0.67	0.15
*Italy**	0.80	0.60	0.70	0.44	0.61
Malaysia	0.20	0.80	0.50	0	0.33
Mexico	0.40	1	0.70	0.67	0.69
S-Africa	0.40	0.60	0.50	0.67	0.56
Spain	1	0.40	0.70	0.22	0.54
Switzerland	1	0.40	0.70	0.44	0.61
UK	0.20	0.40	0.30	0	0.20
USA	1	1	1	0.78	0.93

Very Weak	Weak	Medium	Strong	Very Strong
0–0.19	0.20–0.39	0.40–0.59	0.60–0.79	0.80–1

Multinational systems are in italic.

* Only the strongest SNEs are taken into account in this table.

4 Correlation 0.4307, significance 0.0744***. Up to 0.1 is significant. The lower this number, the more significant.

5 Table 2.2. in *ibid.*, at 100. We consulted the authors of the country reports, but take full responsibility for the final qualification.

the other entities and therefore by definition entails less autonomy for the SNEs. Based on a comparison of the criteria for the two categories, we weighted involvement in the central constitution at half the value of the power to adopt subnational constitutions.[6]

Importantly, the data in Table 20.1 only offers a factual overview. It does not imply that SNEs in multi-tiered or federal systems *should* enjoy strong subnational constitutional autonomy. Federalism is not defined by subnational autonomy alone, but involves a balance between subnational autonomy on the one hand and overall cohesion or integrity on the other.[7] For example, many federal constitutions contain uniformity or homogeneity clauses that require compliance with constitutional provisions and principles that are deemed essential for the integrity or identity of the entire political system. The basic values that underpin the constitutional system would be undermined if SNEs, in their constitutions, could freely adopt other potentially inconsistent principles. In his chapter, Gardner explains that in the US, both the Supreme Court and Congress have shied away from enforcing the 'guarantee clause' for republican government. Yet, the legal guarantee of cohesion through consistency of constitutional values is stronger where a homogeneity clause is present and enforced through an automatic and binding *ex ante* check. Another question is whether this is a legal check, or political in nature. In her country report, Belser mentions that the implementation of a political check is under discussion in Switzerland, with many authors arguing that this competence should be transferred to the Federal Supreme Court.

This points to the difference between law in the books and law in practice. The measures we use to define subnational constitutional autonomy focus on the legal framework of each country. This legal framework consists mainly of legal texts, but also case law. For example, de Araújo shows how the Brazilian Supreme Court has used the symmetry principle to severely reduce the constitutional space available to SNEs. A country's legal framework establishes a particular institutional design which may offer the *promise* of substantial subnational autonomy. In practice, however, SNEs do not always make use of this autonomy and there can be cultural or practical barriers to them doing so. The Argentine SNEs may have considerable legal autonomy, but in practice they are not comparable to the SNEs of Australia, Germany and the US. Moreover, as Fessha points out, the SNEs in Ethiopia have of their own accord made the amendment of provisions on fundamental rights in their subnational constitutions dependent on the central level. Also, the central authorities may be more or less inclined to interfere. As pointed out above, in the UK, the Sewel convention gives the devolved entities a stronger say in practice. There are significant variations among federal countries on all of these points.

Table 20.1 only offers a general picture. By focusing on subnational constitutional autonomy, we are also able to measure the degree of constitutional asymmetry in a country. Not all SNEs enjoy the same amount of subnational autonomy. For example, in Italy, as Delledonne, Martinico and Monti note, the special autonomous entities have weaker procedural constitutional autonomy because their Statutes of Autonomy have to be approved by the central legislature in the form of constitutional laws. In Belgium, the Brussels Region and the German Community have less self-constituent capacity than the other Regions and Communities, especially if the quasi-constitutional organic laws rather than the constitution are selected as a reference point. In India, the state of Jammu and Kashmir had, in theory, a substantial degree of constitutional autonomy denied to other states, but even this has recently been abrogated.

6 Although Table 20.1 shows the calculations down the second decimal point, it needs to be kept in mind that the underlying data measured each component on only 5-point and 9-point scales. We accordingly adopted a broader 5-fold classification of each country's self-constituent capacity as alternatively: very strong, strong, medium, weak and very weak.

7 See *ibid.* at 51–3.

20.2 Explaining variety

So, what explains variety in the extent to which SNEs have self-constituent capacity and enjoy constitutional autonomy in particular? And what explains differences between theory and practice?

These are empirical questions for political scientists, which have not often been explored. Obviously, as Riker pointed out long ago, the political system plays an important role.[8] For example, it is no coincidence that the Western Cape tried to make use of its constitutional autonomy, as reported by Steytler in the South African chapter. This is the only province that is not dominated by the central-governing African National Congress party. In the Brazilian chapter, de Araújo points to the absence of regionalized parties to explain why agendas are mainly focused on central government policies. In Italy, claims for greater subnational constitutional autonomy emerged in the special regions of Trentino-Alto Adige/South Tyrol and to a lesser extent Valle d'Aosta, where strong regional parties, linked to the presence of historic minorities, are active. Similarly, the Basque Country and Catalonia, where nationalist parties have often formed government, played a pivotal role in the latest wave of reform of the Statutes of Autonomy of the Spanish Autonomous Communities.

This book does not seek to propose conclusive explanations for the variety in the design and use of subnational constitutional autonomy in federal countries. Instead, the introduction tendered more modest hypotheses that focus on constitutional origins and underlying multinationality as explanatory factors for the institutional features of each system. Hypothesis 1 suggested that strong SNE powers to adopt subnational constitutions are mainly a feature of coming-together federations, because in such cases the subnational constitutions were pre-existent. Hypothesis 2 predicted weak subnational constitutional autonomy in divided multinational states. In addition, hypothesis 8 factored in the role of compensatory mechanisms: if subnational autonomy is weak, then participation in central constitution-making secures a degree of self-constituent capacity. Other hypotheses formulated in the introduction concentrate on the significance of subnational constitutional autonomy. Hypotheses 3, 4 and 9 address the symbolic value and political salience of subnational constitutions. The assumption is that this is linked with the strength of subnational constitutions: strong subnational constitutions are more likely to have impact. In turn, hypotheses 5, 6 and 7 are mostly concerned with the practical and experimental use and effects of subnational constitutions.

In what follows, the hypotheses are tested based on the country reports in this volume.

20.3 Constitutional origins and underlying multinationality as explanatory variables for strong or weak subnational constitutional autonomy (hypotheses 1, 2, 8)

20.3.1 Constitutional origins (hypothesis 1)

Our first hypothesis was that strong SNE powers to adopt subnational constitutions is mainly a feature of coming-together or aggregative federations. Argentina, Australia, Germany, Switzerland

---

8 William H. Riker, *Federalism. Origin, Operation, Significance* (Little, Brown and Company 1964) 11–16, 51, 91–101, 129–35.

and the USA are strongly aggregative systems.[9] They confirm the hypothesis: they display strong (Switzerland) or very strong overall subnational constitutional autonomy.

Belgium, Italy, South Africa, Spain and the UK are holding-together or devolutionary systems. The remaining countries are hybrids that display mixed characteristics of both aggregative and devolutionary features. In both categories, the picture is more diverse, ranging from very weak to very strong constitutional autonomy.

For example, Bosnia and Herzegovina and Ethiopia have strong subnational constitutional autonomy but have complex origins that are difficult to describe and classify; they appear to display mixed features that are partly coming-together or aggregative and partly holding-together or devolutionary. However, on closer analysis, the apparent anomaly can be explained. As Sahadžić explains in her chapter on Bosnia and Herzegovina, SNE constitutional autonomy is high as a consequence of the 'bottom-up' approach used for the formation of the constitution as well as the multinational character of the federation. Likewise, in his chapter on Ethiopia, Fessha draws attention to the shaping of the constitution by the ethnically based Transitional Government under the control of the Ethiopian Peoples' Revolutionary Democratic Front, a coalition of four ethnically based parties dominated by the Tigray region in northern Ethiopia. While the strong constitutional autonomy attributed to the SNEs in Ethiopia was not based on any pre-existing constitutional status of the regions and ethnicities, the idea that Ethiopia was to be a federation of many 'nations, nationalities and peoples' was a prevailing principle of the constitution.

The rationale behind the original hypothesis was that subnational constitutions were pre-existent in aggregative federations. The expectation was that, in the federal bargain, such SNEs would keep their original constitutional powers, including powers to determine their own constitutions and to legislate on matters not exclusively placed within the jurisdiction of the federation. In this respect, it is important to recognize the possibility that the definition of SNE powers in 'residual' terms may be merely a technical device rather than an outworking of the principle that the constituent states originally possessed a 'fullness' of constitutive and legislative power, aspects of which were conferred upon the federation, with the remaining 'residue' being reserved to those states. As Gamper remarks in this volume, the Austrian *Länder* have residuary competences,[10] but the federal constitution organizes the *Länder* in a way that substantially limits subnational constitutional space. More significant is the pre-existence of subnational constitutions. Subnational constitutions pre-existed the federation in all of the strongly aggregative systems referred to above, while they were partially evident in Austria, Bosnia and Herzegovina, and Canada. In all these countries, overall subnational constitutional autonomy is strong or very strong.

This suggests that the first hypothesis is confirmed, if rephrased to hold that:

> Hypothesis 1.1. SNEs are more likely to have strong powers to adopt subnational constitutions if subnational constitutions based on constitutional autonomy pre-existed the formation of the multi-tiered system.

---

9 In the case of Germany, this is in relation to the Land constitutions adopted before the German Basic Law in 1949. In the case of Switzerland and USA, this is in relation to the cantons and states that existed prior to the formation of the federation in 1848 and 1789 respectively.

10 Article 15 of the Austrian Constitution states that: 'In so far as a matter is not expressly assigned (*übertragen*) by the Federal Constitution to the Federation for legislation or also execution, it remains (*verbleibt*) within the provinces autonomous sphere of competence'.

20.3.2 *Multinational systems (hypothesis 2)*

The second hypothesis predicted that the power to adopt subnational constitutions is especially weak in divided multinational states, because these systems are more easily prone to separatism and will therefore avoid granting or acknowledging powers that can symbolize the existence of sovereign rights to constitutional self-determination and independence. The expectation was that SNEs in these systems will have weak constitutional powers.

According to Stepan's definition, multinational systems are characterized by significant groups that voice important political autonomy claims for territorial entities based on linguistic, religious, cultural or ethnic identities.[11] In our sample of federal countries, ten systems can be identified as multinational: Belgium, Bosnia and Herzegovina, Canada, Ethiopia, Italy, India, Malaysia, South Africa, Spain and the UK.

At first sight, the hypothesis seems not confirmed: five of these countries accord to their SNEs strong (Italy, Spain) or very strong (Bosnia and Herzegovina, Ethiopia and Canada) overall constitutional autonomy. Only two (India and the UK) have weak subnational constitutional autonomy. Interestingly, the Ethiopian SNEs have a right to secede by virtue of the Constitution; in this respect, Ethiopia may be described as an outlier.

Nevertheless, multinationality proves to be an important factor. All systems that have weak or medium overall subnational constitutional autonomy are multinational systems. Also, all non-multinational systems in our sample have strong or very strong subnational constitutional powers. A t-test shows a low average of multinational systems in the group with strong constitutional autonomy (0.3846). Overall, multinationality is a significant factor that distinguishes groups that have strong constitutional autonomy and groups that do not have strong constitutional autonomy.[12]

The same applies for self-constituent capacity. SNEs in some multinational systems have strong self-constituent capacity. However, all non-multinational systems have strong or very strong self-constituent capacity, and all systems where SNEs have weak or medium self-constituent capacity, are multinational. A t-test shows an even lower average of multinational systems in the group with strong self-constituent autonomy (0.38). Multinationality is in this case an even more significant factor that distinguishes groups that have strong self-constituent capacity and groups that do not.[13]

This means that the second hypothesis is confirmed, if rephrased to hold that:

Hypothesis 2.1. Non-multinational systems are more likely to grant strong subnational constitutional powers than multinational systems.

We can also propose as a corollary that says:

Hypothesis 2.2. SNEs in non-multinational systems are more likely to have strong self-constituent capacity than SNEs in multinational systems.

---

11 Alfred Stepan, 'Towards a New Comparative Politics of Federalism, Multinationalism, and Democracy: Beyond Rikerian Federalism' in Edward L. Gibson (ed.) *Federalism and Democracy in Latin America* (John Hopkins University Press 2004) 29, at 39.
12 0.0169★★★. The tables for the t-test can be provided upon request: patricia.popelier@uantwerpen.be
13 0.0049★.

20.3.3 Self-constituent capacity (hypothesis 8)

The introduction distinguished three notions related to subnational constitutionalism: subnational constitutionalism as a principle of legitimized and limited subnational government; self-constituent capacity defined as the power of SNEs to influence the constitutional arrangements that apply to them; and the power of SNEs to adopt a subnational constitution.

The hypothesis formulated in the introduction assumed that if SNEs have only weak or very weak subnational constitutional autonomy, this is compensated through representation. As only two countries have weak or very weak (aggregate) constitutional autonomy, we widen the sample to include countries with medium aggregate constitutional autonomy. Alternatively, we examine countries with weak content autonomy. The reason is that through involvement in the central constitution, SNEs can impact on the content of subnational constitutional arrangements that they are not allowed to regulate on their own.

The assumption was not applied to all multi-tiered systems. Instead, it was expected that at least those systems that self-identify as federal seek a balance between cohesion and subnational autonomy, implying that if SNEs lack substantial constitutional autonomy, they will seek to secure a self-constituent capacity to influence or shape the constitutional arrangements that apply to them.

The hypothesis need not imply that, conversely, SNEs in systems with strong subnational constitutional autonomy are not also strongly involved in central constitution-making. In fact, there is a noticeable correlation[14] between constitutional autonomy and involvement in central constitution-making. All countries with very strong subnational constitutional autonomy also give SNEs strong or very strong involvement in central constitution-making, with the exception of Argentina and Australia where subnational involvement is granted to the subnational electorate rather than the entities in themselves.

The hypothesis is confirmed in three out of five countries: Belgium, India and South Africa, where (very) weak or medium constitutional autonomy is compensated by enabling strong involvement in central constitution-making. If we only look at countries with weak content autonomy, the hypothesis is confirmed in only 2 of 4 countries. We see compensation for weak content autonomy in Belgium and India but not in Malaysia and the UK.

In Belgium, the effect is even stronger, if the Flemish Community is selected as the unit of analysis, and the special majority acts are selected as the 'central constitution'. This can be justified by the fact that these organic laws, rather than the constitution in itself, determine how the SNEs are organized and which specific powers they have. In this procedure, the language groups have a veto right. These groups do not coincide with the SNEs but largely overlap. In particular, the Dutch language group in the Senate consists of 35 senators, the majority of which are representatives of the Flemish Parliament. As a result, the Flemish Community cannot force institutional reform, but it does have the power to veto any change. For the purposes of this chapter, however, we decided to simplify and select the central constitution, which is justified by the fact that it lays down the basic principles of the federal system and determines the categories of community powers.

In his chapter, Steytler confirms that the provinces of South Africa are strongly involved in central constitution-making.

In India, as Singh and Saxena highlight in their chapter, SNEs are likewise well represented in the central constitution-making procedure. Art. 368 of the Indian Constitution requires an

---

14 Correlation 0.3810, significance 0.1188. Up to 0.1 and lower is significant, which means that the correlation is very close to being significant.

absolute majority and a two-thirds majority of the members present and voting in each House, including the Council of States with State representatives. Moreover, specific provisions that affect the States can only be amended if, in addition, the amendment is ratified by the legislatures of not less than one-half of the states. Counter-balancing this, however, is Art. 3, which allows the national Parliament to territorially reorganize any state, including the state of Jammu and Kashmir, which alone of the Indian states had its own subnational constitution until 2019. The autonomy of some tribal areas and tribal states under their 'constitutions within the Constitution' is also subject to unilateral alteration by the Union Parliament.

Nevertheless, it seems that, with these exceptions, involvement in central constitution-making is lower than or, at most, equal to subnational constitutional autonomy.

Here as well, the table only offers a general account. If the tables are completed for each SNE separately, constitutional asymmetries appear. For example, in the Belgian report it is noted that the self-governing capacity of Flemish and French-speaking SNEs is also considerable. This is different for the smaller SNEs, and especially the German-speaking Community.

The results only partially confirm the hypothesis, and support a corollary claim:

Hypothesis 8.1. *Weak constitutional autonomy is likely to be compensated through involvement in central constitution-making, but not necessarily as a rule in all cases.*
Hypothesis 8.2. *SNEs that have very strong constitutional autonomy are also strongly involved in central constitution-making.*

20.4 The significance of subnational constitutional autonomy (hypotheses 3, 4, 9)

The hypothesis that multinational systems are more likely to tolerate only weak subnational constitutional powers is linked with the assumption that constitutions are symbols of self-governance, which is especially delicate in political systems under threat of separatism. This led us to the hypothesis that in multinational systems subnational constitutions have more symbolic value than elsewhere (hypothesis 3). In addition, it was hypothesized that in these systems, regional identity is the most crucial and at the same time the most contentious aspect of constitutional autonomy (hypothesis 4). Where subnational constitutions are not contested, another problem arises, which is the lack of visibility or political salience. To remedy this problem, hypothesis 9 assumes that constitutional review is vital to bring subnational constitutions to life.

20.4.1 The symbolic value of subnational constitutions (hypotheses 3 and 4)

Hypothesis 3 implies a comparison between multinational and non-multinational systems. Clearly, in non-multinational systems, subnational constitutions have low salience and visibility, even if subnational constitutional autonomy is strong. In the Swiss report, Belser calls cantonal constitutions 'Sleeping Beauties'. Likewise, scholars have called the Australian state constitutions 'Cinderellas'.[15]

In multinational systems as well, subnational constitutions do not necessary become politically significant. They are generally a non-topic in Ethiopia, India and Malaysia. Where their existence or content stirs some debate, as in Belgium, Bosnia and Herzegovina, Canada, Italy,

---

15 George Winterton, 'Australian States: Cinderellas No Longer?' in George Winterton (ed.) *State Constitutional Landmarks* (Federation Press 2006) 1.

South Africa and Spain, this remains rather limited. The Belgian, Canadian and South African reports reveal that the issue is especially salient in regions that have a more distinctive regional identity and aspire to more autonomy: Flanders in Belgium, the Republika Srpska in Bosnia and Herzegovina, Catalonia and the Basque Country in Spain, Alberta and Québec in Canada, and the Western Cape and Kwa-Zulu Natal in South Africa. For example, Sahadžić observes in her country report on Bosnia and Herzegovina that the Constitution of the Republika Srpska is 'exploited as a tool to prove statehood in aspirations linked to claims for independence'. Even in Malaysia, where the subnational constitutions have a low profile, subnational identity is strongly asserted by the Malay State constitutions which continue to depict their Malay sultans as heads of the constitutionally established religion of Islam in the context of a federation that became somewhat multinational in character following the entry of Sabah and Sarawak.

These cases suggest we must rephrase the hypothesis:

> Hypothesis 3.1. Subnational constitutions are rarely visible and symbolically significant, except when used to underscore the aspiration to self-governing autonomy of an entity with distinctive regional identity.

Thus qualified, this strengthens the further hypothesis that in divided multinational states, identity clauses are crucial for those SNEs that aspire to adopt their own constitution, and at the same time these are their most contentious aspect (hypothesis 4). To test this hypothesis, we first need to examine whether SNEs in multinational states are free to include identity clauses. Next, we must investigate whether such clauses have been vetoed by central authorities or invalidated by courts.

In non-multinational systems, regional identity clauses are not a topic of discussion. Most SNEs have no need for such clauses. Gardner is very clear in his US country report: 'The practice of using subnational constitutions as vehicles for the assertion of a distinctive subnational identity is essentially non-existent in the United States'. Where they do feel this need—Gamper illustrates this in her Austrian country report—expressions of regional identity are not politically contested because they do not carry any significant implications. The case of Australia also offers an interesting confirmation of this proposition: state constitutions are generally not used as strong markers of regional identity, but they have come to be used to acknowledge the prior occupation of the country by Indigenous peoples, a matter of understandably great importance to them.

In multinational systems, SNEs with pronounced feelings of regional identity are often keen to assert this in their constitutions. Sahadžić reports that this seems a crucial point for the Republika Srpska, where it is 'used in daily political narratives about autonomy claims'. Foo and Lee observe that the Malay States 'strongly project their identity as Malay-Islamic sultanates' but at the same time there is little room for other contrary democratic expressions of state identity. Overall, it seems that SNEs are allowed to include harmless expressions of regional identity, such as flags and anthems, but, as follows from the Spanish and Italian country reports, this stops when claims are made to self-determination. As Carranza notes in his chapter, references to identity in the Statutes of Autonomy 'are prevalent in those [Autonomous Communities] that have strong nationalist identities (Catalonia and Basque Country). But since the Statute's reform era, there has been an "emulation" of these identity claims even in ACs where this issue had not previously been politically evident.' Similarly, the second-generation charters adopted in the Italian ordinary regions after 2001 have generally been replete with identity-related statements with little or no practical effect. Still, not all these statements are treated as harmless. When the regional legislature of Sardinia passed a law that set up an assembly entrusted with writing a draft for the new regional charter in accordance with the principles of regional identity, autonomy and sovereignty, the Italian Constitutional Court struck down this law with no hesitation. Similarly, the Spanish Constitutional Court held that the most controversial passages in the Preamble to the new *Estatut* of Catalonia had no interpretive value. The case of South Africa is no less instructive. As Steytler shows, the drafters of the provincial Constitution of the Western Cape took care to avoid any reference to a provincial identity based on race or ethnicity. Rather, they highlighted some distinctive policy goals of the political party in office in the province, as distinct from the agenda of the federally dominant African National Congress.

In general terms, much depends on how the political system as a whole deals with its multinational character. For example, Fessha notes that in Ethiopia, where the preamble presents the country in terms of 'nations, nationalities and peoples', there is no problem for state constitutions to define their regional identity.

20.4.2 *The value of constitutional review (hypothesis 9)*

A common thread throughout the country reports is that subnational constitutions generally have low political visibility. This is even the case where the demand for subnational constitutional autonomy is high on the political agenda of regional parties, e.g. in Belgium. There, however, this may be due to the very limited space allowed for subnational constitutional development.

Low visibility may be regarded as surprising especially in countries where fully fledged subnational constitutions exist but it is the central constitution, not the subnational constitutions, that is prominent in public debate. Hypothesis 9 suggests that constitutional review helps to bring subnational constitutions to life, by developing subnational constitutional narratives. Such narratives do not emerge where constitutional review is in the hands of a political body, as Fessha reveals in the Ethiopian country report. It was also assumed that this is more likely to occur in dual judicial systems, with separate subnational courts. In fragmenting systems, attempts to establish specialized bodies responsible to interpret subnational constitutional documents and ensure compliance with their provisions testify to the concern behind this hypothesis, that subnational constitutions are not effectively brought to life in the absence of a specialized interpreter. A significant confirmation for this assumption is provided by the constitutions of the two entities in Bosnia and Herzegovina, which established specialized constitutional courts at the subnational level.

This gives rise to a further specification of the hypothesis, that *a dual system of courts, which enables a dedicated body of subnational courts to develop a body of subnational constitutional law, is especially effective in bringing a subnational constitution to life.* This seems to be confirmed by the cases of the United States and Germany, where the existence of a dual judiciary, be it based on specialized constitutional courts or not, has allowed for the emergence of a substantial body of case law based on subnational constitutions. However, while a body of subnational constitutional law exists, the subnational constitutions in those countries are not especially salient in political debate. Another case to consider is Australia, where there are separately established systems of federal and state courts, but the High Court of Australia has general appellate jurisdiction over all state court decisions. In Australia there is an important body of state constitutional law, but its final shape is determined by the highest federal court. Moreover, in Australia, the state constitutions take the form of ordinary statutes, which only bind the legislature to the extent they are entrenched by mandatory 'manner and form' requirements. This determines and limits the role of courts when adjudicating claims based on alleged violations of state constitutions. This obtains even more clearly in Canada, where the relatively weaker and derivative status of the provincial constitutions is further compounded by the relatively centralized structure of the Canadian judiciary.

The dual organization of the judiciary is thus only one of the factors to be considered. In countries with monist judicial systems, such as in Austria, Spain and Italy, subnational constitutions are enforced exclusively by national constitutional courts.

A distinct issue is the political significance of subnational constitutions in countries like Austria, Spain and Italy. In line with what we mentioned in Section 20.4.1, experience from the last two decades shows that the political significance of subnational constitutions will increase, at least in some SNEs, when claims for greater autonomy emerge. Plausible examples are offered by Catalonia and Alto Adige/Südtirol.

The conclusion is that there is no necessary link between the judicial use of subnational constitutions and their capacity to shape public debate. The existence of a dual system of courts, while supportive of the development of a body of subnational constitutional law, is not sufficient to make a subnational constitution politically significant. This suggests a necessary revision to hypothesis 9 in the following terms:

> Hypothesis 9.1. Judicial review on the basis of subnational constitutions may have the potential to bring those constitutions to life, especially when undertaken by subnational courts, but it is not a sufficient condition.

20.5 The use of subnational constitutions (hypotheses 5, 6, 7)

20.5.1 Institutional design at the subnational level (hypothesis 5)

Hypothesis 5 proposes a qualification to the widely held belief that subnational constitutions do not dramatically diverge from national constitutions when it comes to regulating the institutional architecture. The hypothesis suggests that while this may generally obtain, there are three main exceptions. These concern the regulation of the amendment procedure, direct popular participation and the design of the legislature.

A comparative analysis that focuses mainly on aggregative federations confirms this hypothesis. Still, exceptions and nuances deserve mention as well. In the United States, all states have adopted a presidential form of government (state governors) but have generally refrained from imitating the unitary executive model entrenched in the federal constitution, often opting instead for independent election of several lower level executive officials, such as attorneys general and chief financial officers. A presidential form of government is a recurring characteristic of both national and subnational constitutions in Argentina, Brazil and Mexico. Likewise, in Australia, Canada and Germany the constitutions of the federation and the SNEs have adopted parliamentary systems of government. Similar arguments apply to Switzerland: the cantonal constitutions regulate collegial governments; however, in a clear departure from the federal constitution, such governments are elected directly.

Meanwhile, in the United States and Germany, where there is little room for direct democracy at the federal level, the constitutions of the SNEs often display greater openness towards public participation. And in the United States, as well as Australia, while most of the states have bicameral legislatures like the federal congress or parliament, the constitutions of Nebraska and Queensland respectively provide for a unicameral legislature. Furthermore, subnational constitutions are generally easier to amend either because they are ordinary statutes (Australia) or because the amending procedure is far less demanding than the procedure for modifying the federal constitution (United States).

Because state constitutions ordinarily pre-exist the federal constitution of fully aggregative federal systems it is possible, and indeed likely, that the federal constitution will to some extent have been modelled on the state constitutions. However, in some respects, the similarities between the national constitutions and the constitutions of the SNEs are the result of later, near-simultaneous adaptation, often triggered by political developments and changes in political values, especially in the context of a mostly homogeneous political culture. Legal constraints also play a significant role. Homogeneity clauses like the Republican Guarantee Clause in Article IV(4) of the US Constitution and the *Homogenitätsgebot* in Article 28 of the German Basic Law provide for a minimum standard of constitutional homogeneity *among* the several SNEs. At the other extreme, the principle of symmetry between the federal constitution and the state constitution, developed by the Brazilian Supreme Court, is rather an exception. Somewhere in between, the federal constitution may pre-determine the essential elements of the organization of the *Länder* (Art. 95 of the Austrian Federal Constitutional Law) and may leave very little constitutional space for the states (Schedule 8 of the Malaysian Constitution).

In relation to holding-together, fragmenting and multinational systems, the case studies suggest a mixed picture. In Spain, the open-ended nature of the federalizing process has gone hand in hand with a strong push towards homogeneity between the Autonomous Communities, which Carranza describes as a form of 'institutional mimicry', an important counter-point to the heterogeneity of the country. In Italy, the institutional architecture in the ordinary regions is clearly different from what happens at the national level, while, the content of the *statuti* of the fifteen ordinary regions is not dramatically different. Greater differences emerge if attention is drawn to the five special regions, whose institutional frameworks have been regulated in order to address their specific needs. However, the power of these regions to adopt and to amend their *statuti* is placed under state control. Even more telling is the case of the United Kingdom, where the strong asymmetry among the devolved governments is partially expressed in their political institutions, which are all parliamentary systems based on the Westminster model, but which vary from the UK parliament in their mixture of both constituency-based and proportional representation, especially reflected in the carefully designed consociational system implemented in Northern Ireland. In India, Singh and Saxena report that all state constitutions (now including Jammu and Kashmir) are contained in and determined by the federal constitution, which establishes representative systems of parliamentary government that are uniform and are broadly similar to the federal institutions in design, except that most of the smaller states have unicameral legislatures, whereas several of the most populated states are bicameral. In Canada, Malaysia and South Africa, this pattern is even more pronounced, in that all of the subnational legislatures are unicameral, unlike the national legislature, whereas both the national and subnational systems of government are parliamentary.

We conclude that the hypothesis is confirmed at least for aggregative systems and devolutionary systems in which centrifugal forces are less strong. In fragmenting multinational systems, the institutional structure tends to deviate more substantially from the central design. However, divergences in institutional design between the SNEs within some of these systems are more limited. This is interesting in light of the observation that multinational multi-tiered systems are characterized by constitutional asymmetry.[16] This could possibly be explained by the devolutionary nature of such systems: all other things being equal, a centralized constitution-making institution will tend to adopt the same set of guiding principles when designing the constitutions of all subnational units under its authority; divergences will only be likely when

---

16 Maja Sahadžić, *Asymmetry, Multinationalism and Constitutional Law* (Routledge 2020) 83, 88, 95–6.

adaptations to local conditions or aspirations are manifestly necessary. These conclusions give rise to the following theses:

5.1. *Subnational constitutions in aggregative systems and in devolutionary systems with weak centrifugal forces organize powers in the same way as the federal constitution, with the exception of the organization of the legislature, direct participation and the revision of the constitution.*
5.2. *Subnational constitutions in fragmenting multinational systems are less likely to organize powers in the same way as the federal constitution, especially in relation to the organization of the legislature, direct participation and the revision of the constitution.*

20.5.2 Subnational constitutions as laboratories (hypothesis 6)

Hypothesis 6 proposes that subnational constitutions may serve as laboratories for institutional and fundamental rights innovation. While hypothesis 5 assumed a background similarity between central and subnational constitutions, hypothesis 6 frames it more as a *process*. In this process, subnational constitutions introduce innovations, and similarities emerge over time when these innovations are adopted at the central level and by other SNEs.

Several country reports show that subnational constitutions have this potential. Hernández confirms that provincial constitutions have influenced federal constitutionalism in Argentina. Aroney notes that there has been substantial experimentation among the Australian states in relation to the protection of rights and reforms to other institutional arrangements. In the US report, Gardner even uses the term 'constitutional isomorphism'. In the German country report, Reutter remarks that *Land* constitutions have had this effect in particular for post-materialist issues such as gender equality or environmental protection. Serna de la Garza observes that state constitutions have influenced the federal institutional design in Mexico, whereas de Araújo notes that in Brazil subnational constitutions pioneered fundamental rights innovation. Belser explains that in Switzerland the idea of experimental laboratories accounts for the strategy of political parties and civil societies to first test an initiative at the cantonal level. And even where subnational constitutions do not serve as laboratories, occasional success stories point to their potential. For example, Foo and Lee report how in Malaysia, the promotion of freedom of information by Penang and Selangor had briefly led the central government to also consider reforms in this field.

However, it is by no means a general trend that subnational constitutions bring about institutional or fundamental rights innovation at a more generalised or federal level. In most of the countries examined in this volume, no such effects were reported. Of course, much depends on the constitutional space that SNEs have available. For example, de Araújo reveals that in Brazil, the symmetry principle prevents subnational constitutions from functioning as laboratories for institutional innovation. The same applies where the federal constitution largely determines the content of the subnational constitutions. But even where SNEs do enjoy strong constitutional powers, their impact on the federal constitution is limited. As mentioned, in Ethiopia some state constitutions have even gone so far as to make amendments pertaining to fundamental rights conditional to similar amendments in the federal constitution. This closes off the possibility of bringing about innovation from the bottom up.

This suggests that the hypothesis is not generally confirmed. Subnational constitutions do have the potential to serve as laboratories, but they do not necessarily live up to this potential.

Given this result, it seems important to draw a distinction between two aspects of the hypothesis: firstly concerning the influence of one subnational constitution on one another, and secondly concerning the influence of one or more subnational constitutions on the constitution of the federation as a whole. In Australia, for example, there has been significant cross-pollination of constitutional ideas, but most of this has occurred among the states; the only state ideas that have taken root at a federal level have been statutory, rather than constitutional, in nature. In Argentina, Hernández reports how subnational constitutions inspired each other before giving impetus to federal reform in 1994. These cases suggest various reasons why laboratory federalism more readily translates at a horizontal, inter-state level. These include: (a) closer analogies between subnational constitutions than between subnational and federal constitutions; and (b) constitutional change is generally easier, both procedurally and politically, at a subnational level.

Another important potential factor, in relation to both state-state and state-federal borrowing, is the degree of homogeneity or heterogeneity within a federal system. These considerations suggest the following three supplementary hypotheses:

6.1. *Subnational constitutions are prevented from serving as laboratories if their content is largely predetermined by the central constitution.*
6.2. *Subnational constitutions are more likely to serve as laboratories for fundamental rights and/or institutional arrangements for other subnational constitutions than for the federal constitution.*
6.3. *Subnational constitutions are more likely to serve as laboratories for fundamental rights and/or institutional arrangements where the federal system is more homogenous, and cross-pollination of constitutional ideas is most likely to occur among those subnational units within a federal system that are most alike.*

20.5.3 Policy principles (hypothesis 7)

Finally, we hypothesized that subnational constitutions use policy principles to contribute to subnational identity-building by freezing ideological preferences. This hypothesis is not generally confirmed. In some countries, subnational constitutions do not contain any policy principles. In others, they simply copy (Ethiopia) or implement (Brazil) the principles laid down in the federal constitution. Fessha notes that in Ethiopia, the states therefore miss an opportunity to be guided by policy principles that address the needs and preferences of their own populations. While the Austrian *Land* constitutions contain a very large number of directive policy principles, they generally either support principles already established at a federal level or introduce additional principles within the relatively narrow range of *Land* competences.

The most prominent examples of subnational constitutions that make use of policy principles to build subnational identity are found in multinational systems. In his Canadian country report, Gussen stresses the symbolic use of policy principles. Québec in particular has enacted quasi-constitutional statutes that enshrine the principle of *laïcité*, maintain French as the official language of the province and secure a range of social and economic rights not protected by the Canadian Charter of Rights and Freedoms. In Spain, Carranza points to the extensive list of guiding principles for public policy of the Autonomous Communities to reaffirm regional identity. Skoutaris notes the directives contained in the Belfast/Good Friday Agreement pursuant to which the UK Government pledged to impose a statutory requirement on all public authorities in Northern Ireland to promote equality of opportunity without discrimination, particularly on religious or political grounds. Steytler explains that the Western Cape province in South Africa included in its constitution provision for a special Commissioner for the Environment justified in part by the unique natural habitat of the province, together with a series of cultural councils for communities within the province sharing a common cultural and linguistic heritage and a set of Directive Principles of Provincial Policy, which set the province apart from others, both culturally and politically. However, he also notes that the provincial constitution has had little practical effect, illustrating the emptiness of the constitutional promise of provincial constituent power.

These findings provide support for a qualified hypothesis that:

7.1. Policy principles are more likely to be used by SNEs to protect subnational identity and freeze ideological preferences in federal systems that are culturally and politically heterogeneous.

20.6 Conclusion

Our ambition in this volume was to edit a handbook on subnational constitutions and subnational constitutional law which would provide insight into their nature and functions, as well as particularities and controversies that arise within the context of multilevel and federal systems of government. Within this field of research subnational constitutions are generally understood in the context of traditional federal theory and shaped by the assumption, defensible perhaps in relation to the older coming-together or aggregative federations, that subnational constitutional autonomy is an inherent status of subnational entities in federal systems. However, as is well known, there are also holding-together or devolutionary federations in which the constitutional dynamics of the system are fundamentally different.

We developed hypotheses proposing a series of explanatory theses about the status and functioning of subnational constitutions formed and operating under a variety of conditions. These hypotheses turned on two key axes: (a) the formation of the system by processes of aggregation or devolution; and (b) the underlying cultural politics of the system as either uninational or multinational. Acknowledging that these are dichotomies and that particular systems often display mixed characteristics, we formulated hypotheses that would facilitate exploration of the importance of these factors as well as several others relating to the content, operation and significance of subnational constitutions.

Following the testing of our working hypotheses against data contained in the country reports, it becomes clear that subnational constitutions are an integral part of the entire constitutional design of federal and multilevel systems, and that the design of the system reflects, in turn, the social structure and the historical development of each country, understood in its wider regional and global context. This does not mean that all countries are *sui generis* and no useful comparisons can be undertaken. On the contrary, the hypotheses, as refined in this concluding chapter, indicate that patterns develop across different types of multi-tiered system. Many of the revisions to the hypotheses we have proposed in this conclusion concern clearer specification of:

- the conditions (aggregative, devolutionary, mixed) under which a federal or multilevel system has been come into being;
- the ways in which the heterogeneity of a system, especially when its underlying culture and politics is multinational, has a significant impact on the content, functioning and significance of subnational constitutionalism.

Robert Williams, who, to our delight, accepted our invitation to write the foreword to this edited volume, has already made his mark in the field of subnational constitutionalism. Our hope is that this book will be an impetus to the further development of subnational constitutional theory which takes more fully into account the rise of many types of federal and multi-tiered systems in current times. More studies are needed to fully validate our hypotheses, and empirical testing is needed to find extra-institutional variables that account for the variety within a coherent explanatory theory.

APPENDICES

Appendix 1: Indexes

Index 1: The power to adopt subnational constitutions

A. Content

The SNE has no subnational constitutional autonomy	0
The SNE can make non-substantial arrangements in some of the four categories	1
The SNE can make non-substantial arrangements in all four categories	2
The SNE can make substantial arrangements in one of the four categories	3
The SNE can make substantial arrangements in some of the four categories	4
The SNE can make substantial arrangements in all of the four categories	5

(Categories: subnational identity, representative structures and organization of powers, fundamental rights, and policy principles)

B. Procedure

The SNE cannot adopt its own constitution	0
The central authority adopts and amends the subnational constitution after consultation of the SNE	1
The SNE can adopt its own constitution, but the central or other external authorities have a discretionary veto power	2
The subnational constitution can only take effect after a legality test by a central body or the central government can refer it to a central body for a legality test before it takes effect	3
The SNE can adopt its own constitution without central interference according to a procedure designed at the central level	4
The SNE can adopt its own constitution without central interference according to the amendment procedure decided by its own bodies	5

Index 2: Subnational involvement in the central decision-making process

The central government or national electorate can unilaterally change the constitution	0
The subnational electorate or their representatives can delay constitutional reform or create an extra hurdle	1
The SNE can, through collective vote, delay constitutional reform or create an extra hurdle	2
The individual SNE can delay constitutional reform or create an extra hurdle	3
The subnational electorate or their representatives can veto constitutional reform	4
The SNE can, through collective vote, veto constitutional reform	5
The individual SNE can veto constitutional reform	6
The individual SNE can veto reform that applies to this particular SNE or can veto a very specific piece of reform that has an impact on the SNEs	+1
The individual SNE can exclude certain reforms from taking effect in its jurisdiction	+1
The SNE can, individually or through collective vote, propose constitutional reform	+1

Appendix 2: Scores for subnational constitutional autonomy

Country	Dimension	Indicator	Score content	Score procedure
Argentina	Content	The SNE can make substantial arrangements in all of the four categories	5	
	Procedure	The SNE can adopt its own constitution without central interference according to the amendment procedure decided by its own bodies		5
Austria	Content	The SNE can make non-substantial arrangements in all four categories	2	
	Procedure	The SNE can adopt its own constitution without central interference according to the amendment procedure decided by its own bodies		5
Australia	Content	The SNE can make substantial arrangements in all of the four categories	5	
	Procedure	The SNE can adopt its own constitution without central interference according to the amendment procedure decided by its own bodies		5

(Continued)

Country	Dimension	Indicator	Score content	Score procedure
Belgium	Content	The SNE can make non-substantial arrangements in some of the four categories	1	
	Procedure	The SNE can adopt its own constitution without central interference according to a procedure designed at the central level		4
B&H	Content	The SNE can make substantial arrangements in all of the four categories	5	
	Procedure	The SNE can adopt its own constitution without central interference according to the amendment procedure decided by its own bodies		5
Brazil	Content	The SNE can make substantial arrangements in one of the four categories	3	
	Procedure	The SNE can adopt its own constitution without central interference according to a procedure designed at the central level		4
Canada	Content	The SNE can make substantial arrangements in some of the four categories	4	
	Procedure	The SNE can adopt its own constitution without central interference according to the amendment procedure decided by its own bodies		5
Ethiopia	Content	The SNE can make substantial arrangements in all of the four categories	5	
	Procedure	The SNE can adopt its own constitution without central interference according to the amendment procedure decided by its own bodies		5
Germany	Content	The SNE can make substantial arrangements in all of the four categories	5	
	Procedure	The SNE can adopt its own constitution without central interference according to the amendment procedure decided by its own bodies		5

(*Continued*)

Country	Dimension	Indicator	Score content	Score procedure
India	Content	The SNE has no subnational constitutional autonomy	0	
	Procedure	The SNE cannot adopt its own constitution		0
Italy: – Regular SNEs – Special SNEs	Content	The SNE can make substantial arrangements in some of the four categories	4	
	Procedure: Regular SNEs	The central government can refer it to a central body for a legality test before it takes effect		3
	Procedure: Special SNEs	The SNE can adopt its own constitution, but the central or other external authorities have a discretionary veto power		2
Malaysia	Content	The SNE can make non-substantial arrangements in some of the four categories	1	
	Procedure	The SNE can adopt its own constitution without central interference according to a procedure designed at the central level		4
Mexico	Content	The SNE can make non-substantial arrangements in all four categories	2	
	Procedure	The SNE can adopt its own constitution without central interference according to the amendment procedure decided by its own bodies		5
South Africa	Content	The SNE can make non-substantial arrangements in all four categories	2	
	Procedure	The subnational constitution can only take effect after a legality test by a central body		3
Spain	Content	The SNE can make substantial arrangements in all of the four categories	5	
	Procedure	The SNE can adopt its own constitution, but the central or other external authorities have a discretionary veto power		2

(Continued)

Country	Dimension	Indicator	Score content	Score procedure
Switzerland	Content	The SNE can make substantial arrangements in all of the four categories	5	
	Procedure	The SNE can adopt its own constitution, but the central or other external authorities have a discretionary veto power		2
UK	Content	The SNE can make non-substantial arrangements in some of the four categories	1	
	Procedure	The SNE can adopt its own constitution, but the central or other external authorities have a discretionary veto power		2
USA	Content	The SNE can make substantial arrangements in all of the four categories	5	
	Procedure	The SNE can adopt its own constitution without central interference according to the amendment procedure decided by its own bodies		5

Appendix 3: Scores for subnational involvement in central decision-making

Country	Indicator	Additional comment	Score	Total score
Argentina	The subnational electorate or their representatives can veto constitutional reform		4	4
Australia	The subnational electorate or their representatives can veto constitutional reform		4	5
	The individual SNE can veto reform that applies to this particular SNE or can veto a very specific piece of reform that has an impact on the SNEs	State representation and boundaries	+1	

(Continued)

Country	Indicator	Additional comment	Score	Total score
Austria	The SNE can, through collective vote, delay constitutional reform or create an extra hurdle		2	4
	The individual SNE can veto reform that applies to this particular SNE or can veto a very specific piece of reform that has an impact on the SNEs	Federal Council; transfer of competences to the federation	+1	
	The SNE can, through collective vote, propose constitutional reform		+1	
Argentina	The SNEs can, through collective vote, veto constitutional reform		5	6
	The SNEs can propose constitutional reform		+1	
Belgium	The SNE can, through collective vote, veto constitutional reform	This score takes the central constitution into account. If the organic acts are selected as the central acts with constitutional arrangements for SNEs, the score is 6 for the Flemish Community and 0 for the German-speaking Community	5	6
	The SNEs can propose constitutional reform		+1	
B&H	The individual SNE can veto reform	As the seats in the House of Representatives are allocated per entity (2/3 FB&H and 1/2 RS) it is possible that the representatives of the Bosniaks and Croats that predominantly populate the FB&H use their territorial affiliation to veto constitutional reforms	6	7
	The SNE can individually propose constitutional reform		+1	
Brazil	The subnational electorate or their representatives can veto constitutional reform		4	5
	The SNE can propose constitutional reform		+1	

(Continued)

Country	Indicator	Additional comment	Score	Total score
Canada	The individual SNE can veto constitutional reform	For matters falling under S. 41	6	9
	The individual SNE can veto reform that applies to this particular SNE	S. 43	+1	
	The individual SNE can exclude certain reforms from taking effect in its jurisdiction	e.g. S 35	+1	
	The SNEs can propose constitutional reform		+1	
Ethiopia	The SNEs can, through collective vote, veto constitutional reform		5	6
	The SNEs can propose constitutional reform		+1	
Germany	The SNEs can, through collective vote, veto constitutional reform		5	6
	The SNEs can propose constitutional reform		+1	
India	The SNE can, through collective vote, veto constitutional reform		5	6
	The SNE can propose constitutional reform		+1	
Italy	The individual SNE can create an extra hurdle	Art. 138: constitutional referendum	3	4
	The SNEs can propose constitutional reform	Constitutional Court no. 256/1989, 470/1992, 496/2000	+1	
Malaysia	The central government or national electorate can unilaterally change the constitution	2 of the 13 states (Sabah and Sarawak) might have powers for vetoing specific reform but, even then, such powers would have very limited scope	0	0
Mexico	The SNE can, through collective vote, veto constitutional reform		5	6
	The SNE can propose constitutional reform		+1	
South Africa	The SNEs can, through collective vote, veto constitutional reform		5	6
	The individual SNE can veto reform that applies to this particular SNE	Provincial boundaries	+1	

(Continued)

Country	Indicator	Additional comment	Score	Total score
Spain	The SNE can, through collective vote, create an extra hurdle	The Senate is representative of the local entities rather than the regional entities. 1/10 of the Senate can request a referendum. The representatives of the SgC make up about 20% of the assembly. It is up to them to decide whether their representatives have an institutional link or not	2	2
Switzerland	The subnational electorate or their representatives can veto constitutional reform	Art. 142.3: The result of a popular vote in a canton determines the vote of the canton	4	4
UK	The central government or national electorate can unilaterally change the constitution		0	0
USA	The SNEs can, through collective vote, veto constitutional reform		5	7
	The individual SNE can veto reform that applies to this particular SNE	State representation	+1	
	The SNEs can propose constitutional reform		+1	

INDEX